6

Date Due

NOV 1 9 1976			
APR 1 1977			
OCT 1 3 1980			
NOV 2 2 1990			
APR 1 5 1992			
APR 1 5 1992			

Maler

Environmental economics

ENVIRONMENTAL ECONOMICS:
A THEORETICAL INQUIRY

ENVIRONMENTAL ECONOMICS: A THEORETICAL INQUIRY

Karl-Göran Mäler

Published for Resources for the Future, Inc.
by The Johns Hopkins University Press, Baltimore and London

RESOURCES FOR THE FUTURE, INC.
1755 Massachusetts Avenue, N.W., Washington, D.C. 20036

Resources for the Future is a nonprofit corporation for research and education in the development, conservation, and use of natural resources and the improvement of the quality of the environment. It was established in 1952 with the cooperation of the Ford Foundation. Part of the work of Resources for the Future is carried out by its resident staff; part is supported by grants to universities and other nonprofit organizations. Unless otherwise stated, interpretations and conclusions in RFF publications are those of the authors; the organization takes responsibility for the selection of significant subjects for study, the competence of the researchers, and their freedom of inquiry.

This book is the result of one of RFF's studies in environmental economics which are conducted in the quality of the environment program, directed by Allen V. Kneese and Blair T. Bower. It was edited by Ruth Haas. Illustrations were drawn by Clare and Frank Ford.

RFF editors: Mark Reinsberg, Joan Tron, Ruth B. Haas, Margaret Ingram.

CONTENTS

ACKNOWLEDGMENTS

There are many reasons this book has been written. One is my own interest in the environment and the problems connected with environmental quality. Another is my interest in abstract theory and its application to practical problems. (I expect that some readers will find this book too abstract to be practically useful, but I believe that a theoretical approach is necessary in order to develop a conceptual framework, so that we know what we are trying to approximate in our empirical applications.)

In spite of my own interest, however, I do not believe that I would have undertaken this work if I had not been continuously encouraged by other persons. Professor Erik Dahmén and Professor Assar Lindbeck at the Stockholm School of Economics and the University of Stockholm convinced me that environmental economics is a field worth exploring and initiated a research project that ultimately resulted in this book.

Allen Kneese has played a most decisive role in the gestation of this book. He invited me to Resources for the Future where I spent half a year in a stimulating environment completely devoted to research. At RFF I met friends and colleagues who generously gave me advice and comments on early drafts. Blair Bower, Allen Kneese, and Clifford Russell read the entire manuscript and made detailed comments. In the spring of 1972 I presented various chapters in Professor Anders Östlind's research seminar at the Department of Economics, the University of Stockholm, and my colleagues offered many valuable suggestions. In particular

I must mention Guy Arvidsson, Peter Bohm, and Lewis Taylor. The next to final manuscript was reviewed by Kerry Smith and Clifford Russell, both at RFF; by E. Roy Weintraub, Duke University; David Montgomery, California Institute of Technology; and Ingemar Ståhl, University of Lund. Their comments have substantially improved the book.

Ruth B. Haas has edited the manuscript, which included a heavy job of improving my occasionally eccentric English. Miss Dee Stell at RFF and Mrs. Monica Pejne at the Stockholm School of Economics typed preliminary drafts. The final manuscript was typed by Mrs. Monica Pejne, Mrs. Christina Palmer, Miss Gun Wallström, and Mrs. Margareta Modin. They have all been very cautious with me in spite of my wishes to make changes in the manuscript as soon as they were finished. I am very grateful to them all.

I am also grateful to the Ford Foundation and the Riksbankens Jubileumsfond (Bank of Sweden Tercentenary Fund) for financial support.

Although the persons mentioned here in many ways have contributed to improvements in the manuscript, I of course take the whole responsibility for the content of the book and the way it is presented.

Karl-Göran Mäler

Stockholm
September 1973

ENVIRONMENTAL ECONOMICS:
A THEORETICAL INQUIRY

1 INTRODUCTION

1. GENERAL BACKGROUND

In the 1960s the general public in most developed countries began to demonstrate increased concern about the quality of the natural environment. They noticed how lakes, rivers, and even seas had become so polluted that they no longer could be used for recreation. They could smell the odors of the gaseous emissions from automobiles and factories. At the same time, scientists were collecting overwhelming evidence that there were great health hazards connected with continued emissions of large volumes of gaseous, waterborne, and solid residuals [1].* They pointed out the risks for extinction of certain living species and warned of global effects on the climate [2].

Economists also became interested in these problems, and could easily find explanations for these developments. In their view, the natural environment is a public good, a common property. For such a good, there exists no market in which buyers and sellers reveal their preferences, because if one individual is able to buy, for example, better air quality, all other persons in his neighborhood will also benefit from his transaction. Thus, an individual has little incentive to do anything to improve the quality of the environment. (There is also small possibility of effecting such a change because the individual does not have the financial or legal

---

* Numbers in brackets in the text refer to notes listed at the end of the chapter.

1

resources of the firms or municipalities that cause the deterioration of the environment.) But as every individual is motivated by self-interest, no agreements would be reached between those who cause the deterioration and those who suffer from it. The basic cause of environmental degradation is thus the failure of the markets to deal adequately with public goods. In earlier times, when economic activities in the developed countries were less intense than they are today, this market failure did not cause any great problem (although there are many reports in the literature on pollution problems that existed hundreds or thousands of years ago [3]) because the total amount of wastes discharged into the environment was negligible, and direct interference with the environment was on a much smaller scale.

Economic growth means, among other things, that more and more materials are put into circulation, and, as we will show in the next section, this implies an increasing amount of waste that is discharged into the environment until the assimilative capacity of the environment is reached and surpassed.

According to economists, the remedy for this market failure can be found in more active governments, which by a clever environmental policy could give the agents in the economy the proper incentives so that they would regard the environment as a scarce resource. The incentives recommended by economists have mainly been cost-related ones, such as charges on the discharge of wastes into the environment, an idea which goes back to Pigou [4].

In order to determine the proper size of these charges, and to be able to make cost-benefit analyses of the use of the environment, economists have sought methods that can be used to find the consumers' valuation of the quality of the environment. Several methods have been proposed and tried, but it can be stated with some confidence that none has so far proved very successful.

This has been a very brief review of economists' views on environmental problems. The intention of this book is to develop these views somewhat further and to put some of these ideas on a more rigorous basis than currently exists. The discussion, however, will be limited to problems connected with the discharge of residuals. Environmental problems arising from direct intervention in the environment in the form of highway construction, strip mining, hydropower dam construction, will be almost completely neglected. Moreover, except in chapter 3, there is no discussion of the problem of exhaustion of scarce, nonrenewable resources. The rest of this chapter contains a nontechnical, brief, and partial summary of the results obtained in later chapters.

2. A SIMPLE MATERIALS-BALANCE, GENERAL-EQUILIBRIUM FRAMEWORK

In order to obtain a better understanding of how a decentralized market-type economy works and should work, a simple model will be constructed which takes the circular flow of materials into account. The idea is to try to follow the flow of raw materials from the exploitation of deposits in the environment via production processes and consumption processes, back to the environment in the form of wastes. This model is set out in figure 1 [5].

In this diagram five boxes are shown which correspond to production, capital accumulation, consumption, environmental management, and the environment. Before we start discussing details, a few words must be

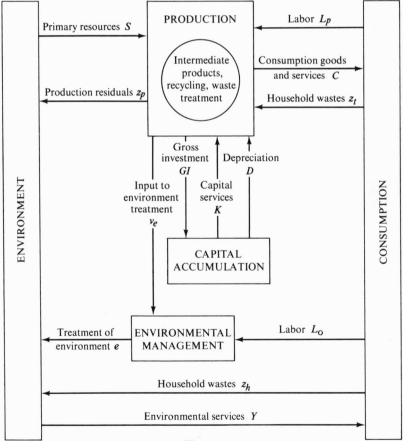

Figure 1

said about the environmental management agency. It is assumed that there is an agency (sometimes identified with the government) whose sole function is to provide protection for the environment. It does this by charging a fee for using the environment for waste disposal and by treating the environment, i.e., by increasing its waste assimilative capacity (through reaeration of water bodies, low flow augmentation, and so on) and by restoring the quality of public lands. It is assumed that this treatment of the environment is paid for by the consumers and that the total profit of the agency is transferred to the consumers as a lump sum. (The profit may be negative, in which case the consumers pay the expenditures of the agency.)

We can follow the flow of materials in the model. In the upper left corner of the diagram is an arrow S which corresponds to the extraction of natural or primary nonrenewable resources from the environment. These resources are used in production as raw material. An arrow L_p from the consumption box in the upper right corner to the production box corresponds to the input of labor in production. The capital accumulation box corresponds to the stock of capital in the economy. This capital stock supplies productive services which are used as a factor of production. The flow of capital services is represented by the arrow K from the accumulation box to the production box.

Consumption in this model consists of consumption of services, either bought directly from the producers of such services or provided by consumption goods. The consumers thus buy a bundle of consumption goods and services C, consume the services that this bundle may yield, and are left with wastes equal in amount to what they bought in the form of consumption goods [6]. These wastes or residuals are either discharged directly into the environment, represented by the arrow z_h from the consumption box to the environment box, or transferred to the production box where the wastes are treated and raw materials recovered.

The capital stock, represented by the capital accumulation box, grows because of gross investments GI, that is, output from the production box set aside for capital accumulation. Owing to physical wear and tear, the capital stock will depreciate, however, and there is a flow of residuals D generated by this depreciation from the capital accumulation box to the production box. This flow D has two economic effects: first it means a decrease in the capital stock, and second it adds to the flow of residuals generated in the economy. In the production box raw materials may be extracted from D and the flow may be recycled.

The environmental management agency buys labor services and goods represented by the arrows L_o and v_e, respectively, and using these inputs treats the environment. The size of the treatment (defined in some way, e.g., the rate of reaeration of a water body) is given by the flow e, represented by the arrow from the environmental management box to the environment box.

Let us now return to the production box. Wastes generated in the consumption and capital accumulation boxes enter this box. In the production processes themselves, residuals are also generated, and the total flow of residuals is treated and recycled. This recycling, together with the circular flow of intermediary products, is represented by the circle inside the production box. It is not in general technologically possible, and it is generally not profitable to recover all the residuals, so there will be a flow of residuals discharged into the environment from the production box z_p.

The quality of the environment is affected by the discharge of residuals and by the treatment of the environment. The environment is regarded as a common property asset which yields a flow of services to the consumers, represented by the arrow Y at the bottom of the diagram. This flow consists of such things as recreation possibilities, aesthetic satisfaction, and clean air. An increase in the discharge of residuals will in general decrease this flow, while an increase in the extent of the environment will in general increase the flow.

Let us now adopt the convention that all flows of materials are measured in tons. Using this convention, we can let the symbol C stand for both the flow of consumption goods and services and the weight of this flow. This ambiguity will not create any difficulties because the meaning will be clear from the context. The same idea applies of course to all other flows as well.

Neither in the production box, the consumption box, nor in the environmental management box are any stocks of goods piled up, so the arrows entering these boxes must be balanced by the arrows leaving them. We thus have

$$S + z_t + D = C + GI + v_e + z_p \qquad \text{for the production box}$$
$$C = z_t + z_h \qquad \text{for the consumption box}$$
$$\text{and } v_e = e \qquad \text{for the environmental management box}$$

Adding these identities yields

$$S + D = GI + z_p + z_h + e \qquad \text{or}$$
$$S - (z_p + z_h + e) = NI$$

where NI stands for net investment: $GI - D$. The net outflow of materials from the environment is thus equal to the net accumulation of the capital stock.

This apparently trivial conclusion is, however, very important because it gives the materials balance in a compact form. That part of the raw materials that is not accumulated in the capital stock will ultimately be returned to the environment. Moreover, another not so trivial conclusion may be drawn. Given the net accumulation of capital, if there are no incentives to keep the discharges of residuals into the environment low, the extraction of natural resources will be too high. If environmental quality is neglected in public policy, then the economy will suffer not only from environmental deterioration, but also from excessive use of natural resources.

It is necessary to introduce some kind of mechanism to allocate resources among different uses in order to derive more theorems. So far the model has consisted only of a set of accounting identities, which is useful as a frame of reference, but inadequate when it comes to explaining the working of the economy.

In almost all economies, centralized or decentralized, prices have been the prime regulator of the allocation of resources. Let us therefore introduce into the model prices, some of which are determined by market forces and others by the environmental management agency.

It will be assumed that all producers and all consumers are price takers, that the prices for all goods and services, except those for environmental quality and ultimate disposal in the environment, are determined by market forces. The prices for ultimate disposal are determined by the environmental management agency. The prices for environmental quality or environmental services are thought of as consumers' demand prices for environmental services. Since environmental quality is a public good, as discussed in the previous section, there are no markets for environmental services, but it is assumed that the environmental management agency has some method to discover the consumers' demand prices (that is, their marginal willingness to pay for these services).

The following symbols will be used:

p = price of consumption goods and services
p_r = price of natural resources
q_t = price for disposing of household wastes to treatment plants
p_K = price of capital goods
p_D = price for disposing of capital residuals by recycling
q = price for ultimate disposal of residuals into the environment
p_e = price of goods used as input in environmental treatment
w = wage rate
π = capital rental rate

v = value of environmental treatment, that is, the cost of giving the environment a unit treatment

δ = demand price for environmental services

Π_p = profit in the production sector

Π_K = profit in the capital accumulation sector

Π_E = profit in the environmental management sector

$z = z_p + z_h$, the total amount of residuals discharged into the environment

NS = consumers' net saving

With this notation, we can now calculate the profits in the three sectors (note that the q prices are prices that the different economic subjects have to pay for the disposal of their wastes):

$$\Pi_p = pC + p_K GI + q_t z_t + q_D D + p_e v_e - wL - p_r S - \pi K - q z_p$$
$$\Pi_K = \pi K - p_K D - q_D D$$
$$\Pi_E = qz + ve - p_e v - wL_e$$

The budget constraint for the consumers is

$$NS + pC + q_t z_t + q z_h = w(L_e + L_p) + p_r S + \Pi_p + \Pi_K + \Pi_E$$

where it is assumed that all profits are transferred to the consumers. Consolidating these four expressions gives the usual saving-investment identity $NS = p_K GI - p_K D$.

Assume now that the relation between residual discharges, environmental treatment, and environmental services is given by the following environmental function

$$Y = Y_o - F(z,e); F(0,0) = 0$$

where Y_o is the environmental quality when no wastes are discharged into the environment and no treatment of the environment is undertaken. We have already assumed that $\partial F/\partial z = F_1 > 0$, $\partial F/\partial e = F_2 < 0$. The total value of environmental services is δY and the value of the disruption of the environment caused by residuals discharge is $\delta(Y_o - Y)$. This is one factor in the social cost of using the environment as a dumping ground. The other factor is the value of environmental treatment ve. The total opportunity cost of using the environment for waste disposal is thus $ve + \delta(Y_o - Y)$. The benefits from using the environment for waste disposal are obviously qz, and the net benefits

$$qz - ve - \delta(Y_o - Y)$$

Maximizing this net social benefit over z and e yields the optimal policy for the environmental management agency (it is assumed that the agency regards the prices q, v, and δ as given):

$$q = \delta F_1 \quad \text{and} \quad v = -\delta F_2$$

The agency should thus allow dumping of residuals to such an extent that the social benefit q from dumping one more unit of waste is equal to the social marginal cost δF_1 of this operation, and the agency should treat the environment to such an extent that the social marginal benefit $-\delta F_2$ equals the social cost v of treatment.

For the other sectors it is assumed that there are perfectly competitive markets in which all decision makers are price takers who maximize their profits or their utilities. In the next chapter it will be shown that given some additional continuity and convexity assumptions, there exists a set of prices and an allocation of resources such that all markets are cleared and profits and utilities maximized, and such that the net social benefit from using the environment for waste disposal is maximized. In other words, there exists an equilibrium for this kind of economy.

Moreover, it will be shown that this equilibrium is a Pareto optimum, in the sense that no person can achieve a better position without leaving at least one other person in a worse position. Finally, it will be shown that all optimal allocations can be represented as equilibrium allocations in this economy. These very important results can be used in analyzing different problems connected with externality theory and policy problems. Some of these will be discussed in the next chapters.

3. CHARGES, BRIBES, AND THE NEED FOR COMPENSATION

There is in the literature on externalities and environmental economics considerable controversy over the nature of the optimal policy. First there is the group that favors Pigou's taxation solution, implying that those who generate external diseconomies should be subject to a unit tax proportional to the damage. Then there is a group that believes that those suffering from the damage should bribe the offending party to take actions to decrease the damage. In addition, there are those like Coase, Buchanan, and Stubblebine who argue that it is not enough to tax the activities that generate external diseconomies, it is also necessary to tax those who suffer from the damages. Finally, there are persons who argue that to achieve optimum, compensation must be paid to those who suffer from the diseconomies [7]. It is now possible to discuss these opinions in view of the general equilibrium model described in section 2 of this chapter and the proofs and theorems given in the next chapter.

Let us start with the controversy on the use of bribes versus charges. A charge is the fee a waste discharger must pay for the right to discharge waste into the environment. In the general equilibrium model, each discharger has to pay a certain amount, represented by the price q, to an environmental management agency for each unit of waste he discharges into the environment. This price q can be interpreted as a unit tax on waste discharges. It would thus seem that the model supports the Pigouvian solution. But it is possible to reinterpret the model so that it will lend support to the bribery argument. We can imagine that the environmental management agency decides to use its revenues (in this case lump sum taxes on the consumers), not for direct transfers to the consumers, but indirectly in subsidies for the waste discharger in such a way that one more unit of waste discharge reduces the subsidy by $\$q$. It is clear that such a mechanism implies a marginal cost of waste discharge equal to q, and that it follows that the equilibrium of the economy when the environmental management agency acts in this way is still a Pareto optimum. In fact, the only difference between the equilibrium when charges are used and when bribes are used is in the income distribution and its consequences for the allocation of resources. As it has been assumed that lump sum transfers are possible, the same income distribution may be achieved, and it is thus seen that bribes and charges are equivalent from a purely theoretical point of view.

The only differences between the two approaches are thus those connected with administration, enforcement, and other such "practical" questions. It must be remembered, however, that the bribes or subsidies must be based on the amounts of wastes discharged and not on any other variable such as the existence of waste treatment processes, the quantity of output, the size of the state tax, or the profit. In Sweden, for example, it is possible for firms to be subsidized by the government for investments in treatment processes. If there is only one way to operate such processes, then such a subsidy may work out well (although some distortions will still be created owing to the absence of incentives to change output). But in most cases, waste treatment processes require very careful supervision, and a subsidy on the investment in treatment processes does not furnish any incentive for such supervision.

A subsidy based on output will not give the proper incentives to invest in residual control processes, since there is no fixed proportion between the amounts of residuals discharged and the quantity of output in a firm. It is obvious that a subsidy based on profits or the size of the corporate tax paid will not provide any incentives for the firms to achieve a residuals control program that can be called optimal, but in the United States and in Sweden depreciation allowances for pollution control activities amount to a subsidy based partly on profits and corporate taxes.

Thus, if the environmental management agency is going to use subsidies or bribes, it must base them on actual waste discharges, and if that is done, the resulting allocation will be optimal. But Kneese and Bower [8] have raised serious doubts about the practicability of using bribes. First, for bribes to produce the same results as charges, it is necessary to continue payment, even if the plant closes down. Second, it may be necessary to pay firms not to locate in certain regions, and, as it is in general very difficult to prove whether a particular firm has serious plans to move into such a region, many firms that never planned such a move will be "bribed" to stay out.

There are, however, situations where charges are not feasible, while bribes are. The use of charges is based on the ability of the environmental management agency to enforce collection of the charges, and in many cases such enforcement is not possible. Such a case would occur when a firm in one country pollutes the water in a river that enters another country downstream. The environmental agency in the latter country cannot, in the absence of international agreement, collect charges from the firm and its only method of dealing efficiently with the pollution problem is to try to bribe the foreign firm to decrease its waste discharges into the river.

Let us now consider the argument that those responsible for environmental deterioration should compensate those who suffer from this deterioration. In equilibrium in the economy characterized by the general equilibrium model, the waste discharger pays the price q for ultimate waste disposal. These charges are collected by the environmental management agency and distributed to the consumers by lump sum transfers. If the agency so wishes, it can make these lump sum transfers proportional to the value of the decrease in the flow of environmental services caused by the discharges of wastes. If the agency acts in this way, consumers are compensated for the environmental deterioration. But the agency may distribute its net revenues in any other way it would like without destroying the optimality of the equilibrium. Such changes in the distribution may of course alter the allocation because of income effects, but the new equilibrium will still be an optimum. It is therefore clear that optimality does not call for any compensation. The way in which the agency chooses to distribute its proceeds from the charges is a matter of equity, not of efficiency in resource allocation.

Finally, let us take a look at the argument raised by Coase and others that in order to achieve optimum it is necessary to tax both parties, the party that generates the externalities and the party that suffers from them. This argument rests on the observation that externalities seem to be symmetrical. If, in Coase's terms, a factory is emitting smoke and thereby damaging the people in the neighborhood, then every action undertaken to decrease this damage by cutting the emissions of smoke is damage to the factory. One more person in the neighborhood increases the damage from smoke and would thus require a further cut in smoke emission. This person will thus create a marginal damage to the factory. To achieve optimum, Coase argues, it is therefore necessary to tax both the factory and the persons living in the neighborhood, so that we end up with both an optimal amount of smoke and an optimal number of persons living in the neighborhood.

The general equilibrium model can be interpreted as covering this case. For example, let z be the emission of smoke from the factory. The demand price δ for clean air in the neighborhood is determined by the sum of the marginal willingness to pay for clean air. For all people living outside the neighborhood, this marginal willingness to pay is probably zero, so it suffices to sum over those persons living in the neighborhood. Consequently, the fee q the factory owner should pay for the smoke emission is determined by the preferences of the population in the neighborhood. If one more person should move into the neighborhood, that would increase δ and so the charge q on smoke emissions would be increased, reflecting an increase in the price of a scarce resource. This is exactly parallel to the case in which the rental price of land rises because one more person demands land. This rent increase will hurt other land renters, but there is no need whatsoever to tax persons because they demand land. There is therefore no need for taxes on persons suffering from smoke either, and the general equilibrium model does not in fact call for such a tax. It is completely sufficient to tax the smoke emissions or to subsidize the factory in such a way that the marginal cost of smoke emissions is equal to q.

4. ECONOMIC GROWTH AND THE ENVIRONMENT

The model outlined in section 2 is in principle an intertemporal model, in which capital accumulation ties the different time periods to each other. When we prove the existence theorem, and the theorems on optimality in chapter 2, this intertemporal aspect will be neglected. Therefore, it seems to be of some interest to try to generalize the results to a real intertemporal model. Another stimulus for undertaking such a study comes from concern about the scarcity of nonrenewable natural resources. Simultaneously with the development of environmental concern, there has been a growing concern about exhaustion of nonrenewable resources in the form of fossil fuels, ores, and arable land, especially in regard to the growing world population [9].

In chapter 3, some simple aggregate intertemporal models are constructed in order to study these problems. The intertemporal aspects of these models are to be found in the production of real capital, the environment's capacity to assimilate wastes, the accumulated use of natural resources, the changes in population, and the intertemporal welfare function. It is assumed that the objective of the economy is to maximize the present value of future utilities or felicities [10] over a finite horizon, where utility in each moment depends on the flow of consumption and on the flow of environmental services. There is a finite amount of natural resources that may be exhausted within the horizon.

The following main conclusions can be drawn from these models.

1. There exists a stationary state, with constant population, constant capital stock, constant quality of the environment, and constant consumption per capita, such that if the horizon is far enough away, the optimal path will tend to this state.

2. In the absence of technological progress, it is desirable to steer the economy toward this stationary state, because this state is such that it can support the highest utility at every moment within the horizon.

3. In the absence of technical progress, this stationary state cannot be extended beyond the horizon, because of the exhaustion of the natural resources.

4. If there is technical progress, and especially if there are inventions that can be used to produce energy (for example, fusion energy) at low constant costs, it may be possible to recycle almost all wastes, and the stationary state may be extended beyond the horizon.

5. If there is technical progress of such a nature that less and less resources are embodied in the material goods and services, a steady state with a growing per capita consumption will be the desired growth objective.

The result in (1) provides weak support for the approach taken in chapter 2, because the general equilibrium model discussed in chapter 2 may be regarded as a description of a stationary equilibrium in an intertemporal model.

5. THE DEMAND FOR ENVIRONMENTAL SERVICES

In the spirit of Pareto optimality, the general equilibrium model of chapter 2 (and of section 2) is constructed on the basis of individual preferences, both for private goods and services and for environmental services. But as was noted in section 2, environmental services are public goods for which there are no markets in which the consumers can reveal their preferences. Moreover, the consumers may have incentives to misrepresent their preferences where environmental services are concerned. It was assumed in section 2 that the environmental management agency has the means for discovering the true preferences of the consumers. To achieve a rational environmental policy, it seems desirable to be able to find such means.

An investigation of consumption theory seems necessary in order to discover methods that can be used to obtain information about consumer preferences. Therefore, chapter 4 is devoted to a basic analysis of consumer behavior. There it is shown that if a consumer's individual demand functions are known, it is possible to reconstruct his preferences completely with regard to private goods on the basis of his Slutsky equations. When some very restrictive conditions are satisfied (one is that the consumers are identical), it is shown that it is possible to reconstruct a community utility function from information on the demand functions. As almost all information we have is about aggregate demand functions, this indicates that it may be impossible to reconstruct the individual utility functions and to use such concepts as consumer's surplus. If, however, it is possible to obtain information on the demand behavior of different social classes, which can be regarded as homogeneous, this difficulty is circumvented. If that is the case, this method of reconstructing preferences can be used to assess the welfare effects of changes in the economy for given ethical beliefs about income distribution.

If it is difficult to reconstruct preferences for private goods, one expects that it would be almost impossible to obtain information for public goods. The analysis in chapter 5 shows that the situation is almost that hopeless. Several methods are discussed there; each has its own weaknesses, and no general method is proposed.

In a cost-benefit analysis of the use of the environment, consumer preferences preferably should be summed to an aggregate marginal willingness to pay for different environmental services. Such a measure indicates how much the consumers together are willing to abstain from consumption to achieve a unit improvement of an environmental service. If the cost (that is, the opportunity cost) for a unit improvement is less than this aggregate marginal willingness to pay, it is clear that the improvement is worthwhile from an economic point of view, provided that the burden of this improvement is distributed over the individuals in a "satisfactory" way.

The most natural approach to obtaining information about consumer preferences on environmental services is, of course, to ask each individual how much he is willing to pay for a unit improvement in the quality of the environment. It has long been recognized, however, that consumers may have very strong incentives to misrepresent their true preferences in their answers. The nature of these incentives is discussed in the first sections of chapter 5 along with methods that can be used to overcome this difficulty. In general, however, there does not seem to be a practicable scheme that would eliminate these incentives completely. On the other hand, there may be situations where it is possible to design the questions in such a way that incentives to overstate the true marginal willingness to pay are balanced against incentives to understate it.

The same incentives may appear when the supply of environmental services is determined by a vote. It is shown, however, that with some a priori information on consumer preferences, it is possible to design the proposal to be voted on in such a way that the outcome is a reasonably good representation of the true preferences.

Voting, questionnaires, and interviews can be regarded as direct methods for obtaining information on consumer preferences. There are also indirect methods based on a priori information on the nature of the environmental services. If, for example, it is known that an environmental service is a perfect complement or a perfect substitute for some private good, and if it is possible to get information about the demand for the private good, it is also possible to compute the aggregate marginal willingness to pay for the environmental service. Admittedly, there are very few environmental services that fall into one of these extreme categories, but there are other kinds of complementarities which can be used to draw the same type of conclusion. One such case discussed in chapter 5 occurs when it is known that the marginal willingness to pay for an environmental service is zero when nothing is consumed of a given private good. (For example, if a person does not use a lake for swimming because it is too expensive, he is probably not willing to pay anything for an increase in water quality in the lake.) Another such case discussed in chapter 5 occurs when changes in environmental quality are reflected in property values. Given these changes, it may be possible to estimate the marginal willingness to pay from a knowledge of the relation between environmental quality and property values.

However, all these methods share a common weakness, namely that they are based on access to complete knowledge of what happens in the environment when residuals are discharged. Furthermore, they presuppose that consumers in general have this perfect information. In reality, our knowledge about ecological relations is very slight, and it follows that the problem for the decision maker is one of uncertainty. This book contains no discussion of uncertainty, however. Instead, it is assumed that the environmental management agency (or the government—we will use these two terms as synonyms) decides on some ambient standards or environmental standards that must be met. The purpose of environmental policy is then to find measures which assume that these standards are met at least cost.

6. ENVIRONMENTAL POLICY

In the general equilibrium analysis of chapters 2 and 3 it is shown that if the environmental management agency has all the necessary information, it is possible to find a set of effluent charges (that is, fees on the discharge of residuals in the environment) such that the resulting allocation is a Pareto optimum. This result implies, among other things, that it is possible to meet any environmental standards at least cost by using effluent charges (provided of course that it is possible to collect these charges).

It appears, however, that no Western countries have chosen to use effluent charges in their environmental policies [11]. It is therefore of some interest to compare effluent charges with other policy measures.

One of the most natural policy measures is an effluent standard, that is, a limit on the amount of a waste a firm, a municipality, or a consumer may discharge into the environment. It is shown in chapter 6 that effluent charges and effluent standards differ only in effects on the income distribution, provided that the environmental management agency has all the information required to set optimal charges or standards and that all flows of residuals are deterministic. It is thus possible to achieve the same environmental objectives with either standards or charges and at the same social costs (neglecting the income distribution). Therefore it becomes of great interest to determine which method requires least information at a central level. The basic conclusion is that the information necessary to set optimal standards is sufficient to set optimal effluent charges, while in general the information necessary to set optimal effluent charges is not sufficient to set standards. In this sense, effluent charges require less information at the central level than effluent standards do.

If the assumption of deterministic residuals flows is dropped, more profound differences between charges and standards will appear. In some cases it is not even possible to achieve the same environmental objectives with standards as with charges. Moreover, the information requirement for standards will in general be much greater than for charges. Furthermore, there is the serious problem of implementing effluent standards when the waste flows are random, while the corresponding problem is much less serious when effluent charges are used.

Both effluent standards and effluent charges require monitoring of the waste discharges. In many cases such monitoring is prohibitively expensive (for example, monitoring some of the solid wastes generated in a household). It therefore becomes important to investigate whether effluent charges can be replaced by some system of standards, charges, subsidies and refunds, which has the same effect on allocations. It is shown that such a system exists for many interesting situations. One can, for example, tax the production of containers that after consumption will create solid wastes, and give a refund if the containers are delivered to certain collection stations.

7. NOTATIONS

Most of the mathematical notations used here are standard and need no comments. R^n is the n-dimensional Euclidean space. If $x \in R^n$, x_i denotes its ith coordinate. For vector inequalities the following notations are used: Let $x \in R^n$ and $y \in R^n$,

$x \leqq y$ means that $x_i \leqq y_i$ $i = 1, \cdots, n$
$x \leq y$ means that $x \leqq y$ $x \neq y$
$x < y$ means that $x_i < y_i$ $i = 1, \cdots, n$

If A is a matrix (or a vector), A^T denotes the transpose of A. The symbol $\{x; P\}$ denotes the set of elements that possess the property P. Set theoretical differences are denoted by $\backslash$, i.e.,

$$A \backslash B = \{x; x \in A, x \notin B\}$$

The following symbols have the same meaning throughout the book:

c = vector of consumption process levels
c^* = compensated demand functions for consumption processes
δ = price vector on environmental qualities
δ^* = vector of compensated demand prices on environmental qualities
e = input vector in environmental treatment
$F(\cdot)$ = environment interaction function
K = stock of capital (although sometimes the number of producers)
$m(\cdot)$ = expenditure function
p = price vector on goods and services
p_r = price vector on raw materials
q = vector of effluent charges
s = imputed price vector on consumption processes
$U(\cdot)$ = utility function
$v(\cdot)$ = indirect utility function
$V(\cdot)$ = indirect social welfare function
$W(\cdot)$ = social welfare function
Y = vector of environmental qualities
z = vector of residuals discharges

Some of these symbols will appear with an index attached to them, for example, c^h is the vector of consumption process levels chosen by consumer h. Sometimes the symbols will be interpreted as scalars.

NOTES

1. See, for example, L. B. Lave and E. P. Seskin, "Health and Air Pollution," *Swedish Journal of Economics*, vol. 73, no. 1, 76–95 (1971).
2. See Carroll L. Wilson and William H. Matthews (eds.), *Man's Impact on the Global Environment: Assessment and Recommendation for Actions* (MIT Press, Cambridge, Mass., 1970). For a useful summary of the most important problems arising from pollution, see the article by Allen V. Kneese: "Background for the Economic Analysis of Environmental Pollution," in *Swedish Journal of Economics*, vol. 73, no. 1, 1–24 (1971). The article also contains a discussion of flows of materials that is of relevance for this book.
3. It is reported that the Romans built their first aqueduct because the ground disposal of filth for generations had finally polluted the ground water. (Percy H. McGauhey, *Engineering Management of Water Quality*, McGraw-Hill, New York, 1968.)
4. As early as 1920 Pigou suggested that taxes on negative external effects and subsidies on positive external effects may be used to correct distortions in the allocation of resources due to externalities. (Arthur C. Pigou, *The Economics of Welfare*, St. Martin's, New York, 1962.)
5. This idea of following the flows of materials and energy has been most carefully stated by Robert U. Ayres and Allen V. Kneese in "Production, Consumption and Externalities," *American Economic Review*, vol. 59, no. 3, 282–297 (1969). Their article gave the direct inspiration for the general equilibrium model in section 2 of chapter 1 and chapter 2 in this book. The substance of this paper can also be found in a most stimulating book by Allen V. Kneese, Robert U. Ayres, and Ralph d'Arge, *Economics and the Environment: A Materials Balance Approach* (Resources for the Future, Washington, D.C., 1972).
6. We neglect here the purchases of consumer capital goods.
7. For a discussion of bribes versus charges, see Allen V. Kneese and Blair T. Bower, *Managing Water Quality: Economics, Technology, Institutions* (Johns Hopkins Press, Baltimore, 1968) and the references given there. Coase's argument is presented in "The Problem of Social Cost," reprinted in William Breit and Harold M. Hochman (eds.), *Readings in Microeconomics* (Holt, New York, 1968). Buchanan and Stubblebine's article, "Externality," has also been reprinted in the same book.
8. Kneese and Bower, *Managing Water Quality*.
9. These concerns have been most explicitly expressed in the so-called World Models produced by a group at Sloan School of Management at Massachusetts Institute of Technology: Jay W. Forrester, *World Dynamics* (Wright-Allen, Cambridge, Mass., 1971) and Donella H. Meadows *et al.*, *The Limits to Growth* (Potomac Associates, Washington, D.C., 1972). These models show that human civilization will either die from shortage of food or natural resources, or pollution

within a hundred years. As these models neglect economic and other social adaptive mechanisms, they are of little value. Moreover, they permit exponential growth of almost all variables except human knowledge, in contrast to experience which has shown that human knowledge may be the variable that has the most rapid growth of all.

10. The term felicity is used by Kenneth J. Arrow and Mordecai Kurz in *Public Investment, the Rate of Return and Optimal Fiscal Policy* (Johns Hopkins Press, Baltimore, 1970) for what is usually called instantaneous utility.

11. It is interesting to note that some socialistic countries have tried effluent charges. In Poland for example, factories discharging more gaseous or liquid wastes than permitted have been charged with a fee, according to the Swedish Embassy in Warsaw. Moreover, every source of sulfur dioxide emission has to share the cost of damage to the forests from air pollution.

2 A GENERAL EQUILIBRIUM MODEL OF ENVIRONMENTAL QUALITY

1. INTRODUCTION

In the preceding chapter, a brief sketch was given of a general equilibrium model that incorporated materials balances and effects of waste discharges on environmental quality. This chapter gives more structure to this sketch by introducing production possibilities, consumption possibilities, consumption preferences, and so on. Not only will we thereby be able to derive useful theorems about the nature of optimal environmental policy, but we will also be able to discuss in more rigorous terms some problems associated with the theory of externalities. The model to be constructed will, however, neglect capital accumulation and aspects of the relations between growth, environmental quality, and the exhaustion of nonrenewable resources. These problems will be discussed in the next chapter. We will thus be concerned with a stationary economy because, among other things, an economy with capital accumulation and population growth most of the time will stay in a stationary equilibrium if it follows some optimal growth path.

This chapter can be conveniently summarized in the following points.

1. The production possibilities in the economy will be stated in terms of activity analysis [1]. It will be assumed that all producers are price takers, and that they maximize their profits. Profit maximizing conditions will be stated.

2. The environmental management agency will be introduced, to-

gether with the environmental interaction function. It will be assumed that the agency behaves in such a way that the maximum possible net benefit from the environment is attained.

3. The consumer preferences and the budget constraints will be introduced. Each consumer is assumed to select that combination of consumption goods and environmental qualities that is best for him in his budget set. This selection establishes demand functions for consumption goods and environmental qualities. It is here assumed that the consumers have to pay a price both for consumption goods and for environmental qualities.

4. The equilibrium of the model will be defined as a feasible allocation such that all markets are cleared and all consumers demand the same amount of environmental services.

5. It will be proved that an equilibrium exists; that this equilibrium is an optimum; and that every optimum can be represented as an equilibrium.

6. The conclusions and the interpretations of the model will be discussed. In particular it will be shown that the assumption in point (3) that consumers pay for environmental services does not support the idea that both parties in an externality relation should be taxed. Before we turn to the production possibilities, a warning is perhaps in order. We will not prove all of the assertions on existence, because the model can be interpreted as a special case of Arrow's and Debreu's general equilibrium model and we can appeal to their proofs. Moreover, one more reason why such an approach has been chosen is that there exist rigorous proofs of existence and optimality for similar models elsewhere in the literature, and these rigorous proofs can be easily adapted to suit our model [2]. The reason that proofs are included at all is that it is hoped these proofs give further insight into the working of the model without bringing in a lot of technical details. Although the model includes externalities, it does not include externalities that affect the production possibilities. In fact, all externalities are thought of as being generated by wastes discharged into the environment, and they only work by changes in the quality of the environment. In principle, it is possible to extend the model to take into account effects on the production possibilities as well, but this will not be done here [3]. Moreover, the external effects are thought of as pure public goods [4], as was discussed in section 1 in chapter 1. This means that the vector of environmental qualities will enter as an argument in the utility functions of all consumers. Private ownership of land and water are not excluded, but the quality of a private piece of land is thought of as a public good. The preferences will, however, generally depend on the distribution of land among individuals, and so in principle we should also

be interested in explaining the distribution of natural resources. That will not be done, however. We take the actual distribution of land as given. Those not interested in the technical details of the model may proceed directly to section 9, where a summary of the model is given.

2. PRODUCTION POSSIBILITIES

The model will contain $n + r + m$ different goods and services. There are n "regular" goods and services, i.e., consumption goods and services, intermediary commodities, raw materials, r residuals, and m environmental services. The discussion of the environmental services is left for the next section. The distinction between "regular" goods and services and residuals is a very subtle one. The idea, however, is that residuals are materials and energy left over in production and consumption processes and discharged into the environment. The extent to which materials are discharged into the environment will in general depend on technological possibilities and relative prices. One good may therefore be regarded as a regular good, say an intermediary product at one relative price configuration, while it may be regarded as a residual at another configuration. In spite of this, let there be a partition of all commodities and services (except the environmental services) into n regular goods and r residuals. If $z \in R^r$ is the vector of net flow of residuals discharged into the environment, and if $z_i = 0$, the ith residual is either not generated at all or it is completely recovered and used as an intermediary good. (In section 8, an alternative model, in which residuals are not distinguished a priori from regular goods and services, is discussed.) A production plan can be described by the vector (S, z) where $S \in R^n$; $z \in R^r$, S is interpreted as the supply of regular goods and services, and z as the flow of residuals. We will use the convention that whenever a component in S is positive, the component is interpreted as the amount of output of the corresponding good, and if it is negative, the amount of input used.

If a component in z, z_i is positive, then z_i of the ith residual must be discharged into the environment. If $z_i < 0$, then the ith residual is recycled in an amount in excess of the amount generated in production. In this case, the deficit is covered by residuals generated in consumption. The total flow of residuals from both consumption and production must never be negative, however.

We now assume that the production possibility set can be described by a closed, convex, polyhedral cone T in R^{n+r} with a vertex at the origin [5]. The economic interpretation of this assumption is the following: The cone property implies that if $(S, z) \in T$, then $(\lambda S, \lambda z) \in T$ for every $\lambda > 0$, that is, the technological possibilities are characterized by constant returns to scale. The intuitive motivation for this is that all goods and services can be regarded as perfectly divisible. That the cone is convex means that if $(S', z') \in T$ and $(S'', z'') \in T$, then $(S' + S'', z' + z'') \in T$. If this is the case, then there are no externalities between the production plans (S', z') and (S'', z''); both plans can be carried out independently of each other. Note here that although the model will be used to analyze externalities, it does not allow for externalities between different production processes. That the cone is closed has no intuitive economic interpretation, and is assumed only because this property facilitates the mathematical analyses. That the cone has a vertex at the origin implies that inaction is feasible, i.e., it is possible to produce nothing using no inputs and generating no residuals. Finally, the polyhedral property implies that there is a matrix A, of the order $(n + r) x N$, such that the production possibility set can be represented as [6]

$$T = \{(S, z) \,|\, (S, z) = Ax, \, x \in R^N, \, x \geqq 0\} \tag{1}$$

The matrix A will be called the technology matrix and the vector x will be called the vector of activity levels. To interpret the matrix, let us denote its columns by $A_j, j = 1, \cdots, N$. Each column may be interpreted as a basic feasible process or activity. The components in A_j give, if negative, the amounts of different inputs necessary, and if positive, the amounts of different outputs obtained from the process if it is operated at the unit level.

We will in the following discussion use representation (1) of the production possibility set. Moreover, we will assume that there is no pair $(S, z) \in T$ such that $S \geqq 0$, and consequently there is no pair $(S, z) \in T$ such that $(S, z) \geqq 0$. The motivation for this assumption is that it is impossible to produce positive amounts of any good without using at least one input.

Let us now partition the technology matrix A into $\begin{bmatrix} A^1 \\ A^2 \end{bmatrix}$ such that $S = A^1 x$, and $z = A^2 x$. Next, prices will be introduced. Let p be a price vector corresponding to "regular" goods, and q a price vector corresponding to residuals. The interpretation of the components of p is straightforward. p_i is interpreted as the amount of dollars the producer gets when he sells one unit of good i, and simultaneously the amount a producer has to pay for one unit of good i to possess that unit. The interpretation of the components of q is similar; q_i is the amount a producer has to pay to be able to dispose of one unit of the ith residual, and the amount that a producer has to be paid to induce him to take care of one unit of residual i.

The profit from one basic process, operated at the unit level, can thus be written

$$p^T A_j^1 - q^T A_j^2$$

where the column A_j has been partitioned in the same way as A was. (The superscript T denotes transposition. A vector without the superscript T attached to it is always interpreted as a column vector, and with the T attached the vector is interpreted as a row vector.)

The aggregate profit in the economy can similarly be written

$$p^T A^1 x - q^T A^2 x$$

We now assume that all producers are price takers, and that they maximize their profits. It is obvious that there may not exist a profit maximum for all prices. If for example,

$$p^T A_j^1 - q^T A_j^2 > 0$$

then the profit from process j can be increased without any limit by increasing the level of operation, x_j. Let A^* denote the cone defined by

$$A^* = \{(p, q) \,|\, p^T A^1 - q^T A^2 \leqq 0\}$$

Note that the set $G = \{(S, -z) \,|\, (S, z) \in T\}$ has no point in common with the positive orthant of R^{n+r}, denoted by R_+^{n+r}, except for the origin, that is

$$G \cap R_+^{n+r} \subset \{0\}$$

As G is convex there exists a vector $(p, q) \geqq 0$ such that

$$p^T S - q^T z \leqq 0$$

for all $(S, z) \in T$ [7]. But this implies that

$$p^T A^1 - q^T A^2 \leqq 0$$

The set A^* is thus nonvoid, and contains points other than the origin. Then if $(p, q) \in A^*$, a profit maximum exists. It is clear from this that the maximum profit cannot be positive. Because of the possibility of inaction, the maximum profit cannot be negative (if a process yields a negative profit, then that process will not be used). We can therefore state the following two conditions for profit maximum

$$p^T A^1 - q^T A^2 \leq 0 \qquad \text{or} \qquad (p, q) \in A^* \tag{2}$$

$$(p^T A^1 - q^T A^2)x = 0 \tag{3}$$

where (2) states that no process can have a positive profit, and (3) states that only processes yielding zero profits will be used.

The profit maximum conditions define supply correspondences, that is, set-valued mappings, defined on A^*. Given $(p, q) \in A^*$, there is a set $\bar{X}(p, q)$ in R_+^N, the positive orthant of R^N, such that all vectors in $\bar{X}(p, q)$ yield maximum profit if the prices are (p, q). Such a set-valued mapping is usually called a correspondence [8]. From the correspondence $\bar{X}(p, q)$ we can define two other correspondences

$$\bar{S}(p, q) = \{S \mid S = A^1 x, \; x \in \bar{X}(p, q)\}$$

$$\bar{z}(p, z) = \{z \mid z = A^2 x, \; x \in \bar{X}(p, q)\}$$

that is, $\bar{S}(p, q)$ is the set of all vectors of net supply of regular goods that are consistent with profit maximization when the prices are (p, q), and $\bar{z}(p, q)$ is the set of all vectors of net supply of residuals that are consistent with profit maximization when the prices are (p, q). However, we will not have any use for these correspondences in the following discussion.

It is now possible to give a more rigorous definition of a residual. A residual is a good that has a "negative" price in the sense that producers and consumers have to pay for the disposal of this good, and must be induced by payment to take care of this good. It is now also obvious that the classification of goods into residuals and regular goods depends on the nature of demand. If, for example, a certain process uses as input a good that is classified as a residual, and if the demand for the outputs of this process increases, then it may happen that the demand for the residual increases to such an extent that the producers are willing to pay a positive price for the possession of this good. The increase in demand has thus changed the classification of goods. It may therefore happen that some of the goods corresponding to components in z may not be residuals but ordinary intermediary products. It is, however, easier to deal with the case when there is an a priori classification of all goods into "regular" goods and residuals, and therefore we will maintain the idea of an a priori distinction between "regular" goods and residuals (but in section 8 we will discard this distinction).

Some of the processes are especially interesting, particularly those for treating wastes. In these processes residuals generated in consumption or in other production processes are used as inputs. These inputs, by the use of energy and other "regular" goods, are transformed into other kinds of residuals, which then are disposed of in one way or another. The revenues associated with the waste treatment process come from the payments made for delivering residuals to this process. The costs arise partly from the use of "regular" goods as inputs, and partly from the cost of disposal of the residuals generated. For a waste treatment process to be profitable (that is, yielding zero profit) the prices of the residuals used as inputs must be higher than the prices of the residuals that are generated. By using such a price differential, the waste treatment process may earn an excess that covers the outlays for inputs in the form of regular goods. In order to make sense, the prices on residuals must in some way reflect the damage to the environment they can cause. Residuals which are more harmful to the environment should thus be priced higher than residuals that are less harmful.

One important point in this connection is that these waste treatment processes do not change the amount of materials involved. The amount of inputs, measured in tons, must be equal to the amount of outputs. This point is valid for every process, not only waste treatment processes. In every process, inputs in the form of physical matter will emerge with approximately the same mass (if we neglect nuclear processes) in the form of outputs of regular goods and residuals. The empirical relevance of this observation is that the sum of masses of all items appearing in a process must be equal to zero. This is the materials balance for the production box in figure 1 in chapter 1.

3. THE ENVIRONMENTAL MANAGEMENT AGENCY

When discussing private goods, it is usually assumed that there is a finite number of well-defined goods, the amount of which can be measured in an objective way. When it comes to a discussion of the quality of the environment, things are not so simple. It is, for example, not generally possible to attach a number to a scenic view and interpret this number as a measure of the quality of that view. What number should be attached to the Grand Canyon of the Colorado? The Grand Canyon consists of an infinite number of details, and it is the composition of these details that makes this canyon so overwhelmingly beautiful. This remark leads to the idea that each detail or point in the Grand Canyon can be represented by a vector S, the components of which describe the quality of that point—color, materials, chemical and physical composition, and so on. To each point in the Grand Canyon we can thus assign a vector S which describes the characteristics of that point and it is the aggregate of all these vectors S that constitutes the particular quality of the Grand Canyon. But this collection of vectors is nothing but a mapping defined on all points in and around the Grand Canyon and with values that describe the quality of each point. The formal definition of environmental quality based on this idea would thus go like this:

Let (x_1, x_2, x_3) be the coordinates of a point in the environment and let t be the chronological time. Let E be a subset of R^3 and let F be some set. The quality over time of the region E in the environment is then defined as a mapping defined on $E \times R$ and with values in F:

$$f : E \times R \ni (x_1, x_2, x_3, t) \to f(x_1, x_2, x_3, t) \in F$$

The environmental quality is thus described as a function, and the set of all possible states of the environment will lead to a study of subsets in a function space, that is, an infinite dimensional space. This is a logical approach to a definition of environmental quality, but it is not an operationally meaningful way of defining environmental quality. It is possible, however, to approximate the f functions by step functions, which are constant over cubes of finite size. These step functions can be represented by finite dimensional vectors, and that is the approach that will be followed throughout this book. We thus assume that there exists a vector $Y \in R^m$, the components of which describe the quality or the state of the environment in any particular region (which can be taken to be the whole planet). One component in Y may measure the oxygen dissolved in a river at a particular location, another component may measure the oxygen dissolved at another location, a third the concentration of sulfur dioxide in the center of a particular city.

This vector Y will alternatively be referred to as the vector of environmental quality, the vector of the state of the environment, or the vector of environmental services.

The vector Y will be thought of as a vector of pure public goods in Samuelson's sense [9], that is, it is assumed that all consumers have preferences over the vector Y. If Y_j is the amount of trash in Mr. Smith's backyard, Mr. Jones, who lives on the other side of the city, will in general be indifferent to changes in Y_j. In spite of this, it is convenient to let Y_j be in the set over which Mr. Jones's preferences are defined.

It is assumed that the supply of environmental services is controlled by a special agency, the environmental management agency. The vector Y is thus determined by this agency. In fact, it is assumed that the agency determines the amount of trash in Mr. Smith's backyard, but it does this in a way that corresponds to Mr. Smith's preferences. If Mr. Smith is the only person who cares about the amount of trash in his backyard, then the policy of the agency is to let exactly that amount of trash be dumped on the yard that Mr. Smith voluntarily would have dumped if permitted. If other persons also care about the backyard, then the optimal policy will differ from Mr. Smith's voluntary actions.

The environmental management agency's ability to act in this way depends on the assumption that the agency knows of some method that can be used to reveal the consumers' preferences for environmental services. This assumption, however, is far from realistic. In fact, we do not know of any satisfactory method of revealing consumer preferences for public goods. But the assumption permits the construction of a logical structure, which can be used in analyzing practical and theoretical problems of importance. Although the assumption is not real, the conclusions that it allows may have great significance for practical problems, and this is the standard defense for assumptions that are felt to be unrealistic.

To be more specific about the agency's actions, we have to introduce an environmental interaction function which shows the factors that affect the environmental services. This function will be written

$$Y = Y_o - F^1 z + F^2 e \tag{4}$$

where z is the vector of the total waste load of residuals discharged into the environment, e is a vector of regular goods and services that are used by the agency for treatment of the environment. Such treatment [10] can include different kinds of reaeration of a water body, construction of dams for low-flow augmentation, or cleaning up grounds (a more fanciful idea is the construction of a gigantic fan to increase the ventilation in the Los Angeles area). It is assumed that z and e have all their components nonnegative, that F^1 is a nonnegative matrix, and that F^2 also is a nonnegative matrix.

The agency charges the producers and the consumers with the price vector q when they discharge wastes into the environment. The agency is also assumed to sell environmental quality to the consumers, but at a different charge to each consumer, so that each consumer demands at most the environmental services actually supplied. If a consumer demands less of a certain service than is supplied, the corresponding price is zero. Let there be H consumers in the economy. The price vector on environmental services that are used in charging consumer h is denoted δ^h. This consumer has thus to pay the agency $\delta^{h^T}Y$ (remember that if the amount of a service, say j, demanded by consumer h is less than Y_j, then $\delta_j^h = 0$).

In the next section it will be assumed that the consumers are price takers and as they cannot independently change the supply of environmental services, $\delta^{h^T}Y$ is in fact a lump sum transfer from consumer h to the agency. The total revenue for the management agency is thus

$$q^T z + \sum_{h=1}^{H} \delta^{h^T} Y$$

and its cost is $p^T e$. The net revenue is thus

$$I = q^T z + \sum_{h=1}^{H} \delta^{h^T} Y - p^T e \tag{5}$$

Let δ denote the total demand price for environmental services, that is

$$\delta = \sum_{h=1}^{H} \delta^h \tag{6}$$

Then the net revenue can be written

$$I = q^T z + \delta^T Y - p^T e \tag{7}$$

In general $\delta \geqq 0$, but it may happen that some component is negative. If we look at the eutrophication of a lake, many people will think that this is a bad thing, and would be willing to pay in order to stop the process. Others may be quite indifferent. But there may be a group that considers eutrophication beneficial, at least in its initial stage, because the growth of nutrients will increase the fish population and thereby increase the joy of sport fishing. This last group will therefore pay to increase the growth of nutrients, and if these payments exceed the payments that are needed for compensating those who are harmed by the eutrophication, the corresponding component in δ will be negative. We will, however, assume that $\delta^h \geqq 0$, $h = 1, \cdots, H$.

Although it is the agency that determines the prices on residuals and on environmental services, we assume that when it has determined the prices it will operate as a price taker and follow a policy that maximizes its net revenue. This corresponds to the case of a public utility charging marginal cost prices.

The agency thus maximizes $I = q^T z + \delta^T Y - p^T e$ subject to the conditions

$$Y = Y_o - F^1 z + F^2 e$$
$$z \geqq 0 \qquad e \geqq 0$$

Exactly as in the case of the producers, a maximum may not exist for all prices (p, q, δ). If we restrict (p, q, δ) to a subset F^* defined by

$$F^* = \{(p, q, \delta) \,|\, \delta^T F^1 \geqq q^T; \, p^T \geqq \delta^T F^2\} \tag{8}$$

a maximum exists. F^* is certainly nonvoid, because it contains $(0, 0, 0)$. Moreover, it can easily be shown that F^* contains other elements than the origin. From now on through this section it is assumed that $(p, q, \delta) \in F^*$.

It is easily seen that at maximum, the following conditions must hold

$$(\delta^T F^1 - q^T)z = 0 \tag{9}$$

$$(\delta^T F^2 - p^T)e = 0 \tag{10}$$

Condition (9) may be interpreted as saying that as long as dumping a residual in the environment decreases the net revenues, then no dumping of that residual should be permitted, and (10) says that if the use of a "regular" good in the treatment of the environment makes only a negative contribution to the net revenue, then this good shall not be used.

The maximum net revenue conditions define certain correspondences on F^*. First we have the supply correspondence of environmental services $\hat{Y}(p, q, \delta)$ which is the set of all vectors that maximizes I when prices are (p, q, δ). Second we have the residual demand correspondence $\hat{z}$ (p, q, δ) which is the set of all vectors z that maximizes I at the same prices. Finally, we have the treatment demand correspondence $\hat{e}(p, z, \delta)$ with a similar interpretation.

If we restrict these correspondences to a compact subset of F^*, it can be shown that the correspondences are closed on this subset [11]. Moreover, it is possible to show that the maximum net revenue $\hat{I}$ is a continuous function of (p, q, δ) [12]. Finally, it is easily seen that the correspondences have convex image sets. The net revenue of the agency is distributed by lump sum transfers to the consumers (again an assumption that is a violation of reality, but as it allows us to study an optimal organization, it will shed light on practical questions).

It can be assumed that each consumer has a share β^h in the agency such that the transfer to consumer h is

$$I^h = \beta^h I \qquad \sum_{h=1}^{H} \beta^h = 1 \qquad \beta^h \geqq 0 \tag{11}$$

Since the consumer payment for the supply of environmental services is a lump sum transfer, we can offset this payment against the consumer's share in the agency's net revenue. It is, however, more convenient to keep these two lump sum transfers separate.

4. CONSUMERS

There are H consumers in the economy. These consumers own the natural resources and the environment, in the sense that the net revenue of the environmental agency is distributed among them. They derive satisfaction by purchasing consumption goods and services and through the supply of environmental services. Their satisfaction from consumption goods and services is not a direct one, however. We will assume that satisfaction is derived from different consumption processes, such as reading a book, eating a good dinner, watching a television show, and so on [13]. The important thing here is that it is not the television show, or the food, or the book, but watching, eating, or reading that gives satisfaction. The book, the food, and the television set are only inputs in these processes. We therefore assume that there is a (finite) number Q of different consumption processes. Each process is characterized by the inputs of consumption goods and services necessary, by the input of time, and by the amounts of different residuals that are generated from the process. Time has entered as one input because eating a dinner, reading a book, or watching a television show require time, and time thus becomes a scarce factor and will have an opportunity cost [14].

We can now formalize these ideas. Let $c \in R^Q$ be Q-vector, let B be a matrix of the order $n \times Q$, D a nonnegative matrix of the order $r \times Q$, and let V be a row vector of dimension Q. The jth column in B and in D, together with the jth component of V, defines a consumption process. The elements in B^j, the jth column in B, are interpreted as the necessary inputs of goods and services for the jth process when it is operated at unit level. The elements in D^j, the jth column in D, are interpreted as the amounts of the different residuals generated by operating the jth consumption process at unit level; and finally the jth component in V, v_j, is interpreted as the time required for operating the jth process at unit level. If the jth process is watching television, then some of the elements in B^j give the energy requirement for the television set, and v_j is the time it takes to watch television one unit. As units we can take hours, so that v_j is equal to one.

We further assume that we can operate these processes at any level, that is, if (B^j, v_j, D^j) is a feasible process, then $(c_j B^j, c_j v_j; c_j D^j) c_j \geqq 0$ is also a feasible process. Moreover, it is possible to operate more than one process during the time period the model ; constructed for, and we assume that (Bc, Vc, Dc) is also a feasible process, such that Bc is the total input of goods, Vc the total input of time, and Dc the total amount of residuals generated during the period. Some processes may correspond to supply of resources. If j is such a process, then $c_j^h \leqq 0$ and $v_j < 0$, reflecting the time worked for others. For this process a natural unit is an hour, the time of work. This assumption does, however, imply that it is impossible to operate two processes simultaneously, for example, watching a television show and drinking coffee. We can, however, define more processes; from the television viewing process and from the coffee drinking process we can define a process called the television viewing and coffee drinking process, which has the same time requirement that the television viewing process has, but is more expensive because of the necessary coffee input. We assume that all such extensions of consumption processes have already been made, and that we still end up with a finite number Q of basic processes.

The balance of materials flow corresponds to the empirically relevant fact that the sum of the weights of all items appearing in a column in the B matrix must equal the sum of the weights of all items appearing in the corresponding column in the D matrix.

The consumers are assumed to have preferences on the vector c^h and the supply of environmental services Y. It would have been possible to introduce the supply of environmental services as inputs in the consumption processes. For example, one process can be sport fishing and one input in this process would then be the quality of the stream, which is used for sport fishing purposes. This approach has not been chosen, however, because it seems more natural, in view of the fact that environmental services are public goods, to let the quality of the stream affect the satisfaction derived from sport fishing.

We now assume that each consumer h is equipped with a consumption set E^h, which is a subset of R^{Q+m}. This set shows the consumption possibilities open to the consumer if we look only at the physiological and biological restrictions on the consumer's supply of services and consumption of private and public goods. We will make the following assumptions concerning E^h:

(i) E^h is convex for each h
(ii) E^h is closed for each h

The first assumption means that any convex combination of possible consumption bundles is also a possible consumption bundle. The second assumption has no economic interpretation, but simplifies the mathematics very much. Not all points in E^h are feasible, however, owing to the limited amount of time every consumer has. Assume the period under consideration has t hours' duration. Then for every consumer, we have the restriction

$$Vc^h \leqq t \tag{12}$$

We now make the assumption that all processes are time consuming. This means that for every $(c^h, Y) \in E^h$,

$$v_i c_i > 0 \text{ if } c_i \neq 0, i = 1, 2 \qquad i = 1, 2, \cdots, Q \tag{13}$$

that is, if process i is a supply activity, then $c_i^h < 0$ and $v_i < 0$.

Denote the set of all c satisfying (12) and (13) by E_c^h. This set is obviously compact. The intersection of the Cartesian product $E_c^h \times R^m$ of E_c^h with the space representing environmental services, with E^h, will be denoted by $\bar{E}^h$. $\bar{E}^h$ is obviously convex and closed, and the intersection of $\bar{E}^h$ and any linear variety obtained by translating R^Q (as a subspace of R^{Q+m}) will be compact (or empty).

The consumers are assumed to have preferences over the set E^h. These preferences are assumed to be represented by continuous utility functions $u^h(c^h, Y)$ defined on E^h and with the following properties [15]:

(iii)   If $c^{h*} \geq c^h$, and if $(c^{h*}, Y) \in E^h$, $(c^h, Y) \in E^h$, then $u^h(c^{h*}, Y) > u^h(c^h, Y)$
(iv)   For each point $(c^h, Y) \in E^h$, there exists at least one point $(c^{h*}, Y^*) \in E^h$, such that $u^h(c^{h*}, Y^*) > u^h(c^h, Y^*)$
(v) u^h is quasi-concave in all its arguments

The first assumption implies that more of each private consumption process is not undesirable. The second assumption implies that the consumers are never satiated. The third assumption is a mathematical formulation of indifference curves convex toward the origin.

Next we make the customary assumption that consumer behavior can be represented by demand and supply functions that are derived from utility maximization. The prices consumer h is faced with are the price vector p on "regular" goods, q on residuals, and δ^h on environmental qualities (note that δ^h will in general be different for different consumers). Let r^h be the vector of resources owned by consumer h and let I^h be his lump sum income. Besides any lump sum transfers among consumers, the only source for the lump sum income is the net revenue of the environmental management agency, because profits are zero, as we saw in the section on producers. The budget set for consumer h is given by

$$M^h = \{(c^h, Y) \mid (c^h, Y) \in \bar{E}^h, \, p^T B c^h + q^T D c^h + \delta^{h^T} Y \leqq I^h + p^T r^h\} \tag{14}$$

It can be shown, however, that the equilibrium prices and quantities will belong to a compact set [16], and therefore we may assume for the present that M^h is compact. (We already know that the intersection of M^h with the linear variety obtained by translating R^Q with the vector Y is compact. The only thing that can create difficulties is thus the flow of environmental services.) As M^h is compact, u^h has a maximum on M^h. The point in M^h that maximizes u^h does not need to be unique. If the preferences can be characterized by strong convexity, that is, if $u^h(c^{h'}, Y') = u^h(c^{h''}, Y'')$ and $(c^{h'}, Y') \neq (c^{h''}, Y'')$ imply $u^h[tc^{h'} + (1 - t)c^{h''}, tY' + (1 - t)Y''] > u^h(c^{h'}, Y')$ for $0 < t < 1$, then the maximizing point will be unique [17]. The set of points maximizing u^h depends on the prices and the lump sum income (p, q, δ^h, I^h), and this dependence establishes a demand correspondence from the set of (p, q, δ^h, I^h) such that M^h is not empty to $\bar{E}^h$. This correspondence will be denoted by

$$\begin{aligned} &\bar{c}^h(p, q, \delta^h, I^h) \\ &\bar{Y}^h(\mathrm{p, q}, \delta^h, I^h) \end{aligned} \tag{15}$$

As the budget set is invariant, if (p, q, δ^h, I^h) is replaced by $(kp, kq, k\delta^h, kI^h)$ where $k > 0$, the demand correspondence will also be invariant for such a multiplication of all the arguments with a positive number. The source of the lump sum transfer is the net revenue of the environmental management agency. The total net revenue is $\hat{I}(p, q, \delta)$ and I^h is (from equation 11) $I^h = \beta^h \hat{I}(p, q, \delta)$. $\hat{I}$ is positively homogeneous of degree 1 in $p, q,$ and δ. If we substitute this expression for I^h in (15) we get

$$\begin{aligned} &c^h \in \tilde{c}^h(p, q, \delta^1, \cdots, \delta^H) \\ &Y^h \in \tilde{Y}^h(p, q, \delta^1, \cdots, \delta^H) \end{aligned} \tag{16}$$

as new expressions for the demand correspondences. As I is positively linearly homogeneous in (p, q, δ), it follows that $\tilde{c}^h$ and $\tilde{Y}^h$ are invariant for a multiplication of all arguments with the same positive number.

However, (16) establishes only demand correspondences for consumption processes and the flow of environmental services. Sometimes demand correspondences for goods and residuals will be needed. These are easily derived from (16) by using the matrices B and D:

$$C^h \in \bar{C}^h(p,\, q,\, \delta^1,\, \cdots,\, \delta^H)$$
$$= \{C^h \,|\, c^h \in \bar{c}^h(p,\, q,\, \delta^1,\, \cdots,\, \delta^H),\, C^h = Bc^h\} \tag{17}$$

Similarly, the supply correspondence for residuals may be derived

$$z^h \in \bar{z}^h(p,\, q,\, \delta^1,\, \cdots,\, \delta^H)$$
$$= \{z^h \,|\, c^h \in \bar{c}^h(p,\, q,\, \delta^1,\, \cdots,\, \delta^H),\, z^h = Dc^h\} \tag{18}$$

The aggregate demand correspondences for goods and services and the aggregate supply correspondence for residuals are

$$C = \sum_{h=1}^{H} C^h(p,\, q,\, \delta^1,\, \cdots,\, \delta^H) \tag{19}$$

$$z = \sum_{h=1}^{H} z^h(p,\, q,\, \delta^1,\, \cdots,\, \delta^H) \tag{20}$$

The problem of consumer choice has been formulated here as the problem of choosing those elements in the budget set that maximize the utility function. Sometimes it is more convenient to work with a different formulation. In this different formulation, one starts with a given utility level and asks what lump sum income is necessary to sustain that utility level. This approach will be used in the proofs that will be given in this chapter, and also in later chapters.

From now on, we assume that the preferences are convex, that is, if $u^h(c^{h'},\, Y') > u^h(c^{h''},\, Y'')$ then with $1 > t > 0$,

$$u^h[tc^{h'} + (1-t)c^{h''},\, tY' + (1-t)Y''] > u^h(c^{h''},\, Y'') \tag{21}$$

Assume that $(c^{h*},\, Y^*)$ maximizes u^h on M^h. This implies that if

$$u^h(c^h,\, Y) > u^h(c^{h*},\, Y^*), \text{ and } (c^h,\, Y) \in \bar{E}^h, \text{ then}$$
$$(p^T B + q^T D)c^h + \delta^{h^T} Y > (p^T B + q^T D)c^{h*} + \delta^{h^T} Y^*$$

because otherwise $(c^h,\, Y)$ would be an element in the budget set and better than the element that maximizes u^h, which is a contradiction. On the other hand, let $(c^{h*},\, Y^*)$ be a point in $\bar{E}^h$ and consider the assumption that $u^h(c^h,\, Y) > u^h(c^{h*},\, Y^*)$ implies

$$(p^T B + q^T D)c^h + \delta^{h^T} Y > (p^T B + q^T D)c^{h*} + \delta^{h^T} Y^*$$

This assumption means that (c^{h*}, Y^*) minimizes the expenditures that are necessary to sustain at least the utility level $\bar{u}^h = u^h(c^{h*}, Y^*)$. If

$$(p^T B + q^T D)c^{h*} + \delta^{h^T} Y^* = p^T r^h + I^h$$

then it can be shown that the utility maximizing point also is a cost minimizing point and vice versa [18]. The expenditure necessary to sustain the utility level $\bar{u}^h$ is obviously a function of prices:

$$m = m^h(p, q, \delta^h, \bar{u}^h)$$

This function will be called the expenditure function [19], and its interpretation is quite clear: the expenditure function gives the least income necessary to sustain a given utility level at different prices.

In later chapters the demand for environmental services will in general be formulated as the amount the consumers are willing to pay to obtain an increase of this flow, and not as a demand function or a demand correspondence. Therefore, the definition of the expenditure function will be altered. The new definition goes as follows: Given the price (p, q) and the flow of environmental services Y, what is the least expenditure (or lump sum income) that can sustain a given utility level? This is equivalent to finding the minimum of

$$\{\gamma \,|\, \gamma \geqq (p^T B + q^T D)c^h, \ (c^h, Y) \in \bar{E}^h, \ u^h(c^h, Y) \geqq \bar{u}^h\}$$

The minimum will obviously be a function of (p, q), Y, and $\bar{u}^h$:

$$m = m^h(p, q, Y, \bar{u}^h)$$

This is the definition of the expenditure function that will be used in later chapters.

Before we leave this section, another concept will be introduced, namely, that of indirect utility function [20]. The indirect utility function v^h is defined by

$$u^h[c^h(p, q, \delta^h, I^h), Y^h(p, q, \delta^h, I^h)] = v^h(p, q, \delta^h, I^h)$$

when we are studying demand correspondences for environmental services, and by

$$u^h[c^h(p, q, I^h, Y), Y] = v^h(p, q, I^h, Y)$$

when we are studying cases where the demand for environmental quality is expressed as willingness to pay. In both cases, the indirect utility function will be well defined on the same set as the demand correspondences.

5. EQUILIBRIUM

In most general equilibrium models, market equilibrium conditions require that the supply for every good or service not be exceeded by the demand; that is, $S \geqq D$ where S is the supply vector and D the demand vector. A strong inequality in some component would then imply that the corresponding price is zero. This condition implies, however, that there is no cost associated with the disposal of the excess supply. This raises the question of whether one should use this notion of market equilibrium in a model in which the disposal cost is a main feature. Should one not use $S = D$ as the notion of market equilibrium instead? If we consider the problem more closely, it is evident that $S_i > D_i$ can hold in equilibrium only if there is no cost associated with the production of the ith good, because if there were, then $S_i = 0$ and there is no disposal cost. The only cases where $S_i > D_i$ implies a disposal cost are thus where good i is jointly produced with one or more other goods with positive prices. If the good i is not demanded at all by the consumer, then it is already listed among the residuals, and $S_i > D_i$ means that the environmental management agency is prepared to allow more dumping of the ith good at zero price than the consumers actually are discharging. The inequality formulation is thus reasonable in this case. But when consumers demand a positive amount of the good at zero price, but not enough to exhaust the supply, it is readily seen that the cost of disposing of this excess supply is not included in the model. Therefore, the inequality formulation of the market equilibrium conditions should be abandoned and equality between supply and demand required. But this raises some complicated mathematical problems because it is much easier to show the existence of an equilibrium with market equilibrium conditions in inequality form. Therefore we will state the market equilibrium conditions such that they require a nonnegative excess supply. One can perhaps justify such an approach by arguing that those goods not listed as residuals and having a positive excess supply are not harmful to the environment (mostly because of the small amounts) and so the disposal cost can be neglected. Moreover, in most empirical problems there is a well-defined class of residuals that is harmful to the environment, and for such problems the chosen approach may be suited.

Admittedly, this is not a logical approach and therefore, in section 8, an alternative model will be sketched in a very brief way which circumvenes these difficulties, and incidentally gives a more rigorous definition of residuals.

Let us now define an equilibrium: Given an economy characterized by the technology matrix A, the environmental interaction function $Y = Y_o - F^1z + F^2e$, the consumption sets $\bar{E}^h$, the utility functions u^h defined on $\bar{E}^h$, the initial resources r^h, $h = 1, \cdots, H$ and the shares β^h. An equilibrium for this economy is a $(6 + 3H)$-tuple

$$(x, z, e, Y, Y^1, \cdots, Y^H, c^1, \cdots, c^H, p, q, \delta^1, \cdots, \delta^H)$$

such that (i) $x \geq 0$ and x maximizes the profit of the producers when the prices are (p, q). (ii) $z \geq 0$, $e \geq 0$ and z and e maximize the net revenue of the environmental management agency when the prices are $(p, q, \delta^1, \cdots, \delta^H)$. (iii) $(c^h, Y^h) \in \bar{E}^h$ and maximizes u^h on the budget set for consumer h determined by the prices (p, q, δ^h) and the share β^h.

(iv) $A^1x + r^h \geq \sum_{h=1}^{H} Bc^h + e$

$$\sum_{h=1}^{H} Dc^h + A^2x \leq z$$

$$Y^h \leq Y \qquad h = 1, \cdots, H$$

with the corresponding price zero when strong inequality holds.

In order to prove that an equilibrium exists, we shall rewrite the model so that it becomes formally identical to the Arrow–Debreu model, and then apply their theorem on the existence of an equilibrium.

First, we will introduce the aggregate technology set X, which can be interpreted as giving the net supply of all goods and services, including residuals and environmental quality. In order to define X, it is convenient to regard Y_o as a resource which will be added to the produced quality $-F^1z + F^2e$. We can now define X by

$$X = \{(S, z^c, y^1, \cdots, y^H) \mid \text{ there exist } x \geq 0, e \geq 0, z \geq 0, \qquad (22)$$

such that $S = A^1x - e$, $z_p = A^2x$, $z^c = z - z_p \geq 0$, $y^h \leq y$

$$h = 1, \cdots, H; y = -F^1z + F^2e\}$$

It is clear that X is closed. Moreover, the origin belongs to X. We will now show that X is convex.

Assume that $(S, z^c, y^1, \cdots, y^H)$ and $(\bar{S}, \bar{z}^c, \bar{y}^1, \cdots, \bar{y}^H)$ are both in X. Let $1 \geqq t \geqq 0$

$$
\begin{aligned}
tS + (1 - t)\bar{S} &= A^1 tx + A^1(1 - t)\bar{x} - te - (1 - t)\bar{e} \\
&= A^1[tx + (1 - t)\bar{x}] - [te + (1 - t)\bar{e}] \\
tz^c + (1 - t)\bar{z}^c &= tz - tzp + (1 - t)\bar{z} - (1 - t)\bar{z}p \\
&= tz + (1 - t)\bar{z} - A^2[tx + (1 - t)\bar{x}] \\
ty^h + (1 - t)\bar{y}^h &= ty + (1 - t)\bar{y} \\
&= -F^1[tz + (1 - t)\bar{z}] + F^2[te + (1 - t)\bar{e}]
\end{aligned}
$$

and as x, $\bar{x}$, e, $\bar{e}$, z^c, and $\bar{z}^c$ are all nonnegative vectors, any convex combination must also be nonnegative. X must therefore be convex. Finally, it is clear that the intersection between X and the positive orthant of R^{n+r+mH} contains only the origin.

The vector S can be interpreted as the net supply of all regular goods, the vector z^c as the supply of waste disposal services, and Y^h as the supply of environmental qualities to consumer h.

Next we will redefine the consumption sets of the consumers by first transforming them into sets of consumption bundles instead of process levels, and then extending them to include the demand for waste disposal services and the demand for environmental qualities from other consumers as well.

Define $\tilde{E}^h$ by

$$
\begin{aligned}
\tilde{E}^h = \{ (C^h, z^h, G^1, \cdots, Y^h, \cdots, G^H) \,|\, (c^h, Y^h) \in \bar{E}^h, \\
C^h = Bc^h, z^h = Dc^h, G^j \in R^m, j \neq h \}
\end{aligned}
\tag{23}
$$

as $\bar{E}^h$ is closed and convex, $\tilde{E}^h$ is also closed and convex.

We can extend u^h from $\bar{E}^h$ to $\tilde{E}^h$ in the obvious way:

$$
\bar{u}^h(C^h, z^h, G^1, \cdots, Y^h, \cdots, G^H) = u^h(c^h, Y^h)
\tag{24}
$$

The initial endowment of resources belonging to consumer h can be written

$$
w^h = (r^h, 0, \cdots, Y_o, \cdots, 0)
\tag{25}
$$

We can now identify our model with the Arrow–Debreu model as it is described by Nikaido [21]. The only thing that needs to be done is to add those further assumptions given for that model in order to establish the existence of an equilibrium. In doing this, a systematic list of all assumptions, new or previously made, will be given. As the starting point, we will take theorem 16.3 in Nikaido [22].

(i) $\bar{E}^h$ is a closed convex set in R^{Q+m}, for each consumer h. We have already seen that this implies that $\tilde{E}^h$ is closed and convex.

(ii) Each E^h has a lower bound (α^h, β^h) which satisfies
$c^h \geqq \alpha^h, Y^h \geqq \beta^h$, for all $(c^h, Y^h) \in \bar{E}^h$
This assumption implies that each $\tilde{E}^h$ also has a lower bound if we introduce artificial lower bounds on G^j.

(iii) Each u^h on $\bar{E}^h$ satisfies the convexity requirement (equation 21) and for each $(C^h, Y^h) \in \bar{E}^h$, there exists $(\bar{c}^h, \bar{Y}^h) \in \bar{E}^h$ such that $u^h(\bar{c}^h, \bar{Y}^h) > u^h(c^h, Y^h)$. If u^h on $\bar{E}^h$ satisfies these assumptions, then the extended utility function $\tilde{u}^h$ on $\tilde{E}^h$ certainly will satisfy the same requirements.

(iv) Each u^h on $\bar{E}^h$ is continuous. Then $\tilde{u}^h$ on $\tilde{E}^h$ is also continuous.

(v) Each consumer has an initial endowment of resources r^h. This implies that each consumer has in the transformed model an initial holding given by equation (25).

(vi) The production technology set T is given by $T = \{Ax \mid x \geqq 0\}$.

(vii) The environmental interaction function is given by $Y = Y_o - F^1z + F^2e$. Together (vi) and (vii) determine the aggregate technology set X as defined in equation (22). X is convex, and satisfies the requirement that it has only the origin in common with the positive orthant of R^{n+s+mH}. Moreover, $X \cap (-X) = \{0\}$.

(viii) Each consumer h has an initial holding r^h such that there exists $(c^h, Y^h) \in \bar{E}^h$ with $C^h = Bc^h \leqq r^h$ with strong inequality for at least some goods or services. In the notations of the transformed model this assumption is equivalent to the existence of a vector f in $\tilde{E}^h$ such that $f < w^h$.

(ix) There exists an allocation such that there is a positive excess supply of all regular goods, all residuals, and all environmental services.

In other words, there exist $x \geqq 0$, $z > 0$, $e \geqq 0$, $(c^h, Y) \in \bar{E}^h$, $h = 1, \cdots, N$, such that

$$A^1x + r^h > \sum_{h=1}^{H} Ec^h + e$$

$$-A^2x + z > \sum_{h=1}^{H} Dc^h$$

$$Y_o = F^1z + F^2e > Y$$

In the notation of the transformed model, this assumption implies the existence of a vector $\eta \in X$, vectors $\zeta^h \in E^h$ such that

$$\eta + \sum_{h=1}^{H} w^h > \sum_{h=1}^{H} \zeta^h$$

Theorem: If (i)–(ix) hold, then there exists an equilibrium for the economy.

Because of the special structure of the production set in the model, it may be possible to weaken the conditions substantially. Debreu has given the following condition [23] that may be substituted for (viii):

$$(w^h + \text{Int } 0^+X) \cap E^h \neq \varnothing$$

where 0^+X denotes the recession cone [24] of X, and Int 0^+X denotes the interior of 0^+X. As X is a cone with vertex at the origin, $0^+X = X$ and the condition reduces to

$$(w^h + \text{Int } X) \cap E^h \neq \varnothing \qquad h = 1, 2, \cdots, H$$

which seems more plausible than (viii).

Some features of the equilibrium are worth a brief discussion. A more thorough discussion will be given later. First, the consumers are supposed to buy environmental services from the agency. However, as we already remarked, the payments for these purchases are lump sum transfers, because no single individual can affect the supply of environmental services.

Second, the lump sum income transfer to a consumer from the environmental management agency is not a fixed portion of the net revenue of the agency, but instead is equal to the value the consumer puts on the environmental services when there are no interventions in the environment in the form of waste discharges and environmental treatment. The total wealth of a consumer h is given by

$$p^T r^h + \delta^{h^T} Y_o$$

which can be seen from (25). This means that the net transfer from the agency to consumer h is

$$\delta^{h^T}(Y_o - Y)$$

and this payment may be interpreted as a compensation to the con-

sumer for the loss in environmental services due to the agency's operations.

But it is quite possible to introduce the idea of a fixed share β^h in the
agency's net revenue. Instead of defining the initial holdings as the vector w^h in (25), we can define the initial holdings as the vector

$$\tilde{w}^h = (r^h, 0, \beta^h Y_o, \cdots, \beta^h Y_o) \tag{26}$$

One can readily prove for oneself that nothing will change in the conditions (i) through (ix) by going from (25) to (26) as the definition of the
initial holding in the transformed model. With $\tilde{w}^h$ as the definition of the
initial holding, the total wealth of consumer h is

$$p^T r^h + \beta^h \sum_{h=1}^{H} \delta^{hT} Y_o \qquad \text{but} \qquad \sum_{h=1}^{H} \delta^{hT} Y_o$$

is the net revenue $\hat{I}$ of the agency, and so we see that the compensation
for the destruction of environmental quality is in no way intrinsic to the
model. The model will have an equilibrium, even if the net revenue of
the agency is distributed in some other way.

6. OPTIMUM

In this section and the next the relations between an equilibrium and an
optimum for the economy discussed in sections 1 through 5 will be discussed. It is possible to apply theorems already proved for the Arrow–
Debreu model in order to obtain results for these relations, but as the
proofs are very easy and shed further light on the nature of the mechanisms involved, they will be given.

Definition: An optimum is a feasible allocation, that is, an allocation
$(x^*, z^*, e^*, c^{1*}, \cdots, c^{H*}, Y^*)$ such that

$$r^h + A^1 x^* \geqq \sum_{h=1}^{H} B c^{h*} + e^*$$

$$z^* \geqq \sum_{h=1}^{H} D c^{h*} + A^2 x^*$$

$$Y^* \leqq Y_o - F^1 z^* + F^2 e^*$$

$$x^* \geqq 0, z^* \geqq 0, e^* \geqq 0, (c^{h*}, Y^*) \in \bar{E}^h \quad h = 1, \cdots, H$$

such that there is no other feasible allocation $(x, z, e, c^1, \cdots, c^h, Y)$
with $u^h(c^h, Y) \geqq u^h(c^{h*}, Y^*)$ for all $h = 1, \cdots, H$ and with

$$u^{h'}(c^{h'}, Y) > u^{h'}(c^{h'*}, Y^*) \text{ for at least one } h'$$

One can prove the following theorem:

Theorem: If all consumers are insatiated, that is, if to every point $(c^h, Y^h) \in \bar{E}^h$, there exists another point $(\bar{c}^h, \bar{Y}^h) \in \bar{E}^h$, which is preferred to (c^h, Y^h), then an equilibrium in the economy is an optimum.

Proof: Let $(x^*, z^*, e^*, c^{h*}, \cdots, c^{H*}, Y^*, p^*, q^*, \delta^{1*}, \cdots, \delta^{H*})$ be an equilibrium. Then it is clear that

$$p^{*T}S + q^{*T}z^c + \sum_{h=1}^{H} \delta^{h*}Y^h \tag{27}$$

is maximized on X (as defined in 22) at the equilibrium point (otherwise the profits of the producers and the net revenue of the environmental management agency would not be maximized in equilibrium).

Assume that the equilibrium is not an optimum. Then there is a feasible allocation $(x, z, e, c^1, \cdots, c^H, Y)$ such that

$$u^h(c^h, Y) \geqq u^h(c^{h*}, Y^*)$$

for all h and with strong inequality for at least one h. But this implies that (c^h, Y) cannot be in the budgets for all consumers, because (c^{h*}, Y^*) maximizes u^h on the budget set. We therefore have

$$(p^{*T}B + q^{*T}D)c^h + \delta^{h^{*T}}Y \geqq (p^{*T}B + q^{*T}D)c^{h*} + \delta^{h^{*T}}Y^*$$

for all h and with strong inequality for at least one h. Summing over all h and noting that

$$p^{*T}B \sum_{h=1}^{H} c^{h*} = p^{*T}S^*, \; q^{*T}D \sum_{h=1}^{H} c^{h*} = q^{*T}z^{c*}, \; \delta^* = \sum_{h=1}^{H} \delta^{h*}$$

yields

$$(p^{*T}B + q^{*T}D)\sum_{h=1}^{H} c^h + \delta^*Y > p^{*T}S^* + q^{*T}z^{c*} + \delta^*Y^*$$

But as c^h, $h = 1, \cdots, H$ is feasible, $S = B\sum_{h=1}^{H} c^h$, $z^c = D\sum_{h=1}^{H} c^h$

and $(S, z^c, Y, \cdots, Y)$ must belong to X. We thus have

$$p^{*T}S + q^{*T}z^c + \delta^{*T}Y > p^{*T}S^* + q^{*T}S^* + \delta^{*T}Y^*$$

in spite of the fact that (S^*, z^{c*}, Y^*) maximizes (26) on X. Therefore we have reached a contradiction, which shows that the equilibrium must be an optimum.

7. REPRESENTATION OF AN OPTIMUM

In the last section it was proved that an equilibrium is an optimum. In this section it will be proved that any optimum may be represented as an equilibrium, or more precisely:

Theorem: If $(\bar{x}, \bar{z}, \bar{e}, \bar{c}^1, \cdots, \bar{c}^H, \bar{Y})$ is an optimum; if $\bar{E}^h$ is convex for each h; if u^h, for each h is continuous on $\bar{E}^h$, and satisfies (21); and if at least one consumer, say consumer h', is not satiated at $(\bar{c}^{h'}, \bar{Y})$, then there exists a price system $(p, q, \delta^1, \cdots, \delta^H)$ such that (i) $\bar{x}$ maximizes $p^T A^1 x - q^T A^2 x$, that is, the profits for the producers; (ii) $\bar{z}, \bar{e}$. and $\bar{Y}$ maximize $q^T z + \delta^T Y - p^T e$, where $\delta = \Sigma \delta^h$, that is, the net revenue for the environmental management agency; (iii) $(\bar{c}^h, \bar{Y})$ minimizes

$$(p^T B + q^T D)c^h + \delta^{h^T} Y^h$$

for all $(c^h, Y^h) \in \bar{E}^h$, such that $u^h(c^h, Y^h) \geqq u^h(\bar{c}^h, \bar{Y})$, $h = 1, \cdots, H$, that is, it minimizes the expenditure necessary to achieve the utility level $u^h(\bar{c}^h, \bar{Y})$.

Proof: Define X as in (22), that is

$$X = \{(S, z^c, y^1, \cdots, y^H) \,|\, \text{there exist } x \geqq 0, e \geqq 0,$$

$$S = A^1 x - e, z^c = z - A^2 x, y^h \leqq y = -F^1 z + F^2 e\}$$

Define G' by

$$G' = \{(\Sigma C^h, \Sigma z^h, Y^1, \cdots, Y^H) \,|\, \text{there exist } (c^h, Y^h) \in \bar{E}^h,$$

$$C^h = Bc^h, z^h = Dc^h, u^h(c^h, Y^h) \geqq u^h(\bar{c}^h, \bar{Y}), h = 1, \cdots, H,$$

$$u^{h'}(c^{h'}, Y^{h'}) > u^{h'}(\bar{c}^{h'}, \bar{Y})\}$$

and w by $w = (\Sigma r^h, 0, Y_o, \cdots, Y_o)$.

Furthermore, define G exactly as G' is defined, except that the condition $u^{h'}(c^{h'}, Y^{h'}) > u^{h'}(\bar{c}^{h'}, \bar{Y})$ is disregarded. It is clear that the closure of G', $C\ell G'$, contains G:

$$G \subset C\ell G' \tag{28}$$

Now define H' by $H' = X + w - G'$ and H by $H = X + w - G$. Because of (28) it is clear that

$$H \subset C\ell H' \tag{29}$$

It has already been proved that X is convex; w is convex because it consists of only one element. Finally, G' and G are convex because of the condition (21); H' as a vector sum of three convex sets is thus also convex.

H' does not contain any positive vectors. If it did, then

$$\Sigma r^h + S - \Sigma C^h > 0$$

$$z^c - \Sigma z^h > 0$$

$$Y - Y^h > 0 \qquad h = 1, \cdots, H, \text{ for}$$

$$C^h = Bc^h, z^h = Dc^h, u^h(c^h, Y^h) \geqq u^h(\bar{c}^h, \bar{Y}),$$

$$u^{h'}(c^{h'}, Y^{h'}) > u^h(\bar{c}^{h'}, \bar{Y})$$

and it would be possible to increase consumer h's consumption of some good without letting anyone else be worse off, and as h' is not satiated, $\bar{c}^h$, $\bar{Y}$ could not have been an optimum.

Thus there exists a hyperplane through the origin [25] such that H' is below the hyperplane. H' then belongs to a closed half space determined by the hyperplane, and in view of (29) H must also belong to this closed half space, and be below the hyperplane. Moreover, it is known that the normal of this hyperplane $(p, q, \delta^1, \cdots, \delta^H)$ is semipositive, that is, it has all its components nonnegative, and at least one component is different from zero. We thus have

$$p^T(S + \Sigma r^h - \Sigma C^h) + q^T(z^c - \Sigma z^h) + \Sigma \delta^{h^T}(Y_o + y - Y^h) \leqq 0 \tag{30}$$

for all $(S + r^h - \Sigma C^h, z^c - \Sigma z^h, Y_o + y - Y^1, \cdots, Y_o + y - Y^H) \in H$

We can, however, rewrite (30) by using the structure of H, and as one result we have

$$(p^T A^1 - q^T A^2)x + (q^T - \delta^T F^1)z + (\delta^T F^2 - p^T)e$$
$$\leqq \Sigma[(p^T G + q^T D)c^h + \delta^{h^T}Y^h - p^T r^h - \delta^{h^T}Y_o] \tag{31}$$

for all $x \geqq 0$, $z \geqq 0$, $e \geqq 0$, $(c^h, Y^h) \in \bar{E}^h$, $u^h(c^h, Y^h) \geqq u^h(\bar{c}^h, \bar{Y})$, $h = 1, \cdots, H$.

We will now show that (31) holds as an equality when $x = \bar{x}, z = \bar{z}$, $e = \bar{e}, c^h = \bar{c}^h$, and $Y^h = \bar{Y}$ by establishing the reverse inequality. As $(p, q, \delta^1, \cdots, \delta^H) \geq 0$, and as the optimum is feasible, that is, the excess supply vectors are nonnegative, we must have

$$p^T(\bar{S} + \Sigma r^h - \Sigma \bar{C}^h) \geq 0 \qquad \text{or} \qquad p^T A^1 \bar{x} - p^T \bar{e} \geq \Sigma(p^T B c^h - p^T r^h)$$

$$q^T(\bar{z}^c - \Sigma \bar{z}^h) \geq 0 \qquad \text{or} \qquad q^T \bar{z} - q^T A^2 \bar{x} \geq \Sigma q^T D \bar{c}^h$$

$$\Sigma \delta^{h^T}(y_o + \bar{y} - \bar{Y}^h) \geq 0 \qquad \text{or} \qquad \delta^T F^1 \bar{z} + \delta^T F^2 \bar{z} \geq \Sigma(\delta^{h^T} \bar{Y}^h - \delta^{h^T} Y_o)$$

Adding these inequalities yields

$$(p^T A^1 - q^T A^2)\bar{x} + (q^T - \delta^T F^1)\bar{z} + (\delta^T F^2 - p^T)\bar{e}$$
$$\geq \Sigma[(p^T B + q^T D)\bar{c}^h + \delta^{h^T} \bar{Y} - p^T r^h - \delta^{h^T} Y_o] \tag{32}$$

Inequality (32) together with (31) yields the desired equality

$$(p^T A^1 - q^T A^2)\bar{x} + (q^T - \delta^T F^1)\bar{z} + (\delta^T F^2 - p^T)\bar{e}$$
$$= \Sigma[(p^T B + q^T D)\bar{c}^h + \delta^{h^T} \bar{Y} - p^T r^h - \delta^{h^T} Y_o] \tag{33}$$

Finally let us subtract (33) from (31)

$$(p^T A^1 - q^T A^2)x - (p^T A^1 - q^T A^2)\bar{x} + (q^T - \delta^T F)z$$
$$- (\delta^T F^2 - p^T)e + (\delta^T F^2 - p^T)\bar{e} \tag{34}$$
$$\leq \Sigma[(p^T B + q^T D)c^h - (p^T B + q^T D)\bar{c}^h + \delta^{h^T} Y^h - \delta^{h^T} \bar{Y}]$$

for all $x \geq 0, z \geq 0, e \geq 0, (c^h, Y^h) \in \bar{E}^h, u^h(c^h, Y^h) \geq u^h(\bar{c}^h, \bar{Y})$

$$h = 1, \cdots, H$$

The conclusions in the theorem follow at once from (34). First choose $z = \bar{z}, e = \bar{e}, c^h = \bar{c}^h, Y^h = \bar{Y}, h = 1, \cdots, H$. Then (34) reduces to

$$(p^T A^1 - q^T A^2)x \leq (p^T A^1 - q^T A^2)\bar{x} \qquad \text{for all } x \geq 0$$

which shows that $\bar{x}$ maximizes the profit.

Second, choose $x = \bar{x}, c^h = \bar{c}^h, Y^h = \bar{Y}^h, h = 1, \cdots, H$. Then (34) reduces to

$$(q^T - \delta^T F^1)z + (\delta^T F^2 - p^T)e \leq (q^T - \delta^T F^1)\bar{z} + (\delta^T F^2 - p^T)\bar{e}$$
for all $z \geq 0, e \geq 0$

which shows that $\bar{z}$, $\bar{e}$ maximizes the net revenue of the environmental management agency.

Finally, choose $x = \bar{x}$, $z = \bar{z}$, $e = \bar{e}$, $c^h = \bar{c}^h$, $h = 1, \cdots, H$, $h \neq h'$. Then (34) reduces to

$$(p^T B + q^T D)c^{h'} + \delta^{h'T} Y^{h'} \geqq (p^T B + q^T D)\bar{c}^{h'} + \delta^{h'T} Y$$

which shows that $(\bar{c}^{h'}, \bar{Y})$ minimizes the expenditures in the set

$$\{(c^{h'T}, Y^{h'}) \in \bar{E}^h \,|\, u^{h'}(c^{h'}, Y^{h'}) \geqq u^{h'}(\bar{c}^{h'}, \bar{Y})\}$$

and the proof is complete.

The expenditure for consumer h in equilibrium is equal to

$$(p^T B + q^T D)\bar{c}^h + \delta^{h^T} \bar{Y} = m^h$$

The total net revenue for the agency is $\hat{I} = \delta^T Y_o$. We assume that $\hat{I} \neq 0$.

If we add w^h over all h (the left-hand side in equation 33 is zero, and the right-hand side must thus also be zero) we find that

$$\Sigma m^h = \Sigma(p^T r^h + \delta^{h^T} Y_o) = \Sigma p^T r^h + \hat{I}$$

Define β^h (which is permitted because we have assumed that $\hat{I} \neq 0$) by

$$\beta^h = \frac{m^h - p^T r^h}{\hat{I}}$$

It is clear that $\Sigma \beta^h = 1$ and $m^h = \beta^h \hat{I} + p^T r^h$. The budget set for the consumer is then

$$M^h = \{(c^h, Y^h) \in \bar{E}^h \,|\, (p^T B + q^T D)c^h + \delta^{h^T} Y^h \leqq p^T r^h + \beta^h \hat{I}\}$$

and from the remarks at the end of section 4, it is clear that $(\bar{c}^h, \bar{Y})$ maximizes u^h on this set. If the distribution of resources r^h is given, it is thus possible to give each consumer a share β^h of the net revenue of the agency (provided the revenue is not zero), so that the optimum can be represented by an equilibrium.

8. AN ALTERNATIVE MODEL

We will in this section fulfill the promise given in earlier sections to present an alternative model which avoids some of the deficiencies connected with the previous model. We will now drop the distinction between "regular" goods and residuals. There are n different goods and services besides the environmental services, and if there is in equilibrium a positive excess supply of one of these goods and services, this excess supply must be discharged into the environment. The effluent charges in this model will appear as negative prices on those goods that appear with a positive excess supply, which after having been discharged into the environment cause a reduction in the flow of environmental services. The model will be further generalized by replacing the linearity assumptions on the production technology and on the environmental interaction function with convexity assumptions.

It is obvious that the model that will presently be discussed is much more general than the previous one. The reason we have put such an emphasis on the less general model is that in the following chapters different models will be used to analyze different environmental problems, and these models will in general be based on an a priori separation between residuals and "regular" goods and services.

We will replace the assumption that the production possibility set is a convex polyhedral cone with the assumption that there is a finite number K of producers and that the production set T^i, $i = 1, \cdots, K$ is such that T^i contains the origin and the total production set $T = \Sigma T^i$ is closed and convex. We assume further that T satisfies $T \cap R^n_+ = \{0\}$, and that $T \cap (-T) = \{0\}$. These last assumptions mean that it is not possible to produce a positive amount of a good unless some input is used and production processes are irreversible.

We will replace the assumption that the environmental interaction function is an affine function of waste discharges and environmental treatment with a concavity assumption; that is, we assume that

$$Y = Y_o + F(z, e)$$

where F is a continuous function, concave jointly in z and e, such that each component of F is nonincreasing in z and nondecreasing in e. These assumptions will be interpreted in section 10.

Since we have dropped the distinction between regular goods and residuals, we have no need for the matrix D used in our consumer theory. The demand for goods and services is thus given by Bc^h for each individual h. The wealth or lump sum income of each individual now equals the value of his initial holdings plus his share in the environmental management agency's net revenue plus his shares in the profits of the producers. We will again denote consumer h's share in the environmental management agency by β^h. His share in producer i's profit is denoted by α_i^h. We assume that all profits are distributed to shareholders so that $\Sigma \alpha_i^h = 1$ for $i = 1, \cdots, K$, and that $\alpha_i^h \geqq 0$.

An equilibrium in this model is defined as a $(K + 3H + 4)$-tuple

$$(\bar{S}^1, \cdots, \bar{S}^K, \bar{e}, \bar{z}, \bar{c}^1, \cdots, \bar{c}^H, \bar{Y}^1, \cdots, \bar{Y}^H, \bar{Y}, \bar{p}, \delta^1, \cdots, \delta^H)$$

such that

(i) $\bar{p}^T\bar{S}^i$ maximizes $\bar{p}^T S^i$ on T^i for all $i = 1, \cdots, K$

(ii) $\bar{z}, \bar{e}, \bar{Y}$ maximizes $\Sigma \delta^{h^T} Y - \bar{p}^T(z + e)$ subject to
$Y = Y_o + F(z, e), z \geqq 0, e \geqq 0$

(iii) $(\bar{c}^h, \bar{Y}^h)$ maximizes $U^h(c^h, Y^h)$ on

$$\{(c^h, Y^h) \in E^h; \bar{p}^T c^h + \delta^{h^T} Y^h \leqq \bar{p}^T r^h + \sum_{i=1}^{K} \alpha_i^h p^T S^i$$

$$+ \beta^h[\Sigma \delta^{h^T} Y - \bar{p}^T(z + e)]\} \qquad \text{for all } h = 1, \cdots, H$$

(iv) $\bar{Y}^h \leqq Y, \delta^{h^T}(\bar{Y} - \bar{Y}^H) = 0 \qquad \text{for all } h = 1, \cdots, H$

(v) $\sum_{i=1}^{K} \bar{S}^i + \sum_{h=1}^{H} r^h = \sum_{h=1}^{H} B\bar{c}^h + \bar{e} + \bar{z}$

It is quite possible to prove the existence of an equilibrium in this model by making some further assumptions similar to those discussed in section 5. In fact, it is possible to reformulate this model so that it becomes identical to the model discussed by Debreu [26] and it is therefore possible to utilize his proof. We will not go into any details, however.

The analysis given in sections 6 and 7 on the relations between equilibrium and optimum can be repeated almost word for word. The main difference is that in the proof that an optimum can be represented as an equilibrium, we cannot find a semipositive price vector; therefore some prices will be negative.

A closer study of condition (ii) in the definition of an equilibrium shows that if $z_i > 0$, then the corresponding price p_i must be nonpositive, and that if $p_i > 0$, then $z_i = 0$. It is therefore clear that residuals discharges (i.e., positive excess supplies) will be priced in a way similar to that in the previous model.

It is now possible to give a rigorous definition of a residual. A residual is a good which in equilibrium is in excess supply, and the discharge of which causes a fall in the value of the environmental services.

9. SUMMARY OF THE MODEL

In the next section, some generalizations and interpretations of the model will be given. But before doing that, it is useful to summarize the structure of the model in a nonformal way. Such a summary will be attempted in this section.

The model is built on Samuelson's public good model [27], with the difference that the production of public goods is specified by an environmental interaction function. The public goods are the environmental qualities. The model follows very closely the outline given in figure 1 in chapter 1, except that capital accumulation is neglected. The decision makers in the economy are thus producers, consumers, and an environmental management agency. The very acts of production and consumption generate residuals which are discharged into the environment, and thereby deteriorate the flow of environmental services. By pricing the waste disposal capacity of the environment and by positive action in the form of treatment of the environment, the management agency may, however, control the environmental damages resulting from dumping wastes.

It is assumed that each producer has a well-defined production set, the elements of which are the possible actions the producer chooses among. The description of such an action includes inputs of labor, energy, raw materials, intermediate products, outputs of goods and services, and outputs of residuals or wastes. An action can thus be described by a vector (S, z) where S is a vector the positive components of which indicate amounts of output of goods and services, and the negative components of which indicate input requirements (S is n dimensional). z is the vector of residuals generated (z is r dimensional).

Given a price system, which can be represented by a vector $(p, q, \delta^1, \cdots, \delta^H)$, where p is the price vector for "regular" goods and services, q the cost of dumping residuals into the environment, and δ^h is the price on environmental qualities consumer h has to pay (there are thus H consumers), the producers choose those actions that maximize their profits. (It is assumed that the producers, like every other decision maker, are price takers.) These profit maximization actions define supply correspondences,

$$S \in \varphi_1(p, q)$$

$$z^p \in \varphi_2(p, q)$$

with the interpretation that if $S \in \varphi_1(p, q)$, $z^p \in \varphi_2(p, q)$, then (S, z^p) maximizes the profits of the producers at the prices (p, q).

Next, let us consider the environmental management agency. It sells waste disposal services z to producers and households. Moreover, it buys goods, represented by the vector e, from the producers, which it uses for treatment of the environment. Finally, it sells environmental services Y (Y is m dimensional) to the consumers. The flow of environmental services Y is related to the discharge of residuals z and to the treatment of the environment e by

$$Y = Y_o - F^1 z + F^2 e \qquad (F^1 \text{ is a matrix of order } m \times r, \ F^2 \text{ is a}$$
$$\text{matrix of order } m \times n)$$

The agency maximizes its net revenue $\delta^T Y + q^T z - p^T e$ where $\delta = \sum_{h=1}^{H} \delta^h$ is the total price vector for environmental services. This maximization yields optimal actions for the agency $(e, z, Y) \in \psi(p, q, \delta)$ where e is the demand for "regular" goods, z the supply of waste disposal services, and Y the supply of environmental quality. The maximal net revenue is $I = \delta^T Y_o$ as can be easily seen. This net revenue is distributed among the consumers in some lump sum way, for example $I^h = \beta^h I$,

where $0 \leqq \beta^h$, $\sum_{h=1}^{H} \beta^h = 1$

Let us now turn to the consumers. It is assumed that each consumer has a preference order over a set of consumption processes. A consumption process is some act that a consumer performs, for example eating dinner or watching a television program. In each such process, consumption goods are used as inputs. The output may be income or satisfaction, but also residuals or wastes, which must be disposed of. Besides deriving satisfaction from consumption processes, the consumers also derive satisfaction from the flow of environmental services they buy from the environmental management agency. The consumers are assumed to behave as if they maximize a utility function. This gives demand correspondences for goods and environmental services

$$C^h \in \zeta_1{}^h(p, q, \delta^h, I^h)$$

$$Y^h \in \zeta_2{}^h(p, q, \delta^h, I^h)$$

but also a supply correspondence for residuals

$$z^h \in \zeta_3{}^h(p, q, \delta^h, I^h)$$

where I^h is the transfer to consumer h from the environmental management agency. (It is assumed that the production sets for the producers are characterized by constant returns to scale, so that the profits are zero; thus the only lump sum income is the net revenue from the agency.)

Different consumers will in general face different price vectors, owing to the public good nature of the environmental quality. For most types of environmental services, δ_j^h will be zero for most consumers because the service j may not affect them directly, and so they will be indifferent to that particular service. Moreover, it is possible within this framework to interpret some of the environmental services as pure private goods, and in that case, δ_j^h is zero for all h except, say, h'.

The equilibrium in the economy can now be defined as an allocation of resources such that all markets are cleared. This means that

$$S \geqq \sum_{h=1}^{H} C^h + e$$

$$z \geqq z^p + \sum_{h=1}^{H} z^h$$

$$Y^h \leqq Y \qquad h = 1, \cdots, H$$

where

$$S \in \varphi_1(p, q)$$

$$z^p \in \varphi_2(p, q)$$

$$(e, z, Y) \in \psi(p, q, \delta)$$

$$I = \delta^T Y_o, \ I^h = \beta^h I \qquad h = 1, \cdots, H$$

$$C^h \in \zeta_1^h(p, q, \delta^h, I^h) \qquad h = 1, \cdots, H$$

$$Y^h \in \zeta_2^h(p, q, \delta^h, I^h) \qquad h = 1, \cdots, H$$

$$z^h \in \zeta_3^h(p, q, \delta^h, I^h) \qquad h = 1, \cdots, H$$

It is now possible to prove that under certain assumptions on the production sets, the consumer preferences, and the consumption sets, an equilibrium exists. This can most easily be seen by transforming the model into an Arrow–Debreu model, which is done as follows.

The environmental agency supplies the vector Y of environmental services to the consumers. We can think of this supply in the following way: The agency supplies each individual separately with the vector Y. There will thus be H markets for environmental qualities, one for each consumer. Although there are only two parties in each market, we maintain the assumption that all parties are price takers, because it is assumed that it is the agency that sets the prices in a way that resembles marginal cost pricing for a public utility.

Although the supply of environmental services on these H markets will be the same, we can at least conceptually regard the model as a model for an economy with n regular goods, s residuals, and Hm environmental qualities and with all goods and services private goods. It is thus possible to apply the theorems derived for the Arrow–Debreu model and an equilibrium will exist. Moreover, by the same reasoning, the equilibrium will be an optimum, and each optimum can be represented by an equilibrium, if certain other assumptions are made.

10. SOME INTERPRETATIONS
AND GENERALIZATIONS OF THE MODEL

The model that has been discussed in the first eight sections of this chapter can be expanded in several directions and interpreted in a more general way than has been done. This section points to some of these generalizations and interpretations.

1. One part of the model that may be regarded as unsatisfactory is the environmental interaction function, and especially the linearity of this function. Before going into a discussion of that problem, it must be noted that the static framework may not be realistic for a discussion of pollution problems because many pollutants will accumulate over time, and consequently the environmental interaction function should be formulated as some kind of dynamic relation, for example, given by a difference or differential equation. That aspect of the pollution problem will be discussed in the next chapter.

The linearity of the environment interaction function may be criticized on an a priori ground, although most empirical models are based on linear functions [28]. One situation in which linearity is not appropriate is when there are synergistic effects. Isolated from each other the pollutants may be quite innocent, but together they can be very harmful to the environment. Mathematically, this means that the interaction function is nonlinear.

Neglect environmental treatment for the moment, and write the interaction function as $Y = Y_o + F(z)$. We maintain the assumption that each component of F is nonincreasing in z and that $F(z) \leqq 0$. A natural way to include synergistic effects between two pollutants z_i and z_k is the following. Let $z' = (z_1, \cdots, 0, \cdots, z_k, \cdots, z_r)$ and $z'' = (z_1, \cdots, z_i, \cdots, 0, \cdots, z_r)$.

Synergism is then said to be present between z_i and z_k on the jth environmental quality if

$$F_j[tz' + (1 - t)z''] < tF_j(z') + (1 - t)F(z'') \text{ for } 0 < t < 1$$

But this is obviously the case if each component of F is a concave function of z.

In section 8 we showed that our general equilibrium model still works if the linear environmental interaction function is replaced by a concave function, and it is therefore true that our model is capable of handling synergistic effects.

One other implication of the concave environmental interaction function is that the marginal physical damage will increase with the size of the waste load. By marginal physical damage on the jth environmental quality caused by the ith residual we mean

$$\triangle Y_j = F_j(z_1, \cdots, z_i, \cdots, z_r) - F_j(z_1, \cdots, z_i + \triangle z_i, \cdots, z_r)$$

The concavity of F_j implies that $\triangle Y_j$ is increasing as a function of z_i. This seems to be a reasonable assumption in most cases.

The concavity of the environmental interaction function with respect to environmental treatment has the same interpretation as the concavity of a production function. In fact, it is possible to interpret the interaction function as a production function with waste loads and environmental treatment as inputs.

2. Let us now turn to a broader interpretation of the model. Up until now z has been interpreted as a flow of materials residuals. It is, however, quite possible to extend the interpretation of the flow z. If, for example, the consumption process v stands for driving an automobile on a certain highway, we could interpret z_k^h as the space occupied by the vehicle operated by the consumer h. Let $1/Y_j$ stand for the time it takes to drive this highway. Y_j depends on $\sum_{h=1}^{H} z_k^h$, that is, the total amount of space occupied by vehicles on the highway. Assume therefore,

$$Y_j = Y_{oj} - F_j\left(\sum_{h=1}^{H} z_k^h\right)$$

where $1/Y_{oj}$ is the time it takes to drive the highway when there is no congestion. It follows that if δ_j is the value the consumers together put on time, the highway authority should charge the drivers with $q_k = \delta_j F_j'$ for operating their vehicles on the highway. This example shows that congestion externalities are included in the model, and that the same pricing mechanism should be applied to these kinds of externalities as to materials residuals.

3. The model is basically a static general equilibrium model. It is, however, possible to interpret the model in a broader sense. If commodities, residuals, and environmental qualities at different dates are regarded

as different commodities, residuals, and environmental services, then the model gives an equilibrium over a set of time periods. Formally, one can therefore say that the model is capable of describing economic growth and the resulting development of environmental services. But owing to the nature of the model, it does not give any deeper insights into the intertemporal allocation problems. Such problems are best discussed within a more explicit dynamic framework, and that will be done in the next chapter.

4. In the model, the waste dischargers pay for the externalities they generate, and the consumers pay for the environmental services. This result seems to support the view held by Coase and others [29] that it is necessary to charge both parties involved in an externality, in order to achieve optimum. Coase's argument goes like this. There is a neighborhood in which there is a factory causing air pollution. Assume it is charged a price reflecting the social cost of its emissions. This fee will depend on the number of persons living in the neighborhood and their preferences. One more person in the neighborhood will thus increase the cost for the factory, and thus in Coase's terminology impose a negative externality on the factory. He concludes there is thus a need for a tax on the individuals living in the neighborhood.

In our model, the tax on the individuals living in the neighborhood corresponds to the price on air quality, and it seems from our model that Coase is right. But, we must not forget that the payment for the environmental services in our model is in the form of lump sum transfers. They are thus not used as incentives, as the objectives of Coase's tax are. If, by some exogenous change, one individual moves from one place to another, he will presumably change his preferences regarding environmental quality, because the quality of the neighborhood he moves into becomes much more important for him than it was before. He therefore is willing to pay a higher price for the quality in the new neighborhood than he did before. But because this payment is a lump sum transfer from him to the environmental management agency, it can be offset by a corresponding lump sum transfer back to him. In fact, in the new equilibrium his net exchange with the agency may be exactly the same as in the old. A change in the size of the transfer will reflect wishes to change the income distribution, but has nothing to do with the achievement of an optimum (it is true that the optimum will change if a person moves from one place to another, because of the aforementioned change in preferences and because of the change in income distribution accompanying the move, but still we will be at some optimum). We can therefore conclude that a tax à la Coase on the consumers is in no way necessary for the achievement of an optimum. The only objective such a tax should have is equity considerations.

Some points in this connection may cause confusion. One is the nature of the vector Y_o, that is, the vector of environmental qualities when no wastes are dumped into the environment and when there is no environmental treatment. Obviously, Y_o depends on the way environmental services are measured. We can choose practically any arbitrary scale for measuring environmental quality. This means that it may be all right to use a scale in which $Y_o = 0$. In this case $I^h = 0$, and $Y \leqq 0$, so that

$$\delta^{h^T} Y \leqq 0$$

that is, the consumers do not pay the agency for the supply of environmental services, but are paid by lump sum transfers, so that they are completely compensated for damages caused by discharges of wastes. If, on the other hand,

$$Y_o > 0, \; I^h \geqq 0, \; \delta^{h^T} Y > 0$$

the consumers have to pay for the supply of environmental services but will receive payment from the agency, owing to their shares in the agency's net revenue. It is therefore clear that the choice of scale is important for equity considerations. Choosing a scale such that $Y_o > 0$ indicates that we are interested in using the environmental management agency's revenues for income redistribution purposes. Choosing a scale such that $Y_o = 0$ indicates that we are not so interested in general income redistributions, but are satisfied with compensating the consumers for their subjective losses caused by environmental disruption.

NOTES

1. See Tjalling Koopmans *et al.* (eds.), *Activity Analysis of Production and Allocation* (Wiley, New York, 1951). For a more elementary discussion, see Robert Dorfman, Paul A. Samuelson, and Robert M. Solow, *Linear Programming and Economic Analysis* (McGraw-Hill, New York, 1958).

2. The model will ultimately be transformed into an Arrow–Debreu kind of general equilibrium model, and references for this model will be given later. For a rigorous discussion of a general equilibrium model with public goods, see Duncan K. Foley, "Resource Allocation and the Public Sector," *Yale Economic Essays*, vol. 7, no. 1, 43–98 (1967), and Duncan K. Foley, "Lindahl's Solution and the Core of an Economy with Public Goods," *Econometrica*, vol. 38, no. 1, 66–72 (1970).

3. There are some serious problems connected with externalities affecting the production possibilities. For a discussion of these, see David Starret: "On a Fundamental Non-Convexity in the Theory of Externalities," *Discussion Paper 115*, Harvard Institute of Economic Research, Harvard University, 1970.

4. The discussion of public goods goes back to the nineteenth century, but not until Samuelson's contributions in the second half of the 1950s was it put on a rigorous basis. For the discussion about 1900 see Richard A. Musgrave and Alan T. Peacock (eds.), *Classics in the Theory of Public Finance* (Macmillan, New York, 1958). Samuelson's contributions may be found in "The Pure Theory of Public Expenditures," *Review of Economics and Statistics*, vol. 36, pp. 387–389 (1954). "Pure Theory of Public Expenditure and Taxation," in J. Margolis and H. Guitton (eds.), *Public Economics: An Analysis of Public Production and Consumption and Their Relations to the Private Sector* (St. Martin's, New York, 1969).

5. For a more complete discussion of the economic interpretation of this assumption, see Samuel Karlin, *Mathematical Methods and Theory in Games, Programming, and Economics* (Addison-Wesley, Reading, Mass., 1959).

6. See Hukukane Nikaido, *Convex Structures and Economic Theory* (Academic Press, New York, 1968), definition 3.8, p. 41.

7. See Nikaido, *Convex Structures*, theorem 3.5, p. 35.

8. See Nikaido, *Convex Structures*, section 4.3, p. 64.

9. See Paul A. Samuelson, *Foundations of Economic Analysis* (Harvard Univ. Press, Cambridge, Mass., 1953).

10. For a discussion of environmental treatment, see Allen V. Kneese and Blair T. Bower, *Managing Water Quality: Economics, Technology, Institutions* (Johns Hopkins Press, Baltimore, 1968), and Robert K. Davis, *The Range of Choice in Water Management* (Johns Hopkins Press, Baltimore, 1968).

11. See Gerard Debreu, *Theory of Value: An Axiomatic Analysis of Economic Equilibrium* (Wiley, New York, 1959), theorem 1.8.4, p. 19.

12. See Debreu, *Theory of Value*.

13. This approach is similar, but not identical, to the approach to consumption theory developed by Lancaster. He does not take consumption processes as the basic building blocks, but different characteristics associated with goods and services. See Kelvin Lancaster, "A New Approach to Consumer Theory," *Journal of Political Economy*, vol. 74, no. 2, 132–157 (1966).

14. For a stimulating discussion of the time element in consumption, see Staffan Burenstam-Linder, *The Harried Leisure Class* (Columbia Univ. Press, New York, 1970).

15. See Debreu, *Theory of Value*, p. 55, for a discussion of conditions under which it is possible to represent preferences with continuous utility functions. These conditions are first, that the consumption set is connected (which is automatically satisfied in our case), and second that for each consumption in the consumption set, the set comprising all consumptions better than or indifferent to this consumption is closed, and the set comprising all consumptions not preferred to or indifferent to this consumption is closed.

16. See Debreu, *Theory of Value*, chapter 5, or Nikaido, *Convex Structures*, chapter V, 16.2, p. 257.

17. See Debreu, *Theory of Value*, section 4.9, p. 65.

18. *Ibid.*

19. The expenditure function is sometimes called the compensated income function. See Karlin, *Mathematical Methods*, section 8.6, p. 265.

20. The concept of indirect utility function was introduced by Harold Hotelling in "Edgeworth's Taxation Paradox and the Nature of Demand and Supply Functions," in *Journal of Political Economy*, vol. 40, no. 5, 577–616 (1932). The term indirect utility function was introduced by Hendrix Houthakker in "Compensated Changes in Quantities and Qualities Consumed," *Review of Economic Studies*, vol. 19, pp. 155–164 (1952). The introduction of the indirect utility function admits a concept of duality in the theory of consumer choice. For a discussion of this duality see Paul A. Samuelson, "Using Full Duality to Show That Simultaneously Additive Direct and Indirect Utilities Implies Elasticity of Demand," *Econometrica*, vol. 33, no. 4, 781–796 (1965).

21. See Nikaido, *Convex Structures*, chapter 5.

22. Nikaido, *Convex Structures*, p. 254.

23. See Debreu, *Theory of Value*, p. 88, and Debreu, "New Concepts and Techniques for Equilibrium Analysis," *International Economic Review*, vol. 3, no. 3, 251–273 (1962). In the last reference, the conditions for existence of an equilibrium are much weaker than what we have used here.

24. The recession cone (or the asymptotic cone) 0^+X of a set X is defined as the set $\{y \mid X + y \in X\}$. See R. Tyrrell Rockafellar, *Convex Analysis* (Princeton Univ. Press, Princeton, N.J., 1970), section 8, for details.

25. See Nikaido, *Convex Structures*, theorem 3.5, p. 35.

26. See Debreu, "New Concepts," *loc. cit.*

27. See Samuelson, "Pure Theory of Public Expenditures," *loc. cit.*

28. The standard example is the steady-state solution to Streeter–Phelps' equations governing the dissolved oxygen in a river. See, for example, Allen V. Kneese, "Background for the Economic Analysis of Environmental Pollution," *Swedish Journal of Economics*, vol. 73, no. 1, 1–54 (1971).

29. See Ronald Coase, "The Problem of Social Choice," in William Breit and Harold M. Hochman (eds.), *Readings in Microeconomics* (Holt, New York, 1968), and James M. Buchanan and William C. Stubblebine, "Externality," in the same collection of readings.

3 ECONOMIC GROWTH
AND QUALITY OF THE ENVIRONMENT

1. INTRODUCTION

In chapter 2 a general equilibrium model for a disaggregate economy was considered. In this model no changes over time were included and only a stationary equilibrium was discussed. The time element will now be added and intertemporal problems will be analyzed for an aggregate model.

There are, however, two kinds of changes over time that can be related to economic models of this kind. First, there are the problems of stability of a static equilibrium; that is, if the economy is out of equilibrium, are there any forces that will steer the economy back to equilibrium? Some aspects of these stability problems will be discussed in a later chapter. Second, there are the problems of intertemporal allocation of resources; that is, how are the resources allocated between different time periods and how should they be allocated over time?

In this chapter, some simple paradigms are presented, which, it is hoped, illustrate the optimal choice over time among consumption, accumulation, and environmental quality. Owing to sometimes unrealistic assumptions, one cannot expect to get "practical results" from these paradigms, but it is hoped that they will give a deeper insight into the connection between environmental quality and economic growth by focusing on the essential variables in the intertemporal tradeoffs.

In popular discussions of the present problems of pollution, many per-

58

sons tend to place the whole blame on the growth of industrial production and population [1]. One of the reasons why the following paradigms may be of interest is that they illustrate, although in a highly abstract manner, the connection between environmental disruption and economic and population growth. Moreover, it seems that the problems connected with irreversible actions can be analyzed with the aid of aggregate optimal growth models.

In all the models to be presented it is assumed that there is a composite commodity which can be used either for capital accumulation or for consumption. In the production of the commodity, three inputs are used—capital, labor, and natural resources. In order to concentrate the analysis on the exploitation of natural resources and the quality of the environment, it will be assumed that the labor force is constant in all but one of the paradigms. The materials balance identity is introduced into the models by assuming that the amount of natural resources exploited ultimately returns to the environment, either in the form of household wastes or as capital depreciation. This flow of residuals back to the environment will affect the quality of the environment, and the relation between the quality and the flow of residuals is assumed to be given by a first-order linear differential equation. It is further assumed that there is only a finite amount of natural resources that can be exploited within the time horizon. An increase in consumption in one time period will thus decrease the amount of natural resources available for future consumption. It will decrease the accumulation of capital and increase the flow of residuals and thereby decrease the future supply of environmental quality.

In studying these models, the main interests will be the existence of steady states in which all variables change at the same rate, and the relation of the optimal time paths of consumption, capital stock, and environmental quality to such steady states. It will be proved that the optimal time paths tend to approach the steady state in the long run (if the steady state exists) and the turnpike property [2] will thus be seen to be valid in these models, in spite of the restrictions on the availability of natural resources.

The models differ from each other in the following respects: the controllability of population, one or more different qualities of the natural resources, and possibilities of recycling residuals. In the first model, population is constant; there is only one quality of natural resources and there is no recycling. In the second model, two qualities of natural resources are introduced. In the third, population can change but is controlled by some authority. Finally, recycling is introduced in the fourth model.

2. THE WELFARE FUNCTION

It is assumed that there is a social choice mechanism that in some way "translates" the preferences of individuals in the economy into aggregate social preferences, represented by the government. The nature of this social choice mechanism will not be studied here; the mechanism is given by the institutions in the economy [3].

It is assumed that these social preferences can be represented in a very simple fashion, namely as an integral over a finite planning period of an instantaneous utility function. The representation of the preferences in the form of a welfare function is thus

$$W = \int_0^T U(C/L, Y)e^{-rt}dt$$

C is the rate of consumption, L is the size of the population, Y is the environmental quality at time t, and r is the rate of time discount. U is a twice continuously differentiable concave instantaneous utility function of per capita consumption and environmental quality. Moreover, it is assumed that

$$U_1 = \frac{\partial U}{\partial\left(\frac{C}{L}\right)} > 0 \qquad U_2 = \frac{\partial U}{\partial Y} > 0$$

$$U_1(0, Y) = \infty, \text{ and that } U_{12} = \frac{\partial^2 U}{\partial\left(\frac{C}{L}\right)\partial Y} = U_{21} > 0$$

The length of the planning period T is of course an element in the social preferences. It is assumed, however, that the government has preferences over the consumption streams and the quality of the environment after the horizon, but that it takes these factors into consideration in a very crude way, namely, that there must be a certain minimum capital stock and a certain minimum quality of the environment at the end of the planning period. Moreover, the economy is not allowed to exhaust all the natural resources during the planning period, but only a certain maximum amount in order to leave to future generations means to achieve at least some standard of living.

The preferences can thus be represented by

$$W = \int_0^T U(C/L, Y)e^{-rt}dt \tag{1}$$

$$K(T) \geq K_T$$
$$Y(T) \geq Y_T \tag{2}$$
$$\int_0^T v(t)dt \leq S$$

Here K is the capital stock and K_T is the minimum level required at the horizon; Y_T is the minimum quality of the environment required at the horizon, $v(t)$ is the flow of natural resources at time t, and S is the maximum exploitation allowed during the planning period.

Notice that this representation of the preferences reflects the choices of the present government and does not involve those of future generations (whose preferences we obviously do not know). The optimal time paths that can be constructed from this welfare function are thus optimal only with respect to the present government and it may very well be that the preferences of future governments will differ from those of the present government. It seems, however, that preferences change very slowly over time and so one can expect that the welfare function will be rather stable, at least for a decade or so. This is important because these intertemporal models are constructed to illuminate future consequences of an optimal decision today on present allocations among consumption, accumulation, and environmental quality. In order to determine present optimal policy, we must know the effects this policy will have on future choices among consumption, accumulation, and environmental quality [4].

The representation of social preferences is in a very special form. First, it assumes cardinal utility. This, however, is not a very serious objection, because we can think of this representation as one out of an infinite number of ordinal representations. More important is the second objection, namely, that it assumes independent utilities. The marginal rate of substitution of consumption between two periods of time is independent of consumption in other time periods. In ordinary theory of consumption decisions, the interdependencies between consumption of different commodities are recognized and do not create any difficulties. In models of intertemporal choice, however, independence is almost necessary in order to make the problem mathematically tractable.

A discount factor is introduced in the welfare function. This factor represents the time preference of the government. People in general are assumed to behave as if they value future consumption lower than today's consumption. It is assumed that the social choice mechanism transmits this time preference to the social preferences. Many authors (i.e., Pigou and Ramsey) have argued that although individuals put a lower value on future consumption, the government should represent future generations also and treat all generations equally, which means that the discount factor is zero [5]. If, however, the present government represents the preferences of the present population, it is hard to advocate that the government should not discount future consumption possibilities relative to present possibilities. In any case, the discount rate represents a subjective value judgment and cannot be interpreted as an objective figure, obtained from free market rates. Moreover, if there is an infinite time horizon, Koopmans has shown that if the time preference is zero, the preferences are insensitive to a change in consumption at at least one point of time [6].

Arrow and Kurz [7] have made a very strong case for weighting the instantaneous utilities with the size of the population and against the formulation of the welfare function used here. They consider a hypothetical country consisting of two islands with fixed population. If the welfare function can be written as the weighted sum of the welfares on the two islands respectively, and if the welfare functions for the two islands are identical functions of per capita consumption, the optimal policy, when the weights are the populations on the islands, is to equalize the per capita consumption. This answer seems very attractive and so one should write the welfare function as

$$W = \int_0^T L(t)U(C/L, Y)e^{-rt}dt$$

But when the population is constant or when it is possible to control the size of the population, the two formulations will yield identical results. These are the only cases that will be discussed in this chapter; therefore the former formulation will be maintained.

3. THE FIRST PARADIGM

As has been stated, there is a composite commodity that can be used for consumption and for capital accumulation. The amount of this commodity is measured in tons. This commodity exists as a nonreproducible natural resource in a certain limited quantity. According to the social preferences, only S tons of this resource may be used within the planning horizon. The resource is used as raw material input in production, where it is transformed into such a form that it can be consumed or invested. The total flow of output of the composite commodity is denoted by Q. It is furthermore assumed that there are no material residuals in production, so that all raw material going into production will come out as output. This means that Q not only measures the volume of output, but also the rate at which the natural resources are exploited.

Production can be described by a neoclassical production function $Q = f(K, L)$ where f is concave, twice co: tinuously differentiable, and with positive first-order partial derivatives.

Since in this first paradigm the population and the labor force are constant, the symbol L in the production function will be suppressed:

$$Q = f(K) \qquad f'(K) > 0 \qquad f''(K) < 0 \tag{3}$$

The required input of the natural resource is then $f(K)$ and the restriction on the exploitation of this resource can be written [8]

$$\int_0^T f[K(t)]dt \leqq S \tag{4}$$

The output Q is allocated to consumption C and to investment. The capital stock is assumed to depreciate owing to physical wear and tear at the rate μ. The net capital accumulation $\dot{K}$ is then given by

$$\dot{K} = x \tag{5}$$

$$x + C + \mu K - f(k) \leqq 0 \tag{6}$$

(Dots over a symbol will indicate the time derivative of the corresponding variable.) If it is assumed that goods already invested in the capital stock cannot be consumed, this means that $C \leqq f(K)$ or $x + \mu K \geqq 0$.

In the consumption process, the commodities are not used up, but transformed into other commodities, residuals. It is assumed (contrary to the discussion in chapter 2) that consumption processes do not require time, so that the consumption goods will be transformed immediately into residuals. The outputs of this process are thus a flow of consumer services and a flow of residuals [9]. Moreover, the wear and tear of the capital stock generates residuals in the amount μK.

The total amount of residuals generated at time t is then

$$z(t) = C(t) + \mu K(t) \tag{7}$$

In this paradigm it is assumed that all residuals are discharged into the environment and that they thereby are lost forever. This is almost certainly true for energy. According to the second law of thermodynamics, recovering lost energy is impossible. However, for minerals it may at least in principle be possible to exploit, although at very high costs, the‧ deposits which the discharges of residuals create.

The discharge of wastes into the environment will affect the quality of the environment. As discussed in chapter 2, there are in general many ways of defining this quality. The way that is chosen here is to consider the ambient concentration of pollutants as a measure of quality. Assume that there is a lake with total water volume A m^3 and an outflow of a m^3 per unit of time. If the ambient concentration of some pollutant is η tons/m^3 and if there is a discharge into the lake equal to z tons of pollutant per unit of time, the following relations must hold:

ηA is the total amount of pollutant in the lake
ηa is the amount of pollutant that is transported away from the lake per unit of time
z is the transportation to the lake of the pollutant and
$-a\eta + z$ is the change in the total amount of pollutant in the lake per unit of time; thus

$$\dot{\eta}A = -\eta a + z \qquad \text{or} \qquad \dot{\eta} = -\frac{a}{A}\eta + \frac{1}{A}z$$

Instead of studying the ambient concentration η, the variable Y, defined by $Y = 1 - \eta$ will be introduced. By a simple calculation it is seen that

$$\dot{Y} = \frac{a}{A}(1 - Y) - \frac{1}{A}z \qquad \text{or with} \qquad \lambda = \frac{a}{A} \qquad \text{and} \qquad \gamma = \frac{1}{A}$$

$$\dot{Y} = \lambda(1 - Y) - \gamma z \tag{8}$$

Y is interpreted as the quality of the water in the lake. This differential equation gives the present quality of the water body as a function of the waste discharges in all previous time periods, including the present.

If $z = \bar{z}$ (constant), the solution to equation (8) is

$$Y = Y(0)e^{-\lambda t} + \left(1 - \frac{\gamma}{\lambda}\bar{z}\right)(1 - e^{-\lambda t})$$

from which it is seen that Y will in the long run approach the steady-state value $[1 - (\gamma/\lambda)\bar{z}]$. If $\bar{z} = 0$, the steady state is defined by $Y = 1$. From this it follows that 1 is an upper bound for environmental quality. This upper bound corresponds to a virgin state in which the environment is not disturbed by the discharge of man-made residuals.

Although equation (8) has been derived only for a very special case, this differential equation will be used as the relation between waste discharges and environmental quality. Note that formally this first-order linear differential equation is identical to the Streeter–Phelps equation, relating the dissolved oxygen deficit to biochemical degradable wastes, but the interpretation is different [10].

The term $\lambda(1 - Y)$ is interpreted as the self-purification of the environment, and in many instances it is possible to change this assimilative capacity by investments in the environment (i.e., mechanical aeration, flow regulation). Such investments will not be considered in this chapter.

When $\lambda = 0$, we have the special case of an absolutely irreversible process, and $\dot{Y} \leq 0$ for all t. This special case will not be discussed, however [11].

The model is now completely specified. The next task is to characterize and investigate the qualitative properties of the optimal time paths for the variables introduced. A feasible time path is a vector (C, K, Y, z) which satisfies the restrictions of the model (2, 4–8):

$$K(T) \geq K_T \qquad Y(T) \geq Y_T \qquad K(0) = K_o \qquad Y(0) = Y_o \qquad (2)$$

$$\int_0^T f[K(t)]dt \leq S, \qquad \left(\text{or } \int_0^T \left\{ f[K(t)] - \frac{S}{T} \right\} dt \leq 0 \right) \qquad (4)$$

$$\dot{K} = x \qquad (5)$$

$$x + C + \mu K - f(k) \leq 0 \qquad (6)$$

$$C + \mu K - z = 0 \qquad (7)$$

$$\dot{Y} = \lambda(1 - Y) - \gamma z \qquad (8)$$

$$x + \mu K \geq 0 \qquad (9)$$

We will assume that K_T, Y_T, and S are chosen in such a way that there exists at least one feasible path. An optimal time path is a feasible time path that maximizes the welfare function

$$W = \int_0^T U(C, Y)e^{-rt}dt \qquad (1)$$

The restriction (9) will be disregarded, however; that is, it is assumed that the capital accumulation is reversible. It has been shown by Arrow and Kurz [12] that in a one-sector model the irreversibility of capital accumulation does not change the basic asymptotic properties, but instead introduces complications in computing the optimal path.

Assuming that there exists at least one optimal time path, the qualitative properties of such paths will be studied with the aid of the Pontryagin maximum principle [13]. According to this principle, there are, associated with the optimal path, multipliers $\bar{p}(t)$, $\bar{\delta}(t)$, nonnegative multipliers $\bar{\alpha}(t)$, $\bar{q}(t)$, and a constant nonnegative multiplier $\bar{p}_r$, such that with the function H defined by

$$H = Ue^{rt} + \bar{p}x + \bar{\delta}[\lambda\,(1 - Y) - \gamma z] - \bar{p}_r\left(f - \frac{S}{T}\right)$$
$$- \bar{\alpha}(x + C + \mu K - f) - \bar{q}(C + \mu K - z)$$

the multipliers and the variables satisfy the following conditions:

$$\dot{\bar{p}} = -\frac{\partial H}{\partial K} = \bar{p}_r f' + \mu\bar{\alpha} - \bar{\alpha}f' + \mu\bar{q} \tag{10}$$

$$\dot{\bar{\delta}} = -\frac{\partial H}{\partial Y} = -U_2 e^{-rt} + \bar{\delta}\lambda \tag{11}$$

$$\frac{\partial H}{\partial C} = U_1 e^{-rt} - \bar{\alpha} - \bar{q} = 0 \tag{12}$$

$$\frac{\partial H}{\partial x} = \bar{p} - \bar{\alpha} = 0 \tag{13}$$

$$\frac{\partial H}{\partial z} = -\gamma\bar{\delta} + \bar{q} = 0 \tag{14}$$

$$\bar{p}_r \int_0^T \left(f - \frac{S}{T}\right) dt = 0 \tag{15}$$

$$\bar{\alpha}(x + C + \mu K) = 0 \tag{16}$$

$$\bar{q}(C + \mu K - f) = 0 \tag{17}$$

$$\bar{p}(T)[K(T) - K_T] = 0 \qquad \bar{p}(T) \geqq 0 \tag{18}$$

$$\bar{\delta}(T)[Y(T) - Y_T] = 0 \qquad \bar{\delta}(T) \geqq 0 \tag{19}$$

These are necessary conditions, which an optimal time path must satisfy. If, however, $\bar{p}(t) \geqq \bar{p}_r$ all $t \in [0, T]$, they are also sufficient in the sense that if a time path satisfies the necessary conditions, the value of the welfare function for this path will not be less than the value for any other feasible time path.

In order to prove this, observe that at an optimal path condition (6) will be effective and that no paths with inequalities in (6) can be optimal. With inequality in (6), it is possible to increase consumption with zero opportunity cost [14]. This implies that x can be solved in (6) and substituted into (5):

$$\dot{K} = f(K) - \mu K - C \tag{5a}$$

Let symbols with an asterisk represent a time path that satisfies the Pontryagin necessary conditions, and let symbols without an asterisk denote an arbitrary feasible path. We then have (with all derivatives evaluated at the optimal path)

$$\int_0^T [U(C, Y) - U(C^*, Y^*)]e^{-rt}dt \qquad \text{(by concavity of } U\text{)}$$

$$\leq \int_0^T [U_1(C - C^*) + U_2(Y - Y^*)]e^{-rt}dt \qquad \text{(by 11)}$$

$$= \int_0^T [U_1(C - C^*)e^{-rt} + (\lambda\bar{\delta} - \dot{\bar{\delta}})(Y - Y^*)]dt \qquad \text{(partial integration)}$$

$$= -\bar{\delta}(T)[Y(T) - Y^*(T)] + \bar{\delta}(0)[Y(0) - Y^*(0)]$$

$$+ \int_0^T [U_1 e^{-rt}(C - C^*) + \lambda\bar{\delta}(Y - Y^*) + \bar{\delta}(\dot{Y} - \dot{Y}^*)]dt$$

(by 2, 19, and 8)

$$\leq \int_0^T [U_1 e^{-rt}(C - C^*) - \gamma\bar{\delta}(z - z^*)]dt \qquad \text{(by 7)}$$

$$= \int_0^T [U_1 e^{-rt}(C - C^*) - \gamma\bar{\delta}(C - C^*) - \mu\gamma\bar{\delta}(K - K^*)]dt$$

(by 14, 12, 13, and 5a)

$$= \int_0^T \{\bar{p}[f(K) - f(K^*)] - \mu(\bar{p} + \bar{q})(K - K^*) - \bar{p}(\dot{K} - \dot{K}^*)\}dt$$

(partial integration)

$$= -\bar{p}(T)[K(T) - K^*(T)] + \bar{p}(0)[K(0) - K^*(0)]$$

$$+ \int_0^T \{\bar{p}[f(K) - f(K^*)] - \mu(\bar{p} + \bar{q})(K - K^*) + \dot{\bar{p}}(K - K^*)\}dt$$

(by 2, 18, 10, and 13)

$$\leq \int_0^T \{\bar{p}[f(K) - f(K^*)] - (\bar{p} - \bar{p}_r)f'(K - K^*)\}dt$$

(by 4 and 15)

$$\leq \int_0^T (\bar{p} - \bar{p}_r)[f(K) - f(K^*) - f'(K^*)(K - K^*)]dt \leq 0$$

because f is concave and because of the assumed nonnegativity of $\bar{p} - \bar{p}_r$. Under this assumption it has thus been shown that

$$\int_0^T U(C,\ Y)e^{-rt}dt \leq \int_0^T U(C^*,\ Y^*)e^{-rt}dt$$

that is $(C^*,\ Y^*)$ is optimal.

The multipliers p, δ, q, and p_r can be interpreted as the present values of the prices for investment goods, environmental quality, waste disposal services, and natural resources. It is, however, easier to analyze the system if the prices are transformed into current prices. Therefore, the following substitutions will be made:

$$\bar{p} = pe^{-rt}$$

$$\bar{\delta} = \delta e^{-rt}$$

$$\bar{q} = qe^{-rt}$$

$$\bar{p}_r = p_r e^{-rt}$$

and (10), (11), (12), and (14) can be written

$$\dot{p} = -(p - p_r)f' + \mu q + (\mu + r)p \qquad\qquad (10a)$$

$$\dot{\delta} = -U_2 + (\lambda + r)\delta \qquad\qquad (11a)$$

$$p = U_1 - q \qquad\qquad (12a)$$

$$q = \gamma\delta \qquad\qquad (14a)$$

If we consider an increase in the capital stock at time t of one unit, this will increase the value of output with pf' but it will increase the cost of production with $p_r f'$ due to the input of raw material, with μp due to depreciation. This unit of capital must thus be worth

$$p = \int_t^T (pf' - p_r f' - \mu p - \mu q)e^{-r(\tau-t)}d\tau + p(T)c^{-r(T-t)}$$

Differentiation with respect to time of this relation yields (12) and so p can be interpreted as the current demand price for capital goods. The same analyses can be made with respect to δ.

$$\delta = \int_0^T (U_2 - \lambda\delta)e^{-r(\tau-t)}d\tau + \delta(T)e^{-r(T-t)}$$

Equation (12) can now be interpreted to mean that the marginal utility of consumption equals the opportunity cost of consumption, which consists of two parts: first, the forgone opportunities of capital accumulation and second, the disposal cost of the consumption residuals. Equation (14) says that the cost of disposal equals the value of the marginal decrement in the quality of the environment caused by the discharge of residuals.

Eliminating q and z, the total system can be written

$$
\left.
\begin{aligned}
&\dot{K} = f(K) - \mu K - C \\
&\dot{Y} = \lambda(1 - Y) - \gamma(C + \mu K) \\
&\dot{p} = (\mu + r)p + \mu\gamma\delta - (p - p_r)f' \\
&\dot{\delta} = -U_2 + (r + \lambda)\delta \\
&U_1 - p - \gamma\delta = 0 \\
&\int_0^T f[K(t)]dt \leqq S
\end{aligned}
\right\}
\tag{20}
$$

Regarding $\bar{p}_r$ as a parameter, the first five equations can be solved for K, C, Y, p, and δ, and by choosing $\bar{p}_r$ appropriately, the last condition will be satisfied.

The system (20) is not autonomous, however, because $\bar{p}_r$ is a constant and $p_r = \bar{p}_r e^{rt}$. This implies, among other things, that there is no singular solution to (20), if $\bar{p}_r > 0$ [15]. The scarcity of natural resources together with a positive time preference thus prevent feasible steady states from being optimal. It is not possible to go much further in the study of (20) if further assumptions are not made. As the main interest in this chapter is in the economics of natural resources, it will be assumed that $r = 0$, in spite of remarks that were made in the previous section. System (20) is then autonomous and may admit a singular solution $(K^*, Y^*, C^*, p^*, \delta^*)$. Such a singular solution must be a solution to system (21):

$$
\left.
\begin{aligned}
&f - \mu K - C = 0 \\
&\lambda(1 - Y) - \gamma(C + \mu K) = 0 \\
&\mu p + \mu\gamma\delta - (p - p_r)f' = 0 \\
&-U_2 + \lambda\delta = 0 \\
&U_1 - p - \gamma\delta = 0
\end{aligned}
\right\}
\tag{21}
$$

It is assumed that (21) has a unique solution that is feasible, that is, the consumption, capital stock, demand price for capital, and demand price for environmental quality are all nonnegative [16]. This solution $(K^*, Y^*,$

C^*, p^*, δ^*) will be called the steady state (although many feasible steady states may exist, there is only one optimal steady state).

A simple calculation shows that $dK^*/dp_r < 0$, and it is therefore possible to choose p_r such that the total amount of the natural resources available for the planning period is sufficient if the economy is steered at the steady state during the planning period. Moreover, at the steady state $(p - p_r)f' = \mu p + \mu \gamma \delta > 0$, so that if the economy happens to be at a steady state at the beginning of the planning period and if the terminal capital stock and environmental quality requirement happen to be at the steady state, it follows that the steady state is the optimal time path.

In order to study the qualitative properties of the optimal time paths, the system will now be linearized. To do that, the restriction on the availability of natural resources will be neglected and p_r will be given an arbitrary positive value. This p_r will then define a steady state and the differential equations will be linearized around this steady state. The idea is the following. If terminal and initial values for K and Y are specified, there is a unique solution to the system, and especially a unique value on p_r. Given this value on p_r, we can neglect the natural resource constraint and we are left with system (20). This same value on p_r defines a steady state (not necessarily feasible), and we linearize the system (20) around this steady state.

The linearized system can be written as follows (all derivatives are evaluated at the steady state):

$$
\begin{aligned}
\dot{K} = {}& (f' - \mu)(K - K^*) + \frac{U_{12}}{U_{11}}(Y - Y^*) - \frac{1}{U_{11}}(p - p^*) \\
& - \frac{\gamma}{U_{11}}(\delta - \delta^*) \\
\dot{Y} = {}& -\mu\gamma(K - K^*) + \gamma\left(\frac{U_{12}}{U_{11}} - \lambda\right)(Y - Y^*) \\
& - \frac{\gamma}{U_{11}}(p - p^*) - \frac{\gamma^2}{U_{11}}(\delta - \delta^*) \\
\dot{p} = {}& -(p - p_r)f''(K - K^*) - (f' - \mu)(p - p^*) + \mu\gamma(\delta - \delta^*) \\
\dot{\delta} = {}& \left(\frac{U_{12}^2}{U_{11}} - U_{22}\right)(Y - Y^*) - \frac{U_{12}}{U_{11}}(p - p^*) \\
& + \left(\lambda - \gamma\frac{U_{12}}{U_{11}}\right)(\delta - \delta^*)
\end{aligned} \right\} \quad (22)
$$

The determinant of the coefficient matrix of the system can be calculated in a routine way, and it is positive. This means that all the eigenvalues of the system are different from zero.

It is well known that linear systems, obtained in this way from the Euler equations to an autonomous problem in the calculus of variations, have the property that the eigenvalues appear pairwise symmetrically around the origin. This property is derived in appendix B in section 9. This means that if κ_1 is an eigenvalue, then so is $-\kappa_1$. Furthermore, simple calculations show that the real parts of all eigenvalues are different from zero. It can therefore be concluded that two eigenvalues have negative real parts and two positive real parts.

This means that the steady state is a saddle point for the linearized system if the utility discount rate is zero. For a system such that the linearized system derived from the original system has a saddle point, the following theorem can be proved [17].

Theorem: For each arbitrary $k > 0$ and $t_1 > 0$, there exist positive numbers ϵ and N such that if $||[K(0) - K^*,\ Y(0) - Y^*]|| + ||[K(T) - K^*,\ Y(T) - Y^*]|| < \epsilon$ and if $T > N$, the solution to the nonlinear system will satisfy

$$||[K(t) - K^*,\ Y(t) - Y^*,\ p(t) - p^*,\ \delta(t) - \delta^*]|| < k\epsilon$$

$$\text{for } t_1 < t < T - t_1$$

Here $||\cdot||$ denotes the Euclidean norm of the vector.

The interpretation of this theorem is clear. If the initial conditions are not too far away from the steady-state configuration and if the same applies to the terminal state, the system will, if the time horizon is long enough, move toward the steady state, then spend most of the planning period in a neighborhood of the steady state and finally, at the end of the planning period, move toward the terminal state. This property of a system to move toward a steady state will be called the turnpike property. What we now have proved is that the optimal paths in this first paradigm have the turnpike property, if the initial and terminal states are not too far away from the steady state. This property implies, among other things, that $p - p_r > 0$ along most of the path, so the sufficiency theorem that was proved earlier can be applied. The solutions to the system of differential equations describe indeed an optimal path. As ordinary existence theories guarantee that there is a solution to our system of differential equations, we have therefore also proved the existence of an optimal path.

The importance of this turnpike property can be derived from two considerations [18]. First, since we know that the optimal time paths will end up in a neighborhood of the steady state, an approximation of the optimal policy in the first time span in the planning period can be made. If the steady state is known, the approximation involved simply choosing the policy that will steer the economy in the shortest time to the steady state. If the present capital stock is smaller than the steady-state capital stock, accumulate; if the environmental quality is less than that in the steady state, decrease the waste discharge.

The second consideration is of more relevance for this book. Since the optimal time path will spend most of the time in a neighborhood of the steady state, the optimal time path can be approximated by the steady state. This is the basic reason why stationary general equilibrium models, like the one presented in chapter 2, may be of interest in an economy where there are accumulations of capital and changes in the quality of the environment. It is possible to look at the stationary equilibrium as a steady state, and if the economy follows an optimal time path, this general equilibrium will be relevant for most of the time. Moreover, it is now possible to study the influence of shifts in the parameters in the model by simply making comparative static studies of the steady state, instead of the very difficult or impossible study of the comparative dynamics of the differential equations of the optimal path. The next task will therefore be to study the comparative statics of the steady state.

It has already been noted that $dK^*/dp_r < 0$. Assume now that (4) is effective. As in the steady state (4) can be written $f(K^*) = S/T$, it is seen that

$$\frac{\partial K}{\partial T} < 0; \frac{\partial K}{\partial S} > 0 \text{ and a fortiori that}$$

$$\frac{\partial p_r}{\partial T} > 0; \frac{\partial p_r}{\partial S} < 0 \tag{23}$$

An increase in the planning period will thus increase the rent accruing to the natural resources and an increase in the availability of natural resources will decrease the rent. These are obvious conclusions. In the same way it can be shown that an increase in the planning period will *ceteris paribus* increase the environmental quality and that an increase in the availability of the natural resources will diminish the environmental quality.

Let us now compare two economies with different assimilative capacities, interpreted as the parameter λ in equation (8). Intuitively, if (4) is effective, consumption will not be affected by a change in λ, but the environmental quality will decrease with a decrease in λ. Owing to diminishing marginal utility for environmental quality, the demand price for environmental quality will increase and so will therefore the "effluent charge" q. The demand for natural resources will thus fall, which means a decrease in the rent p_r. But the decrease in environmental quality means also that the marginal utility for consumption decreases, which further reduces the demand for natural resources. This intuitive conclusion can be seen to be correct if $dp_r/d\lambda$ is solved for:

$$\frac{dp_r}{d\lambda} = \delta\gamma + \frac{1}{f'}\left[(f' - \mu)\left(U_{12} - \frac{\mu\gamma}{\lambda}U_{22}\right) - \frac{\mu\gamma}{\lambda}U_{22}\right](1 - \gamma) > 0$$

Because of this, it may happen that in an economy where the damage to the environment from discharges of residuals is of an almost irreversible kind (that is, λ is very small), the maximal feasible exploitation of natural resources will not be undertaken, owing to the concern for the environment. In that case there will be no scarcity rent accruing to the natural resources, and condition (4) will not be effective.

Before leaving this paradigm, a last exercise on the steady state will be undertaken. In this exercise we will regard the equations defining the steady state, not as describing an optimal path, but as describing a competitive economy in which the government decides on the effluent charge q in an arbitrary way, i.e., zero rather than in accordance with the marginal utility of environmental quality. The equation describing the movement over time for δ will therefore be dropped. We can now analyze the effects changes in the effluent charge q will have on the rent on natural resources, and the effect is $dp_r/dq = -1$.

The zero effluent charge thus results in an overvaluation of the natural resources, besides its obvious effect on the environmental quality. The government can correct for this deviation from optimal behavior either by increasing the effluent charge or by taxing the rents on natural resources. The second method involves an increase in the selling price of natural resources and thus stimulates economizing resources and causes a decrease in the rent.

4. THE SECOND PARADIGM: DIFFERENT QUALITIES OF NATURAL RESOURCES

In the preceding section, it was assumed that there was a single deposit with a finite amount of nonrenewable natural resources of a homogeneous quality. In this second paradigm, two deposits of natural resources with differing quality will be introduced. The difference in quality is thought of as a difference in the real cost of exploiting the deposits. The interesting questions arising from different qualities of natural resources concern the intertemporal exploitation of the deposits. Should the deposits be exploited in order of their qualities, so that the best deposit is exploited first? Or is any other sequence of exploitation better? Economists, since the days of Ricardo, have believed that the best deposits should be exploited first, then the second-best deposits, and so on. It is natural to think that such a time sequence will be followed in any historical development of an economy, but it is quite another thing to state that that sequence is in fact the optimal one. If we consider a time period in which the prices of capital goods are constant and the discount rate is positive, then it is easy to see that the maximum present value of net benefits will be obtained when the low-cost deposits are exploited first and high-cost deposits are exploited later. But it might happen that the prices of capital goods are increasing over time, and if that is the case, it is no longer clear that the best deposits should be exploited first [19].

In order to concentrate on the analysis of this problem of optimal management of nonrenewable resources, considerations of the quality of the environment will be neglected. It is, however, intuitively obvious that it should be possible to derive the same kind of conclusions when environmental quality enters the model.

If, in the above case with constant capital good prices, the discount rate is zero, it becomes a matter of indifference which deposit is exploited first. If it is possible to show that in the absence of a positive time preference the optimal management consists of using the best deposits first, this conclusion is only reinforced if the discount rate is positive. Therefore, it will be assumed that the utility discount rate is zero.

The model that will be used to analyze these problems can now be stated more precisely. Let K_E denote the total capital stock in the economy. This capital stock consists of three parts: the capital stock K used in the production of the composite good, the capital stock used in operating the first deposit, and the capital stock used in mining the second deposit. It is assumed that capital is perfectly malleable, so that capital invested in one deposit can be transferred without any costs to the other deposit or to the production of the composite good. At the end of this section there are some remarks on the nonmalleable case. Moreover, it is assumed that capital depreciates at the same rate in all its uses.

Let v_τ ($\tau = 1, 2$) be the rate of exploitation of deposit τ, and assume that the capital requirement is given by $K_\tau \geqq a_\tau v_\tau$, $v_\tau \geqq 0$, $\tau = 1, 2$. It is assumed that $a_1 < a_2$, so that deposit one is of higher quality than deposit two. The allocation of the total capital stock can then be written

$$K_E \geqq K + a_1 v_1 + a_2 v_2 \tag{24}$$

Exactly as in the previous sections, the natural resources are used as inputs in the production of the composite good. Let μ be, as before, the rate of capital depreciation. We will assume that $1 - \mu a_\tau > 0$, $\tau = 1, 2$; because otherwise one unit of raw material would require that more than one unit of capital be used up in its production.

If $Q = f(K)$ is the production function for the composite good, the raw material requirement can be written

$$v_1 + v_2 \geqq f(K) \tag{25}$$

The two deposits have finite sizes S_1 and S_2, and so the following restrictions must hold:

$$\int_0^T v_1 dt \leqq S_1 \qquad \int_0^T v_1 dt \leqq S_2$$
$$\left[\text{or} \int_0^T \left(v_i - \frac{S_i}{T} \right) dt \leqq 0 \qquad i = 1.2 \right] \tag{26}$$

The accumulation of capital is governed by

$$\dot{K}_E = f(K) - \mu K_E - C \tag{27}$$

The welfare function that is going to be maximized is

$$\int_0^T U(C) dt$$

$$K_E(0) = K_o \qquad K_E(T) \geqq K_T$$

Let p_{r1} and p_{r2} be constant multipliers, π, θ, ϵ_1, and ϵ_2 nonnegative multipliers, p a function of time, and let H be defined by

$$H = U(C) + p[f(K) - \mu K_E - C] - \pi(K + a_1 v_1 + a_2 v_2 - K_E)$$
$$- \theta[f(K) - v_1 - v_2] - p_{r2}\left(v_1 - \frac{S_1}{T} \right) - p_{r2}\left(v_2 - \frac{S_2}{T} \right)$$
$$+ \epsilon_1 v_1 + \epsilon_2 v_2$$

Then the Pontryagin necessary conditions can be written

$$\dot{p} = -\frac{\partial H}{\partial K_E} = \mu p - \pi \tag{28}$$

$$\frac{\partial H}{\partial C} = U' - p = 0 \tag{29}$$

$$\frac{\partial H}{\partial K} = p f' - \pi - \theta f' = 0 \tag{30}$$

$$\frac{\partial H}{\partial v_\tau} = -a_\tau \pi + \theta - p_{r\tau} + \epsilon_\tau - 0 \qquad \tau = 1.2 \tag{31}$$

$$\epsilon_\tau v_\tau = 0 \qquad \tau = 1.2 \tag{32}$$

$$p(T)[K_E(T) - K_T] = 0, \, p(T) \geqq 0 \qquad \text{(the transversality condition)}$$

It is clear that along an optimal path (24) and (25) will be satisfied as equalities.

Obviously, p can be interpreted as the demand price for capital goods, π the rental accruing to capital, θ the price of the raw materials, and $p_{\tau\tau}$ the rent accruing to deposit τ. With this interpretation equations (28)–(32) have clear economic interpretations. Equations (31) and (32) state that if the cost of operating deposit τ is greater than the price of the raw material, then deposit τ will not be used, and that the profit from using deposit τ will never exceed zero (any excess of revenue over cost will be capitalized into a rent $p_{\tau\tau}$). Equation (30) shows that the net value of the marginal productivity of capital equals the capital rental. Equation (29) indicates that the demand price for capital must be equal to the marginal utility of consumption because the composite good can be used for both consumption and investment. Equation (28) finally can be written

$$p(t) = e^{-(T-t)}p(T) + \int_t^T \pi e^{-\mu(\tau-t)}d\tau$$

from which it can be seen that the demand price for capital equals the value at the horizon of the remains of one unit of capital plus the present value of future rentals on this unit.

In order to study the system, the steady state will be investigated. This is a vector $(K_E, K, C, v_1, v_2, p, \pi, \theta, \epsilon, \epsilon_2, p_{r1}, p_{r2})$ constant over time which satisfies conditions (24)–(32) during the planning period. It will be assumed that in the steady state $\epsilon_1 = \epsilon_2 = 0$, because otherwise one of the deposits will not be exploited at all. Then the steady state is defined by

$$
\left.
\begin{aligned}
&\mu p - \pi = 0 \\
&f(K) - \mu K_E - C = 0 \\
&U' - p = 0 \\
&K_E - K - a_1 v_1 - a_2 v_2 = 0 \\
&v_1 + v_2 - f(K) = 0 \\
&pf' - \pi - \theta f' = 0 \\
&-a_\tau \pi + \theta - p_{rr} = 0 \qquad \tau = 1, 2 \\
&\int_0^T v_\tau df = S_\tau \qquad \tau = 1, 2
\end{aligned}
\right\} \tag{33}
$$

Regarding p_{r1} and p_{r2} as parameters, the first eight equations constitute a system in eight unknowns. This system will have a unique solution provided that

$$p_{r1}(1 - \mu a_2) - p_{r2}(1 - \mu a_1) \geq 0 \qquad (34)$$

The validity of this condition depends, of course, on the relative supplies of the two resources and on the time horizon. We will assume that the condition holds for the resource prices p_{r1} and p_{r2} that are associated with the optimal path.

Note that at the steady state

$$p^* = U'[f(K) - \mu(K + a_1 v_1 + a_2 v_2)]$$

an equality that will be useful later on. Furthermore, both deposits will be exploited simultaneously, owing to the constant capital rental π and to the zero discount rate. If the discount rate is positive, no steady-state solution will exist, except if $f(K) = kK$, where k is a constant, and if $U(C)$ is homogeneous of degree two, in which case $U'' > 0$.

The analysis of the nature of the optimal path will now succeed in steps and the results will be illustrated by trajectories in (p, K) space. Note that $p > 0$ because of equation (29).

A. Assume there exists a point of time t', such that $\epsilon_1(t') = \epsilon_2(t') = 0$. Then

$$\theta(t') = p_{r1} + a_1 \pi(t') = p_{r2} + a_2 \pi(t') \text{ or}$$
$$p_{r1} - p_{r2} = \pi(t')(a_2 - a_1) \geq 0 \qquad (35)$$

so that $p_{r1} \geq p_{r2}$, which is intuitively obvious.

As $\pi(t')$ is a constant, it is seen that if $\pi(t)$ is changing over time, (35) and thereby $\epsilon_1 = \epsilon_2 = 0$ cannot hold over an interval with positive length. Moreover, it is obvious that

$$p_{r1} a_2 - p_{r2} a_1 > 0 \qquad (36)$$

B. Assume that $\epsilon_1 = 0$, $v_1 > 0$, $\mu_2 \geq 0$ for a subinterval of $[0, T]$. Then we can solve for π and θ from

$$(p - \theta)f' = \pi - a_1 \pi + \theta - p_{r1} = 0 \text{ and get}$$
$$\pi = \frac{(p - p_{r1})f'}{1 + a_1 f'} \qquad (37)$$

$$\theta = \frac{a_1 p f' + p_{r1}}{1 + a_1 f'}$$

From this μ_2 can be calculated

$$
\begin{aligned}
\epsilon_2 &= p_{r2} + a_2 \pi - \theta \\
&= \frac{p_{r2} - p_{r1} + p f'(a_2 - a_1) - f'(p_{r1} a_2 - p_{r2} a_1)}{1 + a_1 f'}
\end{aligned}
\tag{38}
$$

and $\epsilon_2 \geqq 0$ if and only if

$$p > \psi(K) \equiv \frac{p_{r1} - p_{r2}}{f'(a_2 - a_1)} + \frac{p_{r1} a_2 - p_{r2} a_1}{a_2 - a_1} > 0 \tag{39}$$

where $\psi(K)$ is defined by (39). $p = \psi(K)$ is a curve in (p, K) plane and $\epsilon_2 > 0$ if and only if the point (p, K) is above this curve (in the case $\epsilon_1 = 0$). Moreover, on this curve, $\epsilon_2 = 0$, and as p and K are continuous in time, ϵ_2 will be also. It is obvious that $\psi'(K) > 0$,

$\dot{p} = 0$ if and only if

$$\mu p = \pi = \frac{(p - p_{r1})f'}{1 + a_1 f'} \quad \text{or}$$

$$p = \tilde{p}_1(K) \equiv \frac{p_{r1} f'}{f'(1 - \mu a_1) - \mu} \tag{40}$$

where $\tilde{p}_1(K)$ is defined by (40). $\tilde{p}_1$ will have a discontinuity for $K = \tilde{K}_1$, where $\tilde{K}_1$ is defined by $f'(\tilde{K}_1)(1 - \mu a_1) - \mu = 0$. For $K > \tilde{K}_1$, $\tilde{p}_1 < 0$ and for $K < \tilde{K}_1$, $\tilde{p}_1 > 0$. The curve $\tilde{p}_1(K)$ thus divides the positive quadrant into two parts, with

$$
\begin{aligned}
&\dot{p} > 0 \text{ if } K > \tilde{K}_1, \text{ or } p < \tilde{p}_1 \\
&\dot{p} < 0 \text{ if } K < \tilde{K}_1 \text{ and } p > \tilde{p}_1 \\
&\dot{K} = 0 = f(K) - \mu[K + a_1 f(K)] - C \text{ if and only if} \\
&p = \bar{p}_1(K) \equiv U'[f(1 - \mu a_1) - \mu K]
\end{aligned}
\tag{41}
$$

The curve $p = \bar{p}_1(K)$ has a minimum for $K = \tilde{K}_1$. The curve $\bar{p}_1(K)$ also divides the positive quadrant into two parts and $\dot{K} > 0$ if $p > \bar{p}_1(K)$ and $\dot{K} < 0$ if $p < \bar{p}_1(K)$.

C. $\epsilon_1 \geqq 0$, $v_1 = 0$, $\epsilon_2 = 0$, $v_2 > 0$. In the same way as (36) was derived in **B**, one now gets

$$\pi = \frac{(p - p_{r2})f'}{1 + a_2 f'}$$

$$\theta = \frac{a_2 p f' + p_{r2}}{1 + a_2 f'} \tag{42}$$

and

$$\epsilon_1 = \frac{p_{r1} - p_{r2} + pf'(a_1 - a_2) - f'(p_{r2}a_1 - p_{r1}a_2)}{1 + a_2 f'} \tag{43}$$

and $\epsilon_1 \geqq 0$ if and only if $p \leq \psi(K)$. It is now clear that if

$p > \psi(K)$, then $\epsilon_1 = 0$, $v_1 > 0$, $\epsilon_2 > 0$, $v_2 = 0$

and if $p < \psi(K)$, then $\epsilon_1 > 0$, $v_1 = 0$, $\epsilon_2 = 0$, $v_2 > 0$

$\dot{p} = 0$ if and only if

$$p = \tilde{p}_2(K) \equiv \frac{p_{r2}f'}{f'(1 - \epsilon a_2) - \epsilon} \tag{44}$$

$p_2(K)$ has a discontinuity at $K = \tilde{K}_2$. It is easily seen that $\tilde{K}_2 < \tilde{K}_1$. In the same way as earlier, we have

$\tilde{p}_2 > 0$ for $K < \tilde{K}_2$

$\dot{p} > 0$ if and only if $K > \tilde{K}_2$ or $p < \tilde{p}_2$

$\dot{p} < 0$ if and only if $p > \tilde{p}_2$ and $K < \tilde{K}_2$ $\tag{45}$

$\dot{K} = 0$ if and only if

$p = \bar{p}_2(K) \equiv U'[f(1 - \mu a_2) - \mu K]$

It is readily seen that $\bar{p}_2(K)$ has a minimum for $K = \tilde{K}_2$.

D. We will now show that $\tilde{p}_1$ and $\tilde{p}_2$ intersect in the positive quadrant of the pK plane. We will thus show that the equation

$$\frac{f' p_{r1}}{f'(1 - \mu a_1) - \mu} = \frac{f' p_{r2}}{f'(1 - \mu a_2) - \mu}$$

has a solution K_{12}. The equation can be rewritten into

$$f' = \frac{\mu(p_{r1} - p_{r2})}{p_{r1}(1 - \mu a_2) - p_{r2}(1 - \mu a_1)}$$

Because of assumption (34) this equation has a solution. Moreover, we have that

$$\psi(K_{12}) = \frac{p_{r1}a_2 - p_{r2}a_1}{a_2 - a_1} + \frac{p_{r1} - p_{r2}}{f'(a_2 - a_1)}$$

$$= \frac{p_{r1}a_2 - p_{r2}a_1}{a_2 - a_1} + \frac{p_{r1}(1 - \mu a_2) - p_{r2}(1 - \mu a_1)}{\mu(a_2 - a_1)}$$

$$= \frac{p_{r1} - p_{r2}}{\mu(a_2 - a_1)} = \frac{f'p_{r1}}{f'(1 - \mu a_1) - \mu} = \tilde{p}_1(K_{12}) = \tilde{p}_2(K_{12})$$

As $\psi(K) > 0$, it follows that $\tilde{p}_1(K_{12}) = \tilde{p}_2(K_{12}) > 0$, and thus that $K_{12} < \tilde{K}_2 < \tilde{K}_1$. As the three curves ψ, $\tilde{p}_1$, and $\tilde{p}_2$ intersect at one point, it is clear that this point must be the steady-state configuration.

$$K_{12} = K^*, \quad \tilde{p}_1(K^*) > p^*$$

From (35) and (39) it is seen that

$$\psi(K) = \frac{\pi(t')}{f'} + \frac{p_{r1}a_2 - p_{r2}a_1}{a_2 - a_1}$$

and so

$$\psi'(k^*) = -\frac{\pi(t')}{(f')^2}f'' = -\frac{p_{r1}\mu f''}{f'[f'(1 - \mu a_1) - \mu]}$$

We also have that

$$\tilde{p}_1'(k^*) = -\frac{\mu p_{r1}f''}{[f'(1 - \mu a_1) - \mu]^2} = \frac{f'}{f'(1 - \mu a_1) - \mu}\psi'(K^*)$$

(where the prime indicates the derivative with respect to K) and as

$$\frac{f'}{f'(1 - \mu a_1) - \mu} > 1, \text{ it is clear that}$$

$$\tilde{p}_1'(K^*) > \psi'(K^*) \quad \text{ and so}$$

$$\tilde{p}_2(K) > \tilde{p}_1(K) > \psi(K) \quad \text{ for } K > K^* \quad \text{ and}$$

$$\tilde{p}_2(K) < \tilde{p}_1(K) < \psi(K) \quad \text{ for } K < K^*$$

As (K^*, p^*) has been identified with the steady state, it is clear from (25) and (33) that

$$p^* = U'[f(K^*) - \mu(K^* + a_1 v_1^* + a_2 v_2^*)]$$
$$= U'(f(K^*) - \mu\{K^* + a_1 v_1^* + a_2[f(K^*) - v_1^*]\})$$

If we regard the right-hand side as a function of v_1, it is clear from the assumptions $U'' < 0$, $a_1 < a_2$ that that function is decreasing in v_1. If $v_1 = f(K^*)$, the value of the function is $\bar{p}_1(K^*)$ and so $\bar{p}_1(K^*) < p^*$. In the same way it is seen that $\bar{p}_2(K^*) > p^*$. Moreover, it is easy to see that $\bar{p}_2(K) > \bar{p}_1(K)$ for all K. Finally $\bar{p}_1(K)$ and $\bar{p}_2(K)$ intersect with $\psi(K)$ at $\bar{K}_1$ and $\bar{K}_2$, respectively.

E. It is now possible to depict in a diagram all the constructions that have been made (figure 2). Before doing that, some observations can be made:

1. That part of $\tilde{p}_2(K)$ that is above $\psi(K)$ is not needed because $\tilde{p}_2(K)$ is constructed with the assumption that $\epsilon_1 > 0$, $\mu_2 = 0$, but that cannot be the case for points above $\psi(K)$.
2. Similarly, that part of $\tilde{p}_1(K)$ that is below $\psi(K)$ is not needed.
3. That part of $\bar{p}_1(K)$ that is below $\psi(K)$ is not needed.
4. That part of $\bar{p}_2(K)$ that is above $\psi(K)$ is not needed.

Figure 2 depicts all the possibilities that can arise. Using this diagram, the optimal trajectories can be drawn, and from these trajectories, the

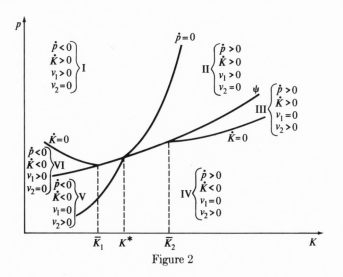

Figure 2

nature of the optimal path can be deduced. The Kp plane has been divided into six regions and the changes in p, K, in the different regions have been indicated. Some cases will be considered.

1. $K_o < K^*$, $K_T > K^*$ (figure 3).

As $K_o < K^*$, $K_T > K^*$, $p(0)$, K_o must be in region I because otherwise K and p would be decreasing all the time. For the same reason, the trajectory cannot enter regions V and VI. The trajectory will thus intersect the curve $\dot{p} = 0$ and enter region II. It cannot intersect ψ for $K < \bar{K}_2$, because in IV $\dot{p} > 0$, $\dot{K} < 0$. It will therefore stay in II or after some time enter region III. In the former case, the second deposit will not be used at all.

If, however, the planning period is long enough, deposit two will be used and the trajectory will enter III or possibly continue along the curve $\psi(K)$, which means that both deposits will be exploited simultaneously. In the former case, at the time the trajectory intersects $\psi(K)$, the first deposit is completely exhausted.

In any case, it is clear that in this growing economy, the deposit with the higher quality will be exploited first. Moreover, it is clear that the optimal trajectory has the turnpike property. Using the same method as Cass, for instance, it is possible to show that if the horizon is long enough, the optimal trajectory will spend most of the time in a neighborhood of the steady state.

2. $K_o > K^*$, $K_T < K^*$ (figure 4).

$p(0)$, K_o must in this case lie in region IV and $p(T)$, K_T must lie in either V or VI. But if $p(T)$, K_T is in V, the best deposit will never be

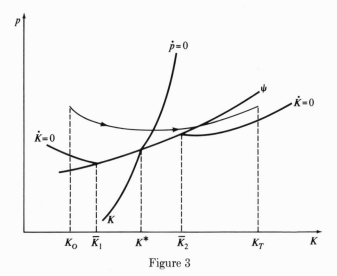

Figure 3

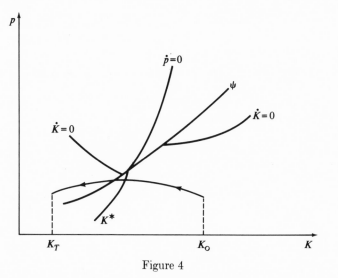

Figure 4

used, which is absurd, so $p(T)$, K_T will in fact be in VI. The turnpike property is seen to hold.

In this contracting economy, the deposit with the lowest quality will be used first, and the deposit with the highest quality will be used at the end. This result can be intuitively explained in the following way. In a contracting economy, capital will become more scarce, which implies increasing marginal productivity and increasing capital rentals. As the capital costs for operating the deposits will increase, the economy would do better to exploit the low-quality deposit first and hold the best deposit for the time when capital costs are higher.

3. $K_o > K^*$, $K_T > K^*$.

If T is small K_o, $p(0)$ may be in region II and only the best deposit will be exploited or at the curve ψ separating II from III and both deposits will be exploited simultaneously (this depends of course on the length of the planning period and the size of the deposits). If, however, T is large enough, such a policy will not be optimal, because K_T will be reached long before the end of the planning period and the economy would end up with a larger capital stock than required and a positive $p(T)$. In this case, the optimal trajectory must start in region IV, approach K^*, p^*, and then cross the ψ curve. The low-quality deposit will thus be exploited first.

The conclusions that may be drawn from this simple paradigm can be summarized as follows. The order in which deposits of different qualities should be exploited in an economy with zero discount rate depends on whether the economy is growing or contracting. If the economy is growing, the best deposits should be exploited first and if the economy is contracting, the best deposits should be spared for the end of the planning period, when the capital rentals are increasing. Moreover, the optimal time path, if the horizon is long enough, approaches a steady state and will stay in a neighborhood of this steady state most of the time. If we do not make the assumption (34), there will not exist a steady state as defined earlier. Optimal trajectories can, however, still be constructed and the same pattern will appear, namely, that the best deposit will be exploited first in a growing economy. We will not go into any details.

If there is a positive utility discount rate, the conclusions for a growing economy will of course be strengthened. The present value of the marginal cost of operating the deposit will now fall with time, not only because of the decreasing price for capital, but also because of the discount rate. In a contracting economy, however, the two forces will counteract each other and the result will in general depend on the rate of contraction of the capital stock.

One assumption basic to the analysis presented in this section must be commented upon. That is the assumption of perfectly malleable capital. In the long run, capital may be viewed as malleable, owing to depreciation and the importance of new investments. One should therefore expect that the conclusions that have been reached are true also when capital is not perfectly malleable, if the horizon is long enough. In the short run, one should on the other hand, expect to find essential differences. A closer analysis shows, however, that even with nonmalleable capital, the optimal trajectories are characterized by using the best deposits if the economy is growing.

Finally, the possibilities of technical progress deserve a remark. Technical progress in a model like this can take different forms: (a) an increase in the productivity of capital in the production of the composite good, (b) a decrease in the raw material requirement in the production of the composite good, (c) a decrease in the capital requirement in exploiting the deposits.

It seems difficult to analyze in detail the nature of the optimal time path in light of ongoing technical progress because it can happen that the low-quality deposit is changed to a high-quality deposit owing to some invention. One conclusion can be drawn, however, without any sophisticated analysis, and that is that technical progress will strengthen the case for using the best deposits first, in the hope that improved techniques will decrease the cost of exploiting low-quality deposits in the future.

Of the three types of technical progress, the second seems to be of particular interest because with this type of progress it seems possible that finite amounts of resources can support production forever. The existence of such technical progress has been reported in the literature, and it is easy to find examples.

However, there may exist a more important device for preventing total depletion of natural resources, and that is recycling of residuals generated in production and consumption. This possibility will be analyzed in the fourth paradigm.

5. THE THIRD PARADIGM: CHANGING POPULATION

So far, population and the labor force have been assumed to be constant. As stated earlier in this chapter, there are many people concerned with the "population bomb" and its consequences for depletion of natural resources and environmental quality. It is obvious that in the preceding models population growth would increase the scarcity of natural resources, decrease the per capita consumption, and possibly deteriorate the quality of the environment (in these models, the total flows of residuals into the environment are determined by the size of the natural resources deposits, so that an increase in population will not necessarily imply an increase in residuals). If exogenous population growth thus means a deterioration of the quality of life, it is natural to ask whether there exists an optimal size of population. The third paradigm is directed to this question.

In order to analyze such a question, one has to assume that it is possible to control the number of people in one way or another. There are only two methods which are supposed to be ethically satisfactory—control of the birthrate, and migration to and from the economy. With migration, it is at least in principle possible to change the population in steps of finite size rather than in a smooth way. On the other hand, it is not considered ethically satisfactory to force people to leave their homes, and economic incentives may therefore be the only instruments that are satisfactory. But, it is not clear that there exist incentives strong enough to induce people to migrate in the desired fashion, although history can give plenty of examples of migration induced by crowding, food shortages, etc. Therefore, migration may not be a feasible way to change the size of the population. Moreover, if we interpret the model as a world model, migration is obviously not a feasible way of changing the population size. The use of the birthrate as a way of controlling the population is even more difficult. First, in almost all societies, it is up to the parents to decide how many children they want to breed. Therefore a system of incentives must be developed in order to get the wanted birthrate. The existence of such a system has not been proved, and it is possible that the birthrate is quite inelastic with respect to economic factors. Second, a change in the birthrate changes the age distribution of the population. A change in population may therefore have as a result a substantial reduction in the productive part of it, the labor force, and an increase in the relative part formed by dependents. Such an unfavorable age distribution, if included in the model, has a stabilizing effect on the birthrate.

In spite of all these difficulties, it will be assumed here that it is possible to control the size of the population without any opportunity costs in the form of unfavorable age distributions. Moreover, it will be assumed that the labor force is a constant fraction of the total population, an assumption that is invalid as soon as the age distribution changes.

In defense of these assumptions, one may argue that the model is constructed for long-run analysis and in the long run it is possible to neglect short-run transitory effects (but the long run must be very long—some hundreds of years—because the short run is so long). This is the same argument that has been used for assuming an aggregate malleable capital stock in an economy with embodied technical progress, except that the time spans are presumably shorter in this case than in the case of changing birthrates. The model can now be described:

Find a maximum of

$$\int_0^T U\left(\frac{C}{L}, Y\right) dt \tag{47}$$

subject to

$$\dot{K} = f(K, L) - C - \mu K \tag{48}$$

$$\dot{Y} = \lambda(1 - Y) - \gamma z \tag{49}$$

$$C + \mu K - z \leqq 0 \tag{50}$$

$$\int_0^T f(K, L) dt \leqq S \tag{51}$$

$$K(0) = K_o \qquad Y(0) = Y_o \tag{52}$$

$$K(T) \geqq K_T \qquad Y(Y) \geqq Y_T \tag{53}$$

The Pontryagin necessary conditions become

$$\dot{p} = -p(f_1 - \mu) + \mu q + p_r f_1 \tag{54}$$

$$\dot{\delta} = -U_2 + \lambda\delta \tag{55}$$

$$\frac{1}{L} U_1 - p - q = 0 \tag{56}$$

$$-\gamma\delta + q = 0 \tag{57}$$

$$\frac{C}{L^2} U_1 = pf_2 + p_r f_2 = 0 \tag{58}$$

$$p(T)[K(T) - K_T] + \delta(T)[Y(T) - Y_T] = 0$$

$$p(T) \geqq 0 \qquad \delta(T) \geqq 0 \qquad \text{(transversality conditions)}$$

where all multipliers have the same meaning as before.

This system of differential equations is assumed to have a singular solution, a steady state for each nonnegative p_r [20]. It is now possible to show, exactly as in section 3, that this singular solution is a saddle point, and that the optimal time path will move, during the first phase of the planning period, to a neighborhood of the steady-state configuration, then stay in this neighborhood for most of the time, and in the final phase leave the steady state and approach the terminal requirement on the capital stock and environmental quality.

There thus exists an optimal population size which, although varying with time, may be approximated by the steady-state population. In the steady state, population will be constant and it is thus proved that in the long run and with limited natural resources zero population growth should be achieved. Even if the rent accruing to the natural resources is zero, indicating that natural resource scarcity is not bounding the total consumption, a steady state exists with zero population growth, but with a higher per capita consumption corresponding to $p_r = 0$. Even in the absence of natural resource scarcity, zero population growth should be aimed at.

6. THE FOURTH PARADIGM: RECYCLING

Up until now, the total flow of residuals generated in production and consumption has been assumed to be discharged into the environment. Such discharges harm the quality of the environment and waste resources.

One of the most important ways in which the quality of the environment can be improved seems to be through the recovery of raw material from residuals [21]. In this way, the scarcity of natural resources will be alleviated also. If complete recovery of raw materials is possible, then a steady state may be sustained forever, and the ultimate depletion of natural resources may lose its significance for the quality of human life.

In this section, recycling and recovery of raw materials from the flow of residuals will be introduced to the model discussed in the first paradigm. As in that paradigm, it is assumed that the population and the labor force are constant and that the utility time discount rate is zero.

The flow of residuals is not a flow of homogeneous residuals in real life. It consists of a large number of different kinds of materials, some of which are easy and cheap to recover and some of which are difficult and expensive to recover. It is obvious that those residuals which are cheap to recover will be processed first, and only if a large part of the total flow of residuals is going to be reclaimed will recovery of the more expensive residuals be undertaken. This means that the cost of recovery is a function not only of the amount recovered but also of the total flow of residuals. Let K_2 be the capital stock allocated to recovery, x the total flow of residuals, and v the flow of raw materials recovered. Remember that x and v are measured in tons, so that there is the restriction $x \geq v$.

The ideas formulated above on the costs of recovering can be formalized in the capital requirement function $K_2 \geq g(v, x)$ where g is a homogeneous function of the first degree, meaning that a proportionate change in the flow of residuals and the amount of raw materials recovered (keeping the rate of recovery v/x constant) causes the same proportionate change in the minimum capital stock. In other words, as long as the rate of recovery is constant, the real average cost of recovery is constant, independent of the amount recovered. It seems that with present technology, it is impossible to recover all raw material in the waste flow. Therefore, it will be assumed that

$$\frac{\partial g(x, x)}{\partial v} = g_1(x, x) = \infty$$

indicating that the marginal cost of recovery increases rapidly with the rate of recovery, and that complete recovery will never be optimal since it requires a too-large investment in recovery processes. It is assumed that g is twice continuously differentiable and that $g_1 > 0$, $g_2 < 0$ and that g is convex.

The difference between x and v, $x - v = z$, is the flow of residuals discharged into the environment. Obviously z must be nonnegative, as must v. Let K_1 denote the capital stock employed in the production of the composite good and let $K = K_1 + K_2$ denote the total capital stock in the economy. The rest of the symbols have the same meaning as before.

The model can now be formulated. Find the maximum of

$\int_0^T U(C, Y)dt$ subject to

$$\dot{K}_1 = f(K_1) - C - \mu K_1 - I_2 \tag{59}$$

$$\dot{K}_2 = I_2 - \mu K_2 \tag{60}$$

$$\dot{Y} = \lambda(1 - Y) - \gamma z \tag{61}$$

$$x = C + \mu(K_1 + K_2) \tag{62}$$

$$x = z + v \tag{63}$$

$$K_2 \geqq g(v, x) \tag{64}$$

$$\int_0^t (f - v)dt \leqq S, \text{ all } t \tag{65}$$

$$z \geqq 0, v \geqq 0 \tag{66}$$

$$K(0) = K_1(0) + K_2(0) = K_o, Y(0) \\ = Y_o, K(T) \geqq K_T, Y(T) \geqq Y_T \tag{67}$$

Some comments on the model are in order before the analysis of the model can begin. First, I_2 is the gross investment in recovery production. I_2 is not restricted in sign, reflecting the assumption of perfect malleable capital.

Second, in (62) and (63) the restrictions are written as equalities, which implies that the multipliers associated with these constraints are not necessarily nonnegative. As the flow of residuals can have two effects—damaging the environment and generating raw materials—it is clear that the price attached to residuals can be of either sign, depending upon the relative strength of these effects.

Third, in (65) it is assumed that it is possible to stock raw materials with no cost. From the materials balance, it is clear that when the capital stock is growing in the economy, raw materials recovered from residuals, even if the rate of recovery is one, are not sufficient for production and so the natural resources or stockpiles of raw materials recovered at an earlier time must be used. If the total capital stock is contracting and the recovery rate is one, more raw material than needed will be recovered and a stock of raw material will be piled up. It is, however, impossible to borrow natural resources from the future, and so the accumulated use of raw materials at any point may never exceed the accumulated recovery of raw materials plus the initial stock S. Let us write

$$R(t) = S - \int_0^t (f - v)dt \tag{68}$$

The time derivative of R is

$$\dot{R} = v - f \qquad R(0) = S \tag{69}$$

and R is restricted to be nonnegative.

$$R \geqq 0 \tag{70}$$

Equation (69) and the equality (70) are equivalent to (65) and will be used in the sequel. Fourth, it is assumed that g is defined only for non-negative v, and that $g_1(0, x) = 0$, so that in optimum $v > 0$. Moreover, as complete recovery is unfeasible, $z > 0$.

It is now possible to use the Pontryagin maximum principle again in analyzing the nature of the optimal time path [22]. Let p_1, p_2, δ, p_r, φ, and q be multipliers, π and Γ, nonnegative multipliers. The Pontryagin necessary conditions then become

$$\dot{p}_1 = -p_1(f' - \mu) + \mu\varphi + (p_r + \Gamma)f' \tag{71}$$

$$\dot{p}_2 = \mu p_2 + \mu\varphi - \pi \tag{72}$$

$$\dot{\delta} = -U_2 + \lambda\delta \tag{73}$$

$$\dot{p}_r = 0 \tag{74}$$

$$U_1 - p_1 - \varphi = 0 \tag{75}$$

$$-p_1 + p_2 = 0 \tag{76}$$

$$-\gamma\delta + q = 0 \tag{77}$$

$$\varphi - q - \pi g_2 = 0 \tag{78}$$

$$-\pi g_1 + p_r + \Gamma + q = 0 \tag{79}$$

$$\Gamma R = 0 \qquad \Gamma(v - f) = 0 \tag{80}$$

$$p(T)[K_1(T) + K_2(T) - K_T] = 0 \qquad p(T) \geqq 0 \tag{81}$$

$$\delta(T)[Y(T) - Y_T] = 0 \qquad \delta(T) \geqq 0 \tag{82}$$

The interpretations of these conditions are straightforward; p_1 and p_2 are the demand prices for capital goods and according to (76) Jevon's law of indifference holds, so that $p_1 = p_2$. Denote the common value p. From (71) and (72) it is seen that $(p - p_r - \Gamma)f' = \pi$. If $p_r + \Gamma$ is interpreted as the price for raw materials, independent of their origin, and π as the capital rental, this is the well-known condition for maximum profit. δ is interpreted as before, namely as the demand price for environmental quality. From (73) and (82) it is seen that this price is always nonnegative. From (77) it is seen that q is nonnegative too. q is obviously the marginal value of the damage to the environment caused by discharges of residuals. φ is interpreted as the marginal value of residuals. This value can obviously be of both signs, as an increase in the amount of residuals will both increase the damage to the environment from waste discharges and decrease the cost of recovering raw materials from residuals. If φ is positive, the damage to the environment outweighs the reduction in recovery costs, and if φ is negative, the opposite relation holds. Condition (75) says that the marginal utility of consumption is equal to the opportunity cost, which consists of capital goods forgone and the value of the residuals generated by a marginal increase in consumption. From (78) it is seen that the marginal value of residuals is equal to the marginal damage from waste discharges plus the reduction in recovery costs πg_2, due to a marginal increase in residuals. In (79) it is seen that the marginal cost of recovery, πg_1, is equal to the price of raw materials plus the value of the environmental damage avoided by increasing the recovery rate.

Since $z > 0$, natural resources must be exploited to meet the raw material requirement, but it can happen that in a subperiod with a contracting capital stock the recovery of raw material is enough to meet this requirement. But even if this would happen, R, the remaining amounts of natural resources, will still in general be different from zero. Only if the contraction of the capital stock occurs in a period when the natural resources are exhausted will R be equal to zero. In an economy that is growing all the time, such a situation cannot occur. From (80) it thus is seen that Γ equals zero for most of the time, and for the whole planning period if the economy is growing or contracting at a slow pace. With this background it is natural to assume that $\Gamma = 0$ for all t.

Since $p_1 = p_2$, it is seen from (71), (72), and (75) that $(p - p_r)f' = \pi \geq 0$.

If K_1, φ, π, x, v, and q are eliminated from the system, if the total capital stock $K = K_1 + K_2$ is introduced, and if we set $p = p_1 = p_2$, the system can be written as

$$\dot{K} = f(K - K_2) - \mu K - C \tag{83}$$

$$\dot{Y} = \lambda(1 - Y) - \gamma z \tag{61}$$

$$\dot{p} = -(p - p_r)f' + \mu U_1 \tag{84}$$

$$\dot{\delta} = -U_2 + \lambda\delta \tag{73}$$

$$g(\mu K + C - z, \mu K + C) - K_2 = 0 \tag{74}$$

$$(p - p_r)f'g_2 - U_1 + p + \gamma\delta = 0 \tag{75}$$

$$(p - p_r)f'g_1 - p_r - \gamma\delta = 0 \tag{76}$$

$$R(t) = \int_0^t [f - (\mu K + C - z)]dt - S \leqq 0 \tag{77}$$

If, as earlier, we regard p_r as a parameter, the first seven equations is a system in seven unknowns. A singular solution to this system, if it exists, is defined by the following equations:

$$\begin{aligned}
&f - \mu K - C = 0 \\
&\lambda(1 - Y) - \gamma z = 0 \\
&-(p - p_r)f' + \mu U_1 = 0 \\
&-U_2 + \gamma\delta = 0 \\
&g - K_2 = 0 \\
&(p - p_r)\,f'g_2 - U_1 + p + \gamma\delta = 0 \\
&(p - p_r)f'g_1 - p_r - \gamma\delta = 0
\end{aligned} \tag{85}$$

In appendix A (section 8), it is shown that this system has a unique solution $(K^*, Y^*, p^*, \delta^*, K_2^*, C^*, z^*)$, the steady-state solution.

As is shown in appendix B (section 9), the eigenvalues to the linearized system occur in parts, symmetric around the origin. If κ_1 is an eigenvalue, so is $-\kappa_1$. It is also clear from appendix B that no eigenvalue is purely imaginary. Two eigenvalues have negative real parts, and two positive real parts. The steady state is thus a saddle point for the system, and the turnpike property is valid for this model. If the planning period is long enough, the optimal time path will approach a neighborhood of the steady state, stay in this neighborhood for most of the time, and finally leave the neighborhood and move so that the terminal requirements on capital and environmental quality are met.

Owing to the possibilities of recovering raw materials from the flow of residuals, the natural resources will not have such a decisive role as they had in the first paradigm. In the first paradigm, the total consumption and capital accumulation during the planning period were determined solely by the availability of natural resources. Recycling residuals, however, allows consumption and capital accumulation to exceed the bounds given by nature. Still, there is a threat that the natural resources will be completely depleted. In the first paradigm, complete depletion of natural resources would mean an immediate end to all economic activities. In this paradigm, however, the exhaustion of natural resources would not result in such a drastic end to mankind. The capital stock will supply a flow of raw materials by its depreciation, and the economy will contract with a continuously decreasing consumption. By reallocating most of the capital stock to recovery processes, the rate of recovery will be increased and the pace at which consumption decreases can be made very small. Such a development can be analyzed within the framework of the model presented in this section. If the planning period is very long, so that total depletion of natural resources is expected, then the steady-state consumption will be very low, the capital stock in the production of the composite good will be very low, but the capital stock in recovery processes will be very high. The economy will move from a high initial consumption level toward the steady state, and stay in the neighborhood of the steady state for a very long time, while the capital stocks are slowly diminishing. If there are no terminal requirements, the economy will at the end of the planning period decrease its capital stocks at a faster pace in a last effort to make life worth living.

It is now clear that it is possible for the economy to survive for even very long periods when there are recycling possibilities, but the quality of life, measured in consumption, will be smaller the longer the time span is. On the other hand, the quality of the environment will be high.

The previous paradigms have promised a decent life until the end of the horizon, and then sudden death. This last paradigm promises almost eternal life, but it is a life of continuously decreasing quality. Obviously, none of these outlooks for the future may be realized; technological innovations may change the picture completely.

7. TECHNICAL PROGRESS

Although the prospects derived in the four paradigms are gloomy, the history of mankind has not yet proved their validity. Barnett and Morse [23], who have carefully studied the empirical relevance of the hypotheses of increasing resource scarcity formulated by Malthus, Ricardo, and other classical economists, concluded that natural resource scarcity has not in general limited economic growth. They started with two hypotheses of increasing resource scarcity—the Malthusian idea of a constant supply of renewable homogeneous resources and the Ricardian idea of an unlimited supply of resources but of a decreasing quality—and added to this the existence of nonrenewable deposits of natural resources. With population growth and an increasing capital stock, increasing resource scarcity is to be expected. But their empirical tests showed very few signs of increasing scarcity of resources, and in the aggregate they could not find any evidence that supported their hypotheses. Their explanation for the breakdown of the classical scarcity doctrine is almost completely based on what they call sociotechnological changes.

The four paradigms studied in this chapter have in common a technological and scientific knowledge that is constant over time. If technical change is so important for the economics of natural resource availability, then the models should be modified to take this factor into account. In this last section this will be done in an informal way and no formalized models will be constructed for an analysis of technological change.

Within the framework of the fourth paradigm, sociotechnological changes can be classified in the following five categories:
1. New discoveries of natural resources.
2. Inventions which make it profitable to use previously unused resources.
3. Inventions which make it possible to increase output of the composite good without increasing the raw material input.
4. Increases in the efficiency in recovery processes.
5. Increases in the productivity of capital in the production of the composite good.

1. New discoveries of natural resources are made almost continuously.

If one looks, for example, at the forecasts of available fossil fuels made at various points of time, many of them have predicted acute shortages of energy some decades or so ahead. But when the times for the alleged shortages have arrived, the net amounts of available fuels have increased in spite of the consumption of fuels. The explanation is, of course, the discovery of new deposits of fossil fuels.

Earlier in history, the discovery of new resources was probably a chance phenomenon, but today discoveries are the results of systematic explorations based on economic incentives. It seems likely that the size of such explorations depends very much on the rent p_r accruing to the natural resources. In the model, this type of technical change should therefore be introduced as an increase in the variable S, the size of the available deposits, and this increase should be a function of the scarcity of natural resources. As the rent in this model is constant, it is to be expected that the size of the explorations will be constant over time. But since the earth's resources are limited, a time will ultimately arrive when all existing deposits are discovered, and this kind of technical change can no longer support economic growth.

2. There are many examples of inventions that have allowed profitable exploitation of unused resources, and they have increased resource availability immensely. Yet, the "big" invention in this field may come in about five decades, namely, when nuclear fusion can supply virtually unlimited amounts of energy. The impact of nuclear fusion processes cannot be overstated. To quote Barnett and Morse [24]: "Once energy becomes available in unlimited quantities at constant cost, the processing of large quantities of low-grade resource material presumably can be undertaken at constant cost without further technological advance, and at declining cost with technological advance and capital accumulation. Hence, the physicist's concept of 'available energy' constitutes a plateau of virtually limitless extent, and one whose availability will tend to reduce virtually all other resource conversion processes to a constant-cost basis as well." With unlimited quantities of energy at constant cost, it may very wel' be possible to recover all the residuals generated in production and consumption, and a steady state is thus possible at which the economy is repeating itself forever. Moreover, if such a situation will arise, the optimal time paths for the economy can be analyzed within the usual optimal growth models where no explicit account of environmental quality and natural resource scarcity is taken. A technical change of this kind is related to the rents accruing to natural resources because the incentives will come from the scarcity of natural resources.

3. Technical progress that increases output without increasing raw material input has the same incentives outlined in point 2. However, the

incentives also arise from the increase in environmental quality, owing to the smaller flow of residuals associated with a flow of consumption goods. By embodying less material in the commodities, this kind of technical progress produces less waste materials. It is thus possible to increase consumption without increasing the extraction of natural resources and without increasing the waste load discharged into the environment. In an economy where no considerations of the environment are taken (that is, where $q = 0$) because of institutional imperfections, the incentives for technical progress will be too small, and the harmful effects will not be limited to the quality of the environment, but will increase the misuse of natural resources.

4. Like the previous kinds of technical change, the incentives for increases in the efficiency of recovery processes will be a function of the resource scarcity and the environmental quality, that is, the prices q and p_r. In an economy that does not face increasing natural resource scarcity, it seems that the incentives to find more efficient processes of recovering raw materials will depend very much on the opportunity cost of not recovering raw materials, that is, the damage to the environment from the discharge of wastes.

If, however, the proper incentives are given, the efficiency of recovering and recycling may increase very rapidly. In fact, the efficiency may grow to such an extent that complete recovery is possible and the economy ends up at a steady state where no discharges of residuals are made.

5. Increase in capital productivity, the last kind of technical change, is the same kind that is usually discussed in aggregate growth models, and requires no further comment.

One of the important points in the above discussion is that technical progress is not something that comes to the economy independent of the actions taken. On the contrary, technical progress should be viewed as endogenous, as something that depends on the incentives and on the actions taken in the economy [25]. It should also be clear that it is possible to direct technological progress to some extent by providing the proper incentives. If the system of incentives is distorted by imperfect markets or a too-short time horizon in a decentralized economy, or for any other reason, it is necessary to correct these distortions if technical changes are to be as beneficial as possible.

One of the major distortions in present capitalistic economies is the lack of revealed concern about the environment. (It seems that most people are concerned about environmental quality but policy measures that can be assumed to reveal such concerns are so far on a very small scale.) There are thus no systematic incentives for producers to develop new methods of recovering and recycling, in spite of their importance for both environmental quality and the supply of raw materials.

8. APPENDIX A

We will in this appendix prove that the system (85) has a unique solution. To do that, we will show that (85) can be identified with the first-order necessary conditions for a constraint maximization problem. It will be shown that this maximization problem has a solution so that (85) has a solution. After that it will be shown that all solutions to (85) correspond to local maxima, and finally that a local maximum must be a global maximum. As the objective function is strictly concave, the global maximum must be unique, and thus the solution to (85) must be unique.

The constrained maximization problem is the following:

$$\max\ U(C,\ Y)$$

$$\text{subject to } -f(K - K_2) + \mu K + C \leq 0$$

$$-K_2 + g(v,\ v + z) \leq 0$$

$$v + z - K - C = 0$$

$$\lambda(1 - Y) - \gamma z \leq 0$$

$$f(K - K_2) - v - S \leq 0$$

$$C \geqq 0,\ K \geqq K_2 \geqq 0,\ z \geqq 0,\ v \geqq 0$$

It is obvious that the constraints are consistent. Moreover, points $(C,\ Y,\ K,\ K_2,\ z,\ v)$ satisfying the constraints are regular points, that is, the Jacobian matrix of the constraints has maximal rank [26].

If the problem has a solution, there exist multipliers p, π, φ, δ, and p_r, all nonnegative except perhaps φ, such that with

$$L = U - p(-f + \mu K + C) - \pi(-K_2 + g) - \varphi(-v - z + \mu K + C)$$
$$- \delta[z - \lambda(1 - Y)] - p_r(f - v - S)$$

the maximum point satisfies

$$\frac{\partial L}{\partial C} = U_1 - p - \varphi \leqq 0$$

$$\frac{\partial L}{\partial Y} = U_2 - \lambda\delta = 0$$

$$\frac{\partial L}{\partial K} = (p - p_r)f' - \mu(p + \varphi) \leqq 0$$

$$\frac{\partial L}{\partial K_2} = -(p - p_r)f' + \pi \leqq 0$$

$$\frac{\partial L}{\partial z} = -\pi g_2 + \varphi - \gamma\delta \leqq 0$$

$$\frac{\partial L}{\partial v} = -\pi(g_1 + g_2) + \varphi + p_r \leqq 0$$

with equality when the corresponding variable is strictly positive. In the fourth condition, we have equality when $K_2 > 0$, and $K - K_2 > 0$. Because of the assumptions we have made on the utility function [U is concave, and $U_1(O, Y) = +\infty$], the production function [$f'' < 0$, and $f'(0) = +\infty$], and the recovery function [g convex, and $g_1(O, x) = 0$], it follows that if a maximum exists, we must have $C > 0$, $K > K_2 > 0$, $v > 0$, and $z > 0$. We can therefore replace all inequalities among the first-order conditions with equalities. This implies, among other things, that $\varphi = \pi g_2 + \gamma \delta \geqq 0$.

Furthermore, at the optimum (if it exists), all constraints except perhaps the first and the last are satisfied as equalities. Assume therefore that $-f + \mu K + C < 0$. This implies that $p = 0$, and hence $-p_r f' - \mu \varphi = 0$. But as $p_r \geqq 0$, $\varphi \geqq 0$, it follows that $\varphi = 0$, $p_r f' = 0$. But $U_1 - p - \varphi = 0$, and thus $U_1 = 0$, implying $C = +\infty$, which is impossible. Thus $p > 0$, and at the optimum $-f + K + C = 0$.

All constraints except perhaps the last one are thus at the optimum satisfied as equalities. But we can select S at will, and therefore we can choose it so small that the last constraint is also satisfied as an equality. If there exist local maxima besides the global maximum, the last constraint may, however, be satisfied as an inequality at those local maxima.

We will now show that the constrained maximum problem has a solution. Y is naturally bounded from above by 1, and C is also bounded from above, which can be seen from $C \leq f - \mu K \leq f(K^*) - \mu K^*$, where K^* is defined as yielding a maximum of $f - \mu K$. As it is assumed that $f(0) = 0$, and $f'(\infty) = 0$, it follows that $f - K$ has a maximum. U is thus defined on a nonempty bounded set in R^2. As all functions appearing are continuous, this set is closed and thus compact. U has therefore a maximum.

This means that the first-order conditions to the constrained maximum problem have a solution. But these conditions can be rearranged to

$$f - \mu K - C = 0$$

$$\lambda(1 - Y) - \gamma z = 0$$

$$g - K_2 = 0$$

$$(p - p_r)f'g_2 - U_1 + p + \gamma \delta = 0$$

$$(p - p_r)f'g_1 + p_r - \gamma \delta = 0$$

$$U_2 - \gamma \delta = 0$$

$$-v - z + \mu K + C = 0$$

$$(p - p_r)f' - \mu U_1 = 0$$

$$f - v - S = 0$$

If we disregard the last equation, and eliminate v, this system is identical to system (85). Moreover, it is clear that we can choose S in such a way that p_r is equal in the two systems. We can therefore conclude that the system (85) has a solution.

Next, we will prove that each solution to (85) corresponds to a local maximum. In order to do that, we will show that the Hessian of the Lagrangian L with respect to C, Y, K, K_2, z, and v is negative definite on the tangent cone defined by the constraints.

The Hessian can be written

$$
L = \begin{bmatrix}
U_{11} & U_{12} & 0 & 0 & 0 & 0 & 0 \\
U_{12} & U_{22} & 0 & 0 & 0 & 0 & 0 \\
0 & 0 & (p-p_r)f'' & -(p-p_r)f'' & 0 & 0 \\
0 & 0 & -(p-p_r)f'' & (p-p_r)f'' & 0 & 0 \\
0 & 0 & 0 & 0 & -g_{22} & -(g_{12}+g_{22}) \\
0 & 0 & 0 & 0 & -(g_{12}+g_{22}) & -(g_{11}+2g_{12}+g_{22})
\end{bmatrix}
$$

The tangent cone is determined by

$$
\begin{aligned}
(-f' + \mu)dK + dC + f'dK_2 &= 0 \\
-dK_2 + (g_{21} + g_{22})dv + g_{22}dz &= 0 \\
-dv - dz + dK + dC &= 0 \\
dz + dY &= 0 \\
f'dK - f'dK_2 - dv &= 0
\end{aligned}
$$

By solving for dC, dY, dK, dK_2, and dz in terms of dv, one arrives at

$$
\begin{aligned}
dC &= \{1 + \mu(g_1 + g_2)\}dv \\
dY &= 0 \\
dK &= -(g_1 + g_2)dv \\
dK_2 &= (g_1 + g_2)dv \\
dz &= 0 \\
dv &= dv
\end{aligned}
$$

or that the tangent cone is determined by vectors of the form

$$
\begin{bmatrix}
1 + \mu(g_1 + g_2) \\
0 \\
-(g_1 + g_2) \\
(g_1 + g_2) \\
0 \\
1
\end{bmatrix} dv
$$

On this tangent cone, the quadratic form defined by the matrix (L) is equal to

$$\{U_{11}[1 + \mu(g_1 + g_2)^2] + 4(p - p_r)f''(g_1 + g_2)^2$$
$$- \pi(g_{11} + 2g_{12} + g_{22})\}(dv)^2$$

Each term is negative, and thus the quadratic form must also be negative for all dv different from zero. We can therefore conclude that all solutions to the first-order conditions correspond to local maxima.

If the feasible region, that is, the set defined by the constraints, is convex, we could conclude that the only solution to the first-order conditions is the unique global maximum. Unfortunately, the feasible region is not convex, and therefore we have to make a careful analysis before we can state that there is a unique solution. Let $X = (C, Y, K, K_2, z, v)$ be a global maximum, and let $X' = (C', Y', K', K_2', z', v')$ be any other solution to (85), which as we have seen corresponds to a local maximum. Assume that X' is such that $f(K' - K_2') - v' < S$. We already know that $f(K - K_2) - v = S$. Then consider the convex combination of the two solutions:

$$tX + (1 - t)X' \qquad 0 \leqq t \leqq 1$$

For such a combination we have

$$S \geqq f[t(K - K_2) + (1 - t)(K' - K_2')] - tv - (1 - t)v'$$

for at least small positive t. There is thus a convex combination of the two solutions that is in the feasible region, and we have

$$U[tC + (1 - t)C', tY + (1 - t)Y'] > tU(C, Y) + (1 - t)U(C', Y')$$

which shows that X' cannot be a local maximum.

We thus have for all solutions equality in the last constraint, or $f(K' - K_2') - v = S$ for all solutions X'. From the constraints we can therefore deduce that $z = C + \mu K - v = f - v = S$, and so z is unique for all solutions. Moreover, $Y = 1 - (\gamma/\lambda)z$, and so Y is also unique for all solutions. In particular, this means that there cannot be two different global maxima, because $U(C, Y) = U(C', Y)$ implies that $C = C'$.

Assume now that X' is a local maximum different from X, and let $K_1 = K - K_2$. Then $f(K_1) - v = S$ defines $K_1 = \psi(v)$ uniquely such that $f[\psi(v)] - v = S$, because $f' > 0$ for all K_1.

We now have

$$C = S + v - \mu[\psi(v) + K_2] = S + v - \mu\psi - g(v, v + S)$$

and C is expressed as a function of v alone. The derivative of this function is

$$\frac{dC}{dv} = 1 - \mu\psi - \mu g_1 - \mu g_2$$

At an optimum (local or global) we must have $dC/dv \leqq 0$, because we know that $z = z' = S$, and that $Y = Y'$.

On the other hand, we can also write C as

$$C = S + v - \mu\psi - \mu(v + S)g\left(\frac{v}{v + S}, 1\right)$$

because g is homogeneous of the first degree, and

$$\frac{dC}{dv} = 1 - \mu\psi' - \mu\left\{g + (v + S)g_1 \frac{S}{(v + S)^2}\right\}$$

If $v' = 0$, it follows that $K_2 = g(O, S) = 0$, but we have already concluded that $K_2 > 0$, and so $v' > 0$.

At an optimum we must therefore have $dC/dv = 0$, and thus

$$\frac{1}{\mu} - \frac{1}{f'} = g + \frac{S}{v + S}g_1$$

If this equation has a unique solution, then any local optimum must be identical to the global optimum [as we have already shown that (27) has a solution, we know that this equation must have a solution]. The left-hand side is decreasing in v because its derivative is $f''/(f')^2 < 0$. The derivative of the right-hand side is

$$\frac{S^2}{(v + S)^2}g_{11} > 0$$

and so the right-hand side is increasing in v. The equation can thus have only one solution. We have thus proved that $v = v'$, and from this it follows that all other variables are uniquely determined also.

9. APPENDIX B

In this appendix we will discuss the variational equations of the Euler–Lagrange equations for an arbitrary autonomous variational problem. In particular, we will show that the eigenvalues for the variational equations will occur pairwise, such that one element in a pair is equal to the other element except that it has the opposite sign.

Let y be an n-vector of state variables and let p be the corresponding n-vector of auxiliary variables, and finally let x be an m-vector of controls. The Hamiltonian to a variational problem is then $H(y, p, x)$. H is linear in p.

The Euler–Lagrange equations can be written

$$
\begin{aligned}
\dot{y} &= \nabla_p H \\
\dot{p} &= -\nabla_p H \\
0 &= \nabla_x H
\end{aligned}
\tag{1}
$$

where ∇_y denotes the gradient of H as a function of y, etc.

If the Hamiltonian is sufficiently differentiable, the system (1) can be written

$$
\begin{aligned}
\dot{y} &= H_{yp}(y - \bar{y}) + H_{pp}(p - \bar{p}) + H_{xp}(x - \bar{x}) \\
&\quad + o(y - \bar{y}, p - \bar{p}, x - \bar{x}) \\
\dot{p} &= -H_{yy}(y - \bar{y}) - H_{py}(p - \bar{p}) - H_{xy}(x - \bar{x}) \\
&\quad + o(y - \bar{y}, p - \bar{p}, x - \bar{x}) \\
0 &= H_{yx}(y - \bar{y}) + H_{px}(p - \bar{p}) + H_{xx}(x - \bar{x}) \\
&\quad + o(y - \bar{y}, p - \bar{p}, x - \bar{x})
\end{aligned}
\tag{2}
$$

where $(\bar{y}, \bar{p}, \bar{x})$ is the singular solution (assuming such a solution exists), H_{yp} is the matrix of partial derivatives of the second order, evaluated at $(\bar{y}, \bar{p}, \bar{x})$, etc., and o are functions of second order of smallness. Note that H_{py} is the transpose of H_{yp}.

We now assume that H_{xx} is nonsingular (which is true in all our applications). Neglecting the o functions, we can solve for $x - \bar{x}$, which substituted in the two first sets of equations yields

$$
\begin{aligned}
\dot{y} &= (H_{yp} - H_{xp}H_{xx}^{-1}H_{yx})(y - \bar{y}) + (H_{pp} - H_{xp}H_{xx}^{-1}H_{px})(p - \bar{p}) \\
\dot{p} &= (H_{yy} - H_{xy}H_{xx}^{-1}H_{yx})(y - \bar{y}) - (H_{py} - H_{xy}H_{xx}^{-1}H_{px})(p - \bar{p})
\end{aligned}
\tag{3}
$$

The characteristic equation derived from these variational equations is

$$\begin{vmatrix} H_{yp} - H_{xp}H_{xx}^{-1}H_{yx} - \lambda & H_{pp} - H_{xp}H_{xx}^{-1}H_{px} \\ -(H_{yy} - H_{xy}H_{xx}^{-1}H_{yx}) & -(H_{py} - H_{xy}H_{xx}^{-1}H_{px}) - \lambda \end{vmatrix} = 0 \qquad (4)$$

By transposing rows, and by changing sign, this equation can be written

$$\begin{vmatrix} H_{yy} - H_{xy}H_{xx}^{-1}H_{yx} & H_{py} - H_{xy}H_{xx}^{-1}H_{px} + \lambda \\ H_{yp} - H_{xp}H_{xx}^{-1}H_{yx} - \lambda & H_{pp} - H_{xp}H_{xx}^{-1}H_{px} \end{vmatrix} = 0 \qquad (5)$$

From (5) it is immediately seen that if λ is an eigenvalue, then $-\lambda$ is also an eigenvalue, because the determinant in (5) is symmetric except for the term λ. We have thus proved that the eigenvalues will occur in pairs, such that the eigenvalues in each pair will have opposite signs.

The characteristic equation can also be written as

$$\begin{vmatrix} H_{xx} & H_{x/} & H_{xp} \\ H_{yx} & H_{y/} & H_{yp} - \lambda \\ H_{px} & H_{py} + \lambda & H_{pp} \end{vmatrix} = 0 \qquad (6)$$

As H is linear in p, $H_{pp} = 0$. In all our applications we have assumed that H is strictly concave in (x, y). This implies that the quadratic form

$$[dx, dy] \begin{vmatrix} H_{xx} & H_{xy} \\ H_{yx} & H_{yy} \end{vmatrix} \begin{vmatrix} dx \\ dy \end{vmatrix}$$

must be negative definite, and in particular for (dx, dy) satisfying $H_{px}dx + H_{py}dy = 0$ (here dx and dy are m- and n-dimensional vectors, respectively). It is well known, however, that this implies that the determinant

$$D = \begin{vmatrix} H_{xx} & H_{xy} & H_{xp} \\ H_{yx} & H_{yy} & H_{yp} \\ H_{px} & H_{py} & 0 \end{vmatrix} \qquad (7)$$

has the same sign as $(-1)^{n+m}$. In particular, this means that $D \neq 0$, and from (6) we see that zero is not an eigenvalue for the variational equations.

By direct computation of the characteristic equation in the three applications we have in this chapter, it can be seen that no eigenvalue is purely imaginary, so that the real parts of all eigenvalues are different from zero.

NOTES

1. See, for example, Paul R. Ehrlich, *The Population Bomb* (Ballantine, New York, 1971). In this book, Ehrlich gives population growth the blame for almost all the major evils in the world today and for those that can be expected in the future.

2. There is a huge literature on turnpike theory, but only that part which deals with consumption turnpike theory is of relevance here. Samuelson seems to be the first who discussed consumption turnpike theory (actually he was the first to comment on turnpike theory at all), and the turnpike theory presented in this chapter has a very close resemblance to Samuelson's commentary in the *American Economic Review*, vol. 55, no. 3, 486–496 (1965). Other important references are David Cass, "Optimum Growth in an Aggregate Model of Capital Accumulation," *Econometrica*, vol. 34, no. 4, 833–850 (1966) and Karl Shell, "Optimal Programs of Capital Accumulation for an Economy in Which There Is Exogenous Technical Change," in Karl Shell (ed.), *Essays on the Theory of Optimal Economic Growth* (MIT Press, Cambridge, Mass., 1967). The mathematical theorems which will be used in this chapter are the Pontryagin maximum principle, standard results from the theory of ordinary differential equations, and a theorem derived in Karl-Göran Mäler, "Studier i intertemporal allokering" (unpublished doctoral thesis, Stockholm University, in Swedish).

For those not acquainted with turnpike theory, a short introduction may be in order. In most of the intertemporal models analyzed by economists, there exist steady states, that is, allocations of capital stocks and consumption in such a way that all essential variables change at the same rate. Among all such steady states, there is in general only one that satisfies the necessary conditions for optimal growth. This steady state will be referred to as the steady state or the optimal steady state. The turnpike theory asserts that given an arbitrary optimal program of capital accumulation, this program will have a tendency to approach the steady state in the long run. Even if the initial capital stocks and the terminal capital requirements are different from the steady state configuration, the optimal program will spend most of the time, if the horizon is long enough, in a small neighborhood of the steady state. The importance of this theory lies in the fact that it allows us to approximate an optimal program by a program that steers the economy toward the steady state and that it allows us to analyze the effects of parameter changes by analyzing the effects on the steady state.

3. The classical reference is Kenneth J. Arrow, *Social Choice and Individual Values* (Yale Univ. Press, New Haven, 1963). Arrow laid down five reasonable conditions that a social choice mechanism should satisfy, and showed that such a mechanism does not exist. Here we do not bother about the existence of a social choice mechanism that is fair in some sense. The important thing is that a mecha-

nism exists, and this mechanism can be based on some voting procedure or it can reflect the preferences of a dictator.

4. See David Gale, "Optimal Development in a Multi-Sector Economy," *Review of Economic Studies*, no. 34, 1–18 (1967).

5. Arthur C. Pigou, *The Economics of Welfare* (St. Martin's, New York, 1962), pp. 24–26; Frank P. Ramsay, "A Mathematical Theory of Savings," *Economic Journal*, vol. 38, pp. 543–559 (1928).

6. Tjalling Koopmans, "Stationary Ordinal Utility and Impatience," *Econometrica*, vol. 28, no. 2, 287–309 (1960).

7. Kenneth J. Arrow and Mordecai Kurz, *Public Investment, the Rate of Return, and Optimal Fiscal Policy* (Johns Hopkins Press, Baltimore, 1970), pp. 13–14.

8. This restriction on the feasibility of growth programs seems not to have been discussed in the literature elsewhere. This condition gives rise to an isoperimetric problem in the calculus of variations, and although the necessary conditions for optimal growth still are very natural from an economic point of view, isoperimetric problems are more difficult to analyze.

9. This corresponds to the discussion in the previous chapter, but with the difference that in that chapter there were many consumption goods, each generating a certain amount of residuals.

10. See, for example, Allen V. Kneese and Blair T. Bower, *Managing Water Quality: Economics, Technology, Institutions* (Johns Hopkins Press, Baltimore, 1968), chapter 1.

11. R. C. d'Arge and K. C. Kogiku in a paper ("Economic Growth and the Natural Environment," Department of Economics, University of California, Riverside) discussed a model similar to ours, but with the difference that they assume that nature cannot purify the wastes. Accordingly, the waste density in their model monotonically increases over time or the environmental quality decreases. Their conclusions on the optimal time profile of effluent charges will therefore differ from the conclusions we are going to derive.

12. Arrow and Kurz, *Public Investment*.

13. In Arrow and Kurz, *Public Investment*, an heuristic derivation of the maximum principle is given. The form used here is from Magnus R. Hestenes, *Calculus of Variations and Optimal Control Theory* (Wiley, New York, 1966), especially theorem 11.1 in chapter 7, p. 347.

14. Assume that (6) is satisfied over a time interval as an inequality. Then $\bar{\alpha}$ is zero over that interval, and from (13) $\bar{p} = 0$. From (10) we have, however, that $\dot{\bar{p}} = \bar{p}_r f' + \bar{q} \neq 0$, and a contradiction is obtained.

15. This is one of the problems integral side constraints create. Still, it can be shown that if $\bar{p}_r$ is regarded as a parameter, for each $\bar{p}_r$ there exists a particular solution (which is not a steady state in the sense that the rate of change of all variables is the same), such that all other solutions with the same value on $\bar{p}_r$ will in the long run approach this particular solution. This means that even in this nonautonomous case there exist optimal trajectories which are attractors to the other optimal trajectories. This property is, however, not so useful.

16. This paradigm may be regarded as a special case of the last paradigm

that will be presented in this chapter. For this larger model, the existence of a unique steady state will be proved, which means that there is a unique steady state in this simpler model, too.

17. In Mäler, "Studier i intertemporal allokering," this theorem is proved. It can also be derived from theorem 4.1, chapter 13 in Earl A. Coddington and N. Levinson, *Theory of Ordinary Differential Equations* (McGraw-Hill, New York, 1955).

18. This result is also of interest in connection with recent discussions about the necessity of a stationary economy due to limited natural resources. These discussions are not directed toward optimal growth problems, however, but take it for granted that the nonrenewable resources will be exhausted if world production continues to grow at the present rate. See Jay W. Forrester, *World Dynamics* (Wright-Allen, Cambridge, Mass., 1971); Donella H. Meadows *et al.*, *The Limits to Growth* (Potomac Associates, Washington, D.C., 1972); Gösta C. H. Ehrensvärd, *Före-Efter, En Diagnos* (Aldus-Bonnier, Stockholm, 1971).

19. In many discussions of the economics of natural resources, it is assumed that there is a single deposit but such that the cost of extracting the resources increases with the accumulated exploitation. For such a case it is clear that the low-cost exploitation must come first; any other policy is not feasible. In this case it is the optimal rate of exploitation that must be determined. For a discussion of these problems see Harold Hotelling, "The Economics of Exhaustible Resources," *Journal of Political Economy*, vol. 39, no. 2, 137–175 (1931). For a simple discussion of determining the rate of exploitation when there are two homogeneous deposits and constant marginal productivity of capital, see Allen V. Kneese and Orris Herfindahl, *An Introduction to the Economic Theory of Resources and Environment* (Merrill, Columbus, Ohio, in press).

20. It is easy to prove, by using the same idea that will be used for the fourth paradigm, that the system has a unique steady state.

21. For the importance of recycling residuals, see George O. Löf and Allen V. Kneese, *The Economics of Water Utilization in the Beet Sugar Industry* (Johns Hopkins Press, Baltimore, 1968); and Allen V. Kneese, Robert U. Ayres, and Ralph C. d'Arge, *Economics and the Environment: A Materials Balance Approach* (Resources for the Future, Washington, D.C., 1972).

22. See Arrow and Kurz, *Public Investment*, p. 42 for a discussion of the maximum principle when there are constraints on the state variables.

23. Harold J. Barnett and Chandler Morse, *Scarcity and Growth, the Economics of Natural Resource Availability* (Johns Hopkins Press, Baltimore, 1963).

24. Barnett and Morse, *Scarcity and Growth*, p. 239.

25. For a discussion of endogenous technical progress, see Kenneth J. Arrow, "The Economic Implications of Learning by Doing," *Review of Economic Studies*, vol. 29, pp. 155–173 (1962); Eyten Sheshinski in Karl Shell, *Essays on Optimal Economic Growth*, pp. 31–52; and Mäler, "Studier i intemporal allokeringsteori."

26. See Hestenes, *Calculus of Variations*, chapter 1 for a discussion of regular constraints and tangent cones.

4 BASIC CONSUMPTION
   THEORY AND WELFARE ECONOMICS

1. INTRODUCTION

In subsequent chapters, we will need some basic facts from consumption theory concerning demand functions, compensated demand functions, demand prices for public goods, expenditure functions, and consumer surplus. Instead of referring the reader to specialized papers or books, a summary of the facts needed will be given in this chapter. No claims are made for originality or new discoveries for the results presented here; they can almost all be found elsewhere in the literature. The reader should examine the classic books by Hicks, *Value and Capital* and Samuelson, *Foundation of Economic Analysis*. The most important difference between the discussion given in this chapter and discussions elsewhere is the systematic use of the expenditure function (for a definition see chapter 2) as a basic tool that can be found here.

This chapter starts with the usual derivation of the Marshallian demand functions from utility maximization subject to the budget constraint. In section 2, the expenditure function is defined as the least lump sum income necessary to sustain a given level of utility. The expenditure function is thus the minimum value of expenditures when consumption is such that the utility exceeds or is equal to a given utility level. The solution to this minimization problem yields compensated demand functions, which show the demand for goods and services when income is so compensated that the individual is on the prescribed utility level.

In section 3 some very useful properties relating the expenditure function, demand functions, and compensated demand functions are proved. One such property is described by the Slutsky equation, which is stated in terms of the expenditure function, and not as is usual, in terms of income and substitution effects.

It is clear that the expenditure function depends on prices and the supply of public goods, for which there are no markets. In section 4 it is shown that the partial derivatives of the expenditure function with respect to the supply of a public good can be interpreted as the demand price or the marginal willingness to pay for this public good.

So far the analysis has been directed to a single consumer. In section 6 it is shown that if some further condition is satisfied, it is possible to aggregate individual expenditure functions in such a way that all the properties discussed in section 3 still are valid.

In section 7, the Slutsky equations are used for computing the expenditure function when the demand functions are known.

In section 8, the expenditure function is applied to a discussion of consumer surplus. The compensating variation and the equivalent variation are defined in terms of the expenditure function, and it is shown that this definition is in certain simple cases identical to the measure of the area under the compensated demand curves. It is proved in section 8 that if the private goods are noninferior, and if the public goods also are noninferior, the equivalent variation is greater than the compensating variation.

In section 9, the analysis is applied to the case where there is a commodity that must be consumed in either one unit or not at all, for example, the services from an amusement park. If the time period is short enough, the consumer must visit the park once, or not at all. It is shown that in this case the compensated demand curve will be identical to the demand curve for the "indivisible" commodity.

The results are all stated in a form that is convenient for subsequent use, which means that sometimes more restrictive assumptions are made than are necessary. Many times differentiability has been assumed, although the same results may be obtained without differentiability. Furthermore, the discussion is not completely rigorous in that continuity problems have been left out.

An elementary presentation of social welfare functions is given in the last two sections of the chapter. The analysis starts with the assumption that there exists an indirect social welfare function, that is, a preference function defined on prices or money incomes of different individuals and the flow of environmental services. It is shown that under certain conditions such an indirect welfare function is equivalent to a Bergson welfare function. It is furthermore shown that if lump sum transfers are feasible, this welfare function can be aggregated into a social utility function defined on the totals of regular goods. This function is then used to discuss the national income concept as a measure of welfare. In particular, it is found that under some conditions it is possible to calculate national income without including the cost of waste disposal in the environment and still obtain an accurate measure of welfare. Finally, the analysis from chapter 2 is used to shed light on the problem of whether expenditures on waste treatment and other environmental protection activities should be deducted from the national income.

2. MARSHALLIAN DEMAND FUNCTIONS

In this and the following sections, we will briefly discuss some aspects of the theory of consumption, and especially consumers' surplus. We will first consider a single consumer. His preferences will be represented by a utility function $u(c, Y)$ defined for nonnegative vectors $c \in R^Q$ and vectors $Y \in R^m$. Here c is the vector of consumption activity levels and Y is the supply of environmental services. Throughout this section we will assume that u is quasi-concave in c and Y, and moreover that it satisfies condition (21) in chapter 2. Sometimes we will restrict the utility function further by imposing differentiability. (It is assumed throughout that u is continuous.) We will assume that u is increasing in c and Y [1].

As the preferences only order different alternatives, we cannot attach any significance to the numerical value of the utility function. This means that if $u(c, Y)$ is any utility function, every property which we have derived by using this utility function must still hold if we replace $u(c, Y)$ with $F[u(c, Y)]$, where $F(u)$ is some strictly increasing function of u. Such a utility concept is usually called ordinal utility.

As in chapter 2, we have the matrices B and D giving the net demand C for goods and services, and the supply z of residuals:

$$C = Bc$$

$$z = Dc$$

We will, however, drop the time element, that is, the vector V. Due to the quasi-concavity of u, the set

$$A = \{(c, Y); c \geqq 0, u(c, Y) \geqq \bar{u}\} \tag{1}$$

is convex. We will also use the set-valued mapping

$$A(Y) = \{c; c \geqq 0, u(c, Y) \geqq \bar{u}\} \tag{2}$$

$A(Y)$ is obviously a convex set.

The price vectors on regular goods and residuals are, as before, p and q. In order to simplify the notation, let us introduce the imputed price vector for consumption activities:

$$s^T = p^T B + q^T D \tag{3}$$

For simplicity, we will assume that the consumption set consists of all vectors (c, Y), with c nonnegative. (Obviously, there are lower bounds on some component in Y. When the air is so polluted that it can no longer be used for breathing, we have a lower bound for at least one component in Y. We assume, however, that the environmental quality never deteriorates to such an extent.)

The budget set is (and we now assume that the only variable the consumer can control is the level of the consumption activities):

$$\{c; c \geqq 0, s^T c \leqq I\} \tag{4}$$

where I is the lump sum income or wealth (including the value of initial endowment). As in chapter 2, it is assumed that the consumer behavior can be represented by choosing that element in the budget set which maximizes the utility function. This maximization problem can be formulated max $u(c, Y)$ subject to

$$s^T c \leqq I \qquad c \geqq 0$$

We assume that $s > 0$. This means that the budget set is compact, and that the utility function has a maximum on the budget set.

Note that if we replace $u(c, Y)$ by $F[u(c, Y)]$, where F is any monotone increasing function of u, the optimal solution will not change. If c' maximizes $u(c, Y)$ over the budget set, $u(c', Y) \geq u(c, Y)$ for all c in the budget set. But as F is monotonically increasing, we also have

$$F[u(c', Y)] \geq F[u(c, Y)]$$

for all c in the budget set, and the optimal solution is invariant for monotone increasing transformations of the utility function.

If it is assumed that u is differentiable in c and that $I > 0$, the Lagrange multiplier technique can be applied. This theorem gives a non-negative multiplier α, such that with L, the Lagrangian, as

$$L = u(c,\, Y) - \alpha(s^T c - I)$$

$$\left.\begin{aligned}
\frac{\partial L}{\partial c_i} &= \frac{\partial u}{\partial c_i} - \alpha s_i \leqq 0 \qquad i = 1,\, \cdots,\, Q \\[4pt]
\alpha(s^T c - I) &= 0 \\[4pt]
c_i\left(\frac{\partial u}{\partial c_i} - \alpha s_i\right) &= 0 \qquad i = 1,\, \cdots,\, Q
\end{aligned}\right\}
\tag{5}$$

are necessary and sufficient conditions for a maximum [2].

If we further assume that the preferences are characterized by strong convexity, that is

$u(c',\, Y) = u(c'',\, Y)$ implies that for all t such that $0 < t < 1$

$$u[tc' + (1 - t)c'',\, Y] > u(c',\, Y) \tag{6}$$

the solution to this system will be unique, because the best vector c in the budget set will be unique.

If the strong convexity assumption (6) holds, we can solve for c in (5) and obtain the Marshallian demand function as point-valued functions of s, I, and Y:

$$c = c(s,\, I,\, Y) \tag{7}$$

If only the weak convexity assumption (21) in chapter 2 holds, we will in general obtain demand correspondences as in chapter 2.

From (7) we see immediately that the demand functions for consumption goods and residuals can be written

$$C = Bc(s,\, I,\, Y) \tag{8}$$

$$z = Dc(s,\, I,\, Y) \tag{9}$$

Quite independent of the validity of (6), we can substitute the demand functions or demand correspondences into the utility function and obtain the indirect utility function:

$$v(s,\, I,\, Y) \equiv u[c(s,\, I,\, Y),\, Y] \tag{10}$$

If u is twice continuously differentiable (and 6 holds) the demand functions $c(s, I, Y)$ will be continuously differentiable (at least in the interior of their domain of definition; this is seen from the implicit function theorem), and so will the indirect utility function $v(s, I, Y)$. It is easy to show that

$$\frac{\partial v}{\partial I} = \frac{\partial u}{\partial I} = \alpha \tag{11}$$

From the definition of the Lagrangian yielding conditions (5), it follows that

$$\frac{\partial v}{\partial s_i} = \frac{\partial L}{\partial s_i} = \sum_{j=1}^{Q} \frac{\partial u}{\partial c_j}\frac{\partial c_j}{\partial s_i} - \alpha s^T \frac{\partial c}{\partial s_i} - \alpha c_i = -\alpha c_i \tag{12}$$

3. COMPENSATED DEMAND FUNCTIONS

Recall the definition of the expenditure function in chapter 2:

$$m(s, Y, \bar{u}) = \inf \{s^T c; c \geqq 0, u(c, Y) \geq \bar{u}\} \tag{13}$$

The expenditure function $m(s, Y, \bar{u})$ gives the least income necessary to achieve the utility level $\bar{u}$, when prices are given by s, and the supply of environmental services is given by Y. The minimum problem in (13) can be written min $s^T c$ subject to

$$u(c, Y) \geqq \bar{u} \qquad c \geqq 0$$

and the Lagrange multiplier technique can be applied.

Note that the solution to this minimization problem is invariant for monotone increasing transformations of the utility index, because the set A (defined in equation 1) is identical to the set

$$A' = \{(c, Y); c \geqq 0, F[u(c, Y)] \geqq F(\bar{u})\}$$

if F is strictly increasing. This means that all properties we derive from the solutions to the utility maximization problem or the cost minimization problem will be invariant for monotone increasing transformations of the utility function. The Lagrangian is $L = s^T c - \beta[u(c, Y) - \bar{u}]$ and if u is differentiable, the necessary and sufficient conditions for a solution are

$$s_i - \beta \frac{\partial u}{\partial c_i} \geqq 0 \qquad i = 1, \cdots, Q$$

$$\beta[u(c, Y) - \bar{u}] = 0$$

$$c_i\left(s_i - \beta \frac{\partial u}{\partial c_i}\right) = 0 \qquad i = 1, \cdots, Q$$

$$c_i \geqq 0$$

(14)

If the condition (6), the strong convexity assumption, holds, this problem has a unique solution, which will be denoted by

$$c^* = c^*(s, Y, \bar{u}) \tag{15}$$

and

$$m(s, Y, \bar{u}) = s^T c^*(s, Y, \bar{u}) \tag{16}$$

The functions $c^*(s, Y, \bar{u})$ will be called the Hicksian compensated demand functions, or simply the compensated demand functions, because they give the demand for the different consumption activities when the consumer's income is so compensated that he is always on the same indifference level.

4. SOME PROPERTIES OF THE EXPENDITURE FUNCTION

We will now prove the following eight facts about the expenditure function and the compensated demand functions. To simplify the exposition we assume throughout that the preferences are characterized by strong convexity and that the utility function is sufficiently differentiable. Some of the theorems are valid without these restrictive assumptions, and for more general proofs, the reader is referred to Nikaido [3], for example.

(i) $\dfrac{\partial m(s, Y, \bar{u})}{\partial s_i} = c_i^*(s, Y, \bar{u})$

(ii) $c[s, m(s, Y, \bar{u}), Y] \equiv c^*(s, Y, \bar{u})$

(iii) $c(s, I, Y) \equiv c^*[s, Y, v(s, I, Y)]$

(iv) m is a concave function in s

(v) $\dfrac{\partial^2 m}{\partial s_i{}^2} \leqq 0$

(vi) $\dfrac{\partial^2 m}{\partial s_j \partial s_i} - \dfrac{\partial c_i[s, m(s, Y, \bar{u})]}{\partial I} \dfrac{\partial m}{\partial s_j} - \dfrac{\partial c_i[s, m(s, Y, \bar{u}), Y]}{\partial s_j} = 0$

(the Slutsky equation)

(vii) $\dfrac{\partial c_i^*}{\partial s_j} = \dfrac{\partial c_j^*}{\partial s_i}$

(viii) m is a convex function in Y

Proofs:

(i) First, it is clear that in (14) $\beta > 0$, and so $u(c^*, Y) \equiv \bar{u}$, which after differentiation with respect to s_i yields

$$0 = \sum_{j=1}^{Q} \frac{\partial u}{\partial c_j} \frac{\partial c_j^*}{\partial s_i} = \frac{1}{\beta} \sum_{j=1}^{Q} s_j \frac{\partial c_j^*}{\partial s_i} \quad \text{or} \quad \sum_{j=1}^{Q} s_j \frac{\partial c_j^*}{\partial s_i} = 0$$

But

$$\frac{\partial m}{\partial s_i} = \sum_{j=1}^{Q} s_j \frac{\partial c_j^*}{\partial s_i} + c_i^* = c_i^*$$

(ii) $m(s, Y, \bar{u})$ is the minimum income necessary to sustain utility level $\bar{u}$ when prices are s and environmental quality Y. Thus (ii) follows. In the same way (iii) is proved.

(iv) Let s' and s'' be two different price vectors, and let $0 < t < 1$. From the minimum property of the compensated demand functions, it follows that

$s^T c^*(\bar{s}, Y, \bar{u}) \geqq s^T c^*(s, Y, \bar{u})$ for all s, and $\bar{s}$, and so

$$m[ts' + (1 - t)s'', Y, \bar{u}] = [ts' + (1 - t)s'']^T c^*[ts'$$
$$+ (1 - t)s'', Y, \bar{u})$$
$$= ts'^T c^*[ts' + (1 - t)s'', Y, \bar{u}] + (1 - t)s''^T c^*[ts'$$
$$+ (1 - t)s'', Y, \bar{u}]$$
$$\geqq ts'^T c^*(s', Y, \bar{u}) + (1 - t)s''^T c^*(s'', Y, \bar{u})$$
$$= tm(s', Y, \bar{u}) + (1 - t)m(s'', Y, \bar{u})$$

and so m is concave in s.

(v) As m is concave in s, and if m is twice differentiable, it follows at once that (iv) holds [4].

(vi) From (i) and (ii) it follows that

$$\frac{\partial m(s, Y, \bar{u})}{\partial s_i} \equiv c_i[s, m(s, Y, \bar{u}), Y]$$

Differentiate with respect to s_j

$$\frac{\partial^2 m(s, Y, \bar{u})}{\partial s_j \partial s_i} = \frac{\partial c_i}{\partial I} \frac{\partial m}{\partial s_j} + \frac{\partial c_i}{\partial s_j}$$

which is (vi).

(vii) From (i) it follows that

$$\frac{\partial c_i^*}{\partial s_j} \equiv \frac{\partial^2 m}{\partial s_j \partial s_i} = \frac{\partial^2 m}{\partial s_i \partial s_j} = \frac{\partial c_j^*}{\partial s_i}$$

(viii) In the proofs of (i)–(vii), we have not used convexity explicitly. In fact, the proofs are still valid if we replace convexity with any condition that guarantees single-valued demand functions. In the proof of (viii), however, we will need the fact that u is quasi-concave. Recall the definitions of the sets A and $A(Y)$ given in (1) and (2). Consider the sets

$A[tY' + (1 - t)Y'']$ and $tA(Y') + (1 - t)A(Y'')$

where t is a real number between zero and one, and where the sum is the ordinary vector sum of two sets.
Assume that
$c \in tA(Y') + (1 - t)A(Y'')$
Then $c = tc' + (1 - t)c''$ such that
$c' \in A(Y')$, and $c'' \in A(Y'')$, and
$u(c', Y') \geqq \bar{u}, u(c'', Y'') \geqq u$
As A is convex,
$[c, tY' + (1 - t)Y''] \in A$ or
$u[c, tY' + (1 - t)Y''] \geqq \bar{u}$ or
$c \in A[(tY' + (1 - t)Y'']$
We have thus shown that
$tA(Y') + (1 - t)A(Y'') \subset A[tY' + (1 - t)Y'']$
Now we use the definition of the expenditure function
$m(s, Y', \bar{u}) = \inf\{s^T c; c \in A(Y')\}$
$m(s, Y'', \bar{u}) = \inf\{s^T c; c \in A(Y'')\}$, and
$m[s, tY' + (1 - t)Y'', \bar{u}] = \inf\{s^T c; c \in A[tY' + (1 - t)Y'']\}$
and so
$tm(s, tY', \bar{u}) + (1 - t)m(s, Y'', \bar{u})$
$$= \inf_{c \in A(Y')} ts^T c + \inf_{c \in A(Y'')} (1 - t)s^T c$$
$$= \inf_{c \in tA(Y') + (1 - t)A(Y'')} s^T c$$
$$\geqq \inf_{c \in A[tY' + (1 - t)Y'']} s^T c = m[s, tY + (1 - t)Y'', \bar{u}]$$
where the inequality comes from the inclusion relation between the sets $tA(Y') + (1 - t)A(Y'')$, and $A[tY' + (1 - t)Y'']$. This inequality shows that m is convex in Y. Exactly as (v) follows

from (vi), it follows from (viii) that

$$\frac{\partial^2 m}{\partial Y_\kappa^2} \geq 0$$

if m is sufficiently differentiable.

These eight properties relating to demand functions, compensated demand functions, and the expenditure function are extremely useful, and will be utilized again and again in the following analysis.

5. DEMAND PRICES FOR ENVIRONMENTAL QUALITY

After having proved the properties (i)–(viii), we will now try to identify the prices for environmental services that were discussed in chapter 2 with concepts introduced in this chapter. Recall how prices on environmental services were introduced in the proof that an optimum can be represented as an equilibrium in chapter 2, section 7. We there looked upon the set of consumption activities and environmental qualities that were better than the allocation ruling at optimum. By that we could find a convex set and a supporting hyperplane to this set. The normal to this hyperplane represented the prices. We can now do the same thing again, but restricting ourselves to one consumer. The normal to the hyperplane we are going to construct will be interpreted as a price vector, and it will then be possible to show the relation between these prices and the expenditure function.

Consider the set A. It consists of all pairs (c, Y) which yield utility at least equal to $\bar{u}$. The set A is convex. Moreover, the point $(\bar{c}, \bar{Y})$ where $\bar{c} = c^*(s, \bar{Y}, \bar{u})$ is not an interior point of A, because otherwise $c^*(s, \bar{Y}, \bar{u})$ would not have minimized $s^T c$ on $A(\bar{Y})$. Accordingly, there exists a supporting hyperplane [5] to A through $(\bar{c}, \bar{Y})$, and with normal (π, δ), such that

$$\pi^T(c - \bar{c}) + \delta^T(Y - \bar{Y}) \geq 0 \text{ for all } (c, Y) \in A$$

If u is differentiable, and $\bar{c} > 0$, this hyperplane is unique.
Let $Y = \bar{Y}$; then

$$\pi^T(c - \bar{c}) \geq 0 \text{ for all } c \geq 0, \text{ such that } u(c, \bar{Y}) \geq \bar{u}$$

But we also know from the definition of $\bar{c}$ that

$$s^T(c - \bar{c}) \geq 0 \text{ for all } c \geq 0, \text{ such that } u(c, \bar{Y}) \geq \bar{u}$$

If the supporting hyperplane is unique, $s = \pi$, and if there is more than one supporting hyperplane to A through $(\bar{c}, \bar{Y})$, we can choose one of them with $s = \pi$. From now on we therefore substitute s for π. (If the hyperplane is not unique, the compensated demand function will be completely inelastic with respect to small changes in the price for one or more goods.)

Let us now choose a different supply of environmental services $\bar{\bar{Y}}$. We can repeat all steps and end up with a new hyperplane, such that

$$s^T(c - \bar{\bar{c}}) + \bar{\bar{\delta}}^T(Y - \bar{\bar{Y}}) \geqq 0 \text{ for all } (c, Y) \in A$$

Especially with $Y = \bar{Y}$, we have

$$s^T(\bar{c} - \bar{\bar{c}}) + \bar{\bar{\delta}}^T(\bar{Y} - \bar{\bar{Y}}) \geqq 0$$

By reversing the roles of $\bar{Y}$ and $\bar{\bar{Y}}$ we can also obtain the following inequality:

$$s^T(\bar{\bar{c}} - \bar{c}) + \delta^T(\bar{\bar{Y}} - \bar{Y}) \geqq 0$$

From the definition of the expenditure function we have

$$m(s, \bar{Y}, \bar{u}) = s^T\bar{c}, \text{ and}$$

$$m(s, \bar{\bar{Y}}, u) = s^T\bar{\bar{c}}, \text{ and thus}$$

$$m(s, \bar{\bar{Y}}, u) - m(s, \bar{Y}, \bar{u}) \geqq -\bar{\bar{\delta}}^T(\bar{\bar{Y}} - \bar{Y}), \text{ and}$$

$$m(s, \bar{Y}, \bar{u}) - m(s, \bar{\bar{Y}}, \bar{u}) \geqq -\bar{\bar{\delta}}^T(\bar{Y} - \bar{\bar{Y}})$$

which entail

$$-\delta^T(\bar{\bar{Y}} - \bar{Y}) \leqq m(s, \bar{\bar{Y}}, \bar{u}) - m(s, \bar{Y}, \bar{u}) \leqq -\bar{\bar{\delta}}^T(\bar{\bar{Y}} - \bar{Y})$$

If we let $\bar{\bar{Y}} - \bar{Y} = (0, \cdots, 0, \Delta Y_j, 0, \cdots, 0)$, the above inequality reduces to

$$-\delta_j \Delta Y_j \leqq m(s, \bar{\bar{Y}}, \bar{u}) - m(s, \bar{Y}, \bar{u}) \leqq -\bar{\bar{\delta}}_j \Delta Y_j \text{ or}$$

$$-\delta_j \leqq \frac{m(s, \bar{\bar{Y}}, \bar{u}) - m(s, \bar{Y}, \bar{u})}{\Delta Y_j} \leqq -\bar{\bar{\delta}}_j \text{ if } \Delta Y_j > 0$$

and

$$-\delta_j \geqq \frac{m(s, \bar{\bar{Y}}, \bar{u}) - m(s, Y, \bar{u})}{\Delta Y_j} \geqq -\bar{\bar{\delta}}_j \text{ if } \Delta Y_j < 0$$

If at each point $[c^*(s, Y, \bar{u}), Y]$, there is a unique supporting hyperplane to A, $\delta_j \to \delta_j$ when $\Delta Y_j \to 0$, and the expenditure function will have partial derivatives with respect to Y_j, $j = 1, \cdots, m$, such that

$$\frac{\partial m(s, \bar{Y}, \bar{u})}{\partial Y_j} = -\delta_j \tag{17}$$

The prices on environmental services can thus be interpreted as the partial derivatives of the expenditure function with respect to environmental services (with the opposite sign). If the supporting hyperplane at $(\bar{c}, \bar{Y})$ is not unique, δ belongs to the subgradient of m at $(s, \bar{Y}, \bar{u})$, as defined by Rockafellar [6].

If the supporting hyperplane is unique, that is, if the utility function is differentiable, and $\bar{c} > 0$, it is easy to see that the vector (s, δ) must be proportional to the gradient of the utility function, evaluated at $(\bar{c}, \bar{Y})$, that is, there exists a positive number β, such that

$$\beta \frac{\partial u}{\partial c_i} = s_i \qquad i = 1, \cdots, Q$$

$$\beta \frac{\partial u}{\partial Y_j} = \delta \qquad j = 1, \cdots, m$$

The first equations are exactly the same as those in equation (14) (as $c > 0$ we have equality in 14). By eliminating β, we see that

$$\frac{\partial m(s, Y, \bar{u})}{\partial Y_j} = -\delta_j = -s_i \left(\frac{\partial u}{\partial Y_j} \middle/ \frac{\partial u}{\partial c_i} \right) \tag{18}$$

that is, the partial derivative of m with respect to Y_j is equal to the value of the marginal rate of substitution between Y_j and any consumption activity.

6. AGGREGATION OVER CONSUMERS

So far we have discussed only a single consumer. To make this analysis useful, we must, however, be able to aggregate over many consumers the concepts we have introduced. It is quite a trivial matter to aggregate the expenditure functions for several consumers in a formal way:

$$m(s, Y, \bar{u}^1, \cdots, \bar{u}^H) = \sum_{h=1}^{H} m^h(s, Y, \bar{u}^h) \tag{19}$$

where m^h is the expenditure function for consumer h, and m is the aggregate expenditure function.

For this aggregation to be useful, the aggregate expenditure function should have most of the properties (i)–(viii) derived for individual expenditure functions in section 4. We can see immediately that properties (i), (iv), (v), (vii), and (viii) are invariant for the aggregation so they hold for the aggregate expenditure function (and the aggregate compensated demand functions). However, those three properties (ii), (iii), and (vi) which involve Marshallian demand functions are not in general invariant for this type of aggregation. This should not be surprising. It is well known that it is impossible to aggregate Marshallian demand functions in a consistent way, unless some further assumptions are satisfied. And if it is not possible to aggregate the demand functions, it cannot be possible to aggregate the expenditure function in a way that leaves properties involving Marshallian demand functions invariant.

In order to be able to aggregate individual demand functions

$$c^h = c^h(s, I^h, Y)$$

in a consistent way to an aggregate demand function

$$c = c(s, I, Y) = \sum_{h=1}^{H} c^h(s, I^h, Y) \tag{20}$$

where

$$I = \sum_{h=1}^{H} I^h \tag{21}$$

one of the following conditions must be satisfied: (a) The income distribution is specified in a fixed way, depending on the total income I: $I^h = \psi^h(I)$. (b) The marginal propensity to demand out of income, that is $\partial c^h / \partial I^h$ must be equal for all consumers.

With one of these conditions satisfied, it is easy to see that the aggregate demand function makes sense. Let us therefore examine whether either one of these conditions is sufficient for a consistent aggregation of the individual expenditure functions.

It can easily be seen that condition (a) is not sufficient for a consistent aggregation of the individual expenditure functions; let us therefore study condition (b) [7]. We assume that

$$\frac{\partial c^h}{\partial I^h} = \frac{\partial c^{h'}}{\partial I^{h'}} = \beta$$

for all h, h', and all distributions of income I^h, $h = 1, \cdots, H$. This condition says that the total demand for consumption activities will be the same for every distribution of the lump sum income I.

As $m = \sum_{h=1}^{H} m^h(s, Y, \bar{u}^h)$ we have

$$\frac{\partial m}{\partial s_i} = \sum_{h=1}^{H} \frac{\partial m^h}{\partial s_i}, \text{ and}$$

$$\frac{\partial^2 m}{\partial s_j \partial s_i} = \sum_{h=1}^{H} \frac{\partial^2 m^h}{\partial s_j \partial s_i} \qquad \text{from (vi)}$$

$$= \sum_{h=1}^{H} \left[\frac{\partial c_i^h}{\partial I^h} \frac{\partial m^h}{\partial s_j} + \frac{\partial c_i^h}{\partial s_j} \right]$$

$$= \sum_{h=1}^{H} \left[\frac{\partial c_i^h}{\partial I^h} \frac{\partial m^h}{\partial s_j} + \frac{\partial c_i}{\partial s_j} \right]$$

Because of our assumption, we can replace the first term with

$$\beta \sum_{h=1}^{H} \frac{\partial m^h}{\partial s_j} = \beta \frac{\partial m}{\partial s_j}$$

Moreover, we see incidentally that condition (a) does not make such a replacement possible, and therefore condition (a) is not enough to guarantee a consistent aggregation of individual expenditure functions. We have now shown that

$$\frac{\partial^2 m}{\partial s_j \partial s_i} - \frac{\partial c_i}{\partial I} \frac{\partial m}{\partial s_j} - \frac{\partial c_i}{\partial s_j} = 0$$

that is, that property (vi) holds for the aggregate expenditure function m.

What is the interpretation of the aggregate expenditure function? $m(s, Y, \bar{u}^1, \cdots, \bar{u}^H)$ gives the minimum total income necessary for sustaining the utility levels $\bar{u}^1, \cdots, \bar{u}^H$, when the price vector is s, and environmental quality is Y. With this interpretation it is clear that properties (ii) and (iii) also hold for the aggregate expenditure function. Note that

$$\frac{\partial m}{\partial Y_j} = \sum_{h=1}^{H} \frac{\partial m^h}{\partial Y_j} = -\sum_{h=1}^{H} \delta_j^h$$

so that the partial derivative of the aggregate expenditure function gives us the sum of all individual demand prices for environmental services, and as we know from chapter 2, it is this sum that is of significance when determining the optimal supply of environmental services.

7. EMPIRICAL ESTIMATION OF THE EXPENDITURE FUNCTION

The significance of property (v) and condition (b) is that they make it possible to estimate m empirically as a function of s. By estimating the Marshallian demand functions by some econometric method, which by the way requires condition (b) because otherwise no aggregate demand functions exist, the Slutsky equations become a system of differential equations in m. By solving this system, one can obtain m as a function of the prices and some constants depending on the utility levels $\bar{u}^1, \cdots, \bar{u}^H$. By choosing some price vector $\bar{s}$ as a basis for all comparisons, it is then possible to determine these constants. Although the utility levels are not known, they represent the welfare of the point $c^h(\bar{s}, Y, I^h)$.

This assumes, however, that there is a solution to the Slutsky equations. For arbitrary specified demand functions there need not exist a solution, unless the demand functions satisfy the so-called "integrability conditions." In order to study these integrability conditions, let us rewrite the Slutsky equations as a system of partial differential equations:

$$\frac{\partial m}{\partial s_i} = c_i^* \qquad\qquad i = 1, 2, \cdots, Q$$

$$\frac{\partial c_k^*}{\partial s_i} = \frac{\partial c_k}{\partial I} c_i^* + \frac{\partial c_k}{\partial s_i} \qquad k = 1, 2, \cdots, Q \tag{22}$$

It is intuitively clear that the classical integrability conditions [8] in consumption theory, that is, the symmetry of the matrix $\partial c_i^*/\partial s_j$ (property vii in section 4), should be sufficient for the existence of a solution. We will prove this now.

Theorem: Suppose that the demand functions satisfy

$$\frac{\partial c_i}{\partial I} c_j + \frac{\partial c_i}{\partial s_j} \equiv \frac{\partial c_j}{\partial I} c_i + \frac{\partial c_j}{\partial s_i} \qquad i, j = 1, 2, \cdots, Q \tag{23}$$

For each price vector s, and each income I, there is a solution to (22), such that

$$m[s, Y, v(s, Y, I)] = I$$

$$c^*[s, Y, v(s, Y, I)] = c(s, Y, I)$$

Proof: Denote the vector $(m, c_1, \cdots, c_Q)$ by y, and the right-hand side of equation (22) by $f_i(s, y)$. Then the necessary and sufficient condition for complete integrability of (22) can be written

$$\frac{\partial f_i}{\partial s_j} + \left(\frac{\partial}{\partial y} f_i\right) \times f_j = \frac{\partial f_j}{\partial s_i} + \left(\frac{\partial}{\partial y} f_j\right) \times f_i, \qquad i, j = 1, 2, \cdots, Q \tag{24}$$

where $(\partial/\partial y)f_i$ denotes the matrix with the partial derivatives of f_i with respect to the components in y as elements [9].

We have only to show that the conditions (24) boil down to (23), when applied to (22).

The left-hand side L.H. of (24) becomes

$$
\text{L.H.} = \begin{bmatrix} 0 \\ \dfrac{\partial^2 c_1}{\partial s_j \partial I}\, c_1^* + \dfrac{\partial^2 c_1}{\partial s_j \partial s_i} \\ \cdot \\ \cdot \\ \cdot \\ \dfrac{\partial^2 c_Q}{\partial s_j \partial I}\, c_n^* + \dfrac{\partial^2 c_Q}{\partial s_j \partial s_i} \end{bmatrix}
$$

$$
+ \begin{bmatrix} 0 & 0 & \cdot\cdot & 1 & \cdot\cdot & 0 \\ \dfrac{\partial^2 c_1}{\partial I^2}\, c_i^* + \dfrac{\partial^2 c_1}{\partial I \partial s_i} & 0 & \cdot\cdot & \dfrac{\partial c_1}{\partial I} & \cdot\cdot & 0 \\ \cdot & \cdot & & \cdot & & \cdot \\ \cdot & \cdot & & \cdot & & \cdot \\ \cdot & \cdot & & \cdot & & \cdot \\ \dfrac{\partial^2 c_Q}{\partial I^2}\, c_i^* + \dfrac{\partial^2 c_Q}{\partial I \partial s_i} & 0 & & \dfrac{\partial c_Q}{\partial I} & & 0 \end{bmatrix} \begin{bmatrix} c_j^* \\ \dfrac{\partial c_1}{\partial I}\, c_j^* + \dfrac{\partial c_1}{\partial s_j} \\ \cdot \\ \cdot \\ \cdot \\ \dfrac{\partial c_Q}{\partial I}\, c_j^* + \dfrac{\partial c_Q}{\partial s_j} \end{bmatrix}
$$

$$
= \begin{bmatrix} \dfrac{\partial c_j}{\partial I}\, c_i^* + \dfrac{\partial c_j}{\partial s_i} \\ \cdot \\ \cdot \\ \dfrac{\partial^2 c_k}{\partial s_i \partial I}\, c_j^* + \dfrac{\partial^2 c_k}{\partial s_i \partial s_j} + c_i^* \left(\dfrac{\partial^2 c_k}{\partial I^2}\, c_j^* + \dfrac{\partial^2 c_k}{\partial I \partial s_j} \right) + \dfrac{\partial c_k}{\partial I} \left(\dfrac{\partial c_j}{\partial I}\, c_i^* + \dfrac{\partial c_j}{\partial s_i} \right) \\ \cdot \\ \cdot \end{bmatrix}
$$

The right-hand side, R.H., becomes in a similar manner

$$
\text{R.H.} = \begin{bmatrix} \dfrac{\partial c_j}{\partial I}\, c_i^* + \dfrac{\partial c_j}{\partial s_i} \\ \cdot \\ \cdot \\ \dfrac{\partial^2 c_k}{\partial s_i \partial I}\, c_j^* + \dfrac{\partial^2 c_k}{\partial s_i \partial s_j} + c_i^* \left(\dfrac{\partial^2 c_k}{\partial I^2}\, c_j^* + \dfrac{\partial^2 c_k}{\partial I \partial s_j} \right) + \dfrac{\partial c_k}{\partial I} \left(\dfrac{\partial c_j}{\partial I}\, c_i^* + \dfrac{\partial c_j}{\partial s_i} \right) \\ \cdot \\ \cdot \end{bmatrix}
$$

Setting the right-hand side equal to the left-hand side yields first

$$\frac{\partial c_i}{\partial I} c_j^* + \frac{\partial c_i}{\partial s_j} = \frac{\partial c_j}{\partial I} c_i^* + \frac{\partial c_j}{\partial s_i} \qquad i = 1, 2, \cdots, Q$$

and these are identical to (23). Furthermore, we have

$$\frac{\partial^2 c_k}{\partial s_j \partial I} c_i^* + \frac{\partial^2 c_k}{\partial s_j \partial s_i} + c_j^* \left(\frac{\partial^2 c_k}{\partial I^2} c_i^* + \frac{\partial^2 c_k}{\partial I \partial s_i} \right) + \frac{\partial c_k}{\partial I} \left(\frac{\partial c_i}{\partial I} c_j^* + \frac{\partial c_i}{\partial s_j} \right)$$

$$= \frac{\partial^2 c_k}{\partial s_i \partial I} c_j^* + \frac{\partial^2 c_k}{\partial s_i \partial s_j} + c_i^* \left(\frac{\partial^2 c_k}{\partial I^2} c_j^* + \frac{\partial^2 c_k}{\partial I \partial s_j} \right) + \frac{\partial c_k}{\partial I} \left(\frac{\partial c_j}{\partial I} c_j^* + \frac{\partial c_j}{\partial s_i} \right)$$

All terms will cancel except

$$\frac{\partial c_k}{\partial I} \left(\frac{\partial c_i}{\partial I} c_j^* + \frac{\partial c_i}{\partial s_j} \right) = \frac{\partial c_k}{\partial I} \left(\frac{\partial c_j}{\partial I} c_j^* + \frac{\partial c_j}{\partial s_i} \right)$$

which is again (23).

The following example will be analyzed to show the use of this theorem. Assume that we are interested in a certain consumption process c_1, with price s_1, and that all other processes are aggregated into a composite process c_2, with price s_2. Assume further that we have estimated the following demand functions:

$$c_1 = \frac{I}{2s_1} - a\frac{1}{2} Y$$

$$c_2 = \frac{I}{2s_2} + a\frac{1}{2}\frac{s_1}{s_2} Y$$

where a is a constant, Y the quality of environment (which is assumed to be one dimensional), and I the income.

The demand functions satisfy the budget constraint, because $s_1 c_1 + s_2 c_2 = I$. Furthermore, they satisfy the integrability condition, because

$$c_2 \frac{\partial c_1}{\partial I} + \frac{\partial c_1}{\partial s_2} = \frac{1}{2} c_2 \frac{1}{s_1} = \frac{I}{4 s_1 s_2} + a\frac{1}{4 s_2} Y, \text{ and}$$

$$c_1 \frac{\partial c_2}{\partial I} + \frac{\partial c_2}{\partial s_1} = \frac{1}{2} c_1 \frac{1}{s_2} + a\frac{1}{2}\frac{1}{s_2} Y = \frac{I}{4 s_1 s_2} + a\frac{1}{4 s_2} Y$$

We are therefore assured that there exists a solution to the Slutsky equations.

Assume now that the environmental quality Y is held constant, and equal to one (in chapter 5 we will study the same example, but when Y varies, and the problem is to estimate the expenditure function as a function of Y). The Slutsky equations become

$$\frac{\partial^2 m}{\partial s_1^2} - \frac{1}{2s_1}\frac{\partial m}{\partial s_1} + \frac{m}{2s_1^2} = 0$$

$$\frac{\partial^2 m}{\partial s_1 \partial s_2} - \frac{1}{2s_2}\frac{\partial m}{\partial s_1} = a\frac{1}{2s_2}$$

By substitution we see that

$$m = \phi_1(s_2)s_1^{\frac{1}{2}} + \phi_2(s_2)s_1$$

is a solution to the first equation. If we substitute this expression for m into the second equation, we get

$$\frac{1}{2}\phi_1's_1^{-\frac{1}{2}} + \phi_2' - \frac{1}{4}s_2^{-1}\phi_1s_1^{-\frac{1}{2}} - \frac{1}{2}s_2^{-1}\phi_2 = \frac{1}{2}s_2^{-1}a$$

Because both ϕ_1 and ϕ_2 are independent of s_1, this gives two equations

$$\phi_1' - \frac{1}{2}s_1^{-1}\phi_1 = 0 \quad \text{and} \quad \phi_2' - \frac{1}{2}s_2^{-1}\phi_2 = \frac{1}{2}s_2^{-1}a$$

The solutions are

$$\phi_1 = As_2^{\frac{1}{2}} \quad \text{and} \quad \phi_2 = Bs_2^{\frac{1}{2}} - a$$

where A and B are integration constants. We thus have

$$m = As_1^{\frac{1}{2}}s_2^{\frac{1}{2}} + Bs_1s_2^{\frac{1}{2}} - as_1$$

The constants A and B can be computed as soon as we fix the point with which we want to make comparisons. Assume, for example, that we take $\bar{u}$ as the value of the indirect utility function when prices are s_1', and s_2', and the income is I. Then we know that

$$m(s_1', s_2', Y, \bar{u}) = I, \text{ and}$$
$$\frac{\partial m(s_1', s_2', Y, \bar{u})}{\partial s_1} = \frac{1}{2}I\frac{1}{s_1'} - \frac{1}{2}a$$

and these two conditions yield

$$A\sqrt{s_1's_2'} + Bs_1'\sqrt{s_2'} - as_1' = I$$

$$\frac{1}{2}A\frac{1}{s_1'}\sqrt{s_1's_2'} + B\sqrt{s_2'} - a = \frac{1}{2}\frac{1}{s_1'}I - \frac{1}{2}a$$

The solution to these two equations is

$$A = \frac{I + as_1'}{\sqrt{s_1's_2'}} \qquad \text{and} \qquad B = 0$$

and so the expenditure function is

$$m[s_1, s_2, Y, v(s_1', s_2', Y, I)] = \frac{I + as_1'}{\sqrt{s_1's_2'}}\sqrt{s_1s_2} - as_1$$

We have thus been able to calculate the expenditure function from a knowledge of the Marshallian demand functions.

Since m is a function of $\bar{u}$, and m in our example is a function of the constant A, it follows that $\bar{u}$ must be a function of A. By choosing the appropriate positive monotone transformation of the utility index, we can identify $\bar{u}$ with A. A must thus be a representation of the indirect utility function if there is only one consumer. From the expression for A, it is then possible to derive the original utility function $u(c_1, c_2)$ (holding $Y = 1$),

$$u(c_1, c_2) = 2(c_1 + a)^{\frac{1}{2}}c_2^{\frac{1}{2}}$$

However, it is not possible to estimate m as a function of Y in this way because there are no markets in environmental services from which the demand functions for Y can be estimated. In the next chapter, some indirect methods will be discussed that can be used to estimate m as a function of s and Y. It will also be shown in a simple example how one can solve the Slutsky equations and determine m completely.

8. CONSUMERS' SURPLUS

There are two reasons why the expenditure function is important in the analysis. First, if it is possible to estimate m as a function of Y, we can immediately calculate the demand prices for environmental services, and make cost-benefit analyses of the use of the environment. Second, the expenditure function is related to the consumers' surplus concept; in fact, the expenditure function is basic to the understanding and the computation of consumers' surplus. We will therefore devote some time to a discussion of consumers' surplus.

To simplify the discussion, we will restrict ourselves to one consumer. If we assume condition (b) of section 6, and the existence of lump sum transfers, then such a restriction only means a saving in symbols, and the result can immediately be generalized to the case of many individuals [10]. Suppose we have a situation characterized by the price vector s', and the supply of environmental services Y', and we are studying the welfare impacts of a change in the economy to a situation where the price vector is s'', the supply of environmental services Y'', and the income unchanged and equal to I. In the first situation, the demand is given by $c = c(s', Y', I)$ (we drop the superscripts referring to consumers because there is only one consumer under study). The utility level is given by the indirect utility function $\bar{u} = v(s', I, Y')$, and the expenditure function satisfies $m(s', Y', \bar{u}) = I$. To be on the same utility level $\bar{u}$, after the change, the income of the consumer must be $m(s'', Y'', \bar{u})$. If this amount is greater than I, the consumer must be compensated for the change and if it is less than I, some of his income can be confiscated without leaving him better or worse off.

We can define $CV = I - m(s'', Y'', \bar{u})$ as a measure of the welfare change in monetary terms. CV is known as the compensating variation, that is, the amount the consumer must be compensated with (if $CV < 0$), or must be made to pay (if $CV > 0$), in order for him to be on the same utility level as before the change.

Let us now look at another variant of consumers' surplus. Assume that we ask how much the consumer is willing to pay to obtain the second situation. In the second situation, his utility is given by $\tilde{u} = v(s'', I, Y'')$, and we have $m(s'', Y'', \tilde{u}) = I$. In order to be at the utility level $\tilde{u}$ when the price vector is s', and the supply of environmental services is Y', the income of the consumer must be $m(s', Y', \tilde{u})$. He is thus willing to pay at most $EV = m(s', Y', \tilde{u}) - I$ for the right to buy consumption activities at the price vector s'', and enjoy the environmental quality Y''.

EV is known as the equivalent variation. When $EV > 0$, EV is the compensation that must be given to the individual when $s = s'$, $Y = Y'$, in order to make the first situation indifferent to the second situation. When $EV < 0$, EV is the amount that can be taken from the individual when $s = s'$, $Y = Y'$, without making him feel worse than in the second situation.

If only prices change between the two situations, we can arrive at the classical idea of the consumer surplus as the sum of areas under the appropriate demand curves. From property (i), we know that $\partial m / \partial s_i = c_i^*$ and so we have

$$CV = I - m(s'', Y, \bar{u}) = m(s', Y, \bar{u}) - m(s'', Y, \bar{u})$$

$$= -\int_{s'}^{s''} \sum_{i=1}^{Q} \frac{\partial m}{\partial s_i} ds_i = -\int_{s'}^{s''} \sum_{i=1}^{A} c_i^*(s, Y, \bar{u}) ds_i \qquad (25)$$

where the integration is performed along some path from s' to s'' (the integral will be independent of the path of integration, because of property vi). Each integral gives the area under the compensated demand curve, and so the consumer surplus can be calculated from the knowledge of the compensated demand curve. By changing u from $\bar{u}$ to $\tilde{u}$, it is seen that EV can also be expressed as areas under compensated demand curves.

To have information on the compensated demand curves, one must in general first estimate the expenditure function, and therefore using the sum of areas under compensated demand curves for computation of consumers' surplus is not the most straightforward way. One exception to this statement is of course when the income effect $\partial c / \partial I$ is zero, because in that case the compensated demand functions are identical to the Marshallian demand functions.

The significance of the compensating variation will now be touched on. Let us assume that the compensations associated with the compensating variation are feasible. Then it is easy to see the relation between the Pareto criterion (a change satisfies this criterion if and only if no one is harmed by the change), and the total compensating variation. Consider two situations with prices s', s'' and environmental qualities Y', Y'', respectively. Let the situation denoted by a single prime be the present situation, in which individual h has utility level $\bar{u}^h (h = 1, 2, \cdots, H)$, and let the other situation be a planned situation. The total compensating variation is

$$CV = \sum_{h=1}^{H} CV^h = \sum_{h=1}^{H} [I^h - m^h(s'', Y'', \bar{u}^h)]$$

If $CV > 0$, it is clear that it is possible to make the change and compensate those who are harmed by the change. The change will thus satisfy the Pareto criterion and is therefore better than status quo (if the change does not exclude future changes that are desirable, the change can be regarded as desirable). If, on the other hand, $CV < 0$, the change will not satisfy the Pareto criterion. If lump sum transfers are feasible, the total compensating variation therefore provides a test of whether the Pareto criterion can be met. The equivalent variation can be used in situations where lump sum transfers are not feasible or are undesirable. This will be discussed in section 11.

9. COMPARISONS BETWEEN CV AND EV

Let us now see if we can say something about the relative size of compensating variation and equivalent variation. Consider again the dual problems:

$$\max u(c, Y) \qquad\qquad \min s^T c$$
$$\text{s.t. } s^T c < I \qquad\qquad \text{s.t. } u(c, Y) \geqq \bar{u} = v(s, I, Y)$$
$$c \geqq 0 \qquad\qquad c \geqq 0$$

It is clear that these two problems will have the same solution, so that property (iii) $c(s, I, Y) \equiv c^*[s, Y, v(s, I, Y)]$. This identity can be regarded as dual to property (ii).

If we write down the Lagrangian for the first problem, with the multiplier α associated with the constraint $s^T c \leqq I$, we know that

$$\frac{\partial v(s, I, Y)}{\partial I} = \alpha$$

and so it follows that

$$\begin{aligned}
\frac{\partial c_i(s, I, Y)}{\partial I} &= \frac{\partial c_i^*[s, Y, v(s, I, Y)]}{\partial I} \\
&= \frac{\partial c_i^*(s, Y, \bar{u})}{\partial \bar{u}} \frac{\partial v(s, I, Y)}{\partial I} \\
&= \alpha \frac{\partial c_i^*(s, Y, \bar{u})}{\partial \bar{u}}
\end{aligned}$$

As α is positive, we see that $\partial c_i(s, I, Y)/\partial I$, and $\partial c_i^*(s, Y, \bar{u})/\partial \bar{u}$ have the same sign.

If we now use the integral expressions for the consumer surplus, and assume that only the prices are different between the two situations, we have

$$CV = -\int_{s'}^{s''} \sum_{i=1}^{Q} c_i^*(s, Y, \bar{u}) ds_i, \text{ and}$$

$$EV = -\int_{s'}^{s''} \sum_{i=1}^{Q} c_i^*(s, Y, \bar{\bar{u}}) ds_i$$

We already know that the integrals are independent of the path of integration (owing to property vi), and so we can assume a parameterized path,

$$s_i = h_i(t) \qquad 0 \le t \le 1$$

$$s_i' = h_i(0)$$

$$s_i'' = h_i(1) \qquad i = 1, 2, \cdots, Q$$

Then we have

$$CV = -\int_0^1 \sum_{i=1}^{Q} c_i^*(s, \, Y, \, \bar{u}) h_i{}'(t) dt, \text{ and}$$

$$EV = -\int_0^1 \sum_{i=1}^{Q} c_i^*(s, \, Y, \, \bar{\bar{u}}) h_i'(t) dt, \text{ and}$$

$$EV - CV = -\int_0^1 \sum_{i=1}^{Q} [c_i^*(s, \, Y, \, \bar{\bar{u}}) - c_i^*(s, \, Y, \, \bar{u})] h_i'(t) dt$$

According to the mean value theorem, there exist $u^1, \cdots, u^Q$, such that u^i is a number between $\bar{u}$ and $\bar{\bar{u}}$, and such that

$$c_i^*(s, \, Y, \, \bar{\bar{u}}) - c_i^*(s, Y, \bar{u}) = (\bar{\bar{u}} - \bar{u}) \frac{\partial c_i^*(s, \, Y, \, u^i)}{\partial u}$$

(u^i depends on t, but that is of no concern), and so we have

$$EV - CV = -(\bar{\bar{u}} - \bar{u}) \int_0^1 \sum_{i=1}^{Q} \frac{\partial c_i^*(s, \, Y, \, u^i)}{\partial u} \, h_i'(t) dt$$

Let us assume that none of the consumption activities, for which prices change, is inferior. Then the partial derivative of the compensated demand functions with respect to the utility level will be nonnegative, as we have just proved. If we furthermore assume that all prices change in the same direction, so that $h_i' \ge 0$ for all i, or $h_i' \le 0$ for all i, we see that $\bar{\bar{u}} - \bar{u}$ has the opposite sign to h_i'. (If no prices decrease, and some increase, then $\bar{\bar{u}} < \bar{u}$, and vice versa.) This means that $EV - CV \ge 0$, or that the equivalent variation is not smaller than the compensating variation when all prices change in the same direction. When some prices increase and some decrease, it is not possible, however, to say anything about the relative size of EV and CV.

We next turn to environmental services, and since they are public goods, there are no markets for them. Therefore, the classification used for private goods—that of inferior and noninferior or superior goods—is not very meaningful. But there is a possibility of classifying public goods in similar categories. Recall the definition of the demand price δ_j for the jth environmental service. From equation (17) we know that

$$\delta_j = -\frac{\partial m(s, Y, v)}{\partial Y_j}$$

where v is the indirect utility function. The interpretation of δ_j is obvious; it is the amount the consumer is willing to pay to obtain one more unit of the jth environmental service. δ_j will depend on income because the indirect utility function depends on income. Note that

$$m[s, Y, v(s, I, Y)] \equiv I.$$

$$\delta_j = \delta_j(s, I, Y) \qquad j = 1, 2, \cdots, m$$

We can also define the compensated demand price δ_j^* as

$$\delta_j^*(s, Y, \bar{u}) = -\frac{\partial m(s, Y, \bar{u})}{\partial Y_j}$$

The difference between δ_j and δ_j^* is that δ_j gives the marginal willingness to pay for Y_j, when income is held constant, while δ_j^* gives the marginal willingness to pay for Y_j when utility is held constant.

If we differentiate δ_j with respect to income we have

$$\frac{\partial \delta_j}{\partial I} = -\frac{\partial^2 m(s, Y, v)}{\partial Y_j \partial u} \frac{\partial v}{\partial I} = \alpha \frac{\partial \delta_j^*}{\partial u}$$

It is now natural to call a public good Y_j noninferior, if the demand price for this public good increases with income, that is, if $\partial \delta_j / \partial I > 0$. If the environmental service Y_j is a noninferior good, then as we have proved, $\partial \delta_j^* / \partial \bar{u} > 0$.

We can now repeat the analysis of the case when only prices change. The compensating variation can be written

$$CV = -\int_{Y'}^{Y''} \sum_{j=1}^{m} \frac{\partial m(s, Y, \bar{u})}{\partial Y_j} dY_j = \int_{Y'}^{Y''} \sum_{j=1}^{m} \delta_j^*(s, Y, \bar{u}) dY_j$$

and the equivalent variation

$$EV = -\int_{Y'}^{Y''} \sum_{j=1}^{m} \frac{\partial m(s, Y, \tilde{u})}{\partial Y_j} dY_j = \int_{Y'}^{Y''} \sum_{j=1}^{m} \delta_j^*(s, Y, \tilde{u}) dY_j$$

Let $Y_j = g_j(t)$, $Y'_j = g_j(0)$, $Y''_j = g_j(1)$, be a path from Y' to Y'. We can, as before, compute the difference between EV and CV.

$$EV - CV = (\bar{\bar{u}} - \bar{u}) \int_0^1 \sum_{j=1}^m \frac{\partial \delta_j^*[s,\, g(t),\, w^j]}{\partial u} g'_j(t)dt$$

If, as we have assumed, $Y'' \geq Y'$, then $\bar{\bar{u}} > \bar{u}$, and $g'_j \geq 0$, so that if all environmental services that change are noninferior goods, $EV > CV$, that is, the equivalent variation is greater than the compensating variation. This is similar to what happened when the prices on private goods changed.

Theorem: When prices and the supply of environmental services change in the same direction, in the sense that no prices increase if the supply of environmental services increases, and vice versa, and if all private and public goods are noninferior, then the equivalent variation is greater than the compensating variation.

10. CONSUMERS' SURPLUS AND INDIVISIBILITIES IN CONSUMPTION

So far we have assumed that all consumption activities have been perfectly divisible. This assumption has made it possible to embed the levels of the activities in the set of real numbers, and thereby obtain powerful mathematical techniques with which to analyze different problems. But this approach has many drawbacks. In many problems there are indivisibilities that must be taken into account. Most people, for example, live in only one place at a time, and if the time period under consideration is short enough, this will create an indivisibility. In the analysis of recreation, it is usually assumed that an individual uses a facility, for example a park, for a whole day, which means that if our time period is one day, we have an indivisibility again.

The general theory of indivisibilities is very difficult because of the combinatorial problem involved, but a simple case will be analyzed in detail. What we will do is to consider a three-good economy in which one good, z, is the numeraire, with price one; one good, Y, the quality of the environment; and one good, x, is assumed to be consumed either entirely within a single time period, or not at all.

We write the utility function $u(z, x, Y)$ where x can take only the values 0 and 1. The good x might for example, be living in a given neighborhood or not living in that neighborhood, or using a park for recreation or not using it. Y stands for the quality of the good x, e.g., the quality of the neighborhood or the quality of the park. Let I be the income of the consumer, and p_x the price of x. The budget constraint is then

$$z + p_x x \leqq I$$

We assume that u has continuous partial derivatives with respect to z and Y. Furthermore, we assume the following generalization of convex preferences.

For each z there exists a unique z', such that $u(z, 1, Y) = u(z', 0, Y)$. This implies that there exists a z'', such that $u(z', 1, Y) = u(z'', 0, Y)$. We assume that $z'' > z' > z$, and $z'' - z' > z' - z$. (26)

This assumption means that the necessary compensation for abstaining from x increases with the consumption of z.

The demand functions are given by

$$\max u(z, x, Y)$$

$$\text{s.t.} \quad z + p_x x \leq I$$

$$x = 0 \text{ or } 1$$

It is obvious that if $p_x = 0$, then $x = 1$, and $z = I$. If p_x increases but still is small, it is also obvious that $x = 1$, and $z = I - p_x$. This follows directly from the assumption above; if p_x is small, then a small reduction in z is still preferred to a reduction in x from 1 to 0. When, however, p_x increases to a certain level p'_x the consumer will switch from $x = 1$ to $x = 0$ and $z = I$. This can be seen from the indifference curve diagram (figure 5).

When $p_x = 0$, the consumer chooses the point C. The points A and B are indifferent, and the decrease in p_x implies a movement along $x = 1$

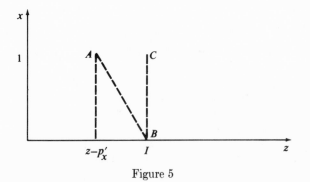

Figure 5

from C to A. When A is reached, it is optimal to switch to B. We therefore see that p'_x is defined by $u(I - p'_x, 1, Y) = u(I, 0, Y)$. The demand functions thus take a very simple form

$$z = \begin{cases} I - p_x & \text{if} & p_x \leq p'_x \\ I & \text{if} & p_x \geq p'_x \end{cases} \tag{27}$$

$$x = \begin{cases} 1 & \text{if} & p_x \leq p'_x \\ 0 & \text{if} & p_x \geq p'_x \end{cases} \tag{28}$$

The demand curves are shown in figure 6.

The expenditure function and the compensated demand curves are found from the solution to the problem

min $z + p_x x$

s.t. $u(z, x, Y) \geq \bar{u}$

$x = 0$, or 1

As before, we see that if $p_x = 0$, then $x^* = 1, z^* = \bar{z}$, where $u(\bar{z}, 1, Y) = \bar{u}$. If p_x increases, x^* is still one, and z^* still $\bar{z}$, until $p_x = p''_x$, where

$$\bar{z} + p''_x = z'' \qquad \text{and} \qquad u(\bar{z}, 1, Y) = u(z'', 0, Y) = \bar{u}$$

The compensated demand functions are thus

$$z^* = \begin{cases} \bar{z} & \text{if} & p_x \leq p''_x \\ z'' & \text{if} & p_x \geq p''_x \end{cases} \tag{29}$$

$$x^* = \begin{cases} 1 & \text{if} & p_x \leq p''_x \\ 0 & \text{if} & p_x \geq p''_x \end{cases} \tag{30}$$

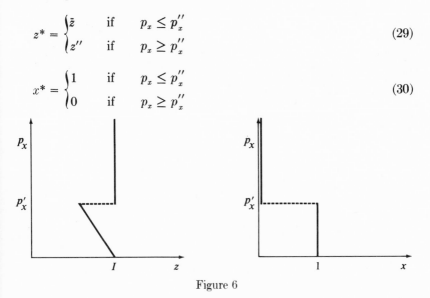

Figure 6

and p''_x, and z'' are given by

$$u(\tilde{z}, 1, Y) = u(z'', 0, Y) = \bar{u}$$
$$p''_x = z'' - \tilde{z}$$

(31)

The expenditure function is then

$$m(p_x, Y, \bar{u}) = z^* + p_x x^* = \begin{cases} \tilde{z} + p_x & \text{if} \quad p_x \le p''_x \\ z'' & \text{if} \quad p_x \ge p''_x \end{cases}$$

(32)

The compensated demand curves are shown in figure 7.

If $\bar{u} = u(I, 0, Y)$, that is, if the initial point represents a situation in which the consumer does not consume x, then the compensating variation can be computed as follows: We have $u(z'', 0, Y) = u(I, 0, Y)$, and thus $z'' = I$. Moreover, p'_x was given by

$$u(I - p'_x, 1, Y) = u(I, 0, Y) = u(I - p''_x, 1, Y)$$

so that $p'_x = p''_x$. In this case, the Marshallian demand function for x is identical to the compensated demand function for x. Note that p'_x is a function of Y, by $u(I - p'_x, 1, Y) = u(I, 0, Y)$.

If Y is the quality of the flow of x, it is natural to assume that

$$u_3(z, 0, Y) = 0$$

(33)

that is, if the consumer does not demand the flow of x, he is indifferent to the quality of that flow. This is an assumption that will be applied many times in the chapter on estimating m as a function of Y (chapter 5).

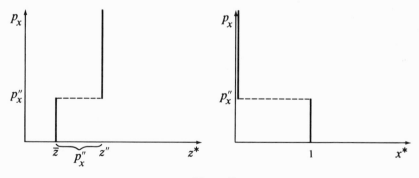

Figure 7

This assumption implies that $u(I, 0, Y)$ is independent of Y, and

$$-u_1 \frac{dp'_x}{dY} + u_3 = 0 \quad \text{or} \quad \frac{dp'_x}{dY} = \frac{u_3}{u_1} > 0$$

that is, an increase in the quality increases the demand reservation price p'_x, or the willingness to pay for x.

The compensating variation variant of the consumer's surplus is then

$$CV = I - m(p_x, Y, \bar{u})$$

$$= \begin{cases} I - \check{z} - p_x & \text{if } p_x \leqq p'_x \\ I - z'' & \text{if } p_x \geqq p'_x \end{cases}$$

but $I = z''$, and $I - \check{z} = z'' - \check{z} = p''_x = p'_x$, and so

$$CV = \begin{cases} p'_x - p_x & \text{if } p_x \leqq p'_x \\ 0 & \text{if } p_x \geqq p'_x, \end{cases} \quad \text{and} \tag{34}$$

$$m = \begin{cases} I - p'_x + p_x & \text{if } p_x \leqq p'_x \\ I & \text{if } p_x \geqq p'_x \end{cases} \tag{35}$$

Since p'_x depends on Y, CV depends on p_x, and Y, and

$$\frac{\partial CV}{\partial p_x} = \begin{cases} -1 & \text{if } p_x \leqq p'_x \\ 0 & \text{if } p_x > p'_x \end{cases} \tag{36}$$

$$\frac{\partial CV}{\partial Y} = \begin{cases} \dfrac{dp'_x}{dY} & \text{if } p_x \leqq p'_x \\ 0 & \text{if } p_x > p'_x \end{cases} \tag{37}$$

CV is also a function of the initial income I, because p'_x is a function of I, and

$$\frac{dp'_x}{dI} = 1 \tag{38}$$

Now, let $\bar{p}_x$ be the initial price of x, and assume that $\bar{p}_x < p'_x$, so that

$$\bar{u} = u(I - \bar{p}_x, 1, Y) = u(z'', 0, Y), \text{ and}$$

$$p''_x = z'' + \bar{p}_x - p''_x$$

This means that the expenditure function can be written as

$$
m = \begin{cases} I + p_x - \bar{p}_x & \text{if } p_x \leqq p_x'' \\ I + p_x'' - \bar{p}_x & \text{if } p_x \geqq p_x'' \end{cases}
\tag{39}
$$

and the compensating variation as

$$
CV = \begin{cases} \bar{p}_x - p_x & \text{if } p_x \leqq p_x'' \\ \bar{p}_x - p_x'' & \text{if } p_x \geqq p_x'' \end{cases}
\tag{40}
$$

Exactly as above we can discuss the dependence of CV on p_x, Y, and I.

Next we will aggregate the demand functions and the expenditure functions over a set of consumers. Let there be a continuum of consumers A, represented by an interval $[0, a]$ on the real line. Each consumer in this set is denoted by the superscript h. Instead of writing $p_x''^h$, and $p_x'^h$, we will simplify these notations to $p_x{}^h$. The meaning of $p_x{}^h$ will be clear from the context. Define the set G by

$$
G = \{h \in A \mid p_x \leqq p_x{}^h\} = G(p_x, Y)
\tag{41}
$$

G is thus the set of consumers that demand a positive quantity of x when the price is p_x and the quality Y.

It is clear that

$$
G(\alpha, Y) \subset G(\beta, Y) \quad \text{if and only if} \quad \alpha > \beta, \text{ and}
$$

$$
G(p_x, Y') \subset G(p_x, Y'') \quad \text{if and only if} \quad Y' < Y''
$$

Let us now assume that $p_x{}^h$ is a measurable function of h [11]. Let μ be the Lebsegue measure on the real line. The function $g(p_x, Y)$ is then well defined by

$$
g(p_x, Y) = \mu(G) = \int_{G(p_x, Y)} d\mu(h)
\tag{42}
$$

It is clear that $g(p_x, Y)$ is the aggregate demand function for x. In view of the inclusion relations above, $g(p_x, Y)$ is decreasing in p_x, and increasing in Y.

The following notations will be useful in aggregating the expenditure functions:

$$G' = G(\bar{p}_x, Y) \cap G(p_x, Y)$$

$$G'' = G(\bar{p}_x, Y) \cap CG(p_x, Y)$$

$$G''' = G(p_x, Y) \cap CG(\bar{p}_x, Y)$$

$$G^{iv} = CG(p_x, Y) \cap CG(\bar{p}_x, Y)$$

where CG denotes the complement of G in A. These four sets are non-overlapping, and their union is A. The interpretation of these sets is straightforward. G' is the set of consumers who demand a positive quantity of x at both the prices $\bar{p}_x$ and p_x, while G'' is the set of consumers who demand a positive quantity of x at the price $\bar{p}_x$, but not at the price p_x.

$\bar{p}_x$ will be interpreted as the current price (or the price in the initial situation), while p_x will be interpreted as an arbitrary price. The aggregate expenditure function can now be written

$$m = \int m^h d\mu(h) = \int_{G'} m^h d\mu(h) + \int_{G''} m^h d\mu(h)$$
$$+ \int_{G'''} m^h d\mu(h) + \int_{G^{iv}} m^h d\mu(h)$$

Note that one of the sets G'', and G''' must be empty, because of the inclusion relations that hold for the sets $G(p_x, Y)$. Assume that $p_x > \bar{p}_x$. Then G'' is empty, $G' = G(\bar{p}_x, Y)$, and $G''' = G(p_x, Y) \backslash G(\bar{p}_x, Y)$. The individual expenditure functions can now be written

$$h \in G' \quad m^h = I^h + p_x - \bar{p}_x,$$

$$h \in G''' \quad m^h = I^h + p_x - p_x{}^h,$$

$$h \in G^{iv} \quad m^h = I^h$$

and the aggregate expenditure function is therefore given by

$$m = \int_{G'} (I^h + p_x - \bar{p}_x) d\mu(h) + \int_{G'''} (I^h + p_x - p_x{}^h) d\mu(h)$$
$$+ \int_{G^{iv}} I^h d\mu(h) = I + (p_x - \bar{p}_x)g(\bar{p}_x, Y) + \int_{G'''} (p_x - p_x{}^h) d\mu(h)$$

where $I = \int I^h d\mu(h)$, that is, the total income.

The following calculations will prove fruitful in interpreting the expression for m.

$$g(s, Y) = \int_{G(s, Y)} d\mu(h) = \int_A C_G d(h)$$

where C_G is the characteristic function of the set G, that is

$$C_G = \begin{cases} 1, \text{ if } h \in G \\ 0, \text{ if } h \notin G \end{cases}$$

We thus have

$$\int_{p_x}^{\bar{p}_x} g(s, Y) d\mu(s) = \int_{p_x}^{\bar{p}_x} \int_A C_G d\mu(h) d\mu(s)$$

According to Fubini's theorem [12] this double integral can be written

$$\int_A d\mu(h) \int_{p_x}^{\bar{p}_x} C_G(s, Y) d\mu(s)$$

$$\int_{p_x}^{\bar{p}_x} C_G(s, Y) d\mu(s) = \begin{cases} \bar{p}_x - p_x & \text{if } p_x{}^h \geq \bar{p}_x, \text{ i.e., if } h \in G(\bar{p}_x, Y) \\ p_x{}^h - p_x & \text{if } p_x \leq p_x{}^h = \bar{p}_x, \text{ i.e., if } h \in G''' \\ 0 & \text{if } h \in CG(p_x, Y) \end{cases}$$

and so

$$\int_{p_x}^{\bar{p}_x} g(s, Y) d\mu(s) = \int_{G(\bar{p}_x, Y)} (\bar{p}_x - p_x) d\mu(h) + \int_{G'''} (p_x{}^h - p_x) d\mu(h)$$

$$= (\bar{p}_x - p_x) g(\bar{p}_x, Y) + \int_{G'''} (p_x{}^h - p_x) d\mu(h)$$

The aggregate expenditure function can therefore be written

$$m = I - \int_{p_x}^{\bar{p}_x} g(s, Y) d\mu(s) \tag{43}$$

The total compensating variation becomes

$$CV = I - m = \int_{p_x}^{\bar{p}_x} g(s, Y) d\mu(s) \tag{44}$$

that is, an area under the aggregate demand curve. This is a natural result because although the aggregate demand function has a positive income elasticity, the individual demand functions have a zero income elasticity [compare equation (38)]. If the commodity x must be consumed in one fixed indivisible unit or not at all, the aggregate demand function will be identical to the compensated aggregated demand function.

When it comes to empirical calculations of consumers' surplus, it is thus necessary to decide a priori whether the good under investigation is indivisible or not. In the latter case it is necessary, as we have seen, to calculate the consumers' surplus by solving the Slutsky equations, while in the former case it is possible to calculate CV directly from the demand function. The result (43) has been derived only for a fall in the price from $\bar{p}_x$ to p_x. It is obvious that (43) is true also for the case of a price increase.

In view of the fact that the compensating demand function is identical to the Marshallian demand function, it is clear that the equivalent variation will be equal to the compensating variation. With this in mind, it is easy to investigate the dependence of m on Y. Assume that we are interested in the maximal amount the consumers are willing to pay for an increase in Y, given that the price p_x is constant.

If Y increases from Y' to Y'', the demand curve shifts from AB to DC in the diagram. The point A represents the current situation. If the price of x is increased to OB, and the consumers are compensated with an amount equal to the area EBA, they are on the same utility level as at A. If the price is increased further to OC, no change in utility will be implied because of assumption (33). If finally the price is decreased to p_x again, and the consumers pay an amount equal to the area ECD, we have ended up at the point D, and no consumer has experienced a change in his utility. The net result of these transactions is that the consumers have to pay an amount equal to the area $ABCD$, which is the maximal amount they

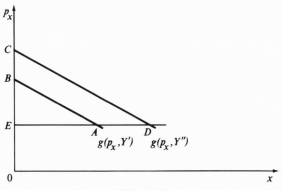

Figure 8

are willing to pay for the increase in Y. In the limit, when Y'' goes to Y', the marginal willingness to pay is given by

$$\delta = \int_{OE}^{OC} \frac{\partial g(s, Y)}{\partial Y} d\mu(s) \tag{45}$$

11. SOCIAL WELFARE FUNCTIONS

Although it is clear from economic theory [13] that the widespread use of national income as an aggregate welfare measure is illegitimate, politicians and persons involved in applied economics continue to use national income as the central or sometimes the only welfare measure. The main criticism from theoretical economists has been that even in an economy without market imperfections, an increase in national income does not necessarily indicate an increase in welfare, defined in some way, because this increase neglects the distributional aspects. But there are, of course, other serious drawbacks with the national income statistics, at least as national income is computed today, such as the neglect of goods that are not priced in any markets. This section and the following discuss different ways in which the computation of national income can be modified to incorporate environmental services. In order to put such a discussion on a firm and rigorous basis, we will assume that lump sum transfers are feasible, so that the distributional effects can be ignored.

Our starting point will be an indirect social welfare function giving the ethical beliefs of the government. Given such a welfare function, one can ask why we should bother with constructing other welfare measures such as the national income statistics. By using the social welfare function it is possible to judge if a change means an increase or decrease in welfare [14], and no other measures are needed. A defense for derived welfare measures may, however, be constructed along the following lines. The preferences of the government are seldom expressed explicitly, and if a third party wants to know if welfare has increased or decreased in the eyes of the government, he must look at the actual development, taking the policy measures initiated by the government as revealing its preferences. This is also the route we are going to follow.

In welfare economics, ethical beliefs are very often represented by a Bergson welfare function

$$W(u^1, \cdots, u^h) \tag{46}$$

where u^h is the utility function of individual h [15].

This is a very abstract formulation, and if one were to ask a member of the government how his ethical beliefs could be represented by such a welfare function, the answer would probably be a laugh. The Bergson welfare function thus does not seem to be of any operational value. Let us therefore try to find a better way to represent the preferences of the government.

To do so, we assume that the economy under consideration is a market economy, and that the basic value is the principle of consumer sovereignty, meaning that the consumer is free to spend his disposable income in whatever way he likes. This assumption precludes some interesting cases, such as compulsory education. However, we will neglect these exceptions because it seems that they really are exceptions to the principle.

The government has preferences concerning the distribution of income. By income is meant the nominal income I^h each consumer receives. But as the purchasing power of the nominal income I^h depends on prices, it follows that the government will have preferences about the prices, too. This means that the ethical beliefs of the government can be represented by the indirect welfare function

$$V = V(s_1, \cdots, s_Q, I^1, \cdots, I^H) \tag{47}$$

The word "indirect" will be explained later on.

It seems that equation (47) is a more realistic description of the preferences of the government than (46). In Sweden, for example, income transfers and taxes are used to change the distribution of nominal income; measures are taken to keep apartment rents low; and earlier at least, there were strong opinions for taxing luxuries, because it was felt that this would contribute to a better distribution of the real income defined in some way.

The main advantage equation (47) has over (46) is that the variables appearing in (47) are easy to interpret and measure, while it is only theoretically conceivable but practically impossible to measure the arguments in (46). However, it is the purpose of the next few paragraphs to show that (46) and (47) are equivalent if the V function satisfies some further conditions. Before we enter into that discussion, environmental services will be introduced. In equation (46), environmental services enter as arguments in the individual utility functions u^h. In equation (47) it seems natural to assume that the government has preferences directly on the vector Y, that is, (47) should be written as

$$V = V(s, Y, I^1, \cdots, I^H) \tag{48}$$

Furthermore, we assume that

$$\frac{\partial V}{\partial I^h} > 0, \ h = 1, \ \cdots, \ H \tag{49}$$

We see that (49) expresses the usual Pareto criterion.

We will now prove the following:

Theorem: If the following two conditions

$$\frac{\partial V}{\partial s_i} = -\sum_{h=1}^{H} c_i^h \frac{\partial V}{\partial I^h} \qquad i = 1, 2, \cdots, Q \tag{50}$$

$$\frac{\partial V}{\partial Y_j} = \sum_{h=1}^{H} \delta_j^h \frac{\partial V}{\partial I^h} \qquad j = 1, \cdots, m \tag{51}$$

are valid, where c_i^h is the level of consumption activity i chosen by consumer h, and δ_j^h is consumer h's demand price for the jth environmental service, there exists a function $W: R^H \ni (u^1, \cdots, u^H) \to R$ such that

$$V(s, Y, I^1, \cdots, I^H) = W[v^1(s, Y, I^1), \cdots, v^H(s, Y, I^H)] \tag{52}$$

where $v^h(s, Y, I^h)$ is the indirect utility function of consumer h.

Remark: If V is defined by (52), it follows that conditions (50) and (51) are satisfied; therefore these conditions are necessary for the existence of the W function.

Proof: If W exists, we get after differentiating (52) with respect to s_i, and I^h

$$\frac{\partial V}{\partial s_i} = \sum_{h=1}^{H} \frac{\partial W}{\partial u^h} \frac{\partial v^h}{\partial s_i} \tag{53}$$

$$\frac{\partial V}{\partial I^h} = \frac{\partial W}{\partial u^h} \frac{\partial v^h}{\partial I^h} \tag{54}$$

According to equation (11) in section 2, we have

$$\frac{\partial v^h(s, Y, I^h)}{\partial I^h} = \alpha^h > 0$$

so it is possible to solve for I^h in $u^h = v^h(s, Y, I^h)$, yielding $I^h = f^h(s,$

Y, u^h). If this function is substituted for I^h in equation (54), the following total differential equation is obtained:

$$\frac{\partial W}{\partial u^h} = \frac{\partial V[s,\, Y,\, f'(s,\, Y,\, u^1),\, \cdots,\, f^H(s,\, Y,\, u^H)]/\partial I^h}{\partial v^h[s,\, Y,\, f^h(s,\, Y,\, u^h)]/\partial I^h} \tag{55}$$

$$h = 1,\, \cdots,\, H$$

It is easy to see (by evaluating the derivatives) that the integrability conditions

$$\frac{\partial}{\partial u^k}\frac{\dfrac{\partial V}{\partial I^h}}{\dfrac{\partial v^h}{\partial I^k}} = \frac{\partial}{\partial u^h}\frac{\dfrac{\partial V}{\partial I^k}}{\dfrac{\partial v^k}{\partial I^k}} \qquad h,\, k = 1,\, \cdots,\, H$$

are satisfied [16].

Thus, there exists a function $W(s,\, Y,\, u^1,\, \cdots,\, u^H)$ which is a solution to (54) such that

$$W(s,\, Y,\, u^1,\, \cdots,\, u^H) = V(s,\, Y,\, I^1,\, \cdots,\, I^H)$$

By differentiating with respect to s_i we obtain

$$\frac{\partial V}{\partial s_i} = \frac{\partial W}{\partial s_i} + \sum_{h=1}^{H}\frac{\partial W}{\partial u^h}\frac{\partial v^h}{\partial s_i} \qquad \text{or (due to equation 54)}$$

$$\frac{\partial W}{\partial s_i} = \frac{\partial V}{\partial s_i} - \sum_{h=1}^{H}\frac{\partial V}{\partial I^h}\frac{\dfrac{\partial v^h}{\partial s_i}}{\dfrac{\partial v^h}{\partial I^h}} \qquad \text{(due to equations 11 and 12)}$$

$$= \frac{\partial v}{\partial s_i} + \sum_{h=1}^{H}c_i^h\frac{\partial v}{\partial I^h} = 0 \qquad \text{(due to equation 50)}$$

In exactly the same way it can be shown by using equation (51) that $\partial W/\partial Y_j = 0$. The theorem is now proved.

Neither of the conditions (50) or (51) seems very realistic. Condition (50) implies that a reduction in the price of one commodity is regarded as indifferent to increases in all individuals' incomes in such a way that the increase in individual H's income is equal to the saving he can obtain from the price decrease. To a certain extent the politicians probably have preferences satisfying this condition, at least if we interpret an individual to mean a homogeneous group of people. The discussion of the tradeoffs between income taxes and indirect taxes indicates this. Therefore we will maintain condition (51). Condition (52) seems unacceptable, however. It requires that the government have information on the individual demand prices for environmental services, but in the next chapter we will show that it is very difficult, if not impossible, to obtain such information.

We will therefore write the social welfare function as

$$W = W[Y, u^1(c^1, Y), \cdots, u^H(c^H, Y)] \tag{56}$$

Next we will aggregate over individuals to obtain a social utility function, with totals of each good as arguments instead of individual net demands. In order to do that, we will follow Samuelson's discussion of community indifference curves [17].

Regard c^h, and c^k, $h \neq k$, as vectors of different consumption activities, and let the corresponding prices be s^h and s^k. Consider now the following problem:

max $W[Y, u^1(c^1, Y), \cdots, u^H(c^H, Y)]$ with respect to c_i^h, and I^h,

subject to $s^{hT}c^h = I^h$, $h = 1, \cdots, H, \sum_{h=1}^{H} I^h = I$

It is here that the assumption that lump sum transfers are feasible enters in, because if such transfers are not feasible, this optimization problem is not meaningful [18]. The solution to this problem can be written $c^h = c^h(s^1, \cdots, s^H, Y, I)$. But $s^1 = \cdots = s^H$, and Hicks' theorem on composite goods can be applied [19]. According to this theorem, the demand for the composite commodity vector

$$c = \sum_{h=1}^{H} c^h$$

will satisfy all the conditions that can be derived from consumption theory. This means that there exists a social utility function $U(c, Y)$ such that the total demand functions

$$c(s, Y, I) = \sum_{h=1}^{H} c^h(s^1, \cdots, s^H, Y, I)$$

can be viewed as generated from the social utility function.

It is this social utility function $U(c, Y)$ that will be used for the rest of this chapter. In view of the important role it will play, it is desirable to summarize the two assumptions on which it is based. First, there is the assumption that condition (50) is valid. Without this assumption, it would not have been possible to translate the indirect social welfare function to a direct social welfare function of the Bergson type. Second, there is the assumption that lump sum transfers are feasible. Without this assumption, it would not have been possible to aggregate over consumers so as to obtain the social utility function from the direct social welfare function.

Before using the social utility function for a discussion of national income and related matters, it may be of interest to sketch the connections between the social utility function and the aggregation of individual expenditure functions. The social expenditure function (social in contrast to total defined as an aggregate of individual expenditure functions, as discussed in section 6) is defined by

$$m(s, Y, \bar{U}) = \min s^T \sum_{h=1}^{H} c^h \tag{57}$$

$$\text{subject to } W[Y, u^1(c^1, Y), \cdots, u^H(c^H, Y)] \geqq \bar{U} \tag{58}$$

The first-order necessary conditions are

$$s_i - \beta \frac{\partial W}{\partial u_i^h} \frac{\partial u^h}{\partial c_i^h} \leqq 0 \qquad h = 1, \cdots, H \qquad i = 1, \cdots, Q \tag{59}$$

Assume that this problem has the solution $\bar{c}^h(s, Y, \bar{U})$, so that

$$m(s, Y, \bar{U}) = s^T \sum_{h=1}^{H} \bar{c}^h(s, Y, \bar{U}) \tag{60}$$

In particular, this solution determines individual utility levels

$$\bar{u}^h = u^h(\bar{c}^h, Y) \qquad h = 1, \cdots, H$$

If the economy is in a state in which the prices are given by the vector s, and the state of environment by the vector Y, the government can by lump sum transfers achieve a situation in which $u^h = \bar{u}^h$. Let m^h be the expenditure function for consumer h. Then it is clear that $c^{h*}(s, Y, \bar{u}^h)$ will satisfy (59), because the first-order necessary conditions for the individual minimum problem will be identical to (59), due to the way in which we have chosen $\bar{u}^h$. We can therefore conclude that

$$m(s, Y, \bar{U}) = \sum_{h=1}^{H} m^h(s, Y, \bar{u}^h), \text{where} \tag{61}$$
$$\bar{U} = W(Y, \bar{u}^1, \cdots, \bar{u}^H)$$

The social expenditure function can thus be obtained by aggregating the individual expenditure functions, and it will tell us how great the least income is which can guarantee the social welfare level $\bar{U}$.

But in general (61) is not an identity in Y, unless condition (51) is satisfied. This means that the "social" demand price for environmental services may differ from the sum of the individual demand prices. To show the connection between the "social" demand price and the sum of the individual demand prices, we differentiate (58) with respect to Y_j.

$$\frac{\partial W}{\partial Y_j} + \sum_{h=1}^{H} \frac{\partial W}{\partial u^h} \left(\frac{\partial u^h}{\partial Y_j} + \sum_{i=1}^{Q} \frac{\partial u^h}{\partial c_i^h} \frac{\partial c_i^h}{\partial Y_j} \right) = 0$$

But

$$\frac{\partial W}{\partial u^h} \frac{\partial u^h}{\partial c_j^h} = \frac{1}{\beta} s_i, \text{ so that}$$

$$\frac{\partial W}{\partial Y_j} + \sum_{h=1}^{H} \frac{\partial W}{\partial u^h} \frac{\partial u^h}{\partial Y_j} = -\frac{1}{\beta} \sum_{h=1}^{H} \sum_{i=1}^{Q} s_i \frac{\partial \bar{c}_i^h}{\partial Y_j}$$

From (60) it is seen that

$$\frac{\partial m}{\partial Y_j} = \sum_{i=1}^{Q} s_i \sum_{h=1}^{H} \frac{\partial \bar{c}_i^h}{\partial Y_j} = -\beta \frac{\partial W}{\partial Y_j} - \beta \sum_{h=1}^{H} \frac{\partial W}{\partial u^h} \frac{\partial u^h}{\partial Y_j}$$

Equation (59) yields

$$\beta \frac{\partial W}{\partial u^h} = \frac{s_i}{\dfrac{\partial u^h}{\partial c_i^h}}, \text{ which entails}$$

$$\frac{\partial m}{\partial Y_j} = -\beta \frac{\partial W}{\partial Y_j} - \sum_{h=1}^{H} s_i \frac{\dfrac{\partial u^h}{\partial Y_j}}{\dfrac{\partial u^h}{\partial c_i^h}} = -\beta \frac{\partial W}{\partial Y_j} + \sum_{h=1}^{H} \frac{\partial m^h}{\partial Y_j}$$

$$= -\beta \frac{\partial W}{\partial Y_j} - \sum_{h=1}^{H} \delta_j^h$$

Define the government's demand price for environmental service j by $\delta_j^g = \beta(\partial W/\partial Y_j)$. Then the social demand price is defined by

$$\delta_j = -\frac{\partial m}{\partial Y_j} = \delta_j^g + \sum_{h=1}^{H} \delta_j^h \tag{62}$$

The social demand price is thus the sum of the government's demand price and all individual demand prices.

Let us now drop the assumption that lump sum transfers are feasible. If we know either the indirect or the direct social welfare functions, it is possible to judge immediately whether a change will increase the social welfare or not, without resorting to expenditure functions and associated consumer surplus concepts. But if the social welfare functions are not formulated explicitly or if we as observers do not know them, some alternative way of judging the welfare effects of a change is desired.

Consider therefore two situations, the present situation characterized by variables denoted by a prime or a bar. The present utility levels of the individuals are denoted by $\bar{u}^h$ ($h = 1, \cdots, H$), and the utility levels in the second situation (in the absence of any compensations), u^h. If the direct social welfare function is written $W = W(u^1, \cdots, u^H)$, the welfare difference between the two situations is

$$\Delta W = W(u^1, \cdots, u^H) - W(\bar{u}^1, \cdots, \bar{u}^H)$$

As W is assumed to be continuously differentiable, the mean value theorem of calculus yields

$$W = \sum_{h=1}^{H} \bar{W}_h \Delta u^h$$

where $\bar{W}_h$ is the partial derivative of W with respect to u^h, evaluated at some point between $(u^1, \cdots, u^H)$, and $(\bar{u}^1, \cdots, \bar{u}^H)$, and $\Delta u^h = u^h - \bar{u}^h$.

The equivalent variations for the change are

$$EV^h = m^h(s', Y', u^h) - I^h$$

As s', and Y' are constant vectors, $m^h(s', Y', u^h)$ is a strictly increasing transformation of the utility function u^h, and is therefore one representation of the preferences of individual h. We can assume that W is defined on this representation of the preferences. The welfare difference can therefore be written

$$\Delta W = \sum_{h=1}^{H} \bar{W}_h [m^h(s', Y', u^h) - m^h(s', Y', \bar{u}^h)]$$

$$= \sum_{h=1}^{H} \bar{W}_h [m^h(s', Y', u^h) - I^h]$$

$$= \sum_{h=1}^{H} \bar{W}_h EV^h$$

The welfare difference between the two situations is thus a weighted sum of the individual equivalent variations [20]. If one has some information on the weights attached to the different individuals, it is therefore possible to calculate changes in social welfare by first estimating the equivalent variations.

Note that $\partial V/\partial I^h = \partial W/\partial u^h$, and it is thus possible to assign the weights $\bar{W}_h$ by asking the government how much they value the nominal incomes of the individual consumers. In practical situations, the analysis can rarely be disaggregated down to the individual level, but stops at different social groups. If it is possible to obtain the information on the relative values on the incomes in these groups, it is thus possible to assess the welfare change by using the equivalent variation.

12. WELFARE MEASURES AND NATIONAL ACCOUNTING

In this section we will use the construction in section 11 to shed light on the use of national income as a measure of welfare or standard of living. The point of departure is the following idea. We assume that the resources in the economy are allocated by means of private markets for private goods and by means of the environmental management agency for environmental services. This means in particular that each consumer is free to spend his disposable income in whatever way he prefers. The government has an indirect social welfare function, and uses lump sum transfers (which thus are feasible) to correct the income distribution. Because of this, an aggregate utility function can be used in the analysis. Assume now that we do not know the aggregate social utility function. This section reconstructs this utility function from information on prices and quantities.

In chapter 2 it was shown that for each distribution of initial resources, including the environmental assets, there corresponds at least one equilibrium. It is clear that the maximum of the aggregate social utility function is attained at one (or more) of these equilibria, if the indirect welfare function satisfies condition (51). If, however, the indirect social welfare function does not satisfy (51), its maximum may be attained at an allocation which is not an equilibrium (or an optimum). But it is easy to reformulate the general equilibrium model in such a way that the maximum of V is attained at an equilibrium. If, instead of calculating the effluent charges q from equation (9) in chapter 2, when δ is the aggregate of individual demand price vectors for environmental services, the environmental management agency calculates q from the total social demand price vector as given by equation (61), it follows that the maximum of V will be attained at an equilibrium. But this equilibrium need not be a Pareto optimum as defined in section 6 of chapter 2.

From the analysis in chapter 2, it follows that the allocation (and distribution of initial resources) that maximizes V is characterized by a price vector p on normal goods, a vector of effluent charges q on residuals, and a vector of social demand prices on environmental services δ. From equation (34) in chapter 2 it is seen that if $(\bar{c}, \bar{Y})$ is a welfare optimum, then

$$s^T \bar{c} + \delta^T \bar{Y} \leqq s^T c + \delta^T \bar{Y}$$

for all (c, Y) such that $U(c, Y) \geqq U(\bar{c}, \bar{Y})$. From this it follows that $s^T c + \delta^T Y \leqq s^T \bar{c} + \delta^T \bar{Y}$ for all (c, Y) such that $U(c, Y) \leqq U(\bar{c}, \bar{Y})$. This implies that $NI = s^T c + \delta^T Y$, the national income, is a measure of welfare if s and δ are the price vectors ruling in the welfare optimum.

This discussion has been essentially static. (It is possible to interpret the supply of environmental services and consumption processes as being dated, and in that sense one can say our discussion has been dynamic.) The national income measure that has been constructed is defined for a certain time period, say a year, and should therefore include an evaluation of the provisions for future consumption that have been made during the period. The simplest way to include such provisions is to assume that the social utility function is a function, not only of the scale of consumption processes c and the supply of environmental services Y during the period, but also of the vector of capital goods K that exists at the end of the period: $U = U(c, Y, K)$.

Such a social utility function can be motivated in exactly the same way as the function $U(c, Y)$. If we regard the vector K^o of capital goods that exist at the beginning of the period as given, K can be written $K = I + K^o$, where I is the vector of net investments during the period. The social utility function can accordingly be written

$$U = U(c, Y, I) \tag{63}$$

The corresponding national income measure is

$$NI = s^T c + \delta^T Y + p^T I \tag{64}$$

This definition of national income will be basic for subsequent discussions.

Our program is now to investigate in some detail the possibilities of applying this definition of national income. First, the relation between

NI and the national income as presently calculated will be studied. Second, some special cases will be studied, namely changing factor supply, changing technology, and changing prices. To simplify the discussion of the second point, only highly aggregate models having one environmental service and one or two consumption goods will be considered.

Let us assume that the environmental interaction function is linear as it was written in equation (4) in chapter 2. Then

$$Y = Y_o - F_1 z - F_2 e, \text{ or}$$

$$\delta^T Y = \delta^T Y_o - \delta^T F_1 z - \delta^T F_2 e$$

By using equations (9) and (10) of chapter 2, it is seen that

$$\delta^T Y = \delta^T Y_o - q^T z + p^T e$$

If this expression for $\delta^T Y$ is substituted into (64) we see that

$$NI = s^T c + p^T I - q^T z + p^T e + \delta^T Y_o$$

The price vector s, however, is a vector of the prices of consumption processes imputed from the price vector p for consumption goods, and the price vector q for residuals, and the relation between these price vectors is given by equation (3): $s^T = p^T B + q^T D$. NI can therefore be written

$$NI = p^T B c + q^T D c + p^T I - q^T z + p^T e + \delta^T Y_o$$

$$= p^T C + q^{Th} z + p^T I - q^T z + p^T e + \delta^T Y_o$$

where $^h z$ denotes the vector of residuals generated by households, while z is the vector of residuals disposed of in the environment. The first three terms give the total cost of consumption and capital accumulation, including the environmental cost of waste disposal. The environmental cost, however, is $q^T z$, which is subtracted, so that the first four terms give the total cost of consumption and capital accumulation, excluding the direct cost of environmental damage from waste disposal. The NI definition thus includes the costs for production and waste treatment, but not the costs arising from waste disposal in the environment. To this should then be added the cost of environmental treatment $p^T e$. This gives the national income, except the term $\delta^T Y_o$. But Y_o is a constant vector, and as long as the demand prices for environmental services remain constant, $\delta^T Y_o$ is constant. This means that if the prices in the economy are the prices ruling in a welfare optimum, national income or net national product, calculated to include the costs for production and waste treatment, will accurately reflect the social welfare function of the government.

The intuitive reason for this result is of course that in welfare optimum, the prices reflect optimal production and consumption processes and therefore also the environmental cost of waste disposal. Processes that generate a lot of harmful residuals will carry low imputed prices. The optimal prices for goods and services will therefore reflect the environmental costs associated with the production.

This analysis has been carried out under the assumption that the environmental interaction function is linear. The same kind of analysis, however, can be applied if we assume that the interaction function F is twice differentiable and convex in z (see chapter 2, section 10, paragraph 1), and if we are interested in changes in national income. In that case we have

$$dNI = s^T dc + \delta^T dY + p^T dI$$

The conditions corresponding to conditions (9) and (10) in chapter 2 are in this case

$$-\delta^T F_1 z = q^T z, \; \delta^T F_2 e = p^T e$$

where F_1 is the Jacobian of partials with respect to z_i, and F_2 is the Jacobian with respect to e_i. The change in national income can therefore be written

$$dNI = s^T dc + p^T dI - q^T dz + p^T de$$

and the analysis proceeds as before.

This means that even if the environmental interaction function is nonlinear, changes in the net national product calculated to include production and waste treatment costs and environmental treatment costs will represent changes in the social welfare function correctly if the prices are the optimal prices. If, however, the welfare optimum changes owing to changes in factor supply or changes in technology, in general the optimal prices will also change, and our net national product concept will fail to represent social welfare. These problems will now be discussed in some detail in a few aggregative models.

If the changes in factor supply or the changes in technology are small, the optimal prices will still give a good approximation of changes in welfare. To see this, recall that the optimal prices can be constructed as

Lagrangian multipliers in the problem of maximizing the social utility function, and that the Lagrangian multipliers have the property that they are equal to the partial derivative of the social utility function with respect to the bounds in the constraints. The price of labor, for example, can therefore be interpreted as the increase in social welfare if the supply of labor increases with one unit. If the factor supply changes, but the change is small, it is thus still possible to estimate the change in social welfare by using the optimal factor prices. The same is true for technological changes also, but in this case it is in general necessary to include the value of environmental damage directly, that is, the effluent charges. To see this, consider the following simple paradigm: A single commodity C is produced by a single factor of production L_1. The production function is $C = G(L_1, \lambda)$ where λ is a technological shift parameter. The consumption and production of this commodity generate residuals which are treated by using L_2 units of the production factor. The resulting amounts of residuals are given by $z = H(C, L_2, \mu)$ where μ is a technological shift parameter.

$$L_1 + L_2 = L$$

The social utility function is $U(c, Y)$, and the optimal allocation must satisfy the following conditions:

$$U_1 - p - qH_1 = 0$$
$$U_2 - \delta = 0$$
$$pG_1 - w = 0$$
$$-qH_2 - w = 0$$
$$q + \delta F' = 0$$

where p, q, w, and δ are Lagrangian multipliers, which are interpreted as prices.

Suppose now that there is a shift in the parameters λ and μ. What happens to social welfare?

$$dU = U_1 dC + U_2 dY = (p + qH_1)dC + \delta dY = dNI$$

By solving for dC and dY one obtains

$$dNI = (-qH_3 d\mu + pG_2 d\lambda)$$

It is thus impossible to calculate dNI without any information about q or δ. This means that the net national product measure which is calculated without any explicit consideration of the cost for the ultimate disposal of residuals in the environment cannot give a correct estimate of welfare changes caused by technological changes, even if the other prices are optimal.

Before we continue the discussion, it may be appropriate to summarize the findings so far. The national income concept as defined above can be used to compare different allocations from a welfare point of view, so long as there are no exogenous changes in the economy. In order to make such comparisons, it is not necessary to know the social cost of waste disposal in the environment; it is enough to know the costs (calculated in the optimal prices) of production and waste treatment. If the optimum changes because of a change in factor supply, the national income will still give an accurate picture of the welfare change, if the change in factor supply is small. But if the optimum changes because of technological change, it is necessary to have information on the environmental cost of waste disposal to estimate the change in national income.

If the changes are large, it is no longer possible to use national income as a measure of welfare, because of the changes in the prices. But even in this case, it is possible for an observer to calculate the change in welfare, although it requires more information. Instead of using the national income, we can use the social expenditure function as defined in section 11. By estimating the demand functions for private goods, and by estimating the functional relationship between environmental demand prices and the supply of these services, it is possible to estimate the social expenditure function by the same method as was used in section 7. We will not go into this subject any deeper, however. It belongs properly to the theory of index numbers.

Up until now we have assumed that the economy is at the optimum. It is in fact not consistent with the approach chosen in this and the previous section to question the optimality of the economy. If the economy is nonoptimal, the constructions that were made in the previous section are no longer possible, and the national income concept loses much of its significance. If one is to analyze an economy which is not optimally organized, one has to be explicit about the imperfections that destroy the optimality. We will study an economy in which the only imperfection is in the environmental management policy. To be more concrete, consider the simple paradigm above, but assume that the environmental management agency has set the effluent charge too low, e.g., equal to zero. In this case the quantities of residuals will exceed those that would be dumped if optimal prices were applied. We can still think of a social utility function $U(C, Y)$ because of the feasibility of lump sum transfers, but there is no connection between national income measured in current prices and this social utility function. In fact, even if current national income increases because of some exogenous change, the social welfare may decrease. The only way out of this problem is to calculate the optimal prices by trying to estimate the incidence of a system of correct effluent charges. If generation of residuals is mainly concentrated in a few sectors, this approach may be possible, but otherwise it may be impossible. In any case, such calculations require information about the environmental cost of waste disposal.

The preferences for environmental services have so far been formulated using social welfare functions, and they have admitted substitution possibilities between environmental services and private goods. In some circumstances, a different formulation may be fruitful. Let us now assume that the government has preferences about private goods, represented by the social utility function $U(c)$, and that they require that the environmental services must never fall below a certain level $\bar{Y}$. Here the environment is regarded as an asset which is never allowed to depreciate below a certain level. It is therefore natural to assume that the national income concept should not include expenditures for activities that keep the flow of environmental services intact, in the same way as expenditures for maintaining the capital stock are not included in the net national income concept. Imagine an economy similar to the economy discussed in chapter 2 but one in which the effluent charges are determined in such a way that the flow of environmental treatment yields the desired flow of environmental services $\bar{Y}$. By using the same type of arguments as before, it is possible to find optimal prices (p, q) for private goods and residuals in such a way that $NI = s^T c + p^T I$ yields a representation of the social utility function $U(c, I)$. It is thus clear that expenditures for direct environmental treatment should not be included in the national income concept. The price vector s includes cost of production, cost of waste treatment, and the imputed cost of environmental damage from ultimate waste disposal. We can therefore conclude that even if the policy aim is to maintain a certain state of the environment, the national income should include expenditures for waste treatment and the imputed cost of ultimate waste disposal, contrary to the intuitive feeling.

The reason for this result is simply that it is the prices that confront the consumer that matter. If we reduce the price of newspaper by an amount that corresponds to the cost of waste disposal in the production of a newspaper, newspapers would be assigned too low a weight in the national income estimate. If all consumers regard newspapers as desirable, and there is an invention that increases the output of newspapers very much, this would mean a very small increase in national income, due to the small weight. But the increase in newspaper supply may mean a great increase in welfare. Therefore, the national income should be calculated in prices that include all costs associated with the supply.

Moreover, the analogy between environmental services as an asset and the capital stock is wrong. The reason we prefer to deduct capital depreciation is that investment is included in the national income concept. If the national income should include the value of environmental services (as we have assumed for the largest part of this section), then expenditures for maintaining the environment should be deducted (which corresponds to the fact that expenditures for environmental treatment were not included in our NI concept).

NOTES

1. Compare note 14 in chapter 2.
2. See Magnus R. Hestenes, *Calculus of Variations and Optimal Control Theory* (Wiley, New York, 1966), p. 36, theorem 10.1.
3. Hukukane Nikaido, *Convex Structures and Economic Theory* (Academic Press, New York, 1968), § 18, pp. 277–304.
4. Let the function f be defined and have continuous derivatives up to the second order on an open convex set $A \subset R^n$. Then f is strictly convex if and only if all principal minors of the Hessian

$$
\begin{bmatrix}
\dfrac{\partial^2 f}{\partial x_1{}^2} & \cdots & \dfrac{\partial^2 f}{\partial x_1 \partial x_n} \\
\vdots & & \\
\dfrac{\partial^2 f}{\partial x_n \partial x_1} & \cdots & \dfrac{\partial^2 f}{\partial x_n{}^2}
\end{bmatrix}
$$

are positive. See Nikaido, *Convex Structures*, § 3.5, pp. 44–51.
5. Nikaido, *Convex Structures*, theorem 3.1.
6. R. Tyrrell Rockafellar, *Convex Analysis* (Princeton Univ. Press, Princeton, N.J., 1970), section 25, p. 241.
7. Aggregation of individual expenditure functions is intimately connected with aggregation of individual utility functions. There are at least two different sets of conditions that make consistent aggregation of utility functions possible. The first, which is equivalent to our condition (b), is that all consumers have identical utility functions which are homothetic (that is, strictly increasing transformations of homogeneous functions). In this case the aggregate utility function is simply $u(\Sigma_h c^h)$, where $u(c^h)$ is the utility function of one individual. The second, which is similar to our condition (a), is that all consumers have

utility functions that are homothetic (but not necessarily identical), and that the income distribution is given by $I^h = d^h I$, where $I = \Sigma_h I^h$, $0 \leq d^h$, and $\Sigma_h d^h = 1$. In this case, the aggregate utility function will roughly be a weighted geometric average of the individual utility functions. The aggregate expenditure function m is related to the individual expenditure functions by the following formula:

$$m = \sum_{h=1}^{H} \left(\frac{1}{d^h} m^h \right) d^u$$

This shows explicitly that condition (a) is not sufficient to guarantee that the aggregate expenditure function can be obtained by summing the individual expenditure functions. Moreover, the formula implies that using aggregate demand functions for estimating the aggregate expenditure function may be quite meaningless, because it is hard to give a clear interpretation of m in this case. What we are interested in is the total income necessary to sustain certain utility levels for the individuals, and this must obviously be the sum of the individual expenditure functions. There is, however, another way one can aggregate individual utility and expenditure functions, which involves explicit use of welfare functions. This method will be discussed in detail in section 11.

8. The usual consumption theory in economics (as presented in sections 2–4 in this chapter) gives a set of restrictions on the demand functions. The integrability problem is about whether demand functions that meet these restrictions can be said to be derived from a utility function. If the Slutsky matrix

is symmetrical, then it can be shown that it is possible to construct a utility function that generates the given demand functions. See Paul A. Samuelson, "The Problem of Integrability in Utility Theory," in *Economica* M.S. 17, pp. 335–385 (1950).

9. For a proof of this theorem of Frobenius, see Jean Dieudonné, *Foundations of Modern Analysis* (Academic Press, New York, 1960), chapter X, section 9, p. 303.

10. In section 11 it will be shown that if lump sum transfers are feasible, and if they are used to achieve an ethical optimum (defined by a social welfare function), condition (b) is not necessary.

11. Measurable means Lebesgue measurable. The use of measure theory in this as well as in later chapters is based on Paul R. Halmos, *Measure Theory* (Van Nostrand, New York, 1950).

12. See Halmos, *Measure Theory*, section 36, theorem C, p. 148.

13. See Samuelson, "Evaluation of Real National Income," *Oxford Economic Papers*, N.S. vol. 2, no. 1, 1–29 (1950).

14. See the discussion on compensation tests in J. V. De Graaf, *Theoretical Welfare Economics* (Cambridge Univ. Press, London, 1957), pp. 84–90.

15. See De Graaf, *Welfare Economics*, and Abram Bergson, "A Reformulation of Certain Aspects of Welfare Economics," *Quarterly Journal of Economics*, vol. 52, pp. 310–334 (1938).

16. See Dieudonné, *Foundations of Modern Analysis*.

17. Paul A. Samuelson, "Social Indifference Curves," *Quarterly Journal of Economics*, vol. 70, no. 1, 1–22 (1956).

18. If some distributional mechanism is specified different from the use of lump sum transfers, a similar analysis can of course be carried out and a social utility function can be derived. But this social utility function will have some very serious defects that decrease its usefulness. The most serious defect is probably that it will not generate demand functions that are aggregates of individual demand functions.

19. John R. Hicks, *Value and Capital* (Oxford Univ. Press, Oxford, 1939), appendix 10.

20. The first time I saw this use of the equivalent variation was in H. Niklasson, "Consumers' Surplus and Related Concepts," Department of Economics, University of Lund (mimeographed).

5 ESTIMATING THE DEMAND
FOR ENVIRONMENTAL SERVICES

1. INTRODUCTION

Because there are no markets for environmental services, the demand for these services is not revealed, as is the demand for private goods. Hence, other ways of determining consumer preferences must be envisaged. In this chapter some of the methods that have been discussed in the literature will be examined.

One can roughly classify the proposed methods into the following four broad categories:

1. Asking the consumers how much they are willing to pay for some increase in the supply of an environmental service.
2. Voting on the supply of an environmental service.
3. Indirect methods, based on relations between private goods and environmental services.
4. Estimating the physical damage from residuals discharge and evaluating this damage by using market prices.

The last method implies that certain components in the vector Y of the flows of environmental services are estimated, and that observable prices exist for these components. For example, if air pollution causes damage to house paint, the damage of the air pollution is estimated to be the cost of maintaining the paint. It is obvious that this method will not in general take into account all the effects of air pollution, and that in particular it will miss the losses in aesthetic values. The method can, however, provide some limits to the range of demand prices for environmental services. We will not discuss this method any further.

The other three approaches will be discussed in greater detail. There is, however, one fundamental problem with the first two approaches, in addition to the problems that will be discussed later on, that will significantly limit their applicability. Up to now, we have assumed that the consumers have complete information on the vector of environmental services and recognize the impact of each component on their own situation. In practice, one has to use rather complicated measurements as proxies for the Y vector. For example, the quality of a water body is often measured by the dissolved oxygen deficit. If there is a proposal to control the flow of degradable organic materials to the water body, the relevant index for water quality is then the dissolved oxygen deficit. But asking people how much they are willing to pay for an increase in the concentration of dissolved oxygen is in most cases meaningless because consumers in general cannot relate the dissolved oxygen concentration to their own conception of the water body. Even if the consumers are furnished information on the effects of the change in dissolved oxygen deficit on fish and plant life, they may still have difficulty relating this to their own perception of the water body. This does not mean that the consumers do not have preferences, but it means that these preferences may very well be defined on variables other than those measured, and the difficulty arises when it comes to constructing a bridge between the two sets of variables. In some important cases, this difficulty will not appear. For instance, when the construction of a hydroelectric power station would destroy a scenic waterfall, the variables may be better defined, and the consumers may therefore reconcile their own conceptions with the technical variables.

The third method, the indirect approach, does not have this difficulty (but has a lot of other difficulties) because it depends on finding out how the consumers have reacted to similar changes in the past. Also, there is no need for any reconciliation between the perception of the consumers and the measured variables.

The first approach will be discussed in sections 2 and 3 with emphasis on incentives to misrepresent the answers. These incentives, first enunciated by Knut Wicksell, have made several economists, especially Paul Samuelson [1], pessimistic about the possibilities of ever being able to deduce anything about the demand for public goods. Section 4 is devoted to voting as a method of determining consumer preferences.

The indirect approach is discussed in sections 5, 6, and 7. In section 5, it is shown that if the elasticity of substitution between a public good and a private good is known a priori, it is possible to calculate the expenditure function as a function of the supply of the public good from a knowledge of the demand for the private good. This is a very strong a priori condition, and it is weakened significantly in section 6 where it is shown that it is possible to calculate the expenditure function if the supply of the environmental service is a matter of indifference for the consumer when the consumer does not consume anything of some private good. In section 7 this condition is used to show some possibilities for obtaining information on the demand price for environmental services from market equilibrium conditions.

The main conclusion of the discussion in this chapter is that there are some possibilities of obtaining information on consumer preferences for environmental services, but these possibilities are very limited. For most of the cases, correct information on such demand will probably never be revealed. However, this negative conclusion does not mean that the framework discussed in earlier chapters is worthless. Although we cannot estimate the demand functions for environmental services in general, we can, by using the methods discussed in this chapter (and methods that will be invented in the future), get some rough ideas of such demand. The information thus gathered can be used to facilitate decisions on environmental and ambient standards by legislatures or other governmen-bodies. Even if the methods discussed cannot yield perfect estimates of the demand, they will probably yield better estimates than pure guess-work, and their use should therefore enable the decision makers in the environmental field to make decisions that bring the economy closer to a Pareto optimum.

2. SURVEYING THE CONSUMERS ON DEMAND PRICES FOR ENVIRONMENTAL SERVICES

The most natural way to obtain information on the demand prices for environmental services is to ask people how much they are willing to pay for these services. But Wicksell [2] observed that the consumers have very strong incentives to conceal their true preferences in order to obtain benefits at the expense of other consumers. In this section, these incentives will be studied, using the formal apparatus developed in chapter 4. For simplicity we will assume that there is only one environmental service (or public good) Y, and that all consumption activities have been aggregated to a composite activity with price p. The point of reference will always be the utility achieved in the situation prior to the change in supply of the public good; that is, we are going to study the compensating variation.

Let $m^{h'}(s, Y, \bar{u}^{h'})$ be the expenditure function for consumer h', whose utility is $\bar{u}^{h'}$ in the present situation. We are interested in

$$-\frac{\partial m^{h'}(s, Y, \bar{u}^{h'})}{\partial Y}$$

the demand price for the environmental service Y.

Let the supply function for the service be

$$Y = G(\delta) \tag{1}$$

where $\delta = \sum_{h=1}^{H} \delta^h$ is the total *stated* marginal willingness to pay for the service (stated in the sense that it is the sum of the amounts the consumers have reported they are willing to pay, in contrast to the theoretical demand price). The stated willingness to pay will obviously depend on how the question is phrased and on how the cost for the environmental service will be distributed among the consumers. We will therefore analyze a sequence of different questions and allocations of the cost.

1. How much are you willing to pay for a unit increase in the supply of the environmental service? The supply of the service will depend on the total stated amounts from all consumers according to the supply function. The willingness to pay you have indicated will be considered as a price, and you will have to pay the total value of the supply, evaluated at this price (i.e., you will have to pay $\delta^h Y$, where δ^h is your marginal willingness to pay, and Y the actual supply of the service).

Assume that each consumer thinks he knows how much all the other consumers together are willing to pay. This is far from realistic, but we will save the discussion of uncertainty and risk for later. Assume furthermore that the consumer believes in the supply function. Then his behavior can be characterized by maximizing his consumer surplus $S^{h'}$

$$S^{h'} = I^{h'} - m^{h'}(s, Y^{h'}, \bar{u}^{h'}) - \delta^{h'} Y^{h'} \tag{2}$$

subject to the constraints

$$Y^{h'} = G\left(\tilde{\delta} + \delta^{h'}\right)$$
$$\delta^{h'} \geqq 0 \tag{3}$$

where $\tilde{\delta}$ is the total amount consumer h' thinks the other consumers are willing to pay ($Y^{h'}$ is the quantity of environmental services consumer h' expects, given $\bar{\delta}$ and his own response $\delta^{h'}$).

The first-order conditions for this problem are

$$-\frac{\partial m^{h'}}{\partial Y^{h'}} - \delta^{h'} - \alpha^{h'} = 0 \tag{4}$$

$$-Y^{h'} + \alpha^{h'}G' \leq 0 \qquad \left(G' = \frac{dG}{d\delta}\right), \text{ with equality when } \delta^{h'} > 0$$

where $\alpha^{h'}$ is a Lagrange multiplier.

These conditions imply that

$$\delta^{h'} \geq -\frac{\partial m^{h'}}{\partial Y^{h'}} - \frac{Y^{h'}}{G'} \qquad \text{with equality when } \delta^h > 0 \tag{5}$$

It is thus optimal for the consumer to understate his demand price for the environmental service. If the individual believes in the supply function, this bias is due to the monopsonistic power the individual has in this situation. We can remove this imperfection but introduce another by asking the individual to state his total willingness to pay and by requiring him to pay this amount. In this case the consumer's surplus is

$$S^{h'} = I^{h'} - m^{h'}(s, Y^{h'}, \bar{u}^{h'}) - A^{h'} \tag{6}$$

where $A^{h'}$ is the amount the individual responds with.

Assume that the supply of the environmental service will come about only if the total revenue $\sum_{h=1}^{H} A^h$ exceeds the total cost for this supply, given by the cost function

$$C = C(Y) \tag{7}$$

If the consumer believes in this cost function, his behavior can be characterized by maximizing his surplus subject to the constraint

$$A^{h'} + \sum_{h \neq h'} A^h - C(Y) \geq 0 \tag{8}$$

The first-order conditions for this problem are

$$-\frac{\partial m^{h'}}{\partial Y^{h'}} - \beta^{h'}C' = 0$$
$$-1 + \beta^{h'} \leq 0 \tag{9}$$

If the consumer believes that his response has some effect on the supply, $\beta^{h'} = 1$, and

$$-\frac{\partial m^{h'}}{\partial Y^{h'}} = C'(Y^{h'})$$

This equation determines the supply of environmental services individual h' expects, $Y^{h'*}$. Given this supply, his response is determined from

$$A^{h'} = C(Y^{h'*}) - \sum_{h \neq h'} A^h$$

Assume that all consumers are identical. The optimum is then characterized by

$$-H\frac{\partial m^h}{\partial Y^h} = C'$$

which shows that a decision based on the individual responses will give a too-low flow of environmental services. If the consumer believes that the supply of the service is independent of his response, he will in the first case regard G' as zero, and in the second case he will regard Y as a constant, independent of his own actions. Consequently, his optimal stated marginal and total willingness to pay is zero.

The responses from the consumers to this type of question thus cannot be used directly for calculating the optimal supply of the environmental service. It may be noted, however, that in the first case if the consumers have perfect information on the supply function (meaning that $\delta^h > 0$ for all consumers), the environmental management agency may calculate the bias by calculating Y/G' for each consumer. By "correcting" the answers for this bias, the agency may then obtain the "true" demand prices. But as the consumers in general will differ in the beliefs of how much all the other consumers are willing to pay, and also in the beliefs of the amount of the environmental service, the corrected demand prices for different individuals are not directly comparable. It is thus not possible to add all the corrected demand prices and use this sum as the optimal total demand price.

If the agency when phrasing the question adds that it has made some estimates of the total willingness to pay, states this estimated total willingness to pay, and says that it wants to check these calculations, it may be possible to make all the consumers have the same belief as to how much all other consumers are willing to pay. If that is the case, the agency can, by repeating the questions several times, obtain information that permits the calculation of the optimal supply of the environmental service. (Note that one round of questions will not be enough, because the corrected total demand price the answers to this question indicate may be very different from the estimate published by the agency and because the individual responses are based on different expected supplies of the environmental service.)

2. How much are you willing to pay for the environmental service? The supply of this service will depend on the total amounts stated. The cost for this service will be covered by "special" funds, and you do not have to pay anything.

It is obvious that the optimal response from the consumer, if he believes the agency, is a very high stated marginal willingness to pay. But he will probably know that the cost must be covered in one way or another, and in some ways these costs will affect him also. If, for example, it has been decided that effluent charges will be part of the environmental policy, then in order to set these charges at the appropriate levels, the marginal willingness to pay must be known. In this case, the consumer will not have to pay anything directly for the flow of environmental services, but only indirectly through effects on prices of consumption goods and the effects on the cost of waste disposal. The connection between his marginal willingness to pay and the cost burden on him is thus very weak, and it seems probable that the consumer will not take into consideration the cost burden falling on him when he responds to the question.

3. How much of the environmental service Y do you want to have, if you have to pay the fraction t^h of the total cost of supplying this service? The total cost is a function $C(Y)$ of the amount of the service.

The consumer's optimal response is determined from maximizing

$$S^h = I^h - m^h(s, Y, \bar{u}) - t^h C(Y) \tag{10}$$

The first-order condition is

$$-\frac{\partial m^h}{\partial Y} - t^h f' = 0 \tag{11}$$

This formula implies that it is possible to calculate $-\partial m^h/\partial Y$ for each consumer, given his response. These estimates of the individual marginal willingness to pay are based, however, on different amounts of the environmental service and are thus not directly comparable. By giving a sequence of questions, each differing in the proportion t^h of the total cost the individual has to pay, it is possible to trace the individual demand functions for the environmental service. By adding these functions vertically it is then possible to obtain the aggregate demand function. This approach depends in a crucial way, however, on the very doubtful assumption that the individual in each round of questions believes that his desired supply of environmental service will be realized. For if that is not the case, the individual will have incentives to misrepresent his preferences. If, for example, he believes that the outcome will be lower than he is going to state, it may be beneficial to him to overstate his demand and thereby indicate a higher marginal willingness to pay than the true one.

In this discussion we have assumed that the amount of environmental services is continuously adjusted to the individual responses, so that the "price" is determined simultaneously with the quantity Y. We will later discuss the case when a unique change in Y is under consideration.

We have also assumed so far that the beliefs the consumers hold are held with certainty. This obviously cannot be the case for the beliefs on the total amount all other consumers are willing to pay. It therefore seems necessary to introduce risk and uncertainty into the analysis. We will start with risk, that is, we assume that although the consumers do not know the final outcome, their beliefs can be represented by probability distributions.

It is intuitively obvious that if the mean of the probability distribution for the amount all other consumers are willing to pay is low, the consumer has stronger incentives to respond with high willingness to pay than if the mean is large (under the assumption that the consumer believes his response has some effect on the supply of the environmental service). If the mean is small, the only chance the consumer has for obtaining a large supply of the service is to respond with a high willingness to pay, but if the mean is large, he believes that he will obtain a large supply owing to the responses of the others.

If the method of payment for the environmental service is not determined, but the consumer believes in a probability distribution over the possible methods of payment, this will influence his response. If he believes there is a high probability that he will not have to pay for the supply of the service, he will respond with a high marginal willingness to pay, but if he believes that the probability that he must pay for the service is very high, he will have incentives to respond with a low marginal willingness to pay.

In order to analyze these incentives, let $g^h(\delta)$ be the density (as consumer h regards it) for the probability distribution of the amount all other consumers are willing to pay, and let α^h be the probability of the consumer's paying the marginal willingness he has indicated, times the total amount of the service supplied. α^h can also be interpreted as the fraction of the response the consumer has to pay. Because of the linearity, both these interpretations make sense. Let us now apply the expected utility hypothesis [3] that is, we assume that the consumer behaves as if he were maximizing the expected value of his consumer's surplus (E denotes mathematical expectation):

$$E[I^h - m^h(s, Y, \bar{u}^h) - \alpha^h \delta^h Y]$$
$$= I^h - \int_0^\infty m^h[s, G(\bar{\delta} + \delta^h), \bar{u}^h] g^h(\bar{\delta}) d\bar{\delta} \qquad (12)$$
$$-\alpha^h \int_0^\infty \delta^h G(\bar{\delta} + \delta^h) g^h(\bar{\delta}) d\bar{\delta}$$

The first-order condition for the maximum problem is

$$-\int_0^\infty \frac{\partial m^h}{\partial Y} G' g^h(\bar{\delta}) d\bar{\delta} - \alpha^h \int_0^\infty (Y + \delta^h G') g^h(\bar{\delta}) d\bar{\delta} \leqq 0 \qquad (13)$$

We assume that the consumer believes that $G' > 0$ (otherwise it is always optimal for him to respond with a zero marginal willingness to pay, so long as $\alpha > 0$). Moreover, let us assume that he responds with a positive marginal willingness to pay so that we have equality in the first-order condition.

Let us solve for the response, δ^h:

$$\delta^h = -\frac{\int_0^\infty \dfrac{\partial m^h}{\partial Y} G' g(\bar{\delta}) d\bar{\delta}}{\alpha^h \int_0^\infty \left(\dfrac{Y}{\delta^h} + G'\right) g(\bar{\delta}) d\bar{\delta}} , \text{ or} \qquad (14)$$

$$\delta^h = -\frac{\int_0^\infty \dfrac{\partial m^h}{\partial Y} G' g^h(\bar{\delta}) d\bar{\delta}}{\alpha^h \left[\dfrac{E(Y)}{\delta^h} + E(G')\right]} \qquad (15)$$

From this we can see that if α^h is very small, δ^h will be larger than the true demand price, but if α^h is large, δ^h will understate the true marginal willingness to pay. In fact, this equation is not valid for α^h near one, because that would mean a negative δ^h, contrary to the assumption that δ^h is positive.

Assume that the supply function is linear in the relevant interval, that is

$$Y = a\delta \doteq a(\delta^h + \bar{\delta}) \qquad (16)$$

Then (15) reduces to

$$\delta^h = -\frac{E\left(\dfrac{\partial m^h}{\partial Y}\right)}{\alpha^h \left[\dfrac{E(\delta)}{\delta^h} + 2\right]} \tag{17}$$

It is clear that there exists some value on α^h which makes the response δ^h and the expected marginal willingness to pay $-E(\partial m^h/\partial Y)$ equal, namely α^h given by

$$\alpha^h = \frac{\delta^h}{2\delta^h + E(\delta)} \tag{18}$$

If there exists an initial estimate of the expected marginal willingness to pay, and if the distribution of δ is known, then α^h may be determined from (18). It may be possible in some situations to make experiments in order to find the distribution and by informing the consumers about this distribution, influence them to act according to this distribution. If α^h is known for each consumer, then it is possible to induce the consumers to reveal their true expected marginal willingness to pay [4].

It seems reasonable to assume that δ^h is small in comparison to $E(\delta)$, and if that is the case, the expression for α^h can be approximated by

$$\alpha^h \sim \frac{\delta^h}{\delta^h + E(\delta)} \tag{19}$$

This shows that the appropriate probability is simply the fraction between consumer h's marginal willingness to pay and the total marginal willingness to pay.

If the consumers are not too heterogeneous, α^h can be approximated by $\alpha^h = 1/H$, where H is the number of consumers. Given that this approximation is sufficiently good, the consumers will be induced to reveal their true preferences. It should be noted that even if this works, it does not provide sufficient information for a decision on the optimal supply of the environmental service, because each consumer's response will in general be based on different expectations of the supply of environmental services. Therefore, several rounds of questions are necessary to permit decisions based on the true preferences of the individuals.

Many conditions must be satisfied in order to use this approach. First, and most basic, the consumer must act according to the expected utility hypothesis. One can argue that when a public agency asks citizens about their preferences, they feel a moral responsibility to respond in a way that is not consistent with the expected utility hypothesis. Second, the consumer must believe in the probability of the fraction α^h, given by the agency. This can be achieved by telling the consumers that the method of payment will be decided by a lottery, in which the payment according to the willingness to pay has a probability equal to α or that the consumer has to pay only the fraction α^h of his response. But in many or rather most cases, this will be impossible. If the environmental management agency has decided to use effluent charges as the main tool in its efforts to control the flows of residuals in the economy, the probability for a payment according to the willingness to pay is zero, and it is not necessary to require the consumers to pay anything from the point of view of allocation. In cases involving conservation of certain pieces of nature, such a lottery may be feasible, but still the consumer knows that in some way or other the cost must be covered. Even if he believes in the lottery, he knows that if he does not have to pay for the conservation directly, chances are great that he is going to pay for it indirectly, by higher prices, by increased taxation, and so on. Moreover, these cases usually involve indivisibilities, so the analysis above is not directly applicable. A study in indivisibilities will be presented later. Third, the agency will get only an estimate of the expected marginal willingness to pay, and if the distribution of $\partial m^h/\partial Y$ has a high variance (either because $\partial m^h/\partial Y$ is sensitive to changes in Y or because of a high variance in the distribution of $\bar{\delta}$), the estimate may not be interesting.

Let us now turn to a discussion of the case where an indivisibility is involved. It can, for example, be the construction of a dam that will destroy the scenic value of a river. We want to know how much the citizens are willing to pay (or the equivalent variation) for preservation of the scenic river.

Let $Y = \bar{Y}$ be the river without any dam, and let $Y = 0$ be the river with the dam. Let $\bar{u}^h$ be the utility in the second situation, that is when $Y = \bar{Y}$, and the consumer has not paid anything for the preservation alternative [5]. Then the compensating variation can be written

$$\sum_{h=1}^{H} [m^h(s, 0, \bar{u}^h) - m^h(s, \bar{Y}, \bar{u}^h)] \tag{20}$$

It is obvious that if the agency asks the consumers for their maximum willingness to pay, they will have incentives to distort their responses in this case as in the previous cases we have discussed. Can we say anything about the bias of these distortions? To analyze that question, let $g^h(\bar{\delta})$, as before, be the density of the probability distribution for the total amount the other consumers are willing to pay, perceived by consumer h.

Assume furthermore that if

$$\sum_{h=1}^{H} \delta^h \quad \text{(the sum of all responses)}$$

exceeds C, the dam will not be constructed, but if

$$\sum_{h=1}^{H} \delta^h \text{ falls short of } C, \text{ the dam will be constructed.}$$

Interpret C as the total cost to the economy if the dam is not constructed (including more expensive electrical power). Assume that the agency announces that each individual h has to pay the fraction α^h of the amount he has stated as his willingness to pay (that is, the individual has to pay $\alpha^h \delta^h$ in case the dam is not constructed). This means, however, that the costs will not be covered in case the dam is not constructed and there is a deficit $D = C - \alpha^h \delta^h - \bar{\alpha}\bar{\delta}$ where $\bar{\alpha}$ is a weighted average of the fractions of the responses the other consumers have to pay. D is a random variable with a distribution given by

$$Pr(D \leqq \bar{D}) = \int_0^{C-\delta^h} g^h(\bar{\delta})d\bar{\delta} + \int_{1/\bar{\alpha}(C-\alpha^h\delta^h-\bar{D})}^{\infty} g^h(\bar{\delta})d\bar{\delta} \tag{21}$$

for $\bar{D} \geqq 0$

The deficit is financed by price increases on electricity and as a consequence the prices on other commodities will also rise. The deficit is thus diffused in the economy and the individual does not know exactly the burden that will fall on him. We assume, however, that he believes in a probability distribution over the fraction t^h of the deficit that will fall on him. Let the density of this distribution be $d^h(t^h)$. We assume that t^h is distributed independently of $\bar{\delta}$ (and therefore also of D). The mathematical expectation of t^h is denoted $\bar{t}^h$. Large consumers of electricity will probably have a higher $\bar{t}^h$ than small consumers. Define B^h by

$$B^h = m^h(s, 0, \bar{u}^h) - m^h(s, \bar{Y}, \bar{u}^h) \tag{22}$$

that is, B^h is the benefit accruing to individual h from conservation of the river.

We assume again that the expected utility rule can be applied. This means that the consumer acts as if he is maximizing

$$E(S) = I^h - m^h(s, \bar{Y}, \bar{u}^h)\int_{C-\delta^h}^{\infty} g^h(\bar{\delta})d\bar{\delta} - m^h(s, 0, \bar{u}^h)\int_0^{C-\delta^h} g^h(\bar{\delta})d\bar{\delta}$$
$$- \alpha^h\delta^h\int_{C-\delta^h}^{\infty} g^h(\bar{\delta})d\bar{\delta} - \int_0^1 t^h d^h(t^h)dt^h \int_{C-\delta^h}^{\infty}(C - \alpha^h\delta^h - \bar{\alpha}\bar{\delta})g^h(\bar{\delta})d\bar{\delta} \tag{23}$$

The first line in (23) gives the expected benefits, the first term on the second line gives the expected payment as a consequence of the response, and the second term the expected burden from financing the deficit.

The first-order condition for a maximum is

$$
B^h g^h(C - \delta^h) - \alpha^h \int_{C - \delta^h}^{\infty} g^h(\bar{\delta}) d\bar{\delta} - \alpha^h \delta^h g^h(C - \delta^h)
$$

$$
- \bar{t}^h \Big\{ [C - \alpha^h \delta^h - \bar{\alpha}(C - \delta^h)] g^h(C - \delta^h) - \alpha^h \int_{C - \delta^h}^{\infty} g^h(\bar{\delta}) d\bar{\delta} \Big\} \leqq 0 \tag{24}
$$

with equality when $\delta^h > 0$. Assume that $\delta^h = 0$. Then

$$
B^h g^h(C) < (1 - \bar{t}^h) \alpha^h \int_C^{\infty} g^h(\bar{\delta}) d\bar{\delta} + \bar{t}^h (1 - \bar{\alpha}) C g^h(C) \tag{25}
$$

The left-hand side is the increase in expected benefits if the individual increases his response from zero to \$1. The first term on the right-hand side is the increase in expected payment deriving from an increase in the response after the consequent reduction in the deficit has been subtracted. The last term gives the increase in the expected burden on individual h arising from the financing of the deficit caused by an increase in the probability for the conservation alternative. The right-hand side thus gives the increase in the expected cost resulting from an increase of zero to \$1 in the response.

If this marginal expected cost is greater than the marginal expected benefit, the consumer will respond with a zero willingness to pay. In the general case we have

$$
B^h \leqq \delta^h - (1 - \alpha^h) \delta^h + \bar{t}^h (1 - \bar{\alpha}) C - \bar{t}^h \delta^h (\alpha^h - \bar{\alpha})
$$

$$
+ (1 - \bar{t}^h) \frac{\alpha^h}{g^h(C - \delta^h)} \int_{C - \delta^h}^{\infty} g^h(\bar{\delta}) d\bar{\delta} \tag{26}
$$

Let us assume for the moment that $\alpha^h = \bar{\alpha}$, and that no individual responds with a zero willingness to pay. Then we have

$$
B^h = \delta^h + (1 - \bar{\alpha})(\bar{t}^h C - \delta^h) + (1 - \bar{t}^h) \frac{\bar{\alpha}}{g^h(C - \delta^h)} \int_{C - \delta^h}^{\infty} g^h(\bar{\delta}) d\bar{\delta} \tag{27}
$$

or if we sum over all h

$$
\Sigma B^h - \Sigma \delta^h = (1 - \bar{\alpha})(C \Sigma \bar{t}^h - \Sigma \delta^h)
$$

$$
+ \Sigma \left[(1 - \bar{t}^h) \frac{\bar{\alpha}}{g^h(C - \delta^h)} \int_{C - \delta^h}^{\infty} g^h(\bar{\delta}) d\bar{\delta} \right] \tag{28}
$$

Let us assume that $\bar{l}^h$ is small in the sense that

$$C \sum_h \bar{l}^h < \sum_h \delta^h$$

If $\bar{\alpha}$ is large enough in (28), the first term will be small and dominated by the second term, which is positive. In this case we thus have

$$B^h - \sum_h \delta^h > 0$$

The responses yield therefore an underestimate of the true benefits. If

$$\sum_h \delta^h > C$$

then the correct decision will be taken in this case, but if

$$\sum_h \delta^h < C$$

then it is still possible that

$$\sum_h B^h > C$$

If α is small, the first term will be negative and dominate the second term, so that

$$\Sigma B^h - \sum_h \delta^h > 0$$

Now the responses yield an overestimate of the true benefits. If

$\sum_h \delta^h < C$, then the correct decision will be taken, but if

$\sum_h \delta^h > C$, it can still be that $\sum_h B^h < C$

This means that if the proportion of the responses the consumers have to pay is large, and if the stated aggregate willingness to pay exceeds the cost, it is possible to make a correct decision concerning the conservation issue. It is also possible to make a correct decision if the proportion of the response that has to be paid is small and if the stated aggregated willingness to pay is smaller than the cost. But in all other cases it is impossible to know what the correct decision is.

Although this analysis has not carried us far concerning the possibilities of obtaining information on the true benefits, it has given us some control over the incentives to distort the responses. It is, for example, possible to create incentives to overstate the benefits by choosing the fractions α^h small, and it is possible to create incentives in the other direction by choosing the fractions α^h large. This possibility of controlling the incentives to a certain degree may be used in a special way to solve decision problems. Peter Bohm has suggested the following approach [6].

Choose two designs of the financial responsibilities A and B such that design A is known to induce overstatements and B understatements of the true benefits. Choose two random samples from the population and confront the first sample with design A and the second sample with design B. Associated with these two samples are two populations (consisting of the same individuals, but differing in the design of the financial responsibilities). It is now possible to test the hypothesis that $\Sigma\delta^h \geqq C$ for the two populations, and if the tests go in the same direction in the two populations (that is, the hypothesis is accepted in both populations or rejected in both), one has sufficient information to make a correct decision. If, however, the hypothesis is accepted in one of the populations but not in the other, the results are not conclusive.

This approach seems very fruitful if it is possible to construct the financial responsibilities in such a way that the differences between the two populations become small, e.g., in such a way as to make the probability of conclusive results large. An experiment Peter Bohm performed showed that in fact there were very small differences between a set of different designs of financial responsibilities.

Let us now return to an analysis of (26). We maintain the assumption that δ^h is positive for all h. Condition (26) can then be written as

$$
\begin{aligned}
B^h = \delta^h &- (1 - \alpha^h)\delta^h + \bar{t}^h(1 - \bar{\alpha})C - \bar{t}^h\delta^h(\alpha^h - \bar{\alpha}) \\
&+ (1 - \bar{t}^h)\frac{\alpha^h}{g^h(C - \delta^h)}\int_{C-\delta^h}^{\infty} g^h(\bar{\delta})d\bar{\delta}
\end{aligned}
\tag{29}
$$

There exists a value on α^h such that the individual is induced to reveal his true benefits. This value is given by

$$
\alpha^h = \frac{(1 - \bar{\alpha}\bar{t}^h)\left(1\dfrac{C}{B^h}\right) + (1 - \bar{t}^h)\left(\dfrac{C}{B^h}\right)}{(1 - \bar{t}^h)\left[1 + \dfrac{1}{B^hg^h(C - B^h)}\displaystyle\int_{C-B^h}^{\infty} g^h(\bar{\delta})d\bar{\delta}\right]}
\tag{30}
$$

It is possible to use (30) in the same way as (18) was used in a previous case. If we have some initial estimates of B^h (known from studies of random samples, for example) and if the distribution of $\bar{\delta}$ and the expectation of t^h is known, it is then possible to compute that fraction of the response that induces the individual to reveal his preferences correctly [7].

This approach can be combined with Peter Bohm's in order to increase the probability of conclusive results. By using an α^h computed by (30) (or some other formula relevant to the actual decision problem) it may be possible to increase greatly the applicability of Bohm's approach.

The conclusion that may be drawn from this discussion of risk is, however, a negative one. There do not seem to exist simple designs of questions and financial responsibilities that may prevent incentives to misrepresent preferences. In some cases, as we have seen, it is possible to weaken these incentives (but these cases require a priori information on the preferences and the consumers' beliefs in probability distributions), but it may be impossible to counteract them completely. The best we can hope for is a control on the direction of these incentives.

There is one strong objection that can be raised against the whole discussion in this section. We are primarily interested in willingness-to-pay concepts, because they tell us what to do in order to satisfy the Pareto criterion. If the total willingness to pay exceeds the cost of supplying a public good, then it is possible to supply this good and finance this supply out of the sums the individual is prepared to pay. But this presupposes that the government really taxes the consumers in amounts equal to their willingness to pay. If this is not done (because the consumers have to pay only the fraction α^h of their responses, for example), the change will no longer satisfy the Pareto criterion. If, however, the government can use lump sum transfers, there is no such problem because then the income distribution can be corrected so that the change becomes Pareto permitted. The main defense for the discussion in this section is thus that the government can affect the income distribution in such a way that an increase in the supply of a public good becomes consistent with the Pareto criterion if the cost of the supply is less than or equal to the aggregate willingness to pay.

Moreover, there is a question whether the consumers really have probability distributions over the different outcomes. In many realistic cases it seems that the consumers know that one of many outcomes will occur but they have no ideas whatsoever on the probabilities for the different outcomes. If that is the case, the above analysis cannot be applied, and we have to search for other principles that can shed light on consumer behavior. One approach is to apply game theory and the formal theory of decisions under uncertainty. This will be treated in the next section.

3. A GAME THEORETIC APPROACH

At the end of the previous section it was assumed that the consumers believed in some probability distributions over the payment methods and over the behavior of all other consumers. This section briefly discusses the case when no such beliefs exist.

Assume that the decision problem under discussion is to choose between two levels of environmental services: $Y = 0$ and $Y = \bar{Y}$. $Y = 0$ represents the present situation and $Y = \bar{Y}$ an improvement of the environment. If the sum of the responses, i.e., if $\sum_h \delta^h$ exceeds the cost C for obtaining the improvement, the change will be realized, while if $\sum_h \delta^h < C$, the present quality of the environment will be maintained. If it is decided that the quality will be improved, the cost for this will be financed either by some fixed taxes t^h, or by letting the consumers pay the amounts they have responded with.

The surplus for consumer h can then be written (with $\bar{\delta}$, as before, the sum of the amounts all other consumers have responded with)

$$S(\delta^h, \bar{\delta}, \epsilon) = \begin{cases} I^h - m^h(s, \bar{Y}, \bar{u}^h) - \epsilon\delta^h - (1 - \epsilon)t^h \text{ if } \bar{\delta} + \delta^h \geq C \\ 0 \text{ if } \bar{\delta} + \delta^h < C \end{cases}$$

$$\epsilon = 0, 1 \tag{31}$$

ϵ is a dummy variable taking the values zero or one, depending on which method of financing the improvement is chosen.

The problem for the consumer is a decision problem under uncertainty, and there are no established theories for consumer behavior in connection with such problems. Therefore a very simple approach will be followed, namely a discussion of the max-min solution [8]. This criterion is conservative, and there is no evidence that consumers actually follow such a simple rule. The criterion, however, is sufficient for our purposes.

The objective is thus to compute

$$\max_{\delta^h} \min_{\bar{\delta}, \epsilon} \ S(\delta^h, \bar{\delta}, \epsilon)$$

Let us first assume that $t^h \leq I^h - m^h(s, \bar{Y}, \bar{u}^h)$. If $\delta^h > I^h - m^h(s, \bar{Y}, \bar{u}^h)$, we have immediately

$$\min_{\bar{\delta}, \epsilon} \ S(\delta^h, \bar{\delta}, \epsilon) = I^h - m^h(s, \bar{Y}, \bar{u}^h) - \delta^h < 0$$

If $\delta^h \leq I^h - m^h(s, \bar{Y}, \bar{u}^h)$, we have

$$\min_{\bar{\delta}, \epsilon} \ S(\delta^h, \bar{\delta}, \epsilon) = 0$$

From this we conclude that

$$\max_{\delta^h} \ \min_{\bar{\delta}, \epsilon} \ S(\delta^h, \bar{\delta}, \epsilon) = 0$$

and that this max-min strategy is achieved by choosing δ^h in the closed interval $[0, \ I^h - m^h(s, \ \bar{Y}, \ \bar{u}^h)]$.

Let us now assume that $t^h > I^h - m^h(s, \ \bar{Y}, \ \bar{u}^h)$. If $\delta^h > t^h$, we have

$$\min_{\bar{\delta}, \epsilon} \ S(\delta^h, \bar{\delta}, \epsilon) = I^h = m^h(s, \ \bar{Y}, \ \bar{u}^h) - \delta^h = A < 0$$

If $\delta^h < t^h$, we have in the same way

$$\min_{\bar{\delta}, \epsilon} \ S(\delta^h, \bar{\delta}, \epsilon) = I^h - m^h(s, \ \bar{Y}, \ \bar{u}^h) - t^h = B < 0$$

Moreover, $A < B$, so that

$$\max_{\delta^h} \ \min_{\bar{\delta}, \epsilon} \ S(\delta^h, \bar{\delta}, \epsilon) = I^h - m^h(s, \ \bar{Y}, \ \bar{u}^h) - t^h$$

This max-min strategy can be achieved by choosing δ^h in the closed interval $[0, \ t^h]$.

In both these cases, correct revelation of the preferences is a max-min strategy, but it is not a unique max-min strategy, and so it is necessary to supplement this criterion with more detailed criteria that discriminate among all the max-min strategies. We will not discuss such extensions. This conclusion seems to supply some (although very weak) support for an idea developed by Peter Bohm [9], namely, that if the consumer is put into a situation characterized by uncertainty of the outcome he may prefer to reveal his preferences correctly.

One of the conclusions obtained in section 2 was that it is in general impossible to obtain information on the willingness to pay by using only one round of questions. If several rounds are permitted, however, it was indicated that correct revelation of the preferences might be possible. Drèze and de la Vallée Poussin [10] have shown that it is possible to construct a tatonnement process that converges to a (pseudo-) equilibrium. At each stage in this process the consumers are asked to reveal their marginal willingness to pay for a public good. On the basis of these responses, new supplies of private and public goods are computed and a plan for their distribution is made such that no one will ever come into a situation that is worse compared to earlier situations. This process means that correct revelation of preferences is the only max-min strategy. Why this is so may be understood by the following argument. The marginal willingness to pay is the same as the value of the marginal rate of substitution. If the consumer responds with a too-high marginal willingness to pay at some stage in the process, the distribution of the private goods calculated according to this response will be unfavorable to him because the high response indicates a high valuation of the public goods. An over-reporting of the marginal willingness to pay may therefore lead to a decrease in the utility of the consumer. On the other hand, an under-reporting might also lead to a decrease in the utility, because the consumer will have fewer public goods.

The same point has been made by Malinvaud [11] in a similar but simpler model. The relevance of these interesting constructions may, however, be very weak. First, the tatonnement process itself seems difficult to apply. Although the notion of a tatonnement process is extremely useful in economic theory, it does not correspond to any feature of the real world. If the population is small, this argument may be neglected, but in realistic cases, the populations are in general large and not so well defined. This means that there may be extremely high administrative costs associated with the process. Second, the process presupposes that lump-sum transfers are feasible. In their original model, Drèze and de la Vallée Poussin discuss an economy in which every decision is made on the central level. In realistic cases, these central decisions on the distribution of private goods have to be replaced by lump-sum transfers. Third, Drèze and de la Vallée Poussin have only proved the convergence of the process for the case with continuous time. In applications, one has to use discrete steps.

The conclusion from this and the preceding section is that the possibilities of obtaining information on the demand for public goods by asking the consumers about their willingness to pay are very slim indeed. But this is a purely theoretical conclusion, and its validity depends on the underlying assumptions. If it can be argued that the consumer behaves in different ways, depending upon whether he is confronted with pure private choices or pure public choices, the conclusion is of course no longer valid. The only way to get information on this question is to make empirical studies of behavior.

4. VOTING

Voting is of course in many economies the usual mechanism by which private preferences are aggregated into collective preferences. Much has been written on this topic [12], and there is no need here to go into any details. Only a few brief points will be made.

It is well known that simple majority voting may lead to arbitrary decisions (in the sense that the social ordering is intransitive) in some cases. Conditions that will preclude this may be found, however. One such condition is the requirement that the individual preferences be single peaked, that is, that it is possible to embed all acts in a one-dimensional space and the preferences of each individual (that is, the utility function) have at most one local maximum.

But even if the preferences are single peaked, it does not follow that the result from the majority voting process is optimal in the sense that it corresponds to a social welfare maximum. It may be shown, however, that if the preferences are in some sense distributed among the consumers in such a way that the median equals the arithmetic average, the outcome of the voting implies that the total demand price for the public good is equal to the marginal cost [13]. In order to see this, recall that the demand price for environmental service Y is given by

$$\delta^h = -\frac{\partial m^h(s, Y, \bar{u}^h)}{\partial Y}$$

Assume that each consumer has to pay a fixed share t^h of the total cost of supplying the environmental service, $\sum_h t^h = 1$. Let $TC(Y)$ be the cost function for Y. As before, the optimal response from consumer h is determined by

$$\max_Y \quad I^h - m^h(s, Y, \bar{u}^h) - t^h TC(Y)$$

A necessary condition for maximum is

$$-\frac{\partial m^h}{\partial Y} - t^h MC = 0 \quad \left(MC = \frac{dTC}{dY}\right), \text{ or } \delta^h = t^h MC$$

If we now assume that for each Y, δ^h is distributed over H consumers in such a way that the arithmetic average $\sum_h \delta^h / H$ is equal to the median, it follows that the outcome of majority voting (which will equal the median in the absence of strategy goals) will be a supply of environmental services such that

$$\delta = \sum_h \delta^h = \sum_h t^h MC = MC$$

This is indeed an attractive feature of majority voting, and the condition on distribution of preferences can be generalized slightly [14], but not very much. We have, however, neglected the strategic aspects, which dominated previous sections. There are also incentives to misrepresent the preferences under a voting scheme, but it is felt that these incentives are somewhat weaker in a majority voting process [15].

Recent studies also suggest that representative democracy with vote trading may give a very good approximation to the social ordering [16]. In any case, voting is used for determining the supply of public goods in all "democratic" societies, and we will therefore take the outcome of this democratic decision process as a starting point in the next chapter when we discuss the means to implement the desired environmental quality.

5. THE ELASTICITY OF SUBSTITUTION AND INDIRECT METHODS OF FINDING THE DEMAND PRICES FOR ENVIRONMENTAL SERVICES

In contrast to the methods explicated in the preceding sections, indirect methods will now be treated. These indirect methods are based on a priori assumptions on the nature of relationships between private and public goods. If, for example, the air quality changes, it may be possible to say something about the willingness to pay for improvements by studying the consumer responses to the changing air quality. In the remaining portions of this chapter, such possibilities will be discussed in great detail.

Let $u(c, Y)$ be the utility function as before (as we will concentrate on one individual, the superscript h will be suppressed). Assume now that there is one activity, say the first activity c_1, and one environmental service, say the first, Y_1, such that the utility function can be put into the form

$$u\{c_2, \cdots, c_Q, Y_2, \cdots, Y_m, [(1 - B)c_1^{1-1/\sigma} + BY_1^{1-1/\sigma}]^{\sigma/\sigma-1}\}$$

where σ is some positive number. It can be shown that [17]

$$\sigma = -\frac{d\frac{c_1}{Y_1} MRS}{\frac{c_1}{Y_1} dMRS}$$

where MRS is the marginal rate of substitution between c_1 and Y_1. σ is called the elasticity of substitution.

Let c' and Y' be the vectors c and Y, with the first components deleted. It can be shown [18] that if $\sigma \to +\infty$, the utility function takes the form $u[c', Y', (1 - B)c_1 + BY_1]$, that is, c_1 and Y_1 are perfect substitutes. If $\sigma \to 1$, the utility function takes the form [19]

$$u(c', Y', C_1^{1-B}Y_1^{B})$$

If $\sigma \to 0$, the utility function takes the form [20] $u[c', Y', \min(c_1, Y_1)]$, that is, c_1 and Y_1 are perfect complements.

As we are working in a partial equilibrium context, we can just as well assume that the prices of all activities except the first are constant. This means that we can aggregate all these other activities to a composite activity which we denote by c'' (note that c'' is a number, the level on which the composite activity is operated). The price index of this composite activity is denoted by s. Furthermore, the supplies of all environmental services except the first are kept constant, so that they can be suppressed both in the utility function and in the expenditure function. Moreover, we can relabel Y_1 to Y.

We are interested in $\partial m(s, s_1, Y, \bar{u})/\partial Y$. Remember from section 5 in chapter 4 that

$$\frac{\partial m}{\partial Y} = -s_1 \frac{\partial u/\partial Y}{\partial u/\partial c_1}$$

If we assume that the elasticity of substitution σ is a constant, independent of c'', c_1, and Y, the two derivatives on the right-hand side can be calculated. Write the utility function as

$$u\{c'', [(1 - B)c_1^{1-1/\sigma} + BY^{1-1/\sigma}]^{\sigma/\sigma-1}\}$$

$$\frac{\partial u}{\partial Y} = u_2 BY^{-1/\sigma}[(1 - B)c_1^{1-1/\sigma} + BY^{1-1/\sigma}]^{1/\sigma-1}, \text{ and}$$

$$\frac{\partial u}{\partial c_1} = u_2(1 - B)c_1^{-1/\sigma}[(1 - B)c_1^{1-1/\sigma} + BY^{1-1/\sigma}]^{1/\sigma-1} \text{ if } \sigma > 0$$

and so

$$\frac{\partial m}{\partial Y} = \frac{-s_1 B}{1 - B}\left(\frac{Y}{c_1}\right)^{-1/\sigma}$$

If the elasticity of substitution σ is known (and is known to be a constant independent of c'', c_1, and Y), and if the constant B is known, then the demand price for Y can be calculated from the formula above.

To apply this approach, one must have some a priori knowledge of the elasticity of substitution. It seems that only the two extreme cases, $\sigma = +\infty$ and $\sigma = 0$, are interesting from this point of view, because in both these cases it is possible to make a priori hypotheses, while it seems impossible to make such hypotheses for cases when $0 < \sigma < +\infty$. One may find examples where an environmental service and a private good (e.g., air quality and an air conditioner) satisfy the same need, and can thus be regarded as perfect substitutes, and in some cases an environmental service may be a necessary prerequisite for enjoying a private good or vice versa. Admittedly, there are probably very few cases which fit into either of these two categories, but the main purpose of the following analysis is to provide an introduction to the next section in which a condition much weaker than that of constant elasticity of substitution is studied.

If c_1 and Y are perfect substitutes, that is, if $\sigma = +\infty$, then the formula for the demand price for Y takes a very simple form $\partial m/\partial Y = -s_1 B$. The constant B must be interpreted as a scale factor, and by measuring Y and c_1 appropriately, B can be taken to be unity. If it is known that c_1 and Y are perfect substitutes, then we can use the price of c_1 as the demand price for Y.

If c_1 and Y are perfect complements, that is, if $\sigma = 0$, things are not so easy any longer. We must obviously have $c_1 \leqq Y$ if $s_1 > 0$, otherwise the consumer would not be maximizing his utility. We can therefore represent the utility function by $u(c'', c_1, Y)$ together with the restriction that $c_1 \leqq Y$. At certain prices and incomes, $c_1 = Y$, but for lower income or higher s_1, $c_1 < Y$. In the first case c_1 will be independent of prices and income, and in the second case c_1 will be independent of the supply of the environmental service.

If we know the demand functions for c_1 and c'', and know the values on prices and income at which $c_1 = Y$, it is possible to calculate the expenditure function as a function of prices and the supply of environmental service. We will not prove this theorem in a general model, but instead show the procedure involved in an example. A general proof, similar to the proof that will be offered in the next section, can be worked out, however.

Example

Let z be the demand for the composite good, and x the demand for the private good complementary to Y. Assume we know the following demand functions

(i) $\quad z = \dfrac{I - p_x Y}{p_z}$

$\qquad x = Y \qquad$ when $\qquad \dfrac{I}{2p_x} > Y$

(ii) $\quad z = \dfrac{I}{2p_z}$

$\qquad x = \dfrac{I}{2p_x} \qquad$ when $\qquad \dfrac{I}{2p_x} \leq Y$

To calculate the demand price for Y, we will solve the Slutsky equations as we did in section 7 of chapter 4. It is easy to see that these demand functions satisfy the integrability conditions.

Let us start with case (i). The Slutsky equation for x takes the form

$$\frac{\partial^2 m}{\partial p_x{}^2} = 0, \text{ which has the solution } m = Ap_x + B$$

We know that the compensated demand function for x is equal to Y, and so $\partial m / \partial p_x = x^* = A = Y$ and thus $m = Yp_x + B$.

To compute B, we make use of the Slutsky equation for z:

$$\frac{\partial^2 m}{\partial p_z{}^2} - \frac{1}{p_z} \frac{m}{\partial p_z} + \frac{m - p_x Y}{p_z{}^2} = 0, \text{ or}$$

$$\frac{\partial^2 B}{\partial p_z{}^2} - \frac{1}{p_z} \frac{B}{\partial p_z} + \frac{B}{p_z{}^2} = 0$$

The general solution to this equation is

$$B = C_1 p_z \log p_z + C_2 p_z$$

where C_1 and C_2 are two constants. This gives

$$m = p_x Y + C_1 p_z \log p_z + C_2 p_z$$

Let us take the point at which $p_x = p_x' = I/2Y$ as our point of comparison, that is, $\bar{u}$ is the value of the indirect utility function at that point. Then the initial conditions give

$$m(p_z', p_x', Y) = p_x'Y + C_1 p_z' \log p_z' + C_2 p_z' = I$$

$$\frac{\partial m}{\partial p_z} = C_1 \log p_z' + C_1 + C_2 = \frac{I - p_x'Y}{p_x'}$$

These two equations show that $C_1 = 0$, and that $m = p_x Y + C_2 p_z$. C_2 is a function of Y, and of $\bar{u}$: $C_2 = C_2(Y, \bar{u})$.

Let us now turn to case (ii). By repeating essentially the same steps as those taken in section 7 of chapter 4, we will find that the expenditure function is

$$m = \frac{I}{(p_x' p_z')^{\frac{1}{2}}} (p_x' p_z')^{\frac{1}{2}}$$

The compensated demand function is accordingly

$$x^* = \frac{1}{2} \frac{I}{(p_x' p_z')^{1/2}} (p_z/p_x)^{1/2}$$

For a low enough price on x, x^* will be equal to Y. We can compute p_x'' as follows:

$$\frac{1}{2} \frac{I}{(p_x' p_z')^{1/2}} (p_z/p_x'')^{1/2} = Y, \text{ and } p_x'' = \frac{I^2 p_z}{4 p_x' p_z' Y^2}$$

Moreover, in case (ii) there is an excess supply of the environmental service; the demand price will be zero, and so

$$\frac{\partial m}{\partial Y} = p_x'' + \frac{\partial C_2}{\partial Y} p_z = \frac{I^2 p_z}{4 p_x' p_z' Y_2} + \frac{\partial C_2}{\partial Y} p_z = 0, \text{ or}$$

$$\frac{\partial C_2}{\partial Y} = -\frac{I^2}{4 p_x' p_z' Y_2}$$

This equation has the solution

$$C_2 = \frac{I^2}{4 p_x' p_z' Y} + C_3$$

This gives us the final expression for the expenditure function

$$m = p_x Y + \frac{I^2 p_z}{4 p_x' p_z' Y} + C_3 p_z$$

The demand price, finally, is given by

$$\frac{\partial m}{\partial Y} = p_x - \frac{I^2 p_z}{4 p_x' p_z'} \qquad p_x \leq p_x'$$

It has thus been possible to compute the demand price for the environmental service from a knowledge of the demand for a private good. The conditions under which this derivation was made are very restrictive indeed. They require that the private good and the environmental service be perfect complements. Therefore, this result is not so promising. In very rare cases can we expect such a strong complementarity between a private good and an environmental service. But note one thing from this example, namely, that the most important step was to use the knowledge that for a certain range of prices on the private good, the demand price for the environmental service is zero. This suggests that perfect complementarity is not necessary in order to apply the same ideas as in this example. In the next section we will show that this is in fact the case. By using far less restricting conditions than perfect complementarity, we can still solve the Slutsky equations so as to obtain the expenditure function as a function of the supply of environmental services.

6. WEAK COMPLEMENTARITY

We saw in the last section that if there is strict complementarity between an environmental service and a private good, it is possible to estimate the demand price for the environmental service from information on the demand function for the private good. It is, however, not necessary that the environmental service and the private good be perfect complements in order to carry out the steps involved in determining the demand price. A much weaker condition of complementarity is the following: if the demand for a private good is zero, then the demand for some environmental service will also be zero. If, for example, the private good is swimming in a lake and the environmental service is the quality of that lake, then it is very reasonable to assume that if a person does not use this lake for recreation, he is indifferent to the quality of its water. Another example is given by the private good of land, where the environmental service is air quality over this piece of land. If a person does not live near this piece of land, he is probably not willing to pay anything for improvement in the air quality. It would therefore seem that this weak complementary condition has very broad applications, although it cannot be applied to cases where option values are involved [21].

In mathematical terms, the condition can be stated as follows: There is an environmental service Y_1 and a consumption activity c_1 such that

$$\frac{\partial u(0, c_2, \cdots, c_Q, Y_1, \cdots, Y_m)}{\partial Y_1} = 0 \qquad (32)$$

(As we will study only one individual, the superscripts indicating individuals are not needed.) We will now show that in many cases this condition will allow estimation of the demand price for the environmental service Y_1 from information on the demand function for c_1. Note first that condition (32) is invariant for monotone transformations of the utility index, so although the condition is stated in terms of marginal utilities, it does not rely on any cardinal utility index.

Note also that condition (32) can be translated into an equivalent condition on the expenditure function, namely

$$\frac{\partial m(s', Y, \bar{u})}{\partial Y_1} = 0 \qquad (33)$$

where s' is a price vector (not necessarily unique) that makes the compensated demand for activity 1 equal to zero. It is not certain, however, that such a price vector exists. For a complete general utility function, it may be that the compensated demand for consumption activity 1 never falls to zero (although the Marshallian demand falls to zero owing to income effects), but for the cases considered here it seems reasonable to assume the existence of such a price vector s'. If the cost of swimming in the above-mentioned lake increases, it seems natural to assume that when the cost has reached a certain size, the person will no longer use the lake for recreation. If the land rents in a region are high enough, people will probably move to another region with lower land rents. With these examples as a justification, we will assume that the compensated demand structure is such that at some prices the compensated demand for activity 1 is zero.

To simplify the notation, we aggregate activities $c_2, \cdots, c_Q$ to a composite activity c, with price s. As all environmental services except Y_1 have been held constant, they will be suppressed in the expenditure function. We can therefore write the condition (33) as

$$\frac{\partial m(s, s_1, Y, \bar{u})}{\partial Y} = 0, \text{ for } s_1 \geq s_1' \tag{34}$$

Assume now that the demand function for c_1 is known:

$$c_1 = c_1(s, s_1, I, Y) \tag{35}$$

As the budget equation holds, (35) defines also a demand function for the composite activity c:

$$c = \frac{1}{s}[I - s_1 c_1(s, s_1, I, Y)] = c(s, s_1, I, Y) \tag{36}$$

We assume that these demand functions satisfy the integrability condition, given in the theorem in section 7 of chapter 4, that is

$$\frac{\partial c_1}{\partial I} c + \frac{\partial c_1}{\partial s} = \frac{\partial c}{\partial I} c_1 + \frac{\partial c}{\partial s_1} \tag{37}$$

If the demand functions are aggregates over the consumers, and if the consumers are heterogeneous, these conditions will not be satisfied (see section 6, chapter 4). Here we assume that the demand functions are either individual functions or aggregates over homogeneous groups of consumers. We will now show that if (34) holds, it is possible to compute

$$\frac{\partial m(s, s_1, Y, \bar{u})}{\partial Y}$$

One can intuitively see from figure 9 why the condition (34) makes it possible to compute the demand price for Y. Consider the compensated demand curve AB for activity c_1. At the price s_1', the consumer demands c_1', and the consumer surplus is the cross-shaded triangle ABC. If the supply of the environmental service increases, the demand curve will shift to the position DE, and the consumer demands $\bar{\bar{c}}_1$. The new consumer surplus is the triangle DEC. How much is the consumer willing to pay for the change in Y, that is, how much is he willing to pay for the induced movement from B to E?

This movement can be divided into three steps:
1. A change in s_1 from C to D. In order not to be worse off, the consumer has to be compensated with the old consumer surplus ABC.
2. A change in Y. If we apply condition (34), this change will not cause any need for compensation.
3. A change in s_1 from D to E. The consumer is willing to pay the new consumer surplus or the area DEC for this change.

The net result is $DEC - ABC$ or the area $BADE$. The amount the consumer is willing to pay for obtaining the change in Y is thus $BADE$.

Note that this calculation is impossible without condition (34). If (34) does not apply, the appropriate transfer in step 2 cannot be determined. This diagrammatic discussion obviously does not prove anything, it only

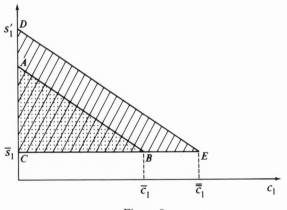

Figure 9

makes it probable that condition (34) together with the demand function should make it possible to calculate the willingness to pay. First there is the problem of determining the compensated demand functions as functions of the supply of environmental services, and second, in the discussion above, the distinction between compensating variation and equivalent variation is blurred. Attacking the problem by the use of Slutsky equations will solve both these difficulties.

Granting the integrability conditions (37), we know that the Slutsky equations have a solution. The Slutsky equation for activity c_1 is

$$\frac{\partial^2 m}{\partial s_1^2} - \frac{\partial c_1}{\partial I} \frac{\partial m}{\partial s_1} - \frac{\partial c_1}{\partial s_1} = 0 \tag{38}$$

This is a second-order differential equation. The solution can be written

$$m = \psi(s, s_1, Y, A, B) \tag{39}$$

where A and B are two integration constants, which in turn are functions of Y, s, and the initial conditions (or $\bar{u}$).

The compensated demand function for c_1 is then given by

$$c_1^* = \frac{\partial \psi(s, s_1, Y, A, B)}{\partial s_1} \tag{40}$$

According to our assumption, there is an s_1', such that for $s_1 \geq s_1'$, the compensated demand for c_1 is zero. We can find this s_1' by using the inverse of the compensated demand function as a function of s_1:

$$s_1 = h(c_1^*, s, Y, A, B); \text{ where}$$
$$c_1^* \equiv \frac{\partial \psi[s_1 h(c_1^*, s, Y, A, B), Y, A, B]}{\partial s_1} \tag{41}$$

Then we have that for $s_1 \geq s_1'$ where s_1' is determined from

$$s_1' = h(0, s, Y, A, B) \tag{42}$$

the compensated demand for c_1 is zero. (We know from property iv in section 3 of chapter 4 that $\partial c_1^*/\partial s_1 < 0$, so that the inverse function exists.) If we substitute this into (39) we get

$$m(s, s_1, Y, \bar{u}) = m(s, s_1', Y, \bar{u})$$
$$= \psi[s, h(0, s, Y, A, B), Y, A, B] \text{ for } s_1 \geq s_1' \tag{43}$$

According to the condition (34), the derivative of this function with respect to Y is zero or

$$
\frac{dm}{dY} = \frac{\partial\psi}{\partial s_1}\left(\frac{\partial h}{\partial Y} + \frac{\partial h}{\partial A}\frac{\partial A}{\partial Y} + \frac{\partial h}{\partial B}\frac{\partial B}{\partial Y}\right)
$$
$$
+ \frac{\partial\psi}{\partial Y} + \frac{\partial\psi}{\partial A}\frac{\partial A}{\partial Y} + \frac{\partial\psi}{\partial B}\frac{\partial B}{\partial Y} = 0
$$

(44)

This is a differential equation in the two unknown functions A and B. We can, however, use (36) to establish a Slutsky equation for the composite activity c. By solving that differential equation, A and B will be determined as functions of s, and we can substitute these solutions into (43). This means that (43) must be an identity in s, and after differentiating (43) with respect to s, a second differential equation in two unknown functions, A and B as functions of Y are established.

By solving this system of equations we finally end up with a solution for the expenditure function. This solution does contain integration constants which can be determined from the initial conditions

$$
m(\bar{s}, \bar{s}_1, \bar{Y}, \bar{u}) = I
$$
$$
\frac{\partial m(\bar{s}, \bar{s}_1, \bar{Y}, \bar{u})}{\partial s} = c(\bar{s}, \bar{s}_1, \bar{I}, \bar{Y})
$$
$$
\frac{\partial m(\bar{s}, \bar{s}_1, \bar{Y}, \bar{u})}{\partial s_1} = c_1(\bar{s}, \bar{s}_1, \bar{I}, \bar{Y})
$$

(45)

We have thus finally obtained an expression for the expenditure function. Well-known theorems on the existence and uniqueness of solutions to differential equations guarantee that the solution is the expenditure function.

The following example shows the steps in the procedure discussed. Let us analyze the example that was used in section 6, chapter 4, with the demand functions

$$
x = \frac{I}{2p_x} - \frac{\theta Y}{2}
$$
$$
z = \frac{I}{2p_z} + p_x\frac{\theta Y}{2p_z}
$$

Here x corresponds to consumption activity 1, and z to the composite activity.

In section 6, chapter 4, the Slutsky equations were solved, although with the unnecessary restriction that $Y = 1$. In the general case we can obtain in exactly the same way the following expression for the expenditure function

$$m = A p_x^{1/2} p_z^{1/2} + B p_x p_z^{1/2} - \theta p_x Y$$

where A and B are functions of Y, and the initial conditions.

The compensated demand function for x is obtained by taking the partial derivative of m with respect to p_x,

$$x^* = \frac{\partial m}{\partial p_x} = \frac{1}{2} A p_x^{-1/2} p_z^{1/2} + B p_z^{1/2} - \theta Y$$

The compensated demand for x is zero when

$$p_x \gtreqless p_x' = \frac{1}{4} \frac{A^2}{Y^2} \frac{p_z}{(\theta - p_z^{1/2} B/Y)^2}$$

For $p_x \gtreqless p_x'$, the expenditure function becomes

$$m(p_x, p_z, Y) = m(p_x', p_z, Y) = \frac{1}{2} \frac{A^2}{Y} \frac{p_z}{(\theta - p_z^{1/2} B/Y)}$$

$$+ \frac{1}{4} \frac{A^2}{Y} \frac{p_z}{(\theta - p_z^{1/2} B/Y)^2} \times \frac{B p_z^{1/2}}{Y} - \frac{1}{4} \frac{p_z}{(\theta - p_z^{1/2} B/Y)^2} \theta Y$$

$$= \frac{1}{2} \frac{A^2}{Y} \frac{p_z}{(\theta - p_z^{1/2} B/Y)}$$

If the condition (34) is valid, then $m(p_x, p_z, Y)$ with $p_x > p_x'$ has to be independent of Y for all p_z. However, this can be true only if $A = CY^{1/2}$, and $B = DY$, where C and D are constants, depending only on the initial conditions. The expenditure function must therefore have the following form:

$$m = C\sqrt{p_x p_z Y} + (D\sqrt{p_z} - \theta) p_x Y$$

The constants C and D can be determined from the initial conditions (45).

$$m(p_x', p_z', Y') = C\sqrt{p_x' p_z' Y} + (D\sqrt{p_z'} - \theta) p_x' Y' = I$$

$$\frac{\partial m(p_x', p_z', Y')}{\partial p_x} = \frac{1}{2} C p_x'^{-1/2} p_z'^{1/2} Y^{1/2} + (D p_z'^{1/2} - \theta) Y = \frac{I}{2 p_x} - \frac{\theta Y}{2}$$

Solving these two equations yields

$$C = \frac{I + p'_x Y'}{\sqrt{p'_x p'_z} Y'} \text{ and } D = 0, \text{ and finally}$$

$$m(p_x, p_z, Y, \bar{u}) = \frac{I + p'_x Y'}{\sqrt{p'_x p'_z} Y'} \sqrt{p_x p_z Y} - \theta p_x Y$$

where $\bar{u}$ is the utility when income is I, prices are p'_x and p'_z, and the supply of environmental service Y', that is $\bar{u} = v(p'_x, p'_z, \bar{Y}, I)$.

The knowledge of the demand functions together with condition (34) has thus made it possible to derive the expenditure function, not only as a function of market prices, but also as a function of the supply of environmental service. This approach is based on some implicit assumptions that may restrict its applicability. First there is the assumption, already stated, that there exist some prices at which the compensated demand is zero. It has already been argued that for most of the cases this seems to be a reasonable assumption. But in connection with this, one must be very careful in specifying the demand structure. Usually we obtain information on demand by econometric analysis. By first specifying the functional form of the demand functions and then estimating the coefficients of these functions from time series or cross-sectional data, a knowledge of the demand pattern is obtained. This approach may be very useful for predictions or analysis of small variations of price because in many cases the predictions are not very sensitive to changes in specifications. In order to estimate the expenditure functions, however, we must have information on the demand functions, not only for a small range of prices, but for all prices above the present price, and our approach will be very sensitive to the specification of the demand functions.

One therefore has to be very careful in employing this method. First, one must be sure that the specification of the demand functions satisfies the integrability conditions in section 7, chapter 4. By choosing demand functions that satisfy these conditions, one implicitly assumes that the preferences of the consumers satisfy the very strict requirements for expenditure function aggregation that were discussed in section 6, chapter 4. The most popular demand function from an econometric point of view is the linear function. But it is easy to show that a linear function does not satisfy these conditions. Let the demand function for c_1 be

$$c_1 = \alpha_{11} s_1 + \alpha_{12} s + \alpha_{13} I + \alpha_{14} Y + \alpha_{15}$$

Then the demand function for the composite commodity c can be derived from the budget equation:

$$c = \frac{1}{s}(I - s_1 c_1)$$

We then have

$$\frac{\partial c_1}{\partial s} = \alpha_{12} \qquad \frac{\partial c_1}{\partial I} = \alpha_{13}$$

$$\frac{\partial c}{\partial s_1} = -\frac{1}{s}(c_1 - s_1\alpha_{12}) \qquad \frac{\partial c}{\partial I} = \frac{1}{s} - \frac{s_1}{s}\alpha_{13}$$

and

$$\frac{\partial c_1}{\partial I}c + \frac{\partial c_1}{\partial s} = \frac{1}{s}\alpha_{13}\frac{s_1}{s}c_1 + \alpha_{12}$$

while

$$\frac{\partial c}{\partial I}c_1 + \frac{\partial c}{\partial s_1} = \frac{1}{s}c_1 - \frac{s_1}{s}\alpha_{13}c_1 - \frac{1}{s}(c_1 - s_1\alpha_{12})$$

But these two expressions are in general different, so that the integrability conditions are not satisfied.

Second, one has to specify the demand functions in such a way that the compensated demand for the good becomes zero for a finite price. If there are substitutes for the good in question, it seems reasonable that the compensated demand will fall to zero for a sufficiently high but finite price, and the demand specification must therefore be such that this will happen.

A further problem is connected with the assumption, implicit in the discussion, that the demand function for c_1 is indeed a function of Y. If this is not the case, it is impossible to calculate the expenditure function as a function of Y. But it is possible to show that if the preferences are such that the demand for c_1 is independent of the supply of Y, the condition (34) is not likely to be realistic.

Let the utility function be $u(c, c_1, Y)$. The demand functions are derived from maximizing u subject to the budget constraint. This yields the usual first-order conditions,

$$u_1 - \alpha s = 0$$

$$u_2 - \alpha s_1 = 0$$

$$sc + s_1 c_1 = I$$

By differentiating these conditions with respect to Y, we will obtain formulas for $\partial c_1/\partial Y$ and $\partial c/\partial Y$.

$$\frac{\partial c}{\partial Y} = -\frac{s_1}{D}(su_{23} - s_1u_{13})$$

$$\frac{\partial c_1}{\partial Y} = \frac{s}{D}(su_{23} - s_1u_{13})$$

where D is a certain determinant. The condition for $\partial c/\partial y = \partial c_1/\partial y_1 = 0$ is therefore $su_{23} - s_1u_{13} = 0$. Owing to the first-order conditions for utility maximization, this can be written

$$\frac{u_1}{u_{13}} = \frac{u_2}{u_{23}}, \text{ or } \frac{\partial}{\partial Y}\log u_1 = \frac{\partial}{\partial Y}\log u_2$$

which gives us $\log u_1 = \log [B(c, c_1)u_2]$, where $B(c, c_1)$ is an arbitrary function of c and c_1. This equation is equivalent to $u_1 - B(c, c_1)u_2 = 0$, which is a partial differential equation of the first order, the characteristic of which is given by

$$dc + \frac{dc_1}{B(c, c_1)} = 0$$

If B is differentiable, this equation has a solution which is given by $\phi(c, c_1) = C$ where C is an arbitrary integration constant. The general solution to the partial differential equation can now be written $u = f[\phi(c, c_1), Y]$ where ϕ satisfies

$$\frac{\partial c}{\partial c_1} = -B(c, c_1)$$

If condition (32) is applied, we find that $f_2[\phi(c, 0), Y] = 0$. Since this relation holds for all c, by differentiating with respect to c we find that $f_{21}\phi_1(c, 0) = 0$. This gives us $\phi_1(c, 0) = 0$. ($f_{21} = 0$ is not a property that is invariant for monotonic transformations of the utility function.) This condition is equivalent to $(\partial/\partial c)u(c, 0, Y) = (\partial/\partial Y)u(c, 0, Y)$, which shows that if consumption of c_1 is zero, then the consumer is indifferent to how much of the composite activity c he consumes. This is a very strong statement about a certain complementarity between c and c_1. The assumption that the demand for consumption activities does not depend on the supply of environmental services combined with condition (32) therefore yields a conclusion which is not likely to be realistic.

7. MARKET RELATIONS

In section 6 we saw that knowledge about how changes in environmental quality affect demand may in some situations allow us to calculate the demand price for environmental quality. A change in the demand function for a private good resulting from a change in environmental quality will in general affect the market price; therefore it may be possible to deduce the demand price from information concerning market reactions to changes in environmental quality.

The reactions of the market, however, depend also on supply conditions, and without information on the relevant supply functions it is not possible to deduce anything concerning the marginal willingness to pay for environmental quality. If, for example, supply is from a constant-cost industry, the price will be determined from cost considerations alone, and changes in environmental quality will not affect the market price. In order to simplify the following discussion, let us make the simplest possible assumption about supply, namely, that supply is completely inelastic to price changes. The supply of land for residential use is usually considered to be constant. Our analysis can therefore be interpreted as an analysis of the market in land, and we will label the variables according to this interpretation [22].

Assume that there are two districts, or regions, or pieces of land which are similar in all respects except some quality variable, for example, air quality. As long as the quality is constant, the consumers will regard these two districts as perfect substitutes, although the rate of substitution will not be unity because of quality differences. Let the supply of land in the two districts be L_1 and L_2, and let Y be the quality of the first district. The marginal rate of substitution between the two kinds of land is denoted by

$$MRS_{12} = B^h(Y) \tag{46}$$

Since the two types of lands are perfect substitutes, this marginal rate of substitution is not a function of the consumption of the land, but it is a function of the quality of the first district. An increase in the quality will in general increase B^h, and thus increase the demand for land in the first district.

Let $x_1{}^h$ and $x_2{}^h$ be the amounts of land demanded by consumer h, and let c be an aggregate of all other consumption activities with price s. Land prices in the two districts are denoted by p_1 and p_2. Let the utility function of a representative individual be

$$u^h(x_1{}^h, x_2{}^h, c^h, Y)$$

The marginal rate of substitution between $x_1{}^h$, and $x_2{}^h$ is given by

$$\frac{u_1{}^h}{u_2{}^h} = B^h(Y), \text{ or}$$

$$\frac{u_1{}^h}{B^h} = u_2{}^h \tag{47}$$

This is a partial differential equation with the characteristic

$$B^h dx_2 - dx_1 = 0 \tag{48}$$

The solution of this equation is

$$C = Bx_1{}^h + x_2{}^h \tag{49}$$

so the solution to the partial differential equation is

$$u = u^h(B^h x_1{}^h + x_2{}^h, c^h, Y) \tag{50}$$

If we apply condition (32) in the previous section, which seems extremely reasonable in this context, we get

$$u_3[B^h(Y)x_1{}^h + x_2{}^h, C^h, Y] = 0$$

or that the utility function can be written

$$u^h = u[B^h(Y)x_1{}^h + x_2{}^h, c^h] \tag{51}$$

Utility maximization subject to the budget constraint gives the following conditions

$$u_1 B^h - \alpha p_1 \leqq 0$$
$$u_1{}^h - \alpha p_2 \leqq 0 \tag{52}$$
$$u_2{}^h - \alpha s = 0$$

where we have assumed that the composite activity c will always be consumed in a positive amount.

Since B^h does not depend on $x_1{}^h$, $x_2{}^h$, or c^h, we can conclude that the amounts of land the consumer demands will be determined solely by the relation between B^h and the relative prices p_1/p_2. If

$B^h > p_1/p_2$, $x_1{}^h > 0$, and $x_2{}^h = 0$, and if
$B^h < p_1/p_2$, $x_1{}^h = 0$ and $x_2{}^h > 0$

We will now make the very restrictive assumption that B^h is the same for all individuals. This assumption is not as restrictive as the assumption that all individuals have the same preferences, but still it means that all consumers must be compensated with the same amount of land for a unit decrease in the quality. Since $B^h = B(Y)$ is the same for all individuals, it follows that if $B(Y) > p_1/p_2$, all consumers will demand land in the first district and the demand for land in the second district will be zero. If

$$\Sigma x_1{}^h > L_1$$

there will be excess demand for land in the first district, and the price will increase. Assuming that there is no excess supply of land, this reasoning gives

$$B = p_1/p_2 \tag{53}$$

as a market equilibrium condition, because when this condition is satisfied, the consumers will be indifferent between land in the two districts. If the condition is violated, all consumers will demand land in one district but not in the other, which is not consistent with market equilibrium.

Denote the relative price p_1/p_2 by n. Then the equilibrium condition can be written

$$B = n \tag{54}$$

By taking the logarithmic derivative of this condition with respect to Y, we get

$$\frac{1}{B} B' = \frac{1}{n} \frac{dn}{dY}$$

We know from section 5 in chapter 4 that the demand price δ^h for environmental quality can be written as

$$\delta^h = s \frac{\dfrac{\partial u^h}{\partial Y}}{\dfrac{\partial u^h}{\partial c}} = s \frac{u_1{}^h x_1{}^h B'}{u_2{}^h} = s \frac{u_1{}^h B}{u_2{}^h} \frac{x_1{}^h B'}{B} \tag{55}$$

But from the first-order conditions we know that the first factor is equal to p_1, and we have just shown that the second factor is equal to $x_1{}^h(1/n)(dn/dY)$.

We thus have

$$\delta^h = p_1 x_1{}^h \frac{1}{n} \frac{dn}{dY} \tag{56}$$

or by summing over all h

$$\delta = p_1 L_1 \frac{1}{n} \frac{dn}{dY} \tag{57}$$

If it is possible to estimate the relative price of the land in the two districts as a function of quality, this formula can then be used to compute the total demand price for quality in the first district.

8. CONCLUSIONS

In this chapter we have discussed some approaches to the problem of revealing the preferences for environmental services. We started with the "natural" approach, that is, asking people how much they are willing to pay for an increase in some environmental service. Our analysis stressed the importance of incentives for individuals to give biased responses to the question. Only when some severe restrictions were introduced concerning the behavior of the individual and the supply of the service was it possible to construct a scheme of questions that might induce the individuals to reveal their preferences correctly. We also mentioned the tatonnement process developed by Drèze, de la Vallée Poussin, and Malinvaud, which in theory may steer the economy toward an optimum. There were some other difficulties associated with this approach, however, the most important being that it is a tatonnement process.

The other approaches discussed exploited some a priori information about the nature of the demand for environmental services, such as complementarities between water quality and demand for water-oriented recreation activities. These approaches have a much narrower scope than the first-mentioned approaches. But for those situations where the a priori information exists, we can be certain from the theoretical discussions that they will work.

We will in the next chapter examine the use of effluent charges in environmental policy, and in this connection some "trial-and-error" processes that might be used for approximating the "correct" effluent charge will be analyzed. One such process is based on the assumption that the responsible public authority (the environmental management agency or the government) has perfect information on the social marginal willingness to pay for environmental quality in each situation that has been realized, but not for potential situations with a different supply of environmental services. This means that the agency has information on some points on the demand curve for environmental quality, but does not know the whole demand curve. Owing to the features of the process, information about the relevant parts of the demand curve will be generated so that the agency can reach the optimal effluent charge after only a few stages. The implication relevant for the discussion in this chapter is that even when the agency has limited information on the demand for environmental quality, it is possible to systemize this information in such a way that the economy may be steered toward an optimum.

In the main, however, our conclusions are negative. There are indeed very few possibilities for obtaining correct information about the demand for environmental services. When we widen the perspective to include more aspects of environmental policy, these conclusions are reinforced. Up to now, we have assumed that the environmental interaction function has been known with certainty. But in real life, we have only very vague ideas of what happens to the residuals when they are discharged into the environment, and for some residuals, the experts do not agree whether the discharge is harmful or not. This means that the individual has much less than the complete information we have assumed and the relevance of the individualistic approach of our discussion is significantly reduced.

When in the next chapter we discuss problems in environmental policy, we will therefore base this discussion on the preferences of the government (or the environmental management agency). In equation (62) of chapter 4 the total demand price for an environmental service was defined as the sum of the government's demand price $\delta_j{}^g$ and the individuals' demand prices $\Sigma \delta_j{}^h$. Our collective approach simply means that the $\delta_j{}^g$ are assumed to swallow the $\sum_h \delta_j{}^h$. Formally, nothing in the theory will change. We still have the optimum characterized by $\delta^g F' = q$. But this optimum will no longer be a Pareto optimum, as was discussed in section 11, chapter 4. In view of what we said above about the uncertainty concerning the interaction function, this characterization of the optimum may be meaningless. In such cases we assume that the "collective" preferences are defined directly on the discharge of residuals. Sometimes these preferences may, in view of these uncertainties, be represented as a maximum limit on the amount of a residual that may be discharged, or as maximum limits on ambient concentrations of pollutants in the environment.

This change from an individualistic approach to a collectivistic approach does not mean, however, that information on individuals' demand for environmental quality is of no value. On the contrary, when reliable information on individual preferences can be obtained, it can be used by the government to determine the social value of environmental changes. Probably such information, if presented to the authorities, would change the environmental policies in several countries radically by showing that the people are willing to abstain from consumption of goods and services in order to obtain an improvement in the environment.

NOTES

1. K. Wicksell, "A New Principle of Just Taxation," in Richard A. Musgrave and Alan T. Peacock (eds.), *Classics in the Theory of Public Finance* (St. Martin's, New York, 1958). Paul A. Samuelson, "The Pure Theory of Public Expenditure," *Review of Economics and Statistics*, vol. 36, pp. 387–389 (1954).

2. See Wicksell, "Principle of Just Taxation," *loc. cit.*

3. For a discussion of the expected utility rule, see Robert D. Luce and Howard Raiffa, *Games and Decisions* (Wiley, New York, 1957), chapter 7. This rule tells us that there exists under certain conditions a utility function defined on the outcomes, such that the behavior of the individual may be represented by maximization of the mathematical expectation of the utility of the outcomes. Here we assume that this utility function may be taken to be identical to the compensating variation, which may not be correct. But we know that there exists a monotonically increasing transformation of the compensating variation unique up to a linear transformation that may be used in connection with the expected utility rule. Such a transformation would, however, destroy the simplicity of the present approach.

4. This approach has also been proposed by Guy Arvidson, who has discussed the idea in an unpublished paper, "A Note on Estimation of Demand for Public Goods" (Department of Economics, Stockholm University). Arvidson restricts his discussion to the case when there is an indivisible supply of the public good.

5. This can obviously be interpreted as a problem whether a small change in the supply of Y should be carried out or not. The analysis of indivisibilities may therefore also be applied to the former case, when the supply of services was assumed to be perfectly divisible.

6. See Peter Bohm, "An Approach to the Problem of Estimating Demand for Public Goods," *Swedish Journal of Economics*, vol. 73, no. 1, 55–66 (1971), and Bohm, "Estimating Demand for Public Goods: An Experiment," *European Economic Review*, vol. 1, pp. 111–130 (1972).

7. See note 5.

8. For a discussion of decision problems under uncertainty, see Luce and Raiffa, *Games and Decisions*.

9. In an experiment reported in Bohm "Estimating Demand for Public Goods," *loc. cit.*, Bohm found that different financial responsibilities did not matter very much for the aggregate willingness to pay. This may be explained by our result that correct revelation of preferences is a min-max strategy.

10. J. H. Drèze and D. de la Vallé Poussin, "A Tatonnement Process for Public Goods," *Review of Economic Studies*, vol. 38, pp. 133–150 (1971).

11. Edmund Malinvaud, "A Planning Approach to the Public Good Problem," *Swedish Journal of Economics*, vol. 73, no. 1, 96–117 (1971).

12. For a survey, see chapter 6 in Richard A. Musgrave, *The Theory of Public Finance* (McGraw-Hill, New York, 1959).

13. See Howard R. Bowen, "The Interpretation of Voting in the Allocation of Economic Resources," reprinted in Kenneth J. Arrow and Tibor Skitovsky (eds.), *Readings in Welfare Economics* (Irwin, Homewood, Ill., 1969), pp. 115–132.

14. See Nicolaus Tideman, "The Efficient Provision of Public Goods," in Selma J. Mushkin (ed.), *Public Prices for Public Goods* (The Urban Institute, Washington, D.C., 1972).

15. See Musgrave, *Theory of Public Finance*.

16. See Edwin T. Haefele, "Environmental Quality as a Problem of Social Choice," in Allen V. Kneese and Blair T. Bower (eds.), *Environmental Quality Analysis: Theory and Method in the Social Sciences* (Johns Hopkins University Press, Baltimore, 1972), pp. 281–332.

17. $MRS = \dfrac{\partial u}{\partial c_1} \Big/ \dfrac{\partial u}{\partial Y_1} = \dfrac{(1 - B)c_1^{-1/\sigma}}{BY_1^{-1/\sigma}}$ and $\dfrac{d\frac{c_1}{Y_1}}{\frac{c_1}{Y_1}} \dfrac{MRS}{dMRS}$

$$= \dfrac{d\frac{c_1}{Y_1}}{\frac{c_1}{Y_1}} \dfrac{\frac{1 - B}{B}\left(\frac{c_1}{Y_1}\right)^{-1/\sigma}}{\frac{1 - B}{B}d\left(\frac{c_1}{Y_1}\right)^{-1/\sigma}}$$

$$= -\dfrac{d\frac{c_1}{Y_1} \cdot \left(\frac{c_1}{Y_1}\right)^{-1/\sigma-1}}{\frac{1}{\sigma}\left(\frac{c_1}{Y_1}\right)^{-1/\sigma-1}d\frac{c_1}{Y_1}} = -\sigma$$

18. $\lim\limits_{\sigma \to \infty} \{(1 - B)c_1^{1-1/\sigma} + BY_1^{1-1/\sigma}\}^{\sigma/(\sigma-1)} = (1 - B)c_1 + BY_1,$ and u is continuous.

19. $\log\{(1 - B)c_1^{1-1/\sigma} + BY_1^{1-1/\sigma}\}^{\frac{\sigma}{\sigma-1}} = \dfrac{\log\{(1 - B)c_1^{1-1/\sigma} + BY_1^{1-1/\sigma}\}}{\frac{\sigma - 1}{\sigma}}$

and l'Hospital's rule gives

$$\lim\limits_{\sigma \to 1} \dfrac{\log\{(1 - B)c_1^{1-1/\sigma} + BY_1^{1-1/\sigma}\}}{\frac{\sigma - 1}{\sigma}}$$

$$= \lim\limits_{\sigma \to 1} \dfrac{(1 - B)c_1^{1-1/\sigma}\log c_1 + BY_1^{1-1/\sigma}\log Y_1}{\sigma^2} \cdot \sigma^2$$

$$= (1 - B)\log c_1 + B\log Y_1 = \log c_1^{1-B}Y_1^{B}$$

$$\lim\limits_{\sigma \to 1}\{(1 - B)c_1^{1-1/\sigma} + BY_1^{1-1/\sigma}\}\frac{\sigma}{\sigma - 1} = c_1^{1-B}Y_1^{B}$$

The result follows because u is continuous.

20. Assume that $c_1 > Y_1$. Then $\frac{c_1}{Y_1} > 1$, and $\{(1-B)c_1{}^{1-1/\sigma} + BY_1{}^{1-1/\sigma}\}^{\frac{\sigma}{\sigma-1}} =$

$$Y_1\left\{(1-B)\left(\frac{c_1}{Y_1}\right)^{1-1/\sigma} + B\right\}^{\frac{\sigma}{\sigma-1}} = Y_1\left\{(1-B)\left(\frac{c_1}{Y_1}\right)^{1-1/\sigma} + B\right\}^{\frac{\sigma}{\sigma-1}}$$

$$\lim_{\sigma\to0}\left(\frac{c_1}{Y_1}\right)^{1-1/\sigma} = 0 \qquad \text{and} \qquad \lim_{\sigma\to0} B^{\frac{\sigma}{\sigma-1}} = 1$$

Hence

$$\lim_{\sigma\to0}\{(1-B)c_1{}^{1-1/\sigma} + BY_1{}^{1-1/\sigma}\}^{\frac{\sigma}{\sigma-1}} = Y_1$$

In the same way it is proved that when $Y_1 > c_1$

$$\lim_{\sigma\to0}\{(1-B)c_1{}^{1-1/\sigma} + BY_1{}^{1-1/\sigma}\}^{\frac{\sigma}{\sigma-1}} = c_1$$

21. This section is based on an article by the author, Mäler, "A Method of Estimating Social Benefits from Pollution Control," *Swedish Journal of Economics*, vol. 73, no. 1, 121–133 (1971). This approach originated, however, with a paper by Joe Stevens, "Recreation Benefits from Water Pollution Control," *Water Resources Research*, vol. 2, pp. 167–182 (1966). Stevens tried to estimate the benefits from water pollution control by using data on recreational demand. He did not discuss the theoretical problems connected with this approach, however, and his results are therefore misleading.

For a discussion of option values, see Krutilla *et al.*, "Observations on the Economics of Irreplaceable Assets," in Kneese and Bower, *Environmental Quality Analysis*, pp. 69–112.

22. The results to be obtained have previously been obtained by Robert H. Strotz by a different method in an unpublished paper.

6 ANALYSIS OF CERTAIN PROBLEMS IN ENVIRONMENTAL POLICY

1. INTRODUCTION

Chapters 2 to 5 have given the general theoretical structure on which the rest of our analysis will be based. The most notable implication of this theoretical structure is that under certain idealized conditions it is possible to support an optimum with prices on waste disposal. This result provides a starting point for a discussion of environmental policy because all other policy measures can be compared with such a pricing mechanism and thereby evaluated in relation to an optimal allocation.

A discussion along these lines will be presented in this chapter. In the next sections, alternative environmental policies will be compared, both with regard to their information requirements and their effects on overall allocation of resources and income distribution. The conclusions are not perhaps very impressive; while it is possible to use limits on discharges as part of environmental policy in such a way as to obtain an optimal allocation, this will in general require more information than a policy based on pricing of ultimate waste disposal. The overall allocation will be different between the two approaches because the income distribution will be different and consequently so will the demand structure.

These conclusions are somewhat modified when the spatial distribution of the residuals is considered. When there is only one agent discharging wastes at each location, and when the diffusion model is of the general form discussed in chapter 2, setting optimal prices on waste disposal will require the same information as setting optimal limits on waste disposal.

If, however, the waste load on the environment is a random variable, there are significant differences between the use of prices and the use of limits in environmental policy. Section 4 discusses the case where it is impossible to counteract the random disturbances by, for example, increasing waste treatment. The law of large numbers implies that the information requirement for setting prices is lower than that for setting limits. When we turn to the more realistic case in section 5, when it is possible to counteract the random disturbances, the situation is radically changed. It may not be possible to set meaningful limits at all on waste discharges.

One objection to pricing ultimate waste disposal is that such a policy requires metering the flow of residuals, which may be prohibitively expensive in certain cases. This objection is discussed with regard to consumption residuals in section 5, and it is shown that there are ways in which the pricing of waste disposal can be modified so as to avoid such an objection.

If the environmental management agency has all the relevant information, it can at least theoretically impose the "optimal solution" directly on the economy, but in general the available information is not enough to permit calculations of the optimal solution. We know from chapter 5 that it is in general very difficult to get estimates on the demand for public goods, and so it is natural to assume that the environmental management agency has limited information on the demand for environmental quality. In sections 7, 8, and 9, some simple paradigms are discussed which are based on such limited information on demand for environmental quality.

Another problem in connection with this information is that the demand for public goods depends on income distribution, and the income distribution will in general depend on the environmental policy. Samuelson has cogently stated the problem, "It is wrong to make, as some have made, a sharp separation between correct public-good decisions and correct redistributional-taxation decisions. Changing public goods does materially affect the distribution of income and all decisions have to be made simultaneously [1]." This problem will be discussed in sections 7 and 9 in relation to a possible adjustment process the agency may want to employ in order to utilize the limited demand information so as to achieve both an optimal allocation and a fair distribution of wealth. In section 8 such processes are applied to the important practical problem of setting effluent charges when the environmental management agency has limited or no information on the costs of improving the environment. This application can be looked upon as an attempt to construct a systematic trial-and-error process, in which the process itself generates information.

2. EFFLUENT CHARGES VERSUS EFFLUENT STANDARDS

So far in the previous chapters, the only policy for controlling waste flows that has been discussed is pricing the discharge of residuals into the environment. Such prices will henceforth be called effluent charges. But in most countries other approaches in environmental policy have dominated. It is therefore of interest to compare some of these other approaches with the result that comes from effluent charges. Such a comparison is especially interesting in regard to the results that were obtained in chapters 2 and 3, namely that it is possible to support an optimal allocation with effluent charges in an otherwise competitive economy. This means that comparisons between effluent charges and other policy measures will reveal the extent to which these other measures can support an optimal allocation also.

The particular alternative approach we will focus on is effluent standards, that is, limits on the discharge of residuals into the environment for each individual unit in the economy. Before discussing this approach, one other alternative will be discussed briefly.

One objection common to both effluent standards and effluent charges is the possibly high costs associated with the necessary monitoring of the waste flows. This objection will be discussed later in this chapter in connection with consumption residuals, and it will be shown that there are ways in which the effluent charge approach can be modified to overcome this objection. Still, it has been a telling one in practice, and in some countries, for example Sweden, other policy measures have therefore been substituted for effluent standards or effluent charges [2]. The implicit argument behind these other measures has been that they in one sense or another approximate the results that would have been obtained by the use of effluent standards.

The most common approach seems to have been to impose requirements that producers and municipal sewage treatment plants make investments in certain waste treatment processes and/or production processes which are known to generate small amounts of residuals. There are, however, at least three problems with this approach. First, there are no guarantees that it will work because, even if a firm has the capacity in the form of capital equipment to reduce its waste flow, it does not follow that it will be profitable for the firm to use this capacity to full extent. If a firm is required to construct a waste treatment plant, but if neither the operation of the plant nor the discharge of waste into the environment is supervised by the environmental management agency, the firm will have very strong incentives to save operating costs in the waste treatment facility. In order to achieve the desired reduction in waste flow, the agency must thus in one way or another monitor the waste flow. If the firm is required to use certain production processes which are known to generate small amounts of residuals, in whatever way the associated machines are operated, this argument loses its importance. But there probably exist very few processes with residuals flows that are independent of the way the processes are operated, and so for most of the producers the argument seems to apply [3]. Therefore, it seems very difficult to control the waste flows without directly monitoring them. Moreover, this leads us directly to the second problem. We want not only to reduce the waste flow, but also to achieve this reduction as cheaply as possible. As technical information tends in most societies to be available principally at the level of the firm, it follows that it may be very difficult for the agency to pick out the optimal processes which should be used, and in most cases we can expect the reduction in the waste flow to be smaller than desired, and of a higher social cost than that connected with effluent charges. It is also clear that if the agency does not have perfect information on the relevant technology, the distribution of waste reduction among different firms will be inefficient. For efficient reduction of waste flow, the marginal cost of reduction should be the same for all waste dischargers. From the optimality of the effluent charge scheme, it follows that the charges will satisfy this condition, while efficient regulation of production and waste treatment requires detailed information on the part of the environmental management agency. The third problem concerns the development of new technology. As discussed in chapter 3, effluent charges will give incentives for development of new production processes that reduce the costs of recycling and recovery of raw materials from the waste flow. But requirements that certain production processes must be used do not give such incentives. Moreover, adoption of a new resource-saving technology must first pass administrative controls, which increases the cost of this technology and may make entrepreneurs hesitate.

It should thus be obvious that administrative regulation of production and waste treatment processes will in general be inferior to either effluent charges or effluent standards. But it must be noted that if monitoring the waste flows is very expensive, it may offer the only possibility of achieving some control of the waste flows [4].

To simplify discussion of effluent charges versus effluent standards, let us introduce here the notion of environmental or ambient standards. In chapter 2 the optimal flow of environmental services was determined by

$$
\begin{aligned}
&\max \delta^T Y + q^T z - p^T e \\
&\text{s.t. } Y + F^1 z - F^2 e \leqq Y_o \\
&\qquad z \geqq 0 \qquad e \geqq 0 \\
&\qquad \delta, q, \text{ and } p \text{ given}
\end{aligned}
\tag{1}
$$

that is, from maximizing the net benefits from the environment. Suppose we know the solution Y^*, z^*, e^* to this linear programming problem [5]. Then the agency can introduce the standards $Y \geqq Y^*$, meaning that the environmental quality must never fall below the optimal level Y^*. Such standards will be called ambient or environmental standards. See also section 8, chapter 5. It is elementary to see that if Y^* is given, the solution to the following problem

$$
\begin{aligned}
&\max q^T z - p^T e \\
&\text{s.t. } -F^1 z + F^2 e \geqq Y^* - Y_o \\
&\qquad z \geqq 0 \qquad e \geqq 0
\end{aligned}
\tag{2}
$$

yields the optimal waste discharge z^*, and the optimal environmental treatment e^*. If the environmental management agency knows the optimal supply of environmental services, it can thus formulate a policy based on environmental standards.

It seems that environmental policy in most countries is formulated with such environmental standards as the basis, although Y^* is determined by a political process, and not by consumers' marginal willingness to pay for environmental quality and cost-benefit analysis of the use of the environment [6]. We will assume that Y^* is given in some way or another for this and the following sections [7]. In a later section we will return to an analysis of environmental standards and show that they are unsatisfactory from some points of view when the waste load and/or the waste assimilative capacity of the environment are exposed to random fluctuations.

Given the environmental standards $Y \geqq Y^*$, we will now compare effluent charges and effluent standards. Assuming that the environmental management agency has all the information needed, it is clear that it can determine the optimal *total* flow of residuals z^* that should be discharged to the environment from the linear program (2). The required information is the vector of optimal effluent charges q and the price vector p.

Given the optimal effluent charges, $q_1, \cdots, q_s$, the *total* flow z^* of residuals is thus determined. However, this flow is the aggregate of flows from several economic units and the information available is not enough to allow separation into individual flows. Such a separation is necessary in order to set up effluent standards that will achieve the same waste reduction at the same cost as effluent charges, particularly when more than one unit is discharging at the same spot. To allocate the total flow of residuals in an efficient way (that is, consistent with optimality, or to lowest social cost), the environmental management agency must also have information on the cost of waste reduction for each discharger. If the agency has this information, it can allocate the total flow so that the marginal cost reduction of each residual will be the same for all units which discharge the residual into the environment, and higher for those which do not discharge the residual at all. Our first conclusion is thus *that information on optimal effluent charges is not in general enough to set optimal effluent standards.*

Assume on the other hand that the agency has the necessary detailed information on the cost for reducing waste discharges at individual units. Assume that this information is available in the form of benefit functions $B^h(z^h)$ for each unit h. These benefit functions give the social benefits from discharging z^h into the environment, given constant prices on all regular goods. Since the only externalities that will be discussed are those that change the environmental quality, we can identify the social benefits with the private benefits and interpret $B^h(z^h)$ as the benefits accruing to the hth unit from discharge of the flow z^h. For simplicity assume that B^h is differentiable. It follows from the production structure discussed in chapters 2 and 3 that B^h is a concave function of z^h. The *ceteris paribus* assumption that prices on regular goods are held constant can be removed at the cost of a more complicated analysis.

The objective for the environmental management agency is then to maximize

$$\sum_h B^h(z^h) - p^T e$$

$$\text{s.t. } F^1 \sum_h z^h - F^2 e \leqq Y_o - Y^* \tag{3}$$

$$z^h \geqq 0 \qquad e \geqq 0$$

thus maximizing the net benefits from using the environment as a dumping ground subject to the condition that a certain environmental quality must be maintained.

The Kuhn–Tucker theorem yields the following necessary and sufficient conditions for an optimal policy:

$$\frac{\partial B^h}{\partial z_j{}^h} - \delta^T F_j{}^1 \leqq 0 \qquad z_j{}^h\left(\frac{\partial B^h}{\partial z_j{}^h} - \delta^T F_j{}^1\right) = 0$$

$$-p^T + \delta^T F^2 \leqq 0 \qquad (-p^T + \delta^T F^2)e = 0 \tag{4}$$

for all h and j. Here δ is a vector of Lagrangian multipliers that can be interpreted as the imputed prices on the environmental standards, and $F_j{}^1$ the jth column in F^1. If Y^* is the optimal supply of environmental services, then δ must be equal to the demand prices for environmental quality. The solution gives directly the optimal effluent standards z^h, but it also gives the optimal effluent charges q from

$$q^T - \delta^T F^1 \leqq 0 \qquad (q^T - \delta^T F^1)\sum_h z^h = 0 \tag{5}$$

Given these effluent charges, the next question is whether they will induce the private decision makers to act in a way that is consistent with the social optimization problem in (3). The private maximization problem can be written as

$$\text{maximize } B^h(z^h) - q^T z^h \tag{6}$$

yielding

$$\frac{\partial B^h}{\partial z_j{}^h} - q_j \leqq 0 \qquad z_j{}^h\left(\frac{\partial B^h}{\partial z_j{}^h} - q_j\right) = 0 \tag{7}$$

as necessary and sufficient conditions for a maximum. Without losing in generality, we can assume that in the social optimum $\sum_h z^h \neq 0$ so that $q^T = \delta^T F^1$.

It is then evident that (7) is identical to the first set of conditions in (4). This implies that a solution to (3) will be a solution to (6), that is, a social optimum will be a private optimum. The reverse implication need not be true, however. It may happen that (6) does not have a unique solution, and in that case some of the solutions to (6) need not be parts of a solution to (3).

If (6) admits several solutions, then these solutions will generate a convex set and B^h will be linear on this set. Let $z^{h'}$ and $z^{h''}$ be two distinct solutions to (6). Then

$$B^h(z^{h'}) - q^T z^{h'} = B^h(z^{h''}) - q^T z^{h''}$$

The concavity of B^h implies that for $0 \leqq \theta \leqq 1$

$$B^h[\theta z^{h'} + (1 - \theta)z^{h''}] - q^T[\theta z^{h'} + (1 - \theta)z^{h''}]$$
$$\geqq \theta[B^h(z^{h'}) - q^T z^{h'}] + (1 - \theta)[B^h(z^{h''}) - q^T z^{h''}]$$
$$= B^h(z^{h'}) - q^T z^{h'}$$

so that $B^h(z^h) - q^T z^h$ is constant on the segment connecting $z^{h'}$ and $z^{h''}$.

It is now clear that if the benefit function B^h is linear over some convex set which contains the optimal solutions to the private maximization problem, the effluent charges may induce the private decision makers to decide on waste discharges that are not consistent with the environmental constraint. The situation is illustrated in figure 10 (which is based on the assumption that there is only one residual under consideration).

If the effluent charge determined by (5) happens to be $\tilde{q}$, the firm is indifferent between the amounts of waste discharges represented by the interval $[z^{h'}, z^{h''}]$. If the effluent standard for this firm is $\bar{z}^h$, it is clear that the use of effluent charges may lead to a violation of this standard. Therefore we can state our next conclusion: *If the benefit functions are not strictly concave, effluent charges may lead to a violation of the environmental standards, while effluent standards will satisfy them* [8]. This objection against effluent charges is relevant even if the supply of environmental services is based on the aggregate marginal willingness to pay, instead of being determined outside the model. If the aggregate marginal willingness to pay for environmental services is known, there is a variant of the

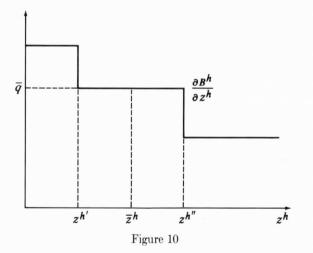

Figure 10

effluent charge approach that will work even if there is only one firm. This variant is simply to assign the total willingness to pay to the firm, instead of the marginal willingness to pay times the quantity of wastes discharged. This seems to be unnecessarily complicated in comparison with the use of effluent standards, however.

The validity of this objection against the use of effluent charges obviously depends on the likelihood of piecewise linear benefit functions. If the production technology is linear, as was assumed in chapter 2, it is clear that the benefit functions B^h are piecewise linear (and piecewise differentiable) and that $\partial B^h / \partial z_j^h$ is piecewise constant. Even if the production technology is nonlinear in general, B^h may be piecewise linear in the cases where there are special waste treatment processes that can be used at constant costs in order to decrease the waste discharges.

All this points toward the conclusion that effluent charges may not be appropriate policy measures. But if the regions in which the benefit functions are linear are small in some sense (that is, if the sets

$$\left\{ z^h; \frac{\partial B^h}{\partial z_j^h} = q_j, j = 1, \cdots, r \right\}$$

are small), the differences in allocation between effluent charges and effluent standards may be very small. As there are usually many opportunities for a firm to reduce its generation of residuals, it seems likely that the possibility of piecewise linear benefit functions can be neglected without imposing any greater costs in the form of misallocation [9], especially with regard to the differences between effluent charges and effluent standards that will be discussed later in this chapter.

Information on each B^h is not necessary to calculate the optimal effluent charges. It is enough if the agency knows

$$B(z^1, \cdots, z^H) \equiv \sum_h B^h(z^h)$$

The separation of B into individual terms is not necessary for calculating the optimal charges. Moreover, if the function

$$B(z) = B(z^1, \cdots, z^H) \text{ where } z = \Sigma z^h \qquad .$$

exists, information on this function is also enough to allow the agency to compute the optimal charges. Therefore there is a basic asymmetry between the information requirement in the two approaches. *It is not possible to calculate the optimal effluent standards from a knowledge of effluent charges, while it is possible to calculate the optimal effluent charges from information on the optimal effluent standards (provided of course that the benefit functions are not piecewise linear).* This difference can be expressed in the following way. To determine optimal effluent standards, it is necessary to know the benefits accruing to each individual unit from waste discharges, while for determining optimal charges, it is only necessary to know the aggregate benefits from waste discharges.

If, however, the only way of knowing the aggregate benefits is through knowledge of individual benefits, there is no difference in the information requirement. Both approaches require detailed knowledge of the benefits accruing to the individual unit. Such a situation may occur if there is only one economic unit discharging wastes at each point. As each residual is defined not only by substance but also by location, it follows that in this case each component of the vector z corresponds to a discharge from only one unit. Even in this case it may happen that effluent charges require less information than effluent standards. Let us consider two cases.

1. Assume, for instance, that the residuals under consideration affect only one environmental quality Y_j. If the environmental interaction function is linear, we have

$$Y_j = Y_j^o - \sum_{i=1}^{m} f_{ji} z_i$$

and assume that $f_{ji} \neq 0, f_{j'i} = 0$ for $j' \neq j$
In this case

$$q_i = \delta_j f_{ji} \quad \text{for all } i \text{ such that } f_{ji} \neq 0$$

This means that (if $f_{j1} \neq 0$)

$$\frac{q_i}{q_1} = \frac{f_{ji}}{f_{j1}} \quad \text{for all } i \text{ such that } f_{ji} \neq 0$$

and consequently that it is only necessary to have information on the effluent charge for the first residual in order to set charges on the other residuals.

This case is not as special as one would believe. In Sweden's case study presented to the United Nations conference on the human environment [10], it was reported that emissions of sulfur dioxide had two different impacts on the environment: first, the local effects caused by high concentrations of SO_2, and second, the more serious regional effects from the deposition of sulfuric acid. It is not necessary to separate out the sources of emission in studying the second effect, and so the environmental interaction function takes the form $f_{ji} = 1$ for all i corresponding to SO_2 emissions.

2. Assume that the objectives for some environmental qualities are set, not by ambient standards, but by demand prices. For some residuals for which it is easy to calculate the value of the damages (e.g., corrosion, the effects on fishing), this approach is the natural one. If these demand prices are constant, the effluent charges can be calculated directly from a knowledge of the environmental interaction function: $q = \delta^T F^1$.

It seems reasonable to assume that it is easier to obtain information on the aggregate benefits than on the individual benefits, simply because besides those methods that can be used for obtaining information on individual benefits (and thus also giving aggregate benefits), methods specialized for aggregate benefits can also be used.

There is another important difference in the two approaches that concerns information. Consider the case when many units discharge the same residual (which implies that all discharges are made at the same location) or when the spatial distribution of discharges does not matter (because of the environmental interaction function). Assume the agency has in some way determined effluent standards which they believe are optimal. If the standards are enforced, and if they are consistent with the environmental standards, the environmental objective will be met. But the agency can never be sure that the effluent standards are in fact optimal, because the markets will never reveal an inefficiency in the standards. On the other hand, if the agency has determined a set of effluent charges and enforces them, it can be sure that the resulting reductions of the waste flows are efficient, but it cannot a priori be sure that the environmental standards will be met. But, after the charges have been levied on the waste dischargers, a violation of the environmental standards will immediately be revealed, and the agency can take the proper steps to correct for this deficiency.

With effluent standards, there is thus no automatic way in which inefficiency will be revealed, but with effluent charges any violations of the environmental standards can be observed in the cases where many units discharge the same residual.

This discussion of information required by the two methods can be summed up as follows: Information required to set correct effluent charges will never exceed the corresponding information requirement for effluent standards. In many instances the information requirement for setting correct effluent charges is less than that for setting standards. This is the case when there is more than one unit discharging wastes at a single point, when only one environmental quality is under consideration, and when the ambient standards are set from given constant demand prices for environmental services. Moreover, inefficiencies connected with effluent standards may never be revealed, while under a system of effluent charges violation of the environmental objectives will be evident. On the other hand, if the private benefit functions are piecewise linear, it may be impossible to implement the desired objectives by using effluent charges.

We will now discuss the incidence of effluent charges versus effluent standards and the effects of the two approaches on the overall allocation of resources. To simplify the discussion, it will be assumed that the agency has all the necessary information required in order to set both optimal effluent charges and optimal effluent standards.

Looking back on the general equilibrium model in chapter 2, it is clear that the agency can achieve the same allocation and income distribution with both approaches by using lump sum transfers to establish the same income distribution, and thus the same demand pattern in the two situations. Since optimal effluent standards are those that achieve the optimum that can be achieved by effluent charges, it is clear that the overall allocation will be the same.

In a more realistic setting, in which lump sum transfers are not possible, the equivalence of effluent standards and effluent charges is not obvious. In the next section it will be demonstrated that the impacts of the same approaches will be the same, but owing to differences in income distribution the demand pattern may change and therefore also the ultimate allocation of resources.

3. COMPARISON OF EFFLUENT CHARGES AND EFFLUENT STANDARDS IN A PARTIAL EQUILIBRIUM CONTEXT

We will in this section compare the incidence of effluent charges and effluent standards. The analysis is based on the assumption that the environmental management agency has the necessary information for setting correct standards and charges. For simplicity, we will study a single competitive industry, consisting of firms generating the same residual. This latter assumption seems to be very restrictive, but it is possible to generalize the analysis to encompass more than one residual (for example, spatially distributed residuals), at the cost of a more complex notation [11].

The classical analysis of a competitive industry is based on the following two assumptions (among others): (1) each firm is so small that it can be neglected in comparison with the total industry supply, and (2) each producer is so small that he cannot affect the market price. The mathematical idealization of these two assumptions is that of a nonatomic measure space. The simplest nonatomic measure space that we may use is the σ field of all Lebesque measurable subsets of an interval on the real line, with the Lebesque measure [12]. In nontechnical language this means that it is possible to represent all producers, including those who already are in the industry, and those who may enter the industry if the profitability rises, by an inverval [0, b]. Let m be the Lebesque measure on the real line. Then $m(G)$, if G is a measurable subset of [0, b], will be interpreted as the number of producers in the subset G. There is, however, one problem with this approach. There is for each subset G, a subset G', such that

$$m(G \backslash G') + m(G' \backslash G) = 0$$

although G and G' are not the same sets. Let us therefore introduce the usual convention of regarding equivalence classes of subsets, instead of the subsets themselves, where the equivalence classes are determined by the equivalence relation between subsets given by

$$m(G \triangledown G') = m(G \backslash G' \cup G' \backslash G) = m(G \backslash G') + m(G' \backslash G) = 0$$

This is a very natural convention because two subsets of producers will be regarded as identical if the measure of the set of producers in the first set only, plus the measure of the producers in the second set only, is equal to zero. One implication of this convention is that identical sets will have the same aggregate output.

Let us next turn to the individual producers and denote the production density at producer h by x^h. The interpretation of x^h is the following. Take a set of producers G, and let X^G be the total output of the producers in G. Then X^G may be represented by

$$X^G = \int_G x^h dm \tag{8}$$

In the same way we can introduce a vector of input densities S^h, and a production function f^h, such that x^h is given by

$$x^h = f^h(S^h) \qquad h \in [0, b] \tag{9}$$

We assume that these production functions have the usual textbook forms. The marginal productivities are all positive, and the average productivities are first increasing and then decreasing. Jointly with x^h, a certain residual or waste is produced. The production function for the residual z^h is assumed to be of the form

$$z^h = g^h(S^h, T^h) \tag{10}$$

This form reflects the idea that the amount of wastes depends on three factors: the amount of output, which is given by S^h, the chosen technology, which is also given by S^h, and the amounts of different input for waste treatment T^h. In the special case when $g^h(S^h, T^h) \equiv f^h(S^h)$, we have a proportional relation between output and the amount of residuals.

Let r be the price vector on inputs. This vector of prices is assumed to be independent of the demand for inputs from our particular industry, and so r will be treated as a vector of constant prices.

Two kinds of cost functions will now be defined. The first gives the minimum total cost of producing x^h when the amount of waste discharge is given by z^h, while the second gives the minimum total cost of producing x^h when the producer has to pay an effluent charge q for the ultimate disposal of his wastes. The first cost function, $C^h(x^h, z^h)$ is defined by

$$C^h(x^h, z^h) = \min r^T(S^h + T^h)$$
$$\text{s.t. } x^h = f^h(S^h) \tag{11}$$
$$z^h = g^h(S^h, T^h)$$

where z^h is given. The second cost function, $TC(x^h, q)$ is defined by

$$TC^h(x^h, q) = \min [r^T(S^h + T^h) + qz^h]$$
$$\text{s.t. } x^h = f^h(S^h) \tag{12}$$
$$z^h = g^h(S^h, T^h)$$

where q is given.

It can be seen immediately that the following relation holds between the two cost functions:

$$TC^h(x^h, q) = \min_{z^h} [C^h(x^h, z^h) + qz^h] \tag{13}$$

A necessary condition for minimum on the right-hand side is that

$$\frac{\partial C^h}{\partial z^h} + q = 0 \tag{14}$$

Furthermore, the following relation also holds between the two cost functions in case there is no restriction on waste discharges:

$$TC^h(x^h, 0) = C^h(x^h, z^h) , \frac{\partial C^h}{\partial z^h} \geqq 0 \tag{15}$$

Let us now turn to the short-run equilibrium of the industry. First assume that there are no restrictions at all on the discharge of wastes. Then the profit for the individual producer is $px^h - TC^h(x^h, 0)$ where p is the ruling market price.

Maximization of the profit yields the individual supply function $x^h(p)$. If G is the set of producers already in the industry, the aggregate supply function is

$$\int_G x^h(p)dm$$

Let the market demand function be $x(p)$. Short-run equilibrium is then given by

$$x(p) = \int_G x^h dm \tag{16}$$

The set of producers may not, however, be in equilibrium, because some of the producers in the industry may operate with losses and some potential producers may enter the industry.

The long-run equilibrium for the industry when there is no waste control is thus defined as such a set G of producers that

$$h \in G \text{ implies } px^h - TC^h(x^h, 0) \geqq 0 \tag{17}$$

and for no $h \notin G$ is it true that $px^h - TC^h(x^h, 0) > 0$, and

$$x(p) = \int_G x^h dm$$

This definition means that in the long run, some firms may earn a differential rent because their production costs are lower than others. The definitions of short-run and long-run equilibrium are unchanged if there is a positive effluent charge. We have only to replace 0 by q everywhere in the argument of the TC^h function.

Let us now turn to the definition of optimum. Optimum will here be defined as such a set of producers that the market is cleared and the total social surplus is maximized. The total surplus is defined as the compensating variation $I - m(p, u)$ plus the value of the product $px(p)$ minus the production costs. Here lump sum transfers are assumed feasible, and m is the social expenditure function [13].

If there is an environmental objective that the total amount of wastes discharged must not exceed some predetermined amount $\bar{z}$, optimum is redefined by requiring that the above maximum be subject to this constraint. Optimum is thus defined by the solution to the following maximization problem:

$$\max I - m(p, u) + px(p) - \int_G C^h(x^h, z^h)dm$$

$$\text{s.t.} \int_G x^h dm = x(p) \tag{18}$$

$$\int z^h dm \leqq \bar{z}$$

and where the maximum is taken over all subsets G, all x^h, z^h, $h \in G$, and p.

Hold G fixed for the moment. Then we can investigate the properties of the short-run optimum by maximizing the objective function over x^h, z^h, $h \in G$, and p. Let $\bar{p}$ and q be Lagrange multipliers and consider the Lagrangian

$$L = I - m(p, u) + px(p) - \int_G C^h(x^h, z^h)dm - \bar{p}\left[x(p) - \int_G x^h dm\right]$$
$$-q\left\{\int_G z^h dm - \bar{z}\right\}$$

Necessary conditions for a maximum are [14]

$$-\frac{\partial m}{\partial p} + x(p) + p\frac{dx}{dp} - \bar{p}\frac{dx}{dp} = 0$$

If u is so chosen that the compensated demand curve $x^*(p)$ passes through the optimal point, $\partial m/\partial p = x(p)$ and

$$p = \bar{p} \tag{19}$$

$$-\frac{\partial C^h}{\partial x^h} + p = 0 \qquad h \in G \tag{20}$$

$$-\frac{\partial C^h}{\partial z^h} - q \leqq 0 \qquad h \in G \tag{21}$$

and with equality when $z^h > 0$. The optimal solutions are functions of the set G, $x^h(G)$, $z^h(G)$, etc.

Assume now that there exists a set G^*, such that

$$h \in G^* \text{ implies that } p(G^*)x^h(G^*) - C^h[x^h(G^*), z^h(G^*)]$$
$$-\dot{\;}q(G^*)z^h(G^*) \geq 0 \tag{22}$$

and

$$h \notin G^* \text{ implies } p(G^*)x^h - C^h(x^h, z^h) - q(G^*)z^h \leq 0$$

If there exists a long-run equilibrium for the industry, we know that at least one set G^* exists, because G^* is exactly the set of producers that will be in the industry in long-run equilibrium.

Assume furthermore that the production functions f^h and g^h are concave. In that case the cost function C^h is convex in x^h, and z^h [15]. We can now show that G^*, $x^h(G^*)$, $z^h(G^*)$, $X(G^*)$ is an optimal solution. Note first that if G^* exists, it will in general not be unique. In the case when the cost functions are the same for all producers, any set with the same measure as G^* will do the job.

Let G be another set of producers, such that at least a subset G' of G with positive measure is such that

$$p(G^*)x^h - C^h(x^h, z^h) - q(G^*)z^h \leq 0 \qquad h \in G' \tag{23}$$

It is intuitively clear that this subset can be chosen so that it contains

$$G \backslash G^* \tag{24}$$

Next choose x^h, z^h, and X with $h \in G$, such that

$$\int_G x^h dm = X \tag{25}$$

$$\int_G z^h dm \leq \bar{z} \tag{26}$$

Let us now study the difference between the values of the objective function for these two sets of producers. In order to simplify the notation, let $X^* = X(G^*)$, $z^{h^*} = z^h(G^*)$, etc. Note that if t is the inverse function of the compensated demand function

$$I - m(p, u) + px(p)$$

$$= \int_{\bar{p}}^{p} \left(-\frac{\partial m}{\partial p} + x + p \frac{dx}{dp} \right) dp$$

$$= \int_{\bar{p}}^{p} p \frac{dx}{dp} dp = \int_{\bar{x}}^{x} h(v) dv$$

The differences in the objective functions for the two sets G^* and G can therefore be written

$$\int_{0}^{X*} t(v)dv - \int_{G*} C^h(x^{h*}, z^{h*})dm - \int_{0}^{X} t(v)dv + \int_{G} C^h(x^h, z^h)dm$$

$\geq$ [because $t'(v) < 0$, and C^h is convex in x^h, and z^h]

$$\geq (X^* - X)t(X^*) - \int_{G*\cap G} \left[\frac{\partial C^{h*}}{\partial x^h} (x^{h*} - x^h) + \frac{\partial C^{h*}}{\partial z^h} (z^{h*} - z^h) \right] dm$$

$$- \int_{G*\backslash G} C^h(x^{h*}, z^{h*})dm + \int_{G\backslash G*} C^h(x^h, z^h)dm$$

(because of 26, 18, 19, 16, 23, and 24)

$$\geq (X^* - X)t(X^*) - p^* \left(X^* - \int_{G*} x^{h*}dm \right) + p^* \left(X - \int_{G} x^h dm \right)$$

$$- q^* \left(\int_{G*} z^{h*}dm - \bar{z} \right) + q^* \left(\int_{G} z^h dm - \bar{z} \right)$$

$$- \int_{G*\cap G} [p^*(x^{h*} - x^h) + q^*(z^{h*} - z^h)]dm$$

$$- \int_{G*\backslash G} C^h(x^{h*}, z^{h*})dm + \int_{G\backslash G*} C^h(x^h, z^h)dm$$

$$= \int_{G*\backslash G} [p^*x^{h*} - C^h(x^{h*}, z^{h*}) - q^*z^{h*}]dm$$

$$- \int_{G\backslash G*} [p^*x^h - C^h(x^h, z^h) - q^*z^h]dm \geq 0$$

because the integrand in the first integral is nonnegative, and the integrand in the second integral is nonpositive.

We have thus shown that G^*, x^{h*}, z^{h*}, and X^* is an optimum. Associated with this solution there are the two multipliers p^* and q^*. It is clear from (19) that p^* is the price on the market in long-run equilibrium, and that q^* is the effluent charge that makes the total flow of residuals from the industry consistent with the environmental goal. In order to make this conclusion more clear, note that (19) says that

$$\frac{\partial C^h(x^{h*}, z^{h*})}{\partial z^h} + q^* = 0, \text{ so that}$$

$$TC(x^{h*}, q^*) = C^h(x^{h*}, z^{h*}) + q^* z^{h*}, \text{ and}$$

$$\frac{\partial TC(x^{h*}, q^*)}{\partial x^h} = \frac{\partial C^h(x^{h*}, z^{h*})}{\partial x^h}$$

so the optimality conditions correspond to a price equal to marginal cost. The effluent charge is equal to the marginal cost of reducing waste discharge, with all firms in the industry having nonnegative profits and all potential producers not in the industry having nonpositive profits if they enter the industry.

In order to achieve this optimum by using regulations instead of an effluent charge, the environmental management agency must restrict the entry to the industry (and if the cost functions differ among firms, select those firms with least costs in optimum), and restrict the waste discharge from each producer. By doing this, it is possible for the agency to achieve the same optimum as can be achieved by an effluent charge, but the income distribution will differ between the two approaches. With the effluent charge approach the individual profits are

$$p^* x^{h*} - C^{h*} - q^* z^{h*} \geqq 0 \qquad h \in G^*$$

for all producers in the industry. Those producers who have a positive profit due to lower costs will therefore earn a differential rent.

With the effluent standards approach, the individual profits are

$$p^* x^{h*} - C^{h*} \qquad h \in G^*$$

which are strictly greater than the differential rents earned under a system with effluent charges. This difference may be interpreted as a differential rent accruing to the producers because of the limited capacity of the environment to assimilate wastes. With effluent charges this rent is transferred to the public (that is, the government).

If there are many residuals, spatially distributed, the same kind of analysis may be applied. In this situation, firms that discharge their wastes at locations with large assimilative capacity, or at locations where the environmental quality is of little concern, may under effluent standards earn a differential rent over firms discharging at places where the social costs of the discharges are high. With effluent charges this kind of differential rent will be socialized. In fact, it is possible to interpret the spatial distribution of the effluent charges as giving a rent gradient for the assimilative capacity of the environment.

In a partial equilibrium analysis, the only difference between charges and regulations is thus in the income distribution. Note, however, that in this example, the environmental management agency needs to have information on the cost functions, not only for the firms already in the industry, but also for every firm that may enter the industry, in order to set the optimal effluent standards [16]. These differences in the distribution of income and wealth will naturally affect the demand functions, and thereby also the allocation of resources. We can therefore expect differences in the overall allocation of resources owing to these differences in income distribution. If lump sum transfers are feasible, the differences in income distribution may be offset by such transfers, and in that case only will the overall allocation be the same when regulation is used as when effluent charges are used.

4. EFFLUENT STANDARDS, EFFLUENT CHARGES, AND RANDOM WASTE LOAD

So far we have compared effluent standards and effluent charges as if the flows of residuals from different firms could be predicted with certainty, given all the relevant information on production technologies, and on prices. These waste flows are, however, in most realistic cases random variables. Mechanical and other failures in plants cannot be foreseen accurately, which means that the resulting waste flow is stochastic. Changes in weather can affect the waste flow to a significant extent, through storm flows in combined sewers. Random fluctuations in demand can cause similar fluctuations in the capacity utilization in some plants, and thereby random fluctuations in waste flows. Moreover, the assimilative capacity of the environment is very sensitive to changes in weather and climate, which means that the environmental interaction function is not a deterministic relation but a stochastic one. Such random fluctuations in the assimilative capacity of the environment may be modeled as random fluctuations in the aggregate waste load (although this approach will not capture all of the interesting features of a stochastic environmental interaction function).

It therefore seems necessary to study the case when the waste flows have random fluctuations, and to compare different tools in environmental policy for this case too. To study this case, let us construct the following model. Assume there are K firms producing different commodities $x^1, \cdots, x^K$, but generating the same residual z. Each firm has a production function of the form

$$x^h = f^h(S^h) \tag{27}$$

$$z^h = g^h(S^h, T^h) + e^h \tag{28}$$

where x^h is the amount produced, S^h input in production (a vector), T^h input in waste treatment (a vector), and z^h the resulting flow of waste. The difference from previous sections is the random variable e^h that is added to the "produced" waste $g^h(S^h, T^h)$. We assume that e^h has a probability distribution with a density $\gamma^h(e)$.

The total waste load is

$$z = \sum_{h=1}^{K} z^h = \sum_{h=1}^{K} g^h(S^h, T^h) + \sum_{h=1}^{K} e^h \tag{29}$$

and the environmental quality Y is given as before by

$$Y = Y_o - F^1(z) \tag{30}$$

(We will neglect environmental treatment because we want to focus on random fluctuations in the individual waste flows. If the stochastic nature of the waste assimilative capacity of the environment is the main object under study, environmental treatment would be a major variable to analyze.)

We assume for simplicity that Y is one dimensional. This can be interpreted as an interest in one special environmental quality. As z is a random variable, Y will also be a random variable, and the formulation of environmental standards as $Y \geq Y^*$ would in general be meaningless. This is because one can always imagine a random fluctuation in the waste load such that the standards would be violated if they were not already set so low that there was in fact no environmental policy. We must therefore reformulate the standards, and one way to do that—a way which has been used in some countries—is the following. Determine a lower limit Y^* on the environmental quality, such that the quality is not below Y^* in more than 100ρ percent of the time. Another way to formulate this objective is to require that

$$Pr(Y \leq Y^*) \leq \rho \tag{31}$$

where $Pr(Y \leq Y^*)$ stands for the probability that $Y \leq Y^*$. This objective implies that we tolerate a low quality of the environment, but only for a short time. For most of the time we require that $Y \geq Y^*$.

An alternative to this formulation of the standards would be a sequence of pairs $\{Y^{*i}, \rho_i\}$, such that $Y^{*i} > Y^{*i+1}$, $\rho_i > \rho_{i+1}$, and

$$Pr(Y \leq Y^{*i}) \leq \rho_i \qquad i = 1, 2, \cdots \tag{32}$$

This formulation implies that a moderate fall in environmental quality can be tolerated for some time, but a large fall in environmental quality may only be tolerated for a very short time. We will come back to this formulation of the environmental standards in the next section, but for the rest of this section, the first, simpler formulation will be used.

The formulation of the environmental standards depends on the probability distribution of Y, or the distribution of z. In some cases this distribution may depend on the environmental policy, for example when it is possible to counteract the random fluctuations in the waste load by fluctuations in the "produced" waste load. This case, which seems to be a very important one, will be discussed in the next section. For this section we assume that when the vectors S^h, T^h of input in the individual firms are once determined, they will not change in response to random fluctuations in e^h.

As we here have assumed a single flow of wastes, and a single quality of the environment, Y and z are scalars, and the inequality $Y \leq Y^*$ can be translated into a corresponding inequality for z, $z \geq z^*$, where $F^1(z^*) = Y^*$. The environmental standard can then be written

$Pr(z \geq z^*) \leq \rho$, or

$$Pr\left(\sum_{h=1}^{K} g^h + \sum_{h=1}^{K} e^h \geq z^*\right) \leq \rho, \text{ or}$$

$$Pr\left(\sum_{h=1}^{K} e^h \geq z^* - \sum_{h=1}^{K} g^h\right) \leq \rho \tag{33}$$

With $\bar{e} = z^* + \sum_{h=1}^{K} g^h$, the standard can finally be written

$$Pr\left(\sum_{h=1}^{K} e^h \geq \bar{e}\right) \leq \rho \tag{34}$$

Here $\bar{e}$ is a function of the "produced" wastes, and accordingly of the input in treatment and production processes. Holding these inputs constant, we can write the density of

$e = \sum_{h=1}^{K} e^h$ as

$$\gamma(e) = \int_{-\infty}^{+\infty} \cdots \int \prod_{h=1}^{K-1} \gamma^h(\tau_h) \gamma^K \left(e - \sum_{h=1}^{K-1} \tau_h \right) \prod_{h=1}^{K-1} d\tau_h$$

if the variables $e^1, \cdots, e^K$ are statistically independent, as we assume they are. Later some brief comments on the case where they are correlated will be offered.

The environmental standard can now be written

$$\int_{\bar{e}}^{\infty} \gamma(e)de = \int_{\bar{e}}^{\infty} \int_{-\infty}^{+\infty} \cdots \int \prod_{h=1}^{K-1} \gamma^h(\tau_h) \gamma^K \left(e - \sum_{h=1}^{K-1} \tau_h \right) \prod_{h=1}^{K-1} d\tau_h de \leq \rho$$

Let the prices on the outputs be $p_1, \cdots, p_K$, and on the inputs $r_1, \cdots, r_n$, respectively. The optimization problem for the environmental management agency can now be described as maximizing

$$\sum_{h=1}^{K} [p_h f^h - r^T(S^h + T^h)]$$

subject to the constraints

$$\bar{e} - z^* + \sum_{h=1}^{K} g^h(S^h, T^h) = 0$$

$$\int_{\bar{e}}^{\infty} \gamma(e)de \leq \rho$$

The Lagrangian to this problem is

$$L = \sum_{h=1}^{K} [P_h f^h(S^h) - r^T(S^h + T^H)] - q \left[\bar{e} - z^* + \sum_{h=1}^{K} g^h(S^h, T^h) \right]$$
$$- \delta \left\{ \int_{\bar{e}}^{\infty} \gamma(\tau)d_\tau - \rho \right\}$$

where q and δ are two Lagrangian multipliers, which can be interpreted as the imputed effluent charge and the imputed value on the environmental constraint.

The first-order conditions for a maximum are

$$p_h f_i^h - r_i - q g^h{}_{S_i} = 0$$
$$-r_i - q g^h{}_{T_i} = 0$$
$$-q + \delta \gamma(\bar{e}) = 0$$

It is clear from these conditions that q can in fact be interpreted as an effluent charge, and that if the environmental management agency imposes on the firm the effluent charge q, the net value of the output of the industry would be maximized subject to the environmental constraint. With perfect information, not only on the production and treatment technologies but also on the probability distribution on the variable $\bar{e}$, the agency can thus achieve optimal allocation by using the effluent charges approach.

Let us now study the effluent standards approach. In that case the agency must determine for each firm a constraint on the amounts of waste the firm may dispose of in the environment. Such standards will take the following form:

$$Pr(z^h \geq z^{h*}) \leq \rho^h$$

The firm will then maximize its profits $p_h f^h - r(S^h + T^h)$ subject to the constraint that

$$\int_{\bar{e}^h}^{\infty} \gamma^h(e^h) de^h \leq \rho^h, \ \bar{e}^h = z^{h*} - g^h$$

yielding the following first-order conditions

$$p f_i^h - r_i - q^h g^h{}_{S_i} = 0$$
$$-r_i - q^h g^h{}_{T_i} = 0$$
$$-q^h + \delta^h \gamma^h(\bar{e}^h) = 0$$

where q^h and δ^h are Lagrangian multipliers. It is clear from these conditions that the agency can choose z^{h*} and ρ^h in such a way that S^h, T^h are the same vectors as in the optimal solution. But as the produced waste flow is the same in this case, and in the optimal situation for every firm, it follows that the overall environmental constraint will be satisfied by the use of effluent standards.

The conclusion is thus the same now as it was in the previous sections:

if all necessary information is available, the only difference between effluent standards and effluent charges is in the income distribution. But let
us now take a closer look at the information requirements. When effluent
standards are used, the environmental management agency must know
the probability distribution for each e^k, that is, the probability distribution for the waste flow from each firm. When effluent charges are used,
the environmental management agency only has to know the probability
distribution of the total waste flow. We have assumed that the individual
waste flows are statistically independent, and so if there are many firms,
the sum of these individual random variables tends to be normally distributed according to the central limit theorem [17]. The importance of
this is obvious. Owing to the central limit theorem, the environmental
management agency already has a lot of information concerning the
probability distribution of the total waste load, without having to study
the individual waste loads. And so, when the individual waste loads are
statistically independent, and there are many firms, the effluent charge
approach requires much less information than the effluent standards
approach.

If the individual waste flows are not independent, but correlated, then
we cannot appeal to the central limit theorem in probability theory. But
if there is some systematic cause (for example, unpredictable weather
changes) behind this correlation, the agency should be able to go directly
toward an estimation of the probability distribution of the total waste
load without first having to estimate the probability distributions of the
individual waste loads. Even if the individual waste loads are not statistically independent, the effluent charge approach will require less information than the effluent standard approach.

When the waste loads are random variables, there is another important difference between effluent standards and effluent charges, namely
a difference in the possibilities of enforcement. With deterministic waste
flows, both approaches require monitoring of the waste flows to the same
extent. But consider a firm faced with effluent standards requiring such
production and waste treatment planning that waste loads on the environment in excess of a certain amount can only appear with a probability
less than a specified number. This firm knows of the difficulties of proving
that an excess waste load is not due to random variations, but to production and treatment planning. It will therefore have incentives to discharge more residuals than is consistent with the effluent standards.
After some time the environmental management agency will obviously
realize that and presumably sue the firm for violation of environmental
regulations, and presumably also sharpen the standards. But as soon as
the agency finds it necessary to tamper with the standards, because some

firms use "stochastic explanations" for their excessive waste load, the efficiency will have been lost. In contrast, the effluent charge approach does not have this drawback, simply because the firms are allowed to discharge any amount of waste, although they have to pay for it. An increase in the waste load, independent of whether it is a "produced" increase in the flow of residuals or a random phenomenon, means that the firm has to pay for the increased burden on the waste assimilative capacity of the environment.

5. COUNTERACTING RANDOM DISTURBANCES IN THE WASTE LOAD

In the preceding section some very distinctive differences between effluent charges and effluent standards were derived when the waste load was a random variable. When we now turn to more realistic cases, when it is possible to counteract random fluctuations in the waste load by changes in the level of waste treatment, much more profound differences will show up.

It is clear that there must be some capacity constraint on the opportunities to counteract the fluctuations in waste load by changes in treatment level, because some of the inputs in waste treatment cannot be changed in the short run. This means that the basic model from the previous sections cannot be applied, but we have to develop a new model for the firm.

Let ζ^h be the vector of flows of untreated residuals resulting from production. This flow is assumed to enter a treatment plant, the technology of which can be described by a linear activity analysis model similar to the model that was used in chapter 2. Let A be the matrix of input coefficients, so if the treatment plant is operated at the level x^h, it can absorb the flow Ax^h. Let B be the matrix of output coefficients, so if the treatment plant is operated at the level x^h, it will generate the flow Bx^h of residuals. If z^h is the flow of residuals discharged into the environment, and if e^h is a random variable, with joint density $\gamma^h(e^h)$ interpreted as the random component in the waste load, the technology of the waste treatment plant can be written

$$I + Ax^h = \zeta^h + e^h$$
$$I + Bx^h = z^h$$

(35)

where I is a slack vector, indicating the amount of residuals discharged into the environment without any treatment whatsoever.

These two relations entail

$$z^h = \zeta^h + e^h - (A - B)x^h = \zeta^h + e^h - Dx^h \tag{36}$$

where $D = A - B$.

Assume that the variable average cost for each treatment process is constant and equal to components in the vector d. Then the variable cost is

$$d^T x^h \tag{37}$$

As soon as the treatment plant has been constructed, it has a certain capacity $\bar{x}^h$, which means that waste loads in excess of the capacity have to be discharged into the environment without being treated. This capacity implies the following constraint

$$x^h \leqq \bar{x}^h \tag{38}$$

The average capacity cost, or the marginal cost of increasing the capacity, is given by the vector $\bar{d}$. The total cost of operating the plant on the level x^h is thus

$$d^T x^h + \bar{d}^T \bar{x}^h \tag{39}$$

We shall now introduce the notion of waste treatment policy. Given the treatment capacity and the waste load ζ^h, a waste treatment policy is a function of the random component e^h

$$x^h(e^h) \tag{40}$$

indicating the level at which the treatment plant is operated for different random waste loads.

The firm can determine (1) the waste load ζ^h, which depends on the output of the firm, and the production process it uses in the production of this output, (2) the treatment capacity $\bar{x}^h$, and (3) the waste treatment policy $x^h(e^h)$. We will for the moment assume that ζ^h is given, and that the only parameters for the firm are the waste treatment capacity and the waste treatment policy. When this is the case, the objective for the firm is to minimize its expected cost for waste disposal, subject to any effluent standards.

We will start by analyzing the implications of effluent standards on treatment capacity and policy decisions. Then we will turn to a similar analysis of effluent charges and compute the effects, and finally, we will study the environmental objectives that are behind effluent standards and effluent charges, respectively

Effluent standards can be formulated as in the previous section:

$$Pr(z_j^h \geq z_j^{h*}) \leq \rho_j^h \qquad j = 1, \cdots, s \tag{41}$$

that is, the probability that the discharge of residual j exceeds a predetermined amount z_j^{h*} is less than or equal to ρ_j^h.

The optimal treatment capacity and treatment policy for the firm is given by the solution to the minimum problem

$$\min \bar{d}^T \bar{x}^h + \int_{-\infty}^{+\infty} \cdots \int d^T x^h(e^h) \gamma^h(e^h) de_1^h, \cdots, de_s^h \tag{42}$$

subject to $z^h = -Dx^h + \zeta^h + e^h$,

$$Pr(z_j^h \geq z_j^{h*}) \leq \rho^h \qquad j = 1, \cdots, s$$

$$0 \leq x^h \leq \bar{x}^h$$

Because the derivation of the distribution of z_j^h is very complicated, we will simplify this problem drastically by assuming that there is only one residual ($s = 1$), and only one treatment process, so that D is a positive scalar, z is a real number, and x^h is a real number. With this simplification, the problem is to minimize

$$\bar{d}\bar{x}^h + \int_{-\infty}^{+\infty} dx^h(e^h) \gamma^h(e^h) de^h \tag{43}$$

subject to $z^h = -Dx^h(e^h) + \zeta^h + e^h$,

$$Pr(z^h \geq z^{h*}) \leq \rho^h$$

$$0 \leq x^h \leq \bar{x}^h$$

Let $\bar{e}^h$ be defined by

$$z^{h*} = \zeta^h + \bar{e}^h \tag{44}$$

When $e^h \leq \bar{e}^h$, the waste load is so small that even if it is discharged untreated, the relation $z^h \leq z^{h*}$ will not be violated. It therefore seems that $x^h(e^h) = 0$ is optimal for $e^h \leq \bar{e}^h$.

Let the capacity be given for the moment. Then there exists a number $\bar{e}^h$, such that

$$-D\bar{x}^h + \zeta^h + \bar{e}^h = z^{h*} \qquad (45)$$

When $e^h > \bar{e}^h$, z^h will exceed z^{h*}, for each feasible capacity utilization level x^h. With $\bar{x}^h$ given, the probability that $z^h \geq z^{h*}$ is thus independent of treatment of waste loads exceeding $\zeta^h + \bar{e}^h$. This leads to the conclusion $x^h(e^h) = 0$ for $e^h > \tilde{e}^h$. For $\bar{e}^h \leq e^h \leq \tilde{e}^h$, let us study the policy

$$x^h(e^h) = \frac{1}{D}(e^h - \bar{e}^h)$$

With this policy, we will have

$$z^h = -e^h + \bar{e}^h + \zeta^h + e^h = \bar{e}^h + \zeta^h = z^{h*}$$

The constraint $z^h \leq z^{h*}$ will thus never be violated with this policy when $\bar{e}^h \leq e^h \leq \tilde{e}^h$. It is obviously not profitable to use more treatment than that given by this policy, because this will not affect the probability that $z^h \geq z^{h*}$. This policy is shown in figure 11.

The proposed policy can be summarized by

$$x^h(e^h) = \begin{cases} 0 & \text{if } e^h < \bar{e}^h \\ \frac{1}{D}(e^h - \bar{e}^h), & \text{if } \bar{e}^h \leq e^h \leq \tilde{e}^h \\ 0 & \text{if } \tilde{e}^h < e^h \end{cases} \qquad (46)$$

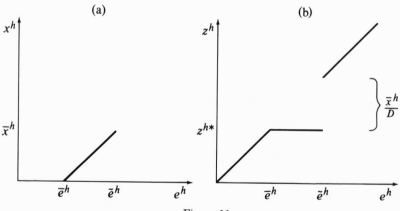

Figure 11

and the capacity $\bar{x}^h$ is given by

$$\bar{x}^h = \frac{1}{D} (\bar{e}^h - \tilde{e}^h) \tag{47}$$

$\bar{e}^h$ is determined by

$$z^{h*} = \zeta^h + \bar{e}^h \tag{48}$$

and $\tilde{e}^h$ by

$$\int_{\tilde{e}^h}^{\infty} \gamma^h(e^h)de^h = \rho^h \tag{49}$$

The expected total cost with this policy is

$$E(TC^h) = \bar{d}\bar{x}^h + d \int_{\tilde{e}^h}^{\bar{e}^h} \frac{1}{D} (e^h - \tilde{e}^h)\gamma^h(e^h)de^h \tag{50}$$

Let us now show that this is in fact the optimal policy for the firm. To do this, note first that if $e^h \leq \tilde{e}^h$, then $x^h(e^h) = 0$ is obviously optimal if $d > 0$. Let us now consider a reduction of treatment in a subinterval around the point e, and with length Δe, in the interval $[\tilde{e}^h, e^h]$. If the treatment is reduced in this subinterval, it should be reduced to zero, because whatever the reduction is, the discharged flow of residuals will be in excess of z^{h*}, and by reducing the treatment to zero, the largest saving of variable cost may be made. The increase in the discharge in residuals from this change is $\Delta z^h = D\Delta x^h = (e - \tilde{e}^h)$ with probability $\gamma^h(e)\Delta e$. The savings in expected variable cost is

$$d\Delta x^h \gamma^h(e)\Delta e = \frac{d}{D} (e - \tilde{e}^h)\gamma^h(e)\Delta e$$

The effluent standard $Pr(z^h \geq z^{h*}) \leq \rho^h$ is violated by this change, however, because the probability for $z^h \geq z^{h*}$ is now

$$Pr(e^h \geq \bar{e}^h) + \gamma^h(e)\Delta e = \rho^h + \gamma^h(e)\Delta e > \rho^h$$

To satisfy the effluent standard, the capacity must increase with $\Delta \bar{x}^h$. This increase in $\bar{x}^h$ leads to an increase in $\bar{e}^h$:

$$-D\Delta \bar{x}^h + \Delta \bar{e}^h = 0, \text{ or } \Delta \bar{x}^h = \frac{\Delta \bar{e}^h}{D}$$

The probability that $e^h \geqq \bar{e}^h + \Delta\bar{e}^h$ is

$$Pr(e^h \geq \bar{e}^h) - \Delta\bar{e}^h\gamma^h(\bar{e}^h)$$

To meet the effluent standard, we must thus have

$$\Delta\bar{e}^h\gamma^h(\bar{e}^h) = \gamma^h(e)\Delta e, \text{ or } \Delta\bar{e}^h = \frac{\gamma^h(e)}{\gamma^h(\bar{e}^h)} \Delta e$$

The needed change in capacity is thus

$$\Delta\bar{x}^h = \frac{1}{D}\frac{\gamma^h(e)}{\gamma^h(\bar{e}^h)} \Delta e$$

and the capacity cost will increase by

$$\frac{\bar{d}}{D}\frac{\gamma^h(e)}{\gamma^h(\bar{e}^h)} \Delta e$$

But the variable cost will also increase with the increase in capacity. From the expression for the total expected cost it is seen that the variable cost will increase with

$$\frac{dE(TC^h)}{d\bar{e}^h} \Delta\bar{e}^h = \frac{d}{D} (\bar{e}^h - \bar{e}^h)\gamma^h(\bar{e}^h)\Delta\bar{e}^h = \frac{d}{D} (\bar{e}^h - \bar{e}^h)\gamma^h(\bar{e}^h) \frac{\gamma^h(e)}{\gamma^h(\bar{e}^h)} \Delta e$$

so that the increase in expected total cost from the capacity increase is

$$\frac{\bar{d}}{D}\frac{\gamma^h(e)}{\gamma^h(\bar{e}^h)} \Delta e + \frac{d}{D}(\bar{e}^h - \bar{e}^h)\gamma^h(e)\Delta e$$

If the change is to be worthwhile, this increase in capacity and variable cost must be less than the savings in variable cost due to the reduction in treatment, or

$$\frac{\bar{d}}{D}\frac{\gamma^h(e)}{\gamma^h(\bar{e}^h)} \Delta e + \frac{d}{D} (\bar{e}^h - \bar{e}^h)\gamma^h(e)\Delta e \leqq \frac{d}{D} (e - \bar{e}^h)\gamma^h(e)\Delta e$$

As $e \leq e^h$, we see that this inequality can be written

$$\frac{\bar{d}}{D}\frac{\gamma^h(e)}{\gamma^h(\bar{e}^h)} \Delta e \leqq 0 \tag{51}$$

that is, the change is worthwhile only if there is no capacity cost, or if the density of e^h at e is zero—two conditions that can be dismissed. Thus the proposed policy is optimal for the firm.

This policy is very peculiar, and does not seem consistent with usual environmental objectives. It implies a waste treatment plant which will be completely utilized with probability zero, and it implies that no waste treatment will be undertaken for large waste loads. The reason for this peculiar behavior is of course the inflexible effluent standard. This standard does not take into account that even in those time periods when the waste load is larger than the predetermined level, society has an interest in control of the discharge of residuals into the environment.

Let us now turn to effluent charges. In most cases it is not practical to let the charge change with random fluctuations in the waste load, so we will consider the case where the firms have to pay a fixed fee per unit of wastes they discharge into the environment. To make the results comparable with those of the effluent standard, we will assume that there is only one residual and only one waste treatment process (although the analysis of effluent charges can be easily extended to cover multidimensional problems).

Let q be the effluent charge. We assume as before that the flow ζ^h is given and constant, so that the firm behaves as if it minimizes the expected cost of waste disposal. The expected cost for waste disposal is

$$
\begin{aligned}
E(TC^h) = \bar{d}\bar{x}^h &+ d \int_{-\infty}^{+\infty} x^h(e^h)\gamma^h(e^h)de^h \\
&+ q \int_{-\infty}^{+\infty} (e^h + \zeta^h - Dx^h)\gamma^h(e^h)de^h
\end{aligned}
\tag{52}
$$

where the first term is the capacity cost, the second the expected variable treatment cost, and the last term the expected payment for discharging residuals into the environment. The firm minimizes this expected cost subject to the following constraints

$$
0 \leqq x^h \leqq \bar{x}^h \tag{53}
$$

$$
0 \leqq e^h + \zeta^h - Dx^h \tag{54}
$$

The expression for the expected total cost can be written

$$
E(TC^h) = \bar{d}\bar{x}^h + \int_{-\infty}^{+\infty} (d - qD)x^h(e^h)\gamma^h(e^h)de^h + q\zeta^h + qE(e^h) \tag{55}
$$

From this we see at once that if

$$
d \geqq qD, \text{ the optimal policy is } x^h(e^h) = 0,\ \bar{x}^h = 0 \tag{56}
$$

The interesting case is when $d < qD$. Assume for the moment that the capacity is given by $\bar{x}^h$. Then the minimizing problem is reduced to

$$\min (d - qD)x^h(e^h) \tag{57}$$

subject to $0 \leq x^h \leq \bar{x}^h$,

$$Dx^h(e^h) = e^h + \zeta^h$$

The solution to this problem is obviously

$$x^h(e^h) = \min\left[\bar{x}^h, \frac{1}{D}(e^h + \zeta^h)\right] \tag{58}$$

For small e^h, we thus have

$$x^h(e^h) = \frac{1}{D}(e^h + \zeta^h) \tag{59}$$

The policy is described in figure 12.
The optimal capacity is determined from

$$\min \bar{d}\bar{x}^h + \int_{-\infty}^{+\infty} (d - qD) \min\left[\bar{x}^h, \frac{1}{D}(e^h + \zeta^h)\right] \gamma^h(e^h)de^h \tag{60}$$

Now we have

$$Pr\left[(e^h + \zeta^h)\frac{1}{D} < \bar{x}^h\right] = \int_{-\infty}^{D\bar{x}^h-\zeta^h} \gamma^h(e^h)de^h \tag{61}$$

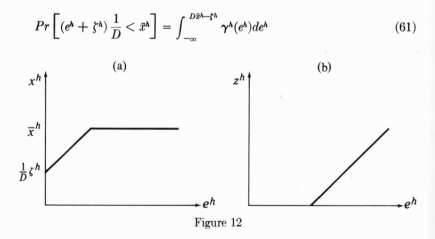

Figure 12

and so (60) can be written

$$d\bar{x}^h + \int_{-\infty}^{D\bar{x}^h - \zeta^h} (d - qD)(e^h + \zeta^h)\frac{1}{D}\gamma^h(e^h)de^h$$

$$+ \int_{D\bar{x}^h - \zeta^h}^{+\infty} (d - qD)\bar{x}^h\gamma^h(e^h)de^h \qquad (62)$$

For a minimum, the derivative with respect to $\bar{x}^h$ must be equal to zero:

$$\bar{d} + (d - qD)D\bar{x}^1\frac{1}{D}\gamma^h(D\bar{x}^h - \zeta^h) - (d - qD)\bar{x}^h\gamma^h(D\bar{x}^h - \zeta^h)$$

$$\int_{D\bar{x}^h - \zeta^h}^{+\infty} (d - qD)\gamma^h(e^h)de^h = 0, \text{ or} \qquad (63)$$

$$\bar{d} = (qD - d)\int_{D\bar{x}^h - \zeta^h}^{+\infty} \gamma^h(e^h)de^h$$

Both the policy and the capacity are now well determined. The policy has an intuitive appeal; when the waste load is small, the capacity utilization is small, and when the waste load is large, all the capacity will be utilized. Moreover, with small waste loads, all residuals will be treated and none discharged directly into the environment. When the load is so large that the capacity of the plant is not enough to treat all wastes, residuals will be discharged directly into the environment. By choosing the effluent charge high enough, it is possible to satisfy the same effluent standard as before, but with less harmful effects on the environment. But the effluent charge does not satisfy the effluent standard at least cost, because the policy implications differ from those we derived for the effluent standard. The difference between the two approaches is simply that they have different environmental objectives. We have seen that the effluent standard is based on an environmental standard $Pr(Y \le Y^*) \le \rho$. What kind of environmental objective is the effluent charge based on?

Assume for simplicity that the environmental interaction function can be written

$$Y = -z = -\sum_{h=1}^{K} z^h \qquad (64)$$

Then we have in the previous notation

$$q = \delta \qquad (65)$$

The total value to society from the environment can then be written

$$-q \sum_{h=1}^{K} z^h - \sum_{h=1}^{K} TC^h \tag{66}$$

where TC^h is the treatment cost in firm h. Maximizing this value is the same as minimizing

$$\sum_{h=1}^{K} (TC^h + qz^h) \tag{67}$$

But as z^h is a random value, this minimization must be interpreted as minimizing the expected value or

$$\min \sum_{h=1}^{K} E(TC^h + qz^h) \tag{68}$$

We have already seen that if the effluent charge q is imposed on the firms, they will minimize $E(TC^h + qz^h)$, and so the total expected value of the environment will be maximized by using the effluent charge.

We can summarize the discussion by the following points:

1. Effluent standards are based on environmental standards of the form $Pr(Y \leq Y^*) \leq \rho$.

2. Effluent standards lead to a waste treatment policy which does not have an intuitive appeal, because when the waste load is very large, no waste treatment will be undertaken.

3. Effluent charges are based on maximizing the total expected value to society of the environment.

4. Effluent charges lead to a waste treatment policy that has an intuitive appeal.

When environmental standards were introduced in the preceding section, a more complicated alternative to the simple formulation was mentioned (see 32). This more complicated alternative consisted of a sequence of pairs (z_i^*, ρ_i), such that

$$z_i^* < z_{i+1}^*, \text{ and } \rho_i > \rho_{i+1}, \text{ and}$$

$$Pr(z \geq z_i^*) \leq \rho_i \qquad i = 1, \cdots$$

By using this more complicated but satisfactory form of the standards, the peculiar form of the waste treatment policy will be less dramatic, and it can be seen that if there are enough numbers of pairs which are close to each other, the optimal waste treatment policy will be similar to that for effluent charges. It is thus possible to achieve the same objective with effluent standards as with effluent charges, but only if one is willing to accept an increasing complexity of the standards. In view of the remarks at the end of section 4 on the difficulties of enforcing standards, it is clear that these difficulties will increase with the complexity of the standards.

6. IMPLEMENTATION OF EFFLUENT CHARGES

It was observed in section 2 of this chapter that one possible objection to using effluent charges is that such charges require metering of waste flows, which can be very expensive. In many cases it is obvious that the costs associated with measuring the amounts of residuals flows would be prohibitively high, and in other cases the costs would be so high that effluent charges may not be the best way to control waste generation and waste discharges.

If we consider residuals generated by households, the problem will become clear. Household wastes consist of a large number of different components. Most of the waste disposed of by sewers is organic matter, suspended or dissolved in water. Some of the organic waste is solid and is disposed of in trash cans. But besides organic matter, many other residuals are generated and disposed of, as for example, phosphorus. In the organic wastes there are generally bacteria which, if not treated carefully, could cause public health hazards. Besides these dissolved or solid residuals, households generate a lot of airborne residuals, such as emissions from automobiles, local heating, and so on.

These different residuals will in general have different effects on the environment. The organic wastes will, if discharged into a watercourse, consume dissolved oxygen and in that way deteriorate the quality of the water. The phosphorus will, if discharged into a watercourse, contribute to the eutrophication of the water body by fertilizing the algae. The increase in the biomass following this fertilizing will increase the oxygen demand (which to some extent is offset by the increased oxygen production by algae), and lead to a decrease in dissolved oxygen. Moreover, the growth of algae will make the water less aesthetically attractive. The increased concentration of bacteria in the water body may, as already mentioned, jeopardize public health. The effects of the airborne emissions are quite different. Increases in ambient concentrations of sulfur dioxide and of nitrogen oxides will affect public health but also plant life, water quality, and so on.

Moreover, there are also large differences in the cost of treatment of these residuals. Conventional sewage treatment plants are designed only to remove organic matter and if one wants to reduce the discharge of phosphorus, one has to use chemical treatment.

The optimal effluent charges should thus be different for these different household components. But such a charge system would require that the sewage for each individual be analyzed periodically, in order to obtain estimates of the flow of residuals on which the charges should be calculated. It is obvious that such monitoring of individual sewage will be prohibitively expensive, and therefore the use of effluent charges is not possible for an important class of waste generators. Moreover, an efficient charge system, even if economically feasible, would probably not be efficient because it presupposes that the consumers know from which goods, and by which activities the different residuals are generated. The average consumer does not have that knowledge, and would therefore not respond to the effluent charges.

The problem in this section is directed to whether the effluent charge system can be modified so that it can withstand the objections raised above. The analysis will be directed toward consumption residuals primarily because it seems to be more economical to meter waste flows from producers than from consumers. To a certain extent the results we will obtain can also be applied to producers.

Let us start with the demand functions that were derived for consumption activities in chapter 4.

$$c^h = c^h(s, Y, I^h) \tag{69}$$

s is the imputed price vector on consumption activities and is given by the following formula

$$s^T = p^T B + q^T D \tag{70}$$

where p is the price vector on consumption goods and q is the price vector on residuals, B the matrix of inputs in the various consumption activities, and D the matrix of the corresponding residuals generated.

The important price concept for consumer behavior is obviously the imputed price vector s on consumption activities. Different price vectors p and q are equivalent to the consumer as long as the imputed price vector s is the same. It therefore follows that the environmental management agency may, instead of levying effluent charges, try to tax the consumption goods and services so as to leave the imputed prices on consumption activities equal to what they would have been with optimal effluent charges.

Let t be a vector of taxes on consumer goods and services. If these taxes are going to be equivalent to the vector of effluent charges, the following equation must be satisfied

$$(p + t)^T B = p^T B + q^T D \tag{71}$$

If p and q are given, this is a system of equations in $t_1, \cdots, t_n$, and if it has a solution, there exists at least one system of taxes that is equivalent to the system of effluent charges. The system can be written

$$B^T t = D^T q \tag{72}$$

$D^T q$ is a vector that gives the cost of waste disposal for each activity, and $B^T t$ is a vector that gives the tax collected for each activity.

In the usual case in consumption theory, B is a unit matrix, and the system has the solution $t = D^T q$. In the general case we cannot expect the existence of a solution, as the following example shows.

Take two beer-drinking activities. The input in each activity is a can filled with beer, while the output is (besides a certain intoxication from beer) an empty beer can and a temporary increase in the weight of the consumer. The empty beer can is disposed of in the trash can in the first activity, and in the second, by throwing it away at a beach. The matrices B and D may look like this

$$B = \begin{bmatrix} 1 & 1 \end{bmatrix} \qquad \text{(beer and a beer can)}$$

$$D = \begin{bmatrix} .9 & .9 \\ .1 & 0 \\ 0 & .1 \end{bmatrix} \qquad \begin{array}{l} \text{(temporary increase in consumer weight)} \\ \text{(empty beer can in a trash can)} \\ \text{(empty beer can on a beach)} \end{array}$$

(Note the materials balance for both activities.) Assume that the residuals resulting from the beer do not impose any external costs on society, so that the corresponding effluent charge is zero.

Let p be the price on beer cans, q_1 the optimal effluent charge on empty beer cans discharged in trash cans, and q_2 the optimal effluent charge on empty beer cans on a beach. Assume that $q_2 > q_1$.

It is in general impossible to collect the effluent charge on empty beer cans thrown away on a beach, and so the effluent charge system is not feasible. And it is not possible to tax beer so that the optimal solution is achieved, because that would require that the following system of equations have a solution

$$t = q_1$$

$$t = q_2$$

But since $q_1 < q_2$, no solution exists.

This example can, however, give us a hint of how we can find a better method of imposing the external costs on the consumers. Tax the beer with 0.1 q_2 per pound beer and beer can, and refund the consumer with $q_1 - q_2$ per pound, for empty beer cans discharged in the trash can (or at some trash collection station). If the consumer throws away the empty beer can on a beach, he will not receive a refund, and so he is paying 0.1 q_2 per beer can discharged on a beach (or q_2 per pound of empty beer cans), and if he throws it into the trash he gets a refund of $q_1 - q_2$ per pound of empty beer cans, which implies that he makes a net payment of q_1 per pound of empty beer cans. This refund system makes it possible to implement the effluent charges without supervising what the consumer is doing at the beach.

This system of taxes and refunds can be generalized, and we will show that there always exists a system of taxes and refunds that is equivalent to optimal effluent charges. Mathematically, the existence of a system of taxes and refunds is the same as the existence of a solution to the following system of linear equations and inequalities.

$$(p + t)^T B + (q - r)^T D = p^T B + q^T D$$

$$r \geqq q \qquad\qquad (73)$$

$$t \geqq 0$$

Here t is interpreted as the vector of taxes on consumption goods and services and r is the vector of refunds for all residuals when discharged at certain collection stations. The condition $r \geqq q$ means that no net effluent charge is collected, but if $r_j > q_j$, a positive refund is given for that particular residual; if $r_j = q_j$, no refund is given.

We will prove the following:

Theorem: Given the materials balances and energy balances for each consumption activity, there exist a positive vector t and a vector r, such that $r \geqq q$, and such that t and q satisfy $B^T t - D^T r = 0$.

Proof: Note first that the materials balance and the energy balance for each activity imply that

$$\sum_{i=1}^{n} b_{ij} = \sum_{i=1}^{s} d_{ij} \qquad\qquad (74)$$

because the sum of those b_{ij} that correspond to materials input must be equal to the sum of those d_{ij} that correspond to materials residuals, and the sum of the rest of b_{ij} is therefore the total energy input in the activity and equal to the rest of the d_{ij} corresponding to energy residuals.

We will now prove that

$$B^T t - D^T r = 0 \qquad\qquad (75)$$

has a solution $(t, r) > (0, 0)$.

According to Stiemke's theorem [18], a necessary and sufficient condition for the existence of such a solution is that

$$\begin{bmatrix} B \\ -D \end{bmatrix} u \geq 0 \qquad\qquad (76)$$

has no solution.

Assume that there is a $\bar{u}$ such that

$$\begin{bmatrix} B\bar{u} \\ -D\bar{u} \end{bmatrix} \geq 0$$

This is equivalent to

$$\sum_{j=1}^{Q} b_{ij}\bar{u}_j \geqq 0 \qquad i = 1, \cdots, n$$

$$-\sum_{j=1}^{Q} d_{ij}\bar{u}_j \geqq 0 \qquad i = 1, \cdots, s$$

with at least one strict inequality.

Summing these inequalities over i and taking (74) into account yields

$$0 < \sum_{j=1}^{n}\sum_{j=1}^{Q} b_{ij}\bar{u}_j = \sum_{j=1}^{Q} \bar{u}_j \sum_{i=1}^{n} b_{ij} = \sum_{j=1}^{Q} \bar{u}_j \sum_{i=1}^{s} d_{ij}$$

$$= \sum_{i=1}^{s}\sum_{j=1}^{Q} d_{ij}\bar{u}_j \leq 0$$

which is a contradiction. Thus (76) has no solution, and there exists a pair $(t, r) > (0, 0)$ which is a solution to (75).

The set of solutions to (75) is a linear manifold, and we can therefore multiply (t, r) with a positive number θ, so that $\theta r \geqq q$, and $(\theta t, \theta r)$ is a solution to (75). If we now take θt, and θr, as t and r, the theorem is proved.

This theorem shows that there always exist taxes on the consumption goods and services, and refunds on residuals discharged at certain places which are equivalent to effluent charges. But unfortunately, the theorem does not solve all problems. For example, one main input in consumption processes is oxygen from the atmosphere used for breathing. If this input is neglected, the materials balance would not be valid, and the theorem would be false. The theorem gives, however, a positive tax on all inputs, which thus would imply that breathing should be taxed, a result that is not satisfactory. Fortunately, the demand for oxygen for breathing is completely inelastic, so the tax on breathing can be replaced by an income tax.

The same objection that was raised against effluent charges can also be raised against a refund system. Sometimes it is impossible to collect the residuals and discharge them at collection stations. A refund for gaseous emissions from fuels for heating is obviously impractical. There are, however, more ways in which the effluent charge system can be modified so as to stand these objections. Instead of relying only on taxes on consumption goods and services, and refunds for residuals, it is possible to increase the number of policy parameters by, for example, taxing certain consumption activities, and by using effluent charges on those residuals for which collection costs are small.

Let residuals $j = 1, \cdots, k$ be those residuals for which effluent charges can be collected, let residuals $j = k + 1, \cdots, h$ be those residuals for which refunds can be given, and let residuals $j = h + 1, \cdots, s$ be those residuals for which neither a charge can be collected, nor a refund given. Furthermore, let $i = 1, \cdots, f$ be those consumption activities that can be taxed, and let $i = f + 1, \cdots, Q$ be those activities that cannot be taxed. As before, let t be the vector of taxes on consumption goods and services. Let r be the vector of refunds, and partition r corresponding to the classification of residuals so that

$$r = \begin{bmatrix} r^1 \\ r^2 \\ r^3 \end{bmatrix} \tag{77}$$

Let N be the vector of taxes on the consumption activities. Partition N into

$$\begin{bmatrix} N^1 \\ N^2 \end{bmatrix}$$

so that N^1 corresponds to those activities that can be taxed. It follows that $N^2 = 0$. Then the existence of taxes, effluent charges, and refunds is equivalent to the existence of a solution to

$$p^T B + q^T D = (p + t)^T B + (q - r)^T D + N^T \tag{78}$$

$$r^1 = 0 \tag{79}$$

$$r^2 \geqq q^2 \tag{80}$$

$$r^3 = q^3 \tag{81}$$

$$N^2 = 0 \tag{82}$$

where the vector q has been partitioned similarly to the vector r, and N is the vector of taxes on all activities, and N^2 thus is the vector of taxes on those activities that cannot be taxed. Equation (78) is the condition that the imputed price vector s on consumption activities is the same in a system with effluent charges as in a system with taxes and refunds. Equation (79) says that for residuals $1, \cdots, k$, it is not necessary to give a refund because effluent charges can be collected. Equation (80) states that for residuals $k + 1, \cdots, h$, a positive net refund may be given, while (81) states that it is impossible either to collect charges or to give a refund for residuals $n + 1, \cdots, s$. Equation (82) finally states that it is impossible to collect taxes on activities $f + 1, \cdots, Q$. If we partition the matrices B and D in the same fashion, the system can be written

$$B^{1T} t - D^{21T} r^2 + N^1 = D^{31T} q^3$$
$$B^{2T} t - D^{22T} r^2 = D^{32T} q^3$$
$$r^2 \geqq q^2$$

This system may or may not have a solution, depending on the coefficients. If, however, q^3 is zero, so that those residuals for which it is impossible to either collect charges or give refunds can be neglected, an argument similar to that used above shows that the system will have a solution. We will not, however, go into that, because in general q^3 will not be zero. If D^{32} is the zero matrix, the system will also have a solution. This condition means that those activities that cannot be taxed generate residuals for which effluent charges can be collected, and refunds can be given. If the system has a solution, it is possible to modify the effluent

charge scheme to take care of any objections that are based upon pro-
hibitive high collection costs.

7. A DYNAMIC LEARNING-BY-DOING PROCESS, WHEN THERE IS ONLY ONE CONSUMER

This section discusses a very simple model of how the environmental
management agency may act in order to approach the optimum in an
economy where there is only one consumer, one environmental service,
and one kind of residual. These assumptions make it possible to discuss
in a very simple manner a process of learning by doing that will be extended to more complicated economies in the next sections. The main
problem is that the agency is assumed to have limited information on the
consumer's preferences for environmental quality, and is therefore in-
capable of calculating directly the optimum price on residuals. However,
by successively adjusting this price in a systematic way, the agency will
accumulate enough information about the response to the demand price
for different supplies of environmental quality to approximate the optimum price on residuals. A method of systematic variation in the supply
of environmental services will be proposed, and it will be shown how new
information on consumer preferences will be generated, and how this
information can be utilized.

The process discussed in this section and the next will probably not
be the most efficient the agency can apply, and we do not claim that it is
an efficient process with respect to speed of convergence, or economizing
with scarce information. The point is simply to show the existence of at
least one process that can be used in a situation where the agency has
limited information on consumer preferences.

Some authors have claimed that without complete knowledge on utility functions of individuals it is impossible to find the optimum, except
in an abstract sense. This is of course true if the optimum is defined by
the maximum of a Bergson welfare function, which depends on the preferences of individuals. But if the optimum is defined by a much more
realistic criterion, it will be shown in the next section that it is possible
to reach the optimum by a learning-by-doing process, or a refined trial-
and-error process.

In order to fix our ideas, let there be one consumer in the economy
with expenditure function $m = m(s, Y, \bar{u})$. Since we have assumed that
there is only one environmental service, Y is one dimensional. Recall
from chapter 4 that the demand price for environmental quality is defined by

$$\delta = -\frac{\partial m[s, Y, v(s, Y, I)]}{\partial Y}$$

and the compensated demand price by

$$\delta^* = -\frac{\partial m(s, Y, \bar{u})}{\partial Y}$$

where $v(s, Y, I)$ is the indirect utility function.

As was shown in chapter 4, section 4, property (vii), m is convex in Y, which implies that $-m$ is concave in Y, so that δ^* is a decreasing function of Y. The effect of an increase in Y on the demand price δ is somewhat more tricky. We have

$$\frac{d\delta}{dY} = -\frac{\partial^2 m}{\partial Y^2} - \frac{\partial^2 m}{\partial Y \partial \bar{u}} \frac{\partial v}{\partial Y} = -\frac{\partial^2 m}{\partial Y^2} + \frac{\partial \delta^*}{\partial \bar{u}} \frac{\partial v}{\partial Y}$$

The first term is positive because m is convex in Y. If Y is noninferior (see the discussion in section 9, chapter 4), the second term is also positive. We henceforth assume that Y is noninferior. Thus, both the demand price and the compensated demand price for Y are decreasing functions of Y.

Next, let us assume a strict partial equilibrium analysis, so that the price vector s is constant throughout this and the next sections. We can now write the demand price and the compensated demand price as functions of Y and I, and Y and $\bar{u}$, respectively.

$$\delta = \delta(Y, I) \qquad \text{and} \qquad \delta^* = \delta^*(Y, \bar{u})$$

Owing to our assumptions, δ is decreasing in Y, and increasing in I, and δ^* is decreasing in Y, and increasing in $\bar{u}$. If, as we will assume, both these functions are differentiable, we thus have

$$\frac{\partial \delta(Y, I)}{\partial Y} < 0 \qquad \text{and}$$

$$\frac{\partial \delta(Y, I)}{\partial I} > 0$$

$$\frac{\partial \delta^*(Y, \bar{u})}{\partial Y} < 0 \qquad \text{and}$$

$$\frac{\partial \delta^*(Y, \bar{u})}{\partial \bar{u}} > 0$$

Next, let us turn to the supply side for environmental quality. As in chapter 2, we assume an environmental interaction function $Y = Y_o - F(z)$. Since we already assumed that there is only one kind of residual, z is one dimensional. In view of the discussion of synergistic effects in section 10, chapter 2, we assume that F is convex in z, so that $-F$ is an increasing concave function of z.

In order to make the assumption of constant price vector s reasonable, we have to assume that the flow of residuals originates in the production sector, and only a limited number of firms generate residuals. Otherwise, if z is generated by consumers also, changes in the effluent charge q on the residual will cause changes in the vector s (remember that $s^T = p^T B + q^T D$), or if a large number of firms are generating z, the supply of goods produced by these firms will change when q changes, and so will the price vector p.

The constancy of the price vector p enables us to introduce the concept of marginal cost for reducing residual generation in an unambiguous way. Let the set of firms generating residuals be denoted by K. Each firm has a production function

$$x^i \leqq f^i(S^i) \qquad i \in K$$

where S^i is the vector of input. Corresponding to the production of x^i is waste generation equal to

$$z^i \geqq g^i(S^i, T^i) \qquad i \in K$$

Some of the firms may produce the same commodity, but with different technology, so that f^i and g^i may vary among firms producing the same commodity (compare section 3). In this way substitution among different waste-generating technologies is taken into account.

The total flow of wastes is

$$\bar{z} = \sum_{i \in K} \bar{z}^i$$

and this is treated in a treatment plant, with the production function $z \geqq H(T^t, \bar{z})$.

Since the economy is completely competitive, except for the market failures induced by environmental qualities, the social value of the production of this group of firms is simply the value of the output minus the value of the input in production and waste treatment. We are thus led to study the following problem

$$\max \sum_{i \in K} p_i x^i - r^T \left\{ \sum_{i \in K} (S_t{}^i + T^i) + T^t \right\},$$

s.t. $x^i \leqq f^i(S^i)$

$$\tilde{z}^i \geqq g^i(S^i, T^i) \qquad i \in K$$

$$z \geqq H(T^t, \tilde{z})$$

$$z \leqq z^*$$

where p_i is the price on output from firm i, r the price vector for input, and z^* the maximum permissible discharge of wastes in the environment. If we make the usual concavity assumptions on the production functions, there are Lagrange multipliers associated with the maximum problem, and the multiplier q associated with the constraint on discharge of residuals in the environment is exactly the marginal social cost of reducing the discharge of residuals in the environment. This is a standard property of Lagrange multipliers; see, for example, Rockafellar, theorem 29.1 [19]. If the constraints are sufficiently "regular" we also know that the multipliers are unique. Another feature of the multipliers is their dependence on the constraints. In our simple problem it can easily be seen that the multiplier associated with the last constraint is a decreasing function of z^*.

The marginal social cost of reducing the flow of residuals is thus a nonincreasing function of the flow of residuals

$$q = q(z) \tag{83}$$

We assume that this function is differentiable. Note that the marginal cost given by $q(z)$ includes substitution of different production activities, increased waste treatment, and a reduction in the output, and that it shows the cheapest way of combining these methods for waste reduction.

We know from the general equilibrium analysis in chapter 2 that in optimum the following relations must hold:

$$\begin{cases} \delta F' = q \\ \quad q = q(z) \\ -\delta = \dfrac{\partial m[s,\ Y,\ v(s,\ Y,\ I)]}{\partial Y} \end{cases} \tag{84}$$

where q is the optimal fee on discharge of residuals in the environment. Let Δ satisfy $\Delta F'(z) = q(z)$. Then we can interpret Δ as the supply price for environmental services, in the sense that if the price on environmental quality is Δ, then the optimal flow of residuals is z. Another way of interpreting Δ is as the imputed value on environmental quality when residuals flow z is being discharged.

Given Δ (which is positive), we know that F' is nondecreasing, and $q(z)$ is decreasing, so if the equation

$$\Delta F'(z) = q(z) \tag{85}$$

has a solution, the solution is unique. The proof of existence of a general equilibrium in chapter 2 showed the existence of at least one solution to this equation, and so we know that for some $\Delta > 0$ there exists a unique solution. We can then write this solution as

$$z = h(\Delta) \tag{86}$$

It is clear from the properties of the functions $F(z)$ and $q(z)$ that $h(z)$ must be decreasing in Δ.

The environmental quality supplied will depend on Δ, by the formula

$$Y = Y_o - F[h(\Delta)] \equiv k(\Delta) \tag{87}$$

and as F is increasing in z, h decreasing in Δ, it follows that $k(\Delta)$ is increasing in Δ.

The revenue collected by the environmental management agency from the effluent charge q is equal to $qz = q(z)z = q[h(\Delta)]h(\Delta)$. The first factor in the last product is increasing in Δ, while the second factor is decreasing. To simplify the analysis without missing any essential points, let us assume that the supply function for residuals is unitary elastic in the relevant range, so that the revenue collected by the environmental management agency from the effluent charge does not vary with changes in the effluent charge. This assumption only simplifies some formulas, and it does not change any of the basic ingredients in the process to be discussed.

Let us summarize the basic functions that we now will use. First, we have the demand price function

$$\delta = \delta(Y, I) \tag{88}$$

giving the demand price for environmental quality for each level of supply. This function is unknown to the agency, but we assume it can observe its values whenever Y is the actual supply of environmental service.

When we discussed the possibilities of estimating the demand price for environmental services in chapter 5, we concluded that there were very few such possibilities, and that it was almost impossible to get enough information on consumer preferences in order to set "optimal" effluent charges. We therefore turned to the government's demand price for environmental quality. The preferences of the government may not be explicated in detail, however. It seems probable that the government can state its demand price for environmental quality (that is, how much the government is willing to offer in order to achieve a unit improvement in environmental quality) in any situation that is realized, but not for hypothetical situations. This means that the agency knows the value of the function $\delta(Y, I)$ for each (Y, I) that has been actually realized in the economy. If a method of revealing the preferences of the consumers has been invented, such that in any realized situation it is possible to get information on the total demand price for environmental quality, then we can interpret $\delta(Y, I)$ as giving the demand price of the consumer. The main point is that the demand price for environmental quality may only be revealed in realized situations.

Second, we have the supply function of environmental services, $Y = k(\Delta)$. It is assumed that the agency knows this function completely. Third, the income I of the consumer is equal to the revenue collected by the agency, and is assumed constant. Finally, the optimum is given by

$$\delta = \Delta \tag{89}$$

For convenience, let us introduce one more function, namely a function that relates the effluent charge q to the demand price Δ for environmental quality. This function φ is defined by

$$q = \varphi(\Delta) \equiv q[h(\Delta)] \tag{90}$$

We can now start discussing different dynamic adjustment paths the agency can apply. The first is simply the following. At time 0, the agency can observe the demand price δ_0 for Y, and calculate the corresponding effluent charge $q_1 = \varphi(\delta_0)$. This effluent charge changes the discharge of residuals to $z_1 = h(\delta_0)$, and the supply of environmental quality to $Y_1 = k(\delta_0)$. After the new allocation has been established, the agency can observe a new demand price, δ_1, calculate a new effluent charge $q_2 = \varphi(\delta_1)$, and so on. The trouble with this process is that there is no guarantee that it will converge. In fact, the process is almost identical to the cobweb pattern discussed in standard textbooks in price theory. It is useful to study the process in a diagram, because this diagram will yield the motivation for the next process we will construct.

In figure 13, the demand price for environmental quality is measured along the vertical axis, and the supply of environmental quality along the horizontal axis. The two curves $\delta(Y)$ and $k(\delta)$ are drawn. Optimum is characterized by the intersection of these curves. The curve $\delta(Y)$ will be called the demand curve, and the curve $k(\delta)$ the supply curve

Assume that the agency initially observes δ_0, and sets $q_0 = \varphi(\delta_0)$. The supply of environmental services will now increase to Y_1. In this new situation, the demand price will have fallen, and the agency will observe δ_1. The supply of environmental quality will, after the charge has been lowered to $q_1 = \varphi(\delta_1)$, decrease to Y_2, and after that fall, the agency can observe δ_2, which in this diagram is higher than δ_0. The process will therefore not converge to the optimum values $\bar{Y}$ and $\bar{\delta}$. This depends of course on how the curves are drawn; with other slopes the process may converge very rapidly to the optimum.

It is clear from figure 13 that the process will show the cobweb pattern, with oscillating prices. One of the main textbook arguments against the cobweb pattern as a realistic description of adjustments in markets is that it neglects completely the fact that producers are capable of learning from past mistakes. As soon as producers know that adjusting supply to

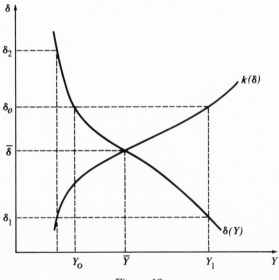

Figure 13

the ruling prices will create excess supply, and a fall in prices, they will adjust to this knowledge and voluntarily restrict output. But the environmental management agency will in general have a memory too, and may therefore be capable of learning something from past mistakes. We will now show that if this learning-adjustment process is accounted for (although in an incomplete way), the process will in fact converge to optimum.

Assume that the initial situation is one with uncontrolled waste discharge in the environment. This corresponds to a zero effluent charge. If the agency observes the demand price for environmental quality in this situation, it can be certain that this demand price is much higher than in optimum. (This follows from the assumption that the preferences are quasi-concave in both consumption of private goods and environmental services, so that the demand curve is falling.)

Although the agency does not know the optimal demand price, it knows that it is lower than the observed price. It can therefore calculate an effluent charge in the first step with this knowledge in mind, meaning that q_1 is set smaller than $\varphi(\delta_0)$. When the waste dischargers have adjusted their discharges to this price, the agency will observe an improved environmental quality, and a lower demand price for environmental services. In this first step, the agency thus knows two points on the curve relating demand price to environmental quality. By using these two points, the agency can obtain a linear approximation of the function $\delta(Y)$. As we have assumed that the agency has complete information on the supply function $Y = k(\delta)$, it can therefore calculate the intersection between the supply curve and the linear approximation, and in that way obtain the effluent charge for the next step. After that next step, the agency can again observe the demand price and approximate the demand curve with a second-degree polynomial (it now has three observations), calculate the intersection with the supply curve, and obtain the new effluent charge. Continuing in this way, using the knowledge generated previously, it seems intuitively clear that the process will converge to optimum.

Instead of proving this conjecture, we will satisfy ourselves with proving the convergence of a process in which the agency does not utilize all the information generated, but only the information from the last two observations. The process works in the following way. In step k, the agency knows the two points A and B on the demand curve (in fact it knows $k + 1$ points, but it only utilizes A and B). The agency now makes a linear approximation of the demand curve, with the requirement that the approximation must go through the two points. This ap-

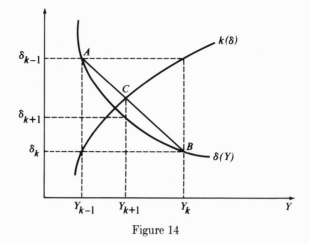

Figure 14

proximation is represented by the line segment AB in figure 14. The equation for this approximation is

$$\delta - \delta_k = \frac{\delta_k - \delta_{k-1}}{Y_k - Y_{k-1}} (Y - Y_k)$$

Here δ_k and δ_{k-1} are the observed demand prices for environmental quality, corresponding to the supplies Y_k and Y_{k-1}, respectively, or

$$\delta_k = \delta(Y_k) \qquad \delta_{k-1} = \delta(Y_{k-1})$$

Then the agency can calculate the intersection between this linear approximation and the known supply curve $Y = k(\delta)$. This intersection is denoted by C in the diagram, and is obtained by solving the equation. Here $\psi(Y)$ denotes the inverse of the supply function $k(\delta)$; due to our assumption that $k(\delta)$ is increasing, there exists an inverse

$$\psi(Y_{k+1}) - \delta(Y_k) = \frac{\delta(Y_k) - \delta(Y_{k-1})}{Y_k - Y_{k-1}} (Y_{k+1} - Y_k)$$

This is a second-order difference equation that describes the process completely. To study the convergence of the process, we only have to study the stability of the solutions to this equation.

Let us make the transformation of variables $Y = x + \bar{Y}$, where $(\bar{Y}, \bar{\delta})$ indicates the intersection of the curves, and the corresponding transformations of the supply and demand functions:

$$a(x) = \delta(x + \bar{Y})$$
$$b(x) = \psi(x + \bar{Y})$$

Then the difference equation can be written

$$b(x_{k+1}) - a(x_k) = \frac{a(x_k) - a(x_{k-1})}{x_k - x_{k-1}} (x_{k+1} - x_k)$$

The equation has the singular solution $x_k = 0$, which corresponds to the optimal allocation. We will therefore study the solutions in a neighborhood of zero.

The equation can now be rewritten into

$$\frac{b(x_{k-1}) - a(x_{k-1})}{x_{k-1}} \frac{x_{k-1}}{x_k - x_{k-1}} = \frac{a(x_{k-1}) - a(x_{k-2})}{x_{k-1} - x_{k-2}} - \frac{b(x_k) - b(x_{k-1})}{x_k - x_{k-1}}$$

and if x_k/x_{k-1} is solved for, we finally obtain [using the fact that $a(0) = b(0)$]

$$\frac{x_k}{x_{k-1}} = 1 + \frac{\dfrac{b(x_{k-1}) - b(0)}{x_{k-1}} - \dfrac{a(x_{k-1}) - a(0)}{x_{k-1}}}{\dfrac{a(x_{k-1}) - a(x_{k-2})}{x_{k-1} - x_{k-2}} - \dfrac{b(x_k) - b(x_{k-1})}{x_k - x_{k-1}}}$$

The terms in the nominator, and the denominator in the fraction in the right-hand side, are difference quotients of the functions $a(x)$ and $b(x)$, respectively. By using the mean value theorem in calculus, we can find numbers θ_1, θ_2, θ_3, θ_4, such that

$$0 \leq \theta_1 \leq x_{k-1}, \text{ or } x_{k-1} \leq \theta_2 \leq 0$$

$$0 \leq \theta_2 \leq x_{k-1}, \text{ or } x_{k-1} \leq \theta_2 \leq 0$$

$$x_{k-2} \leq \theta_3 \leq x_{k-1}, \text{ or } x_{k-1} \leq \theta_3 \leq x_{k-2}$$

$$x_{k-1} \leq \theta_4 \leq x_k, \text{ or } x_k \leq \theta_4 \leq x_{k-1}$$

and such that

$$\frac{x_k}{x_{k-1}} = 1 + \frac{b'(\theta_1) - a'(\theta_2)}{a'(\theta_3) - b'(\theta_4)}$$

We know that $a(x)$ is decreasing, and that $b(x)$ is increasing, and so $a'(x) < 0$, and $b'(x) > 0$, which implies that $x_k/x_{k-1} < 1$. Moreover, if the functions $a(x)$ and $b(x)$ have continuous derivatives, there exists some $N > 0$, such that if $|x_k| < N$, $|x_{k-1}| < N$, and $|x_{k-2}| < N$,

$$\frac{b'(\theta_1) - a'(\theta_2)}{a'(\theta_3) - b'(\theta_4)} > -2$$

and thus that

$$\left| \frac{x_k}{x_{k-1}} \right| < 1$$

for sufficiently small $|x_k|$, $|x_{k-1}|$, $|x_{k-2}|$. But this last inequality means that the process converges to zero, that is, to the optimum allocation. Local stability therefore exists. If the functions $a(x)$, $b(x)$ are such that

$$\sup_{\theta_1,\ \theta_2,\ \theta_3,\ \theta_4} \frac{b'(\theta_1) - a'(\theta_2)}{a'(\theta_3) - b'(\theta_4)} > -2$$

then global stability is ensured. This is, however, an overly strong condition.

We have thus seen that it is possible to construct dynamic behavior on the part of the environmental management agency in such a way that the agency ultimately will approach the optimal allocation, although it does not know the optimal allocation a priori. This whole construction presupposes, however, that the costs associated with the dynamic adjustments can be neglected. If there are investments in durable capital owing to the effluent charge in the first step, and if this charge was set much higher than the optimal charge, the economy will find itself for a long period of time with too much capital in waste treatment, "clean" production processes, etc., in comparison with the optimal amount. Therefore, the initial guess on the effluent charge by the environmental management agency must be a good guess; if not, the economy is going to waste too many resources during the adjustment period.

It is important to note that such waste of resources during periods in which the markets are out of equilibrium is always connected with a decentralized system. In an ordinary market for a private good, the same phenomenon will probably appear with high cost to the society, and it may be that the process outlined here will converge much more rapidly to an equilibrium than the convergence of a price due to market forces. In competitive markets for private goods there are no institutions which pool the information, learn from earlier market behavior, and use this information to force the firms to behave in a rational way.

Finally, let us note that the process outlined can easily be extended to the case when the environmental management agency has very limited information on the supply curve. It can also determine the supply curve simultaneously with the demand curve by a similar process.

8. DIGRESSION ON A TRIAL-AND-ERROR PROCESS

Let us discuss such an extension which may be very important from a practical point of view. Assume that the objective of environmental policy is formulated as an ambient standard that must be met. (We neglect how this standard is set.) Assume also that the agency has no information on the response of waste dischargers to effluent charges. If the agency sets a charge, then it will not know a priori the resulting flow of residuals and consequently it will not know the resulting environmental quality. But after some time, during which the agents have adjusted their waste disposal to the effluent charge, the agency can observe the effect of the charge on environmental quality. It is now quite clear that the process discussed above may be changed to incorporate this kind of ignorance.

As before, let $Y_{t+1} = k(\delta_t)$ be the supply function for environmental services, and let $\bar{Y}$ be the environmental or ambient standard. The process can then be formalized in the following manner. At step t, when the agency has observed $[\delta_{t-2}, k(\delta_{t-2})]$, $[\delta_{t-1}, k(\delta_{t-1})]$, it can approximate the supply function by the linear expression

$$Y - k(\delta_{t-1}) = \frac{k(\delta_{t-1}) - k(\delta_{t-2})}{\delta_{t-1} - \delta_{t-2}} (\delta - \delta_{t-1})$$

The effluent charge that it should apply at step t is then calculated from this expression by setting $Y = \bar{Y}$, or from

$$\bar{Y} - k(\delta_{t-1}) = \frac{k(\delta_{t-1}) - k(\delta_{t-2})}{\delta_{t-1} - \delta_{t-2}} (\delta_t - \delta_{t-1})$$

Make now the change of variables: $\delta = \alpha + \bar{\delta}$ where $\bar{\delta}$ denotes the intersection between $Y = \bar{Y}$ and $Y = k(\delta)$, and $k(\delta) = k(\alpha + \bar{\delta}) = b(\alpha)$. The equation determining δ_t can now be written

$$\frac{\alpha_t}{\alpha_{t-1}} = 1 - \frac{\dfrac{b(\alpha_{t-1}) - b(0)}{\alpha_{t-1}}}{\dfrac{b(\alpha_{t-1}) - b(\alpha_{t-2})}{\alpha_{t-1} - \alpha_{t-2}}}$$

because $\bar{Y} = b(0)$.

As b is increasing, it follows that the right-hand side is less than $+1$. Moreover, if

$$\sup_{\theta_1,\, \theta_2} \frac{b'(\theta_1)}{b'(\theta_2)} < 2, \text{ it follows that } \left| \frac{\alpha_t}{\alpha_{t-1}} \right| < 1$$

and the process converges.

Numerical examples show that the convergence is very fast, and with a good initial guess on the effluent charge, only a few iterations should be needed before a very close approximation of the optimal effluent charge is obtained.

9. DIGRESSION ON INCOME DISTRIBUTION

We will now continue the discussion from section 7. Here we assume that it is the individual preferences that count. The total demand price for environmental quality is thus the sum of the individual demand prices.

Assume there are many consumers in the economy, each with an expenditure function $m^h(s,\, Y,\, \bar{u}^h)$. The aggregate expenditure function is

$$m(s,\, Y,\, \bar{u}^1,\, \bar{u}^2,\, \cdots,\, \bar{u}^H) = \sum_{h=1}^{H} m^h(s,\, Y,\, \bar{u}^h)$$

We maintain from section 7 the assumption that the agency is able to observe $\delta = -\partial m/\partial Y$ for each situation actually realized, but not for hypothetical situations.

It is now clear that if the income distribution is a matter of indifference, the same adjustment process as was discussed in section 7 can be applied. But if the income distribution belongs to the objective of the agency, the problem becomes more difficult. Even if we maintain the assumption of a unitary elastic supply curve for environmental quality, there is the problem of distributing the revenues collected. If in the initial step the revenues are distributed in some way among consumers, the demand price for environmental quality observed in the next step will depend on this distribution. The revelation of this new demand price may, however, affect the desired distribution of the revenues, because the change in environmental quality also means a change in the distribution of the total social income, including the value of environmental services. If such an interaction between the supply of environmental services, the demand price for environmental quality, and the income distribution is recognized, it is obvious that the agency is faced with an extremely difficult problem. A simple general equilibrium model will be constructed to explore this problem.

We assume that there are two private goods, labor and a produced commodity. Moreover, we assume that labor is in inelastic supply. In the production of the private good, residuals are generated which are discharged into the environment, and thereby deteriorate its quality. There are only two consumers, who both supply labor and consume the produced good, and the environmental services. The production function for the produced good is

$$x = f(L') \tag{91}$$

and is assumed to be differentiable, with derivatives $f' > 0, f'' < 0$. L' is the direct input of labor in production. Jointly with x is a residual z produced according to the production function

$$z = g(L'', L') \tag{92}$$

where L'' is the input of labor to control and treatment of wastes. g is assumed to be differentiable, with derivatives $g_1' < 0$, $g_2' > 0$, and g is also assumed to be concave.

Let the price on the produced good x be p, let the effluent charge be q, and let the wage rate be w. Then the profit for the producer is

$$\pi = pf(L') - qg(L'', L') - w(L' + L'') \tag{93}$$

and profit maximization yields the marginal conditions

$$pf' - qg'_2 - w = 0 \tag{94}$$

$$-qg'_1 - w = 0 \tag{95}$$

The two consumers each supply a fixed amount of labor L_1 and L_2. The total supply of labor is thus

$$L = L_1 + L_2 \tag{96}$$

Let the expenditure functions for the two consumers be

$$m^h(p, Y, \bar{u}^h) \qquad h = 1, 2$$

It is assumed that no residuals are generated in consumption.

If $v^h(p, Y, I^h)$, $h = 1, 2$, are the indirect utility functions, the demand for the produced good is given by

$$x = \frac{\partial m^1[p, Y, v^1(p, Y, I^1)]}{\partial p} + \frac{\partial m^2[p, Y, v^2(p, Y, I^2)]}{\partial p} \tag{97}$$

I^1 and I^2 are the lump sum incomes of the two consumers which consist of wage earnings, wL_1 and wL_2, respectively; shares in the profit of the producer, α_1 and α_2, respectively, where $\alpha_1 \geqq 0$, $\alpha_2 \geqq 0$, $\alpha_1 + \alpha_2 = 1$; and shares in the revenues collected by the environmental management agency, qz.

Assume for the moment that the distribution of the revenues of the agency is given by proportional shares $\theta_1 \geqq 0$, $\theta_2 \geqq 0$, $\theta_1 + \theta_2 = 1$. Then we have

$$I^h = wL_h + \alpha_h \pi + \theta_h qz \qquad h = 1, 2 \tag{98}$$

The model now constructed determines the output x, the allocation of the input to production and waste control, the income distribution, and the generation of wastes. If we add the environmental interaction function

$$Y = Y_o - F(z) \tag{99}$$

environmental quality is also determined.

Finally, the aggregate demand price for environmental quality is given by

$$\delta = -\frac{\partial m^1[p, Y, v^1(p, Y, I^1)]}{\partial Y} - \frac{\partial m^2[p, Y, v^2(p, Y, I^2)]}{\partial Y} \tag{100}$$

If the condition

$$\delta F'(z) = q \tag{101}$$

and the assumption that the shares α_h and θ_h give the desired income distribution are added, an optimum is completely characterized.

What is the social marginal cost of supplying a given level of environmental services? It is the amount the consumers must receive as compensation for the decrease in the consumption of the private good that is associated with the necessary decrease in waste discharge. It is thus clear that the social marginal cost for environmental quality will depend on the income distribution, and since the income distribution depends on the method used for controlling the supply of environmental services, it follows that *the social marginal cost for environmental quality depends on the method that is used for achieving the environmental quality.*

The social marginal benefit from environmental quality is defined to be the marginal willingness to pay for environmental quality, and this marginal willingness to pay depends on the income distribution; it follows that *the social marginal benefit from environmental quality depends on the method that is used for achieving environmental quality.*

By using the model, these results can be seen more explicitly. Given that environmental quality is controlled by effluent charges, and that the revenue collected from these charges is distributed in some fixed fashion θ_1 and θ_2, the marginal social cost of waste control can be defined as q^*, where q^* satisfies

$$
\left.
\begin{aligned}
&x = f(L') \\[4pt]
&z = g(L'', L') \\[4pt]
&\pi = pf(L') - q^*g(L'', L') - w(L' + L'') \\[4pt]
&pf' - q^*g_2 - w = 0 \\
&-q^*g_1 - w = 0 \\[4pt]
&L_1 + L_2 = L' + L'' \\[4pt]
&x = \frac{\partial m^1[p, Y, v^1(p, Y, I^1)]}{\partial p} + \frac{\partial m^2[p, Y, v^2(p, Y, I^2)]}{\partial p} \\[4pt]
&I^h = wL_h + \alpha_h\pi + \theta_h q^*z; \; h = 1, 2 \\[4pt]
&\bar{Y} = Y_o - F(z)
\end{aligned}
\right\}
\tag{102}
$$

As only the relative prices are determined by this system, we can choose labor as the numeraire, and put $w = 1$.

These are eleven equations in ten unknowns, but one equation is superfluous, because we have identically $px \equiv I^1 + I^2$. This system yields q^* as a function of Y, or the marginal cost function for waste control. It is obvious that q also will depend on the shares θ_1 and θ_2. If it happens that $\theta_h = \alpha_h$, that is, the revenue collected by the effluent charges is distributed exactly as the profit is distributed, the model can be interpreted as giving the marginal cost of environmental quality when effluent standards are used instead of effluent charges, because the only difference between these two approaches is in the income distribution.

The marginal cost of environmental quality is given by $\delta^* = q^*/F'(z)$ where z is determined from $\bar{Y} = Y_o - F(z)$. It is thus clear that δ^* will be a function of $\bar{Y}$, and all the parameters in the model, and in particular θ_1 and θ_2. Let us therefore write

$$
\delta^* = \delta^*(Y, \theta_1) \text{ (as } \theta_1 + \theta_2 = 1, \text{ only } \theta_1 \text{ appears as an argument)} \quad (103)
$$

The marginal benefit from environmental quality is

$$\delta = \frac{\partial m^1[p,\ Y,\ v^1(p,\ Y,\ I^1)]}{\partial Y} + \frac{\partial m^2[p,\ Y,\ v^2(p,\ Y,\ I^2)]}{\partial Y} \qquad (104)$$

where p, I^1, and I^2 are determined from (102). It is obvious that δ too will be a function of Y, and all the parameters in the model, and in particular θ_1 and θ_2.

$$\delta = \delta(Y,\ \theta_1) \qquad (105)$$

Optimum is given by

$$\delta^* = \delta \qquad (106)$$

if the shares θ_1 and θ_2 correspond to the agency's values on income distribution.

We have now reduced the model to the same model that was discussed in section 7. If it is possible for the environmental management agency to observe the values of the function $\delta(Y,\ \theta_1)$ for each realized situation, it is possible to use the same adjustment behavior as was discussed in the previous section. Given the shares θ_1 and θ_2, the dynamic path will converge to a state in which (106) is satisfied.

If the agency is dissatisfied with the income distribution in that equilibrium, it can start a new adjustment process by changing the shares. Because the agency does not have information on the individual expenditure functions but only on the aggregate expenditure function, it will not in general know how much the shares should change in order to reach the optimum directly. But if the agency holds the view that the first equilibrium income should be transferred from individual 1 to individual 2, it can do this by increasing individual 2's share. This will in general shift both the supply and the demand curve for environmental quality, but by using the same adjustment process as before, a new equilibrium will be reached [20].

The important conclusion of all this is that there is at least a *logical possibility* of achieving an equilibrium such that allocation is Pareto optimal and such that the income distribution is considered satisfactory, even if the environmental management agency has limited information on preferences for public goods.

NOTES

1. Paul A. Samuelson, "Aspects of Public Expenditure Theories," *Review of Economics and Statistics*, vol. 40, no. 4, 332–338 (1958).

2. In Sweden, the *Miljövårdslag* requires that each new investment that in some way will affect the environment must be licensed either by the *Koncessionsnämnd* (a court) or by the environmental management agency. In order to get such a license, the investor must prove that he has taken all such measures that are technically feasible and economically possible in order to prevent environmental damages. There is, however, a change under way toward the use of effluent charges.

3. According to the manager of a Swedish pulp mill, the actual discharge of waterborne residuals is about four times larger than the discharge would have been if the plant had been properly managed from the point of view of pollution.

4. According to some experts, there now exist cheap ways of monitoring most of the waste flows from production processes. There may be some difficulties with old plants with many stacks and sewers, however.

5. Recall from chapter 2 that Y is a vector of environmental qualities that are spatially distributed, and that z is a vector of residuals discharges that also are spatially distributed. The first component in z may therefore be emission of SO_2 at a specific point, while the second component is the emission of SO_2 at another point.

6. Compare the discussion in section 8 of chapter 5 on collective preferences.

7. In these sections effluent charges will be compared with effluent standards, and one result is that the income distribution will in general differ between these two approaches. As the demand prices for environmental quality depend on the distribution of wealth, the optimal supply of environmental services will presumably differ between the two approaches, and if the environmental standards are set as the optimal supply of environmental services, the analysis will not be consistent. We neglect this objection, however. In a later section, the crucial influence of wealth distribution will be studied.

8. This objection against the use of effluent charges has been raised by the Swedish Petrol Institute in discussions on the use of effluent charges to limit the sulfur dioxide emissions in Sweden. The most important method of obtaining a large fall in these emissions is to desulfurize the oil in refineries, and once the refineries have the capacity to do that, they can supply low sulfur oil at constant cost. This means that the total benefit function for Sweden will be linear for a large interval.

9. In view of the observation reported in note 3 it seems that piecewise linear benefit functions are hardly realistic, at least not in pulp mills.

10. Bert Bolin et al., *Air Pollution Across National Boundaries. The Impact on the Environment of Sulfur in Air and Precipitation* (Allmänna förlaget, Stockholm, 1971).

11. A more general analysis can be found in Allen V. Kneese and Karl-Göran Mäler, "Bribes and Charges in Pollution Control: An Aspect of the Coase Controversy," *Natural Resources Journal*, 1973 Symposium Issue (in press).

12. For a mathematical definition of nonatomic measure spaces see Paul R. Halmos, *Measure Theory* (Van Nostrand, New York, 1965).

13. See sections 8 and 11, chapter 4 in this work.

14. These conditions are simply the Euler equations to the variational problem (18). The Euler equations are described in any textbook on calculus of variations. See, for example, chapter 2 in Magnus R. Hestenes, *Calculus of Variations and Optimal Control Theory* (Wiley, New York, 1966).

15. Our earlier assumptions on the production functions imply that f^h, $h \in [0, b]$, are concave on subsets of the form $\{S^h | S^h \geq \bar{S}^h\}$ and that g^h, $h \in |0, b|$ are concave on subsets of the form $\{(S^h, T^h) | S^h \geq \bar{S}^h, \bar{T}^h \geq T^h\}$. As maximum profits will be negative outside these sets, it is no loss in generality to restrict the discussion to these sets and assume f^h and g^h to be concave. This implies that $TC^h(x^h, q)$ is convex in x^h and $C^h(x^h, z^h)$ convex in x^h and z^h on some interval $\bar{x}^h \leq x^h < \infty$, $0 \leq z^h \leq \bar{z}^h$.

16. This is an information requirement that seems to be extreme, and due to the nature of the example. But a closer look at the problems of setting the correct effluent standards reveals that the standards must apply not only to the amounts the present firms are permitted to discharge, but also to the question of which firms should be allowed to start a production activity. The ultimate consequence of the effluent standards approach would therefore be a situation where entries to and exits from an industry and the choices of localization are decided centrally.

17. The relevant form of the central limit theorem is given by William Feller in *An Introduction to Probability Theory and Its Applications* (Wiley, New York, 1966), vol. 2, theorem 3, section 8.4. In loose terms, this theorem states that if e^h, $h = 1, 2, \ldots$, are statistically independent with zero expectations, and variances σ_h^2, and if these variances are bounded (bounded in a special sense), the random variable

$$\sum_{n=1}^{K} e^h \; \Big/ \; \sum_{n=1}^{K} \sigma_h^2$$

tends to be normally distributed with zero expectation and unit variance, when K increases.

18. See theorem 3.7 in Hukukane Nikaido, *Convex Structures and Economic Theory* (Academic Press, New York, 1968).

19. Tyrrell R. Rockafellar, *Convex Analysis* (Princeton Univ. Press, Princeton, N.J., 1970).

20. Here an alternative process will be briefly sketched. The supply side is assumed to be known, that is, the following functions are known

$$Y = Y(\theta, \delta)$$

$$p = p(\theta, \delta)$$

$$q = q(\theta, \delta)$$

$$I^h = I^h(\theta, \delta), \, n = 1, 2$$

The demand price for environmental services δ is a function of θ^1, and Y. With three observations, this unknown function may be approximated with a plane L

$$L: [\delta, \theta, Y] \, E_t^{-1} \begin{bmatrix} 1 \\ 1 \\ 1 \end{bmatrix} + 1 = 0,$$

where

$$E_t = \begin{bmatrix} \delta_{t-1} & \theta_{t-1} & Y_{t-1} \\ \delta_{t-2} & \theta_{t-2} & Y_{t-2} \\ \delta_{t-3} & \theta_{t-3} & Y_{t-3} \end{bmatrix}$$

The intersection of this plane L with the supply function $Y = Y(\theta, \delta)$ determines a curve in (δ, θ, Y) space.

The agency behaves as if L is the true demand function, and can therefore determine the value of the indirect welfare function $V(p, I^1, I^2)$ on this curve. In step t, it selects $\bar{\theta}_t$ and q_t that maximizes V on this curve. This choice will generate new observations for the decision in the next step.

BIBLIOGRAPHY

BIBLIOGRAPHY

d'Arge, Ralph C., and K. C. Kogiku, "Economic Growth and the Natural Environment," Working paper 1, Dept. of Economics, University of California, Riverside.

Arrow, Kenneth J., "The Economic Implications of Learning by Doing," *Review of Economic Studies*, vol. 29, pp. 155–173 (1962).

Arrow, Kenneth J., *Social Choice and Individual Values*. New Haven: Yale University Press, 1963.

Arrow, Kenneth J., and Mordecai Kurz, *Public Investment, the Rate of Return and Optimal Fiscal Policy*. Baltimore: Johns Hopkins Press, 1970.

Arrow, Kenneth J., and Tibor Skitovsky, eds., *Readings in Welfare Economics*. Homewood, Ill.: Irwin, 1969.

Ayres, Robert U., and Allen V. Kneese, "Production, Consumption and Externalities," *American Economic Review*, vol. 59, no. 3, 282–297 (June 1969).

Barnett, Harold T., and Chandler Morse, *Scarcity and Growth, the Economics of Natural Resource Availability*. Baltimore: Johns Hopkins Press, 1963.

Bergson, Abram, "A Reformulation of Certain Aspects of Welfare Economics," *Quarterly Journal of Economics*, vol. 52, pp. 310–334 (February 1938).

Bohm, Peter, "An Approach to the Problem of Estimating Demand for Public Goods," *Swedish Journal of Economics*, vol. 73, no. 1, 55–66 (1971).

Bohm, Peter, "Estimating Demand for Public Goods: An Experiment," *European Economic Review*, vol. 1, pp. 111–130 (1972).

Bolin, Bert *et al.*, *Air Pollution Across National Boundaries. The Impact on the*

Environment of Sulfur in Air and Precipitation. Sweden's case study for the United Nations Conference on the Human Environment. Stockholm: Allmänna förlaget, 1971.

Bowen, Howard R., "The Interpretation of Voting in the Allocation of Economic Resources," in Kenneth J. Arrow and Tibor Skitovsky, eds., *Readings in Welfare Economics.* Homewood, Ill.: Irwin, 1969.

Buchanan, James M., and William C. Stubblebine, "Externality," in William Breit and Harold M. Hochman, eds., *Readings in Microeconomics.* New York: Holt, Rinehart and Winston, 1968.

Burenstam-Linder, Staffan, *The Harried Leisure Class.* New York: Columbia University Press, 1970.

Cass, David, "Optimum Growth in an Aggregative Model of Capital Accumulation," *Econometrica,* vol. 34, no. 4, 833–850 (1966).

Coase, Ronald, "The Problem of Social Choice," in William Breit and Harold M. Hochman, eds., *Readings in Microeconomics.* New York: Holt, Rinehart and Winston, 1968.

Coddington, Earl A., and N. Levinson, *Theory of Ordinary Differential Equations.* New York: McGraw-Hill, 1955.

Davis, Robert K., *The Range of Choice in Water Management.* Baltimore: Johns Hopkins Press, 1968.

Debreu, Gerard, "New Concepts and Techniques for Equilibrium Analysis," *International Economic Review,* vol. 3, no. 3, 257–273 (September 1962).

Debreu, Gerard, *Theory of Value: An Axiomatic Analysis of Economic Equilibrium.* New York: Wiley, 1959.

Dieudonné, Jean, *Foundations of Modern Analysis.* New York: Academic Press, 1960.

Dorfman, Robert, Paul A. Samuelson, and Robert M. Solow, *Linear Programming and Economic Analysis.* New York: McGraw-Hill, 1958.

Drèze, J. H., and D. de la Vallé Poussin, "A Tatonnement Process for Public Goods," *Review of Economic Studies,* vol. 38, pp. 133–150 (April 1971).

Ehrensvärd, Gösta, *Före-Efter, En Diagnos.* Stockholm: Aldus-Bonnier, 1971.

Ehrlich, Paul R., *The Population Bomb.* New York: Ballantine Books, 1968.

Feller, William, *An Introduction to Probability Theory and Its Applications,* vol. 2. New York: Wiley, 1966.

Foley, Duncan K., "Lindahl's Solution and the Core of an Economy with Public Goods," *Econometrica,* vol. 38, no. 1, 66–72 (1970).

Foley, Duncan K., "Resource Allocation and the Public Sector," *Yale Economic Essays,* vol. 7, no. 1, 43–98 (1967).

Forrester, Jay W., *World Dynamics.* Cambridge, Mass.: Wright-Allen Press, 1971.

Gale, David, "Optimal Development in a Multi-sector Economy," in *Problems in the Theory of Optimal Accumulation*, a collection from the *Review of Economic Studies* (January 1967), Edinburgh: Oliver and Boyd, pp. 1–18.

De Graaf, J. V., *Theoretical Welfare Economics*. London: Cambridge University Press, 1957.

Halmos, Paul R., *Measure Theory*. New York: Van Nostrand Reinhold, 1950.

Haefele, Edwin T., "Environmental Quality as a Problem of Social Choice," in Allen V. Kneese and Blair T. Bower, eds., *Environmental Quality Analysis: Theory and Method in the Social Sciences*. Baltimore: Johns Hopkins University Press, 1972.

Hestenes, Magnus R., *Calculus of Variations and Optimal Control Theory*. New York: Wiley, 1966.

Herfindahl, Orris C., and Allen V. Kneese, *An Introduction to the Economic Theory of Resources and Environment*. Columbus, Ohio: Merrill (in press).

Hicks, John R., *Value and Capital*. Oxford: Oxford University Press, 1939.

Hotelling, Harold, "The Economics of Exhaustible Resources," *Journal of Political Economy*, vol. 39, no. 2, 137–175 (April 1931).

Hotelling, Harold, "Edgeworth's Taxation Paradox and the Nature of Demand and Supply Functions," *Journal of Political Economy*, vol. 40, no. 5, 577–616 (October 1932).

Houthakker, Hendrik, "Compensated Changes in Quantities and Qualities Consumed," *Review of Economic Studies*, vol. 19, pp. 155–164 (1952).

Karlin, Samuel, *Mathematical Methods and Theory in Games, Programming and Economics*. Reading, Mass.: Addison-Wesley, 1962.

Kneese, Allen V., "Background for the Economic Analysis of Environmental Pollution," *Swedish Journal of Economics*, vol. 73, no. 1, 1–24 (1971).

Kneese, Allen V., and Blair T. Bower, eds., *Environmental Quality Analysis: Theory and Method in the Social Sciences*. Baltimore: Johns Hopkins University Press, 1972.

Kneese, Allen V., Robert U. Ayres, and Ralph C. d'Arge, *Economics and the Environment: A Materials Balance Approach*. Washington, D.C.: Resources for the Future, 1972.

Kneese, Allen V., and Blair T. Bower, *Managing Water Quality: Economics, Technology and Institutions*. Baltimore: Johns Hopkins Press, 1968.

Kneese, Allen V., and Karl-Göran Mäler, "Bribes and Charges in Pollution Control: An Aspect of the Coase Controversy," *Natural Resources Journal*, 1973 Symposium Issue (in press).

Koopmans, Tjalling et al., eds., *Activity Analysis of Production and Allocation*. New York: Wiley, 1951.

Koopmans, Tjalling, "Stationary Ordinal Utility and Impatience," *Econometrica*, vol. 28, no. 2, 287–309 (April 1960).

Krutilla, John *et al.*, "Observations on the Economics of Irreplaceable Assets," in Allen V. Kneese and Blair T. Bower, eds., *Environmental Quality Analysis*. Baltimore: Johns Hopkins University Press, 1972.

Lancaster, Kelvin, "A New Approach to Consumer Theory," *Journal of Political Economy*, vol. 74, no. 2, 132–157 (April 1966).

Lave, Lester B., and Eugene P. Seskin, "Health and Air Pollution," *Swedish Journal of Economics*, vol. 73, no. 1, 76–95 (1971).

Löf, George O., and Allen V. Kneese, *The Economics of Water Utilization in the Beet Sugar Industry*. Baltimore: Johns Hopkins Press, 1968.

Luce, Robert D., and Howard Raiffa, *Games and Decisions*. New York: Wiley, 1957.

Mäler, Karl-Göran, "A Method of Estimating Social Benefits from Pollution Control," *Swedish Journal of Economics*, vol. 73, no. 1, 121–133 (1971).

Mäler, Karl-Göran, "Studier i intertemporal allokering," unpublished dissertation, Department of Economics, University of Stockholm, 1969.

Malinvaud, Edmund, "A Planning Approach to the Public Good Problem," *Swedish Journal of Economics*, vol. 73, no. 1, 96–117 (1971).

McGauhey, Percy H., *Engineering Management of Water Quality*. New York: McGraw-Hill, 1968.

Meadows, Donella H. *et al.*, *The Limits to Growth: A Report for the Club of Rome's Project on the Predicament of Mankind*. Washington, D.C.: Potomac Associates, 1972.

Musgrave, Richard A., *The Theory of Public Finance*. New York: McGraw-Hill, 1959.

Musgrave, Richard A., and Alan T. Peacock, eds., *Classics in the Theory of Public Finance*. New York: St. Martin's Press, 1958.

Nikaido, Hukukane, *Convex Structures and Economic Theory*. New York: Academic Press, 1968.

Pigou, Arthur C., *The Economics of Welfare*. New York: St. Martin's Press, 1962; London: Macmillan, 1963.

Ramsay, Frank P., "A Mathematical Theory of Saving," *Economic Journal*, vol. 38, pp. 543–559 (1928).

Rockafellar, Tyrrell R., *Convex Analysis*. Princeton, N.J.: Princeton University Press, 1970.

Samuelson, Paul A., "Aspects of Public Expenditure Theories," *Review of Economics and Statistics*, vol. 40, no. 4, 332–338 (1958).

Samuelson, Paul A., "A Caternary Turnpike Theorem," *American Economic Review*, vol. 55, no. 3, 486–496 (June 1965).

Samuelson, Paul A., "Evaluation of Real National Income," *Oxford Economic Papers*, N.S. vol. 2, no. 1, 1–29 (1950).

Samuelson, Paul A., *Foundations of Economic Analysis*, 3rd ed., Cambridge, Mass.: Harvard University Press, 1953.

Samuelson, Paul A., "The Problem of Integrability in Utility Theory," *Economica*, M.S. 17, 335–385 (1950).

Samuelson, Paul A., "The Pure Theory of Public Expenditures," *Review of Economics and Statistics*, vol. 36, pp. 387–389 (1954).

Samuelson, Paul A., "The Pure Theory of Public Expenditure and Taxation," in J. Margolis and H. Guitton, eds., *Public Economics: An Analysis of Public Production and Consumption and Their Relations to the Private Sector*. New York: St. Martin's Press, 1969.

Samuelson, Paul A., "Social Indifference Curves," *Quarterly Journal of Economics*, vol. 70, no. 1, 1–22 (February 1956).

Samuelson, Paul A., "Using Full Duality to Show That Simultaneously Additive Direct and Indirect Utilities Implies Elasticity of Demand," *Econometrica*, vol. 33, no. 4, 781–796 (October 1965).

Shell, Karl, ed., *Essays on the Theory of Optimal Economic Growth*. Cambridge, Mass.: MIT Press, 1967.

Starret, David, "On a Fundamental Non-Convexity in the Theory of Externalities," Discussion Paper 115, Harvard Institute of Economic Research, Harvard University, 1970.

Stevens, Joe B., "Recreation Benefits from Water Pollution Control," *Water Resources Research*, vol. 2, pp. 167–182 (1966).

Tideman, T. Nicolaus, "The Efficient Provision of Public Goods," in Selma J. Mushkin, ed., *Public Prices for Public Goods*. Washington, D.C.: The Urban Institute, 1972.

Wicksell, K., "A New Principle of Just Taxation," in Richard A. Musgrave and Alan T. Peacock, eds., *Classics in the Theory of Public Finance*. New York: St. Martin's Press, 1958.

Wilson, Carroll L., and William H. Matthews, eds., *Man's Impact on the Global Environment: Assessment and Recommendations for Action*. Cambridge, Mass.: MIT Press, 1970.

THE JOHNS HOPKINS UNIVERSITY PRESS

This book was composed in Modern text and Century Black by Monotype Composition Company, Inc. It was printed on Warren's Sebago, 60-lb., regular finish, and bound in Columbia Fictionette, by The Maple Press Company.

Library of Congress Cataloging in Publication Data

Mäler, Karl-Göran.
    Environmental economics; a theoretical inquiry.

    Bibliography: p.
    1. Pollution—Economic aspects. 2. Pollution—
Economic aspects—Mathematical models. I. Title.
HC79.P55M27   333.7   73-19347
ISBN 0-8018-1594-0

Acknowledgements

My thanks are due to the national, regional and local officers of the Campaign for Nuclear Disarmament for providing me with information and facilities which enabled me to carry out a questionnaire survey of CND supporters. I am particularly grateful to the 803 adult and youth supporters who filled in my questionnaires, and to those who gave me information in interviews. My gratitude is due to the London University Central Research Fund for awarding me a travel grant in Summer 1964 which enabled me to visit CND regional and local branches in the North-West, Yorkshire and Midland areas. I benefited from discussions with many sociologists—both in their political and academic guises. I should mention especially Professor S. J. Gould, Professor R. T. McKenzie, Dr C. B. Otley, Mr John Allcock, Mr J. G. H. Newfield and Mr P. M. Jackson (now Labour M.P. for High Peak). My greatest debt is to Dr David Martin who supervised the doctoral thesis (London University, 1966) on which this book is based, and to Professor Peter Worsley who offered many constructive criticisms. Finally, I should like to thank Carole Casey for typing the manuscript.

F. P.

University of Kent at Canterbury

1

Introduction

This is a study of the social bases of support for a political mass movement—the Campaign for Nuclear Disarmament. Opposition to nuclear weapons emerged in Britain in 1955 when the government of the day announced its decision to manufacture a hydrogen bomb, and reached its peak between 1958 and 1963, when CND succeeded in mobilizing support for unilateralism on a mass scale. The political movement which resulted is examined here for the light it throws on certain problems of current interest in the sociology of politics; it is not treated in the form of an historical narrative, neither are its general aims and strategies described and evaluated. In short, it is not CND itself which is of primary interest so much as the theoretical issues it helps to illuminate. For certain of these issues, but not all, some other movement might have served my purpose equally well.

One of the main sets of problems raised for discussion in this study is that presented by the phenomenon of middle class radicalism. Political sociologists have been much preoccupied in recent times with the working class conservative as a 'deviant' political case. McKenzie and Silver, Runciman and, most recently, Nordlinger,[1] have considered in some detail the class characteristics, status perceptions and psychological attitudes of that section of the manual working class which identifies itself politically with the conservatives and so acts against its own 'class interests' as these are commonly perceived. Little if any attention has been directed to the analogous case of that small minority of the middle class which endorses left wing political and social views. This account of the social characteristics of CND supporters—who, as will be later shown, are drawn predominantly from the ranks of the non-manual stratum—is one small attempt to redress the situation.

In the following chapters we shall consider, for example, to what extent there are features present in middle class radicalism which serve to distinguish it from the radicalism characteristic of the working class. It will be suggested that whereas working class radicalism could be said to be geared largely to reforms of an economic or material kind, the radicalism of the middle class is directed mainly to social reforms which are basically moral in content. Again, whereas the former holds out the promise of benefits to one particular section of society (the working class) from which its own supporters are drawn, the latter envisages no rewards which will accrue to the middle class specifically, but only to society at large, or to some underprivileged groups. It is argued in fact that the main pay-off for middle class radicals is that of a psychological or emotional kind—in satisfactions derived from expressing personal values in action. Rewards of this type, unrelated to class or material interests, have less frequently been the focus of attention in studies of political behaviour than those which can be analysed in terms of interest-group politics. The interest-group model treats political behaviour as an instrumental activity—that is, as behaviour geared to the attainment of specific and concrete goals. However,

---

[1] R. T. McKenzie and Allen Silver, 'Conservatism, Industrialism and the Working Class Tory in England', in *Transactions* of the Fifth World Congress of Sociology, Washington, 1962, Vol. III. W. G. Runciman, *Relative Deprivation and Social Justice*, Routledge, 1966. E. A. Nordlinger, *The Working Class Tories: Authority, Deference and Stable Democracy*, McGibbon and Kee, 1967.

politics may also be viewed in terms of its expressive functions, by way of the satisfactions and rewards entailed in the activity itself rather than in the actual outcomes to which the activity is directed. Support for movements like CND is most usefully thought of as behaviour in its expressive aspect. This is not to say that it represents a form of politics which is somehow less 'real' than that which is geared primarily to the attainment of specific goals. For, as Blau argues,

The fact that given actions of people have expressive significance and are not calculated to obtain specific advantages does not necessarily mean that their conduct is irrational but may mean that it is *Wertrational* rather than *Zweckrational*, that is, oriented to the pursuit of ultimate values rather than to the pursuit of immediate rewards. This is not simply a hairsplitting distinction. Expressive social conduct oriented to ideals and absolute values is of great importance in social life, but our understanding of it is not at all advanced by the assumption that it merely reflects idiosyncratic and irrational individual behaviour. Radical political opposition, for example, cannot be explained without taking into account the expressive significance it has for supporters, and failure to do so is a serious shortcoming of formalistically rational models of politics.[1]

It will be seen that involvement in CND was a token not only of an individual's attitude to nuclear weapons but also of his position on a wide array of other radical and humanitarian issues. Identification with CND could be taken to be a capsule statement of a distinctive moral and political outlook, and support for its activities a means of affirming this outlook through symbolic acts.

The profile of middle class radicalism is sketched in further by a consideration of CND supporters' perception of the social structure and their place within it. The question is raised as to whether professional and white collar radicals perceive the social system in terms of a status or consensus model as do the middle class in general, or as a dichotomous or conflict model which, although a characteristically working class picture of society, might be held more appropriate to those of a radical disposition. Along similar lines, information will be presented concerning the class identification of CND'ers in order to evaluate how far middle class radicals emulate working class Conservatives in identifying themselves with members of the 'wrong' social class. This will lead to an examination of certain of the tensions inherent in the combination of high socio-economic status and left wing political commitments, as well as the strategies adopted for minimizing these tensions. Par-

[1] Peter M. Blau, *Exchange and Power in Social Life*, Wiley, New York, 1964, pp. 5–6.

ticular attention is paid to the occupational location of CND'ers, since it can be assumed that political radicals face potential disadvantages in the pursuit of a career, so that the attempt to circumvent these disadvantages becomes a factor of strategic importance in occupational selection. The relationship between occupation and political outlook is also considered from certain other angles, particularly that of Lenski's theory of status crystallization.

CND also provides a useful test case for current propositions in political sociology concerning the sources of recruitment to mass movements. There is a growing literature on the phenomenon of mass politics and movements which attempt to by-pass the orthodoxies of party organization and the parliamentary process in favour of direct modes of political intervention. Much of this literature has expressed concern about the structure of democracy and its vulnerability to this form of politics in modern industrial societies. Factors felt to stimulate the emergence of mass movements are the weakening of individuals' sense of social belonging created by the growth of bureaucracy and urbanization, and their feeling of remoteness from the centres of decision making. Men who experience a sense of powerlessness, an inability to influence events which affect their lives, are felt liable to grow disenchanted with democratic politics and to become susceptible to the appeals of mass movements with a 'direct' political approach. Writers such as Arendt, Kornhauser, Hoffer, Shils and Lederer, among others, have suggested that those who lack moral and social integration into society, and who exhibit the hallmarks of alienation, provide the typical supporters of such movements. This relationship between alienation and recruitment to mass politics will be considered in some detail in Chapter 2, and certain of the assumptions contained in current writings will be tested against the data on the anti-Bomb movement.

It should perhaps be emphasized at this point that a distinction needs to be drawn between disapproval of nuclear weapons and support for the unilateralist movement. Snyder, in his analysis of opinion polls between 1955 and 1962, showed that a sizeable minority of the public expressed disapproval at the manufacture of a British hydrogen bomb—a minority which vacillated over the period between a low point of 19 per cent and a high point of 33 per cent.[1] At the same time, however, the polls showed that many of those who disapproved of the Bomb also disapproved of CND, and

[1] W. P. Snyder, *The Politics of British Defense Policy, 1945–1962*, Ohio State University Press, 1964, p. 59.

Snyder points out that public support for unilateralism tended to decline as CND increased in prominence, particularly during the peak of the civil disobedience demonstrations in the early nineteen-sixties.[1] In the eyes of the public at large the unilateralist movement tended, however unjustly, to be stigmatized as a refuge for 'beatniks' and 'bearded weirdies', as well as for communists or anarchists and other political groups thought to be potentially dangerous. The occasional street scuffles with the police, the 'invasion' of missile sites and the mass arrests—all receiving maximum national publicity—appeared to confirm this impression of the movement's disreputable character. If for no other reason, then, this would have deterred many of those who disapproved of the Bomb from translating their views into active support for CND. Support for unilateralism is thus not to be equated with the more politically and socially 'deviant' stance entailed in support for and involvement in CND. Only the latter is of concern to us in these pages.

In fact, one of the main arguments to be developed is that support for CND is not to be understood wholly as an expression of protest against the Bomb, but as a somewhat more complex affair. It will be claimed that much of the movement's attraction derived from the fact that it also served as a rallying point for groups and individuals opposed to certain features of British society which were independent of the issue of the Bomb, but which the latter served dramatically to symbolize. Organizations which swelled the ranks of CND, such as the Pacifists, the New Left, the Communists and Anarchists, the Quakers, the Labour Left, and so on, were generally less committed to unilateralism as such than to an array of quite distinct aims which were thought to be furthered by support for the Campaign. The nature of certain of these aims, and the way in which CND was seen as a vehicle for attaining them, is described in some detail in Chapters 4, 5 and 6.

CND also provides a useful laboratory for investigating one other set of problems of interest to the political sociologist—namely the involvement of youth in radical politics. The movement against the Bomb was almost unique among political organizations in this country in its ability to attract the younger generation to its ranks. The presence of adolescents and young adults on marches and demonstrations was perhaps the most distinctive feature of CND, as well as one of the most problematic. For given the fact that youth in most western societies has traditionally been apathetic to politics, how is the emergence of a new mood of radicalism and political pro-

[1] Op. cit., p. 61.

test against the government's defence policy to be accounted for? This problem provides the setting for Chapter 7 and is discussed in relation to a number of theories concerning the political involvement of youth—in particular those of family socialization, the 'political generation' and youthful rebelliousness.

Data bearing upon most of the issues outlined here were drawn from questionnaires administered to youth and adult CND supporters. The names and addresses of youth supporters—defined as those between the ages of 15 and 25 years—were collected on the second day of the three-day Easter march held in 1965. Some 550 names and addresses were recorded, comprising an approximate 10 per cent sample of the march, and questionnaires were sent by post in May 1965; a follow-up letter was sent to non-responses two weeks later. In all, 445 usable questionnaires were returned, 81 per cent of the total.[1] The difficulties of attempting to draw an accurate sample from a continuously moving column of marchers will readily be imagined; some people leave the ranks while others join in as the column proceeds, so that its composition is never really constant. No claim can therefore be made that my respondents represent a statistically accurate sample of young marchers, and less so of course of young CND'ers as a whole. Like other sociologists operating on slender resources I have had to choose between imperfect data or no data at all. Despite the disadvantages it entailed the Easter march was considered to be the best means of contacting a reasonable cross-section of young supporters since they were not in the main registered as card-holding members of local CND branches. The march was the one event of the year which brought together supporters from all parts of the country, and was the form of political action most appealing to the younger elements. No other acceptable means of tapping the reservoir of youthful anti-bomb protest seemed feasible.

The sampling of adult supporters presented few difficulties. CND headquarters kindly furnished me with the names and addresses of all local branch secretaries in January 1966. Sixty-four of these (i.e. every third branch) were contacted and requested to send me the names and addresses of local members over the age of 25 years, who were either present supporters or who had been so in the recent past. Forty-two branch secretaries responded favourably and provided me with a total of 505 names and addresses, an average of about twelve supporters per branch. In early March questionnaires were posted to the 505 supporters, and over half were returned com-

[1] A copy of the questionnaire and covering letter will be found in Appendix A.

pleted within ten days. A reminder was sent to non-responses shortly after, and in all 358 usable questionnaires were returned, 61 per cent of the total. The questionnaire was pre-tested in a pilot survey on forty-two members of the Preston, Hereford and Leyton-stone CND branches in February 1966.[1] In addition, a number of interviews were held with branch secretaries and local supporters between 1964 and 1966, mainly in the London, Yorkshire and North-West Regions.

[1] A copy of the questionnaire and letter to branch secretaries will be found in Appendix B.

2

Mass movements and the problem of alienation

A renewed interest in political matters of wide-ranging scope and character has been one of the more notable developments in sociology in recent times. Although early theorists were much preoccupied with the political impact of industrialization and the bureaucratization of major institutions, similar concerns failed to engage the attention of sociologists in the inter-war and immediate post-war years to any notable extent. Political sociology narrowed its focus to the study of voting behaviour in national and local elections, and to largely descriptive accounts of power and influence in small communities. This tendency may have resulted from the comparative stabilization of political struggle in Europe, in which the new mood of consensus and the lessening of class conflict in its more overt forms might have rendered the wider issues less obvious and less appealing objects of study. It may also partly be related to the bureaucratization of knowledge, in that the sociology of politics was originally in the hands of men with a message who were as much interested in changing society as in understanding it, whereas now it is largely an academic discipline and therefore to some extent constrained by the demands of scholarship and the limitations of research.

However this may be, there has more recently developed a renewed interest in macro-politics and new attempts to establish large-scale generalizations about political behaviour. American scholars in particular have increasingly turned their attention to the phenomenon of mass politics and mass movements, providing studies which are very much in the classic European tradition in that they are ultimately concerned with posing questions about the structure of political society and the social bases of democracy. One might hazard a guess that the re-emergence of interest in these questions on the part of Americans has been partly due to the general anxiety in that country about the rise of communism in various parts of the post-war world, which has been perceived as a threat to Western institutions and political freedoms. This could in turn have sparked off an interest in broadbased studies and problems wider in scope than those encompassed by research into community power and voting behaviour. It may also have been prompted by the adverse experiences of American scholars and intellectuals during the McCarthyist period and by their concern at the rise of similar anti-democratic populist movements of the Radical Right.[1] But whatever the intellectual origins of this development, it is one that has made a distinctive contribution to political sociology; so much so that any study such as this, concerned with a political mass movement, inevitably treats it as a source for research cues and theoretical concepts. Consequently, it will be useful to start with a brief examination of some of the central propositions contained in theories of mass movements, and political behaviour in the mass society in general. These will then be tested against empirical material derived from the CND questionnaire. Subsequently, a

[1] See for example, Edward Shils, *The Torment of Secrecy*, Free Press, Glencoe, 1957.

B

number of different propositions will be advanced concerning the social bases of support for mass movements and political radicalism which are prompted by the CND data.

Initially, it is perhaps necessary to clarify the use of the term 'mass' when speaking of mass movements or mass politics. It does not necessarily refer to large numbers, although these may of course often be involved; rather it is a term used to denote political behaviour which is not channelled into formal membership organizations with a bureaucratic authority structure, of the kind a political party or trade union has, for example. Mass movements have 'followings' or 'supporters' rather than members, and their characteristic mode of operation is not through committees or formal procedures, but through the mobilization of supporters in public demonstrations or similar techniques which by-pass the orthodoxies of the political process and democratic machinery.[1] Sometimes a political party is the inspirational force behind a mass movement, but not necessarily or even typically so. Examples would be the Bolshevik or Nazi parties, each comparatively small and close-knit in itself, but capable of raising large-scale support of non-members. More typical of mass movements in general would be the IWW, the Chartists, the Radical Right in America, and of course, CND. All of these lack formal hierarchic structures and paid-up members, but have simply followers who can be mobilized on specific occasions. Mass politics is then usefully thought of as the polar opposite of bureaucratized politics—one of the features in fact which often contributes to its appeal.

Turning now to the various theories of mass behaviour in its political aspect, it is apparent that despite certain differences in content and emphasis there are one or two unifying concepts running through them which can be singled out as the key notions employed in explanation and analysis. The most important of these recurring concepts is that of alienation. Alienation is taken to be the chief characteristic of individuals recruited to mass movements, and the psychological motive force behind their attraction to extremist politics. Whatever else may differentiate the supporters of

---

[1] Thus 49 per cent of CND respondents had either personally taken part in acts of civil disobedience or approved such activities in principle. Just over one third disapproved of this form of politics, whilst the remainder neither approved nor condemned it outright but felt that resort to it depended upon particular circumstances. There was then an overall disposition in favour of by-passing orthodox democratic procedures in certain situations, particularly those felt to require urgency of action. In this context, sharp distinctions between the Committee of 100 and CND are unjustifiable.

mass politics from one another—whether class differences, ethnic, regional or religious differences, the one feature they can be expected to have in common is their sense of estrangement from society; they will be individuals who are *in* society, but somehow not *of* it.

Although alienation is widely used to account for certain types of political behaviour, it has been accorded a number of different meanings, so that the same term is used to describe different social or psychological conditions. In the hands of some writers, alienation and its synonyms take on a somewhat mystical connotation, referring to man's separation from his inner self or from his own true nature—meanings which are too abstract to have much operational value. More generally, however, theorists of mass politics attempt to avoid this metaphysical notion by tying the concept to fairly concrete empirical indices.[1] Even so, different usages do persist and require separate consideration in order to clarify the problems in hand.

Alienation as social isolation

The first, and perhaps commonest, usage of alienation in political sociology is as a term to describe the individual's social isolation. It is a condition in which men are psychologically and socially divorced from society as a result of the lack of ties linking them to the wider community. Hannah Arendt refers to typical supporters of mass movements as being 'atomized', and other writers refer to them as 'uprooted', 'isolated' or 'anomic'.[2] All these synonyms for alienation refer to the factual condition of individuals who are not members of social groups and institutions which are placed intermediate between the family and the state. By the slenderness or absence of their links to the community such individuals are unable to relate themselves in meaningful and satisfying ways to the social system; they are, as it were, socially unanchored and adrift in the world. As a result of this lack of integration they are highly susceptible to the appeals of mass movements, particularly those with a messianic flavour and strong moralistic appeal, and a tendency to favour direct

---

[1] Some writers subscribe to the view that the attempt to harness the alienation concept to empirical indices robs it of its 'true' meaning. See John Horton, 'The Dehumanization of Anomie and Alienation', *British Journal of Sociology*, **15**, 1964.

[2] Hannah Arendt, *The Origins of Totalitarianism*, Harcourt Brace, New York, 1951; William Kornhauser, *The Politics of Mass Society*, Routledge, London, 1959; Emil Lederer, *State of the Masses*, Norton, New York, 1940; E. Hoffer, *The True Believer*, Harper, New York, 1951.

methods of political intervention. It is argued that involvement in this type of movement is functional for the alienated individual in that it provides a sense of purpose and significance to life by creating a feeling that he is perhaps helping to change the course of history, or the fate of the world, or some such purpose of large-scale dimension. The movement provides in other words the very social and psychological satisfactions which for the well-integrated individual are provided by social ties and personal relationships. This particular meaning of alienation stems essentially from a concept of political democracy commonly known as 'pluralism'. It is a theory most usually associated with de Tocqueville, but numerous other political scientists and sociologists have subscribed to it. Briefly, it states that democratic political structures require for their maintenance a well-developed set of intermediate institutions, independent of the state and wider than the network of kinship and family. A pluralist structure ensures that there are strong buffers between the central government and the individual which give stability to the system by providing many points of social anchorage. Durkheim puts the pluralist case in a nutshell in the following passage:

> collective activity is always too complex to be expressed through the single and unique organ of the State. Moreover the State is too remote from individuals; its relations with them too external and intermittent to penetrate deeply into individual consciences and socialize them within. Where the State is the only environment in which men can live communal lives, they inevitably lose contact, become detached, and thus society disintegrates. A nation can be maintained only if, between the State and the individual, there is intercalated a whole series of secondary groups near enough to the individuals to attract them strongly in their sphere of action and drag them, in this way, into the general torrents of social life.[1]

It is possible to single out three different types of function which intermediate bodies are felt to serve, and which give them their key importance in the maintenance of the political structure. These might for convenience be called the normative, the affectual and the interest functions, each of which may be briefly summarized as follows.

The normative function of intermediate bodies is provided in the formal and informal socialization of their members into democratic practices and procedures. That is to say, participation in intermediate organizations such as voluntary associations, trade unions, professional bodies, local community associations, guilds, societies

---

[1] Emile Durkheim, *Division of Labour*, Free Press, Glencoe, 1947, p. 28.

and so on, has the effect of indoctrinating those concerned in an understanding of, and respect for, democratic values, such as elections to office and voting procedure, the public airing of views and conflicting opinions, the willingness to abide by majority decisions, the acceptance of the need for concession and compromise, and so forth. All these attributes of intermediate organizations provide a training in the kinds of values and attitudes which are required for the maintenance of a democratic order, in that institutions of this type are to some extent small-scale versions of the wider political society. A recent British study of Co-operative societies draws particular attention to their contribution to democratic institutions through their normative functions: Participation through these and similar associations

constitutes the mechanism for the recruitment and political education of political men. It provides training in democratic action and access to a forum of oppositional ideas, the toleration and dissemination of which are essential to democratic government. It offers a varied set of opportunities for the nurture and expression of politically and publicly directed energy. Democratic associations constitute the great intermediary foci of loyalties which distinguish the civil from the mass society in which nothing stands between the attachment of a man to his family and to the nation state. In this general sense the Co-operative Movement has played a significant historical role in the development of British democratic institutions.[1]

The second way in which such intermediate groups are functional for democracy is in their affectual aspect. That is, they provide small-scale groupings of a primary kind, which offer the participant a meaningful psychological setting, some means of achieving self-identity and satisfaction through his relationships with others—irrespective of the actual purpose or goals of the organization. Whereas the family is too small to absorb all the emotions and energies of individuals, the state is too large and impersonal. Consequently, it is the social structures between these two institutions which must provide the opportunities and outlets by which a person is able to relate himself to the wider social system. Arnold Rose, in

[1] G. N. Ostergaard, and A. H. Halsey, *Power in Co-operatives*, Blackwell, Oxford, 1965, p. 67. Lipset and his associates in their study of the International Typographical Union, made a similar set of claims with particular reference to trade unions: these and similar organizations serve as 'arenas within which new ideas are generated . . . as communications networks through which people may learn and form attitudes about politics . . . as means of training potential opposition leaders in the skills of politics . . . and as . . . one of the principal means of getting individuals to participate in the larger political arena . . .' S. M. Lipset, et. al., *Union Democracy*, Free Press, Glencoe, 1959, p. 80.

his discussion of voluntary associations in the United States, places particular emphasis on their affectual aspect; according to him, 'the declining influence of the community (and the extended family and the Church) resulted in psychological insecurity, segmentalization of personal relations reducing intimacy, and alienation from once powerful values. The voluntary association is a new structure crescively established to meet these structural needs.'[1]

The third major way in which such intermediate groups contribute to social and political life is through their interest functions. That is, they provide individuals with the means of staking and pressing claims in the allocation of scarce material and social resources, which as individuals acting independently they would be unable to influence. The result of serving men's interests in this way is to diffuse power throughout society and to provide institutional means for the conferral of status within local communities.[2] These interest functions are advantageous not only to group participants but to society as a whole in that they serve to direct individuals' claims and demands into formal channels, such as trade unions and professional bodies, and so prevent potentially disruptive 'mass' pressures on the centres of power. It is argued that without these institutionalized means of establishing demands men would be forced to confront the state directly *en masse*, which would result in political instability and the excesses of populism. In Kornhauser's words:

Intermediate groups, even though they are independent of top elites, operate to protect these elites from arbitrary and excessive pressures by themselves being responsive to the needs and demands of people. In the absence of intermediate groups to act as representatives and guides for popular participation, people must act *directly* in the critical centers of society, and therefore in a manner unrestrained by the values and interests of a variety of social groups.[3]

For this variety of reasons, then, intermediate structures are held to be vital supports of democratic values and practices. It therefore follows logically enough from this that those most intimately in-

[1] Arnold M. Rose, *Theory and Method in the Social Sciences*, University of Minnesota Press, 1954, p. 61.
[2] Bottomore has depicted this process as follows: 'In so far as voluntary organizations take over important functions which the family, or the community as a whole no longer performs, they become centres of power and prestige and the individual's status in the community then comes to depend in a larger degree upon membership of such organizations.' T. B. Bottomore, 'Social Stratification in Voluntary Organizations', in D. V. Glass, *Social Mobility in Britain*, Routledge, London 1954, p. 352.
[3] Kornhauser, op. cit., p. 77.

volved in the network of intermediate groups and relations are more likely to be of a democratic temper and commitment than those who lack such relationships. These latter, the alienated, are consequently more prone to the attraction of mass movements which favour direct modes of political intervention against the state, and are less committed to the orthodoxies of the democratic process. As Robert Nisbet has put it:

> Only through its intermediate relationships and authorities has any State ever achieved the balance between organization and personal freedom that is the condition of a creative and enduring culture ... The individual who has been by one force or another wrenched from social belonging is thrown back upon himself; he becomes the willing prey of those who would manipulate him as the atom citizen in the political and economic realms.[1]

Similarly, in Kornhauser's words:

> The lack of autonomous relations generates widespread social alienation. Alienation heightens responsiveness to the appeal of mass movements because they provide occasions for expressing resentment against what is, as well as promises of a totally different world. In short, *people who are atomized readily become mobilized.*[2]

The concept of alienation and the concept of pluralism are thus welded together to form a general theoretical formula to account for the emergence of mass political movements. Surprisingly enough, however, this theory has rarely been subjected to empirical investigation, but has been argued largely on *a priori* grounds. CND obviously provides a convenient test case for some of the central ideas contained in the theory concerning the sources of recruitment to mass movements. With this view in mind, data were collected bearing upon the issues outlined, in particular information relating to the degree of social integration of CND supporters. One useful and easily constructed index of social integration is that to which frequent reference has been made above—namely the degree of attachment to intermediate groups and institutions independent of the family and the state, of which voluntary organizations are the most obvious examples. Thus, to begin with, respondents were asked to indicate whether they were members of any voluntary associations or similar bodies of a non-political character. The responses are recorded in Table 1 overleaf:

[1] Robert A. Nisbet, *The Quest for Community*, O.U.P., New York, 1953, p. 267.
[2] Kornhauser op. cit., p. 33 (original emphasis).

TABLE I   *Membership in voluntary associations*

		%
Membership in 1 or 2		49
,,	in 3 or 4	24
,,	in 5 or more	11
,,	in none	16
		100 (N = 358)

It proved to be the case that 84 per cent of adult respondents were involved in at least one formal organization, whilst 35 per cent of the total were members of three or more. Only 16 per cent were completely isolated from intermediate groupings of this kind. In order to get some idea of the level of commitment to these associations, information was also sought concerning positions of responsibility held by respondents. It turned out that 46 per cent held, or had recently held, an elected post or position of responsibility of some kind within organizations, 23 per cent having held two or more such positions. Although the various associations mentioned were not systematically coded, a fairly clear picture emerged of the kind generally preferred by CND supporters. These were mainly trade unions and professional associations, and organizations with a decidedly welfare or humanitarian bias; typical examples of the latter type were International Voluntary Services, youth club and church committees of various kinds, Oxfam collection groups, the United Nations Association, Prisoners' Aid Society, The Workers' Educational Association, The Fellowship of Reconciliation, Parent-Teachers' Associations, Women's Guilds, and one or other of the organizations against racial discrimination. In addition to this, 51 per cent were members of a political organization or party—predominantly the Labour Party.

The obvious conclusion to be drawn from this is that CND supporters cannot be thought of as displaying the hallmarks of an alienated sub-section of society in the sense of lacking intermediate links to the social order, as predicted by the pluralist theory of mass politics. The overall impression of CND respondents is that they appear well integrated into a broad range of social activities and institutions of the type felt to provide a buffer against mass movements. It therefore seems clear that involvement in mass politics is fully compatible with social integration in this particular sense and is not necessarily a product of alienation as here defined. A further indirect, but perhaps more crucial, index of respondents' social integration is that provided by data on class composition. Table 2 shows the occupational distribution of the sample as measured by the Hall-Jones scale:

TABLE 2   *Social class composition*

	%
Classes 1 + 2	27
,, 3 + 4	56
,, 5 + 6 + 7	12
No reply	5
	100 (N = 358)

83 per cent of the sample were professional, managerial or white collar workers of various grades (categories 1 to 4) whilst only 12 per cent were drawn from the ranks of the manual working class. This confirms the impressionistic view commonly held by CND supporters—namely, that it is a predominantly middle class movement—a point which is neatly summed up by the presence in the adult sample of more clergymen and university lecturers than unskilled manual workers. Although some degree of working class under-representation could be expected to result from the mailed-questionnaire method of collecting data, non-responses could not plausibly be held to account for differences of this magnitude.[1]

The class position of the Campaign's supporters is obviously a relevant feature in considering their integration into the social system. It may be taken as axiomatic that the middle classes are on the whole more closely integrated into society and its major values and institutions than are lower status groups, a point demonstrated by the greater tendency for deviant sub-cultures to flourish among the latter than the former. Middle class status with all that it implies in the way of material security, favourable home and work environment, high access to valued cultural and welfare resources, and a general ability to control personal environment and life-chances, makes for an overall personality and social type altogether unlike that posited for alienated man. It would appear in fact that generalizations about the relationship between alienation and support for mass movements are drawn almost entirely from the politics of lower status groups. Individuals attracted to mass politics have generally been members of social strata which have experienced relative material deprivation, or whose existing standards of life appeared to be in jeopardy. The Nazi, Communist and Poujadist

---

[1] This was not in any case an unexpected finding since CND was acutely aware of its relative inability to attract working-class support—a point we shall return to later.

movements provide obvious examples of this tendency. The turn to mass politics was characteristically a response mainly of those who were particularly vulnerable to the effects of economic crisis—generally of course lower status groups such as manual workers, small shopkeepers, artisans and the like. At the same time, this is precisely the segment of society which, as a number of empirical studies have demonstrated, is least likely to be involved in intermediate relations of the kind typified by voluntary associations. In all industrial societies for which evidence is available there is a convincing correlation between social class and membership in voluntary associations. With the exception of trade union membership, working class participation in intermediate organizations is minimal; by and large it is a middle class, and especially an upper middle class, affair.[1] It would therefore seem that recruitment to mass movements is not convincingly explained in terms of social isolation, since this is a more or less constant factor in the life situation of lower status groups. It seems far more plausible to explain the latter's attraction to mass politics as a response to material deprivation, especially during periods of economic crisis, rather than to psychological problems created by alienation. The fact that they will be found to exhibit comparatively weak links to the wider community cannot usefully be regarded as a 'cause' of their political involvement, since the weakness of such ties is a product of low social status, and is not a factor which differentiates low status supporters of mass movements from those of similar background who are not drawn to mass politics.[2]

If, as suggested here, the matter of intermediate links is largely irrelevant in influencing support for mass movements, but is simply a reflection of general social status, then it should follow that members of the middle class attracted to mass politics should exhibit the level of social integration common to that class as a whole. And we have seen that this was in fact the case with CND supporters. Similarly, Wolfinger in a recent study of one of the groups comprising the Radical Right, which was also largely middle class in composition, showed that its supporters, far from being socially alienated, were more closely implicated in community and social affairs than the average middle class American citizen. As Wolfinger puts it,

[1] Bottomore, op. cit., C. R. Wright and H. H. Hyman, 'Voluntary Association Membership of American Adults: Evidence from National Sample Surveys, *American Sociological Review*, **23**, 1958.

[2] No evidence is presented by theorists of mass politics that lower status individuals *not* attracted to such movements are better integrated into intermediate associations than those who *are* attracted.

they 'do not seem to be social isolates . . . they have a somewhat higher level of membership in all kinds of organizations—Church committees, civic groups, veterans organizations and so forth—than do business, professional and white collar respondents . . . [in the national sample].'[1] The evidence provided by middle class movements of the Right and Left demonstrates clearly that alienation as defined in pluralist theory is not the characteristic condition of supporters. The ideal-type member of a mass movement as an atomized individual shorn of all social ties, lacking opportunity for the enhancement of self and status, could hardly resemble less the average supporter of CND.

Alienation as powerlessness

A somewhat different usage of alienation is that which treats it as a measure of the individual's powerlessness in the mass society. Alienation is here seen more as a psychological than a social state, the basic ingredient of which is a sense of personal helplessness in the face of powerful political forces which appear remote from, and unresponsive to, individual demands and needs. This in turn encourages disillusionment with the political rules of the game and creates a predisposition for anti-democratic and protest politics. Levin and Eden write:

> The feeling of being wrongfully excluded, powerless, and cheated of one's political birthright is the essential component of political alienation. In a democratic society it may arise from (1) the disjunction between democratic values and perceived political realities—between the roles which democratic man expects he has the right to play and the role he believes he is forced to play, or from (2) actual experience with corrupt politicians. Individuals who believe they have a right to be politically efficacious but who feel politically powerless will feel alienated.[2]

A number of American studies have demonstrated that feelings of political powerlessness (as measured by various attitude tests) are often a dominant factor in individuals' participation in various forms of protest politics against the 'powers that be', both locally and nationally.[3] Because CND may also be represented as an example

[1] R. E. Wolfinger, et. al., 'America's Radical Right: Politics and Ideology', in D. Apter (ed.), *Ideology and Discontent*, Free Press, Glencoe, 1964, p. 276.

[2] M. B. Levin and M. Eden, 'Political Strategy for the Alienated Voter', *Public Opinion Quarterly*, Spring 1962, p. 49. See also Morris Rosenberg, 'The Meaning of Politics in Mass Society', *Public Opinion Quarterly*, Spring 1951, for an early statement of this view.

[3] See especially W. E. Thompson and J. E. Horton, 'Political Alienation as a Force in Political Action,' *Social Forces*, March 1960; and 'Powerlessness and Political Negativism: A study of Defeated Local Referendums,' *American Journal of Sociology*, March 1962. Also, W. A. Gamson, 'The Fluoridation Dialogue: Is it an Ideological Conflict?', *Public Opinion Quarterly*, Winter 1961.

of anti-Establishment politics it was decided to consider this dimension of alienation, and to determine whether support for the Campaign was in any way correlated to a sense of powerlessness in influencing political events. The apparently inevitable drift to nuclear war discerned by those in the movement, and the remoteness of the machinery by which it might be halted, could well be regarded as an extreme example of the 'objective' helplessness of the individual to sway the course of events. The powerlessness theme was occasionally developed by leading figures in the movement and their picture of politics in the mass society closely resembled that of the ideal-type alienated man. Ralph Schoenman's critique, for example:

> The societies we inhabit today are crippling human beings. We are bludgeoned by the devices of authority into a vast paralysis, an inability to affect events, a fear that our anxieties and aspirations must remain private. We know that our values and institutions are terrible confessions of social bankruptcy, yet we feel it pointless to attempt to cope with our social problems. Men are dependent on vast and impersonal societies. These societies are highly ordered, controlled by powerful autocracies, and they are essentially totalitarian in their organization.[1]

In order to discover whether this was also experienced subjectively by Campaign supporters in general, two statements of the kind commonly used in the measurement of powerlessness were put to respondents, who were asked to state their agreement or disagreement. These were (*a*) 'ordinary people cannot hope to change government policies'; and (*b*) 'there will always be war; it's part of human nature'. The responses are recorded in Table 3.

TABLE 3   *Self-perception of political powerlessness*

(a) *Ordinary people cannot hope to*
      change government policies

	%
Agree/Strongly agree	4
Disagree/Strongly disagree	90
Don't know/No response	6
	100 (N = 358)

(b) *There will always be war;*
      it's part of human nature

	%
Agree/Strongly agree	6
Disagree/Strongly disagree	87
Don't know/No response	7
	100 (N = 358)

[1] *Peace News*, 17 February 1961, p. 1.

CND supporters clearly cannot be said to be alienated in the sense of exhibiting feelings that the world is an uncontrollable place and that they are personally unable to influence the course of events. They appear to have a strikingly high degree of optimism about the possibilities of human betterment and their personal political effectiveness, which is quite the reverse of the attitude typically displayed by the subjects in the studies referred to above. The indications are that the unilateralist movement does not seem to have served as a refuge for those overwhelmed by the mass society, even though at first sight its political style might have been thought to be amenable to those who were alienated in this respect.

Alienation from dominant values

Although CND supporters cannot be thought of as being either socially unintegrated or as psychologically unable to come to terms with political realities, there is a further dimension of alienation—or more properly another characteristic which is also given this label—that does appear to distinguish supporters from the population at large, and which is independent of the factors so far discussed. This third and final usage of alienation refers to individuals' non-acceptance or rejection of certain values which may be regarded as central to the social order, and their commitment to alternative values which, simply as a matter of definition, can be classified as deviant. Since the notion of a central value system is a problematic one in sociology, it may be as well if the position adopted here is spelled out a little more fully.

Modern industrial societies are frequently characterized by their lack of uniformity in the normative sphere, and by the existence within any one society of a variety of competing and conflicting values, such that many opposed patterns of behaviour and belief are given the stamp of social acceptibility and legitimacy. However, this absence of a unified and all-embracing system of values, of the kind found in small-scale primitive societies, for example, should not blind us to the fact that even in complex societies there exist certain institutional orders which occupy a key place in the social structure, and the values surrounding which exercise a dominant influence throughout society. Even within a highly diverse and complex normative system it still makes sense to conceive of, on the one hand, a set of dominant values, or core values which are in a way central to the society, which give the society its defining characteristics; and on the other hand a variety of sub-systems which are either opposed to, or in some way deviant from the dominant system. The counter-

argument to this is to claim that conflicting values in our type of
society have equal status and equal weight so that none could be
singled out as being either dominant or deviant, but only different.
Such a view would indeed render the notion of deviance untenable,
since obviously the possibility of deviance implies the existence of
certain commonly accepted standards of conduct and belief in given
spheres of behaviour. Examples of key institutional orders in
British society which could be said to generate dominant values
would include the Established Church, the public schools and the
ancient universities, the elites of the military establishment, the
press and the mass media, the monarchy and the aristocracy, as well
as, perhaps most important of all, the institutional complex of
private property and capitalist enterprise which dominates the
economic sector—post-war experiments with a 'mixed economy'
notwithstanding. Although it would be misleading to consider the
values surrounding these institutions as comprising a coherent and
unified normative system—in the way that Marxism could be said
to be for example—it nevertheless makes sense to suggest that they
are more thoroughly institutionalized in the social order and are
accorded greater legitimacy than those values which embody an
opposing alternative. One reason for the dominant influence of the
former over the latter is, of course, that they are the values which are
embraced by upper strata members of society and which are legitimized by those who exercise a monopoly of power and prestige.
Challenges to dominant institutions characteristically derive from
groups and individuals less favourably placed in the status hierarchy
and who generally have less access to the loci of power. Oppositional values which emerge from this source thus tend to have a
more precarious hold in society than the dominant ones they
challenge. This could perhaps be illustrated by a comparison of the
relative status in British society of the following pairs of dominant
and oppositional or deviant values.

Dominant institutions and values	*Deviant values*
Royalty—monarchism	Republicanism—anti-monarchism
Capitalism—private property	Socialism—nationalization
Church—religion	Anti-clericalism—humanism/atheism
Armed forces—militarism	Pacifism—anti-militarism
Nationalism	Internationalism

To suggest that the array of values listed in the left-hand column
could be classified as being 'dominant' in British society, and those
in the right-hand column as being 'deviant', does not of course

imply any covert ethical judgement. Labelling certain elements in the overall normative order as deviant or oppositional is not to question their *moral* status and legitimacy, or to argue that they are dysfunctional for society by undermining consensus; but serves simply to highlight the point that such values are comparatively marginal to the social order—if only by virtue of the fact that they are not sanctioned by institutional elites and the centres of power. To claim that conflicting political (or other) values carry equal weight, such that the terms dominant and deviant become meaningless is to ignore the unequal distribution of power in society, which ensures that certain values are buttressed more effectively than others. Thus, within a predominantly capitalist economic order, such as exists in present-day Britain, socialist ideals concerning public ownership and workers' control in industry may be regarded as perfectly *legitimate*, but it would nevertheless be highly misleading to infer from this that they therefore occupied parity of status with the opposite ideals centred around private property ownership and commercial enterprise, in terms of the institutionalized means available for their dissemination and practical attainment. Opposing political values such as these can only be conceived of as enjoying parity if attention is focused exclusively on their legitimacy and moral status, and if they are regarded as free-floating entities disembodied from institutional settings. But once values are related to institutional complexes such a view becomes impossible to sustain by virtue of the inequalities of power and status attaching to institutions and the consequent variations in the structural supports for their normative elements.

If it be acknowledged that the notion of dominant values (not necessarily comprising an intellectually coherent 'system') is a valid statement about the normative order of industrial societies, then the alienation concept can usefully be employed as a measure of individuals' rejection of such values. Alienation in this sense would amount to an index of men's lack of commitment to dominant institutional orders and the normative elements they generate and sustain. It is this usage of the concept which is largely implied in references to the 'alienation of the intelligentsia', since it is not estrangement from society—understood as social groupings and structures—which is referred to, so much as estrangement from certain of its normative components. In order to determine to what extent CND supporters could be said to be alienated in this particular sense it was necessary to establish some practical indices of commitment to readily identifiable institutional complexes whose values could be said to exercise a pervasive influence in British society. Three such complexes were singled out for this purpose—the monarchy, the church and the institutional orders of private property and capitalism.

The monarchy, as Shils and Young have argued, can be regarded as a symbolic expression of the national consensus, the institution in which certain sacred and civil attachments to the society as a whole is made manifest.[1] It is not necessary to endorse a wholesale functionalist interpretation of the monarchy in claiming that the values and symbols surrounding it exercise a dominant and pervasive influence throughout all levels of British society. Professor Lipset has commented upon the extent of this influence and its implications for a wide range of social and political behaviour.

The political effects of monarchy and aristocracy were not eliminated when these institutions lost their legislative, administrative and executive prerogatives. The legitimacy of the British Establishment and the existence of deferential voters who believe that those born and trained to lead should in fact lead, who accept the propriety of Government by a party most of whose leaders are products of the public schools and the ancient universities, are in some part to be explained by the widespread acceptance of hereditary privilege, as symbolized in the support given to the institutions of monarchy and aristocracy.[2]

To this extent the value complex surrounding the institution of the monarchy may plausibly be said to be a dominant one in British society, while anti-monarchical values could be represented as deviant.

Secondly, concerning the institutional complex of private property and capitalist enterprise, although it is true that the British economic order does contain an important public sector, there can be little doubt that the dominant practices and values are those generated by the privately owned sector. The extension of public ownership is regarded with disfavour by most sectors of the community, and the pattern of property ownership regarded as 'normal' is that embodying the values of private enterprise. Although anti-capitalist values certainly do command some support in British society they are by no means as pervasive, nor as effectively institutionalized, as those upheld by capitalist enterprise, post-war Labour governments notwithstanding. Values opposing the legit-

---

[1] Edward Shils and Michael Young, 'The Meaning of the Coronation', *Sociological Review*, **1**, 1953.

[2] S. M. Lipset, 'Must the Tories Always Triumph?', *Socialist Commentary*, January 1961, p. 9.

imacy or morality of private property may thus usefully be thought of as deviant in our society.

Thirdly, the values surrounding the religious institutions of the church; it is not suggested that these exert a dominating influence in society in the way that the previous two complexes can be said to, since the evidence of secularization points too strongly in the other direction. What is maintained, however, is that definite elements of religiosity still inform the behaviour of the overwhelming majority of the population in certain specific spheres of conduct and belief, such that in relation to these limited spheres a dominant value orientation could reasonably be said to prevail.

Thus, whilst the majority of people do not attend religious services on a regular basis, widespread importance is still attached to the church's mediation in the life-cycle ceremonies associated with birth, marriage and death, suggesting the continued acceptance of religious values and rituals in certain limited spheres of action. Similarly, self-ascription to 'membership' of religious denominations, and belief in the existence of God is, as Bryan Wilson has pointed out, paradoxically high for a 'secularized' society:

> although church attendance declines in England, and there are fewer people 'on the books' of the Nonconformist Churches and at Easter Communion in the Church of England, there do not appear to be many more people than there were in the past, who are prepared to declare themselves to be non-Christian. The vast majority profess to believe in God. Many of these assert that they 'belong'—in some residual way—to the Church of England. This is one of the discrepancies which persuade some that 'secularization' is a misnomer for what is taking place.[1]

On these grounds, then, it seems plausible to regard the outright rejection of religion, and self-identification as a non-believer, as an index of deviance from values which are given strong institutional and popular support in contemporary Britain.

These three examples provide a starting point in the task of isolating institutions whose values occupy a central or dominant place in the society. This then makes it possible to consider alienation as a rejection of such values in favour of deviant or minority values. Thus, whereas the two previous uses of alienation were measures of social and psychological integration, this final one may be thought of as a measure of normative integration. With this

[1] Bryan Wilson, *Religion in Secular Society*, Watts, London, 1966, p. 4. Michael Argyle, collating a number of opinion surveys on religious membership, puts the figure of those claiming affiliation to a religious denomination at over 90 per cent of the population. *Religious Behaviour*, Routledge, London, 1958, p. 37.

c

distinction in mind, CND respondents were asked questions relating to the three institutions discussed above to determine the extent to which they conformed to, or deviated from, the values in question. Turning first to the matter of the monarchy, respondents were asked to state their measure of agreement or disagreement with the statement that: 'the monarchy is an institution we should be justly proud of'. The responses were as follows, broken down this time into social class categories.

Although respondents in the top two social classes are slightly better disposed towards the monarchy than the remainder, there is a heavy bias against which shows throughout the whole sample. Less than 14 per cent of the total endorse the popular support of royalty

TABLE 4   *Attitudes to the monarchy*

The monarchy is an institution we should be justly proud of	*Respondents' social class*		
	1 + 2	3 + 4	5 + 6 + 7
	%	%	%
Agree/Strongly agree	19	11	11
Disagree/Strongly disagree	72	82	87
Don't know/No response	9	7	2
	100	100	100
	(N = 96)	(N = 201)	(N = 44)

and its symbols, whilst more than 80 per cent express various shades of disapproval. CND supporters may thus be said to be alienated from this particular value complex which is accorded a high degree of esteem among all levels of British society. Turning now to the institution of private property and capitalist ownership, respondents were asked to indicate agreement or disagreement with the statement that: 'all major industries should be nationalised'. The responses are set out in Table 5.

TABLE 5   *Attitudes to nationalization*

All major industries should be nationalized	*Respondents' social class*		
	1 + 2	3 + 4	5 + 6 + 7
	%	%	%
Agree/Strongly agree	65	73	89
Disagree/Strongly disagree	29	21	6
Don't know/No response	6	6	5
	100	100	100
	(N = 96)	(N = 201)	(N = 44)

Again there is clear cut endorsement of the minority view in favour of a large-scale extension of public ownership. Although significant differences occur along class lines, which will be discussed further below, the overall pattern is clear enough, and indicates a strong rejection of values central to the present capitalist economic order.

Concerning finally the field of religion, respondents were asked to state whether they regarded themselves as members of any religious denomination, or whether they fell into one of the various categories of non-believer. This information is recorded in Table 6.

Although there is less unanimity in the matter of religious belief than in the previous two questions, it is nevertheless clear that a good majority of respondents subscribe to no religious denomination, even nominally. 34 per cent describe themselves as atheists or

TABLE 6   *Religious affiliation**

Believers	%	Non-Believers	%
C. of E.	14	Agnostic	19
Quaker	10	Humanist	15
Methodist	5	Atheist	15
Presbyterian	4	Other/None	9
Baptist	2		
Catholic	2		
Jewish	1		
Other	2		
	40		58

(NN = 358)   *2% gave no reply.

agnostics, which may be safely assumed to be greatly in excess of the proportion in the population as a whole. Thus on all three counts respondents came down heavily on the side of oppositional or deviant values even though the three institutions selected were not logically related to one another, in the sense that the rejection of the values associated with one of them necessarily entailed the rejection of the others. Given this overall uniform response, CND supporters may reasonably be said to be alienated from certain central values of British society.

The extent to which dominant values in a society are fully accepted by its members is of course largely a function of the stratification system. Generally speaking, there is a greater commitment to dominant values on the part of higher status groups than among the less materially and socially privileged. In industrial societies for example the integration of the working class into the dominant value system was a long-drawn-out process which only followed upon the full extension of political and citizenship rights. Even so, the process is not a complete one and total value consensus is probably unattainable where social and economic rewards are unequally distributed. Thus to claim that a society has distinguishable complexes of dominant values is not at the same time to claim that all strata are necessarily committed to them in the same degree. Lower status groups in particular often lack strong identification with such values, and this stratum of society may be regarded as structurally amenable to the generation of normative sub-cultures with a high potential for deviance.[1] However, this does not invalidate the argument concerning CND supporters since, as we have seen, they are drawn *predominantly from the middle class* and not from less privileged strata where deviant values are more readily institutionalized. The fact that CND supporters are mainly middle class serves to emphasize their deviance since their value orientations should be compared with those characteristic of the middle class in particular, rather than with those of the overall population. Because the attitude of the middle class towards the monarchy, the church and private property may be safely assumed to be almost wholly favourable, the alienation of CND supporters from such values is thrown into high relief.

To argue that CND supporters are alienated from the values enumerated above does not of course imply that they are alienated from all major values of the society. In the institutions centred around work, family, leisure, culture and so on, they may well endorse the same attitudes and subscribe to the same standards common to the middle class in general. Alienation from values supporting the monarchy, the church and capitalism would appear to be quite compatible with conformity to values which are felt to be independent of these spheres. Indeed, it is not uncommon for deviant political or religious groups to enjoin their members to be particularly conformist with respect to 'neutral' values, as for example in the matters of family life, dress, speech and public demeanour; the purpose of this kind of ultra-conformity is to avoid members being stigmatized as 'cranks', thereby undermining the force of their public message. Thus, a continuous source of annoyance and embarrassment to adult CND members was the outlandish dress often sported by the younger elements in the movement, because this allowed arguments in favour of unilateralism to be dismissed by its opponents as the aberrations of 'bearded weirdies'. Supporters

[1] Robert K. Merton, 'Social Structure and Anomie', in *Social Theory And Social Structure*, Free Press, 1964.

were frequently being urged to dress and behave as conventionally as possible in order to forestall this type of criticism.

Examples of this kind bring out clearly the point that alienation from societal values is by no means necessarily total. Some degree of conformity may be highly functional in sustaining deviance from values which relate to matters of principle and which have important implications for the social structure. The common use of the term 'alienated man' to describe the individual's estrangement from society is therefore misleading and analytically imprecise; it is not usually man in his totality of social roles and attitudes who is at variance with society, but more commonly man in a limited number of spheres only. Because of the possibility of compartmentalizing values and segmenting social roles, alienation in the sense described here is more likely to be a limited and partial phenomenon than a total experience involving the whole personality, as is so often implied. The extent to which alienation from one sphere of values permeates through to others is an empirically open question, and it cannot be assumed *a priori* that alienation from political and religious aspects of the normative order automatically entails alienation from all other aspects. Such a view would come close to positing a notion of alienated man as psychologically disturbed or inadequate, which is a far remove from the perspective adopted here and which in any case would be a highly misleading characterization of the typical CND supporter.[1]

In concluding this discussion of alienation, it may be said that CND supporters' overall position in relation to central societal values points to what might be called a 'deviance syndrome'—that is, the propensity to endorse minority or deviant standpoints on a broad range of public issues. Such an attribute would obviously be an important factor in helping to account for involvement in CND. If the reasonable assumption is made that supporters subscribed to this particular constellation of deviant values before the emergence of the unilateralist movement, then it makes sense to claim that they were, so to speak, 'prepared' for it before the question of nuclear weapons became a major political issue. In other words, an

[1] Even so, it would appear that alienation from societal values is not always compartmentalized, but may affect commitment to popularly accepted standards of an apparently neutral type; to take a trivial example, the wearing of beards did appear to be more common among CND supporters than among men in general; also many respondents indicated they were vegetarians. More significantly, 8 per cent of female respondents were divorced (and an additional 4 per cent separated), a figure which compares with less than 1 per cent for women in the total population. This does suggest that estrangement from certain central values may be conducive to deviance in a wide range of social behaviour.

individual's commitment to CND could to a large extent be said to be determined by his existing predisposition to deviance of the kind outlined. The personal rejection of values associated with the monarchy, religion and capitalism had, as it were, cleared the ground for his acceptance of the kind of appeals initiated by the anti-Bomb movement. Contrariwise, those who believed firmly in these core values would by the same token be highly likely to view the movement in a negative light. Although both sides tended to conduct the debate in terms of rational criteria—presenting plausible arguments for and against nuclear deterrence—this only served to obscure the fact that the individual's ideological position generally came first and the appropriate rational and strategic arguments were adopted to fit it. Attraction to CND appears to have depended not simply on individuals accepting the case against the Bomb and for the Campaign, but rather on their having the kind of prior value orientation which made this case psychologically appealing.[1] Alienation from certain dominant values of British society was a common factor shared by the majority of CND supporters, and therefore helps to explain their recruitment to the movement in a way that other usages of the concept failed to do. This serves to highlight the fact that estrangement from dominant values is quite compatible with the individual's firm integration into society as measured by the usual criteria of social and personal involvement, and that such involvement does not necessarily weaken the appeal of political mass movements.

Although CND supporters may be said to have rejected certain of the values which occupy a central place in the major institutional orders of British society, this is not to say that they are totally alienated from their society and its values. Indeed, such total estrangement would logically produce an attitude of indifference to the country's foreign and defence policies and not a deep resentment that such policies were wrong or immoral. It could be argued in fact that those who were moved to personal protest over the H-bomb issue were individuals who held unusually high expectations of their society, and who had a marked sense of self-identity with its fortunes. Those who demand that their society should be judged by the highest possible standards, and who expect it to adhere in international affairs to the kind of strict moral code relevant to the conduct of individuals are clearly not to be equated with those whose alienation takes the form of withdrawal from the political process

[1] For an elaboration of, and supporting evidence for, this point of view see Chapters 5 and 6.

and a lack of identity between self and society. Individuals who feel personally wounded by their country's actions may be said in fact to be *over*—rather than under-socialized into certain of its basic value premises. This does not run counter to the fact that such individuals, as the CND example shows, may also be those who reject other important institutional features of the society, since it is usually possible to justify such rejection by an appeal to 'higher' values which the society also espouses. As Parsons has pointed out, radical movements derive much of their legitimacy from their ability to exploit the normative ambiguities which inevitably exist in highly complex societies:

Most of the 'ideological issues' which define the difference of value systems concern highly abstract and general formulae which are open to much 'interpretation'. Moreover, many of the abstract formulae, such as the desirability of 'social justice', of 'democracy' or of 'peace' are shared in common. Who is to say whether one interpretation is more legitimate than the other? Movements which exploit the generalities and ambiguities of dominant value-systems and their accompanying ideologies are hence particularly difficult to control by any means which involves depriving them of the claim of legitimacy.[1]

At the same time, Parsons' emphasis on the dysfunctional consequences of this tendency should perhaps be counter-balanced by reference to the point that the ambiguity in general values which results in their being open to different behavioural interpretations also provides a necessary leverage for social change. Those whose commitment to their society is not one of unquestioning acceptance of its major values and institutions are afforded the means of legitimizing their demands for reform—as for example in the insistence that such values should be adhered to in their 'pure' form. Thus, historically, those alienated from certain aspects of the normative order, but who have been committed to societal values in some idealistic form, have often played a key role in the achievement of social reforms and the extension of individual liberties. The dissenting tradition has largely been the contribution of those who have been alienated in the special sense here considered—individuals who, by being partially estranged from the normative order, have been the better placed to comment critically upon it and to crusade against its injustices. These are the individuals who might be said to have followed C. Wright Mills' injunction that 'Alienation must be used in the pursuit of truths.'[2] Total and uncritical

---

[1] Talcott Parsons, *The Social System*, Routledge, 1951, p. 293.
[2] C. Wright Mills, 'The Social Role of the Intellectual', in Irving Horowitz, *Power, Politics and People*, Oxford University Press, 1964, p. 301.

endorsement of society's major values and institutions represents the opposite polar type, and provides the basis for social conservatism, order and continuity. It is no concern of the present study to pronounce upon the relative merits of these different orientations, since in any case a complex society probably benefits from a tension between the two. It is sufficient to reiterate the point that men's relationship to the normative order provides a far surer guide to their support for, or opposition to, CND than any 'rational' considerations of defence or deterrence.

3

Radical politics and social class

The fact that individuals may support political movements because they symbolize the rejection of, or identification with, certain values has not been given the attention it deserves by political sociologists. The bulk of theorizing about political behaviour focuses upon the divisions created by material interests, especially the conflicts over the allocation of scarce material and social resources. Less attention has been paid to the possibility that groups and individuals may be as deeply concerned about the defence or propagation of secular moral values which are quite unrelated to material and economic interests. Daniel Katz has drawn attention to this dimension of activity, which has special relevance to the political behaviour of CND supporters:

Satisfactions also accrue to the person from the expression of attitudes which reflect his cherished beliefs and his self-image. The reward to the person in these instances is not so much a matter of gaining social recognition or monetary rewards as of establishing his self-identity and confirming his notion of the sort of person he sees himself to be. . . . Just as we find satisfaction in the exercise of our talents and abilities, so we find reward in the expression of any attributes associated with our egos.[1]

It will now be suggested that this is the kind of reward which CND supporters chiefly derive from their political activity. Such activities provide compensations which are more psychological than material, and tend to revolve around issues which are more moral than economic in content. These contrasting styles may be analysed in terms of the distinction between expressive and instrumental politics—polar types which are useful in examining certain of the problems under review and to which attention may now be directed.

Instrumental and expressive politics

Instrumental activity may be thought of as that which is directly geared to the attainment of concrete and specific goals, generally of a material kind. Emphasis is placed on the ends to be achieved rather than on the means employed in attaining them. Expressive activity, by contrast, is that which is less concerned with specific achievements than with the benefits and satisfactions which the activity itself affords. The rewards are as much in the action itself as in the ends it is directed to. In the field of politics these two distinctive styles are represented in the contrasting emphases given to the pursuit of power on the one hand and the strict adherence to principle on the other. Instrumental politics is that primarily concerned with the attainment of power to bring about desired ends, even if this means some compromise of principles. Expressive politics is that which is mainly concerned with the defence of principles, even if this means relinquishing power. Most political activity, of course, combines elements of both approaches, and examples of 'pure' types are empirically rare. However, a greater orientation towards one of the two styles is normally discernible, making the distinction a viable and useful one. Such a distinction is essentially that which underlies Max Weber's contrast between the 'ethic of

[1] Daniel Katz, 'The Functional Approach to the Study of Attitudes', *Public Opinion Quarterly*, Summer 1960, p. 173.

responsibility' and the 'ethic of ultimate ends'.[1] The tension between these two political orientations has been at the root of many
of the conflicts within the Labour Party from its foundation until
modern times. Roy Jenkins has contrasted the position of the Labour
Party with that of the Conservative Party in this respect:

> The will to power has always been much stronger in the Conservative
> Party. There it is something to be pursued at almost any cost. The Labour
> Party has quite rightly had a different order of priorities, but its danger is
> that of going too far in the other direction and thinking that it is unsocialist
> and even immoral to desire power. [There is a belief that] the best thing in
> politics is to be a happy few battling against intolerable odds.[2]

Denis Healey too has referred to the Labour Party's tendency to
'discount the power element in politics, seeing it as a specific evil
of the existing system rather than a generic characteristic of politics
as such'.[3] This is not a view which has been confined to the right
wing of the Party; the left have often expressed a similar appraisal,
as the following passage by Crossman indicates:

> parties of the Left can retain their strength and enthusiasm through ex-
> tended periods of opposition, provided that leadership remains committed
> to radical change. But that strength and enthusiasm rapidly ebbs away if
> ever the leadership becomes obsessed by electoral considerations and
> succumbs to the temptation to jettison its radical policies for the sake of
> office . . . it follows that the prime function of the Labour Party . . . is to
> provide an ideology for non-conformist critics of the Establishment . . .
> those who assert that the sole object, or even the main object, of the Labour
> Party today should be to regain office seem to me to misconceive not merely
> the nature of British socialism but the working of British democracy.[4]

This is perhaps simply another way of claiming that political
activity fulfils different needs for different individuals. For the
businessman in local politics, for example, it will typically be a
means to fairly specific material ends, whilst for others it may provide
psychological satisfactions which are not directly dependent on the
achievements of definite goals. It was predicted of CND supporters
that they would hold to a view of politics as an expressive activity
in which the defence of principles was felt to have higher priority
than 'getting things done'. To test this, respondents were asked to
indicate their agreement or disagreement with the following two

[1] From *Max Weber; Essays in Sociology*, translated and edited by H. H. Gerth
and C. Wright Mills, Routledge, 1948, p. 120.
[2] Roy Jenkins, 'British Labor Divided', *Foreign Affairs*, April 1960, p. 494.
[3] Denis Healey, 'Power Politics and the Labour Party', in R. H. S. Crossman
(ed.), *New Fabian Essays*, Turnstile Press, London, 1952, p. 161.
[4] R. H. S. Crossman, *Labour in the Affluent Society*, Fabian Tract 325, June
1960, pp. 5–6.

statements: (a) 'protests and demonstrations which fail to achieve their aims are a waste of effort'; and (b) 'the Labour Party should put principles before power'. Only the responses of Labour Party supporters (73 per cent of the total sample) to this latter statement were recorded.

TABLE 7   *Instrumental vs expressive politics*

(a) *Protests and demonstrations which fail to achieve their aims are a waste of effort*

	%
Agree/Strongly agree	10
Disagree/Strongly disagree	86
Don't know/No response	4
	100 (N = 358)

(b) *The Labour Party should put principles before power*

	%
Agree/Strongly agree	80
Disagree/Strongly disagree	14
Don't know/No response	6
	100 (N = 262)

The great majority of respondents declared themselves in favour of a style of politics in which the achievement of concrete goals is not the prime consideration. From this point of view, politics is concerned with the strict adherence to principles, and the making of gestures felt to be morally right, even though ineffective in practical terms. The rewards of political activity are derived not so much from a sense of accomplishment, at 'getting things done', as from the satisfactions entailed in being 'a happy few battling against intolerable odds'.

In Max Weber's words:

The believer in an ethic of ultimate ends feels 'responsible' only for seeing to it that the flame of pure intentions is not quelched: for example, the flame of protesting against the injustice of the social order. To rekindle the flame ever anew is the purpose of his quite irrational deeds, judged in view of their possible success. They are acts that can and shall have only exemplary value.[1]

Many CND supporters showed themselves well aware that the emphasis upon morality at the expense of expediency entailed them in the dilemma that the principles they upheld might never be

[1] Weber, loc. cit.

translated into practical policies. Written comments on the question-naires frequently drew attention to respondents' acknowledgement of this position and many justified the pure moral standpoint as being the lesser of two evils. The point should perhaps again be underlined that political styles which result in emotional or psycho-logical rewards, rather than practical or material ones, are not use-fully thought of as characteristic of individuals with personality maladjustments. It would be as misleading to suggest that expressive politics was a product of neuroticism as to claim that instrumental politics was a product of greed or power mania. Most forms of politics entail a tension between both orientations, and one cannot be said to be more 'natural' than the other.[1]

Consistent with their expressive commitment is the order of priorities which CND supporters accord to different spheres of politics. Respondents were asked to state which of the three they were personally most interested in—local politics, national politics or international politics. The replies are shown in Table 8.

TABLE 8 *Local, national and international politics: order of priorities*

Most interested in:	%
Local politics	1
National politics	29
International politics	56
No priority/No response	14
	100 (N = 358)

Not unexpectedly, greatest interest was shown in international politics and least in local politics. Local politics with its emphasis on pragmatic and practical matters is obviously the sphere least liable to attract the interest of those disposed to politics as an expressive activity. Conversely, international politics as a major focus of interest is well suited to this particular political style; it is the area in which the possibility of achieving concrete results through individual participation in politics is at its lowest. Instead, it is especially amenable to the making of gestures which stress moral absolutes, but which tend to have little practical effect on outcomes. It is in short the political sphere in which the rewards of personal involvement are almost wholly of an emotional or psy-chological kind.

---

[1] 'an ethic of ultimate ends and an ethic of responsibility are not absolute contrasts, but rather supplements, which only in unison constitute a genuine man —a man who *can* have the "calling for politics".' Weber, op. cit, p. 127.

CND supporters' emphasis on politics as an expressive style is perhaps logically related to the 'deviance syndrome' already referred to in the previous chapter. Those who subscribe to deviant values, particularly of a religious or political kind, will have to seek outlets for their expression and re-affirmation since they are not firmly institutionalized in the social system in the way that dominant values are. Expressive political activity could therefore be regarded as functionally necessary for the maintenance of deviant values. The marches, demonstrations, vigils and so forth which characterize expressive politics provide a means of re-inforcing values which are not securely integrated in the social structure in the sense that they lack the support and the legitimating effect of major institutions. Dominant values by contrast require much less in the way of an expressive commitment since they are taken for granted and appear 'natural' to the mass of the population. Deviants will usually be under various social pressures to conform to dominant values and will therefore have to make more of a conscious commitment to their beliefs than other people if these are to remain intact. An expressive political style helps to serve this purpose by treating all issues as matters of principle so that the minority values are continuously being highlighted and re-affirmed; without this kind of permanent bolstering such values would be in danger of erosion by the conformist pressures of the wider society.

That those who shared a view of politics as an expressive activity should have been drawn to CND is quite understandable. As will be shown in later chapters, involvement in the Campaign was frequently not simply a token of the individual's opposition to the Bomb, but also a capsule statement of his position on a variety of unrelated issues which the Bomb was felt to symbolize. In addition, the average CND supporter would be opposed not only to nuclear weapons, but to capital punishment, Apartheid and racial discrimination, the immigration laws, the monarchy, capitalism and religion —or if religious, the church. He or she would generally be in favour of homosexual law reform, the abolition of censorship, more aid to poorer countries, abortion law reform and so forth. On a wide range of public issues the CND supporter could be expected to have a position well to the left of the population at large. None of the major political parties truly catered for this form of global radicalism. Whilst electorally the majority of CND'ers supported the Labour Party, they made it plain that this was largely *faute de mieux*, and disapproval at the Party's loss of idealism and its cautious political approach—particularly in international affairs—was widespread amongst Campaign supporters.[1] CND thus provided the one single political movement in which 'progressive' values were fully represented in their pure form, and where they could remain untarnished by the demands of electoral expediency. The movement was able to serve as a haven for radicals in the way that the Labour Party, with its commitment to consensus politics, was not able to. To be identified with CND was to be singled out as one who held a constellation of predictably radical attitudes and beliefs quite apart from the matter of the Bomb. This latent function of providing a rallying point and symbol for radicals and their values must be considered an important sustaining force behind CND, and perhaps a more crucial one than its manifest function of attempting to change the government's nuclear weapons policy. The fact that the Campaign was still able to muster mass support for its Easter demonstrations long after its ineffectiveness in changing defence policy had become apparent (as was often freely acknowledged by supporters themselves) indicates the degree of commitment to politics as an expression of minority or deviant values and a form of witness against the values of the wider society.[2]

CND supporters' lack of primary concern with the achievement of concrete political ends may well result in the movement's having a high survival value. From its supporters' point of view the movement can never be said to have 'failed', not merely because of the unpredictability of the future, but also, and mainly, because political activity in support of the values it upholds can be claimed to be beneficial in and of itself. In addition, because it embodies a wide spectrum of radical values the movement is able to shift its emphasis from one set of concerns to another, as and when they become issues of major political importance. As the Bomb becomes a less emotive public issue the Campaign is able to redirect its energies towards those matters which have replaced it in the political arena, particularly of course, in the field of international affairs.

[1] This lukewarm attitude to the Labour Party is borne out by data on respondents' voting intentions. 73 per cent of the sample indicated electoral support for Labour; but of these 42 per cent would not necessarily vote for the Party if a CND candidate were to stand in their constituency— either preferring outright to vote for CND (28 per cent) or being unwilling to commit themselves in advance (14 per cent). That such a large percentage of nominal Labour supporters should consider abandoning their Party allegiance when faced with the choice of a CND candidate does again show—in view of the latter's slender election chances—how much respondents regard political acts as symbolic gestures.

[2] The statement by the Secretary of Crewe CND was not untypical: 'I don't for a moment believe that this country will unilaterally renounce reliance on nuclear strategy, though it is right we should call upon it to do so'. *Peace News*, 20 July 1962, p. 8.

Thus, by the mid-nineteen-sixties the movement's main focus of attention had shifted from nuclear weapons to the war in Vietnam, with protest at American policies, and the British government's support of these policies, supplying the central theme of demonstrations. Given the kind of global radicalism it represents CND would thus appear to have a certain built-in resilience in so far as its continued existence is not directly dependent on the achievement of its pristine aims so much as in its ability to provide a focus for radicalism beyond the scope of the major political parties.

Class differences in radicalism

In the previous section it was suggested that support for CND could usefully be portrayed as an example of expressive politics. It will now be proposed that this characteristic is to a large extent dependent upon the middle class basis of CND, and is one which sets it in contrast to movements drawn predominantly from the working class. The relationship between a movement's social base and its political goals may, it is suggested, be set out as follows. Working class movements have, historically, been devoted primarily to the achievement of aims of a material, bread and butter kind; the Chartists, the IWW, the Communist, Labour and Trade Union movements are examples which obviously spring to mind. They have all been geared to securing a more favourable share of economic wealth or political power and civic rights for their supporters— higher wages, improved working conditions, enfranchisement and so on. In short, their political orientations have been *primarily* instrumental in character, even though some expressive elements may have been discernible. Frequently the ideology underlying their claims has been one involving the repudiation of the *status quo* and its replacement by a new social order based on a different set of property and authority relationships. This has been a common, almost universal, theme of proletarian movements wherever they have emerged—the main variations being not so much in this basic commitment to structural change, but rather in whether the transformation should be carried out by peaceful or revolutionary means. Related to this belief in the need for deep-seated social change, working class movements have generally had a formal ideology of some kind—marxism, socialism, anarchism or the like—which offers its adherents a set of values having explanatory powers of an all-embracing compass.

By contrast to this, radical movements with a middle class base tend to be far less oriented to the achievement of economic or material rewards for their supporters. They are instead more typically concerned with issues of a moral or humanitarian nature—as for example, Anti-Apartheid, the campaign against capital punishment, white support for Negroes' civil rights in the United States, CND and so on. These goals are intrinsically different from those pursued by working class movements in that they offer no particular benefits to those who support them—such benefits are felt to accrue to others (e.g. Negroes, political prisoners) or to society as a whole, rather than to themselves specifically. The main pay-off for such activity is in the emotional satisfaction derived from expressing personal values in action. Again, middle class movements do not generally have an overall ideology purporting to explain the social problems in question by reference to a set of fixed doctrines, as is commonly found in working class movements; instead, such problems are usually considered as social isolates each requiring a particular solution.

That radical movements with a middle class base have a definite bias in favour of moral rather than economic reforms may be illustrated by reference to the CND data. As we have already seen, the great majority of supporters do approve of radical measures in the economic sphere, as indicated by their overall approval of extensive nationalization. Similar support was also shown for a number of other radical proposals which may now be considered. Respondents were asked to express their measure of agreement or disagreement with the following six statements:

(a) Unemployment benefits should be substantially increased.
(b) All major industries should be nationalized.
(c) There should be greater legal protection for trade unions.
(d) The laws against homosexual acts by consenting adults should be repealed.
(e) Britain should give more material aid to poorer countries.
(f) Our present immigration laws should be greatly relaxed.

Although all these proposals are of the type more liable to appeal to those of a left-wing rather than a right-wing disposition, they can usefully be divided into two categories. The first three relate to traditional socialist or Marxist concerns with improved benefits for the working class and with changing the property basis of capitalist society—in short with broad material or class matters. The last three are related to moral or humanitarian issues of a basically non-class character. As will be seen in Tables 9 and 10 below respondents indicated general support for all six proposals, but certain differences in emphasis do emerge along class lines, as predicted.

D

TABLE 9   *Attitudes to economic and class issues*

(a) *Unemployment benefits should be substantially increased*

	Respondents' social class		
	1 + 2	3 + 4	5 + 6 + 7
	%	%	%
Agree/Strongly agree	63	69	70
Disagree/Strongly disagree	23	23	16
Don't know/No response	14	8	14
	100	100	100
	(N = 96)	(N = 201)	(N = 44)

(b) *All major industries should be nationalized*

	Respondents' social class		
	1 + 2	3 + 4	5 + 6 + 7
	%	%	%
Agree/Strongly agree	65	73	89
Disagree/Strongly disagree	29	21	6
Don't know/No response	6	6	5
	100	100	100
	(N = 96)	(N = 201)	(N = 44)

(c) *There should be greater legal protection for trade unions*

	Respondents' social class		
	1 + 2	3 + 4	5 + 6 + 7
	%	%	%
Agree/Strongly agree	43	53	75
Disagree/Strongly disagree	37	27	14
Don't know/No response	20	20	11
	100	100	100
	(N = 96	(N = 201)	(N = 44)

It will be noticed that support for all these measures is greatest amongst working class respondents and least among those in the top two social classes, with classes 3 and 4 occupying the intermediate position. If replies to all three questions are aggregated, among those in agreement with increased unemployment benefits, extension of nationalization and greater protection for trade unions, the following variations in support occur between the different occupational categories; of classes 1 and 2, 57 per cent were in agreement, of classes 3 and 4, 65 per cent and of classes 5, 6 and 7, 78 per cent were in agreement, showing increased support for these measures with declining social status. Disagreement was expressed by 30 per cent of classes 1 and 2, 23 per cent of classes 3 and 4, and by only 12 per cent of classes 5, 6 and 7. This situation may be contrasted with respondents' views on the three moral issues, as presented in Tables 10a, b and c.

TABLE 10   *Attitudes to moral and humanitarian issues*

(a) *The laws against homosexual acts
by consenting adults should be
repealed*

	Respondents' social class		
	1 + 2	3 + 4	5 + 6 + 7
	%	%	%
Agree/Strongly agree	94	87	75
Disagree/Strongly disagree	1	9	9
Don't know/No response	5	4	16
	100	100	100
	(N = 96)	(N = 201)	(N = 44)

(b) *Britain should give more material
aid to poorer countries*

	Respondents' social class		
	1 + 2	3 + 4	5 + 6 + 7
	%	%	%
Agree/Strongly agree	97	93	90
Disagree/Strongly disagree	0	5	5
Don't know/No response	3	2	5
	100	100	100
	(N = 96)	(N = 201)	(N = 44)

(c) *Our present immigration laws
should be greatly relaxed*

	Respondents' social class		
	1 + 2	3 + 4	5 + 6 + 7
	%	%	%
Agree/Strongly agree	67	64	57
Disagree/Strongly disagree	27	27	32
Don't know/No response	6	9	11
	100	100	100
	(N = 96)	(N = 201)	(N = 44)

The extent of support for the three moral reforms is of a reverse order to that pertaining to the economic and class issues. Here it is respondents from the two top social classes who are most completely in favour, whilst the working class respondents show least overall enthusiasm, with classes 3 and 4 again occupying the intermediate position. Support for homosexual law reform, increased aid to poorer countries and the relaxation of immigration laws, was expressed by an aggregate of 86 per cent of respondents in occupational classes 1 and 2, by 81 per cent of those in 3 and 4, and by 74 per cent of manual respondents. Disagreement was expressed by an aggregate of 9 per cent of those in classes 1 and 2, 14 per cent in classes 3 and 4, and by 15 per cent of manual workers. The aggregate differences are not very great, but the direction of the trend in each case is in line with expectations. It was anticipated that the majority of CND supporters would favour all six proposals and that as a result class differences might not be brought out sharply by these particular responses; in addition, therefore, another measure was included with the object of highlighting which *two* of the above six proposals they personally gave most priority to. This resulted in the following scale preference.

TABLE 11   *Economic vs moral issues*

	Respondents' social class		
	1 + 2	3 + 4	5 + 6 + 7
	%	%	%
Economic issues	24	31	48
Moral issues	65	52	32
Don't know/No response	11	17	20
	100	100	100
	(N = 192)	(N = 402)	(N = 88)

(Note: N's are doubled because each respondent had two choices)

This table brings out far more clearly the different overall weighting accorded to the two sets of issues. Twice as many working class respondents gave first priority to economic reforms as respondents in classes 1 and 2, a relationship which was almost exactly reversed in the case of the moral and humanitarian reforms. Consistent with their previous replies classes 3 and 4 were placed between the two extremes, but closer to the top two classes than to the working class. Class differences of a similar kind were also apparent in supporters' main objections to Britain's possession and maintenance of nuclear weapons. Respondents were asked to state which *one* of the four following arguments in favour of abandoning the Bomb carried most weight with them personally:

(a) It is an inefficient means of defence.
(b) It is a waste of economic resources.
(c) It is a fundamentally evil weapon.
(d) It would enable Britain to give a moral lead.

The responses were as follows:

TABLE 12   *Main reasons for urging Britain's abandonment of the Bomb*

	Respondents' social class		
	1 + 2	3 + 4	5 + 6 + 7
	%	%	%
Inefficient means of defence	4	3	5
Waste of economic resources	2	11	25
Fundamentally evil weapon	70	69	50
Would give Britain a moral lead	16	13	16
Don't know/No response	8	4	4
	100	100	100
	(N = 96)	(N = 201)	(N = 44)

It will be seen from this that significant class differences are present in the pattern of respondents' objections to the Bomb. Whilst the importance of arguments as to the effectiveness of the Bomb as a means of defence, or to the moral advantages unilateralism would confer upon Britain, are given roughly the same priorities by all classes, major differences do occur in the objection to nuclear weapons on the grounds of their being either 'evil' or simply a waste of material resources. Although all occupational groups judged the former to be a more important reason than the latter, middle class respondents came out far more strongly in favour of this view than did working class respondents. A quarter of the latter based their main objection to the Bomb on economic grounds, as against only 11 per cent of social classes 3 and 4, and a mere 2 per cent of classes 1 and 2. This does once more seem to underscore the point that although there may appear to be a surface uniformity in the radical outlook, important variations based upon class differences lie beneath the surface. However, given these differences in value orientations among CND supporters, it should be remembered that there is a numerical preponderance of middle class supporters, so that it is their particular constellation of priorities and attitudes which sets its stamp upon the movement as a whole. Thus, whilst CND may certainly be regarded as a radical movement, the radicalism of its followers is centred primarily upon broad moral concerns of a basically non-class kind, rather than on the more traditional left-wing preoccupation with economic change and class conflict. As we have seen, CND'ers do on the whole give the radical answer to questions of this kind, too, but these nevertheless appear to be secondary considerations, rather than the mainsprings of their political commitment. Similarly, of course, working class movements have often declared themselves in favour of certain moral and humanitarian reforms of the kind denoted above, but this does not conceal the fact that their *primary* aims and the political basis of their support have been firmly grounded in the pursuit of material improvement for their members.[1]

[1] The usefulness of such a distinction is denied by Eysenck. In his study of class differences in political and social attitudes he dismisses the 'superficially plausible hypothesis that there are two kinds of conservatism involved, one dealing with economic matters, the other with ideational causes, in such a way that working class people are economically radical and ideationally conservative, while middle class people are economically conservative and ideationally radical.' H. J. Eysenck, 'Primary Social Attitudes as Related to Social Class and Political Party', *British Journal of Sociology*, 2, September 1951, p. 205. However, Eysenck's only grounds for this argument rests on the fact that on a battery of attitude test items more middle class than working class radicals endorsed the *sole* item

This comparative lack of class consciousness on the part of middle class CND supporters also manifests itself in their general perceptual 'model' of the social system. Ralf Dahrendorf, Elizabeth Bott, and Goldthorpe and Lockwood, have produced much material bearing upon differential class perceptions of the authority and opportunity structure of industrial society. They have pointed to the co-existence of two distinct class models of society embodying fundamentally opposed notions of social stratification. The working class model envisages the social system as divided roughly into two main categories—those who exercise power and authority, and those who are subjected to it; society consists of 'them' and 'us' and there is little social traffic between the two. In line with this, the ethic of success and individual achievement has scant relevance; collectivism and solidarity are the dominant concepts, whilst the possibilities for personal advancement are strongly devalued. In contrast to this the middle class model of stratification assumes not a sharp dichotomy, but a graduated hierarchy of authority and opportunity. Society is seen as a ladder which the talented and ambitious can climb; conflicts are not inherent in the social structure but can be avoided by sensible management and good will on all sides.[1] To get some indication whether CND supporters held to the conflict (class) model, or to the consensus (status) model, respondents were asked to state whether they agreed or disagreed with the following statements: (a) 'there is little opportunity for talented people to get on in Britain'; and (b) 'workers and management have common interests and should pull together as a team'. The replies are recorded in Table 13.

It will be seen from these figures that respondents' overall view of British society is one emphasizing its open opportunity structure and the absence of inherent class antagonisms in the industrial sector. In other words respondents subscribe to the status model which is typically held by the middle class in general, but which is less commonly found to characterize the working class's picture of society—as the responses of the working class CND supporters also

---

measuring economic radicalism. All the other items were concerned with moral issues, and on almost all of these the middle class Labour voters took a more radical position than working class Labour voters. For general criticisms of Eysenck's methodology see M. Rokeach and C. Hanley, 'Eysenck's Tender-Mindedness Dimension: A Critique', *Psychological Bulletin*, **53**, March 1956; and, Richard Christie, 'Eysenck's Treatment of the Personality of Communists', ibid.

[1] Ralf Dahrendorf, *Class and Class Conflict in Industrial Society*, Routledge, 1959; John H. Goldthorpe and David Lockwood, 'Affluence and the British Class Structure', *Sociological Review*, Vol. 11, No. 2, 1963; Elizabeth Bott, *Family and Social Network*, Tavistock, 1957.

TABLE 13   *Perceptions of society; class model vs status model*

(a) *There is little opportunity for talented people to get on in Britain*

	Respondents' social class		
	1 + 2	3 + 4	5 + 6 + 7
	%	%	%
Agree/Strongly agree	15	19	40
Disagree/Strongly disagree	79	73	53
No response/Don't know	6	8	7
	100	100	100
	(N = 96)	(N = 201)	(N = 44)

(b) *Workers and management have common interests and should pull together as a team*

	Respondents' social class		
	1 + 2	3 + 4	5 + 6 + 7
	%	%	%
Agree/Strongly agree	64	71	52
Disagree/Strongly disagree	17	24	43
Don't know/No response	19	5	5
	100	100	100
	(N = 96)	(N = 201)	(N = 44)

illustrate. It is intriguing that middle class radicals should share a view of the social order in common with the middle class as a whole, rather than subscribe to the conflict model which, although characteristically working class, might nevertheless be thought to be more appropriate to the radical disposition. It is clear that there is a certain tension in the middle class radical's position in so far as his political sympathies do not lie with his own class and the parties of the right which traditionally represent it, but with the parties of the left which cater largely for the interests of those of a different class from himself. Even more than the working class conservative, the middle class radical may be thought of as a political deviant, supporting policies and parties which are against his own 'class interests' as these are commonly perceived.

Indeed, the middle class radical's position is, in many ways, more extreme than that of the working class Conservative, in the sense that the disjunction between his own values and those of his class as a whole is considerably sharper. In fact, as McKenzie and Silver have argued, it is perhaps misleading to regard the working class Conservative as a political deviant, since in many respects his political outlook is given strong institutional support at the social level, and even amongst his own class this outlook will not necessarily mark him off sharply from Labour voters. As McKenzie and Silver put it:

The organic view of society, promulgated by the great Conservative spokesmen, Burke and Disraeli, finds a responsive echo in the contemporary
urban working class. For such reasons, it is hard to think of working class
Conservatives in Britain as normatively deviant from working-class political culture; on the contrary, they seem to express aspects of a wide national
consensus.[1]

In comparison with the working class Conservative the middle
class socialist or radical is much more out on a limb. Not only is his
position not amenable to an appeal to the 'national consensus'—
which is often the object of his protest—but also the middle class
is much more homogeneous in its (right wing) political outlook
than is the working class, with the consequence that the social
pressures on deviants are likely to be much more concentrated.
Informal interviews with CND supporters certainly suggested that
this was in fact the case. It was common for supporters to refer to
tensions between themselves and their middle class neighbours,
stemming from their different political alignments. 'We're the
black sheep of the neighbourhood', 'they all think we're dangerous
fanatics in this house' and 'anyone in this street who isn't a staunch
Tory is looked upon as a crank', were typical statements which
summed up the political isolation which the average CND'er
would probably experience in his residential community. For
women supporters at home all day the tensions are obviously more
marked, and it would seem that, for many, social relations with their
neighbours are possible only at the price of silence on matters of
politics. As a doctor's wife explained:

They invite me to their homes for coffee, and I've had them back here. If
anything political is discussed I just have to sit mum. They have the most
outrageous and reactionary views, and what is especially annoying is the
way they assume that someone like myself *automatically* agrees with them.
I never say a word, but inside I'm boiling.

An ex-schoolmistress recounted her experience in a commuter
suburb as follows:

We moved into this house about a year ago. To begin with the neighbours
couldn't have been more friendly and helpful. One day I put a Ban-the-
Bomb poster in the window and from then on things changed. They
couldn't have avoided me more if I'd caught the plague.

This may perhaps be an extreme case, but it seems to illustrate the
kind of situation which it is not uncommon for middle class radicals

---

[1] R. T. McKenzie and Allan Silver, 'Conservatism, Industrialism and the
Working Class Tory in England', in *Transactions of the Fifth World Congress of
Sociology*, Washington, 1962 ,Vol. III, p. 197.

to be confronted with. Margaret Stacey, for example, drew attention to similar tendencies in the political life of Banbury. She found that 'when the middle class do come across a member who is a Labour supporter they are surprised and shocked. They avoid social relations with the recalcitrant. When they cannot, as with one who is both a near relative and a business associate, considerable embarrassment is caused.'[1] Stacey records her experience in a middle class household on election day, during a visit of a relative who was a Labour supporter: 'it was impossible to keep politics out of the discussion altogether, it was in the front of everybody's mind, and the awkwardness of the situation was only got round by a good deal of joking and back slapping.'[2]

The comparative isolation of the middle class radical from the political culture of his residential community is to some extent mitigated by the fact that his choice of friends is not primarily based on neighbourhood ties. Whereas working class friendship patterns are heavily influenced by residential factors, the middle class are prone to exercise a much greater degree of selectivity in the choice of friends, and to make compatibility of interests, rather than residential propinquity, the main criterion of this choice. Because of this, the strains entailed for the middle class radical in living in a basically hostile political environment can to some extent be lessened by the strategic selection of friends who share his own convictions.[3] Thus 65 per cent of CND respondents reported that the majority of their closest friends approved of the Campaign, as against 23 per cent whose friends were indifferent, and only 3 per cent whose friends were hostile. The selection of politically like-minded friends seems therefore to be one important means whereby the social constraints towards conservatism in white collar communities may be effectively countered—a process which is facilitated by the middle class tendency to devalue the reference-group function of neighbours. As suggested above, however, this is rather more easily achieved by men than by their house-bound wives.

The ambiguities entailed in being a member of the middle class but identifying with the political aims of the radical left, and thus largely the working class, are brought out clearly in respondents'

---

[1] Margaret Stacey, *Tradition and Change*, Oxford, 1960, p. 53.

[2] Ibid.

[3] Another field of relationships which the middle class radical is liable to find fraught with potential difficulties is of course that of employment. These dilemmas, and the manner in which they tend to be resolved, will be considered at length in Chapter 8.

assessments of their own status positions. They were asked to indicate which social class they considered themselves to belong to, and were presented with the following four possibilities: 'upper-class', 'middle class', 'working class' and 'I do not recognize classes'. The last option was included to provide some additional indication as to whether radicals whose 'objective' position was middle class subscribed to the view of society as class-stratified, or whether in view of their own relatively privileged positions, and the problematic status of the middle class amongst radicals, they would be more likely to disavow altogether the existence of classes. Their responses were as follows:

TABLE 14 *Self-assessed social class*

	Respondents' social class (Hall-Jones scale)		
	1 + 2	3 + 4	5 + 6 + 7
	%	%	%
Upper class/Middle class	50	39	0
Working class	8	22	70
Do not recognize classes/ No response	42	39	30
	100	100	100
	(N = 96)	(N = 201)	(N = 44)

It is immediately noticeable that working class respondents were more certain of their class position than middle class respondents. None of the former identified themselves as members of the middle class—a fact which at once distinguishes them from manual workers in society at large, amongst whom there is a sizeable minority who assess themselves as middle class. In Runciman's national sample, for example, 29 per cent of manual workers classified themselves as middle class, and in Martin's sample of Greenwich and Hertford workers, a total of 24 per cent did so.[1] It would seem therefore that the radical outlook of working class CND supporters predisposes them to devalue the middle class as a reference group more strongly than does the manual sector as a whole. The minority of working class CND supporters who do have doubts about their class location resolve these in favour of non-recognition of classes altogether, rather than identify with the middle class. This serves to underline

[1] W. G. Runciman, *Relative Deprivation and Social Justice*, Routledge, 1966, p. 158; F. M. Martin, 'Some Subjective Aspects of Social Stratification', in D. V. Glass (ed.), *Social Mobility in Britain*, Routledge, 1954, p. 56.

the point sometimes overlooked in studies of the relationship between self-assessed social class and political choice—namely, that the individual's political outlook may well decisively *influence* his class identification, and not simply be a product of that identification.

Table 14 similarly shows that the self-assessed status of middle class CND supporters is also considerably at variance with that common to the non-manual stratum at large. Only half of those respondents in occupational classes 1 and 2 acknowledge membership of the middle class—a figure which contrasts markedly with the 93 per cent who do so in Martin's Greenwich and Hertford sample. Of these latter only 3 per cent replied 'don't know' or 'do not belong' when asked to assess their social class—a finding which squares well with other studies which have shown that the top stratum of the middle class tends to be the most 'class conscious' sector of the population.[1] By contrast, 42 per cent of CND respondents from this stratum claimed not to recognize classes, or could not reply. Similarly, amongst occupational classes 3 and 4, only 39 per cent of CND supporters assigned themselves to the middle or upper class, against 65 per cent of the Greenwich and Hertford sample ; only 3 per cent of the latter could give no answer or claimed not to belong to a class, while the comparable figure for CND respondents was 39 per cent.

Although a refusal to recognize classes is not altogether identical with the claim not to belong to any class, it is sufficiently similar to point up the discrepancy between the status alignments of the middle class in general, and those who support CND. It does again bring out the extent to which middle class status is devalued in the eyes of radicals—not least among those who, by occupational criteria at least, share this status. This was also frequently illustrated by respondents' written comments on the questionnaire; many of those who did in fact allocate themselves to be middle class indicated that they did so with qualifications or reluctance, by entering remarks such as 'by job only', 'middle class in occupation but not in mind', or in one case simply, 'middle class —unfortunately'.[2] The lack of identity which middle class radicals

---

[1] Martin, loc. cit. Runciman's figures are based upon the manual/non-manual division only, and not upon the Hall-Jones scale. 67 per cent of Runciman's non-manuals assigned themselves to middle class categories, as against 45 per cent of all CND non-manuals.

[2] There was little here to support Orwell's scathing comment upon 'the ugly fact that most middle class Socialists, while theoretically pining for a classless society, cling like glue to their miserable fragments of social prestige'. George

feel with their ascribed social status might be expected to convey itself in other ways. A variety of symbolic means are available to individuals who seek to dissociate themselves in some way from the social roles and behaviour patterns which they are constrained to adopt by virtue of their occupational and other statuses. Goffman has coined the term 'role-distance' to describe the behaviour designed to convey an individual's personal withdrawal from activities which are formally required of him in certain social situations.[1] He who personally disapproves of his role obligations is able, through appropriate gestures, intonations, and the like, to fulfil these obligations whilst at the same time conveying to others his dissociation from them; self-respect is preserved by the individual's signals that 'this is not the real me'.

It would appear that, along similar lines, the middle class radical is often prone to exhibit what might be called 'status-distance', by making small symbolic gestures designed to convince others (as well as himself) that, despite his occupation and income, he is not to be thought of as 'bourgeois'. One simple way of conveying this message is by means of dress and personal appearance. Thus, as was mentioned earlier, the wearing of beards was far more common among CND supporters than among men in general. And it is fair to claim that the decision to grow a beard may be taken as a token of the individual's desire to make a personal statement about himself and his individuality—that he is not to be equated with the common herd. The attitude which in our society marks out the wearer of a beard as in some vague and unspecified ways 'different', makes it a readily adaptable symbol for the radical wishing to convey his dissociation from bourgeois values. No doubt differences in dress are able to serve similar purposes. Impressionistically at least it appears that contrasts do exist in the clothing styles of middle class Conservatives and radicals, although this may often be little more than a preference for a more casual appearance on the part of the latter.[2] Whilst matters of dress and appearance are only peripheral

---

Orwell, *The Road to Wigan Pier*, Secker and Warburg, 1959, p. 174. The self-deprecatory attitude of middle class CND supporters was illustrated in much of the heart-searching about the political effectiveness of a radical movement which could not attract industrial workers. See Chapter 4. Mark Abrams' survey of middle class political attitudes showed a similar strong tendency for socialists to undervalue their status positions. Whereas almost 69 per cent of Conservatives classified themselves as Upper- or Middle-Middle Class, only 44 per cent of Labour voters in the same occupational positions did so. 'Politics and the British Middle Class', *Socialist Commentary*, October, 1962, pp. 5–9.

[1] Erving Goffman, *Encounters*, Bobbs–Merrill, 1961.

[2] The connection between political outlook and clothing styles is briefly remarked upon by Goffman in his observation that socialists in their legislative

to an individual's politics it is worthwhile pointing up differences that do exist because of the way they may be utilized by the middle class radical to demonstrate his distance from the middle class in general, and the political and social outlook attributed to it. By the mechanism of 'status-distance' he is able to derive gratification and self-respect from his public disavowal of bourgeois values, without at the same time taking the drastic step of abandoning his middle class status for one lower in the social order. It is perhaps significant in this regard that differences in dress and appearance are not noticeable between Conservatives and radicals in the working class. This would seem to support the view suggested earlier that working class Conservatives are not really deviant within their class in the way that middle class radicals are, and hence feel no need to symbolize their apartness in dress or appearance.

Radical movements and ideology

Finally, the fact that so many CND supporters are able to continue their radicalism with a perception of society in which the prevalence of classes, and hence class conflict, occupies little place, does of course square well with their stronger attachment to humanitarian and moral concerns than economic and class issues. It may in fact be suggested that this particular selection of political priorities seems to mitigate certain of the tensions inherent in the middle class radical's position. Because he is concerned primarily with issues which are basically unrelated to the distribution of economic and material resources, issues in which class interests are brought sharply into focus, the 'inconsistency' between his high socio-economic status and his radical outlook is to some extent reduced. Middle class radicalism which was geared exclusively, or even mainly, to the economic sector would imply far sharper contradictions between politics and social status, and would probably be a more difficult position to sustain. Thus, although the bulk of CND supporters are out of sympathy with the capitalist economic system, and would favour some form of socialist alternative, they do at the same time appear to reserve their strongest disapproval for institutions and practices which are not specific features of capitalism as such, but which could be present in almost any type of society.

---

offices frequently wear open-necked shirts. Goffman, op. cit., p. 145. For general remarks upon the influence of politics upon dress see J. C. Flugel, *The Psychology of Clothes*, Hogarth Press, 1950, pp. 207–8. The wearing of badges of course is perhaps the commonest and most effective device for signalling one's political views to others.

The foregoing has provided some empirical backing for the proposition put forward at the beginning of this section, namely, that the primary concerns of those involved in radical movements will be of two basically different types according to their social class membership. That moral reforms should be more liable to exercise the minds of radical members of the middle class more than the working class is not altogether surprising in view of the different economic and status positions the two groups occupy. The middle classes have, almost as a matter of definition, greater material security and a more favourable share of economic rewards than the bulk of industrial workers. Their jobs are far less jeopardized by recessions and unemployment, with the dislocation of personal and family life which this so frequently entails. Given this greater degree of security which professional and white collar employees enjoy, it is perhaps understandable that they should be less inspired than industrial workers to press for deep-seated changes in the entire economic order. By directing the main focus of grievance on to issues of a moral nature, movements based on the middle class are in a sense able to avoid any direct challenge to the legitimacy of the existing social structure, since solutions to problems of this kind do not usually entail serious readjustments to basic institutions. Such problems can generally be treated as isolated and distinct matters, each of which requires a *separate* solution, rather than as offshoots of one basic problem whose solution requires fundamental social change. Campaigns against hanging, colour discrimination, the Bomb, and so forth, put forward distinct and limited demands, each of which can be met without thorough-going re-adjustments in property or class relationships; they could in fact be aspects of *any* society, and not necessarily a capitalist one, and are treated as such. It is an approach which does not require, and may even be inimical to, any coherent ideology which purports to explain all social ills as epiphenomena of one major evil—such as the oppressive power of the state, or private property relationships. The approach of the middle class radical movement, unlike its working class counterpart, is to treat each evil *sui generis*, and not as reducible to some greater underlying malady which throws into question the legitimacy of the existing order.

These differences in the perceptions of working class and middle class movements would appear to have general applicability, and are thus relevant for comparing not only political, but religious movements also. Religious movements and sects with a working class base could be expected to view the spiritual domain in somewhat different terms from those based on middle class membership. Where religious movements draw predominantly from the working class they may be expected to endorse a spiritual ideology which has as its central idea the complete rejection of human relationships as they exist in secular society, and the promise of a new order in which the underprivileged will cast off their burdens and the high and mighty will be humbled. Although there is a great deal of variation in the ideological content of the numerous sects and movements which have sprung up among lower status groups—Jehovah's Witnesses, Seventh Day Adventists, Primitive Methodists, and the like, it is fair to claim that they have in common the same idea that society is fundamentally oppressive and evil and that sweeping revolutionary changes in human and spiritual affairs are more or less imminent.[1] It is a kind of reflection in the religious sphere of the frustrations and aspirations of the materially underprivileged which are closely paralleled in the secular sphere by the appeals of Marxism and socialism.[2]

Middle class religious sects and movements by contrast, are again much less geared to the notion of a totally wicked society due for imminent destruction by a saviour, in which the meek and the poor will claim their inheritance. More typically, these sects stress the function of religion as a means of attaining a state of grace, of spiritual sanctity and individual redemption. To take two obvious examples, the Moral Rearmament notion of the Quiet Time, in which the religious experience is accomplished by meditation— what has aptly been called the drawing-room conversion; and the very similar Quaker notion of the Inner Light, which again places emphasis on individual contemplation and personal adjustment, rather than on the blood and thunder of messianic teachings.[3] There is, then, a fairly close correspondence in the normative make up of political and religious movements, and one can reasonably predict differences in outlook according to the social strata from which supporters are mainly drawn. Working class movements, have on the whole been dedicated to a vision of deep-seated changes in the human order, whether this be conceived on the material or spiritual plane, in which there will be some kind of

[1] See Werner Cohn 'Jehovah's Witnesses as a Proletarian Movement', *American Scholar*, Summer 1955. Also, J. Milton Yinger, *Religion, Society and the Individual*, Macmillan, New York, 1957, Ch. 7.

[2] Political and religious movements with a strong chiliastic ideology may in fact serve as functional alternatives for under-privileged groups. See S. M. Lipset, *Political Man*, Mercury, London, 1963, p. 108.

[3] Allan W. Eister, *Drawing Room Conversion: A Sociological Account of the Oxford Group Movement*, Duke University Press, 1950.

reversal of existing conditions to the benefit of the underprivileged. Middle class movements, religious and political, are less likely to envisage such drastic changes in things as they are, but will tend to view problems of religion or society as open to solution within the existing framework or relationships and not as a result of the fulfilment of a Grand Design.

CND's lack of a formal ideology which could serve to explain a wide range of social ills was undoubtedly part of its attractiveness, given the political climate of the period. The widespread disenchantment with communism, and the general suspicion of all-embracing systems of thought which characterized the post-war years created a political atmosphere unreceptive to the pursuit of 'causes' on a grand scale. The secular mood following the 'end of ideology' is described by Daniel Bell in his portrayal of the situation of the intellectuals.

In the West, among the intellectuals, the old passions are spent. The new generation with no meaningful memory of these old debates, and no secure tradition to build upon, finds itself seeking new purposes within a framework of political society that has rejected, intellectually speaking, the old apocalyptic and chiliastic visions. In the search for a 'cause', there is a deep, desperate, almost pathetic anger . . . Ideology, which by its nature is an all or none affair . . . is intellectually devitalized, and few issues can be formulated any more, intellectually, in ideological terms.[1]

Given this climate of distrust of grand political doctrines and sweeping theories, the anti-Bomb movement was an ideally acceptable vehicle of radical protest. It provided a focus of opposition to the 'Establishment' by concentrating on a single major issue which could be presented as a straightforward choice between good and evil, but which did not at the same time entail the endorsement of a cumbersome set of doctrines, or a specific world-view. Opposition to the Bomb could be made consistent with a variety of quite different principles—including the rejection of politics altogether. In a word it provided a cause without an ideology. It is probably true to say in fact, that in the secular atmosphere of the period, radical protest could only be expected to develop around single and specific issues of this kind, in contrast to the more diffuse, and in a sense more fundamental radicalism of an age of ideology. John Lehmann, in reviewing the political outlook of intellectuals in the pre- and post-war periods, remarked upon the contrast between the former's ideological and the latter's non-ideological politics. Lehmann was 'struck by certain basic differences between our radica-

[1] Daniel Bell, *The End of Ideology*, Free Press, 1960, pp. 374–5.

lism and theirs', and felt 'dismayed when I observe the objects against which the new radicalism appears to be gathering its forces —the windmills, I feel inclined to say, against which it is tilting'. He contrasted in particular the concern of radicals of his own generation over issues like unemployment and fascism, with the post-war discontents over what he felt to be less fundamental matters; thus, 'when it comes to political realities, I cannot help feeling that the demand for unilateral nuclear disarmament is a lamentably unreal cause as compared with the demands of the intellectuals of the thirties'.[1]

Whilst this contrast between the two generations appears a valid one, the more limited outlook of the post-war radicals was to be expected, given the mood of the times. When so many gods had failed, and scepticism of the grand design had penetrated so deeply, it is understandable that political protest should have been directed to the pursuit of the relatively limited goals of movements like CND. At any rate, it is noticeable that the causes adopted by intellectuals, students and middle class radicals in general, in recent times—such as Negroes' civil rights, the war in Vietnam, and so on, are precisely those single and separate issues which may be supported without reference to any given doctrinal framework or all-embracing theory, but which can be waged as issues *sui generis*.[2] The end of ideology, then, does not necessarily herald the end of radicalism, as has sometimes been implied, but rather casts it in a different, and perhaps somewhat less ambitious, political mould. Because protest of a class or economic kind in the affluent societies of the west has now become comparatively routinized and stabilized, it would appear that the mainsprings of radicalism derive from issues of a progressively 'moral', non-ideological nature. And if the thesis outlined earlier in this chapter is correct, then it could be anticipated that political protest in affluent societies will tend increasingly to have a middle class rather than a working class base. It would be a piquant comment upon Marx's theory of social change if the centre of the political stage were to be vacated by an 'embourgeoisified' working class, only to be replaced by a radical bourgeoisie.

[1] John Lehmann, 'Radicalism, Then and Now', *The Listener*, 9 August 1962, pp. 195-7.
[2] Lipset has remarked that many American civil rights and peace activists 'insist that they are not committed to any ideology. . . . They argue that they are pragmatic, that is, they are issue-oriented. They are concerned with peace, with the Negro and so on. . . . And though willing to work with communists, they reject them politically as ideologists concerned with historic issues.' S. M. Lipset, 'Student Opposition in the United States', *Government and Opposition*, Vol. I, No. 3, April 1966, p. 363.

E

Earlier in this chapter it was suggested that involvement with CND could to some extent be considered as an expression of protest at certain aspects of contemporary British society which were independent of the problem of the Bomb, but which the latter was felt to symbolize. It may be argued in fact that part of the attractiveness of the unilateralist movement lay in its ability to provide a forum for a broad array of disparate 'causes' espoused by religious, political and other groups established long prior to the emergence of the nuclear weapons threat. Many of these were drawn to CND not simply because they were in sympathy with the movement's aims but also, and perhaps mainly, because the Campaign appeared to offer opportunities for the furtherance of their own specific goals and because protest against the Bomb could often stand as an expression of protest against other more fundamental ills of society, even though this connection was not always explicitly made. Thus, most of the groups and organizations attracted to the Campaign could be said to have one distinctive feature in common—namely that they occupied a comparatively marginal position in the social structure in the sense that they espoused certain values not acceptable to the society at large. All could be said to have had an existing predisposition to political deviance in so far as they stood in a relationship of tension—and often hostility—to a society which had rejected their own specific normative framework. Organizations which swelled the ranks of the unilateralist movement, such as the Pacifists, the Communist Party, and the Trotskyists, the Quakers, the New Left, the Anarchists, and the left wing of the Labour Party, could all be broadly characterized as occupying a normatively marginal position in the social order. This is similarly the case, although to a lesser extent, with two other categories of supporters attracted to CND—namely, intellectuals and youth. Whilst it would be sociologically untenable to regard either of these as comprising a formal or homogeneous group—or as necessarily in sharp opposition to the social order—it is plausible to view them as status categories which, as testified by the extensive literature on the 'alienation of the intellectuals', and the problems of adolescence and the 'youth culture', are marked by a certain degree of social marginality. Both have frequently been depicted as being 'in' society but not altogether 'of' it.

It is significant that few political, religious or other bodies which are fully integrated into the social order—in that they fully endorse the value premises upon which major institutions are based —have given support to the unilateralist movement. Most of the groups which were attracted, however, tended to translate the general anxiety arising from the dangers of nuclear war into a full scale critique of contemporary society, or at least those aspects of it most relevant to their traditional concerns. Opposition to the Bomb served for them as a means of symbolizing a variety of other discontents, and support for CND was envisaged as a vehicle for achieving ends not directly related to unilateralism.[1] It is to the documentation of this assertion that we now turn. The following chapter describes briefly the role of the radical Christians, the Communist Party and other Marxist organizations in the Campaign; Chapter 5 considers the part played by intellectuals; Chapter 6 is concerned with the unilateralist conflict within the Labour Party and Chapter 7 with youth involvement in the Campaign.

[1] Socialist parties in capitalist societies appear to have a similar attraction for various fringe groups. Orwell recorded his impression that 'the mere words "Socialism" and "Communism" draw towards them with magnetic force every fruit-juice drinker, nudist, sandal-wearer, sex-maniac, Quaker, "Nature Cure" quack, pacifist and feminist in England'. Orwell, op. cit., p. 173.

4

Symbolic protest—
1: the ideologues

The Christian churches and the Bomb

Like British society itself the churches have been sharply divided in their attitude to the hydrogen bomb and nuclear war, not across denominational lines so much as within the denominations themselves. Indeed the passions and bitterness which this conflict often generates contrasts rather vividly with the tolerance and moderation of the ecumenical dialogue across doctrinal boundaries. One fairly obvious reason why the advent of the atomic and hydrogen bombs could be expected to have created controversy within the churches is that these weapons have activated, in a more extreme way than usual, the pacifist traditions which Christianity has nurtured in this country—particularly within the Nonconformist bodies. Although there has always been a strong minority opposed to armaments of any kind, the emergence of nuclear weapons served to provide it with fresh arguments and a new sense of mission. Traditionally, the Christian rejection of the pacifist view has been based on the concept of the 'just war'—a doctrine proclaiming that Christians are permitted to take up arms provided that certain conditions are fulfilled. One of these conditions is that the use of force must hold out a clear chance of victory and that violence must be kept within controllable limits.[1] Pacifists argue that the hydrogen bomb has rendered the concept of the just war obsolete because these conditions can no longer be fulfilled; destruction is total, and clear victory impossible. To many Christians this is undoubtedly a persuasive argument and one they have found difficult to rebut in a convincing way. This has meant that the traditional boundary separating pacifist from non-pacifist has become blurred, or more correctly perhaps, pushed farther back, so that many who previously placed themselves in the latter category now find themselves in the former. The Christian's rejection of modern weapons no longer has to derive from a literal interpretation of the Sermon on the Mount, but may instead rest on a conviction that their destructiveness does not permit the kind of restraints that previously made war palatable or doctrinally just. Those who accept this view, the 'relative pacifists' as they have been called, could point to the authority of a papal pronouncement which seemed to reach a similar conclusion. In his address on nuclear weapons to the World Medical Association, Pope Pius XII declared:

should the evil consequences of this method of warfare ever become so extensive as to pass utterly beyond the control of man, then indeed its use must be rejected as immoral. In that event, it would no longer be a question of defence against injustice and necessary protection of legitimate possessions, but of the annihilation, pure and simple, of all human life within the affected area. That is not lawful on any title.[2]

[1] For historical treatment of the theory of the 'just war' see R. H. Bainton, *Christian Attitudes toward War and Peace*, Hodder and Stoughton, London, 1960. Also Carl von Weizsacher, *Ethical and Political Problems of the Atomic Age*, SCM Press, London, 1958.

[2] *Acta Apostolicae Sedis*, XLVI, p. 589; Quoted in Mgr. L. L. McReavy and P. E. Hodgson, *Nuclear War*, Catholic Truth Society, London, 1962, p. 15. Many Catholics, however, found the papal pronouncement to be quite compatible with nuclear deterrence. One Jesuit scholar concluded from a detailed examination of the church's teachings that 'nuclear war is not necessarily indiscriminate

Similarly, when the British government announced in 1955 its decision to manufacture the Bomb, Cardinal Griffin declared that 'the use of the hydrogen bomb as a weapon of war would seem to conflict with our well tried principles of the past'.[1] The H-bomb, as non-pacifists themselves concede, has created a climate in which pacifist ideas are received with greater sympathy than they have ever previously enjoyed, so that criticism of the pacifist case is often somewhat cautious and apologetic in tone. The committee set up by the British Council of Churches in 1963 to consider Christian attitudes to the nuclear deterrent arrived at the view that a unilateralist policy would be 'impracticable and even possibly disastrous'. Nevertheless they felt constrained to add that 'the witness of the Christian unilateralist has been—and is—valuable as a protest against the iniquity of the present situation . . . and as a call to end that situation'.[2] The Bishop of Woolwich has also suggested that pacifist ideas have taken on a new force and persuasiveness to Christians in the nuclear age. He concludes a lengthy argument in support of the non-pacifist view by confessing that 'it is increasingly becoming the more difficult case to sustain. I still accept it; I am still not persuaded by the pacifist. But I am in much greater danger . . . of being persuaded by events.'[3]

Although it seems clear that the advent of nuclear weapons has created a greater responsiveness to pacifist ideas, it nevertheless remains true to say that the churches in general have resisted the trend. One of the reasons for this has undoubtedly been the conviction of many Christians that a more serious danger than nuclear war is the possibility of communist domination. When religious life and values themselves are thought to be at stake, then it is seen as a Christian duty to defend them by whatever means available, irrespective of other consequences. The Christians most conscious of this possibility see no moral dilemma in the possession or use of nuclear weapons, and consequently pacifism—even in its milder form—has little persuasive power. The editor of a leading Non-

---

war and that, in consequence, the use of nuclear weapons by a just defendent is not necessarily immoral'. Fr. P. Crane, 'Catholics and Nuclear War', *The Month*, October 1959. See also, C. S. Thompson, *Morals and Missiles*, Clarke & Co., London, 1959; 'The Morality of Nuclear War—A Medieval Disputation', *Blackfriars*, March 1956; 'The Debate on the Morality of Future War', *Clergy Review*, February 1960.

[1] *Manchester Guardian*, 14 March 1955.

[2] *The British Nuclear Deterrent*; Report of the British Council of Churches, SCM Press, London, 1963, p. 28.

[3] J. A. T. Robinson, *On Being in the Church in the World*, SCM Press, London, 1960, p. 54.

conformist weekly gave voice to this view when he wrote: 'In the plainest possible words we believe it would be better for nations to be wiped out than that they should submit to be morally murdered by the poison of Communist totalitarianism.'[1] It is this fact that the potential enemy of the Christianized west does itself have a dynamic ideology fiercely opposed to religious values that acts to restrain pacifist tendencies within the churches. If the potential enemy were itself a Christian country, or at least one that offered no threat to Christian values, then one could predict that the arrival of the hydrogen bomb would have produced an even sharper conflict in the churches than it already succeeded in doing.

Although protest against nuclear weapons is not to be equated with pacifism in the usual sense, it is true to say that the latter contributed heavily to the fortunes of the former by enabling it to draw upon a continuing tradition within the churches, and in providing a seasoned leadership. Leading pacifists in the churches played an active part in sensitizing Christian consciences to the dilemma of the hydrogen bomb, and in encouraging the protest movement against it. At the same time, however, it is worth emphasizing that Christian pacifists and Christian unilateralists are not necessarily the same body of people. Many opponents of the H-bomb would not describe themselves as pacifist on other issues, while many pacifists refuse support to unilateralism because it does not oppose conventional weapons, or because the movement is 'coercive' in spirit.[2] This distinction between the two groups is important for an understanding of the unilateralist movement, for it may be suggested that Christian protest against the Bomb cannot be understood as arising solely from moral anguish about nuclear weapons, but may also be seen as an expression of serious discontent with the role of the church in contemporary society. Protest

---

[1] *Christian World*, 13 March 1958, p. 1.

[2] Although there must obviously be a good deal of overlap between these two groups, the fact that they are not identical is brought out in a survey carried out in the Congregationalist church. The 125 ministers who returned the questionnaire answered two of the questions as follows:

	Yes	No	No answer
Would you describe yourself as a pacifist?	35	86	4
Should GB renounce the H-bomb unilaterally?	65	54	6

Christian World, 13 November 1958, p. 7. A similar survey carried out among Methodist ministers reported comparable distinctions between total pacifists and 'nuclear pacifists'. See John Stacey, 'Christian Pacifism in the Methodist Church', *Prism*, No. 82, February 1964, p. 36.

against the bomb has at the same time represented protest against certain aspects of organized religion and its leaders, and at the circumscribed boundaries of current Christian witness. The attraction of many Christians to this movement is not therefore to be seen simply as the pouring of old pacifist wine into a new bottle, but as a manifestation of other deep-seated divisions within the church.

Thus, it has been a central and recurring complaint of church members who support the unilateralist campaign that the church is failing to have any impact on our society because of its reluctance to confront the major social and political problems of the times; that instead of making its presence felt through forthright pronouncements on controversial issues it counsels caution or avoids discussion altogether. A prominent Methodist exponent of this view, Dr Donald Soper, puts the case as follows:

A Christian Church which fails to assert the basic principles which should inform the political and social life around it, and neglects to make its judgements heard on the actual structure of contemporary society is apostate . . . this is why organized Christianity is not so much opposed today as ignored.[1]

It has been a source of distress to some Christians that the church has appeared more willing to pronounce on matters concerning the personal conduct of the individual than on the affairs of governments and nations. 'We are ready to give the world a lead on the questions of drink and gambling', complained one Congregationalist minister, ' . . . Yet these are not the greatest moral and social problems . . . because . . . overshadowing and dwarfing all other questions is the supreme problem of the nuclear age . . . on which the prophetic voice of the twentieth century Church is all too feeble.'[2] Another Nonconformist minister thought 'it must seem odd to people outside of the Church that we protest so strongly against Bingo, and are so silent in regard to nuclear weapons'.[3] A Catholic writer too has pointed up what seemed to him to be a glaring 'contrast between the readiness of the Bishops to insist on the wickedness of using contraceptives and their extreme hesitation to say anything about the wickedness of the Bomb . . .'[4]

However dissatisfied socially committed Christians had previously been with the church's tendency to restrict its teachings to personal conduct, and to avoid major political issues, it is clear that the

---

[1] *Methodist Recorder*, 27 April 1961, p. 10.

[2] *Christian World*, 14 August 1958, p. 7.

[3] Rev. A. A. Bowyer, 'Bombs and Bingo', *Christian Endeavour*, Jan.–Mar. 1962.

[4] *The Guardian*, 2 April 1964, p. 7.

advent of the H-bomb greatly increased their frustrations. The failure of the church to make an authoritative pronouncement against the Bomb seemed to them to be a betrayal of all that Christianity stood for. Certain members of the Nonconformist churches have been especially sensitive to the fact that the religious dissent which gave birth to their denominations appeared to be much less in evidence in modern times. Methodists and Quakers in particular have expressed concern that they have become too 'respectable', and that the comfort of their members has enervated the radical temper. Envious glances have been cast at the established church which has produced most of the leading social critics within the religious community. But however politically engaged the Anglicans may have appeared to Nonconformists it was not a view shared by the leading militants themselves. Men like Canon Collins, Stanley Evans, Trevor Huddleston and Michael Scott were making the same criticisms of their own church that the Nonconformists were making of theirs. None of them would have disagreed with the view that the church was failing in its mission because of the faint-heartedness of its message and the caution of its leaders; that, to use a recurring expression, Churchianity was killing Christianity.

In the view of this militant minority, of both Anglican and Free Churches, the explanation for the increasing disregard for spiritual values and authority in this country was thus to be found in the conduct of religion itself. The secularization of life is seen not as the result of processes at work outside the church, but of those within it. An explanation in terms of the shortcomings of the church implies, however, that the remedy for the present condition also lies within the hands of Christians themselves, whatever changes might be taking place in society as a whole. The remedy that these critics have in mind is simple and direct. It is that the church should nail its colours to the mast of radical moral protest, and that it should carry its ministry into the political arena without regard to expediency and compromise. Only a church militant of this nature could recapture the disenchanted and regain its rightful place in society.

The Church has proved that the generations when her influence has soared have always been those when there was a growth in concern for men and their conditions of life, i.e. when political controversy has not frightened her leaders into silence.[1]

For Christians whose formula for a revitalized religion prescribed a deeper commitment to political and social matters, the campaign

[1] George Thomas, *The Christian Heritage in Politics*, Epworth Press, London, 1959, p. 19.

against the hydrogen bomb represented a golden opportunity for the church. Here was an issue which raised problems vital to the Christian conscience, which could be argued in moral terms, and which was acknowledged to be one of the most serious facing mankind. If the church was to seize the initiative and place itself at the head of the growing volume of protest, it would infuse new dynamism into religious witness and provide a dramatic opportunity to show the relevance of Christian values to contemporary problems. A Methodist minister, urging his co-religionists to join the campaign declared enthusiastically that

This is one of the great opportunities of the age to preach the Gospel, not in fine sermons, but in action . . . it calls for the Church to give practical witness to the relevance of the Gospel. Unless the Church is represented in this movement, not as an official body, but by convinced individuals, this opportunity will be lost and a generation will be confirmed in their scepticism about the Church.[1]

One Baptist minister felt, similarly, that 'The Christian Church stands to win all or to lose all in this momentous hour', and that 'beyond this world-changing deed [unilateralism] lies the heyday of her personal evangelism of mankind and the victory of Christian morality'.[2]

Many Quakers, too, were fired by the prospect of the campaign's invigorating possibilities and the opportunities for Christian evangelism it presented. One of them wrote to *The Friend*: 'What a help it would be to the Campaign for Nuclear Disarmament if the Society of Friends enthusiastically supported its aims and efforts and helped to fashion them; and what a tremendous release of new life and influx of new members would the Society gain.'[3] One of his co-religionists recorded that in the experience of himself and others, involvement in the campaign against the Bomb afforded 'a point of really united Christian witness, which brings with it a rich reward of new life and light'.[4] Similarly, one of the contributors to a Catholic symposium on nuclear weapons thought highly of the unilateralist movement's regenerating possibilities, asserting that the church's involvement in it would lead to a 'revival of Western religious energies'.[5] Another contributor suggested that the failure to condemn nuclear weapons unequivocally would alienate the

---

[1] *Methodist Recorder*, 17 May 1962, p. 9.
[2] *Baptist Times*, 16 November 1961, p. 10.
[3] *The Friend*, 24 August 1962, p. 1048.
[4] *The Friend*, 21 September 1962, p. 1166.
[5] W. Stein (ed.) *Nuclear Weapons and Christian Conscience*, Merlin Press, London, 1961, p. 151.

present generation from Christianity in the same way that lack of concern over economic problems had alienated the working-class in the nineteenth century. A similar fear was hinted at by a correspondent to the Nonconformist *Christian World*. 'What a pity it would be', he thought, 'if the Christian Church were to miss the boat and a new climate of opinion were to be engineered without the support of Christendom. What would become of the authority of the Church, or what is left of it.'[1] A Quaker unilateralist, urging his co-religionists to support the Campaign, argued similarly that 'if Christians refuse to join with those who make a peaceful protest against preparation for mass murder, then can you blame CND followers if they excise Christianity from their lives for good?'[2]

However much, then, certain Christians may have found themselves drawn to unilateralism on scriptural or humanitarian grounds, the fact that it was presented as a challenging campaign with strong moral overtones made it doubly attractive. For it could be seen not simply as a protest against a perceived evil, but also as a vehicle for stimulating the Christian conscience and creating a resurgence of religious ideals and influence. In the words of one Free Church minister, himself chairman of his local CND; 'if this movement can stir the dry bones, stir the imagination, and help us to take a keener interest in the moral and spiritual issues of the day, *it will not have been in vain*'.[3] It is clear from this viewpoint that the purpose of the campaign was not restricted to the attainment of its manifest goal, but was also thought to have important consequences for the Christian community. As the Rev. Kenneth Rawlings quite openly put it: 'The Aldermaston March is necessary not chiefly to save our skins but to save our souls.'[4] As will be seen later, this wish to harness the moral energies released by the campaign to serve 'private' ends was not an exclusively Christian one, but also preoccupied groups with quite different ideologies.

One notable feature of the campaign against the Bomb which gave additional stimulus to religious participation was the form in which the protest was organized. By largely avoiding orthodox political channels and overt party allegiances in favour of public demonstrations, marches, fasts and vigils, with the physical discomfort or deliberate acts of self-denial they often entailed, responsive chords were touched in those whose religious beliefs had strong

---

[1] *Christian World*, 27 March 1958, p. 8.
[2] *The Friend*, 14 September 1962, p. 1133.
[3] *Methodist Recorder*, 1 February 1962, p. 6. Emphasis added.
[4] *The Junction*, April 1960, p. 5.

puritan roots. The Aldermaston march, in particular with its Easter setting, and its overtones of moral dedication and pilgrimage made a deep impression on socially committed Christians. It provided, too, a handy yardstick against which to measure the shortcomings of the church's own radical witness. A Methodist who had given overnight shelter to a group of marchers confessed he felt 'humbled at their utter devotion to their cause and one wonders how many of us would be willing to sleep rough for three nights a week and march in the pouring rain for our faith'.[1] This tendency to use the Aldermaston march as a stick with which to beat the church was of course difficult for militant Christians to avoid. It was to them intolerable that a secular movement should seem to be displaying a greater concern for the nation's conscience than the religious bodies themselves were doing. 'It is a criticism of the Church and damaging to it in the eye of the world', declared the editor of the *British Weekly*, 'that the lead on this issue is coming more from secular groups—trade unions, groups of young people, non-Christian intellectuals, scientists and writers . . .' instead of from the church.[2] A Presbyterian preacher commenting on the first Easter march drew the inevitable contrast with his own Church.

This was a convincing demonstration of the compulsive power generated by deep conviction, driving ordinary men out of the comfort and security of their personal privacy to proclaim their faith in the open air . . .

By contrast . . . the open air witness of our Churches withers . . . Congregations doze in the relative comfort of the pew. Parsons cling to the protection of the pulpit. The judgement is upon us. We have defaulted in our duty. We must amend.[3]

Those who had themselves taken part in the demonstrations tended to experience them, as others had promised they would, as a means of reaffirming their faith. The editor of *The Friend* remarking upon the large Quaker contingent in 1960 was rapturous about this novel form of religious expression. 'Oh Quakerism!' he begged. 'Stay like this, booted and rucksacked and uninhibited, stepping out on the public road, and hide no more behind minutes and caution and secrecy and high walls.'[4]

The element of open air witness and moral dedication which so commended itself to Christian supporters of the Aldermaston

[1] *Methodist Recorder*, 10 May 1962, p. 6.
[2] *British Weekly*, 26 May 1960, p. 6.
[3] *British Weekly*, 24 April 1958, p. 1.
[4] *The Friend*, 22 April 1960, p. 540. 1,500 Friends were estimated to have taken part in the 1960 Aldermaston march. Friends' Peace Committee *Report*, London Yearly Meeting Proceedings, 1961, p. 159.

march was displayed even more dramatically in the acts of civil disobedience at aircraft bases and in Whitehall. The fact that men were willing to suffer ridicule and imprisonment for their beliefs in an age of materialism came as another sharp jab to the Nonconformist conscience. A new kind of martyrdom seemed to be in the air and Free Churchmen were quick to point up parallels with the persecution of their own religious forbears. 'Is not the spirit that moves the Swaffham demonstrators,' asked one Quaker, '... the same spirit that led to our seventeenth-century ancestors being whipped and stoned and imprisoned? These things cannot be judged in the content of orthodoxy.'[1] Another wondered whether the historian of the future would 'place laurel crowns on the heads of those limp squatters in Whitehall',[2] and Dr Soper, although personally opposed to the tactics of civil disobedience, felt bound to applaud the 'sincere and sacrificial actions exhibited by those who have gone to prison for conscience sake'. He went on to make the familiar criticism that such dedication 'shames the average Christian who, apart from a greedy private interest in salvation, seems apathetic if not cowardly in comparison'.[3]

This willingness on the part of demonstrators to suffer for their cause, to face imprisonment and the hostility of society was a quality that had a cherished place in the hearts of the descendants of Luther, Calvin, Wesley and Fox. Their own religious values had been forged under similar conditions and the spirit of dissent was an attribute that commanded some respect—if only in a nominal, nostalgic fashion. Apart from this particular kind of appeal, the unilateralist movement had another feature that endeared itself to many Christians—its ability to attract the younger generation. Almost all religious denominations had expressed anxiety at their failure to increase, or even to maintain, their congregations by recruiting younger members. Efforts to interest the teenage population in religion had borne little fruit, despite novel and rather bizarre experiments in communication. CND on the other hand was conspicuously successful in recruiting from the younger age-groups of both sexes. This was another object lesson to the church as far as Christian radicals were concerned. It was ample confirmation of their view that unplumbed depths of idealism were waiting to be tapped by a vigorous church leadership. The young supporters of the movement were those 'whom the clichés of the political parties or of organized religion have left untouched', wrote the Rev. J. J.

---

[1] *The Friend*, 23 January 1959, p. 120. [2] *Christian World*, 11 May 1961.
[3] *Methodist Recorder*, 21 September 1961, p. 10.

Vincent in his *Christ in a Nuclear World*. 'The Campaign has given
them something to live and fight for in a day when politics and the
Church seem ingrained with antiquarianism, irrelevance and hope-
lessness.'[1] Canon Collins also thought that the church failed to
attract the young because unlike CND 'it does not offer them an
ideal which fires their imagination and their enthusiasm'.[2]

The comparative success of the campaign in drawing the youthful
to its banner was seen not only as a criticism of the church but also as
an opportunity to carry the gospel to them. By associating with
young demonstrators and sharing their concern over nuclear
weapons Christians could initiate a dialogue with them which could
lead to other things. One minister urged Christians to join the
movement because 'Many of them are young people who are looking
for wise leadership. . . . Unless they have help from the Church they
will become bitter and disillusioned.'[3] Like many others he went on
to urge that only by entering the campaign could Christians hope to
influence the minds of its young supporters. There is little evidence,
however, that church members who did join its ranks were any more
successful in winning the young for Christ than their less militant
brethren had been.[4]

This tendency to regard the unilateralist movement as fruitful
territory for Christian evangelism was given some edge by the
knowledge that other ideologies were also competing for the
allegiance of the young. The presence of communist and other
Marxist groups, in particular, was thought by some to call for even
greater religious participation to combat anti-Christian doctrines.
Vincent reported that 'CND has tended to fall into the hands of
extremists in some area . . . [where] . . . the presence of Christians
would be a great help.' He urged that church members should
'Develop campaigns against nuclear weapons where they do not
exist, and enter them in the name of Christ where they do. The
Communists there, if there happen to be a few, will soon be out-
numbered.'[5] The chairman of Nottingham CND, himself a
Quaker, argued that the presence of communists in the campaign

[1] J. J. Vincent, *Christ in a Nuclear World*, Crux Press, Manchester, 1962, p. 133.
[2] *Christian Action*, Autumn 1961, p. 18.
[3] *Methodist Recorder*, 17 May 1962, p. 9.
[4] The Quakers do seem to have had one small triumph however. A member of
the Friends' contingent on one march recorded that his group 'so impressed the
other young people around them by their friendliness, their sense of purpose, and
their zest for life, that ten of the fellow-marchers who previously knew little of
Quakerism attended our Meeting for Worship . . . last Sunday. What a lesson can
be learnt here in witness and extension work!' *The Friend*, 29 April 1960, p. 590.
[5] J. J. Vincent, op. cit., p. 139.

meant that '*a greater responsibility is laid on us to provide more and more Christian and Quaker influence and not less*'.[1]

Despite these calls to duty, however, the majority of church members did not respond to communist participation in the campaign by joining it themselves. For many, indeed, since the chief danger to the world was not the Bomb but communism itself, there seemed little point in collaborating with the latter against the former. In the eyes of one Friend, for example, CND contained 'the devil that it sought to exorcise'. The movement itself embodied 'the tensions and the suspicions that have created the weapons that the marchers seek to ban'.[2] And if the Bomb was regarded as the surest safeguard against communism it was not merely pointless, but treacherous, for Christians to seek its abolition. Those 'in the pulpit and elsewhere' cried one Congregationalist, 'who are clamouring for unilateral nuclear disarmament by this country should be made to realize that they are furthering the ends of a godless aggression . . . it is deplorable that Christian people—and especially Christian ministers—should be carried away by this Communist inspired panic'.[3] This fear of a dangerous ideological (and military) opponent was clearly one important factor which prevented many Christians from seeing in CND any of the virtues that others so passionately acclaimed. However weighty this consideration was, though, it was not the only, or even the major, restraint to Christian support for the campaign. Even more important perhaps was the belief that the church should not become involved in political controversy of any kind. Religion, from this standpoint, is held to be chiefly concerned with the personal problems posed by the existence of sin, and the state of the soul, and not with solutions to political and social matters; it is seen as a personal affair between man and God, not as a manifesto of public aims. For those to whom this pietistic aspect of Christian belief is of central importance, it is obvious that a movement like CND could have little appeal. Anxiety about nuclear war would in any case appear to be misplaced if the fate of man is in God's hands, far removed from the political hurly-burly. The apparent irrelevance of the unilateralist issue, and the true objects of Christian concern, were clearly set out by a Baptist minister in answer to the arguments of his pro-CND fellow churchmen:

There are issues which confront us Baptists much more vital than this [the H-bomb]. There is the obvious and increasing godlessness of our

---

[1] *The Friend*, 25 May 1962, p. 645. Original emphasis.
[2] *The Friend*, 29 April 1960, p. 590.
[3] *Christian World*, 27 March 1958, p. 8.

nation, the all but universal participation in gambling, the widespread
showing of horror and sadism on the films, and the worship of material and
temporal standards of life . . . In any case material destruction can never
be such a disaster to a Christian as moral and spiritual decay.[1]

To interpret Christianity as a political doctrine is, from this
angle, to misunderstand the true nature and purpose of faith—
which is to provide pathways to personal redemption. To see
political issues in religious terms is 'to confuse and damage both
religion and politics. In fact, it is to mix up things that do not
belong'.[2] That so many of their fellow-believers failed, through
their CND activities, to make such a separation, caused a good deal
of anguish among apolitical Christians. They resented the attempt
to implicate religion in a movement with overtly political aims, and
felt that such activities were bringing the churches into disrepute.
This criticism made itself felt in all the denominations even among
the Quakers, probably the least pietistic of any of the Nonconformist churches, and the one most heavily committed to the unilateralist campaign. Many Friends were especially incensed by the
Society's implication in civil disobedience demonstrations. It was
complained that Quakers were being 'swept off into the activities of
Nuclear Disarmament and join the Teddy Boys, the Income Tax
dodgers and the Algerian "colons" in bringing the law and democratic government into contempt'.[3] A prominent figure in the
Society, Professor Herbert Dingle, gave voice to the feeling shared
by many that 'nine-tenths of our *overt* activities are in association
with non-Christians and anti-Christians in the Campaign for
Nuclear Disarmament and such bodies . . .' In the course of his
analysis of current trends in Quaker life he went on to deplore their
'progressive transformation from the religious to the political
Society of Friends'.[4] For him, as for others, the distinctive contribution of the Quaker testimony was to be found in its ability to
furnish an Inner Light, not a programme of political and social
reform.

Those who shared this view of the nature of the religious life were
critical of their CND co-religionists not only because they confounded religion with politics but because they seemed to be in
danger of worshipping false gods. By pouring their energies into
the unilateralist campaign they had less of themselves to give in the

---

[1] *Baptist Times*, 13 November 1958, p. 6.
[2] *Methodist Recorder*, 10 December 1959, p. 12.
[3] *The Friend*, 9 June 1961, p. 792.
[4] *The Friend*, 27 May 1960, p. 724.

glorification of God and to ordinary church activity. In the words of one disapproving observer, their 'fanaticism' for the campaign against the Bomb 'has for them taken the place of the religion of Christ Jesus'.[1] The suggestion that the movement had tended to become a substitute religion for some of its most ardent Christian supporters is difficult to rebut in view of their own common tendency to describe its mission in religious terms. 'Is not CND in one respect at least "doing His will"?' asked one minister.[2] For those who sought the excitement of a cause it undoubtedly was. 'For many', admitted one Quaker, the Aldermaston march 'has become a modern sacrament, like the Lenten lunch of bread and cheese, a remembrance and re-dedication of ourselves and our way of life.'[3] What the church could no longer offer to those who favoured an activist interpretation of morality, a secular movement could. From this it was only a short step to the possibility that the movement might in any case be the hand of providence working in subtle ways. This at least was the view of the Rev. C. S. Stimson in his pamphlet, *You, Christ and the Bomb*. It was his conviction that because the church was not 'exercising its rightful function in this hour of crisis it is permissible and reasonable to regard the Committee of 100, the CND and other pacifist groups, as *being raised up by God*, and the force of circumstances, to assume this role vacated by the church'.[4] Donald Soper, too, at the climax of the 1959 Easter march, was moved to express similar sentiments. 'Looking at the vast crowd as they chanted "Ban the Bomb" ', he wrote, 'I felt more convinced than ever that in this tremendous demonstration the voice of God was being heard in the voice of the people.'[5]

The prominent role played by clergymen in the CND was particularly noticeable. It was not in the least out of character that three of the movement's leading figures were men of the church—Canon Collins, the Rev. Michael Scott and Dr Soper. Ministers frequently served as chairmen or secretaries of local CND branches, and many played a leading part in demonstrations and organizational activities. It may be suggested that one of the reasons behind the strong attraction of the movement for certain members of the clergy was that it offered them a sense of public mission and leadership within the community which orthodox religious activities were increasingly

[1] *The Friend*, 17 August 1962, p. 1019.
[2] Vincent, op. cit., p. 134.
[3] *The Friend*, 28 April 1961, p. 567.
[4] Rev. C. C. Stimson, *You, Christ and the Bomb*, Committee of 100, London, 1961, p. 4.
[5] *Tribune*, 10 April 1959, p. 4.

failing to do. The minister's role in a highly secularized society is, as Eric Carlton has recently shown, one marked by ambiguity and uncertainty; with many of his traditional functions usurped by outside agencies, the minister is prone to have serious self-doubts concerning his place in, and contribution to, modern society.[1] For many this dilemma was partially solved by involvement in CND. The anti-Bomb movement provided the minister with an opportunity for moral crusading on the pattern established by his forbears, as well as offering leadership roles of a public kind. The strong missionizing flavour of the Campaign was, as we have seen, one greatly to the taste of radical Christians, but it would be doubly so for those of similar outlook who were concerned professionally in the witness of Christian values.[2]

The role of the Free Churches in the H-bomb controversy has been especially singled out since their members have contributed disproportionately to the unilateralist movement. Of the adult CND respondents who claimed affiliation to a religious denomination, 52 per cent were Quakers, Methodists, Presbyterians or Baptists, 34 per cent were Church of England and 4 per cent were Catholics, showing a much higher representation of Nonconformists in CND than in the country as a whole. At the same time, opposition to involvement in the Campaign was also strong in the Free Churches, so that it was within these denominations, rather than among Anglicans or Catholics, that dissension was particularly acute. This paradox can perhaps partly be explained in terms of the structural tensions inherent in Nonconformity which make it especially susceptible to the kind of inner conflicts laid bare by the unilateralist debate. Most of these denominations have an ancestry of dissent, usually stemming from discontent with the established church or with various types of church bureaucracy. Their founders and immediate followers often suffered persecution and other social disabilities accruing to despised minority groups. These antecedents —given the value they tend to be accorded within the denominations—provide a focal point for appeals to radicalism of various kinds. New expressions of social dissent by church members can be legitimized by reference to the conduct of founding heroes and the culturally valued past—to a time when the church put 'principles'

[1] Eric Carlton, *The Probationer Minister*, M.Sc (Econ) thesis, University of London, 1965.
[2] Mary Hocking's novel *The Sparrow* is concerned with an Anglican minister's involvement in the Committee of 100's civil disobedience campaigns as part of his search for a more morally engaging life than that afforded him by his routine parish duties.

before 'expediency'. Counterbalancing this, however, is the fact that Nonconformist congregations are composed mainly of middle-class members, whose own comparative social and material security render them less amenable to radical conduct than their under-privileged forbears. This combination of a dissenting heritage and an economically secure membership provides a permanent basis for controversies over the nature and scope of religious duties, of which unilateralism is only a special case. It is this latent tension between Nonconformist values and middle-class status which enables two sharply different concepts of Christian witness to exist within the same denominational framework. It allows both for a politically engaged interpretation of religious life, and for one which places central emphasis on piety and the problem of sin; the dissenting tradition sustains the former approach, while the restraints implicit in middle-class life help to create a bias for the latter.

It is therefore argued that support for, or opposition to, Christian involvement in the unilateralist movement tended to hinge upon an already existing disposition to interpret Christian duties in either political or pietistic terms. Active protest against the Bomb stem-med, as we have seen, from the exponents of a politicized Christ-ianity, whereas for those whose religion has a more personal and spiritual meaning, support for the unilateralist movement was either opposed or not considered a relevant issue for the church at all. An emphasis on piety focuses Christian values on those matters which apply to individual conduct and personal responsibility, rather than to the collective decisions of governments or political pressure groups. The problems of sin and grace, and 'right relationships' are taken to be the true concerns of the gospel in action, and there is little place in this scheme of things for the affairs of state and con-flicts over the distribution of power and wealth.

It is perhaps understandable that, given their social status, the majority of Nonconformist members would be more inclined to see the scriptures in this light, rather than as a guide to political action. For empirically, it has generally been the case that politicized Christianity has had much more of a radical than a Conservative flavour. With its bias in favour of the dispossessed, its disdain of material wealth, and its charitable view of enemies, Christianity—if applied at key levels of power—would have obvious radical impli-cations for the social structure. By restricting the application of scriptural decrees to lower levels of power, however—and especially to the level of the individual—these implications are largely avoided. When it is man alone who is expected to behave in Christ-like ways, and not collectivities of men and institutions, the socially disruptive potential of religious commands is very much reduced. An approach which confines the burden of Christian duty to personal and family relationships is clearly more acceptable to the majority of church-goers than one which threatens serious dislocation of the social order. Consequently, there is need to urge the separation of religion from politics, and to fail to do so is to 'mix up things that do not belong'.[1]

It is against this tendency to narrow the boundaries of religious decrees that the radical Christian minority is so forcefully opposed. For the latter, the teachings of the gospels are as relevant to the con-duct of the state and other social institutions, as to the conduct of individuals. The Sermon on the Mount is considered to be not simply a doctrine of personal goodness but a charter of government and international relations as well. It is this fundamentally different view of the range of applicability of religious injunctions that was at the root of the cleavage between the radical minority and the churches in general, between the Few and the Many, and conse-quently, between supporters and opponents of the unilateralist campaign. Those who entered CND in the name of Christianity tended to attribute the decline of religion to a failure of nerve on the part of the church, mainly through its reluctance to pronounce a 'Christian solution' to the major social and political problems of the day. Thus, they tended to see the Campaign as providing an oppor-tunity for the church to recapture its waning moral influence and leadership. By harnessing the moral energies released by the move-ment, it was held that organized Christianity could publicly pro-claim the relevance of the gospel to present-day dilemmas. The widespread anxiety over the possibility of nuclear war could thus be turned into account by providing a focal point for effective religious witness.

The attitude of many supporters—clergy and laity alike—pointed to the conclusion also that the movement was, to some extent at least, providing quasi-religious satisfactions of a kind that the church could not. Public witness, self-denial and a sense of martyr-dom in a worthy cause were elements which the Campaign could

[1] Christopher Driver in his critique of recent trends in the activities of the Free Churches was not alone in detecting 'a subtle predisposition to separate religion from life . . . [which] . . . probably helps to account for the corporate laggardli-ness of Dissent in striking to the roots of contemporary social issues. . . . The Free Churches are compelled, or think they are compelled, to see every problem in terms of individual responsibility.' *A Future for the Free Churches?*, SCM Press, London, 1962, pp. 51–2.

offer in abundance, and the parallels with the early Christian church were plain enough for those who wished to draw them. At almost all possible points the unilateralist movement was held up by its Christian supporters as a model of what the church itself should be; its virtues were translated into the church's vices and became fresh ammunition in the hands of those who were at war with 'Churchianity'. Support for CND can therefore be held to derive to a large extent from the radical Christians' inherent opposition to the established religious community, a condition which renders them permanently 'suggestible' to issues and situations which define their position *vis-à-vis* the church in general. For this reason it was the church and its leaders, rather than the government, which were the chief targets of the radical Christians' attack. Participation in the Campaign provided a new and vivid dress for older arguments whose origins are to be found in the two opposing views of the nature and scope of Christian ideals in action. Christian protest against the Bomb and support for CND has therefore symbolized protest against the organized church and its ministry, and the dialogue concerning nuclear weapons has also been a dialogue on the role of religious witness in contemporary Britain.

The Communist Party and the revolutionaries

It was almost inevitable that the unilateralist movement would have a magnetic attraction for the various far left or revolutionary groups and parties which exist on the fringes of British political life. Their banners, slogans and literature were an accepted part of any CND rally and demonstration, and their members active participants in the seemingly endless debates on the future role or correct course of the Campaign. In this section consideration will be given to the part played in the movement by some of the more important of these groups: in particular the Communist Party and other Marxist organizations.

'Mass movements offer excellent opportunities for penetration by totalitarian groups. The Communist party, for example, deliberately creates cadres for the purpose of capturing mass movements.'[1] Kornhauser's assertion would not appear to be an altogether reliable guide to understanding the relationship between the Communist Party of Great Britain and the CND. The Communist Party's role in the unilateralist campaign has been a shifting and ambivalent one, reflecting a general unease towards a movement whose political

[1] Kornhauser, op. cit., p. 47.

position entailed sharp criticism of the Soviet Union no less than of the western powers. The fact that those who protested against nuclear weapons generally drew little distinction between Russian and western varieties was a matter of some concern and embarrassment to the communists, and goes some way towards explaining their reluctance to become involved in the movement during its early stages. Indeed, it is fair to say that initially the official Party line was one of hostility to the idea of British unilateralism, contrary to the frequent assertion that CND was communist-inspired and controlled. Official Party support for unilateralism was in fact withheld until the middle of 1960, and it was not until then that communist influence within the Campaign took on any significance. However, although communists certainly swelled the movement's ranks from 1960 onwards this is not to say either that they succeeded in controlling it or in stamping their own policies upon it. Evidence relating to communist influence in local CND branches is patchy and contradictory, but nevertheless a reasonably clear assessment can be made of the actual impact which the Party made on the Campaign.

Unilateralism was first raised as a major political issue in 1957, when it was the key debate at the Labour Party's annual conference at Brighton. At that conference, in which Aneurin Bevan defended Britain's retention of the hydrogen bomb, the unilateralist motion was heavily defeated, although a motion urging the suspension of British nuclear tests was passed with the support of the platform. The chief supporters of unilateralism were the traditionally left-wing but non-communist unions, such as the Draughtsmen, whereas amongst those opposing it were the unions with communist leadership or fellow-travelling inclinations, such as the ETU, the Scottish miners, and the Boilermakers. As Martin Harrison observed of the occasion, 'The 1957 Conference offered the rare spectacle of the ETU and other Communist-led unions defending the NEC against "irresponsible" unilateralists. When the issues became really heated in 1959 Communist influence helped several [union] Executives rally their conferences to the official line.'[1] At that time the Communist Party was conducting a vigorous campaign of its own calling for the suspension of British tests, in line with the Soviet government's proposal for an international moratorium on all nuclear explosions. The Party's chief immediate concern was to mobilize support for this policy within the Labour

[1] Martin Harrison, *The Trade Unions and the Labour Party since 1945*, Allen and Unwin, London, 1960, p. 237.

movement, and especially within the Labour Party. From the communists' point of view the latter's 1957 conference was regarded with satisfaction since it had gone on record opposing British tests, whereas to the non-communist left the defeat of the unilateralist motion was the event which gave the conference its special, less savoury, flavour. The unilateralist demand was thought by the communists to be a diversion from the main task of securing a test ban as a first step towards meeting the Russians' proposals. 'Whatever one's views about the manufacture of the Bomb by Britain', declared *World News*, 'there can be no substitute for pressure on the Government to change its attitude on international agreement. . . . The most disastrous aspect of the present situation is not that there is no campaign by Labour for unilateral renunciation of the bomb but that there is no campaign for Summit talks.'[1] The left-wing's pressure on the Labour Party not simply for a cessation of tests, but for full-blooded unilateralism was condemned by the communists as 'an utterly wrong action'.[2] Such a radical demand was seen as utopian and disruptive because 'it simply cannot unite the maximum number of people. . . . It is a proposal . . . that would divide those who are today united in demanding that the tests should be stopped.'[3] Communist opposition to the unilateralist line continued throughout 1958 and 1959 and was reflected in the defeat of anti-Bomb motions at conferences of communist controlled unions. Palme Dutt, writing in the Party's theoretical journal *Labour Monthly* in mid-1959 held to the argument that the political issue which caused the greatest concern was 'not the British H-bomb or atom bomb, but the leasing in Britain of the American atom bombers or rocket missile sites'.[4]

The fact that the Communist Party was urging acceptance of the policy advocated by Mr Gaitskell and the NEC, caused much derision among the non-communist left, and a great deal of speculation concerning the motives behind the communists' unusually moderate line. One explanation suggested by a unilateralist Labour MP was that the Soviet Union itself wished Britain to retain the Bomb, since if she abandoned it the United States would probably supply nuclear arms to West Germany—an even worse prospect in the eyes of the Russians.[5] *Tribune*, on the other hand, believed that

[1] *World News*, 15 March 1958, p. 165.
[2] *Daily Worker*, 12 October 1957, p. 1.
[3] *Daily Worker*, 7 October 1957, p. 1.   [4] *Labour Monthly*, June–July 1959.
[5] Tom Driberg in *Reynolds News*, 6 October 1957, p. 6. Driberg's explanation was an attempt to justify Bevan's rejection of unilateralism, rather than the Communist Party's.

the communists' position was due to the Soviet Union's desire to exercise the initiative in test-ban and disarmament proposals, and her unwillingness to see Britain in the role of world peacemaker.[1] But whatever the Party's motives were, it is difficult to accept the official explanation that support for unilateralism would merely fragment the peace movement. For by 1958 the Campaign against the Bomb was already well established, and by 1959 it had reached mass dimensions. By this time, in fact, it is true to say that the Communist Party was the only political body on the far left that was not committed to a unilateralist position—so making its concern for the preservation of unity appear rather unconvincing. The official Party line undoubtedly caused strains within its own rank and file; many individual members certainly ignored the Party line and joined CND demonstrations—but the strength of official disapproval was reflected in the expulsion of three members of the Croydon Party for their involvement in the 1958 Aldermaston March.[2] This opposition to CND was also remarked upon by a young Hull Communist Party member in the course of an interview, in December 1964:

I was active in the Campaign right from the start, and helped to get the local YCND branch set up. Some of the older Party members objected to this and it was raised at the district branch. Everyone felt I should put my first loyalty to the YCL and not to an outside organization. . . . I was disciplined by the Party and warned not to carry on in CND. Yorkshire CND was organizing a coast to coast march from Hull to Liverpool at the time, and I took part in this—and so did quite a few other YCL people. The Party was annoyed and there was some talk of expelling me, but it all blew over. After they realized I would not give up my CND beliefs they more or less tolerated me, but I made several enemies.

The Young Communist League was, as this account suggests, particularly difficult to keep in line, the attractions of the Easter march being stronger for many than Party discipline. It was perhaps realization of the unrest among its own rank and file, particularly the young, that prompted the Party to initiate an 'Aldermaston' of its own—the March for Life, in June 1959. The theme of this demonstration was opposition to American bases and German nuclear arms, the issue of the British bomb being discreetly ignored.[3] This attempt to persuade its own members of its leadership of the peace movement seemed to do little more than highlight the

---

[1] This was also the suggestion put forward by Sir Richard Acland. See *Why So Angry?*, Gollancz, London, 1958, p. 190.

[2] See *Peace News*, 11 January 1963, p. 6.

[3] See the files of *Challenge* and *Peace Campaign* for this period.

Party's isolation from the radical left. As support for unilateralism began to swell in the constituency Labour parties, and in some of the major unions also, the Communists' position was made to appear too sectarian and perverse to be sustained without causing serious opposition from the rank and file, and, in May 1960, the Party finally reversed its line. After three years of consistent opposition to the unilateralist cause the Communists thus became committed to the same policy. No reasons were offered for this sudden switch, which was made directly by the Executive Committee without any internal Party discussion. In the following year, Monty Johnstone, a former editor of *Challenge*, the Young Communist League newspaper, offered the first public admission that the Party had made a tactical error in withholding its support for CND. 'By considering the latter as dividing the movement and diverting it from the main issue,' he wrote, 'we were late in associating ourselves with and giving full support to what has in fact become the key issue on which the left has fought and defeated the Gaitskellite right wing.'[1] Johnstone also took the Party leadership to task for the arbitrary manner in which it had reversed the policy on unilateralism. He complained that

no analysis of the reasons for the change (nor even any recognition that there has been one!), let alone any suggestion that there could have been anything wrong in our previous position, have ever been made to the Party or the public. To do this is ... vital to help dispel a certain distrust towards our Party ... in important sections of the Labour left and the CND, because of our past attitude ...[2]

No such explanation was in fact offered; the Party leadership simply denied that any policy change had taken place or that the Party had ever opposed the unilateralist line. The nearest the leadership ever came to acknowledging that they had erred in their handling of the unilateralist issue was in the General Secretary's admission at the Party's 27th Congress that in advocating a 'generally correct policy' on the Bomb, 'our presentation at times gave rise to misunderstandings, gave opportunities for misrepresentation of our position, and led to some sincere and genuine supporters of nuclear disarmament being misled into thinking that we were against the renunciation of nuclear weapons by Britain. When we clarified our position and put it beyond doubt this contributed to the further recent advances of the peace movement.'[3] These assertions of ideological consistency, however, were made the less convincing by the fact that some Party members were at the same time suggesting

[1] *World News*, 4 March 1961, p. 116.   [2] Loc. cit.
[3] General Secretary's *Report*, 27th Congress of CPGB, 1961, p. 5.

reasons for the Party's initial error in failing to capitalize on the
H-bomb protest. In one such burst of self-criticism it was suggested
that the party 'fell into the right-wing trap of opposing unilateralism
... [because] ... we were, perhaps, so startled that a mass peace
movement could develop in Britain which was not under our
leadership that we concluded that it could not really be what most
people took it to be'.[1]

It seems clear that the main reason behind the Party's policy
reversal on the Bomb was the apparent success of the Labour left in
challenging Gaitskell's leadership. It is significant that the Communist turnabout occurred in mid-1960, immediately after a number of major unions had declared themselves for unilateralism, thus
making Gaitskell's defeat at Scarborough a definite possibility. As
soon as it became evident that the anti-Bomb upsurge in the
Labour Party was not simply, or even primarily, related to the
matter of defence, but to a more embracing inner-party struggle, the
Communists threw their own forces into the movement, this time
on the side of the unilateralists.[2] Once support for unilateralism was
officially sanctioned, the Communist presence quickly made itself
felt in the Campaign. The Communists provided not only an influx
of highly trained political cadres, and a youth movement of their
own, but also threw their weight behind the anti-Bomb cause in the
unions. Those Communist-led trade unions which had voted
unilateralism down at previous annual conferences now switched in
support of it *en bloc*, so contributing to the left's defeat of Gaitskell
at Scarborough. John Gollan, in an assessment of the importance of
this event, declared that 'we can be proud of the part we have
played' in bringing this about, and went on to spell out its wider
implications:

The Scarborough Conference went to the left. This is a start, but only a
start. The Gaitskell right-wing forces are . . . still enormously strong . . . .
The immediate next step is to defeat the right-wing counter-offensive
against the Scarborough decisions . . . to consolidate and extend the
majorities in the trade unions, win over new unions, extend the support in
the Constituency Parties [and] . . . reaffirm the Scarborough decisions
with even more resounding majorities. To do this would bring about
tremendous political developments.[3]

---

[1] *World News*, 18 February 1961, p. 88.

[2] The first official announcement of the Party's new line was made in a policy
statement by the General Secretary; it had the revealing title *Labour and the
Bomb*, CPGB; London 1960. Compare this with the two previous statements by
the Assistant General Secretary: *H-Bomb Tests: End Them Now*, CPGB, London,
1957; and *Close All U.S. Bases*, CPGB, London, 1958.

[3] General Secretary's *Report*, op. cit., p. 16.

There can be little doubt, then, that whatever the official explanation may have been the Communist Party's discovery of the virtues of unilateralism stemmed mainly from the desire to add the Party's weight to the left's attempt to dislodge Gaitskell, and by so doing to end their growing isolation from the radical wing of the Labour movement. Communists now became increasingly in evidence on CND demonstrations (especially when these were directed against American bases and sites) causing some disquiet amongst certain other groups in the Campaign—notably those connected with the church. It was feared too that Communists were having an undue influence in the CND youth organizations, whose newspaper *Youth Against the Bomb* was being edited by a Party member, and which had begun expressing crude anti-German and anti-American sentiments—always a reliable indicator of the Communist presence and one quite out of keeping with the general tone of CND publications. Another indication of this tendency was the satisfaction expressed by the YCL newspaper at what it called the 'growing political consciousness' of the youth CND, whose 'policy has progressed a long way since it stated simply that it was unilaterally against the bomb'.[1] This praise was prompted by the 1962 YCND conference at which a number of resolutions were tabled along Communist Party lines. Alan Clayton, the Secretary of the Scottish YCND, who was a conference delegate expressed alarm at the impact made by the 'confident, well trained speakers of the YCL, swaying young people with the possible horrors of a rearmed Nazi Germany'.[2] The CND London Regional Organizer also drew attention to attempts by Communists Party members to control local groups either by packing meetings with their own supporters and securing the election of Communist officers, or by setting up their own CND branches. He acknowledged that some Party members held posts through hard work for the Campaign, but claimed that others had gained positions by more dubious means and worked for Party ends rather than those of CND.[3] The Secretary of the Scottish Committee of 100 reported that during the anti-Polaris campaigns at the Holy Loch 'the CP were extremely active, and were numerically the basis of the first demonstrations . . .' although this support later diminished.[4]

[1] *Challenge*, July–August 1962, p. 7.

[2] *Counterblast*, July 1962, p. 21. Clayton caused some disturbance by his eventual resignation from CND on the grounds that the Scottish section of the movement had become Communist-dominated. See *Peace News*, 1 June 1962, p. 8.

[3] London Regional Organizer's Report in *Peace News*, 11 January 1963, p. 7.

[4] *Peace News*, 18 January 1963, p. 6.

In South Wales, where cooperation between CND and the CP centred on protest campaigns against the German troops stationed at Castlemartin, the Secretary of CND's Welsh National Council recorded that relations between the two bodies were 'friendly, tolerant and understanding'.[1] In Fulham CND, there was an 'early struggle to convert CND into a branch of the British Peace Committee', which was unsuccessful.[2] In Hornsey CND the chairman and secretary resigned as a result of the activities of the Communist Party members of the branch.[3]

There is little doubt, then, that CP members began to play an active role in the unilateralist movement as soon as the Party leaders had sanctioned the new line, making their presence felt in the trade unions, YCND and in the local branch organizations. But to acknowledge the importance of Communist participation in the Campaign is not to concede that they managed also to dominate it. In fact the evidence suggests that, at the national level at least, Communist influence has been negligible, whether measured in terms of securing representation on the National Committee or in bringing about policy changes in line with the Communist Party position. Party members or fellow travellers have rarely been elected to CND national offices, and indeed rarely presented themselves as candidates for election. Similarly, CND policy decisions have not in any way reflected Communist Party aims and concerns; if anything they have run completely counter to them. CND's 1964 conference decision, for example, calling upon the Soviet Union and the United States to disarm unilaterally, and urging internal resistance to the Bomb in these two countries, clearly was not an echo of the Communist Party's voice, and was indeed deeply embarrassing and exasperating to the Party. The latter's specifically anti-German and anti-American pre-occupations found very little support in the Campaign's policy, a fact which also applies to the YCND. Similarly, even those regional Secretaries most critical of Communist infiltration into local branches acknowledge that this was generally concentrated in a small number of groups and was not typical of CND branches in general. The London Regional Organizer, for example, reported that out of 116 group secretaries in his area only four were known Communists, whilst the number of Communist-controlled branches could be put at seven at most.[4]

---

[1] *Peace News*, 18 January 1963, p. 7.
[2] Personal communication from Secretary, Fulham CND.
[3] Personal communication from Secretary, Hornsey CND.
[4] *Peace News*, 11 January 1963, p. 7. He also stated that a number of other branches harboured strong anti-CP factions.

The Secretary of the Scottish Committee of 100 observed that after the Polaris demonstrations had died away, and the Russians resumed nuclear testing, Communist influence in the region diminished and the Party became 'neither helpful nor harmful, merely irrelevant'.[1] The National Executive of CND, countering allegations by Labour Party spokesmen that Glasgow CND was Communist dominated, issued a statement pointing out that of the forty-nine members of the branch only one was a Communist.[2]

In organizational terms, then, the Communist Party cannot really be said to have made serious inroads into the unilateralist movement, either in the sense of having captured positions at national or local levels, or in effectively shaping CND policy. A number of reasons may be suggested to account for this. In the first place, the possibility of the Communists exerting undue influence was limited by the fact that they were only one of a number of ideologically committed interest groups at work within the Campaign and seeking to use it for their own ends. The usual conditions for a successful takeover of an organization are an apathetic membership and low emotional involvement in the organization's aims; this could hardly be said to characterize CND, one of whose chief features was its tendency to attract a wide variety of deeply committed moral and political radicals. Communist Party strategies and policies would be far more difficult to introduce in an atmosphere of heated ideological debate and conflict than in one of low political temperature. Secondly, Communist supporters entered the movement at a comparatively late stage, by which time other interest groups and factions had become well entrenched. In addition, many of these latter were bitterly hostile to Communist Party policies, and their members often were well acquainted with the Party's methods and personnel. Again, the Communists' initial isolation from and opposition to the unilateralist campaign had earned them the contempt of the whole movement, which inevitably made their position much weaker once they had entered its ranks. Similarly, the Party's strong identification with the Soviet Union and its readiness to defend Russian nuclear policy, including weapon tests, ran completely counter to the general spirit of the Campaign, and was an obvious millstone around the necks of individual Party members. For these reasons alone, any attempt by the Communists to capture the unilateralist movement would have been most unlikely to

---

[1] *Peace News*, 18 January 1963, p. 6.
[2] Only 10 per cent of the adult CND respondents declared themselves to be Communist Party members.

succeed. Although there were certainly small pockets of Communist influence in the Campaign, these were more attributable to the activities of Party members acting as individuals (some of whom were genuine unilateralists and opposed to the official Communist line) than to any explicit policy decision emanating from Party headquarters. In fact the official attitude towards CND seems to have been one of wariness, rather than enthusiasm, suggesting underlying doubts about the wisdom of offering their members to the unilateralist embrace. Close involvement in the Campaign would inevitably expose members to new currents of radical opinion, including criticism of Party policy and the Soviet Union. This might have mattered less if the criticism had come from the right of the Party, since these were the arguments it was accustomed to meeting and dealing with; but the most vocal groups were themselves on the far left—at the Party's exposed flank as it were. Here were to be found an imposing array of political sophisticates, many of them with a communist apprenticeship behind them, who were well equipped to probe the Party's ideological blind spots, and expose its twists and turns on nuclear arms policy. Because the Party's attitude to unilateralism and Soviet policy was so obviously open to attack and ridicule by the left, the Communists' involvement in the Campaign presented as many hazards as advantages. In the company of unilateralists the Communists were in the embarrassing position of appearing to be the most moderate of all groups represented, a fact which squared badly with the Party's claims to represent the vanguard of radicalism. Indeed, the kinds of radical or quasi-revolutionary methods practised among some sections of the movement were looked upon with great disfavour by communist officials who, perhaps mindful of the Party's new parliamentary image, were at pains to dissociate the Party from the civil disobedience campaigns and the activities of the 'Spies for Peace'.[1]

Because of these disadvantages entailed in close cooperation with the Campaign, it appears that the Communists have preferred to avoid any serious organizational involvement, either at local or national levels, but have instead simply used CND marches and demonstrations as opportunities for publicizing their own characteristic policies. It is this tendency to restrict their mass support to the movement's public occasions, rather than attempting to capture the machine, which accounts for the wide discrepancy between the high visibility of Communists in the Campaign, and the latter's decidedly non-communist policies. The Party's own 'peace policies' betray

[1] See for example, *Peace Campaign*, May 1963, p. 1.

little enthusiasm for unilateralism, and concentrate instead on the traditional targets of NATO, American bases and German militarism. Thus as late as 1963 the Secretary of the Party's British Peace Committee declared that 'it is deceptive and dangerous simply to say that Britain should cease to have an "independent nuclear deterrent" when the reality since Nassau is the complete capitulation to the policy of the U.S. . . . [and] . . . the intensified effort of West Germany to secure nuclear weapons'. In his view it was not the campaign against the Bomb, but 'the struggle to bring the most important aspects of the Cold War to the front that is the concern of the peace movement'.[1] It is fairly clear that the Communists' attitude towards the main issues posed by CND was not fundamentally changed, despite the lifting of the official embargo on support for the movement. Like other organizations it has sought simply to use the Campaign as a platform for its own particular policies, neither committing itself to the CND, nor succeeding (and not seriously attempting), to alter that position in line with its own. In so far as they have remained the only group in the campaign not committed to a full unilateralist position their relationship to the rest of the movement is almost as uneasy as that which existed at the outset.[2]

The Trotskyists

Marxist representation in the unilateralist movement was provided not only by the Communist Party but also by a number of smaller independent organizations, chief amongst which were the Socialist Labour League and the International Socialists. Although smaller than the Communist Party they are equally well organized, functioning not as distinct political parties but as pressure groups within the Labour Party and its associated bodies.[3] Unlike the Communist

[1] *Peace Campaign*, May 1963, p. 3. As far as the Party was concerned, 'The peace movement is not political. It seeks to mobilize support for peace from every quarter. It welcomes, for example, the steady pressure from businessmen for more East-West trade, because that is one of the bases for co-existence and therefore a step towards peace', loc. cit.

[2] Events in the mid-nineteen-sixties appear to have caused these tensions to diminish. By 1965 and 1966, the Campaign was increasingly shifting its attention from the Bomb and nuclear weapons policy to the war in Vietnam. CND's policy of opposition to the American presence in Vietnam is clearly far more congenial to the Communist Party line than unilateralism was; consequently, Party cooperation with CND on this front (as for example in the jointly-sponsored Peace in Vietnam committees) is liable to be far more enthusiastic than in the past.

[3] The Socialist Labour League bases itself on the writings of Trotsky, and recruits mainly from among industrial workers. It operates on the assumption of the imminent collapse of the capitalist economic system, and sees its prime

Party, both the SLL and the International Socialists supported the Campaign from its inception—and indeed the resolution which put the unilateralist case at the 1957 conference of the Labour Party was sponsored and moved by Trotskyist members of the Norwood CLP. The Marxists' concern over the Bomb, however, was of a rather different kind from that of other interest groups in the movement. It was regarded not simply as a weapon which could be used in time of conflict with a foreign power, but as a weapon by which domestic power relations could be preserved intact. As the Trotskyists themselves expressed it:

The capitalist class needs the bomb to defend its social system. It would renounce it as readily as it would renounce its position as a ruling class. The bomb is the ultimate custodian of the capitalists' political and economic power.[1]

Similarly, the International Socialists felt that

the Bomb is the most concentrated and the foulest expression of the inhuman class-divided world we live in. Socialism is the social system which alone can remove the danger of the Bomb, and the Bomb is the most compelling argument for abolishing class society.[2]

Marxists were contemptuous of the Communist Party's emphasis on the need for summit talks and international agreement on nuclear disarmament. They represented it as one more sign of the Party's greater willingness to trust in the good faith of governments, and the ruling classes they represented, than in the power of the organized working class. It was only the latter, Marxists argued, who could ever effectively bring about unilateralism. Cliff Slaughter, a Leeds University sociologist, and chief theoretician of the SLL, explained that the League's programme was directed at bringing about 'a struggle for power by the British working class, from which position it will appeal over the heads of their rulers to the workers of other countries to disarm their exploiters ... [The SLL] ... would regard solidarity with the working class movement in every country

---

task as the training of revolutionary cadres to seize control when this crisis comes about. The International Socialists while sharing many of the Trotskyists' premises about capitalist society, see its downfall as a long term rather than an immediate prospect. They tend to be less active on the industrial scene than the SLL and draw their support largely from students and young professional workers. Both organizations are strongly represented in the Young Socialists, the Labour Party's youth organization, which has often provided a battle ground for the waging of bitter political rivalries. For an account of the SLL's main ideas see, George Box, *The Disunity of Theory and Practice: The Trotskyist Movement in Britain since 1945*, B.A. Dissertation, University of Durham, 1964.

[1] *Newsletter*, 28 March 1959, p. 92.
[2] *Young Guard*, September 1961, p. 4.

as its major guarantee of security from attack, rather than the word of any government representative'.[1] Thus, despite their general support for the unilateralist movement, and their presence on anti-Bomb marches and demonstrations, the Marxists were extremely sceptical of the way the Campaign was being waged. They objected to the common tendency within the movement to oppose nuclear weapons on strictly moral grounds, instead of for more fundamental political reasons. They were impatient with the methods advocated by the 'churchgoers, pacifists and political abstainers', and urged instead, the need to 'wage this campaign not in any abstract, humanitarian, above-class way, but as a frankly socialist campaign, with the industrial workers in the lead'.[2] Marxists were apprehensive that the movement would become harmlessly institutionalized and that the Aldermaston marches would serve no more radical purpose than providing 'a yearly catharsis for the middle-class conscience, an act of ritual mortification and sacrifice, till one day good miraculously triumphs over evil'.[3] Demonstrations, petitions and pressure group activities were held to be leading the unilateralist movement into a blind alley; such tactics undermined the cause because they created utopian hopes that the government could eventually be persuaded to relinquish the Bomb of its own accord. Peter Fryer, the editor of the Trotskyist *Newsletter*, and a former correspondent of the *Daily Worker*, explained that 'the statesmen will never surrender the bomb voluntarily. It must be wrenched from their grasps and destroyed by the forces of sanity, by the working people . . .'[4] The way this was to be achieved was by the disruption of industries manufacturing the weapon. Workers were urged to declare 'black' all work and supplies connected with nuclear arms or rocket and bomber bases. Throughout 1958 the SLL was particularly active in attempting to spread this message to workers engaged on military projects of various kinds, and in the same year organized a London conference to coordinate the activities of its supporters in the key industries. The marxists were always at pains to emphasize that the struggle against the Bomb was an integral and necessary part of the struggle against capitalist society, and that opposition to the one was impossible without opposition to the other. The International Socialists summarized this view in their proposal that CND should campaign on the

---

[1] *Labour Review*, Spring 1961, p. 6.
[2] *Newsletter*, 12 April 1958, p. 108.
[3] *Newsletter*, 4 April 1959, p. 100.
[4] *Black the A-Bomb and the Rocket Bases*, A *Newsletter* pamphlet, London, 1958, p. 5.

G

slogan that 'a blow against the bosses is a blow against the Bomb';[1] the Trotskyists spelled out the implications of this in some detail:

The industrial struggle of the working class, the colonial revolutions in Africa, Asia and the Middle East, the fight against the Tory government, the struggle inside the Labour Party for a socialist policy . . . are closely bound up with the campaign against nuclear war. That is why they are brought together in the programme of the Socialist Labour League. . . . It is designed to mobilize the unified opposition ensuing from all the conflicts that break out in capitalist society. To keep these forces separate weakens each one of them. But brought together in a political movement, they will be a force which can sweep away imperialism and end the nuclear threat.[2]

It was not the Bomb as such, then, which was of greatest concern to the Marxists, but the political and economic system they saw it to be a product of. The bomb served as a convenient symbol of capitalist society, a peg upon which to hang long-standing discontents and grievances. They hoped that by attracting industrial workers to the unilateralist movement the political temperature would be raised and class consciousness correspondingly heightened by the fusion of many disparate conflicts into one major conflict. Despite the Marxists' exhortations, however, all attempts to link industrial militancy to the question of the H-bomb proved to be an almost complete failure. Workers could be persuaded neither to 'black' materials or supplies used in the production of nuclear weapons, nor to refuse employment on rocket sites—not least of all because the latter were often located in areas of unemployment, such as East Anglia and Scotland. The one single success registered along these lines was the one-hour token strike of building workers in Stevenage, and this was due more to the efforts of the Direct Action Committee, than to any of the Marxist groups. In trying to follow up this achievement by an intensive drive in the East Midlands, Pat Arrowsmith reported that 'we spoke at about twenty trade union branch-meetings and Trades Councils . . . [and] . . . urged them to follow the example of the Stevenage builders . . . but in vain'.[3] Similar coolness towards the unilateralist campaign was displayed by workers in other parts of the country, and by 1963 the Marxists reluctantly acknowledged that 'no permanent links, even on the smallest scale, have been forged between industrial militancy and the Bomb'.[4]

[1] *International Socialism*, Autumn 1960, p. 1.
[2] *Labour Review*, June–July 1960, p. 43.
[3] *Newsletter*, 17 October 1959, p. 296.
[4] *International Socialism*, Spring 1963, p. 9.

The notable absence of manual workers from the ranks of the Campaign was a fact which continued to haunt, and often to exasperate, those who looked to them as the only force capable of ending the nuclear menace. That the most dramatic display of radicalism in the post-war period should be confined largely to people of professional and white-collar background was not merely disappointing to Marxists, but was felt to be the movement's severest possible handicap. If, it was argued, CND were 'firmly based on working class foundations instead of being a predominantly middle class organization it would be far less respectable, far less acceptable to the Establishment, but far more dangerous. Indeed, the whole fate of the Campaign depends upon ridding it of the obsession of How can we influence the high-ups?, and giving a little more thought to How can we influence the working class?'[1] The absence of manual workers from the Campaign was interpreted not as a rejection of unilateralist aims but as a conspiracy by the movement's leadership to keep them out. As the Trotskyists saw it, 'the CND leaders do not want mass working-class participation, any more than the Communist Party leaders do . . . both rely on agreements between statesmen rather than on working class action'.[2] How industrial workers were dissuaded from entering the Campaign was never explained; the Marxists simply continued to re-iterate that only by mobilizing this section of society could unilateralist aims be achieved. The notion of middle class radicalism had little place in their theoretical schema, and had consequently to be dismissed as impotent and irrelevant—'a voice without lungs'.[3]

The doctrinal contribution of the Marxists to the unilateralist campaign was thus of a purely negative kind; in so far as their ideology placed over-riding emphasis on the crucial role of a class that was never really present in the campaign, Marxists might even be said to have hampered it—in the field of ideas and strategies at least. It may perhaps have been this inability of Marxists to conceive of radical protest outside their conventional class categories that contributed to the flowering of other ideologies whose concepts were more relevant to the unilateralists' situation—most notably anarchism, which found a ready response among the direct action wing of the movement. Significantly enough, the methods of the direct actionists were never fully endorsed by the Marxists, who were rather at a loss to account for this brand of politics. Although they recognized and applauded its potential value as a disruptive force against the state, they nevertheless insisted that it attracted mainly middle class dissidents, who 'because they are middle class . . . see protest as essentially an individual matter. The Quaker tradition of individual protest and suffering is strong among them. They are moved by silence, the struggle within the soul, and against tyranny from without. Of necessity the working class has a different outlook.'[1] To the Marxists, civil disobedience appeared to relegate social conflict to a purely symbolic level, offering opportunities for personal witness against nuclear weapons, but ultimately posing no serious threat to the existing order. Militancy that was not centred in the industrial field was not conceivable in Marxist terms, and was dismissed as a form of harmless shadow-boxing. CND in fact presented Marxists with the puzzling and somewhat disturbing spectacle of a radical movement with an absentee proletariat. As a result, their involvement in it was a rather half-hearted and grudging affair—sustained not through any idealistic commitment to unilateralism as such, but as in the case of so many others, by virtue of the opportunities it appeared to open up for the pursuit of quite different aims.

[1] *Newsletter*, 17 October 1959, p. 296.

5

Symbolic protest—
11: the intellectuals

One of the seemingly vital prerequisites for the establishment of a political mass movement is the leadership and support of an intellectual stratum. Intellectuals are needed to formulate policies and programmes and to create inspirational symbols and appeals. Without an intellectual elite to offer leadership and a coherent set of goals, popular demands or general discontents are rarely able to translate themselves into effective political movements on a mass scale. CND was no exception to this general rule. Both anxiety at, and disapproval of, the British manufacture and testing of nuclear weapons had been latent for several years before the emergence of the Campaign. A number of attempts had been made by radical political groups to harness this discontent into open support for anti-nuclear policies, but with marked lack of success. It was not until a body of nationally known intellectuals, led by A. J. P. Taylor, Kingsley Martin, Bertrand Russell and J. B. Priestley, formally declared their intention of initiating a movement against the Bomb, that CND was created. Without this intervention by intellectuals it is doubtful whether opposition to nuclear weapons would have been lifted out of the hands of small protest groups to form the basis of a nation-wide mass movement.[1] Intellectuals not only took the initiative in originating the Campaign but continued to identify with it publicly, and, in the case of many, to support the civil disobedience programme of the early nineteen-sixties. CND sympathies were particularly strong among the new generation of post-war intellectuals, and the ranks of the Campaign included many of the most celebrated writers and artists of the period.

The tendency for intellectuals to be attracted to radical causes and mass movement has received a good deal of attention from social theorists, and a number of different explanations have been offered to account for it. Several writers have claimed, for example, that the motivating force behind the intellectual's readiness to support extremist politics derives from certain characteristics inherent in the creative role, and the personal tensions and anxieties associated with it. Thus Kornhauser writes:

Intellectuals not only support mass movements; they also originate and promulgate the ideological appeal to fit the mass situation. Those who live for and off symbols—the intellectuals—are least able to suffer a vacuum in the symbolic sphere; at the same time, they are the ones who know how to create the symbols to fill it. *Intellectuals create millennial appeals in response to their own sense of the loss of social function and relatedness in the mass society.*[2]

Hoffer also locates the source of the intellectual's radicalism in his personal anxieties.

Whatever the type, there is a deep-seated craving common to almost all men of words which determines their attitude to the prevailing order. It is a craving for recognition; a craving for a clearly marked status above the common run of humanity. . . . However much the protesting man of words

---

[1] Edward Hyams points particularly to the crucial role of the intellectuals associated with the *New Statesman* in bringing CND into existence. See *The New Statesman: The History of the First Fifty Years, 1913–63*, Longmans, London, 1963, pp. 287-8.

[2] Kornhauser, op. cit., pp. 184-5.

sees himself as the champion of the downtrodden and injured, the grievance which animates him is, with very few exceptions, private and personal.[1]

Karl Mannheim, too, has suggested that 'the fanaticism of radicalized intellectuals should be understood . . . [as] . . . a psychic compensation for the lack of more fundamental integration into a class . . .'[2]

Other theorists have argued that intellectuals are prone to espouse utopian or idealistic causes because of their lack of experience in practical affairs and the decision-making process. To be concerned with power, but to lack first-hand knowledge of its uses and limitations, it is argued, encourages a tendency to champion unrealistic demands of an 'all or nothing' character. Tocqueville, considering the position of French intellectuals at the time of the Revolution, makes this point with force.

Their very way of living led these writers to indulge in abstract theories and generalizations regarding the nature of government, and to place a blind confidence in these. For living as they did, quite out of touch with practical politics, they lacked the experience which might have tempered their enthusiasms. Thus they completely failed to perceive the very real obstacles in the way of even the most praiseworthy reforms, and to gauge the perils involved in even the most salutary revolutions. That they should not have had the least presentiment of these dangers was only to be expected, since . . . they had little acquaintance with the realities of public life, which, indeed, was *terra incognita* to them.[3]

Schumpeter suggests that this reasoning was valid not simply for one particular historical case, but had a more general relevance. 'Intellectuals', he claimed, 'are in fact people who wield the power of the spoken and the written word, and one of the touches that distinguishes them from other people who do the same is the absence of direct responsibility for practical affairs . . . [or] . . . first hand knowledge of them which only actual experience can give.'[4] Similarly, Michels, in his explanation of what he called the 'impossibilism' of the intellectuals, claims that their 'tendency towards extremism arises . . . from the nature of mental work which can be easily dissociated from reality' so making its practitioners unreliable political advocates.[5]

[1] E. Hoffer, *The True Believer: Thoughts on the Nature of Mass Movements*, Mentor, New York, 1964, p. 121–2.
[2] Karl Mannheim, *Ideology and Utopia*, Routledge, London, 1960, p. 141.
[3] Quoted in George B. de Huszar, *The Intellectuals*, Free Press, Glencoe, 1960, p. 13.
[4] Joseph Schumpeter, *Capitalism, Socialism and Democracy*, Unwin, London, 1965, p. 147.
[5] Roberto Michels, 'Intellectuals', in *Encyclopaedia of the Social Sciences*, Vol. VIII, p. 121.

A third, and rather more sympathetic, explanation of the intellectual's apparent attraction to radicalism is offered in terms of the analytical abilities and critical attitudes which his work and training instil in him. Those who live by the exercise of intellect are felt to be less able or willing than others automatically to endorse existing values and the status quo. Indeed it is argued that *only* by remaining detached, and critical of things as they are, is creativity at all possible, and that the intellectual who fails to act as a social critic is not discharging his proper role. 'Only if intellectuals preserve critical intelligence, maintain some remoteness from day to day tasks, and cultivate concern with ultimate rather than proximate values can they serve society fully.'[1]

It will be noted that these theories, different as they are, all attempt to show, with varying degrees of emphasis, that the intellectual's involvement in radical or extremist politics derives from certain features inherent in creative activity. Thus, whether phrased in terms of the personal anxieties and tensions which such work generates, or in terms of the lack of experience in practical politics, or in terms of the critical detachment required by the creative spirit, all the explanations assume intellectuals to be a socially homogeneous category about which generalizations concerning political behaviour can readily be made. The obvious objection to this approach is that by treating the term intellectual as a blanket category it diverts attention away from occupational and status differences, and from possible variations in support for political extremism. Indeed, because attention is focused almost invariably on the dissenting intellectuals it is easy to overlook the fact that these almost always are a minority group, and that political conformity, in the broad sense, is a more typical position of this stratum. Of course, while it is difficult to conceive of a viable social structure in which the great majority of intellectuals were disaffected, there are perhaps differences between societies in the relative status and influence which intellectuals enjoy, and therefore, in the proportionate size of the 'alienated' minority. It has often been pointed out of Britain, for example, that there is no real equivalent of the term 'intelligentsia' commonly used on the continent to denote a specific social stratum—a fact which is taken to suggest the absence of any real gulf between the intellectuals and the rest of society. It is also something of a commonplace that British intellectuals tend themselves to be unwilling to have this, or

[1] Lewis Coser, 'America's Intellectuals: The Twin Temptations', *New Society*, 14 January 1965, p. 13.

any similar, label pinned on them which appears to mark them off as a distinct category.[1] This may well be taken as an indication of the extent to which men of letters and ideas in this country do in fact identify with their society in a way felt to be uncommon among their counterparts on the continent and elsewhere. Through their links with the public schools, the ancient universities, clubs and similar élitist institutions, as well as occasionally through ties of kinship, the British intellectuals do, it has been argued, have ready access to the spheres of influence and prestige often denied to intellectuals elsewhere. Noel Annan has commented upon 'the paradox of an intelligentsia which appears to conform rather than rebel against the rest of society . . . .' an intelligentsia which is 'secure, established and, like the rest of English society, accustomed to responsible and judicious utterance and sceptical of iconoclastic speculation'.[2] Neal Wood, too, has maintained that 'a large body of alienated, discontented intellectuals has never existed in Great Britain. For the most part intellectuals have been solidly middle class, forming a staunch pillar of the status quo.'[3] Wood points out that even in the highly politicized atmosphere of the thirties those who aligned themselves with the communist cause included only a small minority of the intellectuals, a fact which their public 'visibility' and prestige tended to obscure.

Socially unattached intelligentsia

Thus, once it is acknowledged that the majority of intellectuals (in Britain at least) have not in fact been in opposition to major values and institutions, then broad generalizations about the inherent radicalism of the creative or intellectual role are clearly of questionable use. What require analysis are the features which differentiate the minority of dissenting intellectuals from the majority of conformists. Mannheim's concept of the 'socially unattached intelligentsia', also employed by Kornhauser, would appear to be helpful in this task. The 'socially unattached' intellectuals may be regarded as those who are not employed in cultural and educational institutions, but whose general economic position tends to be somewhat marginal and precarious. This category would include freelance journalists, writers, artists, dramatists and others who are expected

[1] For example, Bertrand Russell's celebrated definition: 'I think an intellectual may be defined as a person who pretends to have more intellect than he has, and I hope that this definition does not fit me.' Quoted in Huszer, op. cit., p. 309.
[2] Noel Annan, 'The Intellectual Aristocracy', in J. H. Plumb (ed.), *Studies in Social History*, Longmans, 1955, p. 285.
[3] Neal Wood, *Communism and British Intellectuals*, Gollancz, 1959, p. 28.

to sell their cultural products or services under market conditions, and who are exposed to the frequent incompatibility between the aesthetic considerations of the seller and the commercial considerations of the buyer. Radicalism, rather than being a fixed attribute of the intellectual role, would then be expected to flourish mainly among those of freelance status. By contrast, intellectuals securely entrenched in formal institutional settings such as universities and colleges, publishing houses, the BBC, newspapers and journals, research organizations and the like, generally on a salaried basis, would be held to be less susceptible to the appeal of extremist politics and mass movements. This would be due not simply to the greater economic security and stability afforded by such institutions, but also because of the greater *constraints* which they impose on employees. Intellectuals employed in bureaucracies, as Mills has pointed out, are under certain pressures to conform to orthodox standards of behaviour, and that consequently their public commitments to radicalism may be held in check, not-withstanding their private commitments.[1] Freelance intellectuals, by contrast, are not subjected to bureaucratic restraints and are able to translate their personal views into public stances, however unorthodox. Indeed, under conditions where notoriety and 'having a name' increase the marketability of cultural products, public radicalism may have positive advantages. Some confirmation of this hypothesis appears to be provided by a comparison of the involvement of intellectuals in the nineteen-thirties and in the unilateralist movement. During the former period, as Wood has shown, many of the intellectuals who were attracted to Communism were novelists and poets who were unable to earn a living from their writing, and who were often obliged to take posts as tutors or prep-school teachers, relegating their creative work to spare-time pursuits. Dissatisfaction with a system which failed to reward creative talent may be seen as one of the factors making for their commitment to radical change. However, when CND appeared on the scene some twenty-five years later, this earlier generation of dissenting intellectuals had themselves been integrated into cultural and other institutions, and consequently took no part in this new wave of radical protest. By this time, for example, both Auden and Day-Lewis had held the Chair of Poetry at Oxford; Auden was also a Member of the

[1] C. Wright Mills, op. cit. This same point is implied in Merton's hypothesis that 'bureaucracies provoke gradual transformation of the alienated intellectual into the a-political technician, whose role is to serve whatever strata happen to be in power.' Robert K. Merton, *Social Theory and Social Structure*, Free Press, Glencoe, 1957, p. 214.

American Academy of Arts and Letters, and Day-Lewis was Vice-President of the Royal Society of Literature, and a CBE. Strachey was a Privy Councillor and had held the Ministries of War and Food in the post-war Labour government. Muggeridge was editor of *Punch*, and Stephen Spender was editor of *Encounter* and a CBE, and so on. Edward Shils, contrasting the radical mood of the thirties with the mid-nineteen-fifties, shortly before CND was formed, was able to write:

Never has an intellectual class found its society and its culture so much to its satisfaction. . . . Fundamental criticism of the trend of British society has become rare. . . . The British intellectual has come to feel proud of the moral stature of a country with so much solidarity and so little acrimony between classes.[1]

This transition demonstrates well that radicalism is best thought of not as an inherent feature of creative life, but as contingent upon the structural position of the intellectual, and in particular his degree of integration into cultural and élitist institutions. Since in fact there appears to be a tendency for gifted writers and artists to achieve social recognition and honours over a period of time, it may be presumed that the intellectual's radicalism has something of a limited 'life span'. At any rate, it is certainly the case that men like Kingsley Martin and Victor Gollancz stood out as exceptions to the general rule that those who had flirted with Communism in the thirties were not to be found in CND. Most simply remained aloof and uninvolved, but some, like Strachey and Spender, were hostile to the Campaign. It was in the main, a new generation which responded to the appeal of the anti-Bomb movement and who put their imaginations to work to mirror the political temper of the times.

As with their counterparts of the thirties, these new recruits to radicalism were also heavily drawn from the ranks of the 'socially unattached intelligentsia' rather than from those in established cultural and educational institutions. One noticeable difference however, was that whereas poets seem to have been the chief creative representatives of the earlier period, the archetype figures of the unilateralist movement were actors and playwrights. Many, perhaps most, of the young dramatists associated with the newly emergent school of theatrical realism were supporters of CND and the Committee of 100. Among them were John Osborne, the leading representative of the new school, Arnold Wesker, Doris Lessing, Robert Bolt, Bernard Kops, Shelagh Delaney, John Arden, David

[1] Edward Shils, 'The Intellectuals: Great Britain', *Encounter*, April 1955, p. 7.

Campton, David Mercer, and John Neville and Vanessa Redgrave. Not surprisingly, then, it was through the medium of the stage above all else that literary protest against the H-bomb was most commonly expressed. As early as 1954 Marghanita Laski, a prominent pamphleteer for CND, had treated the theme in her play *The Offshore Island*, which was later produced on television, as was J. B. Priestley's *Doomsday for Dyson;* both attracted widespread comment and publicity. David Campton's plays were almost all concerned with the Bomb in one way or another, the chief among them being *Four Minute Warning, Mutatis Mutandis* and a *View from the Brink*, this latter being performed on the 1960 Aldermaston march. Other writers treated the Bomb, or occasionally CND itself, as a background against which to explore social behaviour and themes of a more universal kind, such as Doris Lessing's *Each in his own Wilderness*, and Robert Bolt's *The Tiger and the Horse*. This latter dealt with the conflict of loyalties of the Master of a university college whose wife's pro-CND activities jeopardized his position.[1] The television playwright David Mercer also wrote a widely acclaimed trilogy, *The Generations*, dealing with the conflicts and final disintegration of a family deeply divided about their attitudes to the Bomb and civil disobedience. Mercer was himself at the time actively involved in the Committee of 100, as were a number of the other writers, for example, Arnold Wesker and Robert Bolt, who were arrested for their part in the Whitehall demonstrations in September 1961.[2] Involvement in the anti-Bomb crusade appeared to carry the same kind of moral imperative that support for Spain had among the intellectuals of the thirties, and sometimes engendered similar conflicts of choice between career and political commitment. Vanessa Redgrave, one of the most dedicated of CND's intellectual supporters, spelled out her dilemma:

I'm hoping to put off answering the question—the choice between my stage career and the campaign—for as long as possible. But the time may come when I shall have to give up the stage for six months, say, so as to devote myself to the Committee. . . . If I'm not prepared to give up the stage, how can I ever ask anyone to make sacrifices again?[3]

---

[1] Vanessa Redgrave, who played the stage role of the CND daughter, claimed that it was this experience which led to her conversion to the unilateralist movement. *Sunday Times*, 17 September 1961, p. 7.

[2] Bolt refused to give assurances to keep the peace and was sent to prison for twenty-eight days. He was at the time working on the film script for *Lawrence of Arabia* and it was only after the personal assurance of the producer, Sam Spiegel, that his absence was jeopardizing production that Bolt finally agreed to be bound over. *The Times*, 29 September 1961, p. 7.

[3] *Sunday Times*, 10 December 1961, p. 1.

The prominence of dramatists amongst the dissenting intellectuals can to some extent be related to the fact that young playwrights were at the forefront of certain changes in cultural values which were occurring at the same time as the debate on the hydrogen bomb and the widespread anxieties about nuclear war. The English theatre of the post-war years had become set in highly conventionalized dramatic forms, characterized most obviously perhaps by the drawing-room comedy, the American musical and the stylized thriller. Very little occurred in the way of experimentation, either in dialogue or theme. In the second half of the nineteen-fifties the existing conventions were challenged with the appearance of a new group of young writers intent on portraying aspects of working-class life in a style of realism which became dubbed as the 'kitchen sink' school, and its practitioners the 'Angry Young Men'.[1] These writers, although they did not really form a close-knit côterie with a specific 'programme' similar to that often proposed by literary movements, nevertheless shared a basic similarity of outlook and ideals as well as a common opposition to reigning cultural norms. No doubt this rough unity of ideas was partly explained by one fact which made them quite unlike any previous generation of British intellectuals: their collectively low-status origins. The intellectuals of the 'thirties derived in the main from prosperous bourgeois families, and were educated at leading public schools and the ancient universities. Many were the descendants of distinguished families, and were not infrequently related to other intellectuals by ties of blood or marriage.[2] In telling contrast to this, the generation of post-war intellectuals in the freelance creative fields were commonly from working-class or lower-middle-class families lacking previous distinction. Wesker, for example, was a pastry-cook, the son of East End Jewish migrants; Shelagh Delaney was a mill hand in Salford; John Osborne was an actor in provincial repertory; Robert Bolt was a schoolteacher in the West Country; Bernard Kops, also from an East End Jewish family, was a docker and casual labourer; the novelists John Braine and Alan Sillitoe were, respectively, a librarian, and a factory hand in the Raleigh works at Nottingham. Most had not been to university, or even grammar

[1] For an account of this development see J. R. Taylor, op. cit., Kenneth Allsop, *The Angry Decade*, Peter Owen, 1958; Kenneth Tynan, *Curtains*, Longmans, 1961; James Gindin, *Postwar British Fiction: New Accents and Attitudes*, Cambridge University Press, 1962.

[2] See Raymond Williams, *The Long Revolution*, Chatto and Windus, London, 1961. (Chapter V: 'Social History of English Writers'.) Also, Annan, op. cit., Wood, op. cit.

school; John Arden, educated at Sedbergh and Cambridge, stood out as a lone exception.

That so many of the new generation of intellectuals derived from low status origins may well have been an additional factor contributing to their common radicalism. Individuals upwardly mobile into the educated middle class are undoubtedly exposed to greater strains and tensions than those born into that class, or than the non-mobile in general. In comparison with the latter they are in particular made more aware of class pressures and status distinctions, arising from their exposure to two different value systems. Certainly these writers were greatly pre-occupied in their works with the question of class, and the personal humiliations and problems which it gave rise to.[1] As Zubaida, in his study of the literati of the nineteen-thirties and nineteen-fifties, points out, 'what the 1950s writers have in common in terms of social experience is that, like their heroes, they lack stable and clear class belongings, they are in marginal and transitional social positions.'[2] He continues:

It can be assumed that all the 1950s writers experienced the strains of marginality and mobility, uncertainty of self-image and identity, conflict and ambiguity in norms and values and styles of life; and that they all suffered the frustrations and humiliations of exclusiveness practised by higher status groups. These strains can, at least partly, account for the discontents of the 1950s writers and for their social criticism. It can also account for the attitudes of hatred and resentment expressed towards the upper classes and the need for self-assertion against upper class styles of life.[3]

Experience of a class structure whose sharp edges they had personally felt might thus be considered as one of the formative influences in predisposing the 'angry young men' to radical politics, and subsequently sensitizing them to the appeals of CND.

One other more immediate factor operating in the same direction was this group's opposition to, and sense of frustration at, the domination of the theatre by commercial interests and the conventional standards already referred to. The reluctance of managements to stage experimental works by new writers, for fear of financial losses, was a continuing theme of discussion and dissatisfaction. The economic grip of 'Shaftesbury Avenue' on the theatre

[1] Most notably, Osborne's *Look Back in Anger*, Wesker's *Chips with Everything* and Braine's novel *Room at the Top*. See also, *Declaration*, ed. Tom Maschler, McGibbon and Kee, London, 1957.

[2] S. D. Zubaida, *Attitudes to Society as Reflected in the English Literature of the 1930s and 1950s*, M.A. Thesis, University of Leicester, 1964, p. 122.

[3] Op. cit., p. 129.

was experienced as alienative and culturally stifling. As Lindsay Anderson put it:

What we run up against is the economic and social framework within which we have to practise our various arts. . . . The framework, the system remains, corrupt and killing, and I doubt whether, within it, the vital theatre . . . will ever be able to find a satisfying means of expression.[1]

Even after the new playwrights had begun to establish a reputation and had succeeded, partially at least, in making some inroads upon the conventional theatre, there remained an uneasy awareness that their foothold was a precarious one and that they were simply being tolerated for their temporary commercial value.

The new movement does not run the theatre, it is *used* by the theatre. The situation is reminiscent of those stately homes where you pay your money and wander freely, feeling as though you owned the place. Come the time when your money (or your talent) is no longer necessary as a bolster, the gracious living will be resumed and everybody else will be out in the cold again. There is a vast difference between working for your own theatre, and working for someone else's profit.[2]

The attitude of the new dramatists was a product of the general tension which may be said to exist in the relationship between the freelance intellectual and the market. When the market is controlled by commercial interests there is an almost inevitable conflict between the artist's demand for his work to be judged solely by aesthetic criteria, and the need for the cultural entrepreneur to judge it in terms of profitability. Bertrand de Jouvenel stated the argument succinctly:

The intellectual's hostility to the businessman presents no mystery, as the two have, by function, wholly different standards. . . . The businessman must say: 'The customer is always right.' The intellectual cannot entertain this notion. A bad writer is made by the very maxim which makes him a good businessman: 'Give the public what it wants'. The businessman operates within a framework of tastes, of value judgements, which the intellectual must ever seek to alter.[3]

Although this is a situation faced by freelance intellectuals in most creative spheres in a non-patronage system, it would appear to be especially acute in the theatre, where the capital outlay on a production is particularly heavy. Under these conditions box office potential must remain an important consideration in entrepreneurial decisions, tending to build up resistance to experimental works or

[1] *Encore*, Nov.–Dec. 1957, p. 5.   [2] *Encore*, Jan.–Feb. 1962, p. 9.
[3] Bertrand de Jouvenel, 'The Treatment of Capitalism by Continental Intellectuals', in F. A. Hayek (ed.), *Capitalism and the Historians*, University of Chicago Press, 1954, pp. 118–20.

any departure from tried formulae. The frustrations engendered by this commercial ethic and the traditionalism of the theatre does go some way towards explaining the presence of so many of the new dramatists in the anti-Bomb campaign. It was hardly fortuitous for example that one of the prominent contingents on the Aldermaston marches paraded under the banner of the Royal Court Theatre, the one major British theatre where new and experimental drama was encouraged and which produced the early works of Osborne, Wesker, Doris Lessing, John Arden, Bernard Kops and other pro-CND writers of the new wave.

The relationship between the unilateralist movement and the contemporary school of drama, not in itself an obviously logical one, was occasionally pointed up by the writers themselves. Charles Marowitz, the director of a small experimental theatre, in defending Osborne's satirical musical *The World of Paul Slickey* against hostile press reviews, felt that 'in knocking *Paul Slickey*, the press is knocking the raucous Ban-the-Bomb enthusiasts who flocked Trafalgar Square. . . . That is why one cannot simply review *Slickey* as an illfated musical by Britain's most important playwright. *Slickey* has triggered the reaction against the anti-Establishment agitators.'[1] Gordon Rogoff, the editor of *Encore*, the journal of the new movement, explained the connection more explicitly. In his view, 'to care about the theatre is to be a critic; to be a critic is to care about life; and to care about life is to care about the bomb'.[2]

Although the dramatists certainly contributed a disproportionate share of CND's intellectuals, other types of creative talent were of course also represented. Leading novelists in the Campaign included J. B. Priestley and John Braine, both of whom were regular platform speakers; Iris Murdoch, Jennifer Dawson, Naomi Mitchison, Alan Sillitoe, a Committee of 100 supporter, Sir Compton Mackenzie, Mervyn Jones, a member of CND National Council, Alex Comfort, D. A. N. Jones, who also served for a period as YCND organizer; and John Brunner, the science fiction writer, who drafted the CND election manifesto in 1964.[3] The poets included Jon Silkin, Adrian Mitchell, a frequent platform speaker, James

[1] *Encore*, Sept.–Oct. 1959, p. 34.
[2] *Encore*, Sept.–Oct. 1959, p. 20.
[3] There were remarkably few literary products with a pro-Bomb or anti-CND theme. The one major exception was Constantine Fitzgibbon's novel *When the Kissing Had to Stop*, which portrayed the success of the unilateralist movement and, with it, Britain's eventual submission to the Soviet Union. For the hostile reactions to this book see, C. Fitzgibbon, *Random Thoughts of a Fascist Hyena*, Cassell, 1963; also, 'Politics and the Novel', *Encounter*, June 1961.

Kirkup and Christopher Logue, whose *Letter to My Fellow Artists*, a polemic against intellectuals who stood aloof from the anti-Bomb struggle, was printed as a CND broadsheet. Among the artists and art critics were Sir Herbert Read, Reg Butler, one of the original Committee of 100 sponsors, John Bratby, John Berger, Henry Moore, an Official CND sponsor, and the cartoonists Abu of the *Observer* and Vicky. The Film and Television Group drew on the services of Anthony Asquith, Miles Malleson, Wolf Mankowicz, Paul Rotha, Kenneth Tynan, Spike Milligan, Basil Wright and Lindsay Anderson. A number of CND documentaries were made under the guidance of this group, the most notable being *March to Aldermaston* (1959), directed by Lindsay Anderson and Anthony Asquith. Some intellectuals aided the Campaign financially, too, by donating it royalties from certain of their works in which the Bomb figured as a theme, such as James Kirkup and Jane Buxton; others offered their services for fund-raising entertainments, including Christopher Logue, Vanessa Redgrave and John Neville, while the concert pianist Denis Matthews performed several recitals in aid of Campaign funds.

Surprisingly, perhaps, there were comparatively few well-known scientists in the Campaign—another point of contrast with the situation in the thirties. Although figures like C. H. Waddington, Kathleen Lonsdale, J. D. Bernal and Antoinette Pirie were associated with CND and wrote pamphlets on the hazards of radiation and nuclear fall-out, scientists never assumed the importance in the movement which might have been expected—given the obvious link between their profession and the Bomb. Any moral and political misgivings scientists in general may have had about the application of atomic research to warlike purposes were not expressed by way of support for CND. As A. J. P. Taylor observed, 'there are far too few nuclear physicists on our platforms. This is surely a disgraceful situation. In America nuclear physicists are leading the campaign. . . . In England most nuclear physicists do just what they are told and regard the Campaign with sceptical disapproval.'[1]

A further factor relevant to an understanding of the intellectuals' involvement in CND is that of Britain's declining political status in

[1] *New Statesman*, 21 June 1958, p. 799. For an account of American scientists' opposition to the H-bomb see Robert Gilpin, *American Scientists and Nuclear Weapons Policy*, Princeton University Press, 1962. It should be noted that this opposition took place almost entirely within the community of professional scientists, and was not translated into political agitation of the CND type. Men like Linus Pauling were exceptional in wishing to translate the moral objections of scientists into a political campaign.

international affairs following the end of the Second World War. The emergence of the United States and the Soviet Union as the two undisputed major powers removed Britain from the position of international leadership which she had exercised for well over a century, added to which was the loss of the Empire following the successful independence claims of former colonies. This sudden loss of international power and prestige inevitably created domestic tensions, as a society accustomed to taking its superiority for granted was required to accommodate itself to a less exalted world role and a humbler conception of itself. Reluctance or refusal to come to terms with this new situation was expressed in a variety of ways and political events.[1] Not least among these was in the founding of CND itself, or more particularly in the nature of the appeal put forward by many of the intellectuals in the movement. This appeal was for Britain to recapture her leadership of the world by renouncing her nuclear weapons, so setting an example to other nations which would prove to be irresistible. It was argued that in the absence of military power and colonial grandeur, Britain could nevertheless regain her rightful position in the world by the sheer weight of moral example. What military power had achieved in the past, moral example could achieve in the present. This was a theme which intellectuals returned to again and again in their arguments against nuclear weapons. Alex Comfort, addressing the inaugural meeting of CND, made this the main theme of his speech: 'We can', he claimed, 'make Britain offer the world something which is virtually forgotten—moral leadership. Let us make this country stand on the side of human decency and human sanity—alone if necessary. It has done so before. If it does so again I do not think we need to fear the consequences.'[2] As early as 1955 the novelist Vera Brittain had made a similar plea. 'Ten years ago this country faced the world as a great power. . . . Today, it has the opportunity to seek another kind of glory: the possession of great moral leadership, of showing the world a third way between the two great powers.' By our possession of the H-Bomb, however, we should lose 'all claim to moral leadership'.[3] Sir Compton Mackenzie, too, felt that 'if Britain disarmed completely I do not believe that any nation in the world would dare to take advantage of her material weakness, because her moral strength would be overwhelming.'[4]

[1] Most obviously perhaps in the attempted invasion of Suez in 1956.
[2] Reprinted in D. Boulton (ed.), *Voices from the Crowd*, Peter Owen, London, 1964, p. 59.
[3] *Peace News*, March 1955, p. 5.
[4] *Peace News*, 24 May 1957, p. 9.

Even Sir Stephen King-Hall, who generally based his support for CND on strategic grounds, upheld the contemporary relevance of Milton's injunction, which was a favourite closing line of Campaign speeches: 'let not England forget her precedence in teaching the nations how to live.'[1] Similarly, A. J. P. Taylor, in defending CND against Labour party criticisms, protested that 'we are not seeking to disrupt the Labour Party. . . . We are seeking to win it over. We offer it the moral leadership of the world.'[2] The central place which this theme occupied in the arguments for unilateralism quite clearly stemmed from an unwillingness to adjust to Britain's diminished international status and to acknowledge that others did not necessarily look to this country as a model for the conduct of their own affairs. This appeared to be particularly true of the older intellectuals attracted to CND, who were, of course, more inclined to take great-power status for granted than those who had come to maturity in the post-war years. J. B. Priestley, perhaps more eloquently than any other writer, captured the mood of this older generation as they faced the prospect of a world in which Britian, and therefore to some extent themselves too, no longer made the most important decisions, at a time when these decisions had never seemed more vital. His long article in the *New Statesman*, 'Britain and the Nuclear Bombs', appeared towards the end of 1957, and was influential in bringing CND into being. It concluded as follows:

Our bargaining power is slight; the force of our example might be great . . . we could begin to restore the world to sanity and lift this nation from its recent ignominy to its former grandeur. Alone, we defeated Hitler; and alone we can defy this nuclear madness. . . . There may be other chain-reactions besides those leading to destruction; and we might start one. The British of these times, so frequently hiding their decent, kind faces behind masks of sullen apathy or sour, cheap cynicism, often seem to be waiting for something better than party squabbles and appeals to their narrowest self interest, something great and noble in its intention that would make them feel good again. And this might well be a declaration to the world that after a certain date one power able to engage in nuclear warfare will reject the evil thing for ever.[3]

This passionate belief in the possibility of Britain's assumption of the moral leadership of the world—what David Marquand has

[1] Stephen King-Hall, *Defence in the Nuclear Age*, Gollancz, London, 1958.

[2] *New Statesman*, 21 June 1958, p. 800.

[3] *New Statesman*, 2 November 1957, p. 556. This was later reprinted as a CND pamphlet. After the Campaign was well established Priestley suggested that part of its drawing power had rested on the fact that 'We British no longer have any bright image of ourselves. And perhaps, among other things, we went campaigning for that image.' *New Statesman*, 19 May 1961, p. 786.

dubbed the 'white man's burden school of unilateralism',[1] does not altogether square with the stereotype of the radical intellectual's alienation from society. As suggested in Chapter 2, alienation as a condition of dissociation between self and society cannot meaningfully be attributed to those who endorse a political appeal based upon traditional notions of British supremacy and national grandeur. Estrangement from society would more logically have entailed indifference to the country's declining status and not a sense of deep concern. As with unilateralist supporters in general, in fact, the radicalism of CND intellectuals is more usefully understood as stemming from an excessively high, rather than low, commitment to certain aspects of the normative order. And in this respect it could be predicted, in line with Tocqueville's and Schumpeter's arguments, that highly idealistic expectations concerning national conduct would be most likely to flourish among those intellectuals divorced from institutional settings which inculcate a more pragmatic and cautious approach to the affairs of men and states, and which also, it may be added, deter their employees from the kind of political activism liable to jeopardize their career prospects. The freelance, or 'socially unattached intelligentsia', with no bureaucratic careers to consider are thus not simply more predisposed, but are also far freer to engage in the type of public radicalism associated with movements like CND.

In Chapters 4 and 5 we have seen that support for CND on the part of a variety of different groups and individuals could be interpreted as a form of symbolic protest, in the sense that their involvement in the Campaign did not derive solely, or even mainly, from opposition to nuclear weapons. Instead, protest against the Bomb was often a thinly-veiled protest at certain other aspects of the social order which were independent of the Bomb, but which the latter appeared dramatically to highlight. To campaign against the Bomb was thus to a great extent also to campaign against other perceived ills of society. It was shown, for example, that the involvement of Christians in CND could in large part be understood as stemming from their radical interpretation of the scope of religious witness, and their belief that the church's participation in and leadership of the anti-Bomb protest would revive its flagging moral authority. Support for the Campaign was not seen simply in terms of achieving unilateralist goals but also as having the more important func-

---

[1] David Marquand, 'Bombs and Scapegoats', *Encounter*, January 1961, pp. 43–8.

tion of revitalizing the Christian community. For the Marxists, on the other hand, participation in CND was useful chiefly as a means of stimulating revolutionary activity and sharpening men's consciousness of the coercive powers of the state. They were openly sceptical of the Campaign's ability to achieve its goals but supported it mainly for the disruptive potential it appeared to open up. The Communist Party's role was far less radical and was concerned mainly with using CND as a platform for publicizing its own non-unilateralist policies. The intellectuals' involvement derived from two distinct sources: those of the post-war generation—the dramatists in particular—were radicalized largely as a result of the sharp discontents they experienced in attempting to introduce new cultural standards into a traditional setting dominated by a commercial ethic, and by the status conflicts they were exposed to by virtue of their lowly social origins. The older intellectuals were drawn to CND because they saw in unilateralism the makings of a grand moral gesture which would redress Britain's loss of military and economic power by bestowing upon her the mantle of world moral leadership. To suggest that these varieties of anti-Bomb protest were symbolic in character is not of course to claim that those involved were totally unconcerned with unilateralism; it is, however, to claim that sole attention to this rather obvious and overt aspect of their support fails to grasp the full range of its significance. The final example of symbolic protest to be considered is that provided by the unilateralist conflict within the Labour Party, and it is to a discussion of this that the following chapter is dedicated.

6

Symbolic protest—
III: unilateralism and the
Labour movement

That the Labour Party should have figured as one of the chief *dramatis personae* of the unilateralist movement was perhaps inevitable in view of its long-standing sympathies with pacifism and anti-war movements. More correctly, of course, it has not been the Party as a whole which has been identified with the rejection of violence in international affairs, so much as a prominent minority on the Left. However, although the leadership of the Labour Party have never, except during Lansbury's brief tenure, officially endorsed the pacifist view, there has always been an attitude of regard and respect towards individual pacifist members. Despite the fact that Labour's foreign and defence policy has varied little in essentials from that of its main rivals in recent times it still remains the only major party in which those of pacifist or near-pacifist temperament can find a political environment amenable to their ideas and influence.[1] Given a sympathetic attitude towards the pacifist or 'pacifistic' line of reasoning, it was perhaps readily predictable that the anti-Bomb movement should have touched deeply responsive chords within the Party, and that many of its members should have provided much of the movement's impetus and leadership. But that the inner-party debate should have generated as much upheaval and bitterness as it succeeded in doing is not altogether attributable to the traditional divisions between pacifist sympathizers and those committed to the use of violence in international conflict. Certain other controversies were made manifest in the issue of the Bomb and succeeded in giving a sharper edge and significance to the controversy than it would otherwise have had. In this chapter it will be shown to what extent factors independent of the usual anti-military sentiments of the Left helped to shape the arguments of the unilateralists, and the way that these tended to change in line with shifts in the Party's fortunes and balance of forces.

The Party and the Bomb before 1959

Although unilateralism reached its climax within the Party in the early nineteen-sixties the matter of nuclear weapons had become an issue well before this time, and easily pre-dated the launching of CND. As early as 1954 a small group of Labour MP's under the chairmanship of Fenner Brockway formed the Hydrogen Bomb National Campaign Committee. It included among its numbers George Craddock, Anthony Wedgwood Benn, Sydney Silverman and Anthony Greenwood, some of whom were later to become prominent figures in the unilateralist movement. Apart from holding poster demonstrations in Whitehall, and addressing a few small meetings, the Committee was not noticeably active or successful in its aim of arousing public opinion and interest in the Bomb. Shortly after its inception it was wound up, £600 in debt.[2]

---

[1] This relationship is explored in detail in David Martin's *Pacifism: An Historical and Sociological Study*, Routledge, London, 1965, Chapter Six.

[2] Fenner Brockway, *Outside the Right*, Allen and Unwin, 1963, Chapter XIII.

Nuclear weapons policy was also the cause of stormy scenes within the Parliamentary Labour Party early in 1955. Aneurin Bevan and some sixty of his followers abstained from voting for an opposition motion on the government's defence White Paper—in which the decision to produce a British hydrogen bomb was first stated. Bevan had the whip withdrawn and only narrowly escaped expulsion from the Party. It was perhaps ironical that Bevan should have been the spearhead of this early dissension in the Party over the question of the Bomb, since it was precisely on this issue that he was later to break with his supporters, so putting a dramatic end to the 'Bevanite' movement. Bevan's views on the Bomb were in fact remarkably inconsistent, appearing to change suddenly over short periods of time, and even from speech to speech. In April 1955 he declared himself to be 'profoundly opposed to the manufacture of the bomb'[1] while more generally he seemed content to reiterate official Party policy, which opposed nuclear tests only. As late as May 1957, shortly before he was to come out strongly in support of the nuclear deterrent he was still arguing the unilateralist case.[2]

In a way, Bevan's uncertain and ambiguous position on nuclear weapons reflected a personal dilemma at a crucial stage of his political career. His high prestige within the Party rested very largely on the support of the rank and file in the constituencies, who appeared to favour a radical policy on the Bomb. But power, as against mere prestige, depended on winning the support of the Parliamentary Labour Party and trade union leaders, who favoured a more cautious approach. Bevan's ambiguity might therefore be seen as reflecting the conflicting demands put upon him by opposite wings of the Party. In a celebrated speech to Annual Conference in 1957 he finally decided in favour of 'multilateralism' and derided as an 'emotional spasm' the unilateralist position which he had himself so recently flirted with, and which was almost certainly closer to his own radical inclinations.[3] In realistic terms, this was perhaps another way of declaring that he had chosen for himself a place of actual power in the Party (and potentially the country)

[1] Quoted in D. E. Butler, *The British General Election of 1955*, Macmillan, 1955, p. 90.

[2] In a major speech at Reading he urged that Britain should declare that 'We can make the H-bomb, but we are not going to make it. We believe that what the human race needs is leadership in the opposite direction, and we are going to give it. We are going to prove there are influences and principles in the world that rise superior to those that attach still to the story of barbarism.' *The Times*, 6 May 1957, p. 4.

[3] *Proceedings of Labour Party Annual Conference*, Brighton, 1957.

rather than the semblance of power as a figurehead of the militant rank and file. The debate on the Bomb was a watershed in Bevan's career, signifying in the eyes of the political élites his transition from 'rebel' to 'statesman'.[1]

It is not Bevan's career as such which is of primary interest here, however, so much as the way in which this brief but crucial phase of it serves conveniently to highlight the *leitmotif* of this chapter; namely, the manner in which the conflict in the Labour Party over the Bomb has concerned itself not simply with matters of defence but, more importantly, with questions of power within the Party. Stated crudely, decisions for or against unilateralism have served mainly to provide a language and a dressing to cover other deep-seated conflicts unrelated to defence or nuclear weapons policy. Although the divisions in the Party over the question of the Bomb were apparent by 1959, the decisive confrontation between the leadership and the unilateralists did not occur until after the Party's defeat at the general election of that year. From this point on, the controversy changed in character as a number of new elements entered into it which made it far more disruptive and rancorous than it had ever previously been.

The Party and the Bomb after 1959

The Party's defeat in 1959 was its third in succession and the period which followed it was one of deep-seated unrest as various factions attributed its electoral unpopularity to different internal maladies. The right-wing view, with which Gaitskell, the Party leader, was closely associated, was that the socialist principles on which the Party constitution was based required fundamental revision to render them more relevant and appealing to a comparatively affluent welfare state. It was suggested that the emphasis on nationalization of the industrial sector as the basis of a socialist programme should be abandoned; instead, more attention should be paid to improvements in general welfare benefits and the extension of citizenship rights. The left wing on the other hand, claimed that the Party had forfeited its appeal because it had increasingly become a pale image of its Conservative opponents, and that what was needed was an extension of public ownership and radical policies rather than a diminution of them. It was against the background of this important controversy that the unilateralist conflict, which

---

[1] For highly personalized accounts of Bevan's career at this stage see E. Hunter, *The Road to Brighton Pier*, Barker, 1957; and M. Krug, *Aneurin Bevan: Cautious Rebel*, Yosseloff, New York, 1961.

had been muted during the election period, was re-opened with new vigour. From here on the dispute over nuclear weapons became incorporated into the more general and deep-seated disagreement over the future role and ideology of the Party. The leading protagonists in the 'revisionist' conflict were largely the same groups and individuals who were also lined up against one another on the issue of unilateralism. Because these two contending factions faced each other in hostility over two crucial policy matters simultaneously, a new element of fierceness was injected into the dispute over the Bomb which succeeded virtually in paralysing the Party as an effective opposition from late 1959 until the end of 1962. These animosities centred with particular vehemence around the leadership of Gaitskell who had identified himself firmly with the revisionists and anti-unilateralists. In 1959, following the election defeat, Gaitskell attempted unsuccessfully to have Clause Four of the Party constitution (pledging social ownership of the means of production) replaced by a statement of wider aims similar to those adopted by social democratic parties on the continent. His commitment to this goal, which aroused strong opposition from the trade unions, provoked the Left into openly questioning his fitness to lead the Party in view of the acknowledged discrepancy between his conception of socialism and that of the majority of Party members. This discontent with the leadership blossomed into outright opposition in 1960, following the unilateralists' victory at Annual Conference. Instead of accepting this verdict, as he had done in the defeat over Clause Four, Gaitskell chose to 'fight and fight and fight again'. The Party leader's open defiance of the Scarborough decision against the Bomb brought upon his head the full anger of those who believed that the Parliamentary Labour Party was bound by the Party constitution to accept the broad lines of policy as determined by Annual Conference. Although, as Professor McKenzie has shown, *de facto* power over policy matters has resided in the PLP, the Party constitution appears to confer this power *de jure* to Annual Conference.[1] This potentially conflictful situation had not resulted in a head-on clash in the past because of the willingness of the PLP and its leaders to pay lip-service to the ideals of the constitution, while quietly ignoring those conference decisions which were not felt to be compatible with the realistic demands of parliamentary government. The fact that the clash eventually occurred over the matter of the Bomb was due it would seem, not

[1] R. T. McKenzie, *British Political Parties*, Heinemann, London, 1963 (2nd edition).

simply to the fact of its being a major policy issue, but mainly because of the wilful determination of the leading protagonists that there should be a final showdown. Thus, it was no accident that the debate on the constitutional powers of Conference took place in the same year (1960) as the unilateralists achieved their victory. It had been known by the middle of the year, after four of the six largest unions (TGWU, AEU, USDAW and NUR) had adopted unilateralist policies, which way the voting was likely to go at Scarborough. Consequently, there had been a good deal of speculation concerning the leadership's reaction to a defeat; in particular it was wondered whether Gaitskell would resign (as the Left hoped) or whether he would stay on and simply ignore the Conference decision. In an attempt to forestall this latter possibility, a number of unilateralists sponsored resolutions 'reaffirming' the sovereignty of Conference as the Party's policy-making body. Had Conference passed the resolution in the form moved by John Stonehouse, a unilateralist MP, Gaitskell's position might well have become unsupportable, since the Left could have claimed full legitimacy in their campaign for his removal. In fact, however, the motion finally accepted had a number of conditions attached which succeeded in stripping it of its basic intention, so leaving the constitutional position as ambiguous as ever.[1]

It should be pointed out that it was not only the Left which was anxious for a showdown on this vexed question of policy-making in the Party. A number of Gaitskell's close supporters also welcomed the confrontation, since they felt that the emasculation of Conference would facilitate their attempts to wean the Party away from traditional socialist doctrines. Anthony Crosland, a leading revisionist, writing in the American *New Leader* shortly before the Scarborough conference, felt that if Gaitskell were bold enough to challenge its decision on the Bomb

> The Parliamentary leadership would have asserted at least some degree of independence and the policy-making role of the Conference would be to some extent devalued. . . . Paradoxically, therefore, a defeat for the leadership at the conference might not be unmitigated disaster—for from the resulting crisis and confusion there might, eventually, emerge a much altered radical Labor party attuned to the new realities of the 1960s.[2]

[1] For a full discussion see R. T. McKenzie, op. cit., pp. 617–20. The Left could still point to certain authoritative, non-partisan interpretations of the constitution which appeared to support their position, namely that of Sir Ivor Jennings *Party Politics*, vol. II, *The Growth of Parties*, C.U.P., 1961, p. 366.

[2] C. A. R. Crosland, 'British Labor's Crucial Meeting,' *The New Leader*, 3 October 1960, p. 8.

Thus, this separate but crucial issue of the distribution of power within the Party became interlocked with the controversies over revisionism and the Bomb. And because there tended to be a close (though not exact) correspondence between the views an individual held on one issue and those he held on the others, the position he took on the more 'established' conflict over the Bomb served conveniently to define his attitude towards the other areas of disagreement.[1] The case for unilateralism henceforth became not merely the case for ridding the country of the Bomb, but for ridding the Party of Gaitskell and the revisionist and anti-Conference tendencies with which he was identified. It was mainly for this reason that the unilateralist conflict was conducted with such venom and bitterness throughout the early nineteen-sixties in comparison with the period before Labour's election defeat. The disagreement during the earlier period, although certainly spirited at times, had little of the fierce rancour of the later years, when the anti-Bomb movement was used to carry so much extra ideological cargo. No Party leader since Macdonald can have been subjected to such a barrage of criticism and personal abuse from his own followers as Gaitskell was during this period. Even as late as May 1962, only ten months before his death, he had to be given a police escort to ensure his safe conduct from the Glasgow May Day rally, when unilateralists in the crowd turned upon him.[2] The party unilateralists' attitude towards Gaitskell contrasted markedly with their attitude towards Bevan when he had opposed them in the previous confrontation in 1957. Although Bevan's defence of the Bomb certainly created a sense of shock and disappointment among the Left, it did not engender the kind of hostility which was loosed upon Gaitskell. Perhaps this demonstrates clearly enough the extent to which the unilateralists' campaign against the Party

---

[1] The main exceptions to this generalization were the trade union leaders, most of whom opposed both revisionism and unilateralism.

[2] One unilateralist MP, Judith Hart, referring to the state of feeling in the Party at the time, recorded that 'There's such bitterness: I can't visit some of my friends now. Once defence or Scarborough or Gaitskell come up our arguments are nasty. We can't talk to each other any more.' *Tribune*, 18 November 1960, p. 5. A reading of the left-wing press for this period suggests that the sentiments of many Labour unilateralists were expressed by the Young Socialist who, when asked in a recent political study to name the event which had given him greatest pleasure that year, replied 'the death of Hugh Gaitskell'. Quoted in P. Abrams and A. Little, 'The Young Activist in British Politics', *British Journal of Sociology*, **16**, December 1965, p. 328. John Osborne, a leading anti-Bomb dramatist, also carried 'a knife in my heart for . . . you Gaitskell, you particularly'. John Osborne, 'A Letter to my Fellow Countrymen', in D. Boulton, *Voices from the Crowd*, Peter Owen, 1964, p. 154.

leader was based not simply on opposition to his stand on nuclear weapons. For the difference was that Bevan, unlike Gaitskell, was not associated with revisionist and anti-Conference views, but tended in fact to identify himself with the Left on these matters. His position was thus less vulnerable because he was able to face the unilateralists on a single and isolated issue. It was only when the anti-Bomb movement inside the Party became linked with the defence of traditional socialism and Party democracy (the threat to which was symbolized in the person of Gaitskell) that it became powerful enough to mount a definite challenge to the leadership.

The unilateralists' vendetta against Gaitskell caused a certain amount of misgiving amongst CND supporters proper, who did on the whole confine their attacks to Labour policy, and avoided personalities. Indeed, suspicion of the Left's passionate espousal of unilateralism began to mount as it became clearer that the anti-Bomb movement was being used as a convenient stick with which to beat the Party leader. The Labour-Left centred around *Tribune* was often a source of acute irritation to non-Party CND'ers because of its tendency to view the anti-Bomb campaign almost exclusively in terms of an inner-Party struggle. They were continuously being urged to join the Party's ranks and lend their weight to the Left's opposition to the leadership. 'The Labour Party', *Tribune* declared in a typical editorial, 'is now the real battlefield. Help us to consolidate our position. And help us to achieve the power that alone will enable us to translate our aspirations into action.'[1] Because the Left was so concerned to make the Party a 'battlefield' it tended to be impatient of CND supporters who held aloof from party politics and so failed to make any contribution to the broader conflict within the Party. Non-Party CND'ers became increasingly mistrustful of the Left as it became clearer that their prime concern was with Party affairs, and not with a 'pure' commitment to unilateralism, as such. This suspicion, which proved to be amply justified by subsequent events, was occasionally made explicit when relations between the two groups became particularly strained. George Clark, a leading non-Party figure on the CND National Council, in the course of a complaint against the Left's refusal to support a civil disobedience campaign, declared that 'because we were not attacking the leadership of Mr Gaitskell it was not your campaign. In which case you should cease pretending to lead the fight against nuclear weapons and raise the standard which shows that you are

[1] *Tribune*, 14 October 1960, p. 4.

really only opposed to the present leadership of the Labour Party.'[1]

Although the Labour Left found the anti-Bomb movement to be a useful vehicle for conducting a more general campaign, it would be misleading to suggest that the dissension within the Party was based simply on the opposition of organized militants to a moderate leadership. In the first place, misgivings about Mr Gaitskell's handling of the unilateralist issue were not confined to the radical rank and file, but were shared by certain of the Party's senior members—including some members of the shadow cabinet. For example, Harold Wilson, the then shadow chancellor, decided 'under strong pressure from many colleagues'[2] to oppose Gaitskell in the 1960 election for the Party leadership. Wilson, putting himself forward as a 'unity' candidate, was easily defeated but nevertheless caused Gaitskell the humiliation of being the first elected Labour leader to have his position challenged in a subsequent contest. Similarly, Anthony Greenwood, a prominent unilateralist, resigned from the shadow cabinet because, as he wrote to Gaitskell, 'I do not believe that under your leadership it is any longer possible, in spite of your great qualities, to safeguard that unity which the Party so desperately needs . . .'[3]

The split provoked by the issue of the Bomb, then, clearly represented something rather different from the traditional rebellion of an extreme left-wing minority against a moderate centre leadership. Moderation in fact was no more noticeable among the leadership than among the Left. If, indeed, it was true that the unilateralists employed the anti-Bomb campaign as a lever to oust Gaitskell, it was hardly less true that Gaitskell himself chose to make his stand on nuclear policy a means of reasserting his dominance over the Party. His rigidity on the matter of the Bomb, and his response to the Scarborough decision, strongly suggest that he was not simply defending multilateralism and the NATO alliance (since the moderates wished to preserve these also) but that he had decided to make defence policy a test case for re-establishing his authority as Party leader, which had been badly undermined by his recent defeat on Clause Four. Both sides, in fact, tended to use the language of nuclear strategy to cloak what was essentially a struggle for internal power. In Gaitskell's case this led to the emphatic rejection of all compromise proposals on defence policy which the

[1] *Tribune*, 3 March 1961, p. 10. The paper dismissed the demonstration as the activities of a 'lunatic fringe'. 7 April 1961, p. 4.
[2] *The Times*, 21 October 1960, p. 12.
[3] *The Times*, 14 October 1960, p. 14.

Party moderates put forward to reconcile the protagonists. The most important of these proposals was that drawn up by Richard Cross-man and Walter Padley. The Crossman-Padley document was one of three circulating in the Party in early 1961—the other two being Frank Cousins's unilateralist statement, and the official draft policy, later known as *Policy for Peace*. The latter document re-iterated a number of previously made points in the Party's defence policy; namely that Britain should cease to become an independent nuclear power, that there should be a non-nuclear zone of controlled dis-armament in Central Europe, and that NATO strategy should not be based on a threat to use the H-Bomb first in the event of war. The Crossman-Padley draft also argued for staying in NATO, and accepted most of the main proposals of *Policy for Peace*. It differed from the latter on one point only, namely, that NATO strategy should not be based on the threat of a first nuclear strike, either of H-bombs or *strategic* nuclear weapons, which the official policy appeared by implication to allow. Cousins's document, which although unilateralist in intent, was by no means as extreme as its opponents were inclined to suggest. It too, for example, argued in favour of Britain's remaining in NATO and attempting to 'reform' it from within. Where it differed from the other two statements was in its insistence that NATO strategy should be based on conventional rather than nuclear weapons, and its call for the removal of American nuclear bases from Britain.

Between the official draft policy and the Crossman-Padley pro-posal there was an almost complete measure of agreement. So much so in fact that the latter was hardly a compromise at all, since it conceded all the major points of Gaitskell's policy and made nought but the slimmest of concessions to the unilateralists. (This did not go unnoticed by the unilateralists themselves, of course. Konni Zilliacus, for example, dismissed the Crossman-Padley draft as 'the last hope of the more astute opponents of Scarborough'.)[1] With their joint acceptance of the need for collective security through a NATO armed with nuclear weapons, as well as of the present need for American bases in Britain, it could hardly be maintained that the two documents represented anything other than a difference in nuance of the same basic 'multilateralist' policy. *The Times* underlined the same point, arguing that whereas the document 'attributed to Mr Cousins is obviously at odds with the official principles', the same 'cannot be said of Mr Crossman's version. Here the differences appear to be of a nicety that would

[1] *Tribune*, 21 April 1961, p. 8.

become disputatious schoolmen better than practical politicians in the throes of a party crisis.'[1] This was particularly so given the ever-changing nature of defence strategy and the great flexibility the Party had adopted to it in the past. Harold Wilson had staked his challenge to Gaitskell's leadership precisely on this point, arguing that an intransigent stand was unrealistic because 'defence policy . . . by the very nature of things changes from year to year and even from month to month'.[2] Interestingly enough, although Gaitskell refused to accept the 'compromise' proposal, leading unilateralists in the Party were willing to consider it with some favour, despite the fact that they would have been conceding almost the whole of their case. Thus, Michael Foot, while expressing a personal preference for the Cousins' statement, felt nevertheless that 'a major step forward . . . would be achieved if either the Crossman document or the Cousins document could secure the general backing of the Labour Party'.[3] *Tribune* itself went so far as to claim that 'the document drafted by Richard Crossman . . . goes much farther [than official policy] in accepting many of the unilateralists' arguments',[4] which was of course patently untrue. Leading Party unilateralists showed a surprising willingness to abandon their own policy in order to support the compromise plan—bringing them as a result under sharp fire from the CND.[5] The editors of the *New Left Review* also pointed out that 'many CND'ers were suspicious of the speed with which Labour Party unilateralists turned to the Crossman compromise'. They felt that while 'it may have been tactically correct to isolate the leadership in this way . . .', it was nevertheless 'unacceptable as the basis of a policy'.[6] Frank Cousins, Tom Driberg and Anthony Greenwood were among those who threw their weight behind it in the NEC deliberations on defence at which the various drafts were discussed. The resultant union of unilateralists and moderates against the Right saw the defeat of the Crossman-Padley draft by a very narrow margin, fifteen votes to thirteen.[7]

[1] *The Times*, 23 February 1961, p. 13.   [2] *The Times*, 21 October 1960.
[3] *Tribune*, 3 March 1961, p. 7.   [4] *Tribune*, 24 March 1961, p. 3.
[5] Michael Foot, in particular, came in for heavy censure from delegates to the 1961 CND conference for his endorsement of the Crossman proposal. Report of CND Conference in the *Observer*, 5 March 1961.
[6] *New Left Review*, March–April 1961, p. 6.
[7] Driberg afterwards wrote of the NEC discussion that he found it 'hard to believe that if Mr Gaitskell had come down strongly for acceptance of this draft he would have been unable to convince even one of his friends that he was right.' *The Times*, 28 February 1961, p. 5. Crossman, too, felt it an absolute tragedy that Hugh Gaitskell found it impossible to accept the compromise plan'. *The Times*, 27 February 1961, p. 7.

This apparent softening of the unilateralists' attitude was not due to signs of their impending defeat at the 1961 Conference. The three documents on defence were being canvassed at a time when the outcome was by no means certain, particularly since none of the major unions had yet then met in conference. If anything, the general feeling during this period was that the unilateralists seemed likely to repeat their Scarborough success.[1] Nevertheless, it appears likely that, at this stage, they would have been satisfied with a token victory over Gaitskell, which the latter's acceptance of the Crossman draft could have been represented as being, despite the fact that it was hardly less 'multilateralist' than the Gaitskell policy they were supposed to be fighting. Once again, the Left's readiness to adopt this tactic suggests how little they were actually committed to unilateralist goals as such, and how much simply to the struggle against Gaitskell.

The Party leader himself did not approach the defence issue with greater rationality and dispassion. To accept the Crossman-Padley compromise, which was a compromise in name only, was the price required to lessen the conflict. Gaitskell's refusal to do so, and to insist on the total acceptance of the official document, ensured that the civil war in the Party would continue unabated. The Left were now forced to abandon the more moderate stance they had been willing to adopt in favour of their original unilateralist position. Cousins, for example, who had felt that the 'Crossman draft provided a genuine basis for restoring party unity' confirmed later that had it been accepted 'I should not have felt it necessary to prepare my own draft.'[2] Gaitskell thus chose to polarize the conflict and to ensure that the struggle would be resolved in a clear-cut way, either by his defeat or by outright victory. As Professor Epstein, referring to Gaitskell's tactics at the time put it: 'plainly he was sharpening the issue between himself and the unilateralists instead of trying to conceal it. He thereby cut off his chance of subsequent retreat and compromise if unilateralism triumphed again at annual conference.'[3] Ostensibly, this decision to reject the smallest compromise was

---

[1] See for example the detailed assessment of unilateralist strength in the trade unions by Alan Fox, in *Socialist Commentary*, February 1961.

[2] *The Times*, 28 February 1961, p. 5.

[3] Leon D. Epstein, 'Who Makes Party Policy?', *Midwest Journal of Political Science*, Vol. VI, No. 2, May 1962, p. 176. Roy Jenkins also confirmed that Gaitskell had definitely 'faced in his own mind the distinct likelihood that in six months' time he might have to go—probably to retire completely from politics'. 'Leader of the Opposition', in W. T. Rodgers (ed.), *Hugh Gaitskell*, Thames and Hudson, 1964.

concerned with the varying merits of the different defence proposals, but in fact it is fairly clear that these had taken on something
of the quality of totemic symbols, representing little more than the
alignment of forces within the Party. Both the leadership and the
Left were, in the words of the *New Statesman*, using 'slogans as a
means of covering up a struggle which has very little to do with
disarmament or defence and a great deal to do with an internal
struggle for power'.[1] Thus, the commonly presented picture of the
Party leader standing up against the intransigent and extremist
'Pacifists, Unilateralists and Fellow-Travellers' (as he called them in
the Scarborough debate), in defence of NATO and the western
alliance against neutralist policies is not an accurate description of
the situation as it had developed in 1961. The frantic attempts
which had been made since Scarborough to bridge the gulf between
the two sides had created new conditions not unfavourable to a
solution which would have left the Party's basic commitment to
NATO unimpared. All the unilateralists asked for in exchange was
that the Party leader should be seen to have abandoned his own rigid
position in favour of a nominal compromise. His refusal to grant
them this token satisfaction, so deliberately prolonging the conflict,
makes it difficult to disagree with Richard Crossman's subsequent
verdict that 'Hugh Gaitskell exploited the Labour Party's divisions
in his fight to retain the leadership.'[2]

Although at the 1961 Annual Conference Gaitskell duly won the
victory he had staked so much on, it may be doubted whether leadership of such an inflexible kind was really in the best interests of the
Party. A leader of any mass political party is generally expected to
be able to balance off the contending interest groups and opinions
which inevitably develop within its ranks, rather than openly to
identify himself with one particular faction. This would seem to be
especially necessary in an organization like the Labour Party in
which there are semi-institutionalized divisions between Left and
Right. Leadership under these conditions requires skill in political
brokerage, in the ability to reconcile and compromise, and not a
rigid adherence to matters of 'principle'. It requires, too, a feeling
for, if not necessarily a belief in, the traditional myths, symbols and
values which any party accumulates over time, and which have the
function of distinguishing it from other parties in the eyes of its
members (a factor which may have heightened importance in periods
when the actual *policies* of the major parties differ very little). Mr

[1] *New Statesman*, 31 March 1961, p. 501.
[2] *The Guardian*, 5 July 1963, p. 24.

Gaitskell during his tenure of office gave slight indication that his skills lay in this direction. From the outset he was closely identified with a small caucus of intellectuals well to the Right of the Party, who showed little sympathy for, or understanding of, the militant, radical impulses which have provided the inspirational bases of the Labour movement. This was perhaps demonstrated most clearly in the somewhat maladroit attempt to re-write the Party constitution by stripping away traditional socialist objectives. Other Party leaders, before and since, generally appreciated better than Gaitskell that the constitution is a cherished part of Labour mythology, having little relevance to the conduct of present-day affairs but nevertheless not to be tampered with. Similarly, his open denigration of the powers of Annual Conference ruptured another tacit and long-standing convention that leaders should pay lip-service to the ideals of inner-Party democracy, even though it is generally recognized that these are disregarded in practice. On these important matters, as well as on the question of the Bomb, Gaitskell showed himself to be more concerned with defending his personal integrity and point of view than with using his power to reconcile Party conflicts. Strict adherence to 'principle' and the conviction of personal rightness may, after all, be interpreted also as inflexibility and dogmatism; these are hardly desirable traits in a Party leader, particularly when issues as uncertain and fluid as defence policy are under consideration.[1] It was this disposition of Mr Gaitskell as much as the militancy of the Left which was responsible for the Party's complete disruption in the early nineteen-sixties. It would be uncharitable to deny that the Party leader's stand against, and ultimate victory over, the unilateralists demanded high personal courage, since it put his political career at stake. What is more open to question, however, is whether his victory was due to his having convinced the Labour movement of the rightness of his case, or to other factors.

Organized efforts to spread the multilateralist case were certainly made inside the Party throughout 1961. The Campaign for Democratic Socialism, under the leadership of W. T. Rodgers, the former Secretary of the Fabian Society, and Denis Howell, set out to

---

[1] Roy Jenkins wrote of Gaitskell's stand on the common market that 'Like all his political positions it was fixed partly by logic and partly by emotion. And once fixed he held to it with great tenacity.' Jenkins, loc. cit. David Martin has drawn my attention to the fact also that Gaitskell's strained relations with the Party stemmed partly from his tendency to interpret his role as that of an alternative prime minister, with an emphasis on caution and responsibility, instead of that of an *opposition* leader. For a full critique of this position see Bernard Crick, 'Two Theories of Opposition', *New Statesman*, 18 June 1960, pp. 882–3.

capture key positions in the constituencies and union branches with the aim of reversing the Scarborough decision. The organization was not dedicated solely to the triumph of multilateralism, but also to the general revisionist policies which usually went with it. CDS was in fact very much a mirror image of the unilateralist movement in the Party, in the sense that it too tended to make its position on the Bomb a convenient focal point in campaigning for a more diffuse set of goals and values—particularly those relating to the leadership. As the *Guardian* tartly commented, CDS 'gives the impression that the multilateralist wing of the Labour Party cares as much about keeping Mr Gaitskell as party leader as it cares about keeping Britain in NATO'.[1] It is difficult to be certain how influential CDS actually was in the 1961 reversal of unilateralism. The organization claimed an impressive membership in the constituency parties of 3,000 supporters, (which belied Michael Foot's dismissal of it as a 'squalid little conspiracy'[2]) but there is no real evidence to suggest that without CDS's intervention the Blackpool decision would have been very different. Although it may well have tipped the balance in a handful of constituencies, it is most doubtful that it played the decisive role attributed to it by some commentators, since, according to Hindle and Williams' estimate, *fewer* constituencies supported multilateralism in 1961 than in 1960, before CDS had entered the scene.[3] Similarly, there is little ground for believing that the organization had any real impact on the trade unions. The latter's rejection of unilateralism was obviously a key factor in Mr Gaitskell's victory at Blackpool; however, this would appear to be less attributable to the zeal of a right-wing pressure group than to another more important factor—namely, the unions' growing concern about the extent of the civil war in the Party. The evidence suggests that the unions' support for the Party leader on defence resulted not so much from a mass conversion to Gaitskellite principles and multilateralist arguments, as from the willingness of many unilateralists to swallow their convictions in the over-riding interests of Party unity. It is to an elaboration of this point that we now turn.

The Trade Unions and the Bomb

As in the case of the Labour Party, a number of leftish trade unions, for example USDAW and the AESD, were expressing opposition

---

[1] *The Guardian*, 13 January 1961, p. 10.

[2] *Tribune*, 18 August 1961, p. 4.

[3] K. Hindle and P. Williams, 'Scarborough and Blackpool: An Analysis of Some Votes at the Labour Party Conferences of 1960 and 1961', *The Political Quarterly*, Vol. 33, No. 3, July–September 1962.

to the Bomb in one form or another as early as 1955. But more generally, nuclear weapons policy was rarely accorded high priority at union conferences before 1959; and whenever the matter was raised it hardly ever centred on demands for British renunciation. More usually, motions were concerned with expressing condemnation of all nuclear weapons and their testing, and with urging the government to press for disarmament negotiations under United Nations supervision. When specifically unilateralist demands were framed they gathered very little support. According to Harrison, even by 1957 and 1958 unilateralists in the major unions could generally muster only between 200,000 to 300,000 votes, according to the terms of the motion.[1]

Part of the reason for the meagreness of support for the anti-Bomb campaign in the unions was that the Communist Party was at this time also opposed to British renunciation. Consequently, those unions with strong Communist influence tended to throw their weight behind 'orthodox' defence policies, so creating an alliance with the Right which was almost always powerful enough to defeat the unilateralists on the non-Communist Left.[2] The swing to unilateralism on any scale did not begin until 1959, when it was endorsed by two of the largest unions, the Transport Workers and the Municipal and General Workers. The latter's decision, however, was something of a freak, since the NUGMW was one of the most unquestioningly loyal supporters of Mr Gaitskell; the conference was recalled later in the year and the decision duly reversed. Although this was a clumsy and even unnecessary manoeuvre—since the reversal could easily have been delayed until the following year—it was by no means untypical of the cavalier attitude the unions in general were to display towards nuclear arms policy.

The shift towards unilateralism which had started slowly in 1959 had by the following year developed into almost a landslide. In quick succession, the annual conferences of USDAW, the AEU and the NUR rejected the official defence line in favour of anti-Bomb policies. Only two of the six big unions, the Municipal Workers and the Miners, were committed to support Gaitskell. It was perhaps not altogether fortuitous that this sudden and surprising

---

[1] Martin Harrison, *The Trade Unions and the Labour Party Since 1945*, Allen and Unwin, 1960, p. 237.
[2] This was especially apparent at the 1957 Labour Party Conference when unions like the ETU, the Boilermakers, and the Foundry Workers, noted for pro-communist sympathies, voted with the NEC against the unilateralists.

swing to unilateralism coincided with the change in the Communist Party line on the Bomb. Communist union members who had organized opposition to unilateralism prior to 1960, were now mobilizing support for it and voting with their natural allies on the Left. But although the Communists certainly contributed to the unilateralist victories it is unlikely that their intervention was as crucial as their opponents, and they themselves, were prone to claim. This is shown most clearly by the fact that although they were no less active in the campaign the following year the decisions were mostly reversed. Although many complex factors were obviously involved in the unions' massive defection from the Party's official defence policy, one may be singled out here as being of particular relevance; namely the hostility towards the Party leader then current among trade unionists, arising from his recent attempt to jettison traditional socialist doctrines. The unions' resistance to the abandonment of Clause Four, and to the revisionist arguments in general, was sharp and decisive. Even unions otherwise noted for political moderation were unwilling to sanction any tampering with the sacred commitment to social ownership; and it was this opposition of course which forced Gaitskell to abandon the proposal. Significantly, it was during the same round of annual conferences at which revisionism was soundly condemned by the unions that unilateralism was also endorsed. It may not be too fanciful to suggest, then, that the resentment which had been built up against Gaitskell over the Clause Four controversy was carried over to the debate on nuclear policy. The rejection of the official line on the Bomb, with which the Party leader was closely identified, might thus be seen as a vote of disapproval of him and his policies on a matter of greater immediate concern to trade unionists.[1] The suggestion that the vote against the Bomb was a vote against Gaitskell and revisionism, rather than for a particular defence policy, is given extra credence by the fact that the decision was reversed in one union after another the following year, although defence and foreign policy considerations were precisely the same. The reason unilateralism was dropped in 1961, although the unions offered no reason themselves, were not inspired by changes in the international situation or Britain's military needs, but by the domestic crisis in the Labour Party. As has been shown in the previous section, the Party was by 1961 at the height of its internal dissension, with its two

---

[1] Occasionally the connection between the two controversies was made quite explicit, as by the General Secretary of the Garment Workers' Union: 'It is now quite evident that the defence issue for political purposes is, in fact, related to the clause 4 issue.' *The Garment Worker*, July 1961, p. 99.

major wings confronting one another in a spirit of deep animosity. To many it appeared that a situation was approaching in which the Party might either destroy itself altogether, or else create such permanent disunity within its ranks that it would forfeit any real chance of electoral victory for many years. Those trade unions which had voted against Gaitskell in 1960 were thus faced with the choice of confirming unilateralist decisions and so prolonging the conflict, with all that this implied for the Party's future; or of throwing their support behind the leadership and thereby crushing the unilateralist revolt. Given the traditional emphasis placed by the trade-union movement on the need for unity, above all other considerations, as well as their over-riding concern with the material advantages felt to be derived from a Labour government, it is not surprising that they moved back behind Gaitskell and abandoned unilateralism as readily as they had embraced it the previous year. Whereas in 1960 a vote against the Bomb entailed a salutary rap on the leader's knuckles for his revisionist flirtations, a similar vote in 1961 would have entailed the complete disruption of the Labour Party.

In the process of dropping unilateralism it was made clear that support for the Labour leadership was not due to a sudden conversion to Gaitskell's arguments and principles; rather, such support was offered solely in the interests of Party unity and *despite* the leader's ideological position. The somewhat grudging nature of this support showed itself in the decisions of the three largest unions which switched from unilateralism to multilateralism in 1961, thereby playing the key role in the whole episode; these were USDAW, the NUR and the AEU.[1] The decisions arrived at by these unions, as with some less powerful ones, were not framed in terms of a clear-cut mandate for the official defence policy, but sought generally to establish some kind of compromise acceptable to both wings of the Party. The resolution moved by the USDAW executive, for example, read partly as follows:

Believing that the restoration of Party unity on a policy representing maximum agreement is an essential condition of achieving a Labour Government by 1964 . . . this ADM instructs the Executive Council and the Union's delegations to National Conference to regard the re-establishment of Party unity on the basis of the Crossman-Padley draft as the first priority in implementing the decisions of the ADM on Foreign Policy and Defence.

---

[1] A complete list of unions and their voting records at the Labour Party conferences in 1960 and 1961 is given by Hindle and Williams, op. cit.

This motion was easily carried, 153,000 votes to 80,000.[1] Walter
Padley, the USDAW President, informed delegates that the 'unity
resolution' would be submitted to the Labour Party conference
provided that other big unions endorsed similar compromise proposals. 'The aim', he declared, 'is not to get a majority of one vote for
the Crossman-Padley document' at the Party conference, but to get
a big majority behind it.[2] If other unions showed reluctance to take
a similar compromise position at their conferences, then the USDAW
motion would not be submitted, and the union would vote on either
a straight multilateralist or unilateralist ticket. Consequently,
delegates were asked to state a second preference, in the event of the
union's delegation to Blackpool having to support one of the 'extreme' positions. On this voting, a unilateralist motion was defeated
by 139,000 to 93,000, while a multilateralist one was passed by
103,000 to 98,000. Multilateralism thus became the union's *second*
preference, and by no means an unequivocal endorsement of the
official Party line. Subsequently, the USDAW executive decided
against submitting the 'unity resolution' to Party conference on the
grounds that it appeared unlikely to command a decisive majority.
As a result, the union's votes reverted automatically to Mr Gaitskell.
This decision of the union's executive not to press their own resolution at Blackpool caused much resentment among those unilateralists who had swallowed their first preference in order to back the
Crossman-Padley compromise, only to find they had let the multi-
lateralists in by the back door.[3] While it seems unlikely that this had
been the executive's intention all along, as their critics suggested,
the reason given for their failure to sponsor the unity resolution—
that other big unions were not similarly inclined—is difficult to
sustain. Both the AEU and the NUR were in fact in a similar
position to USDAW in that they had refrained from making an
unequivocal decision one way or the other. The resolution put
before the AEU National Council, and carried easily by thirty-
seven votes to twelve, instructed the union to 'request the Labour
Party and the TUC to consider ways and means of formulating a
Defence and Foreign Policy capable of uniting the Party and
sufficiently flexible to take full cognizance of changing circumstances

---

[1] *Report of Proceedings of 15th A.D.M., Union of Shop, Distributive and Allied
Workers*, Bournemouth, 1961, p. 94.
[2] Op. cit., p. 108.
[3] What one delegate afterwards referred to as a 'Tammany Hall get out' which
would 'stink in the nostrils of intelligent trade unionists for a long time'. *New
Dawn*, 8 July 1961, p. 448.

peculiar to defence and foreign affairs'.[1] This demand, kept deliberately vague in order to attract broad support, was essentially the same as the USDAW motion in its concern to make Party unity the prime consideration of defence policy. It is therefore difficult to see why the USDAW executive failed to be encouraged by it. Here too, the AEU's decision could not be read as a vote of confidence in the official, multilateralist line. Indeed, at the same conference a resolution phrased in general terms about the need for world peace, ended with the words: 'we further demand the multilateral renunciation of the testing, manufacture, stock-piling and basing of all nuclear weapons in the world'. Had this been carried, it could have been taken as indicating the union's firm commitment to the official Party policy, but in fact an amendment was moved specifically deleting the 'multilateralist' clause, and carried by forty-four votes to six. This would seem to demonstrate clearly enough that the union's intention was not to throw its weight behind Mr Gaitskell, but to seek out a middle path which could unite the Party.

The situation in the NUR was not altogether different. At the 1961 conference the voting on the official *Policy for Peace* resulted in a tie, thirty-eight to thirty-eight. This motion was therefore effectively lost. The unilateralist motion was also narrowly defeated, thirty-seven votes to thirty-nine. The union had thus failed to commit itself to either policy, thereby prompting the suggestion that the union's 1960 decision, in favour of unilateralism, was still in force. A further decision by the 1961 AGM would appear to have strengthened the unilateralists' claim. This arose from a statement (Decision No. 941) issued by the NUR executive the previous month (June 1961) endorsing the official Labour Party-TUC policy on defence, despite the fact that the declared policy of the union, as determined by the 1960 conference, was for unilateralism. At the 1961 conference, therefore, a number of resolutions were tabled censuring the NUR executive for their statement and challenging its legality. This challenge was upheld by forty votes to thirty-six, so formally cancelling Decision No. 941.[2] This appeared to make clear enough the union's rejection of official Labour defence policy, even though the status of unilateralism was somewhat ambiguous. The NUR executive, however, notwithstanding its recent defeat on the matter, issued a statement in August 1961 declaring that 'in view of all the circumstances we reaffirm our previous Decision No. 941 of June 1961', that is, pledging support for *Policy for Peace*.[3]

[1] AEU *Journal*, July 1961, p. 207.
[2] *Railway Review*, 11 July 1961.   [3] *Railway Review*, 11 August 1961.

Thus in none of the three major unions which switched from unilateralism to multilateralism at the 1961 Blackpool conference, so ensuring victory for Mr Gaitskell, had a clear-cut preference for the latter's position on defence been expressed by their respective conferences. In the AEU and USDAW the delegates had declared themselves unmistakably in favour of a compromise policy, while the NUR had reached deadlock. That their combined voting strength should have been thrown behind the Party leader for a policy document based on the rejection of all compromise could hardly have inspired faith in the unions' democratic process.

The fact that the unions' swing from unilateralism in 1961 was due mainly to the desire to end the strife in the Labour Party was reflected not only in the 'unity' resolutions, which had little to do with defence as such, but also in the debates themselves. The predominant attitude to the problem was summed up by the Barrow delegate to the USDAW conference:

All we have been discussing here in the way of conditions and wages, etc., will be so much vapourising if we cannot have what we need to implement the return of a Labour Government.... Accepting [the Crossman-Padley compromise] will enable us to re-dedicate ourselves to our main objective, the return to power of a Labour Government, because until we heal the split, gone for ever is the chance of the Labour Party to become again the Government of this country.[1]

Even many of those who described themselves as convinced unilateralists were willing to swallow their convictions for the sake of this over-riding need for unity. The Edinburgh delegate to the 1961 AEU conference, for example, who had moved the unilateralist motion the previous year, stated that he would support the unity resolution and vote against the unilateralist and multilateralist motions.[2] The Newcastle delegate, also a unilateralist, reluctantly adopted a similar position, explaining that 'we have either got to compromise or accept the destruction of the Labour Party'.[3] The *Guardian*'s industrial correspondent at the AEU conference suggested that 'it was the older Labour Party members who tipped the scales. Some of them had voted unilateralist last year and many were mandated by their divisions to vote that way again this year. But when it came to it, they put their loyalty to the Labour Party above all other loyalties.'[4] The editor of the AEU *Journal* put a similar interpretation on the vote. 'The decision', he wrote, 'was a direct

[1] *Report of Proceedings, 15th A.D.M. USDAW*, 1961, p. 104.
[2] *The Times*, 5 May 1961.
[3] The *Guardian*, 5 May 1961.
[4] Loc. cit.

mandate from the committee that not only the Union leadership but the leadership of the national Movement should put unity first and that there should be an end to quarrels which benefit only the Tories.'[1] Thus the debates in 1961 were almost wholly dominated by concern for the state of the Party, and hardly at all with the merits of opposing nuclear policies.[2] Unilateralism was defeated ultimately because sufficient members of those committed to it were willing to relinquish their support in the interests of Labour unity and not because, as McKenzie suggests, 'they were put to rout . . . by a very modest (if highly skilful) effort by a small group of dedicated anti-unilateralists . . .' in CDS.[3]

The fact that the abandonment of unilateralism by the major unions could not be construed as outright support for Mr Gaitskell and the official defence policy is equally well illustrated by their even firmer rejection of an integral part of that policy—namely the establishment of Polaris missile bases in Britain. The provision of facilities for American nuclear bases as part of Britain's contribution to the NATO alliance was a central part of Labour defence policy. Bearing in mind the Party's then recent commitment to abandon the British 'independent deterrent', the question of facilities for American nuclear weapons could be said to have been more crucial and relevant than that of the British hydrogen bomb. Consequently, to reject this policy would, if such decisions had the least significance for the formulation of defence policies, have undermined the Party's pro-NATO position no less effectively than endorsement of unilateralism would have done. Notwithstanding this, the majority of big unions rejected the official line on Polaris (the AEU did so unanimously) and so ensured its subsequent defeat at the Party conference, despite Mr Gaitskell's plea for its acceptance.[4] The stiffening attitude towards Polaris, occurring as it did precisely when anti-Bomb sentiments were softening in favour of a compromise position, was a source of annoyance to the Party leader, aware as he obviously

[1] AEU *Journal*, June 1961, p. 165.

[2] Occasionally it was made quite explicit that the various compromise proposals put before delegates had little relevance to the problem of defence. The Area Organizer of USDAW, for example, freely acknowledged that 'The Padley-Crossman document is a means to an end. What is the end? Simply this; that we stop destroying the Labour Party.' *USDAW Proceedings*, op. cit., p. 102.

[3] McKenzie, op. cit., p. 627. Lipset also places exaggerated importance on the role of CDS. See his Introduction to Robert Michels' *Political Parties*, Collier Books, 1962, p. 31.

[4] The voting was 3,611,000 to 2,739,000. The platform was also defeated on a motion protesting at the training of West German NATO forces in Britain, 3,519,000 to 2,733,000.

was of the connectedness of the two issues. In his fraternal address
to the General and Municipal Workers he referred to the unilateralists' opposition to Polaris and the shift of emphasis away from
the Bomb. 'It suggests,' he said, 'that they are less concerned . . .
to fight on issues of principle than they are to secure some kind of
prestige victory over the leadership. It suggests that they are more
inclined to win on some issue or other and less concerned about the
precise subject on which they win.'[1] Although this was undoubtedly
true, it was a strategy to some extent forced upon unilateralists in
the trade unions by the Labour leader's own tendency to regard the
specific issue of the Bomb as a test case of his command over the
Party. Because Gaitskell had deliberately chosen to elevate this into
a question of confidence in his leadership it became impossible for
union members to press the unilateralist case without at the same
time bringing to a head the crisis in the Labour Party which they
obviously wished to avoid. Their rejection both of unilateralism and
Polaris was a way out of the dilemma. By dropping their anti-Bomb
demands they confirmed Gaitskell in his position as leader, and
thereby avoided plunging the Party into the deeper turmoil which
would almost certainly have followed his defeat. At the same time,
by rejecting the official policy on Polaris they made it plain that
their major commitment was to Party unity and not to the leader's
declared views on defence. Because Gaitskell had not staked so much
personally in getting Polaris accepted, its defeat would not be
regarded as a serious blow to his standing in the Party in the way
that defeat on the H-bomb issue would certainly have done. Contradictory voting on defence policies was thus a non-disruptive way of
expressing dissatisfaction with the Party leadership, similar to that
which had been shown the previous year by the endorsement of
unilateralism.[2] Gaitskell was considered victorious and the Party
'saved' because he had been succesful on the H-bomb vote; his
defeat on Polaris was regarded as little more than a minor irritant.
Had these two controversies been genuinely concerned with defence
then the rejection of Polaris should have caused greater concern to a
Party already committed to abandoning the British H-bomb, in
favour of offering facilities for American missile sites in this country.

[1] *Report of Proceedings of 46th Congress of the National Union of General and
Municipal Workers*, Hastings, 1961, p. 368.
[2] This dissatisfaction was also expressed more directly by some unions.
USDAW, for example, carried without opposition a motion declaring that 'Public
advocacy of opposition to democratically decided conference decisions is in-
compatible with any claim to retention of a position of formal leadership.' 1961
Conference proceedings, op. cit.

Unilateralism after Gaitskell

The defeat of unilateralism at the Blackpool conference firmly established Mr Gaitskell's position as Party leader, much in the way he had gambled it would. However, it did not end the controversy over nuclear weapons policy nor heal the rift between the leadership and the Left. Some six months after Blackpool, as has previously been mentioned, Gaitskell was roughly treated by Labour supporters at the Glasgow May Day Rally, ostensibly for his failure to oppose the Polaris base as demanded by Conference. Shortly before this, too, in February 1962, he was at the centre of another storm as a result of his public support for the American Government's decision to resume nuclear testing in response to a similar announcement by the Soviet Union. The Blackpool conference had also gone on record as being *unanimously* opposed to nuclear testing by any country, and called on 'all the powers concerned to refrain from any further nuclear tests and to concentrate with renewed energy on negotiations [for disarmament]'.[1] For the Left this was further evidence of the Party leader's fondness for openly defying Conference decisions. To make matters worse, it was, as Michael Foot reminded him, defiance 'not of a resolution passed by some narrow majority composed of "pacifists, unilateralists and fellow-travellers", but of one sponsored by himself . . .'[2] A number of unilateralist MP's tabled a motion 'deploring' the American decision on testing, and *Tribune* at once organized a campaign against the leadership, culminating in a demonstration outside Transport House at the end of March. (The slogan of the campaign—'Test Gaitskell, not the Bomb'—nicely highlighted how far the two were almost synonymous in the eyes of the Left.) If, as has been maintained in this chapter, opposition to the Party leader was one of the chief sustaining factors of the unilateralist campaign inside the Party, then it may be doubted whether the issue of nuclear weapons policy would have ceased to be a major rallying point for the Left. As long as Gaitskell remained leader, symbolizing as he did the spectre of revisionism and Party autocracy, anti-Bomb activity would almost certainly have

---

[1] *Report of 60th Annual Conference*, The Labour Party, Blackpool, 1961, p. 162. George Brown, moving the resolution, openly faced the possibility that it might be necessary to criticize the American government. 'Sir, let us not mince words here, either,' he told delegates. 'We must condemn the resumption of nuclear tests . . . no matter who resumed them, the British public must know that in these respects British democratic socialists do not change their course according to whom they have to speak out against,' op. cit., p. 165.

[2] *Tribune*, 2 March 1962.

persisted among a large section of radical Labour supporters.[1] Although he did not live long enough for this assertion to have been put to the test, its underlying reasoning is vindicated most forcibly by the events following his sudden death and the succession of Harold Wilson. Under a new Party leader whose political record and attitudes were far more attractive to the Left, the latter with surprising haste dropped their militant posture on the Bomb and became apologists for the same defence policy they had opposed under Gaitskell. Because the new leader was not identified with groups and attitudes inimical to traditional socialist doctrines and inner party democracy, the main impetus behind the nuclear weapons campaign was removed. Unilateralism, considered solely on its appeal as an anti-Bomb campaign, failed to generate the same enthusiasm inside the Party. The Left now tended to regard the field of foreign policy and defence as fraught with complexities and problems which could not be reduced to simple moral absolutes and sloganizing. Raymond Fletcher, *Tribune*'s defence correspondent, identified the new mood in his analysis of the resolutions submitted in the 1963 Conference, few of which were straight unilateralist demands. He found that

The main preoccupation of the Labour Party now, as shown in the motions, is not to register moral abhorrence. It is to spell out in detail the practicable steps by which the weapons that provoked the abhorrence can be got rid of. And the rank and file, with their usual instinctive wisdom, have emphasized that the first steps toward peace have already been agreed upon by the party as a whole.

Fletcher forbore to point out that the 'steps toward peace' which were now found to be acceptable were precisely the same as those which had been vigorously opposed in the preceding years. Whereas under Gaitskell organized protest campaigns were felt to be the most effective way of influencing policy on the Bomb, Fletcher now urged that the rank and file should 'let time and the disarmament conference provide the solutions that cannot be found at the moment'.[2] The annual conferences of both the Labour Party and the TUC reflected the transformation in the clearest way possible—

---

[1] Norman Birnbaum, who was himself closely involved in CND, commented upon the fact that 'The Labour Left has seized upon the CND and used it as a very effective weapon of intra-party warfare', and underlined the point that even after Gaitskell's Blackpool victory 'nuclear disarmament remains an effective focus of many sorts of intra-party discontent'. Norman Birnbaum, 'Great Britain: The Reactive Revolt', in M. A. Kaplan, *The Revolution in World Politics*, Wiley, New York, 1962, p. 60.

[2] *Tribune*, 26 July 1963, p. 5.

by agreeing not to debate defence policy at all.[1] The sudden defection of the Left from the unilateralist cause was underlined in various ways throughout 1963. Most importantly perhaps, three leading unilateralist MP's, Michael Foot, Judith Hart and Anthony Greenwood, declined to stand for re-election to CND's National Council, with which they had been associated since the movement's early days. Although these resignations were claimed not to be inspired by policy differences, they were nevertheless a serious blow to the prestige and self-confidence of CND from which it never really recovered. Further signs were the decision in May 1963, less than three months after Gaitskell's death, of Victory for Socialism, the pro-unilateralist ginger group, voluntarily to wind itself up; and *Tribune*'s removal in August of its front page banner proclaiming its leadership of the anti-Bomb struggle, which it had carried in various forms for the previous five years. This was merely a symptom of the complete turnabout in the journal's approach to nuclear weapons policy, which at times read like a caricature of the cautious, 'statesmanlike' approach it had denounced in the past as a betrayal of socialist idealism. Michael Foot's re-evaluation of the issue was not untypical of the general mood.

One truth about the situation [he wrote after Wilson's first year as leader] is that foreign policies cannot be defined in the same detailed terms which are satisfactory and workable in domestic affairs. A party in opposition may give a general impression of what it intends to do in government in the realm of foreign politics. But circumstances alter, the prophets are confounded, and what one government can do depends partly on what other governments do. . . . How fast and how far a new Government could move in assisting this [unilateralist] policy would partially depend on the reactions of other governments—that is on circumstances which cannot be defined in advance.[2]

Not surprisingly, the Left's relationship with CND, never an easy one, now became distinctly strained, as the former discovered previously hidden virtues in Labour's defence policy. A group of CND'ers attending the Party's 1963 Conference to promote the unilateralist cause complained that 'some of our erstwhile colleagues pretended not to know us',[3] while David Boulton, the editor of CND's *Sanity*, also attending the conference, recorded that

---

[1] David Boulton, the editor of *Sanity*, who was covering the TUC conference, reported that the TGWU voted with the platform *against* an emergency resolution urging the discussion of defence policy. Boulton suggested that unilateralists would 'justifiably draw the conclusion that Mr Cousins has sold CND down the Aldermaston Road'. *Tribune*, 13 September 1963, p. 10.

[2] *Tribune*, 3 April 1964, p. 3.

[3] *Sanity*, October 1963, p. 2.

'whereas in previous years the Labour Left has been glad to join and support CND's conference activities, this year large sections of the Left . . . registered marked embarrassment'. The reason being that 'for a large part of the Labour Left the Campaign for Nuclear Disarmament has ceased to be of any high priority'.[1] Party members who had allied themselves with the unilateralist campaign in Gaitskell's time, now tended to rationalize their defection from the cause by claiming that it was Labour's defence policy rather than themselves which had undergone fundamental change. In particular they found themselves impressed by the Party's proposal to abandon the independent nuclear deterrent, although this had been official policy since 1960. Previously, this had been considered more as a diversion from unilateralism than a step in its direction, particularly because of the implied reliance on American nuclear strength instead (which was of course no less the case in 1963). Labour 'unilateralists' tended to become impatient, as a result, with CND's insistence on its pristine aims and its watchful criticism towards the Party under Wilson. *Tribune* sternly remonstrated against them that 'with so much of the CND's policy statement *Steps towards Peace* now incorporated in Labour's policy, some jubilation from CND would be in order; a half-contemptuous attitude towards the party is not'.[2] In fact of course jubilation on CND's part would have been completely unwarranted. Mr Wilson's position on defence was identical with that of his predecessor, a point which both he and the non-Party unilateralists were quick to emphasize.[3] Had the Left been less pre-occupied with using the unilateralist movement as a lever to prise Gaitskell out of office, and more genuinely concerned with the issue of the Bomb as such, they would have been more troubled by the continuity of policy on nuclear weapons, and less eager to proclaim support for the 'new' line. 'You have shown', wrote one justifiably angry CND supporter, 'that you were more interested in CND as a platform for getting rid of Gaitskell than for a moral crusade against the lunacies of nuclear war.'[4]

[1] *Tribune*, 11 October 1963, p. 10.

[2] *Tribune*, 4 October 1963, p. 4. The Rev. Donald Soper too reacted in similar spirit to the Committee of 100's Easter demonstration, about which he had said warm things in the past. He wished the demonstrators would 'be their age and realize that what may have been an entirely appropriate demonstration five years ago is both irrelevant and unseemly now.' *Tribune*, 24 May 1963, p. 4.

[3] The editor of *Peace News* declared he did not 'believe that Labour foreign policy is different in any fundamental way now from what it was under Mr Gaitskell. We believe it was rational to oppose Mr Gaitskell in 1960, and that it is rational to oppose Mr Wilson now.' Letter to *New Statesman*, 18 October 1963, p. 526.

[4] *Tribune*, 14 June 1963, p. 11.

As the general election approached, the Left became increasingly inclined to stress Party unity under the new leader before all other considerations. The Bomb was hardly thought of as presenting a political problem at all, and it was never really raised as an important election issue by Labour members. Indeed, in contrast to the previous two elections, it was the Conservatives who made nuclear weapons policy an important topic in 1964. *Tribune*, whose 'Notes for Speakers' during the election campaign failed to mention the Bomb at all, declared that 'If the issue has been neglected it is because the electorate want it to be. They are in fact bored with the bomb. All the public opinion polls . . . confirm that the question of defence and deterrence interests fewer and fewer voters as polling day draws near.'[1] It was not merely the public but the Left which was now bored with the Bomb. The public had expressed no greater interest in it in 1959, but *Tribune* then would have been quick to dismiss the relevance of opinion polls as guides to political action.[2]

Following Labour's election victory with its precarious majority of five (soon to fall to three) the emphasis even more than before was on the need to avoid 'rocking the boat'. The 'unilateralist' MP's were well represented in the new government, and even in the cabinet—through Frank Cousins, Barbara Castle, Gerald Gardiner and Anthony Greenwood. So pervasive was their presence felt to be in fact that the following year a Conservative MP, Neil Marten, moved an opposition motion regretting 'the influence which the supporters of the Campaign for Nuclear Disarmament have had upon the Government's policies'.[3] This influence, however, was less real than imaginary. The Labour government's defence policy made no concessions to unilateralist principles, which in any case were never seriously pursued by the Left. If the latter had wished to press the anti-Bomb case with one fraction of the persistency they had shown under the previous leadership they would, given the

---

[1] *Tribune*, 11 September 1964, p. 16.

[2] Ian Mikardo, for example, denounced in 1958 what he felt to be Labour's 'pandering to the electorate' by formulating policies 'not on their merits but almost entirely on an estimate of their electoral popularity . . . The formula seems to be "Find out what Johnny wants and give it to him".' *Tribune*, 12 September 1958, p. 5.

[3] See *House of Commons Debates*, Vol. 716, No. 152, Cols 291–358, 13 July 1965. Marten suggested that a third of Labour members were CND sympathizers, which was certainly an over-estimate. CND itself put the figure at approximately seventy-three—thirty-seven of whom were in 'close touch' with the Campaign and thirty-six in some agreement. For a full list of names see *Sanity*, September and November 1964.

K

government's tiny majority, have constituted a formidable pressure group. Their unwillingness to do so was not surprising. The comparative docility of unilateralist MP's was a good indication of the general lack of enthusiasm for the anti-Bomb crusade which had permeated the Party since Wilson's succession to the leadership. With the Left more closely integrated into the main body of the Party than at any time since the early nineteen-fifties, the dominant mood was one of consensus rather than conflict. With the closing of the gulf between Left and Right, and a leadership more sensitive to the traditional values of the rank and file, the discontents which had provided the footholds for unilateralism inside the Party were suddenly smoothed away. The movement, as we have seen, derived its main motive power from the opposition built up against Gaitskell over issues separate from that of the Bomb. Unilateralism was a convenient issue on which to concentrate this opposition, and to keep it perpetually on the boil, as it were, independently of the actual aims of the movement. The Left were not as deeply committed to these aims as their words and deeds suggested, so that potentially some other ready-made large scale protest campaign might have served the purpose equally as well. As Sir William Carron, the AEU President, observed: 'the battle centres around nuclear disarmament as a fulcrum to move the present leadership— we should be fools indeed not to admit this feature . . . and it is just as obvious that the battle could have taken place on any other issue had it presented itself more opportunely'.[1] The Left underlined this point more forcibly than any of its critics could have done by their rapid defection from the unilateralist cause after the succession of Harold Wilson to the Party leadership. The anti-Bomb crusade in the Labour Party died with Hugh Gaitskell and the open challenge to traditional socialist concepts with which he was identified.[2] Thus the struggle on the part of the Labour Left, as with that of other

[1] Presidential address to the National Committee of the AEU, 1961, AEU *Journal*, June 1961, p. 175. It is perhaps an exaggeration to say that *any* issue could have served this purpose; clearly, the Left is more readily mobilized where there is an *intrinsic* commitment to the issue involved as well as an instrumental one.

[2] Interestingly enough, a recent account of the Norwegian CND (KMA) suggests that it too was harnessed to similar purposes by militants in the Norwegian Labour Party. Nils Peter Gleditsch recorded that the major aim of the Left in the Norwegian CND 'was to rock the boat in the Labour Party, to bring a new policy, and with it possibly a new leadership. . . . The nuclear issue was used as a platform on which the party leadership could be weakened or even defeated.' See 'What Happened to the Norwegian CND', *Peace News*, 30 August 1963, p. 5.

groups involved in the Campaign, represented a form of symbolic politics in that it was concerned less with achieving its declared aims than with playing out a quite unrelated political drama for which the unilateralist movement provided a convenient national stage.

7

Youth involvement in CND

One of the most characteristic and surprising features of CND—
and one singled out by most observers for special comment, was its
success in mobilizing adolescents and young adults behind a
political cause. The Campaign's ability to attract the youthful to its
ranks was something of a new phenomenon in British political life,
in so far as the general attitude of the younger generation towards
politics has traditionally been one of apathy and disinterest. A
number of studies of adolescent values and behaviour in the United
States and Europe have indicated that teenage preoccupations centre
primarily around sporting, entertainment and peer group activities,
with politics being regarded as an exclusively adult sphere of in-

terest. A recent study of the political attitudes of the young in Britain found that

The majority leave school at 15 ignorant of the workings of the political system and content to be so . . . 90 per cent find politics a bore. They have no generalized empathy for public affairs. They are aware of certain issues but not powerfully involved in them. . . . Sixty per cent believe it will make little or no difference to their lives which party is in power.[1]

Given this picture of the traditional apathy of youth towards political involvement, how is the appearance of comparatively large numbers of adolescents and young adults on marches and demonstrations against the Bomb in the late nineteen-fifties and early nineteen-sixties to be accounted for? It is the discussion of this problem with which this chapter is mainly concerned.

The political generation

One type of explanation for the emergence of political radicalism among young people is that contained in the concept of the 'political generation'. The basic postulate of this notion is that an individual's political and social outlook is heavily influenced by the character of the age in which he grew to maturity, and more specifically by the degree of his exposure to, or isolation from, dramatic national and international political events. Generally speaking, young people whose formative years were spent in a period of political crises and instability are held to be more likely to exhibit political awareness (usually of a radical kind) than those whose early years coincided with a period of stability and order. Rudolf Heberle states the generation thesis succinctly as follows:

Certain experiences during the most formative period of life tend to be of decisive effect on the development of the individual's social philosophy and on his political attitudes. People of approximately the same age will be influenced by the same experiences. These experiences may therefore be called the decisive experiences of a political generation.[2]

The view that young people's politicization, as manifested in support for CND, was a response to the acute anxieties and crises of the times was one commonly canvassed in contemporary political journals—not surprisingly, perhaps, since it could scarcely be

[1] P. Abrams and A. Little, 'The Young Voter in British Politics', *British Journal of Sociology*, Vol. XVI, No. 2, June 1965, p. 95. For studies of adolescent leisure pursuits and values see, *The Adolescent in Britain*, The Social Survey, Central Office of Information, 1950; F. Musgrove, *Youth and the Social Order*, Routledge, 1964; Thelma Veness, *School Leavers*, Methuen, 1962.
[2] Rudolf Heberle, *Social Movements*, Appleton, New York, 1951, p. 120.

doubted that the years between 1955 and 1962 were remarkable for a succession of national and international events of a dramatic and far-reaching kind. The period encompassed the British government's decision to produce a hydrogen bomb, the denunciation of Stalin at the 20th Congress of the CPSU, the uprisings in Poland and Hungary, the invasion of Suez—and with it a major political crisis at home, as well as the conflict over the Cuban missile sites in which nuclear war between the major powers was only narrowly averted. This cluster of events, experienced on top of the other more or less permanent world tensions, could be said to have created a distinctive political ethos similar to that which existed in Europe in the nineteen-thirties. Those who were reaching maturity at this time were thus felt to have been exposed to a highly politicized climate sufficient to account for a general radical awakening and involvement in a movement of mass protest.

Whilst this explanation does have a certain amount of plausibility and appeal, the general assumptions on which it rests, and which are contained in the notion of the 'political generation', have by no means been fully validated by empirical research. The problem is a notoriously difficult one to handle operationally, and the attempts which have been made to do so are strikingly inconsistent in their findings. A number of American writers have argued in favour of the explanatory powers of the generation concept. Richard Centers, for example, in his study of social class in the United States found that men in his national sample between the ages of 40–49 years were consistently more radical in outlook than all other age-groups, and he attributes this to the effects of the depression which this group would have experienced as young men in the nineteen-thirties.[1] He makes the same point with greater force in his explanation of the high degree of collectivist and radical attitudes found in all social classes of a sample of post-war adolescents. This is accounted for by reference to the fact that the latter were raised during the New Deal period when state intervention in the economy and in welfare measures created an atmosphere favourable to the acceptance of collectivist values.

Born in depression, reared in unemployment and insecurity, constantly exposed to the ideology of three Roosevelt administrations, witnessing dramatic victories of welfare legislation, T.V.A., etc., and probably in numerous instances personally and tangibly and perceptively benefiting

---

[1] Richard Centers, *The Psychology of Social Classes*, Princeton University Press, 1949, pp. 167–8.

from welfare measures, could one expect a result other than just what we have in these youth?[1]

Berelson and his colleagues adopt a similar line of reasoning to explain age-related differences in support for the two parties in the 1952 presidential election. They suggested that New Deal experiences were an important factor in accounting for disproportionate support for the Democrats among certain age-groups.[2] More recently, Maurice Zeitlin found in his study of Cuban workers' attitudes to political events in their country that levels of support for the Revolution and Castro's government varied significantly from one generational group to another. The most enthusiastic supporters were drawn from amongst that category of workers who were between 18 and 25 years of age at the time of the Revolution—precisely the stage in the life cycle which Zeitlin singles out as being the most decisive for the formation of lasting political and social attitudes.[3]

A number of other studies have appeared, however, which do not support the explanatory claims of the generation hypothesis. Arthur Kornhauser and his colleagues, for example, in their investigation of American automobile workers, found that union members who had lived through the depression years and the pre-war periods of intense industrial conflict were *less* radical in their political outlook than members who were too young personally to have experienced either.[4] Similarly, Toch in his comparison of pre-war and post-war opinion polls of social and political attitudes in the United States found no significant differences in the degree of liberalism among members of different generations, despite notable contrasts in the political ethos to which each had been exposed in youth.[5] A recent British study of the same problem produced findings echoing a similar lack of discrepancy between the political outlook of younger and older generations. Abrams and Little in their examination of NOP surveys of political attitudes showed that on a wide variety of issues the views of the young closely mirrored those of their seniors.

[1] Richard Centers, 'Children of the New Deal: Social Stratification and Adolescent Attitudes', *International Journal of Opinion and Attitude Research*, Vol. 4, 1950, p. 325. On the basis of his 1947 findings Centers predicted that American society would shift well to the left when the adolescents later became voters.

[2] B. Berelson, et. al., *Voting*, University of Chicago Press, 1954, pp. 59–60.

[3] Maurice Zeitlin, 'Political Generations in the Cuban Working Class', *American Journal of Sociology*, Vol. LXXI, No. 5, 1966.

[4] A. Kornhauser, et al., *When Labor Votes*, University Books, New York, 1956, p. 220.

[5] H. Toch, 'Attitudes of the "Fifty-Plus" Age Group: Preliminary Considerations towards a Longitudinal Survey', *Public Opinion Quarterly*, Vol. 17, 1953.

It was the extent of conformity to, rather than deviance from, the outlook of the older generation which proved to be the remarkable feature of the politics of the young.

Our general conclusion would be that the young in Britain, having been offered no new politicizing experiences, vote in the same way, for the same reasons and on the basis of similar political attitudes as *the old*. If it is 'decisive political experiences' that make political generations then for some reason Suez, Hungary, the emergence of Africa and China, the spread of nuclear weapons, have failed to provide such experiences.[1]

Thus, whilst CND, and youth involvement in it, obviously had its origins in certain major political events in the second half of the nineteen-fifties, it would be misleading to interpret this as a straight-forward relationship between *Zeitgeist* and generation. In the first place, whereas the events referred to clearly had the same overall implications for all young people in Britain, only a fairly small minority became involved in CND. The great majority failed to respond to the crises of the times by allying themselves with the movement against the Bomb. Indeed, it is by no means certain (as so many commentators have suggested) that the problem of the Bomb has weighed particularly heavily on the young, in the sense that they regard it as the major issue confronting them in modern times. The NOP data cited by Abrams and Little showed that the 'independent deterrent' came near to the bottom of the list of problems felt by young people to be of most political importance—well after items like the cost of living, housing, unemployment, education and even pensions.[2] This ordering of priorities—placing material, bread-and-butter concerns above apparently more momentous defence and foreign policy issues—is clearly in line with adult views, as recorded in numerous studies of electoral politics.

It should be clear from all this, then, that large-scale political and social events, even those as overwhelming as the threat of nuclear war, cannot be said to affect a generation in the same overall way. A generation of any age-group is not usefully thought of as a *tabula rasa* on which events are able to make a standard imprint. Such events do, rather, tend to be perceived in different ways according to individual or group values and dispositions. Mann-heim injected a greater degree of sophistication into the generation concept by distinguishing between generation as 'location', i.e. shared temporal position, and generation as 'actuality', i.e. a common consciousness and identity of outlook. He suggested that the

---

[1] Abrams and Little, op. cit., p. 108.
[2] Abrams and Little, op. cit., p. 104.

latter would not automatically derive from the former but that generations would be sub-divided into 'generation-units', that is, collectivities which would perceive the same political and social realities of the period in distinctive ways, according to their particular interests and dispositions.[1] Seen from this angle, as far as the present study is concerned, the problem becomes one of seeking to account for the tendency of one such 'generation-unit', composed of a minority of young people, to interpret the political events of the period in a way which led to their involvement in a radical mass movement.

Family socialization into radicalism

One approach to this problem is that opened up by evidence relating to family socialization into politics. This provides an alternative mode of explanation for political behaviour to the generation concept in that its major postulate declares that political attitudes and loyalties are formed at a relatively early age, through childhood exposure to parental influences, direct and indirect. These influences, it is argued, have a decisive effect on the individual's political outlook throughout his adult life.[2] Thus, whereas the generation thesis locates the source of political behaviour in events and experiences emanating from the wider society, the family socialization thesis locates it within the family unit, considered independently of society at large. The former implies potential political dissensus between the generations arising from their exposure to different experiences and atmospheres, while the latter implies strong political consensus between generations as a result of the success of the old in socializing the young.

The transmission of political values from parents to children has most frequently been documented in studies of voting behaviour, and has thus been examined in the setting of orthodox political conflict of a party kind. Radical mass movements like CND have less often provided the focus for such studies, so posing the question as to whether parental socialization is as effective in providing recruits for non-party organizations, especially those of a 'deviant' kind, as for the more conventional and legitimate political parties. Is, in other words, political deviance 'inherited' in the same manner as political orthodoxy, or does it derive more from extra-familial institutions? Even more, did CND represent a *reaction against* family

---

[1] Karl Mannheim, *Essays in the Sociology of Knowledge*. Routledge, 1952.
[2] Much of the empirical data on family influences upon political outlook is brought together in H. H. Hyman, *Political Socialization*, Free Press, 1959.

influences by attracting those young people who were resentful of adult or parental authority and who saw in the movement a means of rebelling against such authority? Data bearing upon these and other matters were collected through postal questionnaires administered to 550 CND supporters between the ages of 15 and 25.[1]

Concerning firstly the matter of family influences and attitudes towards CND, respondents were asked to indicate whether their parents themselves supported or approved of the Campaign, or whether they disapproved of it, or whether they expressed no opinion on the matter. The replies are set out in Table 15.

TABLE 15   *Parental attitudes to CND*

	%
At least one parent supports or approves of CND	62
Neither parent supports or approves of CND	35
Don't know/No response	3
	100 (N = 445)

From this it will be seen that the great majority of respondents have at least one parent who is sympathetic to the Campaign, either in the sense of being an active supporter, or in approving its aims and methods. Only about a third of the sample could expect no such support from the home, either because the parents were indifferent to CND or because they were opposed to it for a variety of reasons. Given the fact that there was comparatively little public approval for the policies and methods of the movement, any encouragement offered from the home would be an especially important source of support, and particularly so in the case of young people for whom parents are still likely to provide a meaningful point of reference. The nature of this support was of course open to some variation; it might take the form of parental encouragement to join the Campaign or, more frequently it would seem, parents simply endorsed an 'independent' decision of the child himself. This is made clear by many of the respondents in their remarks about their parents' attitudes. Some typical written comments were as follows:

My parents have always been extremely active politically and they encouraged me to become active in CND. (nineteen-year-old girl, Swansea.)

My involvement in CND springs directly from that of my father as do most of my socio-political opinions . . . (Languages student, Sevenoaks.)

My mother used to support CND right at the beginning. Both parents

---

[1] For details see Introduction.

assist me in CND activities when I'm home; e.g. car lifts to marches; mother also buys at CND bazaars . . . (Sociology student, Amersham.)

Both my parents agree entirely with my belonging to CND and encourage me to a great extent. (Laboratory technician, Hull.)

Both my parents are very active and have run local groups with a few others for several years. Father also supports the Committee of 100. (Grammar school girl, Sidcup.)

More specific evidence concerning parental support for CND activities is provided by a comparison of attitudes expressed by respondents' mothers and fathers separately, as shown in Table 16.

TABLE 16   *Individual parental attitudes to CND*

	Respondent's mother	Respondent's father
	%	%
Active supporter	11	8
Approves of CND, but is not active	42	33
No opinion	24	23
Disapproves of CND	19	29
Don't know/No response	4	7
	100	100
	(N = 445)	(N = 445)

It is noticeable that respondents' mothers were considerably more sympathetic to CND than were their fathers; 53 per cent of mothers gave it active or nominal support, as against 41 per cent of fathers. Conversely, only 19 per cent of mothers expressed disapproval, compared with 29 per cent of fathers. Thus, although the majority of supporters in the sample had at least one parent behind them—usually the mother—there was not necessarily an overall consensus in the home on this issue. Some respondents made it clear in fact that CND could be the focus of political tensions in the home when their parents held opposing views.

My father tends to regard CND as completely naive and also as being a dangerously Communist or extremist orientated organization. My mother would be active in support (from a moral viewpoint) but fears the row in the family if she did. (Politics undergraduate, Oxford.)

Mother expresses sympathy towards CND and Committee of 100 demonstrations. . . . Father is greatly hostile—he equates nuclear disarmament with 'appeasement' and 'cowardice'. Mother will do such things as making coffee for meetings, sewing banners, typing notes, etc. (Clerk, Liverpool.)

My mother is always pleased to see 'people who stand up for what they believe in' and says if she were 20 years younger she would join. My father

... sees CND as a collection of long-haired, banjo-swinging nits. (Grammar school girl, Bath.)

It is perhaps somewhat surprising that respondents' mothers displayed more sympathy for the Campaign than their fathers did. This is especially so in view of the findings of a number of studies in Britain and Europe as to the greater degree of Conservatism in political and social attitudes that women in general display compared with men. However, when it comes to the question of politics in general, rather than CND specifically, respondents' mothers were not shown to be significantly more radical than their fathers. 61 per cent of mothers and 58 per cent of fathers supported the Labour or Communist parties, while 31 per cent of mothers and 30 per cent of fathers were Liberal or Conservative voters. Measured by the yardstick of orthodox party politics then, CND homes do not appear to be more heavily weighted towards radicalism on the maternal side; the great majority of respondents come from families in which there is some level of commitment to left-wing politics on the part of both parents.[1] Furthermore, when the *salience* of politics for the parents is compared, respondents' fathers are seen to be more involved and interested than mothers.

TABLE 17   *Parental attitudes towards politics*

	Mother %	Father %
Very active in politics	10	13
Definitely interested, but not really active	35	47
Only mildly interested	40	29
Completely uninterested	13	7
Don't know/No response	2	4
	100	100
	(N = 445)	(N = 445)

As might be expected, the degree of parental interest in politics is rather high, certainly when judged against that of the population in general, and this would no doubt be another feature contributing to the activism of their children.[2] Concerning the mothers, although

[1] These voting preferences refer to mothers and fathers taken as aggregates for purposes of comparison, and not *husbands* and *wives*. However since only in 13 per cent of cases do husbands and wives vote on opposite sides of the Right-Left dichotomy these figures give a good indication of the degree of *joint parental support* for the Left.

[2] Abrams' national survey showed that only 21 per cent of men and 8 per cent of women were 'very interested' in politics. The number of activists is, of course,

the level of involvement may be high for women in general it is less than that shown by fathers. This means that the greater sympathy and support for CND which mothers show is not a simple artefact of a stronger predisposition for radical ideas and actions of a broader political kind. If anything their CND sympathies flourish in the face of a commoner tendency to devalue the importance of politics. The fact, too, that considerably more mothers support the two parties of the Right than disapproved of CND, implies that the Campaign was for many of them 'above' politics in the sense that their evaluations of it were distinctly out of line with orthodox party values—especially so of course in the case of Conservative voters. The relationship between electoral choice and support for CND on the part of respondents' parents is shown in Table 18.

TABLE 18 *Electoral choice and parental attitude to CND*

Parental attitude to CND	Parent's vote							
	Communist		Labour		Liberal		Conservative	
	Mo.	Fa.	Mo.	Fa.	Mo.	Fa.	Mo.	Fa.
	%	%	%	%	%	%	%	%
Active support or approval	100	95	60	50	42	39	26	11
Disapproval	—	—	12	20	18	35	53	62
No opinion	—	5	26	28	38	23	21	24
Don't know								
No response	—	—	2	2	2	3	—	3
	100	100	100	100	100	100	100	100
N =	(37)	(40)	(234)	(219)	(62)	(31)	(76)	(103)

Although there is a definite relationship between voting behaviour and support for CND the relationship is not altogether clear-cut. However, the overall pattern is plain enough; the farther to the Left of the political continuum parents are located the likelier will be their sympathy for CND; the farther to the Right the likelier their

---

much smaller. See Mark Abrams, 'Social Trends and Electoral Behaviour', *British Journal of Sociology*, **13**, September 1962, p. 233. These figures obviously are not altogether comparable in so far as the table above records respondents' *assessment* of parental interest in politics. However, being political activists themselves it is likely that respondents will tend to under—rather than over—state their parents' level of interest.

Not unexpectedly, there was a strong relationship between the level of political interest and support for the Left. 72 per cent of parents who were 'very active' or 'definitely interested' in politics were Labour Party or Communist Party supporters. The majority of Liberal and Conservative parents were only 'mildly' or 'completely uninterested' in politics.

disapproval. But when party choice is held constant it is noticeable that mothers invariably exhibit friendlier attitudes to the Campaign than fathers—so that even among Conservative mothers 26 per cent express their approval. Although differences in attitude to CND certainly vary more by party allegiance than by the sex of the parent, the latter discrepancy is the more interesting, if only because it was somewhat less predictable. It is perhaps possible that anxiety about the Bomb and atmospheric tests was felt more acutely by women, and especially mothers, than by men. Public controversies concerning the possibly harmful effects of radiation on the reproductive process and childbirth enjoyed major prominence at the time of CND's emergence, and were of course given additional publicity by the Campaign itself. In so far as women have a deeper emotional involvement in matters affecting childbirth, it may well be that they were rather more troubled by the idea of nuclear testing, and had a correspondingly greater sympathy for CND's aims. Significantly enough, a number of other studies have shown a greater degree of opposition to nuclear weapons on the part of women. Solomon and Fishman found in their research on the American peace movement that the mothers of student demonstrators were more than twice as likely as fathers to be in agreement with their children's attitudes towards nuclear weapons. The authors suggest that American women in general are more concerned about this problem than are men.[1] Similarly, Putney and Middleton in a study of students' attitudes towards nuclear war (in a sample drawn from sixteen American colleges and universities) showed that, on every single index, female students were significantly more prone than male students to endorse an anti-war or pacifist position.[2] Again, for Britain, Bealey and his associates, in their study of politics in a local constituency, found that Labour Party women members were more in favour of unilateral nuclear disarmament than were male members—a sex discrepancy which was paralleled in most of the polls on university students' attitudes to the Bomb.[3] However, this apparently greater degree of anxiety felt by women over nuclear weapons should not be equated with endorsement of CND, since a great

[1] Frederic Solomon and J. R. Fishman, 'A Psychosocial Study of Student Peace Demonstrators in Washington DC', *Journal of Social Issues*, October 1964, p. 63.
[2] Snell Putney and Russell Middleton, 'Some Factors Associated with Student Acceptance or Rejection of War', *American Sociological Review*, Vol. 27, No. 5, 1962.
[3] F. Bealey, et al., *Constituency Politics*, Faber, 1965, p. 282. See also the New Society Survey of readers' opinions, *New Society*, 16 May 1963, p. 12.

many of those who were opposed to the Bomb were opposed to CND also. Existing radical dispositions would seem to be a far surer guide than female status in predicting support for, or involvement in, CND.

An alternative explanation for the differences between maternal and paternal support for CND may reside in the fact of the fathers' greater degree of commitment to political parties. Since none of the four parties unambiguously endorsed CND demands, any support for the Campaign would have cut across allegiance to the party and its own policy on the Bomb. Mothers sympathetic to unilateralism would have been in less of a dilemma on this score because their involvement and interest in party politics was a good deal weaker; consequently the pull of competing loyalties would have been much reduced for them, so allowing even nominal Conservatives to harbour pro-CND sympathies.

A third, theoretically more intriguing, possibility is that radically-minded youths tend to come from mother-oriented rather than father-oriented families. In so far as respondents appear to identify more with their mothers' views on CND than with their fathers', this might be taken as an index of closer attachment to the female parent. The suggestion that there may be a somewhat greater tendency for radicalism to take root among children from mother-centred families is not a too fanciful one, since there is a well-established connection in the reverse direction between extreme right wing or authoritarian attitudes and the experience of father-dominance in childhood. It may well be that political predispositions tend to be of the opposite kind when the mother is the dominant figure in the family. McKinley has suggested the possibility of such a relationship in his analysis of data on the American family:

a powerful and hostile father leads to the son's having a reactionary political position, while a powerful and overly controlling (and perhaps hostile) mother coupled with isolation from peers leads to extreme Liberalism or Marxism. This would also fit in with interpretations of the association between the power of the German father and the rise of reactionary ideology in Germany, with the findings of Strodtbeck (that Jewish mothers are more dominant) and Lenski (that Jewish voters, despite their high economic and occupational status, are quite liberal in their political beliefs.)[1]

A similar relationship is hinted at by Frenkel-Brunswick, following her findings that male subjects who scored high on the F-scale

[1] D. G. McKinley, *Social Class and Family Life*, Free Press, 1964, p. 191.

reported coming mainly from father-dominated families.[1] Unfortunately, so far as the CND data are concerned, this problem was not clearly formulated in advance, and consequently no independent measures of parent-child and other family relationship were made. Although we can only speculate here on the possible relationship between family structure and political beliefs, this could well prove to be a fruitful line of enquiry in future studies.

Parental opposition and political rebelliousness

The emphasis of this chapter so far has been on the degree of parental support available to respondents in their involvement in CND. We have seen that, by and large, young supporters tend to have home backgrounds conducive to their own radical, activist orientations. But of course many parents were less enthusiastic about CND, and their children's part in it, and it is now necessary to balance the picture so far presented by considering the fact of parental opposition. This opposition, as Table 18 shows, is roughly associated with support for parties of the Right, but there are also minorities among Labour parents who also disapproved. This was sometimes due to the latter's own political activism and the feeling that CND presented a threat to the party:

> My parents believe that everything Harold Wilson says is the Word of God, and would only support CND if it also meant not going against the Labour Party and Harold in particular. As far as my involvement is concerned they have tried to convert me—without success. (Journalist, Chiswick.)
> My parents feel that I am betraying the Labour Party, which I was brought up to support, and that I am the victim of Russian agents, if not a Russian agent myself. (Trainee teacher, Middlesbrough.)

Other parents, although not themselves approving of CND, were somewhat resigned to their children's participation in it, rather than openly hostile. This tolerance seemed mainly due to the feeling that it was an ephemeral, transitory affair which they would quickly abandon with adolescence.

> They regard my involvement in CND as merely a phase that I will grow out of. They do not take my support of it seriously. (Grammar school girl, Great Missenden.)

---

[1] Else Frenkel-Brunswick, 'Parents and Childhood as Seen through the Interviews', in T. Adorno, et al., *The Authoritarian Personality*, New York, 1950, pp. 370–1. Interestingly enough, pro-CND dramatists have frequently singled out the mother as the dominant character in radical families. Obvious examples are Sarah Kaln in Wesker's *Chicken Soup with Barley*, Frieda Waring in David Mercer's *A Climate of Fear* and Myra Bolton in Doris Lessing's *Each in His Own Wilderness*.

Though they express no obvious opinion about CND they tend to regard it as unrealistic and idealist, and point out that young people grow out of such ideas. (Sociology student, Rugby.)

They feel it is just a phase I am passing through and since they think I will soon grow out of it they are fairly tolerant of my present activities. (Schoolboy, Feltham.)

They think it is a laugh. (Office girl, Bedford.)

To a minority of parents, however, it was anything but a laugh. To these CND, or at least their children's connections with it, was something of a family disaster and was obviously capable of generating a great deal of bitterness and discord in the home. Their opposition to it appears to have been on two main grounds: status and ideological. The former expressed itself in concern about the (supposed) social characteristics of the movements supporters, as well as in the more practical fears about the possible jeopardy to future employment as a result of arrest or imprisonment:

My father thinks the Campaign contains too many bad elements—anarchists, sex-maniacs, etc. (Girl librarian, Romford.)

My parents are completely intolerant of CND: it does not conform with their idea of well ordered (Victorian) society. (Student nurse, Slough.)

Mother thinks they are all cranks, pagans, show-offs and dirty students—also because she is a Roman Catholic she no longer speaks to me. (Furniture salesman, Bath.)

Mother is worried in case I get arrested again 'with those untidy fools'. (Politics undergraduate, Clydebank.)

Where the disapproval of CND rested on ideological grounds, as for example in the belief that it was Communist-dominated, or that it was a threat to cherished political values, then parental opposition appears to have been sharpest of all. Fathers once again were singled out as expressing hostility on these grounds, whereas mothers seemed more troubled by the 'beatnik' image than by political objections:

Father, being an ex-RAF pilot thinks I am 'a communist, cowardly rat'. Mother says father knows best. (Draughtsman, South Shields.)

My father, after 27 years in the army, thinks we ought to be put behind bars. (Salesman, Manchester.)

My father was a policeman and hence his attitude was extremely hostile. Eventually I left home because of this and became involved in direct action. (Sub-editor, Oxford.)

Both my parents disapprove: father is an ex-serviceman and therefore considers the movement as traitors. Mother simply because she doesn't want me to be imprisoned. She's worried about my future employment. (Public schoolboy, Warwick.)

L

Clearly, then, young people's involvement in CND is not to be understood wholly as the inheritance of political radicalism from their parents. As the above extracts make clear, many respondents, far from reflecting family views, were in the movement in the face of parental disapproval or even hostility. This raises the question of whether, for a minority of supporters at least, CND may also have served as an outlet for rebelliousness against parental authority. That is, whether for some, it may have represented a reaction *against* family socialization rather than an expression of its effectiveness. The possibility of this will now be considered in the light of relevant data.

Politics, on the whole, would seem to offer a somewhat unattractive outlet for youthful rebellion. As Lane has suggested, adolescents in modern society generally have more effective means of flouting their parents' values than by cross-voting or joining radical movements.[1] Nevertheless, there is some evidence that a minority do occasionally act along these lines, allowing political behaviour to be dictated more by personal antagonisms than by 'rational' considerations. Maccoby and her colleagues, for example, in a study of the electoral choices of young people in Cambridge, Massachussetts, found the usual high degree of political consensus between parents and their children. However, agreement on party choice was significantly weaker for that group of young voters whose parents had exercised strict control over them during childhood and adolescence. Parent-child consensus in political choice was greatest where parents had been light on discipline, and at its lowest where they had been authoritarian. Maccoby interprets this greater tendency to vote 'against' the parents as a form of protest against a strict upbringing—that is, political rebellion in the classic sense.[2] With these findings in mind, CND supporters were also questioned about parental controls to determine whether similar relationships existed. Respondents were asked to indicate which of the following statements applied to their own experiences of parental authority during their teenage years.

(a) They allowed me to make very few of my own decisions.
(b) They gave me guidance, but did not interfere in my life too much.
(c) They gave me a completely free hand in everything.

---

[1] Robert E. Lane, 'Fathers and Sons: Foundations of Political Belief', *American Sociological Review*, August, 1959.

[2] Eleanor Maccoby, et al. 'Youth and Political Change', *Public Opinion Quarterly*, Spring, 1954.

The replies were then matched against parents' attitudes to CND in order to determine whether those who supported the Campaign in defiance of parental opposition were more likely to have experienced a stricter upbringing than those whose parents either approved of it or held no clear opinion one way or the other. Obviously, only those whose parents disapproved of CND would be in a position to 'use' the Campaign as an outlet for rebellion against the family. The replies are set out in Table 19.

TABLE 19   *Parental authority and attitudes to CND*

Experience of parental authority	Support/approve of CND %	No opinion/ neutral %	Disapprove of CND %
Authoritarian	4	8	20
Moderate control	83	78	70
Libertarian	11	13	7
Don't know/No response	2	1	3
	100	100	100
	(N = 198)	(N = 111)	(N = 98)

The most commonly reported type of parental control was the happy medium between authoritarianism and libertarianism, and this held true irrespective of parents' attitudes to CND. However, within this overall orientation, certain important variations do occur. In particular, it is significant that those respondents whose parents disapproved of CND, and who constitute the only group for whom the Campaign could have served as an outlet for rebellion, are also the ones most likely to have experienced authoritarian control in the home. They are five times more likely to have reported a strict upbringing than those whose parents agreed with them on CND, and two and a half times more likely to do so than those whose parents were indifferent or of mixed views.[1] This relationship may be illustrated more clearly in a comparison of the two polar minority groups reporting an authoritarian or libertarian upbringing, and Table 20 shows the extent to which those respondents who experienced strict discipline in the home supported CND in the face of parental disapproval. They were far more likely to be in political opposition to their parents than those respondents who felt free of the burden of parental discipline. For this minority, then, CND might well have been serving as an outlet for rebellion against

[1] Parents were classified as 'neutral' when they held opposing views on CND; when only *one* parent held an opinion, for or against, this was classified as parental approval or disapproval respectively, since this could be taken as representing the dominant viewpoint in the home.

TABLE 20   *Libertarianism, authoritarianism and parental attitudes to CND*

Parental attitude to CND	Authoritarian upbringing %	Libertarian upbringing %
Support/approve of CND	20	49
No opinion/neutral	26	35
Disapprove of CND	54	16
	100	100
	(N = 37)	(N = 42)

disciplinarian parents in the manner suggested by Maccoby. Perhaps support for a radical movement like CND, in opposition to parents' views, would be a more effective reaction than voting for a different political party. The secrecy of the ballot and the comparative rarity of the occasion are factors in voting which may tend to diminish its usefulness as a form of symbolic protest. The unilateralist movement, with its minority group status and permanent opposition to authority, would offer a far more effective outlet for those who wished to express rebellion in political terms, and especially so of course for those too young to vote.

Having drawn attention to the relationship between authoritarianism and parent-child disagreement on CND, a caveat must be entered regarding its interpretation as an index of rebelliousness. It is possible that attitudes towards CND and attitudes towards family discipline are closely linked, forming part of the same psychological syndrome. If parents who are prone to be strict in dealings with their children are also more liable to be hostile to movements like CND, and vice versa for those with a more liberal approach, then we should not be measuring two distinct variables but two aspects of the same one. A number of studies have demonstrated a connection between the degree of tolerance in personal relationships and placement on the radical-conservative continuum. Although there are certain variations in the findings, the general pattern is one denoting a link between disciplinarianism and extreme conservatism on the one hand, and personal tolerance and political liberalism on the other.[1] It could therefore be argued that those parents who disapproved of CND have, *ipso facto*, a somewhat greater tendency to be stronger on family discipline than those who approved of it. This would then explain the relationship

[1] T. W. Adorno, et al., op. cit.; also, J. G. Martin and F. R. Westie 'The Tolerant Personality', *American Sociological Review*, **24**, August 1959.

observed in Tables 19 and 20, in a way that would not require the rebelliousness hypothesis. Both explanations are feasible but in any event this hardly poses a serious dilemma because the issue of rebelliousness, however valid, is relevant for only a fairly small minority of the sample.

The problem of rebelliousness as so far discussed has related to conflict between parents and children, as manifested in the latter's support for CND. However, conflict may also be considered along a different dimension—namely, that between older and younger generations in society at large, rather than within the framework of the family. It is quite feasible that those who are in basic agreement with their parents' political and social views may nevertheless express resentment at certain aspects of the adult world in general. This is particularly so in complex societies where the young are frequently called upon to play subordinate roles in adult institutions which are quite distinct from the family. The exercise of authority over the young by non-familial personnel commonly engenders adolescent resentment towards adult society, which does not necessarily entail rebellion against parents. Indeed, in so far as parental authority is tempered by strong affective bonds, which are generally absent in non-familial settings, it may be suggested that adolescent hostility towards bureaucratic authority figures is bound to be stronger than that felt towards parents. This would then explain the 'paradox' of adolescent conflict with older generations being combined with a close identity of outlook between parents and children, so frequently demonstrated by empirical studies. It has been necessary to labour this point somewhat because discussions of youthful rebelliousness often fail to distinguish between these two different targets.

Concerning CND supporters, it does seem clear that much of the movement's appeal for the young did derive from the anti-adult, anti-authoritarian character which the Campaign frequently assumed. The Bomb could be, and was easily held up as a symbol of the older generation's moral and political bankruptcy, the supreme example of adult wickedness and folly. In refusing to condone the terrible new weapon the young could demonstrate their own political purity and high moral purpose and contrast these with the apparently less altruistic and less moral attitudes of their seniors. More than any other political issue the Bomb could be shown to symbolize the troubled and menacing world which the older generation had created for the young to live in. Thus, to protest against the

Bomb was also in large part to protest against much of adult society in general; it was a telling way of making manifest certain of the latent tensions inevitably present between the generations.[1] It is undeniable that many of those attracted to CND were simply against authority or the 'powers that be', and would have found it difficult to give expressly political reasons for their support for the Campaign. This was well recognized by many of the politically dedicated CND members; as one YCND branch secretary expressed it in the course of an interview:

We got a lot of young people who joined us because this was the thing to do among teenagers. They came on Aldermaston or wore the CND badge because they thought this would annoy the grown-ups. A lot of these types were in it for the kicks—they couldn't give you any reason for being against the Bomb. Some of them stayed in the Campaign and became good members, but a lot drifted off in search of new thrills. It's getting harder to attract teenagers now because CND has become too respectable and square.

Nominal support for CND was, for many teenagers, a more or less commonly accepted feature of the youth culture; like the preference for folk music, outlandish clothes and the like, it was a way of drawing a line of demarcation between adolescent and adult values. Christopher Farley, an adult CND supporter, drew attention to this apparently superficial attachment to the Campaign on the part of many of the young, and the way it was linked with other typically youthful concerns. In his report of the Beaulieu Jazz Festival for *Peace News* he estimated that

about 30 per cent—roughly—of the festival audience wore CND badges, yet very few of them thought or cared much about the Campaign or its development . . . They wore badges to indicate they were against the Bomb but there was nothing very special about nuclear weapons—they were simply against them in the same way that they rejected much else of society, except that the Bomb was everything else writ large.[2]

Another CND supporter suggested that, for the young, the slogan Ban the Bomb 'canalises, and gives group support, to the general and diffuse adolescent anger against authority; the phrase becomes a form of swearing, a secular blasphemy'.[3]

Undoubtedly, too, a further attraction of the Campaign for the young was its preference for political activity by way of marches and

[1] This self-awareness at being a distinct social category set apart from adults was reflected in the choice of title for one of the movement's prominent journals—*Our Generation Against Nuclear War*. Lipset has pointed to a similar tendency among young American peace and civil rights activists. S. M. Lipset, 'Student Opposition in the United States', op. cit.

[2] *Peace News*, 4 August 1961, p. 5.   [3] *Peace News*, 19 April 1963, p. 10.

demonstrations, which contrasted favourably with the highly bureaucratized and authoritarian methods of the youth organizations of the political parties. The excitement of a four-day march, with its attendant personal sacrifices and discomforts suffered for the sake of a cause, the fellowship and conviviality, and the creation of *Gemeinschaft* relationships, combined to create an appeal which could not be matched by the daily round of routinized politics. The Aldermaston march was one of the few 'institutions' which represented a distinctively adolescent presence in political life and moral commitment; it provided the one occasion when the radical young stood for a brief moment at the centre of the stage of national politics. Bryan Wilson has described some of the social and psychological satisfactions enjoyed by adolescents from events of this kind:

Boredom becomes momentary excitement, frustration is replaced by stimulation, and the sense of powerlessness is eclipsed by sudden, if evanescent, power in the modern marching movements of youth—CND, Anti-Apartheid, the Vietnam Protest and the Oxfam movement. Clearly there is good will involved, and some of these are causes which moralists might applaud, but there is in the form which support for these causes takes, something else—the prospect of excitement and power of a generational movement when young people come together in a spirit of moral commitment. There is an echo of the revivalism of Moody and Sankey, and the incidental functions which they fulfil seem not essentially dissimilar. Young people may not understand the real causes of the malaise they suffer but they organize against recognizable symptoms of the ills of the world.[1]

This tendency on the part of young people to express discontent with aspects of the adult world by aligning themselves with CND is not of course to be explained simply as an outcome of structured tensions between the generations. Generally, such frustrations as are felt by the young tend to find outlets in quite other directions— as, for example, in certain forms of juvenile delinquency. CND supporters would appear to be untypical of youth in general in their manner of making manifest the latent antagonisms between generations. This is partly due to the particular kind of value orientations which young CND'ers have concerning society and their place in it, especially their attitudes towards spheres of public and private involvement. Adolescents in industrial societies are commonly characterized by their privatized modes of life, resulting from certain of the strains inherent in the transitional phase between childhood and adult status. This phase is one in which problems such as the selection of a marriage partner, and the area of sexual relations in

---

[1] Bryan R. Wilson, *The Social Context of the Youth Problem*, 13th Charles Russell Memorial Lecture, October, 1965, p. 17.

general, the choice of occupation, and the related problem of moving out of the parental home and establishing independence, come together and create a situation felt to be sufficiently absorbing to encourage young people to withdraw into the realm of the personal and private, and to make them indifferent to the issues of the wider world. Leisure activities, friends, family, career concerns and the like are the main objects of involvement for the great majority of young people. Even among university students who are exposed to a climate more favourable to the development of broader social horizons the situation is not altogether different. One recent survey of student attitudes in American universities, for example, came to the conclusion that 'the present generation of college students . . . is politically disinterested, apathetic and conservative. Social movements and social philosophies do not arouse their interest or command their commitment. . . . In the slogan of their own campus culture they "play it cool".'[1] In Britain the picture is not dissimilar. L. F. Douglas, in his study of London University undergraduates, asked them to indicate which of a number of items they felt personally most concerned with. 50 per cent gave their first choice as family, 23 per cent as career, 16 per cent as leisure and friends, and only 9 per cent stated 'Community and world betterment' to be the object of primary interest.[2] In order to determine to what extent, if any, Campaign supporters differed from other young people in their public and private orientations, respondents were similarly asked to indicate which of the following issues they personally held to be of greatest importance:

settling down and raising a family
the plight of the hungry nations
finding oneself a good job
improving relations between the different races
enjoying oneself with friends
working for a more just and humane society

Respondents' personal and social priorities are illustrated in Table 21 opposite.

It is clear that young CND'ers were overwhelmingly more oriented to concerns of a public kind than to those of a more personal and private character. The matters which are felt to be of greatest moment to the bulk of young men and women, particularly marriage, family and career, were relegated by CND supporters to

[1] R. K. Goldsen, et al., *What College Students Think*, Van Nostrand, Princeton, 1960, p. 199.
[2] L. F. Douglas, *Types of Students and their Outlook on University Education*, Ph.D. thesis, London University, 1964. Compiled from p. 430.

TABLE 21   *Public vs. private orientations*

Most important issues	%
Working for a more just and humane society	39
Improving race relations	23
The plight of the hungry nations	15
Settling down and raising a family	6
Enjoying oneself with friends	5
Finding oneself a good job	4
Don't know/No response	8
	100 (N = 445)

a very definite second place, after the problems which confront society and the world at large. This does not necessarily mean of course that the more personal aspects of life are irrelevant and meaningless to CND supporters; undoubtedly they are caught up in these affairs much in the way that others of their age are. It is rather that, at this stage of their lives at least, they have a propensity to identify themselves emotionally with certain remote events as well, which most of their peers are less keenly sensitized to. Significantly, this particular disposition has been seen by some sociologists to be strongly associated with support for political mass movements. Kornhauser, in particular, has argued that individuals who relate themselves to large-scale social events, rather than to the more 'proximate' concerns of family, community, occupational group and so forth, may be more susceptible to the appeal of extremist politics.

Where proximate concerns are meaningful, people do not spend much time or energy seeking direct gratification from remote symbols. They may try to understand and influence the course of distant events, but they do so by means of and in relation to their face-to-face relations, at home, in the neighbourhood, at work, in their club or union, and so forth. But when these proximate relations fail to serve major interests or to provide personal gratifications, people are likely to turn away from their local world to the 'great society' in their search for new ways to satisfy their needs. . . . In the absence of proximate sources of gratification and restraint, individuals may become highly responsive to the appeal of mass movements bent on the transformation of the world.[1]

Whilst it may be true that an overriding concern with large scale societal issues in preference to more proximate and personal matters is conducive to recruitment to mass movements, it would be a harsh judgement which concluded that such an orientation is necessarily dangerous to democratic institutions and the liberal spirit. The ability to be moved by the plight of others, and a

[1] W. Kornhauser, op. cit., p. 60.

general concern for the improvement of man's lot, have after all inspired many of the great social reforms and movements of the past, and have been responsible for many of the freedoms and privileges of modern democratic society. Young CND supporters tended to be highly committed to a variety of humanitarian aims and activities, which were very much in this same tradition. They appeared to be more involved than adolescents in general in organizations such as Oxfam, and other famine relief groups, VSO, Adventure Playgrounds, anti-Apartheid and similar anti-racialist organizations, voluntary welfare agencies, and the like. It is difficult to see where these and similar humanitarian concerns would spring from if not from among those who faced outwards to society rather than inwards to a purely personal and private world. Indeed, privatization carries political dangers of its own, and does not automatically commend itself as the outlook best fitted to the young citizen—any more than the enervation of the radical temper would necessarily be the unmixed blessing suggested by the advocates of consensus politics.

CND and youth politics

So far in this chapter young CND supporters have been treated as a politically homogeneous category, united by a single attitude towards the Bomb. But the actual composition of the movement was of course somewhat more complex than this, especially in so far as members of various political youth organizations were represented in its ranks, providing different bases of commitment to its aims. It is therefore necessary to examine some of the ways in which these differences were expressed. To begin with, respondents were asked to specify which, if any, political organizations apart from CND they were members of; the replies they gave are shown in Table 22.

TABLE 22   *Membership in political organizations—CND youth*

	(N)	%
Young Socialists	105	24
Young Communist League	71	16
Anarchists	45	10
Other	24	5
None	200	45
	445	100

In all, 55 per cent of the sample were members of political groups well to the left of centre; there were only two Young Liberals and no Young Conservatives, although electoral supporters of these two parties were present among the remaining 45 per cent of 'non-politicals'. This rather large number involved in radical politics beyond CND is not perhaps surprising, although it does raise the question of whether support for the unilateralist movement was an outcome of such involvement or whether participation in the movement itself acted as a spur to wider political activity. Certainly this latter process was felt to be at work by political activists themselves who looked upon the Campaign as a fruitful source of recruitment. A commonly felt view among the latter was that young people's protest against the Bomb served to sensitize them to the problem of state power and other political realities in a way that could be usefully capitalized upon. Although it is always difficult to sort out the various factors which go towards shaping an individual's commitment to politics it does seem true to say that CND did in fact serve as a transmission belt into radical politics of a wider kind for some young people who might otherwise have held aloof. In the first place, among all those in the sample who were members of a political group, 62 per cent stated that they had joined *after* they had become involved in CND. Protest against the Bomb was, for many, their first major political experience, and one which thrust them dramatically into the midst of the ideas and personnel of the radical left.[1] And since many of the latter were deliberately engaged in the recruitment of young CND'ers to their own organizations it would have been surprising if no such transition had taken place. Although it is not possible to make any quantitative estimate of this process, the general sequence of events it comprised was made clear in the course of interviews with those who had been recruited to political groups via CND. A Young Communist League member described his own experience as follows:

I took part in CND for the first time in 1961. I hitch-hiked from Manchester to join the Aldermaston march—more out of curiosity than anything. My parents are completely unpolitical and thought I was crazy. I mixed with all sorts on the march—everyone had a different line and you didn't know who to believe. On the last day I met some people with a Manchester banner and they offered me a lift back in their coach. They turned out to be Communist Party members, and we discussed politics all the way back. I wasn't convinced by everything they said, but they invited me to come to some of their meetings. I went for about three months regularly. No one

---

[1] This was due partly of course to the absence of any age qualification involved in support for CND. The youth organizations of the political parties do not normally accept members below the age of 15, whereas it was not uncommon to find youngsters under this age in CND. Of the present sample, 55 per cent had been active in the Campaign from the age of 15 and below.

asked me to join anything, but gradually I came to see that they were talking more sense than anyone else. I joined the YCL and now I'm fairly active in the branch and in my union. I still go on CND marches but I'm not really active in the Campaign.[1]

A similar process of recruitment earned new members for the Young Socialists and the Anarchists; indeed, the actual group a previously non-committed youngster moved into seems often to have been a matter of chance contacts. The political transition of another, highly articulate, young man was described thus:

I first joined CND as a Baptist purely on the moral issues alone, not knowing or thinking much about the political and economic implications of the arms race. I was of the opinion that God wouldn't let 'them' use it anyway. Through talking to people in my local CND group and listening to the speakers at meetings I soon found it necessary not only to question my value judgements, but to rethink them entirely. I have therefore since become an atheist and a member of the Young Socialists. This transformation was mainly due to the people I met within CND, especially the local group who became my friends, and who eventually formed what you sociologists would call my peer group.

Sometimes the transition into radical politics via CND was a rather more complicated affair, with several stages involved, as the experience of an eighteen-year-old girl illustrates:

After being in the CND for some time, from the age of 15 in fact, I joined the Young Communists—mainly because the friends I'd made in CND were also in it. I was a moderately active member for a time, and also began to take part in Committee of 100 demonstrations. Since this was not compatible with the Party line I left and devoted myself to the Committee of 100. I was then very much influenced by the Anarchists in the Committee, and I now regard myself as a total Anarchist.

Clearly, then, the unilateralist movement did serve to baptize some young people into a wider political radicalism, and to provide the previously uncommitted with a definite ideology of one kind or another. At the same time, it would be unrealistic to suggest that experiences in CND were the main influences behind the membership of *most* young supporters in political organizations. Although, as we have seen, the majority of respondents joined such organizations subsequent to their participation in CND, there is little doubt that many, or perhaps most, would have done so if the unilateralist movement had not appeared on the scene, simply as a result of family influences guiding them in this direction.[2] This

[1] Kenneth Newton, currently studying membership of the British Communist Party, also states that several younger members he has interviewed entered the Party through CND (Ph.D., Cambridge, in preparation).

[2] Thus, Abrams and Little found that 4 out of 5 of their young activists came from families with a record of political activity. Abrams and Little, op. cit., p. 330.

is shown in the tendency for those respondents who were politically involved *before* joining CND to come more frequently from politically active homes than those who became involved only *after* their CND experiences. This suggests that the Campaign's stimulus to wider political activity was less important for those whose parents were themselves activists, than for those whose parents were politically apathetic.

In a sense, it could be said that where parental involvement in left-wing politics was weak, CND served as a substitute form of socialization into more radical ways. This would seem to be especially true of the Anarchists. Very few of the latter's parents were politically engaged—proportionately fewer in fact than the parents of the 'non-political' respondents. This, coupled with the fact that only 13 per cent of respondents were Anarchists *before* entering CND (the comparable figures for the Young Socialists and Young Communists being 37 per cent and 31 per cent respectively), does point very strongly to the independent influence of the Campaign in drawing them into the Anarchist movement.[1] The parents of Anarchists were very rarely themselves Anarchists, and would not therefore be in a position to influence their children's politics directly, in the way that Marxist and socialist parents have certainly done. It is interesting to note, too, that the parents of Anarchists were considerably less approving of CND than were the parents of members of the other two political groups. Indeed, *opposition* to parental views, rather than socialization into them, appears to be the distinguishing trait of Anarchist supporters. Their adherence to libertarianism and CND signifies a sharper deviance from parental views than that displayed by Young Socialists and Young Communists, who tend on the whole to be in conformity with their parents' outlook. Similarly, this greater degree of rebelliousness on the part of the Anarchists is matched by the fact that 20 per cent of them reported an authoritarian upbringing as against only 3 per cent of Young Socialists and 8 per cent of Young Communists. This may well indicate that young CND supporters who were in rebellion against their parents did not subsequently enter one of the three other political organizations on a completely random basis, but did in fact find themselves more attracted to the Anarchists—

---

[1] The importance of CND in introducing young people into the libertarian movement was often acknowledged by Anarchists themselves. CND officials were aware of this also. The North-West Regional Organizer, in the course of an interview, commented that the Manchester Anarchist group were continually poaching members from YCND branches in the district, and were much more of a threat in this respect than the Young Socialists or Young Communists.

perhaps because they were the most nihilistic and anti-authoritarian of the three, thereby serving the needs of the rebellious more adequately.

Education and radicalism

The central theme of this study has been that support for CND, and similar movements of a moralistic kind, represents a brand of radicalism which is distinctively middle class in character. We have seen that adult supporters of the movement were drawn predominantly from the ranks of the white collar and professional classes, and that manual workers were conspicuously under-represented. The question arises therefore as to whether a similar pattern of class representation is mirrored among younger CND supporters. The answer to this is set out in Table 23, showing respondents' social class as measured by father's occupation.

TABLE 23   *Social class of young CND respondents: by father's occupation*

Father's occupational category	%
1 + 2	32
3 + 4	30
5 + 6 + 7	33
Don't know/No response	5
	100 (N = 445)

62 per cent of respondents have middle class social origins as measured by the conventional criterion of father's occupational status. One third derive from working class backgrounds; it was more than twice as likely in fact that the father of a young CND supporter in the present sample would be of managerial, executive or professional status (1 + 2), than that he would be an unskilled or semi-skilled worker (6 + 7). The ideal-type young CND supporter could thus be said to come from a middle class home with radical leanings—having in essence the type of parents who share much in common with adult CND supporters. Although father's occupation is a useful index of a young person's social class, it needs to be supplemented with information about the class attributes and attainments of the individual himself. Since education plays a key role in the placement of individuals in the stratification order of industrial society, the type of secondary schooling received may be taken as a further indicator of class position—or at least potential class position—of respondents. The following table shows the type

of secondary education received by CND youths in comparison with that of young people in England and Wales in general.

TABLE 24   *Secondary education of CND youth*

	CND respondents	Population of England and Wales (aged 13 in 1956)
	%	%
Secondary Modern	14	65
Grammar	48	20
Technical	12	4
Comprehensive	9	1
Public	13	10
Other/No response	4	—
(N = 445)	100	100

Clearly, the type of secondary education enjoyed by CND youths was a good deal more favourable than that experienced by their peers in the country at large. Whereas 65 per cent of young people in the total population had received their education in the secondary modern schools, this fate had befallen only 14 per cent of CND respondents. Some 61 per cent of the latter had attended, or were at the time attending, grammar and public schools, in contrast to the 30 per cent of young people in England and Wales as a whole who had been to such schools. Since the grammar and public schools generally serve as avenues to universities and the professions, we may take this as additional evidence of the potential middle class status of the bulk of supporters. This point is more forcibly brought out when the present occupations of those between 18 and 25 years of age are examined, since this is a more decisive period in the determination of future life-chances. 73 per cent of the sample were in this age group, and their occupations are shown in Table 25.

TABLE 25   *Occupations of CND supporters between 18 and 25 years*

	%
Receiving full-time education	55
Non-manual occupation	32
Manual occupation	10
Other/No response	3
	100 (N = 327)

The majority of 18-plus respondents were receiving full-time education, either in the sixth forms of public and grammar schools, or in universities, CATs, Teacher Training Colleges, and similar institutions. Again, one need hardly stress the fact that this is greatly in excess of the proportion of young people as a whole undergoing full-time education at 18-plus, and is also greater than that of middle class youths in general. Similarly, among respondents of this age-group in full-time employment the number of those holding non-manual jobs considerably out-weighs the number in manual occupations. All in all, then, the predominantly middle class status of the respondents' parents has been more than adequately preserved by the respondents themselves—whether measured in terms of occupational or educational criteria.[1]

The high level of educational attainment typical of young CND supporters may be considered a further factor contributing to their radical disposition. The process of education is, among other things, one in which the cherished values and ideals of society are implanted in the young in a fairly systematic way, so that the longer an individual spends in formal education the more thorough this socialization process is likely to be. Those who have been exposed to higher education—at university in particular—are therefore liable to be more deeply imbued with society's highest ideals and values in their 'pure' form than are most individuals. Consequently, when adult society, and especially governments, fail to act in accordance with these ideals, but engage instead in compromise and concession, students are prone to exhibit radical reactions. The discrepancy between ideals and performance may seem all the more glaring and reprehensible to students in so far as they are not themselves embroiled in adult roles and responsibilities, with the need for compromise which this often entails. As Lipset has expressed it:

if some University students are inclined to be irresponsible with respect to the norms of adult society, they are also inclined to be idealistic. They have not established a sense of affinity with adult institutions; experience has not hardened them to imperfection. Their libidos are unanchored; their capacity for identification with categories of universal scope; with mankind or the oppressed or the poor and the miserable, is greater than it was earlier or than it will be in later life. Their contact with the articulated moral and political standards of their society is abstract; they encounter them as principles promulgated by older persons, as impositions by authority, rather than as maxims incorporated into and blurred by their own practice. . . .

---

[1] In view of the comparative success of young CND supporters in these two fields there would seem to be little basis for Professor Rex's contention that the Campaign tended to be an attraction to those resentful of the lack of education opportunities and the possibility of youth unemployment. See John Rex, 'The Sociology of CND', *War and Peace*, Jan.–March 1964, p. 54.

Educated young people everywhere, consequently tend disproportionately to support idealistic movements which take the ideologies or values of the adult world more seriously than does the adult world itself.[1]

Universities and similar institutes of higher learning provide a favourable milieu for those with nonconformist and radical views, and also help to generate such views through the educational process. That is to say, exposure to the liberating and critical influences of the universities can have the effect of creating liberal or radical dispositions in those of previously more orthodox or conservative outlook. This process has been demonstrated in a number of studies which have shown that students' political and social attitudes frequently undergo definite changes with exposure to university education, and that these changes are almost always in a leftward direction, indicating a tendency to adopt a more critical or detached attitude towards established values. Selvin and Hagstrom, for example, in their study of Berkeley students' attitudes to civil liberties showed that 'Libertarianism increases steadily from year to year among the undergraduates. The proportion highly libertarian almost doubles, from 21 per cent among the first year students to 40 per cent in the last year, and the proportion only slightly libertarian drops from 32 per cent to 14 per cent in the same period.'[2] Graduate students proved to be most libertarian of all, some 54 per cent of the total sample falling into the highly libertarian category. The authors point to the fact, too, that it is the most academically successful students who tend to increase in libertarianism, and suggest that this process is the result of accumulated learning. Lipset, in an earlier study of Berkeley students' attitudes towards the 'loyalty oath' controversy, reported similar findings. It was again the senior and graduate students who held the most radical and liberal views and whose opposition to the loyalty oath was strongest.[3] Lipset suggests that this could be explained by the greater exposure of these students to the libertarian outlook of university teachers. The more junior students would not have been socialized to the same extent into the social and political values dominant in the academic community, but would still have adhered to the more illiberal views commonly held outside the university.

[1] S. M. Lipset, 'University Students and Politics in Under-Developed Countries,' *Minerva*, **3**, Autumn 1964, p. 31.
[2] Hanan C. Selvin and Warren O. Hagstrom, 'Determinants of Support for Civil Liberties,' *British Journal of Sociology*, **11**, March 1960, p. 58.
[3] S. M. Lipset, 'Opinion Formation in a Crisis Situation', *Public Opinion Quarterly*, **17**, Spring 1953.

M

The evidence for Britain points in a similar direction. As a number of studies have shown, there is a significantly greater tendency for members of the middle class who have undergone higher education to vote for parties of the left, than is the case among those whose education ended in the grammar or public school.[1] Abrams' survey of middle class political attitudes, carried out in the early nineteen-sixties, showed that of respondents from what he classified the 'Upper Middle Class' and 'Middle Middle Class', only 9 per cent of Conservative supporters were university graduates, as compared with 26 per cent of Labour supporters. Similarly, among the 'Lower Middle Class' sample, only 2 per cent of Conservative supporters were graduates, as against 9 per cent of Labour supporters. Of all Lower Middle Class university graduates 33 per cent were Labour voters.[2] Concerning students specifically, Richard Rose demonstrated a greater degree of political support for the Left among Manchester University undergraduates than was found among their parents.[3] Whereas their parents were predominantly Conservative, the students themselves were more evenly divided—34 per cent being Labour supporters and 33 per cent Conservative. University life was shown to have greater corrosive effects on the political loyalties of those from Conservative homes than on those from Labour homes. Of students with Labour fathers, 70 per cent themselves supported Labour, whereas of students with Conservative fathers, only 51 per cent also supported the Conservatives. This shift to the left which university experience stimulates among middle class students who enter higher education with the inherited Conservatism of their parents is also confirmed by a survey of Nottingham University undergraduates. Barnes and Paton, in their 1962 study, reported that 51 per cent of first-year students supported the Conservatives, and 21 per cent Labour, whereas among third-year students support for the Conservatives fell to 45 per cent, and support for Labour rose to 37 per cent.[4]

---

[1] Cf. Richard Rose, *Politics in England*, Faber, 1965, p. 69. Also, 'How Much Education Makes a Tory?', *New Society*, 1 November 1962.

[2] Mark Abrams, 'Politics and the British Middle Class', *Socialist Commentary*, October 1962, pp. 5–9.

[3] Richard Rose, 'Students and Society', *New Society*, 2 January 1964, p. 22.

[4] Neil Barnes and George Paton, 'Redbrick Student', *Socialist Commentary*, November 1962, pp. 23–6. Eysenck found in his study of political attitudes in the middle class that university-trained socialists were 'very significantly more radical than the non-university trained'. H. J. Eysenck, 'Primary Social Attitudes—1: The Organization and Measurement of Social Attitudes', *International Journal of Opinion and Attitude Research*, 1, September 1947, p. 68.

The authors state that, in all, one-fifth of Nottingham students reported a change in political allegiance since entering the university, and of these three times as many had moved Left as had moved Right.

The disparate pieces of evidence brought together here, then, do appear to support the contention that higher education has something of a radicalizing effect on many of those who experience it. It would seem that those who have been exposed to a rigorous intellectual regime are somewhat less likely to give automatic endorsement to the conventional political and social attitudes commonly held among the middle classes. The great majority of the latter have not been educated beyond the grammar or public school level, and would not have had their accepted values and standards seriously challenged or questioned as a part of the learning process. Secondary education can, by and large, be characterized as the absorption of received information; the presentation of knowledge is given a heavy 'factual' bias, in contrast to the doubts, ambiguities and conflicting views surrounding any given subject with which the university student is confronted. Whereas education in the grammar and public schools may be thought of as a straightforward socialization process into middle-class norms and values, higher education—particularly at university—can be conceived of, in part at least, as a 'de-socialization' process in so far as it inculcates a questioning and critical attitude to certain values which the average middle-class student would previously have taken for granted. Extended exposure to the educational system could thus be said to socialize the young more thoroughly into the society's abstract ideals—such as 'democracy', 'equality', 'freedom', and the like— while at the same time creating a sharper awareness of the apparent discrepancies between these ideals and actual realities. It is not therefore surprising that movements like CND should draw so heavily from among those with high educational attainments.

The tendency for advanced education to make inroads upon young people's acceptance of middle class political values is more marked in some fields of study than others. In general, the process would seem to be especially marked in the social sciences and humanities, and least so in fields like engineering, technology and other applied sciences. Rose, for example, in his previously cited study, found that among Manchester students, engineers supported the Conservatives by a ratio of 2 : 1, while social scientists supported Labour by a ratio of 3 : 1.[1] Selvin and Hagstrom similarly showed that at

[1] Rose, op. cit.

Berkeley, men in the social sciences and humanities were about twice as likely to be highly libertarian as those in engineering, education and business administration.[1] The data on CND respondents conform to the same overall pattern; of those in higher education, 70 per cent were specializing in either humanities or social sciences, while only 17 per cent were in pure or applied sciences. This relationship between politics and field of study is partly explained by the fact that those who opt for subjects which encourage intellectual criticism and social analysis are often already sympathetic to the liberal or nonconformist outlook *before* entering university. Thus, of those CND'ers still in sixth forms who indicated an intention to enter further education the same heavy bias in favour of the humanities and social sciences was present, suggesting that the process of self-selection was already at work. But even so, granted some degree of self-selection among young radicals, it is still the case that these particular fields of study do independently foster the kind of attitude disposition which has much in common with the middle-class radical outlook, as is attested by the leftward swing of students in these subjects during their stay at university. This is of course one of the main reasons why universities and colleges were chief sources of CND support, since these were the milieux which encouraged the type of intellectual and moral attitudes which lay at the centre of the Campaign's appeal. Sociology students, in particular, appear to have been especially well-disposed to CND, and frequently provided the leadership and organizational core within universities. This was often true of sociology teachers too. In London and the provinces, sociology teachers played a noticeably prominent role in mobilizing student opinion behind CND on a national and local basis. It would seem in fact that support for CND during its peak years was almost a culturally prescribed norm among large sections of the student body, and one that was given additional legitimacy through its acceptance by prestige and authority figures among the academic staff. It would not be stretching matters too much to suggest that in these particular settings, opposition to CND would have been almost a deviant stance to take and one that might have been difficult to sustain in the face of reference group pressures.[2] How-

[1] Selvin and Hagstrom, op. cit., For similar findings see Douglas, op. cit., also Sanford, *The American College*, Wiley, New York, 1962.

[2] On the importance of university reference groups in encouraging a leftward shift among students, see T. Newcomb, 'Attitude Development as a Function of Reference Groups: The Bennington Study', in E. E. Maccoby, et al., *Readings in Social Psychology*, Methuen, 1961.

ever much the unilateralist movement may have been unfavourably regarded by the public at large, therefore, this would have had little effect on its standing among students, since the latter's normative frame of reference would be the distinctively liberal and tolerant one of the academic community. It could be said in fact that university and college settings gave students a certain degree of immunity from the adverse opinions of CND held by the public at large. To this extent students were better provided than most other sectors of the population with the social and psychological buttresses necessary to sustain a commitment to public non-conformity, which may be suggested as a further reason why the student presence was always a readily identifiable feature of any CND activity.

In conclusion, it is instructive to contrast the activities of young CND supporters with more common forms of deviance amongst the young—most obviously the increasing tendency towards juvenile delinquency. Although delinquency is a more characteristic outlet for youthful non-conformity than political radicalism, it is a pattern most commonly associated with lower status groups in society. Theories of juvenile delinquency frequently make use of Merton's paradigm of deviance, which points up the discrepancy in achievement-oriented societies between the institutionalized goals of success and material rewards and the limited means of attaining them. Delinquency is conceived of partly as an alternative to the achievement of desired objects by legitimate means, and partly as a response to the frustrations imposed upon the young members of lower status groups by an inegalitarian educational and occupational system. The sporadic outbreaks of teenage violence and the more regular occurrence of crimes against property are perhaps inevitable forms of deviance among working class youth marked out by society from an early age as 'failures'.

Young CND supporters, by contrast, are characterized by their success in the educational system, with all that this implies in terms of future occupational attainments and income and status rewards. Deviance on their part thus expresses itself not as a reaction against social and material deprivation, but against society's failure to live up to certain professed ideals in other spheres. Ironically enough, although the economic and status positions of young CND'ers are on the whole assured by their educational attainments, their exposure to this system—higher education in particular—has rendered them highly critical of the discrepancy between society's ideals and practices. Philip Abrams has argued this point as follows:

The school-leaver most likely to disaffiliate himself spiritually or politically from adult society is not the one who is not bothered about society but the one who has been too effectively taught, who has really taken over the values of democracy and intellectual independence as his or her own and who is forced on looking at the world to recognize the gulf between those values and most of what actually goes on. . . . It is the child in whom the overt aims of education, liberal values, critical intelligence and an understanding of society are actually achieved who repudiates society as it is; the educational failures, conversely, contribute simply to its maintenance . . .

In so far as we do teach children about their society in ways that realize the educationalist's professed aims we are going to produce impassioned critics of society, 'irresponsible beatniks', 'marchers', 'socialist fanatics' and so forth.[1]

Thus, whilst high educational achievement may serve to prevent adolescents and young adults from engaging in deviant behaviour of the delinquent kind, it tends to foster instead the kind of spirit which is conducive to the radical appeal of movements like CND. This is perhaps a measure of the extent to which successful middle class youths are able to identify with their society and its fortunes and values, in contrast to the less privileged whose own social and moral integration is more problematic. For, as has been suggested in an earlier chapter, to protest against the government's defence policy and international conduct is in a sense to state one's ego-involvement with British society; and it is understandable that individuals who feel this degree of self-identity with society are more liable to be drawn from the ranks of those who have won an acceptable place within it, than from among those who feel they have much less to be grateful for.

[1] Philip Abrams, 'Notes on the Uses of Ignorance', *Twentieth Century*, Autumn 1963, pp. 76–7.

8

The occupational location of
middle class radicals

The educated middle class

Throughout this study frequent use has been made of the term 'middle class' to describe the social composition of CND. Although this is a convenient shorthand description of a particular segment of society, and of heuristic value for the illumination of certain sociological problems, it lacks the analytical precision necessary for considering issues which cannot be posed in terms of class polarization. The concept of the middle class is useful mainly in making contrasts with other social strata, particularly of course the working class. However, it is obviously of little help when the focus of attention shifts to questions concerning differences within the non-manual stratum itself. It then becomes an inconvenient blanket term concealing certain crucial distinctions between white collar groups which it is necessary to make in handling some kinds of problems. As far as the present study is concerned, it seemed apparent at an early stage in the research, largely on impressionistic grounds, that CND supporters were not drawn randomly from all sections of the middle class, but tended to be concentrated heavily in certain occupational fields. These initial impressions were later worked into more rigorous propositions which could be tested by data from the questionnaires, and the discussion of which forms the main subject matter of this final chapter.

Before confronting these issues head-on, however, it may be useful to introduce here some factual material relating to the educational standards of CND respondents, which has a bearing on the discussion which follows. It was seen of the young CND supporters considered in Chapter 7 that their educational standards were well above average for the population of their age, and even above those for the middle class considered separately. The immediate question of interest was whether adult supporters would be more typical of their class as a whole in their level of educational achievement, bearing in mind that most would have completed their secondary education before the reforms introduced by the 1944 Education Act had come into effect. Tables 26, 27 and 28 show that adult respondents are also an exceptionally well-educated group, another feature which distinguishes them from the bulk of the middle class.

TABLE 26   *Secondary schooling*

	%
Secondary Modern/Elementary	20
Technical	6
Grammar	47
Public/Boarding	21
Other	3
No response	3
	100 (N = 358)

Thus, 68 per cent had attended grammar school, or one of its private equivalents. Only one fifth of respondents had attended secondary modern school—fewer in fact than the number attending public or boarding schools. In line with this finding is the information concerning terminal education age.

TABLE 27   *Terminal education age*

	%
15 and below	25
16–18	30
19 and over	43
No response	2
	100 (N = 358)

Only a quarter of respondents terminated their education at the age of 15 or earlier, in comparison with over 80 per cent of the population at large. Similar large scale discrepancies occur in the field of further education.

TABLE 28   *Further education*

	%
Teacher Training	11
CAT	3
University	30
Other	10
None	44
No response	2
	100 (N = 358)

A total of 54 per cent of respondents had had some form of higher education, either at a university, teacher-training college, a CAT, or a college of art, music, architecture, and the like. This figure is well in excess of that for the middle class as a whole. The Robbins Report showed that of the young post-war middle class (i.e. children of non-manual workers) 12 per cent had taken degree courses, 7·5 per cent had had some other type of full-time education, and 5·5 per cent had experienced part-time further education, a total of 25 per cent.[1] Since these figures refer to the educational standards of young middle class men and women who had benefited from the 1944 reforms, the overall higher achievements of the adult CND sample is all the more striking.

One may then say of CND supporters that they are drawn not simply from the middle class, but from the ranks of the *educated middle class*. This introduces the first of the distinctions necessary for breaking down the classification of 'middle class' into more useful research categories. The concept of the educated middle class

[1] *Report of the Committee on Higher Education*, HMSO, 1963, Appendix 1, Table 1, p. 39. 61 per cent of adult CND respondents were over the age of 40, and would have completed their education before the end of the war.

would appear to be a viable one in so far as it denotes a social segment which may be shown to have behavioural characteristics noticeably at variance with the overall middle class pattern. Evidence available from a variety of sources appears to support this contention. In the field of politics for example, as we saw in the previous chapter, the non-manual sector as a whole gives heavy backing to the parties of the Right, whereas those of highest educational standards, and particularly university graduates, are significantly less inclined to do so; proportionately they are much more liable to support left-wing parties than those of similar status but less education. Similarly, Stouffer's research on civil liberties in the United States shows that level of education is the best single predictor of political tolerance and liberalism, and one that points up significant differences of outlook between the well educated and the less educated members of the middle class.[1] Again, in the field of religion there is a greater tendency for middle class individuals exposed to higher education to shed their beliefs than among those not so exposed.[2] The reason for the propensity of the educated middle class to exhibit somewhat different behavioural traits to non-manuals in general is perhaps, as already suggested, related to the 'liberalizing' effects of higher education, particularly in its emphasis on the adoption of analytical attitudes and a questioning frame of mind. The argument was advanced in Chapter 2 that British society, as indeed any industrial society, could be said to have certain values which occupied a dominant position in the normative order, in the sense that they were the values upheld by the major institutions of society. While there is an overall tendency for acceptance of these values to be more complete among higher social strata than among lower, it seems clear that exposure to certain forms of advanced education has the effect of undermining such total acceptance among middle class members. To this extent, it could be said that the minority of the non-manual stratum which has undergone formal intellectual training beyond the sixth form constitutes a permanent source of potential opposition to certain commonly accepted socio-political values, and therefore provides also a source of potential recruits to movements like CND.

[1] Samuel A. Stouffer, *Communism, Conformity and Civil Liberties*, Wiley, New York, 1955.

[2] See H. Webster et al., 'Personality Changes in College Students', in N. Sanford, *College and Character*, Wiley, New York, 1964. It is significant in this respect that the British Humanists are also mainly members of the educated middle class. See Colin B. Campbell, 'Membership Composition of the British Humanist Association', *Sociological Review*, November 1965.

There is, however, an additional reason why this segment of the middle class might be expected to be more amenable to the appeals of radicalism, apart from the liberalizing influence of education. The educated middle class is that stratum whose social position and life chances rest primarily upon its intellectual attainments and professional qualifications, and not upon the ownership of property or inherited wealth. They represent in advanced form the new and expanding professional and scientific middle classes brought into being by the increasing rationalization and bureaucratization of modern industrial society, and whose status positions are not dependent upon wealth or capital ownership. The educational system has for them provided the means for achieving high placement and social and economic security which property provided for the traditional middle class. This independence from property ownership in the achievement of high social status may be considered as one important factor which, although it cannot of course be said necessarily to generate a predisposition to radicalism, could be held to be one necessary for its emergence. By contrast, those whose class position rests primarily on the exercise of property rights or inherited wealth are liable to be least disposed to a political outlook which deviates from the Conservative norm. The political values of the Right, with their strong emphasis on the sanctity of private property, carry an obvious imperative for this segment of the middle class to an extent which they do not for the professional and technical middle class. The latter are in a sense 'freer' in their choice of political allegiance in so far as their talents and expertise are at a premium in highly industrialized societies, and their rewards and privileges more or less guaranteed, no matter what the reigning political ideology. Property ownership on the other hand lacks this functional necessity; it is much more of an arbitrary value whose legitimacy and usefulness can be questioned in a way that the technicians' and the professional experts' cannot. Under these circumstances, conservative political values represent the only real safeguard for those whose social and material security rests upon property.

For these reasons, then, the main basis of support for CND is located mainly in the educated middle classes with professional or scientific training of one kind or another. However, this is still a fairly large and heterogeneous category which may be narrowed down further still. It is possible to do this by drawing a distinction between those professional employees who are engaged (1) in the world of business and commerce—for example in accounting, insurance, banking, sales, marketing, personnel and managerial or supervisory posts in business enterprises; and (2) those engaged in the welfare and creative professions—for example, social work, medical services, teaching, the church, journalism, art, architecture, scientific research, and so on. The latter are occupations in which there is a primary emphasis upon either the notion of service to the community, human betterment or welfare and the like, or upon self-expression and creativity. The former type occupations, on the other hand, are set in the framework of values of the business world, with its over-riding concern with profitability and efficiency, and whose rewards are primarily of a material kind. Parsons has referred to this distinction as follows:

> the dominant keynote of the modern economic system is almost universally held to be the high degree of free play it gives to the pursuit of self interest. It is the 'acquisitive society', or the 'profit system' as two of the most common formulas run. But by contrast with business in this interpretation the professions are marked by 'disinterestedness'. The professional man is not thought of as engaged in the pursuit of his personal profit, but in performing services to his patients or clients, or to impersonal values like the advancement of science.[1]

It was hypothesized that middle class CND supporters would be located predominantly in the welfare and creative professions, and only minimally in the commercial professions. The following table shows the occupations of the 163 male respondents in classes 1 to 4, divided into these two major categories and one residual category.

TABLE 29   *Occupational breakdown of middle class males*

Commercial		Welfare and creative		Other	
Office Managers and		Schoolteachers	40	Engineers and	
Supervisors	8	Clergymen	11	Draughtsmen	10
Advertising & Sales	8	Physicians	10	Civil Servants	
Accounting & Banking	4	Scientists	10	and LGOs	9
Company Directors	3	Architects	9	TU & Co-op	7
Self employed	8	University and		Mature students	2
		College lecturers	8		
		Social Workers	5		
		Journalists	5		
		Artists/Novelists	3		
		MPs	2		
		Librarians	1		
	31		104		28

[1] Talcott Parsons, *Essays in Sociological Theory*, Free Press, Glencoe, 1964, p. 35.

As expected, the heaviest concentration was in professional occupations of the welfare and creative variety, with teaching as the dominant example; clergymen, medical and social workers, architects and scientists were also well represented. Although the various professional, managerial and white-collar posts of a commercial kind are key areas of employment for middle class males in the country at large, only a comparatively small minority of the CND sample were to be found in them.[1]

Occupation and political values

One type of explanation for the clustering of middle class radicals in this particular range of professions is that which posits a causal relationship between occupational values and political outlook. Some writers have suggested that certain professions inculcate in their members a set of values and attitudes which have implications beyond the occupational sphere—not least in the field of politics. Glazer, for example, in his analysis of the membership of the American Communist Party, found that disproportionately large numbers were drawn from the professions of teaching, librarianship and social work. He explains this by suggesting that these occupations, particularly social work and teaching, confront their members with an awareness of pressing social problems (which most middle class people have little first hand experience of) so creating attitudes favourable to programmes of social change and political reform.[2] Similarly, CND supporters often formed themselves into occupational groups of various kinds—teachers' section, architects' group, social workers' group, etc.—which frequently justified their support for the movement in terms of the compatibility between its goals and the humanistic values of their respective professions.[3]

A somewhat different slant on the relationship between occupation and politics, and one which has sparked off some controversy in sociology, is that entailed in Lenski's concept of status crystallization. Lenski, in a series of papers, has suggested that the relationship between social stratification and political behaviour is

[1] Because so many of the female respondents classified themselves as housewives or part-time workers it was decided not to include them in the table. However, amongst those who were employed, a pattern similar to that of male respondents was found—with teaching again being by far the commonest occupation.

[2] Nathan Glazer, *The Social Basis of American Communism*, Harcourt Brace, New York, 1961, pp. 138–48.

[3] For example, the statement by a group of CND social workers that 'We believe that many social workers, who protest as individuals against the envisaged use of nuclear weapons will feel as we do that their personal beliefs are inseparable from their attitude to human beings which leads them to be social workers.' *New Statesman*, 27 June 1959, p. 895.

most usefully seen not so much as a function of the individual's class position in a vertical hierarchy of material and status rewards, as of the degree of congruence or incongruence between the various key statuses which any individual holds in a complex society. Briefly, Lenski's hypothesis is that individuals whose different statuses (e.g. ethnic, occupational, economic, educational) are out of line with one another, in the sense that they rank high on one but low on others, will be more inclined to endorse left of centre political attitudes than those whose various statuses are roughly congruent in their rank order.[1]

Apparently the individual with a poorly crystallized status is a particular type of marginal man, and is subjected to certain pressures by the social order which are not felt (at least to the same degree) by individuals with a more highly crystallized status. . . . In recent years political observers have reported relatively strong support for liberal political programmes from such diverse groups as college professors, Jewish businessmen, Hollywood actors and the Protestant clergy. All four of these categories of persons, it must be noted, are characterized by a relatively low degree of status crystallization. Professors and clergymen enjoy high occupational and educational rank, yet their income is sometimes less than that of skilled manual workers. Screen stars frequently combine high income rank with low educational rank, and sometimes with low ethnic rank as well. Jewish businessmen combine high income and occupational rank (and often high educational rank) with low ethnic rank. If the foregoing analysis is sound, one would be led to expect a relatively high frequency of liberal biases among the members of such groups, and for the same fundamental reasons.[2]

The relevance of this argument to the problem under review is clear enough. It suggests that a further cause of radicalism among the 'lower professional' or welfare occupations in which CND adults are predominantly found may be traced to the discrepancy between their high educational status and low economic status. It is characteristic of these occupations that they demand fairly high educational qualifications as a condition of entry, but that in comparison with white-collar occupations in the business and commer-

[1] Gerhard E. Lenski, 'Status Crystallization: A Non-Vertical Dimension of Social Status', *American Sociological Review*, **19**, August 1954.
[2] Op. cit., p. 412. For attempted refinements of Lenski's theory see R. E. Mitchell, 'Methodological Notes on a Theory of Status Crystallization', *Public Opinion Quarterly*, Summer 1964; also, Edward E. Sampson, 'Status Congruence and Cognitive Consistency', *Sociometry*, **26**, June 1963; A. C. Brandon, 'Status Congruence and Expectations', *Sociometry*, **28**, September 1965. For general critiques of Lenski's approach see W. F. Kenkel, 'The Relationship Between Status Consistency and Politico-Economic Attitudes', *American Sociological Review*, **21**, June 1956; also K. D. Kelly and W. J. Chambliss, 'Status Consistency and Political Attitudes', *American Sociological Review*, **31**, June 1966.

cial world they command relatively low salaries. Indeed, it is commonly argued that the salaries of those in welfare professions *should* be comparatively low, in order that the 'right sort' of people be attracted to them, and not those mainly concerned with material rewards. It may be suggested that the attempt to justify the lower incomes derived from this type of work by stressing its 'vocational' aspects does to some extent reflect the priorities inherent in industrial societies, priorities which favour higher rewards to those involved in the productive sphere than to those far removed from this sphere. Although this might be said to be a characteristic of all industrial societies because of the high premium placed on material production, it is perhaps especially true of capitalist type societies because of their somewhat greater tendency to relate rewards to some criterion of profitability. Judged in these terms, professions like teaching, social work, the church and so on, are inevitably less well rewarded than those white-collar occupations requiring the same, or even lower, educational standards, but which are more closely involved in material production or commercial gain. An interpretation of this kind seems warranted in the light of Hodge's comparison of the average incomes of occupational groups in the United States in relation to their incumbents' educational status. He showed that business managers were far more likely than professional workers to be receiving incomes in excess of that which could be expected on the basis of their level of education—suggesting that white-collar rewards were differentially allocated in favour of those in the commercial and production sectors.[1] The growing discontent with salaries expressed among welfare professions in Britain in recent years—the schoolteachers in particular—suggests that the disparity between rewards and education in this sector of the middle class is becoming more acutely felt. Discontent has been voiced not only at low salaries but at what has been felt to be the generally depressed level of facilities and services available for carrying out professional duties—again in contrast with those commonly provided in commercial organizations. In social work

Working conditions are bad. Hours are too long, with little organized compensation for evening work. . . . In many agencies, offices and waiting rooms are uncomfortably furnished and in dingy surroundings. There is a serious lack of modern aids such as dictaphones, and often inadequate clerical assistance. If these were common features of commercial organizations they would soon cease to make profits.[2]

---

[1] Robert W. Hodge, 'The Status Consistency of Occupational Groups', *American Sociological Review*, **27**, June 1962.

[2] John Haines. 'Satisfaction in Social Work', *New Society*, 5 January 1967, p. 18.

Schoolteachers, too, have with increasing frequency drawn attention to the unfavourable conditions in their own work situation—crowded classrooms, old buildings, lack of amenities, and so on—which, like their salaries, seem to compare badly with those of business enterprises. Linked with this is the fact that teachers tend to be more radical in politics than most other sectors of the middle class—one manifestation of which is the growing militancy of their trade unions in recent times. This is also displayed in teachers' attitudes towards a variety of social and political attitudes, as recorded in the *New Society* survey of readers' opinions.[1] Rachel Powell, in her secondary analysis of the published tables, found that 'teachers are way out on a limb, and, in comparison with other groups occupy an exposed radical position'.[2] She pointed out that, concerning issues which lent themselves to the adoption of a radical or conservative position, 'over the whole complex of socio-political questions, the teachers maintain a leftward displacement of round about 5 per cent . . . . Where social workers tend to divide in proportion of 4–1 against the bomb, and 6–1 against hanging, teachers . . . are 6–1 against bombs, 7–1 against hanging.'[3] The contrast between teachers and other middle class occupational groups was of course even greater.[4]

Thus, given the discrepancy between material and educational statuses which characterizes so many of the service professions, and given the relationship between status inconsistency and radicalism posited by Lenski, the fact that these professions provide the bulk of CND supporters appears readily explained. However, although it may be the case that the conflicting expectation deriving from status inconsistency may predispose some members of the service professions to adopt a more radical outlook than that commonly found among the middle class as a whole, it seems unlikely that this is the main explanation for the concentration of CND'ers in these occupations. An alternative and more satisfactory hypothesis may be suggested; namely, that middle class radicals are necessarily

[1] R. P. Kelvin, 'What Sort of People', *New Society*, 16 and 23 May 1963.

[2] 'Are Teachers Radical?' *New Society*, 30 May 1963, p. 28.

[3] Loc. cit.

[4] Interestingly enough, the tendency for teachers to combine professional status with left-wing views appears to be acknowledged by the public at large in the uncertain political image they have of this occupational group. Birch, in his study of politics in Glossop, recorded that his respondents expressed marked uncertainty about the political party which teachers were thought to vote for—in contrast to the fairly definite views they held about the conservative allegiances of other professional groups. A. H. Birch, *Small Town Politics*, Oxford, 1959, p. 90.

highly selective in their choice of occupation, and that the welfare professions provide the kind of milieux most amenable to their political orientations. That is, the connection between these particular occupations and political radicalism is to be explained not in terms of the strains created by status inconsistency, nor as a result of individuals adopting the humanistic values generated within the professions, but rather as a result of the tendency for individuals who are *already* radical to enter these fields of employment rather than others. As a number of writers have demonstrated, men are strongly motivated to seek out occupations which are most compatible with the values they hold at a more general level. As Morris Rosenberg has put it:

Whenever an individual makes a selection from a given number of alternatives, it is likely that some value is behind the decision. An occupational choice is not a value, but it is made on the basis of values. . . . When an individual chooses an occupation, he thinks there is something 'good' about it, and this conception of the 'good' is part of an internalized mental structure which establishes priorities regarding what he wants out of life. To ask what an individual wants out of his work is to a large extent to ask what he wants out of his life.[1]

Rosenberg isolated two distinct and opposing sets of attitudes which correlated both with occupational choice and political outlook. Individuals who scored high on a 'faith in people' scale, i.e. those who expressed high confidence in the honesty, goodness and trustworthiness of people in general, were prone to select occupations of the type referred to above as having a welfare or creative bias; they were characterized as being 'people oriented' and tended to devalue the notion of success and personal advancement. Those who scored low on this scale were more prone to prefer occupations in sales, finance, advertising, and the general field of business and commerce, and to put great stress on the importance of 'getting ahead'. Again, those who expressed high 'faith in people' were also much more liberal in their political attitudes than those low on the scale, displaying views on racial discrimination, nuclear weapons and civil liberties similar to those held by CND supporters.[2] It seems clear, then, that on *a priori* grounds middle class radicals could be expected to enter those occupations which they felt to be most compatible with their political and social outlook. And as Rosenberg's study, as well as the actual location of CND supporters, confirms, these

---

[1] Morris Rosenberg, *Occupations and Values*, Free Press, Glencoe, 1957, p. 6.
[2] Rosenberg, op. cit., pp. 25–35; see also, Rose K. Goldsen, *What College Students Think*, Van Nostrand, New York, 1960, pp. 23–59 and pp. 148–52.

N

are primarily the professions with a heavy welfare or creative bias. It would be especially important for radicals to enter occupational fields in which there was a greater emphasis on community service or creativity than on material success or 'getting ahead'. This, apart from other factors, could be expected to arise from the disadvantages which radicals would probably face in a competitive situation with more orthodox rivals. Recent studies of large organizations have drawn attention to managements' increasing concern with the private lives of employees when considering them for positions of responsibility.[1] Bearing in mind the general political ethos surrounding top management it seems unlikely that an employee known to be involved in CND would not be at a disadvantage with his peers in the race for promotion. Handicaps of this kind entailed in being a known radical were sometimes made explicit by respondents themselves, as some of the following extracts from the questionnaires make clear:

After many controversial activities I received a firm 'certainly not' from the editor of a local evening newspaper in reply to my job application. He is of course totally antagonistic to CND. (Journalist, Lancashire.)

A hostile headmaster resorted to unprofessional conduct in order to have me reprimanded by the school governors. (Secondary Modern teacher, Herts.)

I believe, and indeed I know unofficially, that my radical opinions have completely negated my advancement. I have no regrets—indeed I expected this. (Engineering Draughtsman, Harlow.)

I was seen by my matron in a demonstration. She did not wish to know me after that. (Nurse, North London.)

I have been absent without leave twice as a result of having been arrested and having to attend magistrates' court next morning. My boss dictated a letter (which I typed!) reprimanding me and making vague threats about what might happen if I did it again. (Secretary, North London.)

I was called a coward when the matter arose during an interview for another job. (Dairy Inspector, Somerset.)

Other respondents reported minor upsets with their employers which, though not serious enough to lead to their dismissal, nevertheless made working life a little more difficult. Some also declared that they were careful not to mention their politics at work for fear of adverse repercussions. Having said this, however, it should be emphasized that the great majority of respondents stated that they had experienced no difficulties whatsoever in this respect, even when their views and activities were fully known to their employers. In a few cases their politics put them at a slight advantage:

[1] W. H. Whyte, *The Organization Man*, Doubleday, New York, 1956.

The principal of the local Training College heard me lecture to CND on genetics, then invited me to join the staff part-time. (Lecturer, Herts.)

The owner of the paper I work on is a Labour Councillor, and his wife is a prospective Party candidate; both active in CND. (Journalist, Cumberland.)

Science fiction and radical or progressive views are highly compatible and I have even managed to sell stories set in a unilaterally disarmed Britain. (Writer, Hampstead.)

The fact that most respondents were not felt to be at a handicap as a result of their political views and activities would appear to confirm the suggestion that they were in the main in occupations which did not conflict with these. In other words, CND supporters are clustered in a comparatively narrow range of occupations not simply because of a preference for 'people-oriented' work but also because these are the occupations in which their political radicalism entails least disadvantage. Discrimination against known radicals, although potentially liable in almost any occupation, is obviously likely to be least in those spheres of employment which embody values not sharply at variance with left-wing politics. This is perhaps a round-about way of saying that the occupational location of radicals results from their desire to avoid direct implication in the capitalist economic system. Whilst it is true to say that the notion of capitalism generally implies not merely a particular type of economy but an entire social system, it is nevertheless within the framework of economic relationships that the defining characteristics of the system are at their most intrusive. The fields of commerce and private industrial enterprise are almost synonymous with capitalism in a way that teaching, medical and social work, scientific research and the like are not. The political radical's involvement in one of these latter occupations would therefore be a way of escaping direct implication in capitalist economic relations. One could say in fact that the professions serve as a kind of 'sanctuary' for the middle class radical in that they allow him to achieve a high degree of self-identification with his work without creating serious strains between his personal and occupational values such as would be set up if he worked directly in the sphere of business enterprise.

This distinction between professional and commercial worlds, useful as it is, cannot be made too clear cut, however, because of the increasing tendency for professional workers to become employees in commercial enterprises. Nevertheless, the fact that their general orientations remain crucially different is demonstrated by the conflicts to which such employees are exposed due to the contradictory demands of commercial and professional life. Scientists in private industry, for example, are generally under pressure to give priority to the immediate commercial possibilities of their research rather than to its purely theoretical aspects as required by the values of science. This situation, as a number of recent studies have shown, tends to result in serious tensions between scientists and managers. Kornhauser has put the argument in a nutshell:

Professional science favors contributions to knowledge rather than to profits; high quality research rather than low-cost research; long range programs rather than short term results; and so on. Industrial organization favors research services to operations and commercial development of research. These differences breed conflict of values and goals.[1]

That professional employees are often to be found in commercial settings does to some extent cut into the argument presented above, in that professional values may be tempered by commercial pressures, so rendering their practitioners less immune to the ethic and atmosphere of the business world than was suggested. It is therefore not sufficient to claim merely that middle class radicals will be found in the professions as a sanctuary shielding them from direct involvement in capitalism (narrowly defined) since professional workers are increasingly found in the employment of private industry. Instead, it must further be predicted that radicals will seek to offer their professional services to organizations and institutions of a non-commercial, non-profit-making type, and will avoid employment in settings where professional values are threatened by the business ethics of capitalism. Consequently, respondents were asked to state which category their employers fell into; the responses —males only—were as follows in Table 30, including for comparative purposes those of working class male respondents.

Middle class male CND supporters are to be found predominantly in the employment of state and local authorities, independent bodies such as churches and universities, various non-profit-making organizations including trade unions and Cooperative societies, or in freelance professions. Only about a quarter were employed in private industry and commercial organizations, as compared with 67 per cent of working class male respondents. Perhaps this demonstrates with greater force the argument that the clustering of radicals in the welfare and creative professions is not best explained as a product of status inconsistency, but as the result of occupational

[1] William Kornhauser, *Scientists in Industry: Conflict and Accommodation*, University of California Press, 1962, p. 25. Also, Steven Box and Stephen Cotgrove, 'Scientific Identity, Occupational Selection and Role Strain', *British Journal of Sociology*, **17**, March 1966.

TABLE 30   *Commercial and non-commercial employment (Male respondents)*

	Respondents' social class		
	1 + 2 %	3 + 4 %	5 + 6 + 7 %
Commercial, profit-making organizations	19	32	67
Non-commercial, non-profit-making organizations, and Freelance.[1]	79	61	31
No response	2	7	2
	100	100	100
	(N = 53)	(N = 110)	(N = 39)

self-selection on the part of radicals, stemming from their desire to avoid direct employment in capitalist economic institutions. The fact that status inconsistency (between educational and income ranking) may also be present could be said to derive from the tendency, remarked upon earlier, for relatively higher material rewards to be allocated to those closely involved in the production and distribution process; and since in Britain (as in other western countries) this generally entails employment in commercial enterprises, to avoid these latter almost inevitably means taking an occupation where salaries are lower in relation to the level of education required. Radicals in our society do thus appear to make some kind of agreement with themselves to accept less-well-paid jobs than they could command in commerce or private industry in exchange for other, non-material, satisfactions.

An alternative proposition to this which could also help to account for the occupational location of middle class radicals is that they do initially enter a much wider range of white collar and professional jobs, in commercial as well as non-commercial settings, but that those in the former come under severer pressures than those in the latter to jettison their political beliefs. If an individual's career exposes him to strains created by the conflict between his political and occupational values, he may be expected to follow one of two courses of action; either to change his occupation for one more compatible with his political outlook, or to remain in his occupation and modify his politics accordingly. This latter process

[1] The main non-commercial organizations were: State and local authorities, churches, universities, regional hospital boards, trade unions and Co-operative societies.

does certainly occur to deplete the ranks of radicals, and is one which is described differently according to whether it is viewed with approval or disapproval. In the eyes of those who approve it is characterized as becoming 'mature' or 'responsible', the process by which idealists are converted to realists by the hard facts of life and the exigencies of earning a livelihood. Those who disapprove see it simply as a case of 'selling out', the abandonment of cherished political beliefs in exchange for material rewards or personal advancement. There would seem to be in fact a process at work analogous to 'natural selection', in so far as radicals seem able to withstand the pressures making for political conformity more successfully in some occupations than others. It could be suggested that CND supporters are found more frequently in the welfare professions than in commercial enterprises because those radicals who do initially enter the latter tend ultimately either to leave them for more congenial settings, or to tailor their political beliefs so that they conflict less with the ethos of the business world. To pursue the Darwinian metaphor, the environment of capitalist enterprise would select against radicals more severely than the environment provided by the welfare and creative professions; so that assuming radicals were to enter occupations on a more or less random basis, the different degrees of 'survival value' the occupations afforded would lead to the kind of uneven distribution that we find among CND supporters. Undoubtedly this process does partly account for the occupational location of respondents, although it is probably less important than the fact of self-selection discussed earlier. This is suggested by the data on young CND supporters. Those respondents still at school or university who indicated their intended future occupations showed a range of preferences closely similar to those of adult supporters, with teaching and varying kinds of social work being the predominant choices. This again underlines the extent to which radicalism is carried into these and similar professions, rather than being generated internally by the conflicts to which incumbents are said to be exposed.

The strain towards compatibility between occupational and political values would seem to be applicable mainly to the middle class, and much less so to industrial workers. A salient distinction between manual work and white collar or professional work is that the latter entails the individual in a much greater degree of self-identification and moral involvement with his occupation than does the former. Consequently, it is amongst the non-manual rather than manual workers that the need to reconcile personal and occupational values is especially relevant. This is not only because of the former's greater ego-involvement in the work situation, but also because of the availability of a range of career choices sufficiently differentiated to make this a relevant consideration in white collar occupational selection. In other words middle class occupations embrace a spectrum of values wide enough to provide niches compatible with almost any set of attitudes and beliefs. Considerations of this kind have little relevance for industrial workers since the types of jobs open to them are comparatively undifferentiated in the values they embody. Occupational selection would thus be relatively uninfluenced by personality needs or political and social attitudes. But the fact that radical manual workers are therefore more likely to be employed in capitalist enterprises than radical middle class workers does not produce in them the strains which the latter would be exposed to. This is firstly because manual work unlike most professional work stresses extrinsic rather than intrinsic rewards, and can therefore be performed with the minimum amount of ego-involvement and commitment to the organization. Secondly, industrial workers tend in any case to have a well developed sub-culture whose overall framework of values is generally overtly anti-capitalist in content or at least amenable to certain forms of political radicalism. Thus, industrial workers with radical views can be directly employed in capitalist concerns without the least degree of commitment to organizational goals and values and hence experience no strains between the latter and their personal political values—a feat which would be far less possible for radical white collar employees. Using terms recently made familiar by Etzioni, industrial workers have merely a 'calculative' involvement with their employers, implying no necessary value consensus; whereas white collar and professional employees have more of a 'moral' involvement with the organizations they work for, implying a certain harmony of values.[1] And, as the above table confirms, it is those of highest occupational status who are liable to have the strongest moral commitment to the organization, and who would therefore be under most strain if there were any serious incompatibility between personal and occupational values. Thus, among the middle class male respondents alone, only 19 per cent of those in the two top social classes are found in commercial organizations, as against 32 per cent of those in classes 3 and 4. It is thus for the middle class—and especially the upper middle class—radical

[1] Amitai Etzioni, *Complex Organizations*, Free Press, Glencoe, 1961.

rather than for his working class counterpart that the area of employment imposes the necessity of making a definite strategic choice, and which accounts for the occupational pattern we find amongst CND supporters. This being so, it could be said that the welfare and creative professions provide acceptable sanctuaries to those who wish to avoid direct involvement in capitalist enterprises by affording outlets for the exercise of their talents which entail no compromise of political ideals.

Appendix A

May 1965

Dear CND Supporter,

On the recent Easter March you kindly agreed to fill in a postal questionnaire in connection with a study we are doing at Hull on the CND. We are enclosing one of these for you now. It takes about 15 minutes to complete, most answers requiring only a tick in the appropriate place. If you feel you would like to amplify your answers perhaps you could write them on the back of the questionnaire, or on a separate piece of paper.

Please do not write your name and address on the questionnaire. Each one has been given a code number which we can refer to in case it is necessary to send reminders to those who are late in returning them. You may be quite sure that this information will be treated as highly confidential.

We should be most grateful if you could return the completed questionnaire as soon as possible, preferably within three or four days if you can. This is because we should like to finish analysing the returns before the end of the present University term.

Very many thanks for cooperating with us in this way.

Yours sincerely,
Frank Parkin,
CND Survey.

CND SURVEY

Age...... Male......
Female......

Which part of the country are you from?
Town............... County...............
Is there an *active* branch in your district? Yes...... No......

What type of school/college have you attended? Please tick where appropriate

(a) Secondary Modern...... (e) Grammar......
(b) Technical...... (f) Teachers' Training College......
(c) Comprehensive...... (g) CAT......
(d) Public/Boarding...... (h) University......
   (i) Other (please state)......

What is your present job?.............................

If you are a student what is your main subject?...............................

What kind of job do you hope to get after completing your studies?

....

In which year did you first begin to support CND?

     1958......   1962......
     1959......   1963......
     1960......   1964......
     1961......   1965......

Are you a member of any of the following:

    (a) Young Socialists......   (d) Anarchists......
    (b) Young Liberals......   (e) Socialist Labour League......
    (c) Young Communist League......   (f) Any other political group......
                                      (please state)

If you belong to one of the above did you join *before* or *after* you began to support CND?

    Before CND......
    After CND......
    I joined both at the same time......

Are you a practising member of any religious denomination?

                                           Yes...... No......

If 'yes' please tick the appropriate one:

    (a) C of E......   (d) Quaker......
    (b) Methodist......   (e) Roman Catholic......
    (c) Jewish   (f) Other (please state)......

Are you a member of a trade union?   Yes...... No......

Could you state briefly what other organizations you are a member of—e.g. college or university societies, clubs, voluntary associations, etc.

If a General Election were now held which party would you vote for?

(If you are not yet of voting age, assume that you are.)

    Labour......   Conservative......   Other......
    Liberal......   Communist......   None at all......

If a CND candidate were to stand in your constituency would you vote for him or still vote as above?

    Vote as above......
    Vote for CND candidate......

If a General Election were now held which party do you think your parents would vote for? Please tick for each parent.

	Mother	Father
Labour	......	......
Liberal	......	......
Communist	......	......
Conservative	......	......
Other	......	......
None at all	......	......

How do your parents feel about CND? Please tick for each parent.

	Mother	Father
(a) Is an active supporter of CND	......	......
(b) Approves of CND but is not active	......	......
(c) Expresses no opinion about CND	......	......
(d) Disapproves of CND	......	......

Please write in any remarks you would like to make about your parents' attitude towards CND, or your involvement in it.

What is your parents' attitude towards politics in general?

	Mother	Father
(a) Is very active in politics	......	......
(b) Is definitely interested, but not really active	......	......
(c) Is only mildly interested	......	......
(d) Is completely uninterested	......	......

How do most of your closest friends feel about CND?
  (a) Most of them either support or are sympathetic to CND......
  (b) Most of them are not really concerned one way or the other......
  (c) Most of them are hostile to CND......

Here are four commonly given reasons for urging Britain to give up the Bomb. Although you may agree with all of them, please tick the *one* which carries greatest weight with you personally.
  (a) Because it is an inefficient means of defence......
  (b) Because it is a fundamentally evil weapon......
  (c) Because it is a waste of economic resources......
  (d) Because it would enable Britain to give a moral lead......

Which of the following issues do you think a young person should be mostly concerned about today? Please tick the two you yourself consider to be the most important.
  (a) Settling down and raising a family......
  (b) The plight of the hungry nations......
  (c) Finding oneself a good job......
  (d) Enjoying oneself with friends......
  (e) Working for a more just and humane society......

(Now could you please mark with a *cross* the one you personally consider to be the *least* important.

Which of the following measures would you most like to see implemented by the present parliament? Please tick *two* only.
  (a) Increased unemployment benefits......
  (b) Nationalization of major industries......
  (c) Abolition of capital punishment......
  (d) Greater legal protection for trade unions......
  (e) More material aid for poorer countries......
  (f) Repeal of the laws against homosexuality......

Here are five statements, each expressing a particular point of view. Could you please tick each one to indicate your level of agreement or disagreement with it.

	Strongly agree	Agree	Disagree	Strongly disagree
The class struggle is an out-dated notion which is irrelevant to our present-day problems	......	......	......	......
In Britain today there is plenty of opportunity for talented people to get on in life	......	......	......	......
The most urgent need in this country today is not to distribute wealth more evenly but to eradicate all forms of violence from our lives	......	......	......	......
Obedience and respect for authority are the most important virtues that children can learn	......	......	......	......
Parents these days allow their children too much freedom	......	......	......	......

Concerning this last question, what were your own parents' attitude towards you as a teenager?

(*a*) They allowed me to make very few of my own decisions......

(*b*) They gave me guidance but did not interfere with my life too much......

(*c*) They gave me a completely free hand in everything......

What is your father's job? (If retired or dead, what was his job?)

....

Mother's occupation.............................

Which of the three social classes do you place yourself in?

Upper Class......

Middle Class......

Working Class......

Finally, apart from the question of the Bomb, what other aspects of life in Britain today are you most critical of?

Thank you for taking the trouble to fill this in. Could you please make sure you have answered all the questions, and return it in the enclosed stamped addressed envelope to the CND Survey, Department of Sociology, The University, HULL, Yorks.

Appendix B

To all CND Branch Secretaries

February 1966

Dear

We are carrying out a survey of CND and would be most grateful for your assistance. Our aim is to send out anonymous questionnaires to adult Campaign supporters in the local branches in order to get information about the general composition of the membership, of which very little is at present known. As well as collecting factual information about age, occupation and so on, we shall seek members' opinions on certain political and social questions, as well as their views on the Campaign itself.

Could we ask you to cooperate with us in this venture by sending us the names and addresses of your branch members over the age of 25 who have played a fairly active part in local campaign affairs within the past two or three years—either in supporting CND demonstrations, selling literature, organizing fund-raising schemes and the like. It is not necessary that they should be active at present, so long as they have made a definite contribution to the branch's work some time in the recent past. One of the reasons for including past activists as well as present ones is that we hope to find out why some supporters drop out. We are restricting the present survey to those over the age of 25 because a separate study is being made of young supporters between the ages of 15 and 25.

It should perhaps be said that this project is being carried out with the full knowledge and approval of CND headquarters, from whom your address was obtained, although it is not of course an 'official' Campaign undertaking. Our aim is to try and get the questionnaires sent out by the end of January, so it would be most helpful if you could send your list in the enclosed stamped addressed envelope within about seven days or so.

Thank you in advance for your cooperation.

Yours sincerely,
Frank Parkin,
CND Survey.

March 1966
Dear CND Supporter,

I am carrying out a study of the post-war peace movement in Britain, with special reference to CND, and would be most grateful for your help. In order to get some information about the composition of the Campaign's membership I am circulating a questionnaire to past and present supporters in local branches throughout the country. Your name was supplied by your branch secretary as one of the members who has played a role in CND affairs within the fairly recent past; consequently I am enclosing a questionnaire which I hope you will be kind enough to complete.

As you will see, much of the information sought is of a straightforward factual kind, such as age, sex, occupation, and so forth, although I am also seeking supporters' views about certain current social and political matters. Most of the answers require simply a tick in the appropriate place, but one or two ask for your written comments; if there is not enough space for these please continue on the reverse side of the sheet. The questionnaire is anonymous and the information will form the basis of statistical tables from which it will not be possible to identify the answers of any individual. The code number in the corner is to enable me to identify non-returns in order to send out reminders. You may be quite sure that your replies will be treated in the strictest confidence.

I should perhaps say that although this is not an 'official' CND project it is being carried out with the full knowledge and approval of national, regional and local sections of the Campaign. Indeed, it would not have been possible for me to have contacted you without the active cooperation of many groups and individual members at all levels. I am hoping now that I can also count on your goodwill in filling in and returning the questionnaire in the stamped addressed envelope provided—within, if at all possible, the next seven days. Please let me emphasize that for the purpose of this survey it is not necessary that you should be currently active in the Campaign.

Many thanks in advance for your help.

Yours sincerely,

Frank Parkin.

P.S. If you would like to know the results of the survey please indicate this on the last page of the questionnaire.

CND SURVEY

1. Male......   2. Age: Under 21......   3. Single......
   Female......   21–25......   Married......
                                 26–30......   Divorced......
                                 31–40......   Separated......
                                 41–55......   Widowed......
                                 Over 55......

4. Name of local CND Branch.............................

5. In which year did you first begin to support CND:
   1958......   1962......
   1959......   1963......
   1960......   1964......
   1961......   1965......

6. About how long have you lived in your present branch area:
   ......years.

7. In comparison with when you first joined the Campaign has your level of activity now
   (a) increased......
   (b) decreased......
   (c) remained about the same......

8. If it has *decreased* is this because of:
   (a) a changed attitude towards nuclear weapons......
   (b) discontented with CND......
   (c) pressure of work/domestic reasons......
   (d) other political activities......
   (e) Other reasons (please state)......

9. Type of Secondary Schooling received:
   (a) Secondary Modern/Elementary......
   (b) Technical......
   (c) Public/Boarding......
   (d) Grammar......
   (e) Other (please state)......

10. Further Education, if any:
    (a) Teacher Training......
    (b) CAT......
    (c) University......
    (d) Other (please state)......
    (e) None......

11. At what age did your *full time* education end:......

12. If a General Election were now held which party would you vote for:
    (a) Labour......   (c) Conservative......   (e) Other......
    (b) Liberal......   (d) Communist......   (f) None......

13. If a CND candidate were to stand in your constituency would you vote for him or still vote as above:
    (a) Vote as above......   (b) Vote for CND candidate......

14. Are you a member of any political party or political organization other than CND or the Committee of 100.
    (a) Yes......   (b) No......
    If 'yes' which one......

15. Are you a member of any religious denomination:
    (a) Yes......   (b) No......

    If 'yes' please indicate which:
    (a) C of E......   (d) Methodist......
    (b) R.C.......   (e) Quaker......
    (c) Jewish......   (f) Other......
                        (please state)

    If 'no' are you
    (a) a Rationalist or Humanist......
    (b) an Agnostic......
    (c) an Atheist......

16. Have you ever participated in civil disobedience/direct action campaigns:
    (a) Yes......
    (b) No......

    If 'no' do you
    (a) approve of them......
    (b) disapprove of them......

17. What non-political organizations have you been a member of within the last few years (e.g. T.U., Professional Association, Clubs, Women's Guilds, Charitable Organizations, etc.)
    1.
    2.
    3.
    4.
    5.

    If you have held an elected post in any, please indicate:
    1.
    2.
    3.
    4.
    5.

18. Are you interested in
    (a) Local Politics   Yes......   No......
    (b) National Politics   Yes......   No......
    (c) International Politics Yes......   No......

    Could you now please number these from 1 to 3 in the order in which they most interest you, if at all.

19. What is your occupation (if Housewife, your husband's occupation). Please be as specific as possible—e.g. if Teacher, what kind of school, if Civil Servant, what grade, etc..

20. Salary (If housewife, husband's salary)
    (a) Below £500....   (d) £901–£1200....   (g) £1701–£200....
    (b) £500–£750....   (e) £1201–£1400.... (h) £2001–£2500....
    (c) £751–£900....   (f) £1401–£1700.... (i) Over £2500....

21. Are you employed by: (If Housewife, is your husband employed by:)
    (a) A Commercial organization......
    (b) The State or Local Authority......
    (c) Self Employed or Freelance......
    (d) Other (please state)......

22. Some supporters experienced difficulties with their employers because of their CND activities and beliefs. Has this ever happened to you? Could you please write in any remarks you would care to make about your own experience in this matter. (Continue overleaf if necessary.)

23. What have you found to be the general attitude towards CND of the following groups. Please tick for each group as appropriate:

	Mostly approved of CND	Mostly indifferent to CND	Mostly hostile to CND
(a) Your closest friends	......	....	......
(b) Your family	......	....	......
(c) Your colleagues at work	......	....	......
(d) Your employers or their representatives	......	....	......

24. Which social class do you place yourself in:
    - (a) Upper class......
    - (b) Middle class......
    - (c) Working class......
    - (d) I do not recognize classes......

25. Which *one* of the four following arguments against the Bomb carries greatest weight with you personally:
    - (a) It is an inefficient means of defence......
    - (b) It is a fundamentally evil weapon......
    - (c) It is a waste of economic resources......
    - (d) It would enable Britain to give a moral lead to other nations......

26. Here are a number of statements expressing a point of view about current social and political issues: could you please indicate your measure of agreement or disagreement with each of these.

	Strongly agree	Agree	Dis-agree	Strongly disagree
(a) Unemployment benefits should be substantially increased	......	....	......	......
(b) All major industries should be nationalized	......	....	......	......
(c) The laws against homosexual acts by consenting adults should be repealed	......	....	......	......
(d) There should be greater legal protection for trade unions	......	....	......	......
(e) Britain should give more material aid to poorer countries	......	....	......	......
(f) Our present immigration laws should be greatly relaxed	......	....	......	......
(g) The class struggle is an outdated notion which is irrelevant to our present-day problems	......	....	......	......
(h) There is little opportunity for talented people to get on in Britain	......	....	......	......
(i) The monarchy is an institution we should be justly proud of	......	....	......	......
(j) Workers and management have common interests and should pull together as a team	......	....	......	......

(k) Commercial advertising debases
human values   ....
(l) There will always be war; it's
part of human nature   ....
(m) Ordinary people cannot hope
to change government policies   ....
(n) The Labour Party should put
principles before power   ....
(o) Protests and demonstrations
which fail to achieve their aims
are a waste of effort   ....

27. The first six of these statements (*a* to *f*) are all possible measures of government. Could you now please mark with a cross the *two* which, if any, you personally would most like to see implemented.

28. Apart from the matter of the Bomb and defence policy, are there any other aspects of British society today of which you are critical:

29. Were any of your parents or close relatives associated in their time with 'radical' religious, or political movements—e.g. ILP, CP, Quakers, Pacifists, Labour Left, etc.
    (*a*) Yes......   (*b*) No......
    If 'yes' could you please give brief details:
    Mother   Other close
    Father   relatives

Thank you for filling this in. If you would like to know the results of the completed survey please put a cross here.

Index